Life
the continuous process

Readings in Human Development

Freda Rebelsky

Boston University

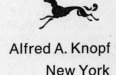

Alfred A. Knopf
New York

THIS IS A BORZOI BOOK
PUBLISHED BY ALFRED A. KNOPF, INC.

First Edition

987654321

Copyright © 1975 by Alfred A. Knopf, Inc.

Library of Congress Cataloging in Publication Data
Main entry under title:

Life, the continuous process.

  Includes bibliographies and indexes.
  1. Developmental psychology—Addresses, essays, lectures.
I. Rebelsky, Freda, 1931–
[DNLM: 1. Psychology—Collected works. BF713 F931]
BF713.5.F76   155   75–12808
ISBN 0–394–31979–6

Manufactured in the United States of America

preface

Today's student does not have to read far in recent research on human development to realize that many previous biases about aging are now being called into question. Over and over, cherished assumptions about the strength of youth and the debility of age are challenged by data. These challenges, however, have not yet been presented in clear form. A book of readings that can provide a framework for new thought on the processes of human development over the life span is sorely needed.

The present book of readings is, in fact, the direct result of our dissatisfaction with what has thus far been available to students who wanted to study postchildhood development. The idea of this book occurred in two stages, the first being the recognition that the dissatisfaction we felt was a reality. Much of the current material in books seemed meaningless or overwhelmingly difficult, and we had to comprehend that this was not due to our failures, our stupidities. That first realization freed us to recognize a second possibility: that we were capable of creating a more useful, eye-opening way of looking at human development over the life span.

The selections in this book have been chosen from an enormous, disparate literature (ranging from research articles to songs and stories) to reflect the excitement and knowledge about both the content and processes of human growth and development over the life span. We hope our readers will gain a sense of the richness of human development, an awareness of their own biases about aging, and an ability to use new ideas and feelings to enrich the full development of themselves and others.

We also hope that this book will be generative to a generation of students, enabling them to "free up" from their old viewpoints. We think two of the major purposes to any education are to learn that there are interesting new things in the world worth thinking about and to learn that one is capable of thinking about these new things. We think this book will introduce many new ideas to readers; we hope that it also enables them to feel smart enough to want to learn more and create more knowledge in this very important area of human development. Though we now know a great deal more about human development over the life span than we did even a decade ago, there is a great deal more to learn. This book could not have been written a decade ago; and it is exciting to think about the knowledge that a new generation of students can discover by asking the new questions. A decade from now, present readers of this book will, we hope, be adding new chapters to this developing field.

acknowledgments

We acknowledge with gratitude the authors who gave us permission to reprint their work in this volume. We also thank Lynn Dorman and Kathie White, who used our materials in their courses and made helpful suggestions. Bernice Neugarten and Richard Kalish also made useful, critical comments about our book.

The collaborators who worked on this book add the following acknowledgment:

It is a rare event for a group of ex-students to collaborate with their former professor on a book of edited readings. In many ways this book represents a synthesis of academic work and personal conviction. It was only through Freda's motivating influence and unwavering faith in us that the fantasy of this publication became a reality. Individually and collectively we salute her and offer our thanks for providing us with this unique opportunity.

contents

part two   socialization issues

THE CIRCLE GAME

JONI MITCHELL

Yesterday a child came out to wonder,
Caught a dragonfly inside a jar.
Fearful when the sky was full of thunder,
And tearful at the falling of a star.

(CHORUS)

And the seasons, they go round and round
And the painted ponies go up and down.
We're captive on the carousel of time.
We can't return, we can only look behind
From where we came
And go round and round and round
In the circle game.

Then the child moved ten times round the seasons,
Skated over ten clear frozen streams.
Words like, when you're older, must appease him,
And promises of someday make his dreams.

(CHORUS)

Sixteen springs and sixteen summers gone now,
Cartwheels turn to carwheels thru the town.
And they tell him, take your time, it won't be long now,
Till you drag your feet to slow the circles down.

(CHORUS)

So the years spin by and now the boy is twenty,
Though his dreams have lost some grandeur coming true,
There'll be new dreams, maybe better dreams, and plenty
Before the last revolving year is through.

(CHORUS)

introduction

The mental images people live with affect the way they actually live. Whether they view growing old as meaning getting enfeebled and stupid or attaining greater strength and intellectual skills, their expectations help, to some extent, to shape their behaviors.

Developmental psychologists have committed themselves to uncovering the "facts" of human development and the various forces, both inside and outside the person, that influence these facts. As we shall show through the introductory sections and readings in this book, many of the facts about the changes that occur in people over the life span are as yet undiscovered. We hope the reader will agree with us that the major task we propose, to be able to think more clearly and openly about the data and processes of development, is an interesting, mind-opening one.

Life expectancy at birth in the United States has increased significantly during this century. In 1900 it was 47.3 years. At present it is 71.0 years. In addition, survival of infancy and adolescence extends life expectancy. Thus, if you were twenty in 1974 your life expectancy is between seventy-three and seventy-four. And if you were sixty-five in 1974, your life expectancy was over fifteen more years!

This longer life brings with it new potentials and problems. For example, a forty-year-old professor, teaching for ten years, could learn an entire new field at age forty and devote more time to the new field than he gave to the first one. Women who have opted to stay home until their children are grown are now able to be ready for entire new careers at an age when, at the turn of the century, mothers were dead or still having babies.

These statements are meant to help the reader recognize how erroneous many time-honored images of aging are and how vital it is to explore, clarify, and reevaluate these images; for they can shape behavior to the destruction of potential and even, as Howard Nemerov's "Wolves in the Zoo" suggests, to the destruction of a species and its growth.

> They look like shaggy dogs, but wrongly drawn,
> And a legend on their cage tell us there is
> No evidence that any of their kind
> Has ever attacked man, woman, or child.

Now it turns out there were no babies dropped
In sacrifice, delaying tactics, from
Siberian sleds; now it turns out, so late,
That Little Red Ridinghood and her Gran

Were the aggressors with the slavering fangs
And telltale tails; now it turns out, at last,
That gray wolf and timber wolf are nearly gone,
Done out of being by the tales we tell

Told us by Nanny in the nursery—
Young sparks we were, to set such forest fires
As blazed from story into history,
And put such bounty on their wolfish heads

As brought the few survivors to our terms,
Surrendered in happy Babylon among
The peacock dusting off the path of dust,
The tiger pacing in the striped shade.

If you ask a young child to describe an old person, he might say "wiser," "weaker," "taller," and be talking about a twenty-five-year-old, who seems very old to a six-year old. When is old age to you? What are the words you would use to define people of different ages?

In several classes at Boston University, students (mainly in their twenties) were asked to use three words to describe each decade. Descriptives and categories frequently used included the following:

10–19 energetic, optimistic, unformed, immature, growing, searching, insecure, young
20–29 school, work, searching, unsure, idealistic, worried, deciding
30–39 adjusting, marriage, job, active, organized, achieving, secure, maturing
40–49 happy, worried, maturity, reassessing, mellow, routine, middle-age, children
50–59 reassessing, freedom, physically aging, parents, political
60–69 retired, health problems, mellowed, aging, enjoying, scared, settled, retrospective, grandchildren
70–79 slower, death of others, physical infirmities, contentment, grandchildren, resting, secure, lonely, troubled

Students reported that it was easiest to think of words for their own decade, or for the decade they had just passed through, and that the later decades (especially 40–49 and 50–59) were most difficult to describe. It was as if there were a large period of life yet to come which was indescribable, followed by a period in which health problems and inevitable decline were most salient. Perhaps most important though some of the images are mixed, these students believed that *education, work, marriage, children, grandchildren, participation in political life, and retirement* were clearly age-related.

Interviewing people about their views of life also confirms this; we have some concensus about the "right" age for some aspects of development. Yet frequently enough to cause consternation, there are people doing their thing at the "wrong" age: fifty-year-olds in school, seventy-year-olds getting married, sixty-year-olds starting new careers. In addition, some issues, like physical disability or death, are felt with greater ease by seventy-year-olds than by twenty-year-olds. Repeatedly, students reported their shock at finding eighty-year-olds, sick in bed, discussing plans for a trip a few years hence to see new parts of the world or discussing plans for death with seeming ease. Throughout life, people *live*: they think about the past, present, *and* future; they deal actively with the world around them. Thus Luria, a Nobel prize winner in physiology, in his book, *Life: The Unfinished Experiment* (1973), concludes:

As most human beings painfully realize in their own life experience, the . . . mind places on men, alone among all living beings, an almost unbearable burden: the consciousness of one's individual transience, the awareness of inevitable death, what existentialist philosophers have called the "absurd" of the human condition. Yet most men do not despair. They do not rush into suicide to escape the anguish of life's absurdity. In the words that Voltaire in *Candide* (1759) put in the mouth of an old woman, raped, mutilated, a hundred times defiled: *"Je voulais cent fois me tuer, mais j'aimais encore la vie"* [A hundred times I wanted to kill myself, but I still loved life].

Humankind is justified, I believe, in suspecting that once again blind evolution has operated with subtle wisdom. While fashioning consciousness and exposing man to the ultimate terror, it may by natural selection have also brought forth in the human mind some protective compensatory features. Human evolution may have imprinted into man's brain an intrinsic program that opens to him the innermost sources of optimism—art, and joy, and hope, confidence in the powers of the mind, concern for his fellow men, and pride in the pursuit of the unique human adventure. [p. 150].

Using This Book

The Written Word Is Not the Final Word

We recognize that many readers tend to accept published material written by experts as "truth." We are presenting these articles as examples of the varieties of interest, research design, and findings about human beings. However, you should be aware that even the best article can present only the data of a specific time as seen by a specific person. And we believe that all observers of data are biased by their interests and training. This certainly does not mean that the articles are not worth reading. A major reason for the selection of the material in this book is to help you see phenomena in different ways than you did before. We want to open your eyes, not close your mind.

Reading Specific Articles

We think people learn more when they are actively involved in their own learning than when they are passive recipients. Our students have found that outlining an article enables them to summarize it thoroughly and easily, and, in addition, forces them into a critical attitude.

For your own sanity, and to help you to compare articles later, we suggest that abstracts be done with some uniformity. It seems to make little difference what size paper you use, or even how much you write about an article. What does matter is consistency, the same ordering of material and the same size paper.

Many of our students start off thinking that criticism of an article means tearing it apart, criticizing all of its parts. They feel obligated to comment on sample size, statistics used, and so forth. Abstracting and criticism then become frustrating tasks, since most undergraduate students simply do not have the background and working knowledge of the field that are required to do this sort of criticism adequately. On the other hand, even without extensive knowledge of the subject of an article, a thoughtful reading of it will at times allow a reader to see data more clearly than the author did. Research readings are not "hard facts" to be interpreted in only one way. You may disagree with the author's discussion as to *why* the results came out as they did and *what* the results mean in more general terms. This is fine, it is how new research is generated. But even if you disagree with the interpretations, you should accept the author's actual data or results.

Most research is done carefully and systematically. The results obtained and the results of statistical analyses are, in most cases, acceptable. Results are results are results. You may certainly question why certain statistical tests are used or why the author thinks some measure is actually measuring the stated phenomenon, but, again, you should spend your time criticizing other things than the results of the measurement. We suggest this because many students get so involved in questioning the results that they do not bring their intelligence to bear on the major problems in many studies, that of interpretation of the results. By raising questions yourself about the research, you are able to bring your own training and experience to bear on someone else's thinking. You thereby establish a real dialogue on an equal level with the author.

There are articles in this book that may seem to you "silly," "dull," "obvious," "brilliant," or whatever. (These were some of the words used by our own students, but you may have your own descriptions!) The interesting thing is that an article described as useless by one student is often thought of as brilliant by another student in the same class.

When reading an article, everyone fits it into his or her current background of information. If you already know much about an area, articles in that area may seem obvious. If you do not like or are not particularly interested in that area, those articles may seem silly or useless to you. If the article excites you in some way, you may think of it as brilliant. All we can ask is that you try to be fair to each article as you read it. Each selection was published because the editors of a journal in the field thought it was important for *some* reason. The reason was not always that it was the first research done in an important area. It might have been that the methodology was unique or the discussion and rationale seemed useful to others. And we selected the articles to provide you with a chance to see the breadth of current research interests and methods.

Before reading an article, look at the date that it was originally published. This may help you in your appraisal of the article. Also read the introduction to each chapter before reading the articles contained in it. You may disagree with us—and you certainly would not be alone in that—but at least you will have some idea of our thinking on the topics, and this may give you a point of reference from which to argue.

An outline that we find useful for abstracting articles is presented below, though you may find a better way to organize the material you read.

RESEARCH ARTICLES
Problem: General statement of previous research. Author's hypothesis or hypotheses.
Method: Instruments used (their validity and reliability). Experimental procedure.
Sample: Relevant variables, for example, age, sex, socioeconomic status.
Results: Author's findings and interpretation.

In addition to the abstract of the research article, you should attempt to

1. evaluate the article
2. offer alternative interpretations
3. comment on the implications for classroom and/or behavior

THEORETICAL ARTICLES

Imagine what it would be like if all the authors were in a room together. How would they interpret each other's data? Where would they agree or disagree? What would you say? Arguing for the positions of the various authors also helps one to understand that there is no one answer to the questions asked by the authors.

Brief summary of major points.

Author's interpretation and implications.

In addition to this abstract of the theoretical article, you should attempt to

1. evaluate the theoretical position (or compare to another)
2. comment on the implications for research and/or behavior

These abstracts need not be long. They are for your own benefit: to encourage you to think about what you read, to help you write better critical papers, and to participate more effectively in class.

Relating Articles Within a Chapter

After you have read a few articles within a chapter, you will start to notice several things

1. that different authors approach the same topic from very different points of view
2. that different conclusions are possible within the same topic
3. that you emotionally, from your own training and biases, tend to accept or reject certain findings

Bring to the articles a sense of intelligent curiosity. Study them, think about them, put yourself into them. Evaluate their conclusions. Do they make sense to you? Do you agree? Consider other research or evidence on the topic.

Relating Articles Across Chapters

After you read several chapters you will begin to realize that the human being is extremely complex and that the whole person is made up, at the least, of the material presented in chapters 1 to 10 in this book. For example, if you are reading an article on the prime of life, depending on which chapters you read before it, you might ask what would happen if the person had a good job, a bad marriage, or lived in China. You will probably find yourself designing research along new lines, something few of our students initially think themselves capable of doing. Students are, in fact, quite capable of designing research, but most of them brush off their ideas with a statement to the effect that if they have thought of it, it must obviously have been done already.

Use of Supplementary Readings

After reading some of the articles or complete chapters, you may find that you wish to read further on a certain topic. We have suggested further readings on each topic at the end of the chapters but not everyone may find these to be enough. We therefore are including the names of some general reference books that can be used for searching the literature on a given topic. Chapters in most of these general references will often tell you what others have thought about the topic, and what others have learned about it. All of this information is useful to you as you read or perhaps design a study on the topic.

Statistics

In reading some of the articles, you will undoubtedly come across those things that many have come to feel dumb about: numbers, data, statistical tests, and so forth. Do not feel dumb, and do not skip the tables, graphs, and figures either. They are there to help you understand the research and they are important. Yes, the author may say some of these things in words, but you must also learn to read them in figure form. For that reason, and because we do not believe in mathematical blocks, especially in college students, we have included the following brief aid to reading statistics.

Mean: Usually the same as the mathematical average.

Standard deviation: A measure of the variability of the scores. The more spread out, or variable, the scores are, the larger the standard deviation.

Normal curve: Represents the distribution of many psychological characteristics in the general population. When the distribution is not normal, the data are sometimes transformed via some procedure to approximate normality.

Correlation: The relationship between variables. When there is a tendency for variable A to always go with variable B, in the same direction, we speak of a positive correlation. An example is height and weight in children. When two variables go together but in opposite directions, we speak of a negative correlation. For example, the relationship between income and family size is negative. Large families tend to have small incomes and small families tend to have larger incomes.

Level of confidence: You will most often read things such as that a factor is significant at the .01 level or p .05. These all refer to the "goodness" of the results obtained. A level of .05 means that the results could have happened by chance only 5 times out of 100; .01 means that chance could account for the results only 1 time out of 100. The present level of confidence acceptable to psychologists is .05.

Chi square, t-test, and analysis of variance: The names of various statistical tests that we use for examining our data to see if they answer the questions asked. We are not going to explain the various tests, but we want to familiarize you with their names. You will come across an assortment of letters, both English and Greek, that are used for naming what one student once called baroque statistics. Some of the letters you will encounter are X^2, F, r, U. You will also read sentences that have phrases like this in the middle of them: ($t = 2.69$, p .01), or ($F = 5.32$, p .005). What they mean is that the statistical test, represented by the first letter, yielded a final number (in the above cases these are the 2.69 and the 5.32) which was significant at the given level of confidence (here they were significant at .01 and .005 respectively). The results, thus, are likely not to be due to chance.

Use of Indexes

There are also two indexes in this book. The first is of the authors of the articles in this book and of authors mentioned in all references (boldface type indicates the page on which an author's article begins). The second is an index of concepts. The concept index can be useful in helping you relate articles to each other.

part one developmental issues

chapter one
general
problems

Freud believed that love and work *(Liebe und Arbeit)* are the adult products of healthy human development. If adults could not love and work, no human society could exist.

Development may be viewed as directional. Freud saw it as a movement upward toward an adult capacity for love and work. Erikson's final stages of life posit *generativity vs. stagnation* and *ego integrity vs. despair*. Many present-day American students view development as an inverted-U curve; first there is the movement upward toward increasing intellectual and physical abilities, and then somewhere (19? 29? 39? 49? 59?), a change in direction toward the inevitable decline.

Development, for many developmental psychologists, is always up, directed toward maintenance of integrity of the self, individuation, and self-actualization (Flavell, 1972). Throughout life, we find increasing differentiation and growth of abilities to deal effectively with the complex interaction of person and world. In that sense, the higher levels of development are not reducible to lower ones. Thus, an older person has not only seen *more* of life because of his greater number of experiences; he also has seen and felt a different life and is, thereby, a different

3

person, not only older but more "experienced."

The readings in this chapter should help the student focus on some major developmental issues:

1. Why have early experiences rather than later experiences been the subject of so much thought and study?
2. Is there ever such a thing as a "particular" experience, or does experience always depend on one's age, stage, time of life, prior experiences, and so forth?
3. How can the changes that occur throughout life be explained? Is there an adequate explanatory principle to explain development?

Everyone brings to the study of human beings strong, though sometimes unstated, theories about the nature of development. But we do think it is very useful for students to state, out loud to themselves, what *form* they think development takes (a straight line, inverted U, etc.), what they see as the likely "end product" of development (death, increasing competence, ability to love and work, etc.), and *why* they think development occurs (new problems occur daily, the organism is trained by a certain age, etc.). Only then can students begin to recognize some of the reasons behind their "theory of development" and understand that others may see the world with very different theoretical lenses.

Gerald Levin (1973) stated several major dichotomous dimensions of development, asking his students to place themselves on these dimensions. We have included his table, substituting the word "person" wherever he used the word "child." Try to fill out the form. Then read the articles that follow. We hope you will find yourselves beginning to raise good questions about your own view of development. We also hope you will recognize that you bring a viewpoint to the study of human development, a viewpoint

that you may never have admitted even to yourself. As Mandler and Kessen (1959) have said so well:

Atoms do not study atoms, stars do not investigate planets, paramecia presumably do not have a general theory about the behavior of paramecia; but man studies, investigates, and theorizes about man. . . . the fact that man studies himself . . . puts a major stumbling block in the path of scientific psychology.

Levin's section on theory follows:

One good way to learn about theories of developmental psychology is to start with the main arguments. Theoretical writing is largely polemic, or argumentative. Theoreticians usually have an alternative view in mind. Much of what they say and much of the research they do can best be understood when you know what the argument is about.

Most of the important arguments in developmental psychology revolve around a few central issues. Most of these issues are old and predate scientific study. The central arguments endure because child development is incredibly complex and because superficially contradictory generalizations about people are true. The seven paradoxes summarized below each give rise to a central issue, an axis of conflict. Try to see the wisdom in both positions on each issue. Learn to see where different writers take their stand.

Paradox 1. The person's psychological functioning changes so radically during the course of development that it is useful to regard developmental changes in behavior as fundamental—as basic and profound as the developmental changes in physical structure that start when the ovum is fertilized and end when the human body is physically mature. (The developmental position.)

However, it also is useful to assume that the person's psychological characteristics are essentially constant. The obvious changes in behavior can be regarded as superficial. For example, it can be argued that babies learn and remember as we do, but cannot show it because of secondary factors such as sleepiness, poor muscular control, and difficulty in understanding what we want them to learn.

Apparent improvement in learning performance can be attributed to progress in these peripheral areas, rather than to basic changes in psychological functioning. (The non-developmental position.)

Paradox 2. Developmentally, changes in behavior can be seen as a continuous series of minute changes. While the cumulative product of these tiny changes is dramatic, the process should be thought of as analogous to the height changes between birth and maturity. All the person gains is "more of the same," rather than something different. (The continuity position.)

However, the most important changes in behavior can usefully be thought of as qualitative and discontinuous in nature. Like the physical difference between a fertilized ovum and a newborn baby, some psychological differences involve a dramatic transformation from one stage of development to another. (The discontinuity position.)

Paradox 3. Development involves tremendous biological changes and the realization of potentials inherent in the genes. The helplessness of infancy, language, and heterosexual behavior, for example, are all products of evolution. To understand normal development and its deviation, you must put the person in biological perspective. (The biological position.)

However, development involves a tremendous amount of learning, the acquisition of forms of behavior that are passed on from generation to generation through culture. The helplessness of infancy provides humans with an almost unique opportunity for learning. Language, like other aspects of culture, must be learned through interaction with the human environment. Even seemingly biological matters such as sex take on a human character only as a result of the social context in which they are developed. To understand normal development and its deviations, you must put the person in sociological perspective. (The sociological position.)

Paradox 4. A central feature of human beings is the way that the person is molded by powerful influences that are beyond his control. Driven by forces such as hunger from within, and initially helpless in solving the problems of survival, the person is almost completely dependent on the others around him. As they take care of him, they shape his behavior in a thousand ways, obvious and subtle, deliberately and accidentally creating a figure in their own image. (The view of the person as passive.)

However, it is remarkable that the human is so active in teaching himself and in seeking out ever more difficult problems. Even the baby likes to "do his own thing" and frustrates his parents' efforts to feed him by playing with the food, deliberately spilling the milk, and seeking out endless diversion. Most of the really important achievements of childhood, such as learning to walk and talk, come more from the child's constant curiosity and desire to master the world than from any interest in pleasing his parents. The well-fed child does not lapse into a state of pleasurable sloth but instead burns up tremendous amounts of energy in actively exploring the world. (The view of the person as an active agent.)

Paradox 5. The best vantage point in understanding people is to understand what motivates them, what determines why they select one reaction rather than another. As the poets have long known, "feeling is first." We must first focus on the emotional-motivational side of development. (The affective position.)

However, it is essential to understand how the person knows the world around him. The "environment" is only what he makes of it, how he sees it. Only careful study can reveal what situation he actually responds to. Similarly, only a scrutiny of how he thinks and what he can remember makes it possible to understand his motives and emotions. Since the person's cognitive functioning changes so radically during the course of development, we must start by understanding cognitive development. (The cognitive position.)

Paradox 6. The essence of developmental psychology is the study of the broad patterns and features of behavior that take years to develop. By standing off from the confusing and unimportant minute-to-minute details, we can see the "forest"—the major trends and what influences them. (The macroscopic position.)

However, if we want to understand the dynamics of development—the underlying processes of change—we must look at the "fine grain" of children's behavior and see how the changes take place. To stand off from these details is to remain but a spectator and never learn about the forces behind the scenes, the ones that run the show. (The microscopic position.)

Paradox 7. People all are essentially similar, despite the apparent differences among them. This similarity should be the central focus of developmental psychology. We must search for the basic principles that apply to everyone. (The general psychology position.)

People all are different, despite the superficial resemblances among them. This wonderful variety should provide our starting point. Only after we have adequately explored this diversity and found useful means for categorizing the varied "species" of humans and learning how and when the differences appear, will we be ready to search for important similarities. (The differential psychology position.)

Where do you stand on these seven controversies? Draw your own "theoretical profile" by checking the appropriate point on each scale in the following table:

Are the seven arguments really independent? For example, does your stand on the continuity-discontinuity issue limit your freedom to take stands on other issues? Which dimensions, if any, do you think cluster together?

This book contains a section on one major theory of individual development, that of Erik Erikson. A brief explanation should enhance the reader's ability to see that Erikson's theory is presented, not because it is "truth" or "right," but because it states clearly how a theoretician can think about life stages. Erikson is now an "old man," yet he still is generative: his books on youth, on identity crises, on the development of individuals such as Gandhi, are still issuing from his pen. He is a man who has tried many things. He does not have the usual educational degrees; in fact, his formal schooling ended during high school, when he became a traveler and artist. He has experienced in himself the shifts of interest and abilities that occur throughout development and

Theoretical Profiles

	1	2	3	4	5	6	7	
Developmental:	__	__	__	__	__	__	__	:Nondevelopmental
Continuity:	__	__	__	__	__	__	__	:Discontinuity
Biological:	__	__	__	__	__	__	__	:Social
Activity:	__	__	__	__	__	__	__	:Passivity
Cognitive:	__	__	__	__	__	__	__	:Affective
Microscopic:	__	__	__	__	__	__	__	:Macroscopic
General:	__	__	__	__	__	__	__	:Differential

has had the time and nerve to reflect on these.

Erikson sees life as a series of resolutions of conflict within the self. Individuals at every age are faced with the very conflicts that were stated in the quotation from Luria given in the Preface: How does one handle the human dilemma of life and death? Quite clearly, for Erikson

and for all human beings, these conflicts must be understood differently at different ages, and yet they are always representations of the age-old conflicts between hope and despair. Almost all mythologies have presented us with a heaven and a hell. The reality of life is that both exist within ourselves, and the resolution of these opposite elements is the process through which we are propelled to maturity.

To love and to work is to live. To live richly and fully, a person must deal, at each point in his life, with hope and despair. This effort at resolution *is* work and requires love of self and others. Erikson's theory makes explicit his view of what the conflicts of each age are and how and when they should be resolved. His article will be one way of using your own "theoretical profile" and experiences to reflect on your ideas about human development.

References

FLAVELL, J. An analysis of cognitive-developmental sequences. *Genetic Psychol. Monogr.*, 1972, *86*, 279–350.

LEVIN, G. *A self-directing guide to the study of child psychology.* Monterey, Calif.: Brooks-Cole, 1973. Pp. 24–26.

MANDLER, G., and KESSEN, W. *The language of psychology.* New York: Wiley, 1959. p. 29.

1. CONTINUITIES AND DISCONTINUITIES OF PSYCHOLOGICAL ISSUES INTO ADULT LIFE

BERNICE L. NEUGARTEN

I have chosen to play the devil's advocate . . . , for despite the title of [this] paper . . . , I am impressed more by the discontinuities than the continuities in the psychological issues that have thus far been preoccupying developmental psychologists who are concerned with the lifespan.

We shall not understand the psychological realities of adulthood by projecting forward the issues that are salient in childhood—neither those issues that concern children themselves, nor those that concern child psychologists as they study cognitive development and language development and the resolution of the Oedipal.

Many of those investigators who have been focusing upon infancy and childhood are dealing with issues that are not the salient issues to adults. To illustrate very briefly, and not to dwell upon the obvious:

In the adolescent we are accustomed to thinking that the major psychological task is the formation of identity. For the period that immediately follows, Kenneth Keniston has recently suggested the title "youth," distinguishing it from young adulthood, as the time when the major task for the ego is the confrontation of the society, the sorting out of values, and making a "fit" between the self and society.

In young adulthood, the issues are related to intimacy, to parenthood, and to meeting the expectations of the world of work, with the attendant demands for restructuring of roles, values, and sense of self—in particular, the investment of self into the lives of a few significant others to whom one will be bound for years to come.

In middle age, some of the issues are related to new family roles—the responsibilities of being the child of aging parents, and the reversal of authority which occurs as the child becomes the decision-maker for the parent . . . the awareness of the self as the bridge between the generations . . . the confrontation of a son-in-law or daughter-in-law with the need to establish an intimate relation with a stranger under very short notice . . . the role of grandparenthood.

Some of the issues are related to the increased stock-taking, the heightened introspection and reflection that become characteristic of the mental life . . . the changing time-perspective, as time is restructured in terms of time-left-to-live rather than time-since-birth . . . the personalization of death, bringing with it, for women, the rehearsal for widowhood, and for men, the rehearsal of illness; and for both, the new attention to body-monitoring.

Some of the issues relate to the creation of social heirs (in contrast to biological heirs) . . . the concomitant attention to relations with the young—the need to nurture, the care not to overstep the delicate boundaries of authority relationships, the complicated issues over the use of one's power—in short, the awareness of being the socializer rather than the socialized.

And in old age, the issues are different again. Some are issues that relate to renunciation—adaptation to losses of work, friends, spouse, the yielding up of a sense of competency and authority . . . reconciliation with members of one's family, one's achievements, and one's failures . . . the resolution of grief over the death of others, but also over the approaching death of self . . . the need to maintain a sense of integrity in terms of what one has been, rather than what one is . . . the concern with "legacy" . . . how to leave traces

of oneself . . . the psychology of survivor-
ship. . . .

All these are psychological issues which
are "new" at successive stages in the life
cycle; and as developmental psychologists
we come to their investigation ill-equipped,
no matter how sophisticated our approaches to child development.

The issues of life, and the content and
preoccupation of the mental life, are different for adults than for children. Furthermore, as psychologists, we deal in a
sense with different organisms. Let me
illustrate again, only briefly, that which we
all know:

As the result of accumulative adaptations to both biological and social events,
there is a continuously changing basis
within the individual for perceiving and
responding to new events in the outer
world. People change, whether for good
or for bad, as the result of the accumulation of experience. As events are regis-
tered in the organism, individuals inevitably abstract from the traces of those
experiences and they create more encompassing as well as more refined categories
for the interpretation of new events. The
mental filing system not only grows larger,
but it is reorganized over time, with infin-
itely more cross-references. This is merely
one way of saying that not only do the
middle-aged differ from the young because
they were subject to different formative
experiences, but because of the unavoid-
able effects of having lived longer and of
having therefore a greater apperceptive
mass or store of past experience.

Because of longer life histories, with
their complicated patterns of personal and
social commitments, adults are not only
much more complex than children, but
they are more different one from another,
and increasingly different as they move
from youth to extreme old age.

More important, the adult is a self-pro-
pelling individual who manipulates the
environment to attain his goals. He creates
his environment, more or less (and varying in degree, of course, by the color of

his skin and the size of his own or his
father's bank account). He invents his future self, just as he re-creates or *reinvents*
his past self. We cannot go far in understanding adult psychology, then, without
giving a central position to purposive behavior, to what Charlotte Buhler calls in-
tentionality, or to what Brewster Smith
has called the self-required values, or to
what Marjorie Lowenthal refers to as the
reassessment of goals as itself the measure
of adaptation.

These are not new ideas, but because
they are such striking features of the adult
as compared to the child, they create special problems for the student of the life
cycle when he turns to problems of prediction, for we do not yet know how to
capture the phenomena of decision-making.

Another factor is the adult's sense of
time and timing. The adult, surely by middle age, with his highly refined powers of
introspection and reflection is continually
busying himself in making a coherent story
out of his life history. He reinterprets the
past, selects and shapes his memories, and
reassesses the significance of past events
in his search for coherence. An event
which, at the time of its occurrence, was
"unexpected" or arbitrary or traumatic
becomes rationalized and interwoven into
a context of explanation in its retelling
twenty years later.

The remembrance of things past is continually colored by the encounter with the
present, of course; just as the present is
interpreted in terms of the past. To deal
with both the past and the present simultaneously is a unique characteristic of
human personality. It is a set of mental
processes which vary according to the
sensitivity of the individual, probably with
his educational level and his ability to
verbalize, but a set of mental processes
which probably also follow a distinguishable course with increasing age. In a study
presently under way in Chicago, for instance, the data seem to show that middle-
aged people utilize their memories in a
somewhat different fashion than do old

people. The middle-aged draw consciously upon past experience in the solution of present problems; the old seem to be busy putting their store of memories in order, as it were, dramatizing some, striving for consistency in others, perhaps as a way of preparing an ending for that life-story.

There is another way in which issues of time and timing are of central importance in the psychology of adulthood: namely, the ways in which the individual evaluates himself in relation to socially defined time. Every society is age-graded, and every society has a system of social expectations regarding age-appropriate behavior. The individual passes through a socially regulated cycle from birth to death as inexorably as he passes through the biological cycle; and there exists a socially prescribed timetable for the ordering of major life events: a time when he is expected to marry, a time to raise children, a time to retire. Although the norms vary somewhat from one socioeconomic, ethnic, or religious group to another, for any social group it can easily be demonstrated that norms and actual occurrences are closely related.

Age norms and age expectations operate as a system of social controls, as prods and brakes upon behavior, in some instances hastening an event, in others, delaying it. Men and women are aware not only of the social clocks that operate in various areas of their lives; but they are aware also of being "early," "late," or "on time" with regard to major life events.

Being on-time or off-time is not only a compelling basis for self-assessment with regard to family events, but also with regard to occupational careers, with both men and women comparing themselves with their friends or classmates or siblings in deciding whether or not they have made good.

Persons can describe ways in which being on-time or off-time has other psychological and social accompaniments. Thus, in a study of Army officers (the Army is a clearly age-graded occupation, where ex-

pectations with regard to age and grade are formally set forth in the official Handbook) the men who recognized themselves as being too long in grade—or late in career achievement—were also distinguishable on an array of social and psychological attitudes toward work, family, community participation, and personal adjustment.

When factors such as these are added to the inexorable biological changes, the individual develops a concept of the "normal, expectable life cycle"—a phrase which I have borrowed from Dr. Robert Butler and which owes much, of course, to Hartmann's "normal, expectable environment." Adults carry around in their heads, whether or not they can easily verbalize it, a set of anticipations of the normal, expectable life cycle. They internalize expectations of the consensually validated sequences of major life events—not only what those events should be, but when they should occur. They make plans and set goals along a time-line shaped by these expectations.

The individual is said to create a sense of self very early in life. Freud, for example, in describing the development of the ego, and George Mead, in describing the differentiation between the "I" and the "me," placed the development of self very early in childhood. But it is perhaps not until adulthood that the individual creates a sense of the life cycle; that is, an anticipation and acceptance of the inevitable sequence of events that will occur as men grow up, grow old and die—in adulthood, that he understands that the course of his own life will be similar to the lives of others, and that the turning points are inescapable. This ability to interpret the past and foresee the future, and to create for oneself a sense of the predictable life cycle differentiates the healthy adult personality from the unhealthy, and it underlies the adult's self-assessment.

The self-concept of the adult has the elements of the past contained within it. The adult thinks of himself in the present in terms of where he has come from; what he has become; how content he is at fifty compared to the time when he was forty.

All this differentiates the adult as subject from the psychologist as observer. The adult has a built-in dimension of thought that is the present-relative-to-the-past— but the psychologist has not yet created dimensions of this type in capturing the psychological realities of the life cycle and in studying antecedent-consequent relations. In fact, it is the specific aim of most investigators to keep separate Time 1 from Time 2 observations and evaluations, on the premise that to do otherwise is to contaminate the data.

To put this differently, to the subject, the blending of past and present is psychological reality. To the investigator, validity (and therefore, reality) lies in keeping time segments independent of each other.

Thus, to repeat, some of the problems that face us in attempting to build a psychology of the life cycle stem from the facts that the salient issues of the mental life are different for adults than for children; the underlying relations of the individual to his social environment are different; the relations of the investigator to his subject are different; and the salient dimensions psychologists use to describe and measure mental and emotional life *should* be different.

I am suggesting, then, that our foremost problem in studying the lifespan is to create a frame of reference and sets of dimensions that are appropriate to the subject matter, and that are valid in the sense that they are fitting ways of capturing reality. To do this, it might be added, we need first a great wealth of descriptive studies, based on various methods that stem from naturalistic observational approaches.

Let me turn now more specifically to the studies which are emerging in which the attempt is made to relate findings on childhood and adulthood in the lives of the same individual—in short, to longitudinal studies which form the foundation of a psychology of the life cycle.

The longitudinal studies may be seen, in overly simplified and overly dichotomized terms, as being of two major types: first are those I shall refer to as "trait" or "dimension" oriented, studies addressed to questions of stability and change along given dimensions of ability and personality; second are those I shall call "life-outcomes" oriented, those which pose such questions as these: What kind of child becomes the achieving adult? The middle-aged failure? The successful ager? The psychiatric casualty? What constellation of events are predictive of outcomes?

In the first type of research, the investigators have been preoccupied with such problems as whether or not the individual who is aggressive at age three is aggressive at age thirty, or whether the high I.Q. child turns out to be the high I.Q. adult. There are also studies in which the ipsative approach is taken, and in which the stability of personality types is the question being pursued—the difference being, that is, that attention is focused upon the patterns of traits rather than individual traits, and the degree to which these patterns show stability or change.

In such studies, the investigator is plagued with questions of validity of his measures over time—is the concept of aggression or intelligence the same concept for three- and thirty-year-olds? Are we measuring the same phenomenon? These studies have proceeded without regard to the events of the life cycle, and the passage of calendar time is itself taken to be the sufficient variable. As in Kagan and Moss' studies from birth to maturity, or Nancy Bayley's studies of cognitive development, or Oden's latest follow-up of the Terman gifted group, the presumption seems to be that the same changes can be expected between age three and thirty whether or not marriage has intervened, or parenthood, or job failure or widowhood. "Time" is treated as independent from the biological and social events that give substance to "time," and independent from the events that might be regarded as the probable psychological markers of time.

In studies of life-outcomes, we need, of course, studies of traits and dimensions; but we are in particular need of studies aimed at determining which life events produce change and which do not—which ones leave measurable traces in the personality structure, and which ones call forth new patterns of adaptation.

Let me illustrate: parenthood might be presumed to be an event that has a transforming effect upon the personality, whether one reasons from psychoanalytic theory, or role theory, or learning theory; and whether one conceptualizes the event in terms of elaboration and differentiation of the ego, or in terms of adjustment to a major new set of social roles, or in terms of the development of new sets of responses to the demands of a new significant other. Yet we have no systematic studies of the effects of parenthood upon personality development; and no good evidence that parenthood is more significant, say, than college attendance or marriage or widowhood.

To take another example: some of my own work on middle-aged women has led me to conclude that the menopause is not the transforming event in personality development that puberty is; nor is the departure of children from the home of the same importance as parenthood.

We need to establish which life events are the important ones, but we need to study also when the event occurs, in terms of its social "appropriateness." (To marry at age thirty is a different psychological event than to marry at age sixteen; and to be widowed at age forty may be more significant than to be widowed at age sixty-five, for in either case, the event comes off-time and does not fit the anticipations of the normal, expectable life cycle.)

Among the longitudinal and long term follow-up studies presently available, investigators have taken both prospective and retrospective approaches. They begin with a group of infants or young children and follow them forward in time; or they begin with a group of adults and look backward in their life histories to identify the predictors or antecedents of present adult status. In both instances, what is most striking is the relative lack of predictability from childhood to adulthood with regard to life-outcomes. To mention only a few very recent studies: Hoyt's review of the literature indicates that we cannot predict from school success to vocational success . . . Robins' study of deviant children grown up shows that while anti-social behavior in childhood is predictive of sociopathic behavior in adults, the withdrawn personality characteristics of childhood are not associated with later adult pathology of any kind . . . Rogler and Hollingshead's study in Puerto Rico indicates that experiences in childhood and adolescence of schizophrenic adults do not differ noticeably from those of persons who are not afflicted with the illness . . . Baller's follow-up of mid-life attainment of the mentally retarded shows low predictability from childhood, with persons of below-70 I.Q. faring vastly better than anyone anticipated.

I recognize that, in some ultimate sense, we may never be able to make satisfactory predictions regarding life-outcomes, no matter how well we chose our variables or how well we manage to identify the important and unimportant life events, for we shall probably never be able to predict the changes that will occur in an individual's social environment, nor the particular contingencies and accidents that will arise in an individual life, nor—equally important—the ways his life cycle is affected by those of the significant others with whom his life is intertwined. Furthermore, the psychologist, no matter how sophisticated his methods, will need the sociologist, the anthropologist, and the historian, to say nothing of the developmental biologist, to help him. Thus the study of lives will flourish only to the extent that a truly interdisciplinary behavioral science is created. Perhaps we shall have to leave the field to the creative writer, the philosopher, or the archivist for a long time still to come, and decide that the life cycle as a unit of study in the behavioral sciences is one with which we are not yet prepared to deal.

Yet we developmental psychologists are not likely to abandon the subject matter that intrigues us; and in the immediate future, as we work in our own areas, we can probably gain enormously in our ability to predict outcomes if we focus more of our attention upon the things that are of concern to the individuals we are studying—what the subject selects as important in his past and in his present; what he plans to do with his life; what he predicts will happen; and what strategies he elects —in short, if we make greater use of the subject himself as the reporting and predicting agent.

I am reminded in this connection that Jean McFarlane recently told me that after her intensive and intimate study of her subjects over a thirty-year period, she was continuously surprised to see how her people turned out. In going back over the data that she and Marjorie Honzik had painstakingly amassed, she found that much of what her subjects told her had been important to them when they were children or adolescents was not even to be found in her records—in other words, that which the investigators had regarded as important and had bothered to record was not the same as that which the subjects themselves had regarded as important at the time.

I suggest therefore that in future studies we pay more attention to gathering systematic and repeated self-reports and self-evaluations, and in doing so, to utilize what I shall call the "clinical" as well as the "observer's" approach. In the one case, the clinical psychologist tries to put himself into the frame of reference of his patient or client and to see the world through that person's eyes. In the other case, the "observer" psychologist brings his own frame of reference to the data and interprets according to his own theories.

We need to gather longitudinal data of both types (as by collecting autobiographies from our subjects at repeated intervals, and by creating a set of dimensions and measures that are appropriate to that data). We need, in other words, to use a double perspective: that of the observer and that of the person whose life it is.

In conclusion, I have been drawing attention to the discontinuities between a psychology of childhood and a psychology of adulthood, between the perspectives of the investigator and that of the subject himself, between the stances of the clinician and the psychometrician. If . . . we have presently available only a few elements of a lifespan developmental psychology, I am suggesting a few of the elements that are conspicuously missing.

2. THE LIFESPAN AS A FRAME OF REFERENCE IN PSYCHOLOGICAL RESEARCH

NANCY BAYLEY

The study of change in persons over time is recognized as an important aspect of psychological research and theory, concerning both children (development) and the elderly (decline). There is less heed paid, however, to the evidence that the processes of change over the lifespan are continuous even during the relatively stable adult years. Such evidence indicates that any segment of the lifespan should be considered appropriate for the investigation of psychological change in relation to age. Furthermore, these investigations may appropriately be directed toward practically all major fields of psychology: experimental, learning, personality, emotions, social, clinical, educational, and very obviously in such areas as intelligence and motivation.

Certain methods and procedures of study, it is true, are age-specific; and to this extent the particular tools and procedures to be applied in studying changes over time must differ with the age of the subjects. Yet the tools that have been devised for the study of the young, the middle-aged or the old can often be adapted for other ages, or they can be used in ways that facilitate the observation of changes with age. What I should like to propose, therefore, is that investigators in the various fields of psychology seriously undertake to include in their research designs, and more particularly in their theoretical constructs, one frame of reference that is concerned with the processes of change with age.

The Concept of Maturity

Actually, many who study either children or the aging are interested in the entire lifespan. Questions are repeatedly raised about what a given developmental trend will lead to; or what may have preceded a given adult behavior pattern. There are also questions of the rates at which children approach mature status in a given function, and whether changes in senescence parallel, or are of the same character as, changes in childhood. For those whose interests are primarily with adults, much of the recent emphasis in research is on the nature of changes from mature to old, that is, the process of aging. This kind of research implies a concept of the mature condition as a point of reference against which the processes of growth and of aging can be juxtaposed for comparison.

If this is so, then we should inquire into the nature of such a reference point, to consider just what is meant by the term "mature" as is applies to behavioral processes and functions. This consideration leads to the further questions of when, under what conditions, and in what ways a person is to be considered mature. Maturity as a general concept applied to human adults is neither a specific point in time nor a static condition that extends over a span of years, but is rather a complex series of ever-changing processes. There may, however, be long periods of relative stability in a given process or function once that function has reached its full development.

For many behavioral functions it is difficult to know just when they become mature. It is difficult because there are individual differences at all ages in the degree, or quality attained in most kinds of behavior. For such characteristics we cannot tell whether a person has reached his own most mature functioning in a given structure or function except in relation to his own performances at other periods of his life. For example, with few exceptions the epiphyses in the long bones of the hand and arm close toward the end of the second decade of life, and for certain purposes, this condition may be called "mature." When we measure intelligence, however, there is no point or stage of adult functioning which is reached by all persons, no level to which one can point and say that now the person's intelligence is mature. If a point is picked arbitrarily, there will be many who never reach it, and many who will go far beyond.

Furthermore, there is evidence that different abilities and qualities of the personality become mature at different times in the life of the individual. Each characteristic may be thought of as having its own schedule. Some functions mature early in life, others late. For example, the well-known studies of Lehman (1953) show differing ages at greatest intellectual achievement for mathematicians, for poets, for historians, and for philosophers. Some abilities, including those that draw heavily upon vocabulary and upon accumulated knowledge, maintain a high degree of efficiency for a long time. Others tend to deteriorate rapidly after reaching an early peak. This latter course of rapid growth and decline tends to be true of certain kinds of physical or athletic abilities that require a combination of strength, speed, and skill. For some behaviors (that is, such personality factors as emotional independence) it is doubtful whether the term "mature" can be applied, even though reference is often made to persons' maturity or immaturity in respect to them. To the extent that maturational changes do occur in these respects, they may be very subject to environmental conditions that determine when, indeed whether, they ever mature.

This train of thought leads to the necessity, for a comprehensive approach to the study of behavior, that we consider the whole life process as a frame of reference.

Any behavior that is being studied, if it is to be adequately interpreted, must be seen in reference to the age or ages of the individuals under study and to their probable status in the developmental cycle. For example, in studying learning, not only the fact that the subject is animal or human, but also the fact that he is six months, six years, twenty-six years, or sixty years old will determine the conditions of the experiment, the kinds of behaviors to be studied, and the selection of suitable rewards or punishments. In general, change is most rapid and most obvious at the two ends of the lifespan, in infancy-childhood and in old-age senility. However, even though it tends to be forgotten, and even though the various behavioral functions of the young adult are often treated as stable, change is continuous, right through the "mature" adult period. The processes of maturation of growth and subsequent decline never cease, whatever the structure or function being considered.

Age as a Variable

For many practical reasons, it is useful and convenient in psychological experiments to study a function in its current condition, and to put aside for the time being any consideration of change over time. The nature of the function itself is the object of study. An experiment is set up to investigate learning, or perception, or agression, or fear, or maternal behavior, or peer-group interactions; and the experiment is carried out on some selected population, usually all of whom are about the same age. This is obviously a procedure to be encouraged. It is important and necessary, and it provides the bulk of the experimentation in psychology. Psychological processes are so complex that they must at certain stages in knowledge be broken down into small, meaningful segments that can be studied in relative isolation.

A serious limitation of much of this type of research, however, is that the investigator often forgets to take into account the context from which he has abstracted. He continues to study various aspects of a specific bit of behavior, using essentially the same population of subjects for each new experiment. He then presents his findings as isolated items of information; or (often by implication only) he generalizes his findings and assumes that what he has learned, for instance, about group leadership in twenty-year-old males, or about shock avoidance learning in a given strain of albino rats, will apply equally to humans of all ages.

The inadequacy of this form of reasoning seems obvious when it is pointed out. Nevertheless, it tends to persist in practice. What is needed, perhaps, is a broader interpretation of the concept of comparative psychology. This term is usually applied to the study of animals as it throws light upon human behavior. To this end our animal experiments and observations are compared with pertinent aspects of human behavior. Investigators must be careful in making comparative interpretations to take account of the differences as well as the similarities between the animal under study and the human. Consistent with this reasoning, it should be kept in mind that if we study, for example, certain social responses of college sophomore men, then the results of such a study may apply to other male college sophomores, but not necessarily to populations who are older or younger, or females, or differently educated, or from a different cultural or ethnic group.

The relevant characteristics of a population to be studied for a given psychological function are legion. It should go without saying that if these relevant characteristics are not controlled or accounted for, the experimenter's conclusions may go far astray. If, then, the investigator is constantly alert to seek out and to identify these relevant factors, he will continue to find new and often unexpected ones that must be taken into account.

The earlier studies on the effects of environment on mental growth, for example Bayley and Jones (1937), were concerned with obvious variables such as years of schooling, and types of occupation. They took no cognizance, however, of some of the more subtle variations such as emotional climate in the home, or the impact of different cultural value systems upon intellectual motivation. Such factors as the latter are now regularly considered to be environmental variables with which one must reckon. The monograph of Sontag, Baker, and Nelson (1958) is a good example of a study in which parental attitudes and behaviors were included in investigating the causes of change in I.Q.

We are only beginning to be aware of the possible effects on various kinds of mental functioning of *age differences* in such things as motivation, the quality of the subject's education, and of his accumulated life experiences. This is an area that is open for much exploration and one that has great potentialities. We have learned through experience with infants and young children to adapt experimental procedures to their interests and capacities. We find, for example, that children usually cannot be motivated for learning tasks with the same lures as are used for monkeys; and that the verbal incentives used to encourage school children to strive for success in intellectual tasks are inapplicable with six-month-olds. We have not yet considered very seriously the need to find out, or to utilize in our experimental designs, what we already know about pertinent aspects of older persons' motivations, preoccupations and physical limitations.

For example, in studying the nature of intellectual functions and in developing tests for measuring intelligence we have become aware of the need to adapt the specific test items and procedures to the different cultural and socioeconomic populations to be studied. In the same way, we need to make the test items and procedures age-appropriate, to make them more relevant to the motivations, the life situations, and the goals of persons at each period in the lifespan. In this respect we have done fairly well with infants, children, and youths, but we have been remiss with intelligence tests for older people. It is customary to apply to older populations those tests that were originally designed for young (usually college-age) adults. In doing so, we have overlooked important areas in motivation, preoccupations, and daily experiences that are most common in older people. Consequently our interpretations of the intellectual processes and capacities of older people may well be faulty.

Pressey has been concerned with this problem, and he and Demming (Demming and Pressey, 1957) have devised tests of intelligence that are especially designed for measuring the abilities of older persons. Their results show consistently higher scores for populations over thirty than are found with the conventional intelligence tests. As has been noted before, whether measured intelligence decreases, increases, or remains unchanged after age of twenty-five is at least in part a function of the tests used. We should keep in mind the question whether the tests are equally "fair" (in terms of meaningfulness and motivating power) at all ages.

The foregoing is but one way in which psychological researchers need to gain sophistication about the conditions that may be important in determining behavior. Let us consider some others which could profitably be reviewed through a lifespan orientation.

When measuring a behavior out of context, as in an "unnatural" laboratory environment, we may inadvertently change the relevant aspects of the conditions for response so that the particular responses are not representative of the behaviors we started out to measure. This has been pointed out by anima ecologists, who have shown many differences between the behavior of the rat or the monkey, for example, when in its natural "wild" environments and when in its laboratory cages. It is often necessary repeatedly to check the results of laboratory experiments by returning to natural life situations for further observations of the behaviors under study. What is more, the relative importance of the laboratory–natural life differences may shift with the populations under study, and with the age at which an animal started his life in a cage.

The point to be made here is that we have tended to neglect the important environmental differences that are related to the age of the persons under study. Some of these differences are obvious; others are less so; and some may not become evident until revealed by further studies. Let us consider some of the factors, both external and internal, as they relate to the infant under one year, the preschooler, the school-age child, the adolescent, the young adult, the middle-aged, the elderly, and the senescent. Within the organism itself there are such age-related variables as sensory acuity, energy, motor coordination and agility, knowledge and experience (or apperceptive mass), awareness of and outlook toward life expectancies, and attitudes toward other people. Also, as Barker and his associates (1955) have shown, social interactions and roles change markedly with age. Many of these conditions are related, as both cause and effect, to the attitudes toward and treatment of these individuals by those persons with whom they interact.

Cultural stereotypes attribute different characteristics to the different age groups, but an individual may not see himself as having these conventionally assigned attributes. Depending on the nature of the problem, any of these and other variables could, if not controlled or taken into account, influence the data of an experiment.

Longitudinal Studies

Nothing has thus far been said about long-itudinal studies, in which the same subjects are remeasured or retested at successive intervals as they grow up or grow older. The points already mentioned could apply to either cross-sectional or longitudinal studies. However, some kinds of inquiry are better adapted to one or the other of these methods.

There are certain kinds of information, of particular relevance to the lifespan frame of reference, that can be obtained only by means of longitudinal studies. Fortunately, a longitudinal study need not span the entire life cycle of any group of persons. Of necessity, we deal with portions and segments usually a few years, of our subjects' lives. The longer the time period over which the researcher can reassess the same population, the more we can learn about individual patterns of growth and change. By studying the same persons over time, we can begin to see sequences of etiological complexes. We become alerted to dynamic interactions between the organism and his environment. When a person is studied only once, as he appears in relation to the rest of the sample, there is a tendency to make static interpretations and evaluations. Subject X, for instance, on the basis of a single set of observations and tests, is defined as being anxious, as lacking in energy, as having an average I.Q., as having a slow reaction time. Observed repeatedly over time, this same subject will be seen to change in many of these respects. We find we must look for the reasons for the change both in X and in his environment. Why, for example, was he anxious at one time, but less so at another time? We become able to note such things as the effects of long-continued emotional climates as they operate to decrease or to enhance intellectual functions.

Just such a study as this was made recently by Sontag and his associates (1958) on records from the Fels Institutes pop-ulation. By observing growth changes over time, we learn something of the processes of maturation of inherent characteristics, and we are able to study the effects of specific kinds of experiences on the course of development. Another study relevant to this point is that of Macfarlane, Allen, and Honzik (1954) in which the incidence of problems reported in a longitudinal sample was found to change over time with the age and relative maturity of the children. A series of studies by Bayley and Schaefer, so far published only in part (Schaefer and Bayley, 1963; Bayley and Schaefer, 1960a, 1960b), indicate changes in both maternal behaviors and child behaviors over time.

As already mentioned, most studies of this kind have been made for those parts of the lifespan in which change is most rapid. We now have a considerable accumulation of data on development of the child, and we are rapidly getting data on some aspects of the retrogressive processes in the elderly. Examples of the latter are the studies of Kallmann and his associates (1951, 1961) of aged twins.

The processes of change and of adaptations during the middle years are much less adequately documented. However, several populations who were studied as children are now being studied as young adults. Perhaps the pioneer study in this respect is Terman and Oden's series of reappraisals of gifted children as adults (1947, 1959). With many of these subjects being studied again at an average of about fifty-five, the study has covered a span of almost forty-five years in the lives of these subjects. In several studies, such as those of Lowell Kelly (1955) and of Owens (1953), adult populations have been remeasured after long intervals. Other follow-ups of adult populations first studied as children are based on research programs that were started somewhat more recently, and most of the subjects, therefore, are at present in their thirties. These include the three growth studies at Berkeley, California (for example, Tuddenham, 1959), the Minnesota adult studies of populations studied as school children (Anderson and Harris, 1959) and, to some degree, the continued observations of subjects at the Fels Institute and at the University of Colorado. In most of these studies there are large accumulations of records, including both mental and physical data.

From these various populations, we should soon be getting much valuable information about relationships and growth trends between childhood and adulthood for both mental and physical characteristics. The very fact that these are longitudinal studies gives assurance that the research programs will be oriented toward processes of change with age. There will be an effort made to discover relationships between adult mental processes (both intellectual and emotional) and all available childhood records that might be relevant, concerning both the children themselves and their childhood environments.

Considerable thought and effort should be put into the planning of adult follow-up programs. For example, there is the importance, in assessing intelligence, of maintaining continuity by use of the same instrument at different ages. The fact that the test is objectively the same (for example, the Terman Group Test, or the Stanford-Binet, or even the Wechsler Scales) does not insure that the tests tap the same, or the most relevant, intellectual functions at all ages. In order to study age changes in intellectual capacity, it will be necessary to devise and standardize (on a cross-sectional sample) a series of tests that are designed to secure high motivation and to be valid measures of ability for several different adult age-groups. If we can devise and standardize such a series of age-appropriate scales, which for convenience may be referred to as tests B, C, D, and E, then in longitudinal studies it might be possible to evaluate changes in intellectual functions by giving these tests in a succession of partial repetitions. That is, if, in the original study, some standard

test, A, had been given at age sixteen and earlier, the first of the adult follow-ups might include test A and the new test B. Subsequent rounds of testing could follow some such pattern as: tests B and C, A and C, B and D, D and E, and C and E. Such a procedure would keep the testing sessions from becoming too long at any one time, and would have the further advantage of dealing with test material that would always be appropriate for the subjects.

There may be less of a problem in adapting, for age-appropriateness, such instruments as projective tests and other measures of emotional and personality variables. However, it is pertinent to investigate this aspect of any test one plans to use. Again it may be pointed out that this kind of age-adjustment in personality tests has been considered more often in making adaptations for young children than for older adults.

Relations Between Growth and Decline

Because the beginning and end of the life cycle are both periods of rapid change, there is a tendency to compare the two periods and to look for similarities in them. Also, because the deterioration in abilities makes the older person more dependent and in many ways more "childlike," there is the temptation to consider these deteriorative processes as direct reversals of developmental processes. There are, however, many differences. The young nervous system and the entire anatomy of the child are very different from those of the aged individual. The reasons for less than mature or optimal functioning are very different in the young and the old. The processes of change have different rates, and they appear to be controlled by very different, perhaps quite uncorrelated, conditions.

An area of research that has been little explored, but that could prove to be very fruitful, is that of comparisons between infancy and senescence—or, to expand the range, the total period of growth and of decline. We may inquire into the nature of individual differences in rates of growth versus rates of decline, and ask what are the determinants of these opposing processes. In what ways do they seem to be intredependent? Do those persons who mature early in a function show earlier decline, possibly a shorter lifespan, a shorter span of mature function, or a more rapid decline once the senescent process has started? It is possible that the rates of change in the three stages (growth, maturity, and decline), are quite unrelated, or that there are differently correlated rates in different processes.

Across species there is clear evidence that animals with shorter lifespans have relatively rapid growth and early decline. Whether or not this is true within a given species is another question, although it seems plausible that this might be so. We can find in humans some meager evidence that seems to support such a hypothesis. For example, in several longitudinal studies of early behavior development (Bayley, 1933; Furfey and Muehlenbein, 1932), there is a slight negative correlation between mental test scores earned in the first six months of life and scores earned after three years. A study of Bantu infants (Geber and Dean, 1957) reports great precocity, by our test standards, in infants under six months; but this precocity diminishes with age, and disappears by the time the children are two or three years old. There is some evidence that children who by school-age score highest in intelligence often start slowly, and are relatively retarded in the first six or eight months of life. At the other end of the lifespan, a number of investigators (Jones, 1955) have found relatively greater decrement in scores earned by those persons in the lower educational and occupational levels. None of these studies has been carried out with sufficient controls to give clear-cut answers to the question of possible relations between rates of change and levels of ability. Some full lifespan studies may

be necessary before we can know whether those slow-starting babies are the same persons who continue to be intellectually alert in old age. Other conditions, such as adult life experiences, could be the important determinants of rates of senescent decline.

Constancies of Personality

Another recurring concern of those who study the same persons over time is to identify those basic, underlying constancies of personality that characterize the individual, and to chart the course of their developmental changes. Many behaviors, as well as physical characteristics, change with age. Being age-specific, a behavior that is appropriate at one stage of development is often very inappropriate at another. A two-month-old is expected to communicate his wants by crying; a four-year-old, by gestures and words. An age-reversal of these behaviors would certainly be remarkable. The manner of expressing one's emotions changes with age, and in order to evaluate degrees of "emotionality" at different ages, we must work out a means of relating these emotional behaviors to scales of intensity that include the age-appropriateness of each behavior pattern.

In many respects there appears to be no continuity in traits or reaction-tendencies, and no possibility of predicting from observations made at one age what can be expected in the same person a few years later. Yet in spite of the fact that our measures often indicate little or no consistency, we intuitively feel, and believe that we recognize, constancies of personality and behavioral tendencies. The problem is to be able to devise ways of documenting and scoring these characteristics so that they may be compared, evaluated, and used to predict later patterns of behavior.

This is an important and baffling problem, for example, in studies of the etiology of schizophrenia and other mental disorders. Studies of run-of-the-mill behavior problems in childhood (for example, Macfarlane, Allen, and Honzik, 1954) have shown that for the most part problems tend to be age-limited. Certain problem behaviors occur at certain ages, and not at other ages. One set of problems is "outgrown," and replaced by another set. The occurrence of a problem in a child at one age does not usually signify that this child will continue to have problems, even in a different guise, at his next stage of development.

However, some basic reaction-tendencies, or deviations in patterns of sensitivity, seem to make some people more and others less vulnerable to environmental hazards. If these individual differences in sensitivity or vulnerability persist, perhaps they can be measured and studied in relation to their age-related manifestations, and to tendencies toward given patterns of pathology. The framework within which to look for these underlying constancies may be available in Freudian theory, or in some variant conception of dynamic developmental processes; or it may be found in such physical variables as hormonal or biochemical balance, or in inherent genetic characteristics. Schaefer and Bayley (1963), for example, found for the Berkeley Growth Study children that most consistent behaviors observed were activity and speed of action. These behaviors in the first two years were correlated with positive task-oriented behaviors in boys through age twelve, but for girls the r's were negative with task-oriented behaviors in childhood, though positive with adolescent extraverted, aggressive behaviors. These correlational trends point to the further probability of sex differences in the processes of change or stability over time.

There is thus the hope that we may find persistent underlying attitudes and reaction-tendencies that determine indentifiable sequences of age-related or maturity-related behavioral patterns. In the past, the efforts to identify such tendencies and patterns have been mostly by means of retrospective studies of the mentally ill or the emotionally disturbed. This approach has been found inadequate because of both the atypical selection of subjects, and the selective biases in the subjects' memories. Researchers in this field are now turning more often to longitudinal studies (which are prospective rather than retrospective), or to the records of extant studies, to check their hypotheses.

In the analysis of personality factors and of mental pathologies the age-specific behavior tendencies may well be studied profitably by cross-sectional methods. But the durability and persistence of the basic personalities can be learned by the more tedious longitudinal process.

In this paper I have touched upon a variety of ways in which it seems to me that psychological research will benefit when it is planned, carried out, and interpreted within the frame of reference of the lifespan and of the continuous processes of change that characterize all behavior. This frame of reference will affect our understanding of the concept of maturity; it will emphasize the relevance of changing functions, experiences and motivations for any particular behaviors under consideration; and it will help direct attention to ways of improving various testing instruments.

The longitudinal studies lend themselves to investigation of many important questions that can only be answered definitely by observations of the same persons over time. We should continue to explore ways in which to utilize more fully the data from the longitudinal studies that are now in progress, as well as to institute new ones. One relatively unexplored field in longitudinal research is the comparison of the processes of development with those of decline. Another important but difficult problem is to identify underlying persistent and predictable qualities of personality, to chart their course over the lifespan, and to study their causes and their responsiveness to re-education. And, of course, the last word has by no means been said about age-trends in intellectual capacities. Better tools can give us much better information about the nature of intelligence.

Let us hope that there will be others, in addition to those whose research is specifically oriented toward processes of change in the young and the old, who will work within this frame of reference in carrying on their researches. More adequate knowledge of the processes of behavioral change with age should serve to improve both the science and the practice of psychology.

Summary

Psychological theory and research will benefit in many ways if the research is planned, carried out, and interpreted within the frame of reference of the lifespan and the continuous processes of change that characterize all behavior. This frame of reference will affect our understanding of the concept of maturity; it will emphasize the relevance of changing functions, experiences, and motivations to any particular behaviors under consideration; and it will help direct attention to ways of improving various testing instruments. It is of relevance both to cross-sectional and longitudinal studies. Not only are cross-sectional studies needed for age-specific normative data. All behavioral research, including studies of restricted and atypical populations and behaviors, should be oriented in regard to the subjects' age or stage of development as well as their other characteristics. Longitudinal studies lend themselves to investigation of many important questions that can only be answered definitely by observations of the same subjects over time. Questions to be explored by this method include comparisons of the processes of development with those of decline, the identification of underlying persistent and predictable qualities of personality, and individual age-trends in intellectual capacities.

References

ANDERSON, J. E. and D. B. HARRIS. *A survey of children's adjustment over time: a report to the people of Nobles County.* Minneapolis: University of Minnesota, 1959.

BARKER, R. G., and H. F. WRIGHT. *Midwest and its children.* Evanston: Row, Peterson, 1955.

BAYLEY, NANCY. "Mental growth during the first three years. A developmental study of sixty-one children by repeated tests." *Genet. Psychol. Monogr. 14:* No. 1, 1933.

BAYLEY, NANCY, and H. E. JONES. "Environmental correlates of mental and motor development: a cumulative study from infancy to six years." *Child Develpm. 8:* 329–341, 1937.

BAYLEY, NANCY, and E. S. SCHAEFER. "Relationships between socioeconomic variables and the behavior of mothers toward young children." *J. Genet. Psychol. 96:* 61–77, 1960a.

BAYLEY, NANCY, and E. S. SCHAEFER. "Maternal behavior and personality development: data from the Berkeley Growth Study." *Psychiatric Res. Rep. 13:* 155–173, 1960b.

DEMMING, J. A., and S. L. PRESSEY. "Tests 'indigenous' to the adult and older years." *J. Counsel. Psychol. 4:* 144–148, 1957.

FURFEY, P. H., and J. MUEHLENBEIN. "The validity of infant intelligence tests." *J. Genet. Psychol. 40:* 219–223, 1932.

GEBER, M., and R. F. A. DEAN. "The state of development of newborn African children." *Lancet i:* 1216, 1957.

JONES, H. E. *Age changes in mental ability. Old age in the modern world.* London: Livingstone, 1955, pp. 267–274.

KALLMANN, F. J. "Genetic factors in aging: comparative and longitudinal observations on a senescent twin population." In: Hoch, P. H., and J. Zubin (eds.), *Psychopathology of aging.* New York: Grune & Stratton, 1961.

KALLMANN, F. J., LISSY FEINGOLD, and EVA BONDY. "Comparative adaptational, social, and psychometric data on the life histories of senescent twins." *Amer. J. Hum. Genet. 3:* 65–73, 1951.

KELLEY, E. L. "Consistency of the adult personality." *Amer. Psychologist 10:* 659–681, 1955.

LEHMAN, H. C. *Age and achievement.* Princeton: Princeton University Press, 1953.

MACFARLANE, JEAN W., LUCILE ALLEN, and MARJORIE P. HONZIK. *A developmental study of the behavior problems of normal children between twenty-one months and fourteen years.* University of California Publications in Child Development, 2; p. 222. Berkeley: University of California Press, 1954.

OWENS, WILLIAM A., JR. "Age and mental abilities: a longitudinal study." *Genet. Psychol. Monogr. 48:* 3–54, 1953.

SCHAEFER, E. S., and NANCY BAYLEY. "Maternal behavior, child behavior and their intercorrelations from infancy through adolescence." *Monogr. Soc. Res. Child Develpm. 28:* 1963.

SONTAG, L. W., C. T. BAKER, and V. L. NELSON. "Mental growth and personality development: a longitudinal study." *Monogr. Soc. Res. Child Develpm. 23:* 1958.

TERMAN, L. M., and M. H. ODEN. *The gifted child grows up: twenty-five years' follow-up of a superior group, genetic studies of genius.* Stanford, Calif.: Stanford University Press, 1947.

TERMAN, L. M., and M. H. ODEN. *The gifted group of midlife: thirty-five years' follow-up of the superior child, genetic studies of genius.* Stanford, Calif.: Stanford University Press, 1959.

TUDDENHAM, R. D. "Constancy of personality ratings over two decades." *Genet. Psychol. Monogr. 60:* 3–29, 1959.

3. EIGHT AGES OF MAN

ERIK H. ERIKSON

1. Basic Trust vs. Basic Mistrust

The first demonstration of social trust in the baby is the ease of his feeding, the depth of his sleep, the relaxation of his bowels. The experience of a mutual regulation of his increasingly receptive capacities with the maternal techniques of provision gradually helps him to balance the discomfort caused by the immaturity of homeostasis with which he was born. In his gradually increasing waking hours he finds that more and more adventures of the senses arouse a feeling of familiarity, of having coincided with a feeling of inner goodness. Forms of comfort, and people associated with them, become as familiar as the gnawing discomfort of the bowels. The infant's first social achievement, then, is his willingness to let the mother out of sight without undue anxiety or rage, because she has become an inner certainty as well as an outer predictability. Such consistency, continuity, and sameness of experience provide a rudimentary sense of ego identity which depends, I think, on the recognition that there is an inner population of remembered and anticipated sensations and images which are firmly correlated with the outer population of familiar and predictable things and people.

What we here call trust coincides with what Therese Benedek has called confidence. If I prefer the word "trust," it is because there is more naïveté and more mutuality in it: an infant can be said to be trusting where it would go too far to say that he has confidence. The general state of trust, furthermore, implies not only that one has learned to rely on the sameness and continuity of the outer providers but also that one may trust oneself and the capacity of one's own organs to cope with urges; and that one is able to consider oneself trustworthy enough so that the providers will not need to be on guard lest they be nipped.

The constant tasting and testing of the relationship between inside and outside meets its crucial test during the rages of the biting stage, when the teeth cause pain from within and when outer friends either prove of no avail or withdraw from the only action which promises relief: biting. Not that teething itself seems to cause all the dire consequences sometimes ascribed to it. . . . the infant now is driven to "grasp" more, but he is apt to find desired presences elusive; nipple and breast, and the mother's focused attention and care. Teething seems to have a prototypal significance and may well be the model for the masochistic tendency to assure cruel comfort by enjoying one's hurt whenever one is unable to prevent a significant loss.

In psychopathology the absence of basic trust can best be studied in infantile schizophrenia, while lifelong underlying weakness of such trust is apparent in adult personalities in whom withdrawal into schizoid and depressive states is habitual. The re-establishment of a state of trust has been found to be the basic requirement for therapy in these cases. For no matter what conditions may have caused a psychotic break, the bizarreness and withdrawal in the behavior of many very sick individuals hide an attempt to recover social mutuality by a testing of the borderlines between senses and physical reality, between words and social meanings.

Psychoanalysis assumes the early process of differentiation between inside and outside to be the origin of projection and introjection which remain some of our deepest and most dangerous defense mechanisms. In introjection we feel and act as if an outer goodness had become an inner certainty. In projection, we experience an inner harm as an outer one: we endow significant people with the evil which actually is in us. These two mechanisms, then, projection and introjection, are assumed to be modeled after whatever goes on in infants when they would like to externalize pain and internalize pleasure, an intent which must yield to the testimony of the maturing senses and ultimately of reason. These mechanisms are, more or less normally, reinstated in acute crises of love, trust, and faith in adulthood and can characterize irrational attitudes toward adversaries and enemies in masses of "mature" individuals.

The firm establishment of enduring patterns for the solution of the nuclear conflict of basic trust versus basic mistrust in mere existence is the first task of the ego, and thus first of all a task for maternal care. But let it be said here that the amount of trust derived from earliest infantile experience does not seem to depend on absolute quantities of food or demonstrations of love, but rather on the quality of the maternal relationship. Mothers create a sense of trust in their children by that kind of administration which in its quality combines sensitive care of the baby's individual needs and a firm sense of personal trustworthiness within the trusted framework of their culture's life style. This forms the basis in the child for a sense of identity which will later combine a sense of being "all right," of being oneself, and of becoming what other people trust one will become. There are, therefore (within certain limits . . . defined as the "musts" of child care), few frustrations in either this or the following stages which the growing child cannot endure if the frustration leads to the ever-renewed experience of greater sameness and stronger continuity of development, toward a final integration of the individual life cycle with some meaningful wider belongingness. Parents must not only have certain ways of guiding by prohibition and permission; they must also be able to represent to the child a deep, an almost somatic conviction that there is a meaning to what they are doing. Ultimately, children become neurotic not from frustrations, but from the lack or loss of societal meaning in these frustrations.

But even under the most favorable circumstances, this stage seems to introduce into psychic life (and become prototypal for) a sense of inner division and universal nostalgia for a paradise forfeited. It is against this powerful combination of a sense of having been deprived, of having been divided, and of having been abandoned—that basic trust must maintain itself throughout life.

Each successive stage and crisis has a special relation to one of the basic elements of society, and this for the simple reason that the human life cycle and man's institutions have evolved together. [Here] we can do little more than mention, after the description of each stage, what basic element of social organization is related to it. This relation is twofold: man brings to these institutions the remnants of his infantile mentality and his youthful fervor, and he receives from them—as long as they manage to maintain their actuality—a reinforcement of his infantile gains.

The parental faith which supports the trust emerging in the newborn has throughout history sought its institutional safeguard (and, on occasion, found its greatest enemy) in organized religion. Trust born of care is, in fact, the touchstone of the *actuality* of a given religion. All religions have in common the periodical childlike surrender to a Provider or providers who dispense earthly fortune as well as spiritual health; some demonstration of man's smallness by way of reduced posture and humble gesture; the admission in prayer and song of misdeeds, of misthoughts, and of evil intentions; fer-

vent appeal for inner unification by divine guidance; and finally, the insight that individual trust must become a common faith, individual mistrust a commonly formulated evil, while the individual's restoration must become part of the ritual practice of many, and must become a sign of trustworthiness in the community.[1] [It has been] illustrated how tribes dealing with one segment of nature develop a collective magic which seems to treat the Supernatural Providers of food and fortune as if they were angry and must be appeased by prayer and self-torture. Primitive religions, the most primitive layer in all religions, and the religious layer in each individual, abound with efforts at atonement which try to make up for vague deeds against a maternal matrix and try to restore faith in the goodness of one's strivings and in the kindness of the powers of the universe.

Each society and each age must find the institutionalized form of reverence which derives vitality from its world-image—from predestination to indeterminacy. The clinician can only observe that many are proud to be without religion whose children cannot afford their being without it. On the other hand, there are many who seem to derive a vital faith from social action or scientific pursuit. And again, there are many who profess faith, yet in practice breathe mistrust both of life and man.

2. Autonomy vs. Shame and Doubt

In describing the growth and the crises of the human person as a series of alternative basic attitudes such as trust vs. mistrust, we take recourse to the term a "sense of," although, like a "sense of health," or a "sense of being unwell," such "senses"

---

[1] This is the communal and psychosocial side of religion. Its often paradoxical relation to the spirituality of the individual is a matter not to be treated briefly and in passing (see *Young Man Luther*). (E.H.E.)

pervade surface and depth, consciousness and the unconscious. They are, then, at the same time, ways of *experiencing* accessible to introspection; ways of *behaving*, observable by others; and unconscious *inner states* determinable by test and analysis. It is important to keep these three dimensions in mind, as we proceed.

Muscular maturation sets the stage for experimentation with two simultaneous sets of social modalities: holding on and letting go. As is the case with all of these modalities, their basic conflicts can lead in the end to either hostile or benign expectations and attitudes. Thus, to hold can become a destructive and cruel retaining or restraining, and it can become a pattern of care: to have and to hold. To let go, too, can turn into an inimical letting loose of destructive forces, or it can become a relaxed "to let pass" and "to let be."

Outer control at this stage, therefore, must be firmly reassuring. The infant must come to feel that the basic faith in existence, which is the lasting treasure saved from the rages of the oral stage, will not be jeopardized by this about-face of his, this sudden violent wish to have a choice, to appropriate demandingly, and to eliminate stubbornly. Firmness must protect him against the potential anarchy of his as yet untrained sense of discrimination, his inability to hold on and to let go with discretion. As his environment encourages him to "stand on his own feet," it must protect him against meaningless and arbitrary experiences of shame and of early doubt.

The latter danger is the one best known to us. For if denied the gradual and well-guided experience of the autonomy of free choice (or if, indeed, weakened by an initial loss of trust) the child will turn against himself all his urge to discriminate and to manipulate. He will overmanipulate himself, he will develop a precocious conscience. Instead of taking possession of things in order to test them by purposeful repetition, he will become ob-

sessed by his own repetitiveness. By such obsessiveness, of course, he then learns to repossess the environment and to gain power by stubborn and minute control, where he could not find large-scale mutual regulation. Such hollow victory is the infantile model for a compulsion neurosis. It is also the infantile source of later attempts in adult life to govern by the letter, rather than by the spirit.

Shame is an emotion insufficiently studied, because in our civilization it is so early and easily absorbed by guilt. Shame supposes that one is completely exposed and conscious of being looked at: in one word, self-conscious. One is visible and not ready to be visible; which is why we dream of shame as a situation in which we are stared at in a condition of incomplete dress, in night attire, "with one's pants down." Shame is early expressed in an impulse to bury one's face, or to sink, right then and there, into the ground. But this, I think, is essentially rage control against the self. He who is ashamed would like to force the world not to look at him, not to notice his exposure. He would like to destroy the eyes of the world. Instead he must wish for his own invisibility. This potentiality is abundantly used in the educational method of "shaming" used so exclusively by some primitive peoples. Visual shame precedes auditory guilt, which is a sense of badness to be had all by oneself when nobody watches and when everything is quiet—except the voice of the superego. Such shaming exploits an increasing sense of being small, which can develop only as the child stand up and as his awareness permits him to note the relative measures of size and power.

Too much shaming does not lead to genuine propriety but to a secret determination to try to get away with things, unseen—if, indeed, it does not result in defiant shamelessness. There is an impressive American ballad in which a murderer to be hanged on the gallows before the eyes of the community, instead of feeling duly chastened, begins to berate the on-lookers, ending every salvo of defiance with the words, "God damn your eyes." Many a small child, shamed beyond en-durance, may be in a chronic mood (al-though not in possession of either the courage or the words) to express defiance in similar terms. What I mean by this sinister reference is that there is a limit to a child's and an adult's endurance in the face of demands to consider himself, his body, and his wishes as evil and dirty, and to his belief in the infallibility of those who pass such judgment. He may be apt to turn things around, and to consider as evil only the fact that they exist: his chance will come when they are gone, or when he will go from them.

Doubt is the brother of shame. Where shame is dependent on the consciousness of being upright and exposed, doubt, so clinical observation leads me to believe, has much to do with a consciousness of having a front and a back—and especially a "behind." For this reverse area of the body, with its aggressive and libidinal focus in the sphincters and in the but-tocks, cannot be seen by the child, and yet it can be dominated by the will of others. The "behind" is the small being's dark continent, an area of the body which can be magically dominated and effectively invaded by those who would attack one's power of autonomy and who would desig-nate as evil those products of the bowels which were felt to be all right when they were being passed. This basic sense of doubt in whatever one has left behind forms a substratum for later and more verbal forms of compulsive doubting; this finds its adult expression in paranoiac fears concerning hidden persecutors and secret persecutions threatening from be-hind (and from within the behind).

This stage, therefore, becomes decisive for the ratio of love and hate, cooperation and willfulness, freedom of self-expression and its suppression. From a sense of self-control without loss of self-esteem comes a lasting sense of good will and pride; from a sense of loss of self-control and of foreign overcontrol comes a lasting pro-pensity for doubt and shame.

If, to some reader, the "negative" po-tentialities of our stages seem overstated throughout, we must remind him that this is not only the result of a preoccupation with clinical data. Adults, and seemingly mature and unneurotic ones, display a sensitivity concerning a possible shameful "loss of face" and fear of being attacked "from behind" which is not only highly irrational and in contrast to the knowledge available to them, but can be of fateful import if related sentiments influence, for example, interracial and international policies.

We have related basic trust to the in-stitution of religion. The lasting need of the individual to have his will reaffirmed and delineated within an adult order of things which at the same time reaffirms and delineates the will of others has an institutional safeguard in the *principle of law and order*. In daily life as well as in the high courts of law—domestic and in-ternational—this principle apportions to each his privileges and his limitations, his obligations and his rights. A sense of rightful dignity and lawful independence on the part of adults around him gives to the child of good will the confident expec-tation that the kind of autonomy fostered in childhood will not lead to undue doubt or shame in later life. Thus the sense of autonomy fostered in the child and modi-fied as life progresses serves (and is served by) the preservation in economic and political life of a sense of justice.

3. Initiative vs. Guilt

There is in every child at every stage a new miracle of vigorous unfolding, which constitutes a new hope and a new respon-sibility for all. Such is the sense and the pervading quality of initiative. The cri-teria for all these senses and qualities are the same: a crisis, more or less beset with fumbling and fear, is resolved, in that the child suddenly seems to "grow together" both in his person and in his body. He appears "more himself," more loving, relaxed and brighter in his judgment, more activated and activating. He is in free possession of a surplus of energy which permits him to forget failures quickly and to approach what seems desirable (even if it also seems uncertain and even dangerous) with undiminished and more accurate direction. Initiative adds to autonomy the quality of undertaking, planning and "attacking" a task for the sake of being active and on the move, where before self-will, more often than not, inspired acts of defiance or, at any rate, protested independence.

I know that the very word "initiative," to many, has an American, and industrial, connotation. Yet, initiative is a necessary part of every act, and man needs a sense of initiative for whatever he learns and does, from fruit-gathering to a system of enterprise.

The ambulatory stage and that of infantile genitality add to the inventory of basic social modalities that of "making," first in the sense of "being on the make." There is no simpler, stronger word for it; it suggests pleasure in attack and conquest. In the boy, the emphasis remains on phallic-intrusive modes; in the girl it turns to modes of "catching" in more aggressive forms of snatching or in the milder form of making oneself attractive and endearing.

The danger of this stage is a sense of guilt over the goals contemplated and the acts initiated in one's exuberant enjoyment of new locomotor and mental power: acts of aggressive manipulation and coercion which soon go far beyond the executive capacity of organism and mind and therefore call for an energetic halt on one's contemplated initiative. While autonomy concentrates on keeping potential rivals out, and therefore can lead to jealous rage most often directed against encroachments by younger siblings, initiative brings with it anticipatory rivalry with those who have been there first and may, therefore, occupy with their superior equipment the field toward which one's initiative is directed. Infantile jealousy and rivalry, those often embittered and yet essentially futile attempts at demarcating a sphere of unquestioned privilege, now come to a climax in a final contest for a favored position with the mother; the usual failure leads to resignation, guilt and anxiety. The child indulges in fantasies of being a giant and a tiger, but in his dreams he runs in terror for dear life. This, then, is the stage of the "castration complex," the intensified fear of finding the (now energetically erotized) genitals harmed as a punishment for the fantasies attached to their excitement.

Infantile sexuality and incest taboo, castration complex and superego all unite here to bring about that specifically human crisis during which the child must turn from an exclusive, pregenital attachment to his parents to the slow process of becoming a parent, a carrier of tradition. Here the most fateful split and transformation in the emotional powerhouse occurs, a split between potential human glory and potential total destruction. For here the child becomes forever divided in himself. The instinct fragments which before had enhanced the growth of his infantile body and mind now become divided into an infantile set which perpetuates the exuberance of growth potentials, and a parental set which supports and increases self-observation, self-guidance, and self-punishment.

The problem, again, is one of mutual regulation. Where the child, now so ready to overmanipulate himself, can gradually develop a sense of moral responsibility, where he can gain some insight into the institutions, functions, and roles which will permit his responsible participation, he will find pleasurable accomplishment in wielding tools and weapons, in manipulating meaningful toys—and in caring for younger children.

Naturally, the parental set is at first infantile in nature: the fact that human conscience remains partially infantile throughout life is the core of human tragedy. For the superego of the child can be primitive, cruel, and uncompromising, as may be observed in instances where children overcontrol and overconstrict themselves to the point of self-obliteration; where they develop an overobedience more literal than the one the parent has wished to exact; or where they develop deep regressions and lasting resentments because the parents themselves do not seem to live up to the new conscience. One of the deepest conflicts in life is the hate for a parent who served as the model and the executor of the superego, but who (in some form) was found trying to get away with the very transgressions which the child can no longer tolerate in himself. The suspiciousness and evasiveness which are thus mixed in with the all-or-nothing quality of the superego, this organ of moral tradition, make moral (in the sense of moralistic) man a great potential danger to his own ego—and to that of his fellow men.

In adult pathology, the residual conflict over initiative is expressed either in hysterical denial, which causes the repression of the wish or the abrogation of its executive organ by paralysis, inhibition, or impotence; or in overcompensatory showing off, in which the scared individual, so eager to "duck," instead "sticks his neck out." Then also a plunge into psychosomatic disease is now common. It is as if the culture had made a man overadvertise himself and so identify with his own advertisement that only disease can offer him escape.

But here, again, we must not think only of individual psychopathology, but of the inner powerhouse of rage which must be submerged at this stage, as some of the fondest hopes and the wildest fantasies are repressed and inhibited. The resulting self-righteousness—often the principal reward for goodness—can later be most intolerantly turned against others in the form of persistent moralistic surveillance, so that the prohibition rather than the guidance of initiative becomes the dominant endeavor. On the other hand, even moral man's initiative is apt to burst the boundaries of self-restriction, permitting him to do to others, in his or in other lands, what he would neither do nor tolerate being done in his own home.

In view of the dangerous potentials of man's long childhood, it is well to look back at the blueprint of the life-stages and to the possibilities of guiding the young of the race while they are young. And here we note that according to the wisdom of the ground plan the child is at no time more ready to learn quickly and avidly, to become bigger in the sense of sharing obligation and performance than during this period of his development. He is eager and able to make things cooperatively, to combine with other children for the purpose of constructing and planning, and he is willing to profit from teachers and to emulate ideal prototypes. He remains, of course, identified with the parent of the same sex, but for the present he looks for opportunities where work-identification seems to promise a field of initiative without too much infantile conflict or oedipal guilt and a more realistic identification based on a spirit of equality experienced in doing things together. At any rate, the "oedipal" stage results not only in the oppressive establishment of a moral sense restricting the horizon of the permissible; it also sets the direction toward the possible and the tangible which permits the dreams of early childhood to be attached to the goals of an active adult life. Social institutions, therefore, offer children of this age an *economic ethos*, in the form of ideal adults recognizable by their uniforms and their functions, and fascinating enough to replace, the heroes of picture book and fairy tale.

4. Industry vs. Inferiority

Thus the inner stage seems all set for "entrance into life," except that life must first be school life, whether school is field or jungle or classroom. The child must forget past hopes and wishes, while his exuberant imagination is tamed and harnessed to the laws of impersonal things—even the three R's. For before the child, psychologically already a rudimentary parent, can become a biological parent, he must begin to be a worker and potential provider. With the oncoming latency period, the normally advanced child forgets, or rather sublimates, the necessity to "make" people by direct attack or to become papa and mama in a hurry: he now learns to win recognition by producing things. He has mastered the ambulatory field and the organ modes. He has experienced a sense of finality regarding the fact that there is no workable future within the womb of his family, and thus becomes ready to apply himself to given skills and tasks, which go far beyond the mere playful expression of his organ modes or the pleasure in the function of his limbs. He develops a sense of industry—i.e., he adjusts himself to the inorganic laws of the tool world. He can become an eager and absorbed unit of a productive situation. To bring a productive situation to completion is an aim which gradually supersedes the whims and wishes of play. His ego boundaries include his tools and skills: the work principle (Ives Hendrick) teaches him the pleasure of work completion by steady attention and persevering diligence. In all cultures, at this stage, children receive some *systematic instruction*, although . . . it is by no means always in the kind of school which literate people must organize around special teachers who have learned how to teach literacy. In preliterate people and in nonliterate pursuits much is learned from adults who become teachers by dint of gift and inclination rather than by appointment, and perhaps the greatest amount is learned from older children.

Thus the *fundamentals of technology* are developed, as the child becomes ready to handle the utensils, the tools, and the weapons used by the big people. Literate people, with more specialized careers, must prepare the child by teaching him things which first of all make him literate, the widest possible basic education for the greatest number of possible careers. The more confusing specialization becomes, however, the more indistinct are the eventual goals of initiative; and the more complicated social reality, the vaguer are the father's and mother's role in it. School seems to be a culture all by itself, with its own goals and limits, its achievements and disappointment.

The child's danger, at this stage, lies in a sense of inadequacy and inferiority. If he despairs of his tools and skills or of his status among his tool partners, he may be discouraged from identification with them and with a section of the tool world. To lose the hope of such "industrial" association may pull him back to the more isolated, less tool-conscious familial rivalry of the oedipal time. The child despairs of his equipment in the tool world and in anatomy, and considers himself doomed to mediocrity or inadequacy. It is at this point that wider society becomes significant in its ways of admitting the child to an understanding of meaningful roles in its technology and economy. Many a child's development is disrupted when family life has failed to prepare him for school life, or when school life fails to sustain the promises of earlier stages.

Regarding the period of a developing sense of industry, I have referred to *outer and inner hindrances* in the use of new capacities but not to aggravations of new human drives, nor to submerged rages resulting from their frustration. This stage differs from the earlier ones in that it is not a swing from an inner upheaval to a new mastery. Freud calls it the latency stage because violent drives are normally dormant. But it is only a lull before the storm of puberty, when all the earlier drives re-emerge in a new combination, to be brought under the dominance of genitality.

On the other hand, this is socially a most decisive stage: since industry involves doing things beside and with others, a first sense of division of labor and of differential opportunity, that is, a sense of the *technological ethos* of a culture, develops at this time. We have [elsewhere] pointed . . . to the danger threatening individual and society where the schoolchild begins to feel that the color of his skin, the background of his parents, or the fashion of his clothes rather than his wish and his will to learn will decide his worth as an apprentice, and thus his sense of *identity*—to which we must now turn. But there is another, more fundamental danger, namely man's restriction of himself and constriction of his horizons to include only his work to which, so the Book says, he has been sentenced after his expulsion from paradise. If he accepts work as his only obligation, and "what works" as his only criterion of worthwhileness, he may become the conformist and thoughtless slave of his technology and of those who are in a position to exploit it.

5. Identity vs. Role Confusion

With the establishment of a good initial relationship to the world of skills and tools, and with the advent of puberty, childhood proper comes to an end. Youth begins. But in puberty and adolescence all samenesses and continuities relied on earlier are more or less questioned again, because of a rapidity of body growth which equals that of early childhood and because of the new addition of genital maturity. The growing and developing youths, faced with this physiological revolution within them, and with tangible adult tasks ahead of them, are now primarily concerned with what they appear to be in the eyes of others as compared with what they feel they are, and with the

question of how to connect the roles and skills cultivated earlier with the occupational prototypes of the day. In their search for a new sense of continuity and sameness, adolescents have to refight many of the battles of earlier years, even though to do so they must artificially appoint perfectly well-meaning people to play the roles of adversaries; and they are ever ready to install lasting idols and ideals as guardians of a final identity.

The integration now taking place in the form of ego identity is, as pointed out, more than the sum of the childhood identifications. It is the accrued experience of the ego's ability to integrate all identifications with the vicissitudes of the libido, with the aptitudes developed out of endowment, and with the opportunities offered in social roles. The sense of ego identity, then, is the accrued confidence that the inner sameness and continuity prepared in the past are matched by the sameness and continuity of one's meaning for others, as evidenced in the tangible promise of a "career."

The danger of this stage is role confusion.[2] Where this is based on a strong previous doubt as to one's sexual identity, delinquent and outright psychotic episodes are not uncommon. If diagnosed and treated correctly, these incidents do not have the same fatal significance which they have at other ages. In most instances, however, it is the inability to settle on an occupational identity which disturbs individual young people. To keep themselves together they temporarily overidentify, to the point of apparent complete loss of identity, with the heroes of cliques and crowds. This initiates the stage of "falling in love," which is by no means entirely, or even primarily, a sexual matter—except where the mores demand it. To a considerable extent adolescent love is an attempt to arrive at a definition of one's identity by

[2] See "The Problem of Ego–Identity." *J. Amer. Psa. Assoc.*, 4:56–121.

projecting one's diffused ego image on another and by seeing it thus reflected and gradually clarified. This is why so much of young love is conversation.

Young people can also be remarkably clannish, and cruel in their exclusion of all those who are "different," in skin color or cultural background, in tastes and gifts, and often in such petty aspects of dress and gesture as have been temporarily selected as *the* signs of an in-grouper or out-grouper. It is important to understand (which does not mean condone or participate in) such intolerance as a defense against a sense of identity confusion. For adolescents not only help one another temporarily through much discomfort by forming cliques and by stereotyping themselves, their ideals, and their enemies; they also perversely test each other's capacity to pledge fidelity. The readiness for such testing also explains the appeal which simple and cruel totalitarian doctrines have on the minds of the youth of such countries and classes as have lost or are losing their group identities (feudal, agrarian, tribal, national) and face worldwide industrialization, emancipation, and wider communication.

The adolescent mind is essentially a mind of the *moratorium,* a psychosocial stage between childhood and adulthood, and between the morality learned by the child, and the ethics to be developed by the adult. It is an ideological mind—and, indeed, it is the ideological outlook of a society that speaks most clearly to the adolescent who is eager to be affirmed by his peers, and is ready to be confirmed by rituals, creeds, and programs which at the same time define what is evil, uncanny, and inimical. In searching for the social values which guide identity, one therefore confronts the problems of *ideology* and *aristocracy,* both in their widest possible sense which connotes that within a defined world image and a predestined course of history, the best people will come to rule and rule develops the best in people. In order not to become cyni-

cally or apathetically lost, young people must somehow be able to convince themselves that those who succeed in their anticipated adult world thereby shoulder the obligation of being the best. . . .

6. Intimacy vs. Isolation

The strength acquired at any stage is tested by the necessity to transcend it in such a way that the individual can take chances in the next stage with what was most vulnerably precious in the previous one. Thus, the young adult, emerging from the search for and the insistence on identity, is eager and willing to fuse his identity with that of others. He is ready for intimacy, that is, the capacity to commit himself to concrete affiliations and partnerships and to develop the ethical strength to abide by such commitments, even though they may call for significant sacrifices and compromises. Body and ego must now be masters of the organ modes and of the nuclear conflicts, in order to be able to face the fear of ego loss in situations which call for self-abandon: in the solidarity of close affiliations, in orgasms and sexual unions, in close friendships and in physical combat, in experiences of inspiration by teachers and of intuition from the recesses of the self. The avoidance of such experiences because of a fear of ego loss may lead to a deep sense of isolation and consequent self-absorption.

The counterpart of intimacy is distantiation: the readiness to isolate and, if necessary, to destroy those forces and people whose essence seems dangerous to one's own, and whose "territory" seems to encroach on the extent of one's intimate relations. Prejudices thus developed (and utilized and exploited in politics and in war) are a more mature outgrowth of the blinder repudiations which during the struggle for identity differentiate sharply and cruelly between the familiar and the foreign. The danger of this stage is that intimate, competitive, and combative relations are experienced with and against the selfsame people. But as the areas of adult duty are delineated, and as the competitive encounter, and the sexual embrace, are differentiated, they eventually become subject to that *ethical sense* which is the mark of the adult.

Strictly speaking, it is only now that *true genitality* can fully develop; for much of the sex life preceding these commitments is of the identity-searching kind, or is dominated by phallic or vaginal strivings which make of sex-life a kind of genital combat. On the other hand, genitality is all too often described as a permanent state of reciprocal sexual bliss. This, then, may be the place to complete our discussion of genitality.

For a basic orientation in the matter I shall quote what has come to me as Freud's shortest saying. It has often been claimed, and bad habits of conversation seem to sustain the claim, that psychoanalysis as a treatment attempts to convince the patient that before God and man he has only one obligation: to have good orgasms, with a fitting "object," and that regularly. This, of course, is not true. Freud was once asked what he thought a normal person should be able to do well. The questioner probably expected a complicated answer. But Freud, in the curt way of his old days, is reported to have said: "Lieben und arbeiten" (to love and to work). It pays to ponder on this simple formula; it gets deeper as you think about it. For when Freud said "love" he meant *genital* love, and genital *love*; when he said love *and* work, he meant a general work-productiveness which would not preoccupy the individual to the extent that he loses his right or capacity to be a genital and a loving being. Thus we may ponder, but we cannot improve on "the professor's" formula.

Genitality, then, consists in the unobstructed capacity to develop an orgastic potency so free of pregenital interferences that genital libido (not just the sex products discharged in Kinsey's "outlets") is expressed in heterosexual mutuality, with full sensitivity of both penis and vagina, and with a convulsion-like discharge of tension from the whole body. This is a rather concrete way of saying something about a process which we really do not understand. To put it more situationally: the total fact of finding, via the climactic turmoil of the orgasm, a supreme experience of the mutual regulation of two beings in some way takes the edge off the hostilities and potential rages caused by the oppositeness of male and female, of fact and fancy, of love and hate. Satisfactory sex relations thus makes sex less obsessive, overcompensation less necessary, sadistic controls superfluous.

Preoccupied as it was with curative aspects, psychoanalysis often failed to formulate the matter of genitality in a way significant for the processes of society in all classes, nations, and levels of culture. The kind of mutuality in orgasm which psychoanalysis has in mind is apparently easily obtained in classes and cultures which happen to make a leisurely institution of it. In more complex societies this mutuality is interfered with by so many factors of health, of tradition, of opportunity, and of temperament, that the proper formulation of sexual health would be rather this: A human being should be potentially able to accomplish mutuality of genital orgasm, but he should also be so constituted as to bear a certain amount of frustration in the matter without undue regression wherever emotional preference or considerations of duty and loyalty call for it.

While psychoanalysis has on occasion gone too far in its emphasis on genitality as a universal cure for society and has thus provided a new addiction and a new commodity for many who wished to so interpret its teachings, it has not always indicated all the goals that genitality actually should and must imply. In order to be of lasting social significance, the utopia of genitality should include:

1. mutuality of orgasm

2. with a loved partner

3. of the other sex

4. with whom one is able and willing to share a mutual trust

5. and with whom one is able and willing to regulate the cycles of
   a. work
   b. procreation
   c. recreation

6. so as to secure to the offspring, too, all the stages of a satisfactory development.

It is apparent that such utopian accomplishment on a large scale cannot be an individual or, indeed, a therapeutic task. Nor is it a purely sexual matter by any means. It is integral to a culture's style of sexual selection, cooperation, and competition.

The danger of this stage is isolation, that is the avoidance of contacts which commit to intimacy. In psychopathology, this disturbance can lead to severe "character-problems." On the other hand, there are partnerships which amount to an isolation à deux, protecting both partners from the necessity to face the next critical development—that of generativity.

7. Generativity vs. Stagnation

. . . [The term "generativity"] encompasses the evolutionary development which has made man the teaching and instituting as well as the learning animal. The fashionable insistence on dramatizing the dependence of children on adults often blinds us to the dependence of the older generation on the younger one. Mature man needs to be needed, and maturity needs guidance as well as encouragement from what has been produced and must be taken care of.

Generativity, then, is primarily the concern in establishing and guiding the next generation, although there are individuals who, through misfortune or because of special and genuine gifts in other directions, do not apply this drive to their own offspring. And indeed, the concept generativity is meant to include such more popular synonyms as *productivity* and *creativity*, which, however, cannot replace it.

It has taken psychoanalysis some time to realize that the ability to lose oneself in the meeting of bodies and minds leads to a gradual expansion of ego-interests and to a libidinal investment in that which is being generated. Generativity thus is an essential stage on the psychosexual as well as on the psychosocial schedule. Where such enrichment fails altogether, regression to an obsessive need for pseudo-intimacy takes place, often with a pervading sense of stagnation and personal impoverishment. Individuals, then, often begin to indulge themselves as if they were their own—or one another's—one and only child; and where conditions favor it, early invalidism, physical or psychological, becomes the vehicle of self-concern. The mere fact of having or even wanting children, however, does not "achieve" generativity. In fact, some young parents suffer, it seems, from the retardation of the ability to develop this stage. The reasons are often to be found in early childhood impressions; in excessive self-love based on a too strenuously self-made personality; and finally (and here we return to the beginnings) in the lack of some faith, some "belief in the species," which would make a child appear to be a welcome trust of the community.

As to the institutions which safeguard and reinforce generativity, one can only say that all institutions codify the ethics of generative succession. Even where philosophical and spiritual tradition suggests the renunciation of the right to procreate or to produce, such early turn to "ultimate concerns," wherever instituted in monastic movements, strives to settle at the same time the matter of its relationship to the Care for the creatures of this world and to the Charity which is felt to transcend it.

. . . .

8. Ego Integrity vs. Despair

Only in him who in some way has taken care of things and people and has adapted himself to the triumphs and disappointments adherent to being, the originator of others or the generator of products and ideas—only in him may gradually ripen the fruit of these seven stages. I know no better word for it than ego integrity. Lacking a clear definition, I shall point to a few constituents of this state of mind. It is the ego's accrued assurance of its proclivity for order and meaning. It is a postnarcissistic love of the human ego—not of the self—as an experience which conveys some world order and spiritual sense, no matter how dearly paid for. It is the acceptance of one's one and only life cycle as something that had to be and that, by necessity, permitted of no substitutions: it thus means a new, a different love of one's parents. It is a comradeship with the ordering ways of distant times and different pursuits, as expressed in the simple products and sayings of such times and pursuits. Although aware of the relativity of all the various life styles which have given meaning to human striving, the possessor of integrity is ready to defend the dignity of his own life style against all physical and economic threats. For he knows that an individual life is the accidental coincidence of but one life cycle with but one segment of history; and that for him all human integrity stands or falls with the one style of integrity of which he partakes. The style of integrity developed by his culture or civilization thus becomes the "patrimony of his soul," the seal of his moral paternity of himself ("...pero el honor/Es patrimonio del alma": Calderón). In such final consolidation, death loses its sting.

The lack or loss of this accrued ego integration is signified by fear of death: the one and only life cycle is not accepted as the ultimate of life. Despair expresses the feeling that the time is now short, too short for the attempt to start another life and to try out alternate roads to integrity. Disgust hides despair, if often only in the form of "a thousand little disgusts" which do not add up to one big remorse: *"mille petits dégôuts de soi, dont le total ne fait pas un remords, mais un gêne obscure"* (Rostand).

Each individual, to become a mature adult, must to a sufficient degree develop all the ego qualities mentioned, so that a wise Indian, a true gentleman, and a mature peasant share and recognize in one another the final stage of integrity. But each cultural entity, to develop the particular style of integrity suggested by its historical place, utilizes a particular combination of these conflicts, along with specific provocations and prohibitions of infantile sexuality. Infantile conflicts become creative only if sustained by the firm support of cultural institutions and of the special leader classes representing them. In order to approach or experience integrity, the individual must know how to be a follower of image bearers in religion and in politics, in the economic order and in technology, in aristocratic living and in the arts and sciences. Ego integrity, therefore, implies an emotional integration which permits participation by followership as well as acceptance of the responsibility of leadership.

Webster's Dictionary is kind enough to help us complete this outline in a circular fashion. Trust (the first of our ego values) is here defined as "the assured reliance on another's integrity," the last of our values. I suspect that Webster had business in mind rather than babies, credit rather than faith. But the formulation stands. And it seems possible to further paraphrase the relation of adult integrity and infantile trust by saying that healthy children will not fear life if their elders have integrity enough not to fear death.

9. An Epigenetic Chart

... The foregoing conception of the life cycle ... awaits systematic treatment. To prepare this, I shall conclude . . . with a diagram. In this, . . . the diagonal represents the normative sequence of psychosocial gains made as at each stage one more nuclear conflict adds a new ego quality, a new criterion of accruing human strength. Below the diagonal there is space for the precursors of each of these solutions, all of which begin with the beginning; above the diagonal there is space for the designation of the derivatives of these gains and their transformations in the maturing and the mature personality.

The underlying assumptions for such charting are (1) that the human personality in principle develops according to steps predetermined in the growing person's readiness to be driven toward, to be aware of, and to interact with, a widening social radius; and (2) that society, in principle, tends to be so constituted as to meet and invite this succession of potentialties for interaction and attempts to safeguard and to encourage the proper rate and the proper sequence of their enfolding. This is the "maintenance of the human world."

But a chart is only a tool to think with, and cannot aspire to be a prescription to abide by, whether in the practice of child-training, in psychotherapy, or in the methodology of child study. In the presenta-

tion of the psychosocial stages in the form of an *epigenetic chart* . . . , we have definite and delimited methodological steps in mind. It is one purpose of [mine] to facilitate the comparison of the stages first discerned by Freud as sexual to other schedules of development (physical, cognitive). But any one chart delimits one schedule only, and it must not be imputed that our outline of the psychosocial schedule is intended to imply obscure generalities concerning other aspects of development—or, indeed, of existence. If the chart, for example, lists a series of conflicts or crises, we do not consider all development a series of crises: we claim only that psychosocial development proceeds by critical steps—"critical" being a characteristic of turning points, of moments of decision between progress and regression, integration and retardation.

It may be useful at this point to spell out the methodological implications of an epigenetic matrix. The more heavily-lined squares of the diagonal signify both a sequence of stages and a gradual development of component parts: in other words, the chart formalizes a progression through time of a differentiation of parts. This indicates (1) that each critical item of psychosocial strength discussed here is sys-

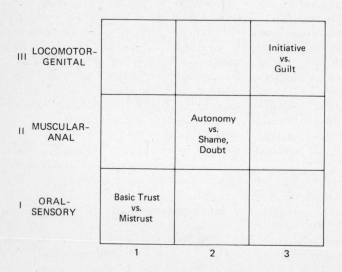

Figure 3.1

	1	2	3
III LOCOMOTOR-GENITAL			Initiative vs. Guilt
II MUSCULAR-ANAL		Autonomy vs. Shame, Doubt	
I ORAL-SENSORY	Basic Trust vs. Mistrust		

tematically related to all others, and that they all depend on the proper development in the proper sequence of each item; and (2) that each item exists in some form before its critical time normally arrives.

If I say, for example, that a favorable ratio of basic trust over basic mistrust is the first step in psychosocial adaptation, a favorable ratio of autonomous will over shame and doubt, the second, the corresponding diagrammatic statement expresses a number of fundamental relations that exist between the two steps, as well as some facts fundamental to each. Each comes to its ascendance, meets its crisis, and finds its lasting solution during the stage indicated. But they all must exist from the beginning in some form, for

every act calls for an integration of all. Also, an infant may show something like "autonomy" from the beginning in the particular way in which he angrily tries to wriggle himself free when tightly held. However, under normal conditions, it is not until the second year that he begins to experience the whole *critical opposition of being an autonomous creature and being a dependent one*; and it is not until then that he is ready for a decisive encounter with his environment, an environment which, in turn, feels called upon to convey to him its particular ideas and concepts of autonomy and coercion in ways decisively contributing to the character and the health of his personality in his culture. It is this encounter, together with the resulting crisis, that we have tenta-

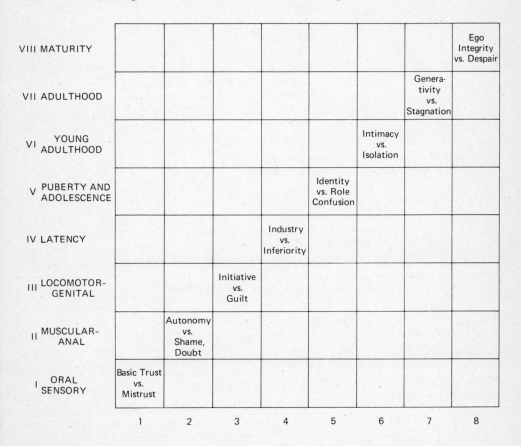

	1	2	3	4	5	6	7	8
VIII MATURITY								Ego Integrity vs. Despair
VII ADULTHOOD							Genera-tivity vs. Stagnation	
VI YOUNG ADULTHOOD						Intimacy vs. Isolation		
V PUBERTY AND ADOLESCENCE					Identity vs. Role Confusion			
IV LATENCY				Industry vs. Inferiority				
III LOCOMOTOR-GENITAL			Initiative vs. Guilt					
II MUSCULAR-ANAL		Autonomy vs. Shame, Doubt						
I ORAL SENSORY	Basic Trust vs. Mistrust							

Figure 3.2

tively described for each stage. As to the progression from one stage to the next, the diagonal indicates the sequence to be followed. However, it also makes room for variations in tempo and intensity. An individual, or a culture, may linger excessively over trust and proceed from I 1 over I 2 to II 2, or an accelerated progression may move from I 1 over II 1 to II 2. Each such acceleration or (relative) retardation, however, is assumed to have a modifying influence on all later stages.

An epigenetic diagram thus lists a system of stages dependent on each other; and while individual stages may have been explored more or less thoroughly or named more or less fittingly, the diagram suggests that their study be pursued always with the total configuration of stages in mind. The diagram invites, then, a thinking through of all its empty boxes: if we have entered Basic Trust in I 1 and Integrity in VIII 8, we leave the question open, as to what trust might have become in a stage dominated by the need for integrity even as we have left open what it may look like and, indeed, be called in the stage dominated by a striving for autonomy (II 1). All we mean to emphasize is that trust must have developed in its own right, before it becomes something more in the critical encounter in which autonomy develops—and so on, up the vertical. If, in the last stage (VIII 1), we would expect trust to have developed into the most mature *faith* that an aging person can muster in his cultural setting and historical period, the chart permits the consideration not only of what old age can be, but also what its preparatory stages must have been. All of this should make it clear that a chart of epigenesis suggests a global form of thinking and rethinking which leaves details of methodology and terminology to further study.[3]

be avoided. Among them is the assumption that the sense of trust (and all the other "positive" senses postulated) is an *achievement,* secured once and for all at a given state. In fact, some writers are so intent on making an *achievement scale* out of these stages that they blithely omit all the "negative" senses (basic mistrust, etc.) which are and remain the dynamic counterpart of the "positive" ones throughout life. The assumption that on each stage a goodness is achieved which is impervious to new inner conflicts and to changing conditions is, I believe, a projection on child development of that success ideology which can so dangerously pervade our private and public daydreams and can make us inept in a heightened struggle for a meaningful existence in a new, industrial era of history. The personality is engaged with the hazards of existence continuously, even as the body's metabolism copes with decay. As we come to diagnose a state of relative strength and the symptoms of an impaired one, we face only more clearly the paradoxes and tragic potentials of human life.

. . .

I have since attempted to formulate for Julian Huxley's *Humanist Frame* (Allen and Unwin, 1961; Harper and Brothers, 1962) a blueprint of essential strengths which evolution has built both into the ground plan of the life-stages and into that of man's institutions. While I cannot discuss here the methodological problems involved (and aggravated by my use of the term "basic virtues"), I should append the list of these strengths because they are really the lasting outcome of the "favorable ratios" mentioned at every step of the [discussion of] psychosocial stages. Here they are:

Basic Trust vs. Basic Mistrust: Drive and *Hope*
Autonomy vs. Shame and Doubt: Self-Control and *Willpower*
Initiative vs. Guilt: Direction and *Purpose*
Industry vs. Inferiority: Method and *Competence*
Identity vs. Role Confusion: Devotion and *Fidelity*
Intimacy vs. Isolation: Affiliation and *Love*
Generativity vs. Stagnation: Production and *Care*
Ego Integrity vs. Despair: Renunciation and *Wisdom*

The italicized words are called *basic* virtues because without them, and their re-emergence from generation to generation, all other and more changeable systems of human values lose their spirit and their relevance. Of this list, I have been able so far to give a more detailed account only for Fidelity (see *Youth, Change and Challenge,* E. H. Erikson, editor, Basic Books, 1963). But here again, the list represents a total conception within which there is much room for a discussion of terminology and methodology. (E.H.E.)

---

[3] To leave this matter truly open, certain misuses of the whole conception would have to

4. ADULT STATUS OF CHILDREN WITH CONTRASTING EARLY LIFE EXPERIENCES: A FOLLOW-UP STUDY

HAROLD M. SKEELS

Introduction

A follow-up study that covers a span of some 30 years will inevitably bracket changes in psychological concepts and practices. In the early 1930s when the subjects of this report were identified as infants, the prevailing concept of intelligence held by psychologists, social workers, and educators was that intellgence is a fixed individual characteristic. It was believed to be related to parental genetic traits that were inferred from the parents' occupational and educational achievements, to show little fluctuation from early childhood to maturity, and to be relatively uninfluenced by the impact of environment. Assessment of the intelligence of young children, while difficult, was regarded as not impossible. It was believed that knowing a child's mental level facilitated planning for his future, since the developmental quotient was considered to be an acceptably stable predictor of his future development. In the absence of reliable measures for an infant, for example, the parents' educational achievement, occupational classification, and general sociocultural status were considered to be predictive of the child's potentialities.

In developing plans for dependent children, social workers in the more sophisticated agencies placed considerable emphasis on details of family history. The resulting assessment of potential was used as a basis for matching children and prospective adoptive parents or for making other plans for the child. When such information was not available, or was unfavorable, the child was held for observation until his development could be assessed. For some children this meant several years of observation. Since foster homes were relatively scarce, most children in this category were detained in orphanges during the observation period.

At the same time, some agencies were not influenced by the prevailing, academically accepted concepts of intelligence and of prediction of future development. In these agencies, a variety of practices was found ranging from indiscriminate placements in adoptive homes to early diagnosis of retardation.

The validity of what were then regarded as desirable practices had never been empirically tested, nor was there evidence to contradict them. Conducting planned and carefully designed research in the area was out of the question for both financial and humanitarian reasons. However, the possibility of observing and studying the results of existing practices was completely feasible. The natural-history approach of observing, measuring, recording, and interpreting data without intervention in the practices that produced them was basic to the initial reports in the so-called Iowa Studies. Included among them were the follow-up studies of the mental development of children who had been placed in adoptive homes in infancy and in later childhood (Skeels, 1936, 1938; Skodak, 1939; Skodak & Skeels, 1945, 1949), and the study of the mental growth of children who had been in inadequate homes for varying periods (Skeels & Fillmore, 1937). Later, studies were made of the effects of specific intervention, such as the influence of language training (Dawe, 1942) and the effect of a nursery-school program (Skeels, Updegraff, Wellman, & Williams, 1938; Wellman, 1938).

The present study is a report on the status as adults of two groups of children originally encountered in the Iowa institutions. One group experienced what was then regarded as the normal course of events in a childcaring institution, while the other experienced a specifically designed and implemented intervention program. Reports on the development of these children have appeared in two previous publications. The first (Skeels & Dye, 1939) described the original experimental period, and the second (Skeels, 1942) reported a follow-up some two years later. The study was not planned nor the data gathered in a way to form the basis for studies of personality structure in depth. The findings reported here, therefore, are concerned with the question of whether and for how long a time mental development is affected by major changes in early environment and, specifically, with the factors significantly associated with deflections in mental development. It is hoped that these findings will contribute to the growing body of evidence on the effects of deprivation and poverty on the young child's ability to learn.

Mention may be made that this report summarizes one unit of a series of studies that were the center of much controversy over the years. In addition to its historical interest, it is hoped that it will have contemporary value and support for workers in the applied fields of child development. Comparisons with the growing body of literature on early childhood development and on the impact of environment on children are left to the reader.

The Original Study

All the children in this study had become wards of the orphanage through established court procedures after no next of kin was found able to provide either support or suitable guardianship. Of the 25 children, 20 were illegitimate and the remainder had been separated from their parents because of evidence of severe neglect and/or abuse. Then as now, the courts were reluctant to sever the ties between child and parents and did so only when clearly presented with no other alternative. All the children were white and of north-European background.

The orphanage in which the children were placed occupied, with a few exceptions, buildings that had first served as a hospital and barracks during the Civil War. The institution was overcrowded and understaffed. By present standards, diet, sanitation, general care, and basic philosophy of operation were censurable. At the time of the study, however, the discrepancies between conditions in the institution and in the general community were not so great and were not always to the disadvantage of the institution. Over the past 30 years, administrative and physical changes have occurred that reflect the economic and social gains of our society. The description of conditions in the institution in the 1930s, therefore, does not apply to the present.

At the time the original study was begun, infants up to the age of 2 years were housed in the hospital, then a relatively new building. Until about 6 months, they were cared for in the infant nursery. The babies were kept in standard hospital cribs that often had protective sheeting on the sides, thus effectively limiting visual stimulations; no toys or other objects were hung in the infants' line of vision. Human interactions were limited to baby nurses who, with the speed born of practice and necessity, changed diapers or bedding, bathed and medicated the infants, and fed them efficiently with propped bottles.

Older infants, from about 6 to 24 months, were moved into small dormitories containing two to five large cribs. This arrangement permitted the infants to move about a little and to interact somewhat with those in neighboring cribs. The children were cared for by two nurses with some assistance from one or two girls,

10 to 15 years old, who regarded the assignment as an unwelcome chore. The children had good physical and medical care, but little can be said beyond this. Interactions with adults were largely limited to feeding, dressing, and toilet details. Few play materials were available, and there was little time for the teaching of play techniques. Most of the children had a brief play period on the floor; a few toys were available at the beginning of such periods, but if any rolled out of reach there was no one to retrieve it. Except for short walks out of doors, the children were seldom out of the nursery room.

At 2 years of age these children were graduated to the cottages, which had been built around 1860. A rather complete description of "cottage" life is reported by Skeels et al. (1938) from which the following excerpts are taken:

Overcrowding of living facilities was characteristic. Too many children had to be accommodated in the available space and there were too few adults to guide them. . . . Thirty to thirty-five children of the same sex under six years of age lived in a "cottage" in charge of one matron and three or four entirely untrained and often reluctant girls of thirteen to fifteen years of age. The waking and sleeping hours of these children were spent (except during meal times and a little time on a grass plot) in an average-sized room (approximately fifteen feet square), a sunporch of similar size, a cloakroom, . . . and a single dormitory. The latter was occupied only during sleeping hours. The meals for all children in the orphanage were served in a central building in a single large dining room. . . .

The duties falling to the lot of the matron were not only those involved in the care of the children but those related to clothing and cottage maintenance, in other words, cleaning, mending, and so forth. . . . With so much responsibility centered in one adult the result was a necessary regimentation. The children sat down, stood up, and did many things in rows and in unison. They spent considerable time sitting on chairs, for in addition to the number of children and the matron's limited time there was the misfortune of inadequate equipment. . . .

No child had any property which belonged exclusively to him except, perhaps, his toothbrush. Even his clothing, including shoes, was selected and put on him according to size. [pp. 10–11]

After a child reached the age of 6 years, he began school. His associates were his cottage mates and the children of the same age and opposite sex who lived on the other side of the institution grounds. Although the curriculum was ostensibly the same as that in the local public school, it was generally agreed that the standards were adjusted to the capabilities of the orphanage children. Few of those who had their entire elementary-school experience in the institution's school were able to make the transition to the public junior high school.

The orphanage was designed for mentally normal children. It was perpetually overcrowded, although every opportunity to relieve this pressure was exploited. One such relief occurred periodically when new buildings were opened at other institutions, such as the schools for the mentally retarded. It was not uncommon for a busload of children to be transferred on such occasions. A valued contribution of the psychologists was the maintenance of lists of children who, on the basis of test scores and observable behavior, were regarded as eligible for transfers.

The environmental conditions in the two state institutions for the mentally retarded were not identical but they had many things in common. Patient-inmates were grouped by sex, age, and general ability. Within any one ward, the patients were highly similar. The youngest children tended to be the most severely disabled and were frequently "hospital" patients. The older, more competent inmates had work assignments throughout the institution and constituted a somewhat self-conscious elite with recognized status.

Personnel at that time included no resident social workers or psychologists. Physicians were resident at the schools for the mentally retarded and were on call at the orphanage. Administrative and matron and caretaking staffs were essentially untrained and nonprofessional. Psychological services were introduced in the orphanage in 1932 when the author, on the staff of the Iowa Child Welfare Research Station, State University of Iowa, became the first psychologist to be employed by the Iowa Board of Control of State Institutions. Over the years this proved to be a happy marriage of service and research related to the care of dependent children.

Identification of Cases

Early in the service aspects of the program, two baby girls, neglected by their feebleminded mothers, ignored by their inadequate relatives, malnourished and frail, were legally committed to the orphanage. The youngsters were pitiful little creatures. They were tearful, had runny noses, and sparse, stringy, and colorless hair; they were emaciated, undersized, and lacked muscle tonus or responsiveness. Sad and inactive, the two spent their days rocking and whining.

The psychological examinations showed developmental levels of 6 and 7 months respectively, for the two girls, although they were 13 and 16 months old chronologically. This serious delay in mental growth was confirmed by observations of their behavior in the nursery and by reports of the superintendent of nurses, as well as by the pediatrician's examination. There was no evidence of physiological or organic defect, or of birth injury or glandular dysfunction.

The two children were considered unplaceable, and transfer to a school for the mentally retarded was recommended with a high degree of confidence. Accordingly, they were transferred to an institution for the mentally retarded at the next available vacancy, when they were aged 15 and 18 months, respectively.

In the meantime, the author's professional responsibilities had been increased to include itinerant psychological services to the two state institutions for the mentally retarded. Six months after the transfer of the two children, he was visiting the wards at an institution for the mentally retarded and noticed two outstanding little girls. They were alert, smiling, running about, responding to the playful attention of adults, and generally behaving and looking like any other toddlers. He scarcely recognized them as the two little girls with the hopeless prognosis, and thereupon tested them again. Although the results indicated that the two were approaching normal mental development for age, the author was skeptical of the validity or permanence of the improvement and no change was instituted in the lives of the children. Twelve months later they were re-examined, and then again when they were 40 and 43 months old. Each examination gave unmistakable evidence of mental development well within the normal range for age.

There was no question that the initial evaluations gave a true picture of the children's functioning level at the time they were tested. It appeared equally evident that later appraisals showed normal mental growth accompanied by parallel changes in social growth, emotional maturity, communication skills, and general behavior. In order to find a possible explanation for the changes that had occurred, the nature of the children's life space was reviewed.

The two girls had been placed on one of the wards of older, brighter girls and women, ranging in age from 18 to 50 years and in mental age from 5 to 9 years, where they were the only children of preschool age, except for a few hopeless bed patients with gross physical defects. An older girl on the ward had "adopted" each of the two girls, and other older girls served as adoring aunts. Attendants and nurses also showed affection to the two, spending time with them, taking them along on their days off for automobile rides and shopping excursions, and purchasing toys, picture books, and play materials for them in great abundance. The setting seemed to be a homelike one, abundant in affection, rich in wholesome and interesting experiences, and geared to a preschool level of development.

It was recognized that as the children grew older their developmental needs would be less adequately met in the institution for the mentally retarded. Furthermore, they were now normal and the need for care in such an institution no longer existed. Consequently, they were transferred back to the orphanage and shortly thereafter were placed in adoptive homes.

At this point, evidence on the effects of environment on intelligence had been accumulated from a number of studies. Skeels and Fillmore (1937) had found that older children who came from inadequate nonnurturant homes were mentally retarded or borderline but that their younger siblings were generally of normal ability, which suggested that longer residence in such homes had a cumulatively depressing effect on intelligence. Children also became retarded if they remained for long periods in an institution (1930-style) supposedly designed for normal children (Skeels, 1940). However, if children were placed in adoptive homes as infants, or even as young preschoolers, their development surpassed expectations, and improvement continued for long periods following placement (Skodak, 1939). In even more extreme cases, seriously retarded children were able to attain normal levels of functioning when placed in a setting officially designed for the mentally retarded (Skeels & Dye, 1939). The consistent element seemed to be the existence of a one-to-one relationship with an adult who was generous with love and affection, together with an abundance of attention and experiential stimulation from many sources. Children who had little of these did not show progress; those who had a great deal, did.

Since study homes or temporary care homes were not available to the state agency at that time, the choice for children who were not suitable for immediate placement in adoptive homes was between, on the one hand, an unstimulating, large nursery with predictable mental retardation or, on the other hand, a radical, iconoclastic solution, that is, placement in institutions for the mentally retarded in a bold experiment to see whether retardation in infancy was reversible.

By the time these observations were organized into a meaningful whole and their implications were recognized, individual psychological tests were available for all children in the orphanage. As part of a continuing program of observation and evaluation, all infants over 3 months of age were given the then available tests (Kuhlmann-Binet and Iowa Test for Young Children), and were retested as often as changes seemed to occur. Retests at bimonthly intervals were not uncommon. Older preschoolers were re-examined at 6- to 12-month intervals; school-aged children, annually or biennially. Children who were showing marked delay in development were kept under special observation.

Children whose development was so delayed that adoptive placement was out of the question remained in the orphanage. The only foreseeable alternative for them was eventual transfer to an institution for the mentally retarded. In the light of the experiences with the two little girls, the possibility was raised that early transfer to such an institution might have therapeutic effects. If not all, then at least some of the children might be able to attain normal mental functioning. In the event they did not, no significant change in life pattern would have occurred, and the child would remain in the situation for which he would have been destined in any case.

This radical proposal was accepted with understandable misgivings by the administrators involved. It was finally agreed that, in order to avoid the stigma of commitment to a state school for the retarded, children would be accepted as "house guests" in such institutions but would remain on the official roster of the orphanage. Periodic re-evaluations were built into the plan; if no improvement was observed in the child, commitment would follow. Insofar as possible, the children were to be placed on wards as "only" children.

In the course of time, in addition to the two little girls who have been described and another transferred to the second of the two institutions at about the same time, 10 more children became "house guests." The transfers were spaced over a year's span in groups of 3, 3, and 4. All went to one institution for the mentally handicapped, the Glenwood State School. Unfortunately, the number of "house guests" exceeded the number of "elite" wards of older girls and necessitated the use of some environments that were less desirable. Consequently, in some wards there were more children, or fewer capable older girls, or less opportunity for extra stimulation, with a resulting variation in developmental patterns.

Experimental group.   The experimental group consisted of the 13 children who were transferred from an orphanage for mentally normal children to an institution for the mentally retarded, as "house guests." All were under 3 years of age at the time of transfer. Their development had been reliably established as seriously retarded by tests and observation before transfer was considered.

The identification and selection of the children who constituted the experimental group can perhaps be best explained by a description of the procedures that were normally followed. County or welfare agencies, faced with the problem of care for an illegitimate or ward-of-the-court child, applied to the Board of Control and/or the Iowa Soldiers' Orphans' Home, as it was then known. When accepted (rejections occurred rarely and only under most unusual circumstances, such as obvious multiple handicaps identifiable at

birth), the child was brought to the institution and placed in the hospital for observation. During the first few days he was given routine medical examinations and was observed for abnormalities or infections, etc. Within two to four weeks after admission he was also given a psychological examination. The legal commitment, available social history, and other information were collated and at the monthly assignment conferences decisions were made regarding the child. These conferences were attended by the superintendent of the institution, the Director of the Children's Division of the State Board of Control, and the psychologist. On call also were the head nurse or the pediatrician and any other staff member who could supply pertinent information. If no legal, medical or developmental impediments to adoptive placement were found, the child was assigned to an adoptive home, largely on the basis of requested sex, coloring, and religious background.

Decisions on the children who were unplaceable for legal, medical, or developmental reasons were reviewed at each subsequent monthly conference until a resolution was attained. Consequently, the children who remained in the pool of unplaced infants or toddlers became very well known to the conference participants.

As the evidence from the research studies accumulated, concern about the future of these children increased and led to the decision that some radical measure was justified. Coincidentally, a change had occurred in the administration of the state institution for the mentally handicapped which created a favorable climate for social experimentation. Those children who happened to be in the infant to 3-year-old age range, were not ineligible for placement for legal reasons, were not acutely ill, but who were mentally retarded, became members of the experimental group. The entire project covered a span of some three years and was terminated when a change in the administration of the state school reduced the tolerance for such untidy procedures as having "house guests" in an institution. The onset of World War II and the departure of the principal investigator for military service effectively closed the project.

A project such as this could not be replicated in later years because infants were no longer kept exclusively in the orphanage. Temporary boarding homes came to be utilized prior to adoptive placement or for long-term observation and care.

The experimental group consisted of 10 girls and 3 boys, none with gross physical handicaps. Prior to their placement as "house guests," the examinations were routinely administrated to them without any indication that they would or would not be involved in the unusual experience.

At the time of transfer the mean chronological age of the group was 19.4 months (SD 7.4) and the median was 17.1 months, with a range of from 7.1 to 35.9 months. The range of IQ's was from 35 to 89 with a mean of 64.3 (SD 16.4) and a median of 65.0. Additional tests were made of 11 of the 13 children shortly before or in conjunction with the pretransfer tests reported in Table 4.1, using the Kuhlmann-Binet again or the Iowa Test for Young Children, and the results corroborated the reported scores.

The children were considered unsuitable for adoptio 1 because of evident mental retardation. For example, in Case 1, although the IQ was 89, it was felt that actual retardation was much greater, as the child at 7 months could scarcely hold up his head without support and showed little general bodily activity in comparison with other infants of the same age. In Case 3, at 12 months, very little activity was observed, and the child was very unsteady when sitting up without support. She could not pull herself to a standing position and did not creep. Case 11 was not only retarded but showed perseverative patterns of behavior, particularly incessant rocking back and forth. Cases 5, 8, and 13 were classified at the imbecile level. In present-day terms, they would have been labeled "trainable mentally retarded children."

Table 4.1 lists for each child the pretransfer test findings and ages at time of transfer; also shown are posttransfer test results, length of experimental period, and changes in IQ from first to last test.

Contrast group.   Since the original purpose of the experiment was to rescue for normalcy, if possible, those children showing delayed or retarded development, no plans had been made for a control or comparison group. It was only after the data had been analyzed that it was found that such a contrast group was available because of the tests that were routinely given to all children in the orphanage. To select such a contrast group, therefore, records were scrutinized for children who met the following criteria:

1. Had been given intelligence tests under 2 years of age.
2. Were still in residence in the orphanage at approximately 4 years of age.
3. Were in the control group of the orphanage preschool study (Skeels 1938).
4. Had not attended preschool.

The Skeels et al. (1938) study had included two groups of children matched in chronological age, mental age, IQ, and length of residence in the institution, of which one group had the advantages of the more stimulating environment of preschool attendance while the other group, the controls, experienced the less stimulating environment of cottage life. Since the purpose of the contrast group in the present study was to provide data on children in a relatively nonstimulating environment, those who had attended preschool were not included. Such limitations, however, did not constitute a selective factor as far as the characteristics of the children were concerned.

Table 4.1. Experimental group: mental development of children as measured by Kuhlmann-Binet Intelligence Tests before and after transfer

Case Number[a]	Sex	Before Transfer Test 1 Chronological Age, Months	IQ	Chronological Age, Months, at Transfer	After Transfer Test 2 Chronological Age, Months	IQ	Test 3 Chronological Age, Months	IQ	Last Test Chronological Age, Months	IQ	Length of Experimental Period, Months	Change in IQ, First to Last Test
1	M	7.0	89	7.1	12.8	113	...	...	12.8	113	5.7	+24
2	F	12.7	57	13.1	20.5	94	29.4	83	36.8	77	23.7	+20
3	F	12.7	85	13.3	25.2	107	...	...	25.2	107	11.9	+22
4	F	14.7	73	15.0	23.1	100	...	...	23.1	100	8.1	+27
5	F	13.4	46	15.2	21.7	77	32.9	100	40.0	95[b]	24.8	+49
6	F	15.5	77	15.6	21.3	96	30.1	100	30.1	100	14.5	+23
7	F	16.6	65	17.1	27.5	104	...	...	27.5	104	10.4	+39
8	F	16.6	35	18.4	24.8	87	36.0	88	43.0	93	24.6	+58
9	F	21.8	61	22.0	34.3	80	...	...	34.3	80	12.3	+19
10	M	23.3	72	23.4	29.1	88	37.9	71	45.4	79	22.0	+7
11	M	25.7	75	27.4	42.5	78	51.0	82[b]	51.0	82[b]	23.6	+7
12	F	27.9	65	28.4	40.4	82	...	...	40.4	82	12.0	+17
13	F	30.0	36	35.9	51.7	70	81.0	74[b]	89.0	81[b]	52.1	+45

[a] Arranged according to age at time of transfer.
[b] Stanford-Binet IQ.
Source: Adapted from H. M. Skeels & H. B. Dye (1939, Table 1).

A total of 12 children were selected on the basis of the criteria and became the contrast group. The mean chronological age of the group at the time of first examination was 16.6 months (SD 2.9), with a median at 16.3 months. The range was from 11.9 to 21.8 months. The mean IQ of the group was 86.7 (SD 14.3) and the median IQ was 90. With the exception of two cases (16 and 24) the children had IQ's ranging from 81 to 103; the IQ's for the two exceptions were 71 and 50, respectively. When the children were examined, it was not known that they were or would become members of any study group. The re-examinations were merely routine retests that were given to all children.

At the ages when adoptive placement usually occurred, 9 of the children in the contrast group had been considered normal in mental development. All 12 were not placed, however, because of different circumstances: 5 were withheld from placement simply because of poor family histories, 2 because of improper commitments, 2 because of luetic conditions, 2 because of other health problems, and 1 because of possible mental retardation.

The subsequent progress of the children in both the experimental and the contrast groups was influenced by individual circumstances. The groups were never identified as such in the resident institution; the members of each group were considered together only in a statistical sense. A child in the experimental group remained in the institution for the mentally retarded until it was felt that he had attained the maximum benefit from residence there. At that point, he was placed directly into an adoptive home or returned to the orphanage in transit to an adoptive home. If he did not attain a level of intelligence that warranted adoptive plans, he remained in the institution for the mentally retarded.

The contrast-group members remained in the orphanage until placement. One was returned to relatives, but in most instances the children were eventually transferred to an institution for the mentally retarded as long-term protected residents. A few of the contrast group had been briefly approved for adoptive placement, and two had been placed for short periods. None was successful, however, and the children's decline in mental level removed them from the list of those eligible for adoption.

Table 4.2 lists the chronological ages and test findings for the children in the contrast group over the experimental period and the changes in IQ that occurred.

Summary and Implications

In the original study, the 13 children in the experimental group, all mentally retarded at the beginning of the study, experienced the effects of early intervention, which consisted of a radical shift from one institutional environment to another. The major difference bewteen the two institutions, as experienced by the children, was in the amount of developmental stimulation and the intensity of relationships between the children and mother-surrogates. Following a variable period in the second institution, 11 of the 13 children were placed in adoptive homes.

The contrast group of 12 children, initially higher in intelligence than the experimental group, were exposed to a relatively nonstimulating orphanage environment over a prolonged period of time.

Over a period of two years, the children in the experimental group showed a marked increase in rate of mental growth, whereas the children in the contrast group showed progressive mental retardation. The experimental group made an average gain of 28.5 IQ points; the contrast group showed an average loss of 26.2 IQ points.

The first follow-up study was made 2½ years after the termination of the original study. The 11 children in the experimental group that had been placed in adoptive homes had maintained and increased their earlier gains in intelligence, whereas the 2 not so placed had declined in rate of

Table 4.2. Contrast group: mental development of children as measured by repeated Kuhlmann-Binet Intelligence Tests over an average experimental period of two and one-half years.

Case Number[a]	Sex	Test 1		Test 2		Test 3		Last Test		Length of Experimental Period, Months	Change in IQ, First to Last Test
		Chronological Age, Months	IQ	Chronological Age, Months	IQ	Chronological Age, Months	IQ	Chronological Age, Months	IQ		
14	F	11.9	91	24.8	73	37.5	65	55.0	62	43.1	−29
15	F	13.0	92	20.1	54	38.3	56	38.3	56	25.3	−36
16	F	13.6	71	20.6	76	40.9	56	40.9	56	27.3	−15
17	M	13.8	96	37.2	58	53.2	54	53.2	54	39.4	−42
18	M	14.5	99	21.6	67	41.9	54	41.9	54	27.4	−45
19	M	15.2	87	22.5	80	35.5	74	44.5	67	29.3	−20
20	M	17.3	81	43.0	77	52.9	83[b]	52.9	83[b]	35.6	+ 2
21	M	17.5	103	26.8	72	38.0	63	50.3	60	32.8	−43
22	M	18.3	98	24.8	93	30.7	80	39.7	61	21.4	−37
23	F	20.2	89	27.0	71	39.4	66	48.4	71	28.2	−18
24	M	21.5	50	34.9	57	51.6	42	51.6	42	30.1	− 8
25	M	21.8	83	28.7	75	37.8	63	50.1	60	28.3	−23

[a] Arranged according to age at first test.
[b] Stanford-Binet IQ.
Source: Adapted from H. M. Skeels & H. B. Dye (1939, Table 2).

mental growth. Over the three-year post-experimental period, the children in the contrast group showed a slight mean gain in IQ but were still mentally retarded to a marked degree. In those children that showed gains in intelligence, the gains appeared to be associated with improved environmental experiences that occurred subsequent to the original study.

In the adult follow-up study, all cases were located after 21 years.

The two groups had maintained their divergent patterns of competency into adulthood. All 13 children in the experimental group were self-supporting, and none was a ward of any institution, public or private. In the contrast group of 12 children, 1 had died in adolescence following continued residence in a state institution for the mentally retarded, and 4 were still wards of institutions, 1 in a mental hospital, and the other 3 in institutions for the mentally retarded.

In education, disparity between the two groups was striking. The contrast group completed a median of less than the third grade. The experimental group completed a median of the twelfth grade. Four of the subjects had one or more years of college work, one received a B.A. degree and took some graduate training.

Marked differences in occupational levels were seen in the two groups. In the experimental group all were self-supporting or married and functioning as housewives. The range was from professional and business occupations to domestic service, the latter the occupations of two girls who had never been placed in adoptive homes. In the contrast group, four (36%) of the subjects were institutionalized and unemployed. Those who were employed, with one exception (Case 19), were characterized as "hewers of wood and drawers of water." Using the t test, the difference between the status means of the two groups (based on the Warner Index of Status Characteristics applied to heads of households) was statistically significant ($p < .01$).

Educational and occupational achievement and income for the 11 adopted subjects in the experimental group compared favorably with the 1930 U.S. Census figures for Iowa and for the United States in general. Their adult status was equivalent to what might have been expected of children living with natural parents in homes of comparable sociocultural levels. Those subjects that married had marriage partners of comparable sociocultural levels.

Eleven of the 13 children in the experimental group were married; 9 of the 11 had a total of 28 children, an average of 3 children per family. On intelligence tests, these second-generation children had IQ's ranging from 86 to 125, with a mean and median IQ of 104. In no instance was there any indication of mental retardation or demonstrable abnormality. Those of school age were in appropriate grades for age.

In the contrast group, only two of the subjects had married. One had 1 child and subsequently was divorced. Psychological examination of the child revealed marked mental retardation with indications of probable brain damage. Another male subject (Case 19) had a nice home and family of 4 children, all of average intelligence.

The cost to the state for the contrast group, for whom intervention was essentially limited to custodial care, was approximately five times that of the cost for the experimental group. It seems safe to predict that for at least four of the cases in the contrast group costs to the state will continue at a rate in excess of $200.00 per month each for another 20 to 40 years.

Implications of Study

At the beginning of the study, the 11 children in the experimental group evidenced marked mental retardation. The developmental trend was reversed through planned intervention during the experimental period. The program of nurturance and cognitive stimulation was followed by placement in adoptive homes that provided love and affection and normal life experiences. The normal, average intellectual level attained by the subjects in early or middle childhood was maintained into adulthood.

It can be postulated that if the children in the contrast group had been placed in suitable adoptive homes or given some other appropriate equivalent in early infancy, most or all of them would have achieved within the normal range of development, as did the experimental subjects.

It seems obvious that under present-day conditions there are still countless infants born with sound biological constitutions and potentialities for development well within the normal range who will become mentally retarded and noncontributing members of society unless appropriate intervention occurs. It is suggested by the findings of this study and others published in the past twenty years that sufficient knowledge is available to design programs of intervention to counteract the devastating effects of poverty, sociocultural deprivation, and maternal deprivation.

Since the study was a pioneering and descriptive one involving only a small number of cases, it would be presumptuous to attempt to identify the specific influences that produced the changes observed. However, the contrasting outcome between children who experienced enriched environmental opportunities and close emotional relationships with affectionate adults, on the one hand, and those children who were in deprived, indifferent, and unresponsive environments, on the other, leaves little doubt that the area is a fruitful one for further study.

It has become increasingly evident that the prediction of later intelligence cannot be based on the child's first observed developmental status. Account must be taken of his experiences between test and retest. Hunt (1964, p. 212) has succinctly stated:

In fact, trying to predict what the IQ of an individual child will be at age 18 from a D.Q. obtained during his first or second year is much like trying to predict how fast a feather might fall in a hurricane. The law of falling bodies holds only under the specified and controlled conditions of a vacuum. Similarly, any laws concerning the rate of intellectual growth must take into account the series of environmental encounters which constitute the conditions of that growth.

The divergence in mental-growth patterns between children in the experimental and contrast groups is a striking illustration of this concept.

The right of every child to be well born, well nurtured, well brought up, and well educated was enunciated in the Children's Charter of the 1930 White House Conference on Child Health and Protection (White House Conference, 1931). Though society strives to insure this right, for many years to come there will be children to whom it has been denied and for whom society must provide both intervention and restitution. There is need for further research to determine the optimum modes of such intervention and the most appropriate ages and techniques for initiating them. The present study suggests, but by no means delimits, either the nature of the intervention or the degree of change that can be induced.

The planning of future studies should recognize that the child interacts with his environment and does not merely passively absorb its impact. More precise and significant information on the constitutional, emotional, and response-style characteristics of the child is needed so that those environmental experiences that are most pertinent to his needs can be identified and offered in optimum sequence.

The unanswered questions of this study could form the basis for many lifelong research projects. If the tragic fate of the 12 contrast-group children provokes even a single crucial study that will help prevent such a fate for others, their lives will not have been in vain.

References

DAWE, HELEN C. A study of the effect of an educational program upon language development and related mental functions in young children. *Journal of Experimental Education*, 1942, *11*, 200–209.

HUNT, J. MCV. The psychological basis for using preschool enrichment as an antidote for cultural deprivation. *Merrill-Palmer Quarterly of Behavior and Development*, 1964, *10*, 209–248.

SCHENKE, L. W., & SKEELS, H. M. An adult follow-up of children with inferior social histories placed in adoptive homes in early childhood. Study in Progress, 1965.

SKEELS, H.M. The mental development of children in foster homes. *Pedagogical Seminar & Journal of Genetic Psychology*. 1936, *49*, 91–106.

———. Mental development of children in foster homes. *Journal of Consulting Psychology*, 1938, *2*, 33–43.

———. Some Iowa studies of the mental growth of children in relation to differentials of the environment: a summary. In *Intelligence: its nature and nurture*. 39th Yearbook, Part II. National Society for the Study of Education, 1940, pp. 281–308.

———. A study of the effects of differential stimulation on mentally retarded children: a follow-up report. *American Journal of Mental Deficiency*, 1942, *46*, 340–350.

———, & DYE, H. B. A study of the effects of differential stimulation on mentally retarded children. *Proceedings & Addresses of the American Association on Mental Deficiency*, 1939, *44*, 114–136.

———, & FILLMORE, EVA A. The mental development of children from underprivileged homes. *Journal of Genetic Psychology*, 1937, *50*, 427–439.

———, & SKODAK, MARIE. Techniques for a high-yield follow-up study in the field. *Public Health Reports*, 1965, *80*, 249–257.

———, UPDEGRAFF, RUTH, WELLMAN, BETH L., & WILLIAMS, R. M. A study of environmental stimulation: an orphanage preschool project. *University of Iowa Studies in Child Welfare*, 1938, *15*, No. 4.

SKODAK, MARIE. Children in foster homes: a study of mental development. *University of Iowa Studies in Child Welfare*, 1939, *16*, No. 1.

SKODAK, MARIE, & SKEELS, H. M. A follow-up study of children in adoptive homes. *Journal of Genetic Psychology*, 1945, *66*, 21–58.

———. A final follow-up study of one hundred adopted children. *Journal of Genetic Psychology*, 1949, *75*, 85–125.

U.S. BUREAU OF THE CENSUS, 1960. *Methodology and scores of socio-economic status*. Working Paper No. 15. Washington, 1963, p. 13. (a)

———. U.S. Census Population, 1960, Vol. I. *Characteristics of the population*. Part 17, Iowa. Washington: U.S. Government Printing Office, 1963. Table 103, pp. 17–333. (b)

———. U.S. Census Population, 1960. *Detailed characteristics, United States summary*. Final Report PC(L)–1D. Washington: U.S. Government Printing Office, 1963. Table 173, pp. 1–406. (c)

WARNER, W. L., MEEKER, MARCHIA, & EELLS, H. *Social class in America: the evaluation of status*. New York: Harper's Torchbooks, 1960.

WELLMAN, BETH L. Our changing concept of intelligence. *Journal of Consulting Psychology*, 1938, *2*, 97–107.

WHITE HOUSE CONFERENCE ON CHILD HEALTH AND PROTECTION. *Addresses and Abstracts of Committee Reports, 1930*. New York: Appleton-Century, 1931.

5. THE PRIME OF LIFE

PATRICIA DANIEL and MARJORIE LACHMAN

What do people of different ages in the life span consider to be their "prime of life"? The few studies which are relevant to this topic have found that older people are not as happy or productive in their later years as they were when younger, or that young people do not look forward to their later years as being happy or productive (Alston and Dudley, 1973; Kastenbaum, 1959; and Landis, 1942).

Neugarten (1968) dubbed the middle adulthood years as the prime of life, for respondents aged 40–60 considered themselves to be at maximum capacity and ability to handle themselves and the environment. However, somewhat contradictory are the findings of Alston and Dudley (1973), who asked 1380 working people between 20 and 50+ if their lives are exciting. Over half of those between 20 and 39 said their lives are exciting, but less than half of those between 40 and 50+ said so.

One set of questions relevant to a choice of prime of life centers on the issue of happiness. A study by Landis (1942) asked 450 people over age 65 what the happiest period in life is. Only 5% of the respondents selected middle or old age as being the happiest age. In another study, Kuhlen (1968) observed that happiness decreases on the average, and thus unhappiness seems to increase, as people move beyond middle age. It is not made clear by these investigators what middle or old age is considered to be, only that it is not the happiest period.

The issue of what age periods means is a significant one. As has been pointed out by activity theory (Havighurst, Neugarten, and Tobin, 1968) and by other studies (Bloom, 1961; Tuckman and Lorge, 1954a and 1954b), many people have different conceptions of what middle age

and old age are. In fact, according to the findings of these researchers, many people well into their 70s consider themselves to be middle-aged. Thus, the categorization of prime of life into young, middle, and old age is lacking in precision and generalizability; further research on the topic might do better to categorize according to actual chronological age.

Do the studies cited above allow us to arrive at some conclusion as to when most people feel their prime of life is? Probably not. The ambiguity in interpreting age periods has already been mentioned as one source of difficulty in interpreting these studies. Another problem is the fact that different questions (e.g., pertaining to happiness, productivity, excitement) have been asked by different investigators. Still, it is reasonable to ask what people consider to be their prime of life, for the phrase appears in popular as well as professional sources (Neugarten, 1968). However, if we are to learn what period people consider to be their prime, we may need to ask them directly.

The present study asks the question "What do you consider to be your prime of life?" of people from teen-age to the 80s. The question was part of a general interview used by students in a course on the topic of postchildhood development. The purpose of this study was to investigate responses to the prime of life question as part of a larger study in the area of life-span development.

Responses were coded for when the prime occurs and for the time span or length of prime, and findings were analyzed for age and sex differences. Regarding the issue of "when," one possible prediction from previous research is that young people think their primes will take place in the future, while older people reflect back on their primes, considering them to have occurred at an earlier age. Regarding the second issue, the time span, a pilot study (Daniel and Kauffman, unpublished data) indicated that as age increases, the noted time span or length of prime increases as well.

Method

Three hundred and eighteen males and females between the ages of 13 and 85 were interviewed. (See Table 5.1 for a breakdown by age group and sex.) The subjects were interviewed in a variety of settings by a large number of interviewers. As part of a longer interview, subjects were asked, "What would you consider to be your prime of life and why?" Each interviewer read this question aloud to individuals in each of the age categories and wrote down the respondent's actual words.

In looking at "when" people at different ages said their prime was or would be, the responses were categorized as either "past," "now," "future," "always," or "more than one response." A subject's response to when his prime occurs was categorized as "past" if the person indicated the prime to have occurred, but now to be over; the "present" if the subject indicated that he is in his prime now, but will not be much longer; the "future" if the subject indicated that his prime will occur at some later point in time; "always" if the individual indicated that he was, is, and forever will be in his prime; and "more than one response" if the respondent gave multiple answers that could have been placed in two or more of the above categories. Subjects' responses were scored as "no data" if there was no indication as to when the prime occurs.

For "length of prime," responses were categorized as quantitative if a specific time span was given (e.g., "age 20–25" or "the 40s") or as nonquantifiable. Nonquantifiable answers took the form of *events* designating prime (e.g., "my prime was when my children were growing up");

"always" (e.g., "there is no one prime, it is always"); and "present" (e.g., "my prime is now"). Some responses were classed as "no data," for various reasons (e.g., subject did not understand the question or there was no indication of a prime length).

Two coders achieved better than 80% reliability on both the "when prime occurs" and "length of prime" scoring.

Results

The responses were grouped according to the subjects sex and age (divided into seven groups by decade—teens through 70s and older), and percentages were then computed within each of the categories for "when prime occurs" and "length of prime."

Figure 5.1 shows percentages of subjects by age group, responding to the different categories for when the prime occurs. For the category of prime in the past, the 70s groups had the highest percentage of responses (66%), whereas only 4% of the adolescent group said their prime had already occurred. The 40s and 50s age groups had the largest percentage of responses (37% of 40s and 35% of 50s), indicating prime in the present; the 70s and older had the lowest percentage of responses (13%) in this category. Although 35% of the 50s group indicated their primes to be in the present, it is interesting to note that 39% of this group said their prime was in the past. For the future category, the group that had the largest percentage of those who indicated that their primes still lie ahead of them were the adolescents (61%), and the lowest percentage of this category was in the 70s (0%). Of those who said their prime is always, the 20s had the largest representation (20%), with the 60s and 70s having the fewest giving that response (3%). No consistent sex differences were evident in the analysis of "when the prime occurs." (See Table 5.2 for a breakdown

Table 5.1. Distribution of subjects by age group and sex

	Teens			20s			30s			40s			50s			60s			70s+			Totals		
	M	F	T	M	F	T	M	F	T	M	F	T	M	F	T	M	F	T	M	F	T	M	F	T
	20	37	57	40	18	58	25	23	48	23	26	49	23	19	42	13	19	32	19	13	32	163	155	318

Table 5.2. When prime of life occurs by age group and sex

Response		Teens			20s			30s			40s			50s			60s			70s+		
		M	F	T	M	F	T	M	F	T	M	F	T	M	F	T	M	F	T	M	F	T
		(20)	(37)	(57)	(40)	(18)	(58)	(25)	(23)	(48)	(23)	(26)	(49)	(23)	(19)	(42)	(13)	(19)	(32)	(19)	(13)	(32)
Past	N	1	1	2	2	2	4	5	5	10	4	3	7	8	9	17	9	10	19	11	10	21
	%	5	3	4	5	11	7	20	22	21	17	11	14	35	47	39	69	53	59	58	77	66
Now	N	3	11	14	7	4	11	9	5	14	9	9	18	10	5	15	1	6	7	1	3	4
	%	15	30	25	17	22	19	36	22	29	39	35	37	43	26	35	8	32	22	5	23	13
Future	N	12	23	35	19	9	28	6	4	10	8	5	13	1	0	1	0	1	1	0	0	0
	%	60	62	61	47	50	48	24	17	21	35	19	27	4	0	2	0	5	3	0	0	0
Always	N	1	1	2	8	3	11	1	6	7	0	6	6	1	3	4	0	0	0	1	0	1
	%	5	3	4	20	17	19	4	26	15	0	23	12	4	16	10	0	0	0	5	0	3

Note: "More than one response" and "no data" categories are not included in the table. Total percentages in these categories are 3% and 9%, respectively.

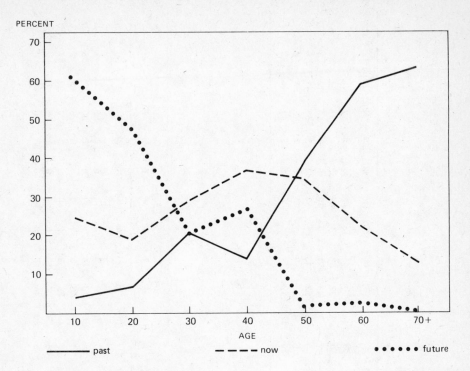

PERCENT

Figure 5.1. When prime of life thought to occur: percentage of respondent by age group

of all age groups and categories for "when prime occurs.") The trend appears to be a movement of the occurrence of the prime from future to present to past as one looks across the life span.

The results for the quantitative vs. the nonquantifiable analyses are shown in Table 5.3. For those subjects who gave a specific time span for prime, analysis of variance and mean number of years were computed for each age group and for sex differences in age groups. For all age groups, more subjects gave time spans than nonquantifiable answers, although the 40- and 60-year age groups had nearly equal quantitative and nonquantifiable responses. These data must be interpreted with caution, for the question as stated in the interview did not demand that the respondent give a time span, and not all interviewers probed for the information if it was not volunteered. In spite of this

difficulty, the response can be suggestive of trends and questions for future research.

Table 5.4 contains the nonquantifiable category. No clear age trends are apparent in the comparisons of the subcategories of events, "always" and "present." For those subjects who gave a particular time span for prime length, mean number of years in the time span was calculated for each age group and for sex differences in each age group. Spans over 40 years were omitted from the analysis in order to avoid distortion of mean scores. Table 5.5 depicts the findings for this analysis. For both sexes combined, the longest mean time span was 14 years for the 60s group; the shortest was 6.1 years for the teen-age group. No clear trends are apparent over the ages for this overall analysis. Dividing the responses by sex, however, reveals an interesting finding: for all ages, the mean time span is shorter for females than for males.

Table 5.3. Time span vs. nonquantifiable responses by age group and sex

Response		Teens			20s			30s			40s			50s			60s			70s+		
		M	F	T	M	F	T	M	F	T	M	F	T	M	F	T	M	F	T	M	F	T
		(20)	(37)	(57)	(40)	(18)	(58)	(25)	(23)	(48)	(23)	(26)	(49)	(23)	(19)	(42)	(13)	(19)	(32)	(19)	(13)	(32)
Time span	N	11	24	35	19	12	31	14	10	24	14	7	21	14	8	22	7	7	14	10	7	17
	%	55	65	61	48	67	53	56	43	50	61	27	43	61	42	52	54	37	44	53	54	53
Nonquant. response	N	8	10	18	15	5	20	6	11	17	5	16	21	8	10	18	3	10	13	3	5	8
	%	40	27	32	38	28	34	24	48	35	22	62	43	35	53	43	23	53	41	16	38	25
No data	N	1	3	4	6	1	7	5	2	7	4	3	7	1	1	2	3	2	5	6	1	7
	%	5	8	7	15	6	12	20	9	15	17	12	14	4	5	5	23	11	16	32	8	22

Table 5.4. Nonquantifiable responses by age group and sex

Response		Teens			20s			30s			40s			50s			60s			70s+		
		M	F	T	M	F	T	M	F	T	M	F	T	M	F	T	M	F	T	M	F	T
		(8)	(10)	(18)	(15)	(5)	(20)	(6)	(11)	(17)	(5)	(16)	(21)	(8)	(10)	(18)	(3)	(10)	(13)	(3)	(5)	(8)
Events	N	5	4	9	2	0	2	2	1	3	0	3	3	2	3	5	2	2	4	1	3	4
	%	62	40	50	13	0	10	33	9	18	0	19	14	25	30	28	67	20	31	33	60	50
Always	N	1	1	2	9	3	12	2	6	8	2	6	8	1	3	4	0	3	3	0	0	0
	%	13	10	11	60	60	60	33	55	47	40	38	38	12	30	22	0	30	23	0	0	0
Present	N	2	5	7	4	2	6	2	4	6	3	7	10	5	4	9	1	5	6	2	2	4
	%	25	50	39	27	40	30	33	36	35	60	44	48	63	40	50	33	50	46	67	40	50

Table 5.5 Mean number of years in length by age group and sex

	Teens			20s			30s			40s			50s			60s			70s+		
	M	F	T	M	F	T	M	F	T	M	F	T	M	F	T	M	F	T	M	F	T
(n)	(11)	(24)	(35)	(17[a])	(12)	(29)	(14)	(9[b])	(23)	(14)	(7)	(21)	(14)	(8)	(22)	(7)	(7)	(14)	(10)	(7)	(17)
	8	5	6	11	6	9	10	5	8	12	7	11	12	8	10	16	12	14	11	6	9

Note: Means are rounded off to nearest whole number. Main effect for sex was significant, $p < .0003$.
[a] Two males in the 20s age group were excluded from the means calculations for exceeding 40-year cutoff for prime length. Responses of these subjects were 80 and 64 years.
[b] One female in 30s age group was excluded from means calculations for exceeding 40-year cutoff for prime length. Response of this subject was 51 years.

For females, the mean time span ranges from a low of 5 years in the teens to a high of 12.4 in the 60s; for males the range is from 8.4 years in the teens to 15.6 years in the 60s.

A 7×2 analysis of variance with factors age and sex was performed on the time-span data. Age and age × sex interaction were not significant. The main effect for sex, however, was significant ($F = 14.3827$, $df = 1$ and 147, $p < .0003$).

Discussion

One clear-cut finding of this study was that the younger groups expect the prime of life to occur at some time in the future, the middle groups say their primes are in the present, and the older age groups reflect back on its occurring in the past. These findings are not totally consistent with other research. Alston and Dudley (1973), Kastenbaum (1959), and Landis (1942) all found that the middle and older years were not considered to be attractive times, whereas this study found that for many people the prime of life falls somewhere between ages 30 and 60. If people in this middle age bracket consider themselves to be in their primes, then an important question to ask is, Why do so many people look unfavorably on these years?

The fact that the length-of-prime analysis revealed no significant age differences is not consistent with the suggestion by Fraisse (1964) that as one gets older, he perceives time durations as shorter. The finding of sex differences in the perception of how long the prime lasts is not consistent with some studies cited by Fraisse (1964) which found that females estimate durations to be longer than do men. An interesting question for future research on this topic would be why males consistently view their primes as lasting a longer time than do females. Could the difference be related, for example, to career vs. family orientations, or to optimistic vs. pessimistic personality characteristics?

Those individuals who did not give a time span for the prime of life most often gave a specific event or described a situation during which their primes occurred or would occur. Many subjects who gave a time span also mentioned events. It would be worthwhile to explore further the situations and events that people use to characterize their primes, and to see whether these vary with age. For example, many teen-agers in this sample mentioned college and marriage as features of their primes, whereas people in the 60s and 70s often mentioned their good health or the period when their children were growing up as reasons for their choice of "when" the prime occurs.

The questions of what events or situations characterize the prime raises the broader issue of the meaning of the concept "prime of life." Gitter and Mostofsky (1973) have suggested categories for use in constructing a social indicator for the quality of life, which refers to "the condition of a person's day-to-day existence" (p. 290). They outline various "aspects of life"—for example, physical environment, health and illness, participation and alienation, and aspects of personal relations—that can be used to assess both objective, factual information and subjective evaluations of the quality of life. This scheme would be useful, not only in investigating age and personality correlates of reported levels of quality of life, but also in examining what constitutes the *prime* of life. A person's prime may be characterized by a particular configuration of levels of quality and relative importance of the different aspects of life. People at different ages may place different values on the different aspects when describing their primes.

An interesting response that was given most often by those in the 20s and second most often by those in the 30s was that everyday is the prime; the prime is always. Who are these people who have such an outlook? Why do so few teen-agers and persons in the 60s and 70s give this response? One hypothesis for future research (Kathleen White, personal communication, July 1974) is that a person's assessment of the prime of life may be related to the issue of control. Those persons who feel they have control over their lives may feel that their prime is always, whereas those who feel controlled by external circumstances may see their primes as being at some time in the past or future. An individual's locus of control may shift with age or other factors, and changes in assessment of prime of life may coincide with these shifts. For example, people who are forced to retire may feel more externally controlled than do younger people whose decisions about career and family are made personally. This hypothesis could be tested by correlating performance on the Internal-External Locus of Control Scale (Rotter, 1966) with responses to questions about the prime of life.

The cross-sectional design of this study and its implications for inferring developmental trends illustrates a recurrent problem in life-span research. The age vs. cohort issue can be seen in the following example. The highest percentage of responses in the 40s age group was in the "present" category for the "when" of prime. We do not know, from these data, whether the adolescents sampled in this study would give the same responses, when in their 40s themselves, as those in that age bracket sampled in this study. Historical events may have differentially affected different age groups, confounding the age variable. In other words, it cannot be inferred from this study that as a developmental trend, as an individual gets older he thinks that he moves closer to his prime, then that he has passed it. In order to make such a statement, a longitudinal or sequential (Schaie, 1965) design would be necessary.

It is possible, however, to use these cross-sectional data to generate hypotheses for future research. For example, this study found that 35% of those in the 50s age group said their prime are in the present, and 39% of that same group chose a time in the past. Since most people in the

two age groups younger than the 50s chose the present and an overwhelming percentage of those in the 60s and older groups chose the past as the time when their primes occurred, the responses of the 50s may be suggestive of a period of transition. These data cannot confirm this prediction, however; it remains for a longitudinal study to discover any changes in attitudes toward the quality of life during the 50s and why such changes occur.

In order to come closer to answers about the prime of life and other issues in life-span development, more rigorous analyses must be performed. The present study represents an attempt to explore the issue of prime of life in order to suggest appropriate questions and methods for further research. A major flaw in this study was the open-endedness of the question, allowing for a diversity of answers that were not always codable into discrete categories. Further research on this topic should investigate the precise time given for prime of life, incorporating "always" as a legitimate alternative response. In addition, some system such as the social indicator model (Gitter and Mostofsky, 1973) should be used for classifying reasons for choice of prime.

In an era when average length of life span is increasing, it seems worthwhile to look further into the possibilities of enjoying life to its fullest at all ages. This means understanding not only what people at different ages feel about themselves and their peers but also what they think about other age groups as well. Perhaps with more research in this area, using improved methods for studying the person and incorporating a fuller perspective, we can understand better the ups and downs of the life cycle and help to create a predominance of periods on the upside.

Summary

Three hundred and eighteen subjects between the ages of 18 and 85 were asked, "What do you consider to be your prime of life and why?" The responses were scored for length of span and for when the prime was thought to occur. Age trends were found for when prime occurs: in the future for young respondents; the present for middle-aged respondents; and the past for the oldest respondents. No consistent age trends were found for length of prime, but a significant sex difference did emerge: men chose longer time spans for the prime than women did.

References

ALSTON, J. and DUDLEY, C. Age, occupation, and life satisfaction. *The Gerontologist*, 1973, *13*, 58–61.

BLOOM, K. Age and self-concept. *American Journal of Psychiatry*, 1961, *118*, 534–538.

FRAISSE, P. *The psychology of time*. London: Eyre & Spottiswoode, 1964.

GITTER, A. G., and MOSTOFSKY, D. I. The social indicator: An index of the quality of life. *Social Biology*, 1973, *20*, 289–297.

HAVIGHURST, R., NEUGARTEN, B., and TOBIN, S. Disengagement and patterns of aging. In B. L. Neugarten (Ed.), *Middle age and aging*. Chicago: University of Chicago Press, 1968.

KASTENBAUM, R. Time and death in adolescence. In H. Feifel (Ed.), *The meaning of death*. New York: McGraw-Hill, 1959.

KUHLEN, R. G. Developmental changes in motivation during the adult years. In B. L. Neugarten (Ed.), *Middle age and aging*. Chicago: University of Chicago Press, 1968.

LANDIS, J. What is the happiest period in life? *School and Society*, 1942, *55*, 643–645.

NEUGARTEN, B. The awareness of middle age. In B. L. Neugarten (Ed.), *Middle age and aging*. Chicago: University of Chicago Press, 1968.

ROTTER, J. B. Generalized expectancies for internal vs. external control of reinforcement. *Psychological Monographs*, 1966, *80* (1, Whole No. 609).

SCHAIE, K. W. A general model for the study of developmental problems. *Psychological Bulletin*, 1965, *64*, 92–107.

TUCKMAN, J., and LORGE, I. Classification of the self as young, middle-aged or old. *Geriatrics*, 1954a, *9*, 534–536.

TUCKMAN, J., and LORGE, I. Old people's appraisal of adjustment over the life-span. *Journal of Personality*, 1954b, *22*, 417–422.

CHAPTER ONE: SUGGESTED FURTHER READINGS

BALDWIN, A. L. *Theories of child development*. New York: Wiley, 1968.

HARRIS, D. B. (ed.). *The concept of development*. Minneapolis: University of Minnesota Press, 1957.

KAGAN, J. The three faces of continuity in human development. In D. A. Goslin (ed.), *Handbook of socialization theory and research*. Chicago: Rand McNally, 1969. Pp. 983–1002.

KAGAN, J., and MOSS, H. A. *Birth to maturity: A study in psychological development*. New York: Wiley, 1962.

KESSEN, W. Research design in the study of developmental problems. In P. H. Mussen (ed.), *Handbook of research methods in child development*. New York: Wiley, 1960, Pp. 36–70.

STEVENSON, H. W. (ed.). Concept of development. *Monogr. Soc. Res. Child Develop.*, 1966, *31*, No. 5 (Serial No. 107).

WOHLWILL, J. F. *The study of behavioral development*. New York: Academic Press, 1973.

In addition to the above readings, Academic Press has published three volumes on Life-Span Developmental Psychology, edited by several authors, which contain reviews of various topics on this subject.

chapter two
physiology

My father has Addison's pernicious anemia. It crept up on him. In fact, his anemia crept up on me and his doctor.

At 89, many of his symptoms could be explained as being part of the aging process. For example, he felt depressed and was weak or tired most of the time. He didn't lose much weight, but his once hardy appetite had waned. He complained that food didn't taste right and that his sore tongue made eating painful. He became terribly forgetful, but then he's been a little absent minded for as long as I can remember. He has had arthritis for years and his left knee joint is badly damaged. When his gait became unsteady and his feet numb, it all seemed part of the degenerative process.

My father spends much of his time outdoors, and he didn't look pale. But when, on a hunch, I peeked at the inside of his lower lid, it showed not a trace of pink. I'd like to report that at the sight of that pale membrane, I proclaimed, "aha, you are of Scandinavian ancestry, and you have the classical symptoms of pernicious anemia.

I did no such thing. Because I didn't know enough about the disease, I only suggested a simple anemia and reported my guess to my father's doctor. Blood work showed a drop in hemoglobin and red cell count, and iron was prescribed. When, in a month's time, there was little improvement, I suggested to the physician that I'd seen vitamin B-12 used with success in the anemia of old age (still not knowing why). The doctor, a reasonable and bright fellow, allowed that it was certainly worth a try. When my father began to improve within the week, it was the physician who put everything together and exclaimed, "aha!" [Stern,1973].

The physiological process of growth, maturity, and gradual decay confuses and worries many people. The belief that by age eighty we will be bent, white-haired, and feeble does nothing to weaken this anxiety. Yet many of the characteristics people proclaim as facts of life, like white hair, are not simply the result of living to an old age. The above episode clearly shows how detrimental our stereotypes of aging can be, for we tend to disregard the illnesses of the elderly by lumping them into the category "due to old age." When a person reaches "old age," not only are illnesses shrugged off, but even death becomes something different. Death is said to be of "natural causes." But what are the "natural" causes of death or aging? Are physiological changes responsible for a gradual decay of the body? or is the deterioration of physical and mental skills controlled by the interactions between the environment and man's physiology? Scientists in biology, chemistry, and psychology have only recently begun to grapple with these questions, leaving the interested student with a paucity of answers.

We cannot divide our lives into different stages when we look at physiology, because each change in the physiological process is interrelated to many changes that precede and follow. It appears easy to note the physiological changes among females of nine, twenty-nine, forty-nine, and sixty-nine. Yet the comparison cannot illuminate the continuous growth and change in each of their bodies, nor can it provide an explanation of why these changes have occurred. Are the changes related to different living patterns, diet, and expectations?

One of the myths that many people believe to be fact is that people shrink as they get older. Cross-sectional studies com-

paring twenty-year-olds, forty-year-olds, and eighty-year-olds tended to support this thesis. However, a longitudinal study by Tanner (1970) revealed that

in Western Europe men increased in adult height little if at all between 1760 to 1830, about 0.3 cm (.0762 in.) per decade from 1830 to 1880, and about 0.6 cm (.1564 in.) per decade from 1880 to 1960.

Old people do not shrink at all; they merely seem smaller because the young grow up without recognizing how much they have grown. Thus the myth develops out of the change from the childhood perception of grandparents being "tall as trees" to the adult perception of a small, frail grandparent.

Another myth that people believe is that the gradual decrease in sexual activity in older people was attributed to physiological changes. Popular wisdom might have led one to believe that women lose the urge for sex after menopause and that older men are incapable of sexual activity. However, recent studies by Masters and Johnson (1966) and others have done much to dispel this myth. Women, in fact, feel freer and more active in sex after menopause, and men can enjoy active sex lives well into their older years. These studies also note that the sex drive in men and women is different. Men reach their peak in the early twenties and gradually taper off. Women gradually build to a peak between thirty and forty. Once again one can see that the process is dynamic and continuous over a life span and that the data we have are limited by our culture and expectations.

The aging process is, then, not simple but extremely complex. We are not born with a set pattern laid out for us. Life is not set in our genes, waiting for us to be its slave. Rather we are everchanging organisms gradually progressing through time. That first gray hair or that first wrinkle does not just "pop out," but is part of the day-to-day, minute-to-minute process of life.

References

MASTERS, W. H., and JOHNSON, V. E. *Human sexual response.* Boston: Little, Brown, 1966.

STERN, P. APA: Insisious foe of an aging Swede: Addison's pernicious anemia. *Amer. J. of Nursing,* 1973, *73,* 111–112.

TANNER, J. M. Physical growth. In P. Mussen (Ed.), *Carmicheal's manual of child psychology.* (3rd ed.) New York: Wiley, 1970.

6. COMMENTARY ON THE DREAM OF SCIPIO (1472)

MACROBIUS

. . .

Again, seven is the number by which man is conceived, developed in the womb, is born, lives and is sustained, and passing through all the stages of life attains old age; his whole life is regulated by it.

. . .

...after seven days [the child] casts off the remnants of the umbilical cord, after two weeks its eyes begin to move towards light, and after seven weeks it freely turns its pupils and whole face to moving visible objects. After seven months the teeth begin to appear in the jaws, and after fourteen months the child sits up without fear of falling. After thrice seven months its babbling takes the form of words, and at twenty-eight months it stands firmly and walks.... After seven years the teeth that first appeared yield their place to new ones better adapted to chewing solid foods. By the seventh year, too, the child speaks plainly.... By the fourteenth year the child reaches the age of puberty. ... After thrice seven years a beard covers the cheeks. This year also marks the limit of increasing stature. After four times seven years the body ceases to grow broader. At the thirty-fifth year the man attains the full vigor of his physical powers; no one is able to increase his strength later....

And now we must call attention to the fact that the number seven multiplied by itself produces the age which is properly considered and called perfect, so that a man of this age, as one who has already attained and not yet passed perfection, is considered ripe in wisdom and not unfit for the exercise of his physical powers. When the decade, which has the highest degree of perfection of all numbers, is joined to the perfect number seven, and ten times seven or seven times ten years are reached, this is considered by natural philosophers the goal of living, and terminates the full span of human life. When anyone exceeds this age he is retired from active duty and devotes himself solely to the exercise of his wisdom ...

. . .

7. PRISONERS OF PREJUDICE

THOMAS C. DESMOND

His hair is snow white, and mountains of wrinkles ridge his bony hands. But he is as young as a college senior. For the storms of life have not battered down his spirit, nor have the passing years shriveled his soul. Each day his face gleams with excitement, as he eagerly awaits new challenges and new experiences. His puckish humor brightens his neighborhood and his philosophic insight enriches his friends.

And he says, "It's great to be only 83."

There is youth in old age, and beauty too—if we had but the eyes to see them.

There is zest in later years, and gayety too—if we had but the understanding to recognize them.

And there is peacefulness that stems from ripe maturity—if we had the inner resources to appreciate it.

Why then do we think of old age as the years of crabbed wretchedness, of infirmity heaped upon infirmity, of useless rusting away and of community ostracism?

Attitudes and Our Aged

Because we are prisoners of stereotypes. The rigid, irrational views society holds are stripping millions of aged of a rich finale in the drama of life.

We see a pathetic old man so we say old age is pathetic. Our old folks feel old because society expects them to feel old. And our old men and old women act as society thinks old men and old women should act.

But now at last, a unique linking of science and man's faith is opening up an opportunity to party Time's thrusts at our aged.

Out of the psychological laboratories is coming new understanding of the prejudices and mythology of old age. We are beginning to learn how to attack intergeneration conflicts.[1]

From the surgeon's operating table comes new appreciation of the hardiness

of aging tissues. And out of the new enlightenment of many of the aged themselves is coming a demonstration of the agelessness of human spirit.

Old age is preventable. Not the outward signs, the weathering of skin or the dimming of the eyes' focus, or the tiring of the legs. But the inner self that largely determines one's own *true* age.

The thermostat of true aging is set by one's mind.

By serenity of spirit. By continued "growth." By purposeful activity. And underlying these, financial security.

These are, for the most part, responsibilities of the self. One cannot legislate peace of mind, nor can youthfulness be allocated like roads and bridges and post-offices by legislative fiat.

Role of Government

Where then is the responsibility of government?

The answer to this question is being found by inquiries such as have been made by [the New York State Joint Legislative Committee on Problems of the Aging]. There are many specific "solutions" to overt difficulties of older persons, ranging from increased social security and specialized job counselling and housing for the aged. But our aged will remain society's neglected step-children until a basic readjustment is made in our attitudes toward our aged, until we recognize and examine our stereotypes about the aged and alter them. This is a job that government, in cooperation with private groups, must do. The task ahead is to unshackle the aged from the prejudices of society, and guide them to new understanding of opportunities in old age.

---

[1] See *Living Without Hate*, by Alfred J. Marrow, Harpers, New York City, 1951, pp. 51–58, for an account of how an industrial psychologist broke down employer and supervisor prejudices against older workers.

8. AGE DIFFERENCE IN REACTION TIME: AN ARTIFACT?

JACK BOTWINICK and LARRY W. THOMPSON

A fact as solid as any in the psychological study of aging is that, as adults grow older, they become increasingly slow in responding to environmental events. It is not necessary here to refer to the substantial literature bearing on this fact except, perhaps, to indicate that the literature goes back to the earliest days of modern experimental psychology. Psychologists are interested in the slowing in older age, not only because of its importance in psychomotor skills, but also because of its presumed reflection of central nervous system (CNS) functioning (Botwinick, 1965).

We never doubted this fact of slowdown with age, having contributed to the literature establishing it. However, we wonder about it now. In carrying out a study that may be reported at some future date we made a chance observation which, while not refuting unequivocally the fact of age differences in reaction time (RT), challenges, or at least requires an elaboration of, theories relating to age deficits in CNS functioning.

Young Athletes and Nonathletes

In the course of simultaneously recording heart rate (EKG) and RT[1] from both elderly men (68–86, M = 74.1 years) and young men (18–27, M = 19.5), we thought we discerned that a succession of several young subjects had unusually slow heart rates and, perhaps, unusually quick RTs. When we inquired about these subjects, our assistants identified some of them as Duke University team athletes. We seemed to have had a run of these subjects and we wondered why. Upon questioning we learned that because we were collecting data toward the end of the school year when the athletic seasons were over, the athletes had more time to serve as subjects. They needed to do this in order to fulfill their requirements for their psychology courses.

Recognizing that this sampling bias may be important to control, we decided to call back all the subjects we had tested up to that time to question them about their habits of exercise. All subsequent young subjects were similarly questioned. On the basis of their reports, the young subjects were categorized into two groups: (a) those who were team athletes committed

heart cycling was involved in the timing of the stimulus.

Each subject was comfortably seated in a soft lounge chair and pressed a telegraph key on a side table to initiate the RT sequence. The subject was forewarned of the stimulus by the occurrence of a tone (400 cycles/second, 65 db, lasting 0.5 seconds) preceding the stimulus tone. The time between the warning tone and the stimulus tone, i.e., the preparatory interval (PI), was a constant, set at just over 1.0 seconds. However, both the heart cycling and the apparatus contributed to some small variation of the PI. Small as it was, it was necessary to contend with it since it made for a group difference in mean PI, and thus, conceivably, in RT itself. More will be said about this in the text, in the concluding part of the section, "Age Differences and Similarities: Results."

---

[1] We were carrying out an experiment to determine whether RTs varied in relation to when in the cardiac cycle the stimulus calling for a response occurred. The apparatus was designed such that the subject's own R-wave (peak amplitude of the cycle) triggered the stimulus (a 1,000-cycle/second, 85db tone, terminated by a finger lift response). The R-wave triggered the stimulus immediately (zero latency), 0.2 seconds, 0.4 seconds, or 0.6 seconds later, according to a prearranged schedule. For the purpose of the present study, these periods of stimulus occurrence were disregarded and all RT data were grouped; the subject had no idea that his own

to continuous exercise, or those who were not team athletes but who exercised or played ball regularly, four to five days of each week; (b) those who exercised irregularly or not at all. When subjects exercised as much as three times during some weeks but their exercise pattern was either not regular or not taken seriously, it was difficult to place them in one of the two categories. Almost always these subjects were placed in the nonathletic category rather than in the athletic category. The numbers for the athlete and nonathlete groups were 20 and 17, respectively.

Age Differences and Similarities: Results

We compared the RTs of elderly subjects with those of the athletes and nonathletes, and the results were very clear, unequivocal, and—to us at least—surprising. While the older subjects were significantly slower than the young athletes, they were not significantly slower than the young nonathletes. These results suggest that a reexamination, or at least an elaboration, of one of the basic "facts" of aging is in order.

The remainder of this section involves a more technical presentation of these results. Those who are not interested in the technical details may procede without loss of concept to the next section, "Fact or Artifact: Discussion."

Each subject had 120 RT trials. All these trials were with regular PIs during which there were 16 irregularly spaced catch trials (only a warning signal was presented, no stimulus). A short, 5–10 minute break was given at the half-way point of the 120 trials.

Each subject was characterized by his mean and median RT, and the group means of these are shown in Table 8.1. This table also shows the group standard deviations (SD), the number of subjects (N), and the results of t-test group comparisons of RT. The only place in Table 8.1 in which the results of individual mean and median RTs are different is with the combined samples of young subjects. A statistically significant age difference was found with the mean RTs, not with the medians.

The measures in which the individual subjects contributed to their respective groups may be seen in Figure 8.1. In Figure 8.1, each elderly subject and each young athletic and nonathletic subject is

Table 8.1. Mean and standard deviation (SD) of individual subject mean and median reaction time (RT)

	Elderly (E)	Young athletes (A)	Young nonathletes (N)
Mean RT			
Mean	176.15	148.14	165.06
Median	157.00	137.45	155.76
SD			
Mean	23.88	20.31	48.65
Median	24.50	18.91	51.45
N	13.00	20.00	17.00

t test of mean difference of individual means.
  E vs. A: $t = 3.37$, $p < .01$.
  E vs. N: $t = .79$, $p > .05$.
  E vs. (A+N): $t = 2.18$, $p < .05$.
  A vs. N: $t = 1.30$, $p > .05$.
t tests of mean difference of individual medians.
  E vs. A: $t = 2.36$, $p < .05$.
  E vs. N: $t = .08$, $p > .05$.
  E vs. (A+N): $t = 1.16$, $p > .05$.
  A vs. N: $t = 1.35$, $p > .05$.

PERCENT

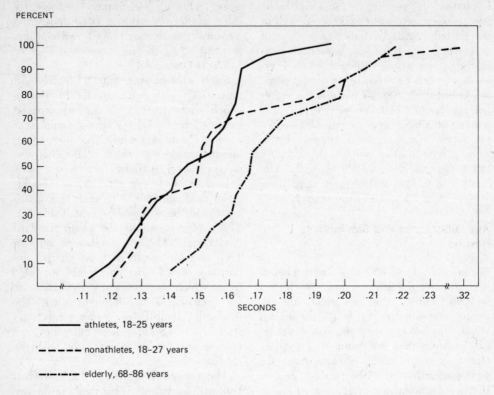

Figure 8.1. Cumulative percentage of subjects in each of three groups who have mean reaction times indicated on the abscissa

represented as a percentage of his group having a particular mean RT. These percentages are cumulated such that, for example, Figure 8.1 may be read as follows: approximately 7 percent of the elderly subjects had mean RTs of 0.14 seconds, 15 percent had RTs approximately 0.15 seconds or less, and 100 percent had mean RTs approximately 0.22 seconds or less. Similarly, 100 percent of the young athletes had RTs approximately 0.20 seconds or less, but only 82 percent of young nonathletes performed this well. In Figure 8.1 it may be seen that the nonathletes may really be composed of two subgroups: one similar to the athletes, and one different, being much slower and comparable to slower older people (5 of 17 subjects, nearly 30 percent). This idea is also reflected in the relatively large standard deviations of the nonathlete group, seen in

Table 8.1. One young nonathlete had a mean and median RT of 0.32 and 0.33 seconds, respectively—so slow that he may belong in a category by himself. When the data of this subject were eliminated from the analysis, the overall results and conclusions were not changed in any important way.

The apparatus controlling the PI (interval between the warning signal and the stimulus) was set at approximately 1.0 second. In the usual RT experiment, this is considered sufficient to describe the PI, but since the original purpose of the investigation was to examine RT relationships with cardiac function while keeping the PI controlled, we had a more precise measurement of the PI than usual. For each subject, we measured 120 RTs. While the PIs were approximately 1.0 seconds in duration, there were differences among them due to variations in the functioning of the apparatus and in the cardiac cycle which triggered the stimuli.

Because we kept such a fine control and record of the PI, we were able to test for group differences in the PI. We know that RT is a function of the PI (e.g., Botwinick & Thompson, 1966), and, thus, if groups differ in the PI this can account for the extent of group differences in RT.

PIs were found significantly different between elderly and nonathletic young subjects—the PIs of the elderly subjects were longer. To adjust for this, the longest PIs and their associated RTs of five elderly subjects and the shortest PIs and their associated RTs of one nonathlete were eliminated. In this way, elderly and nonathletic young subjects had PIs which were not significantly different. When this equating was accomplished, the age comparisons of the RTs remained the same, i.e., elderly and nonathletic young subjects were not significantly different in RT.

Fact or Artifact: Discussion

We do not think that the present data refute the "fact of aging"—the often demonstrated decline in speed to respond with increasing adult age.[2] We do think the present data open up the need for more investigation and, perhaps, broader and modified views of the significance of speed to respond. Most important, the present data emphasize that just as individual differences must be controlled or evaluated in aging samples they must also be considered in the younger controls to which the elderly are compared. We know that matters such as health and sickness in old age determine the extent of age differences in the statistical comparisons (e.g.,

Botwinick & Birren, 1963). We now suggest that matters such as physical fitness in young age also determine the extent of age differences. It is not suggested here that these physical items are all that we need to monitor; on the contrary, we believe that they are but one class of items, perhaps not even the most important class.

Although the present data may alert us to the need for a much finer analysis of the age-RT literature, we do not believe that the present data showed that all of the slowness to respond in later life is an artifact of exercise. First, we really do not know how typical or atypical our subject samples may be. Second, since we did not start out doing this particular study, we categorized some of the subjects only after viewing the data and suspecting a relationship between RT and cardiac function (with athletes tending toward slower heart rates). This may have unduly influenced the results. We do not know at this time how repeatable the present study may be, but we do know that it is not easy to schedule athletes and nonathletes for testing. Thus the present data may best be regarded as suggestive, demonstrating a direction of analysis. Third, the present results may be less general than we would like to believe, and more unique to the specific procedures. Table 8.1 and Figure 8.1 show that as RTs go, those in this study are not especially fast. Our subjects were not seated in an alert position at a desk or table, but they were seated in a deep, soft, lounge chair. Furthermore, both the warning signal and the stimulus were tones. We have a hunch that it is more difficult to be quick with two tones (one alerting and one as stimulus) than with an alerting light and a tone stimulus. If this is correct, then perhaps only the most able of subjects, i.e., young athletes, were able to overcome this disadvantage. Perhaps a less demanding RT situation would more easily differentiate elderly subjects from young nonathletes. Fourth, and perhaps most important, it may be seen in Figure 8.1 that some age differ-

---

[2] The distinction between speed to respond and speed of carrying out the response must be recognized. This distinction is frequently phrased in terms of reaction time and movement time. The present study has to do *only* with reaction time.

ence in RT is inherent even in the present data.

Figure 8.1 shows that the very fastest old person had a mean RT of 0.14 seconds. Seven of the 20 athletes (35 percent) and 6 of the 17 nonathletes (also approximately 35 percent) had faster RTs than this. In addition, as already indicated, the lack of significant difference between the elderly and nonathletic subjects was due principally to 5 slow nonathletes. Figure 8.1 shows that these 5 nonathletes (29 percent of sample) plus 1 or 2 athletes (5–10 percent) may belong to a special yet-to-be-described category, one that is much more specific and indicative of the underlying mechanisms than the crude categories of athlete and nonathlete.

The major point here is that rather than representing different age groups simply by means, medians, and the like, they may be more meaningfully represented by percentages in combination with these measures of central tendency. For example, Figure 8.1 shows that of the 37 subjects in the total young group, 11 (or 30 percent) were slower in RT than a third of the elderly subjects. We wager that if all age comparisons were made on the basis of such a combination of percentage and central tendency statistics much of the age difference which may seem impressive at first would lose its interest. An obvious disadvantage of such indices is that they do not lend themselves to parametric statistical tests of significance.

A Final Note and Summary

The contribution of the present report may lie less in the specific considerations of reaction time than in its broad methodological sampling implications. When we identified a college population subsample of 16–19 percent whose performances were no different, probably were worse, than the performances of an elderly sample, implicit questions were raised regarding the relation between a person's history and his aging patterns. To make more

meaningful our conceptions of aging processes we need to control or to evaluate individual differences in a large variety of factors. This is as true for aging samples as for their younger controls.

In this study, we separated our young adult subjects into athlete and nonathlete categories because, as a portion of the data was being collected, we thought that heart rate may be related to RT, and that both these variables may differentiate the two categories of subjects. It is important to note that the categorization was made independent of either heart rate or RT, and in the final analysis, athletes and nonathletes were not very different in these measures. During the course of the experiment, mean heart rate of athletes was 70.14 beats per minute, and of nonathletes, 76.96. Although the difference was in the direction of expectation, it was not statistically significant ($p > .05$). The corresponding mean heart rate of the elderly subjects was 71.58, not significantly different from either young group.

Despite these nonsignificant relationships, categorizing young adult subjects into groups of athlete and nonathlete proved interesting. The often-demonstrated age difference in RT was seen again with athletic young subjects but not with nonathletic young subjects, which suggests that exercise or its lack may be a factor in the slowing with age: we can expect that young people overall exercise more than elderly people. Although this may pose difficulties for CNS theories explaining the age-related slowdown, it is well to recognize that the diminution with age in the amount of exercise may be more a co-function of CNS deficits than it is an antecedent or cause of the slowdown.

In any case, as was indicated, the data of the present study emphasized the need to control or to evaluate individual differences in a large variety of factors, not only habits of exercise. Furthermore, emphasis on individual differences ought to be complemented with a similar emphasis on individual differences with respect to the main measures of study, as for example. RT in the present study. This emphasis may best be made by referring to per-centage in combination with measures of central tendency.

References

BOTWINICK, J. Theories of antecedent conditions of speed of response. In A. T. Welford and J. E. Birren (Eds.), *Behavior, aging, and the nervous system.* Springfield, Ill.: Charles C Thomas, 1965, pp. 67–87.

BOTWINICK, J. and BIRREN, J. E. Cognitive processes: mental abilities and psychomotor responses in aged men. In J. E. Birren, R. N. Butler, S. W. Greenhouse, L. Sokoloff, and Marian R. Yarrow (Eds.), *Human aging: a biological and behavioral study.* U.S. Government Printing Office, 1963, pp. 143–156.

BOTWINICK, J. and THOMPSON, L. W. Components of reaction time in relation to age and sex. *J. Genet. Psychol.,* 1966, *108,* 175–183.

9. MOVEMENT AND AGING: A PSYCHOLOGICAL APPROACH

HANS KREITLER and SHULAMITH KREITLER

Complaints of old people about bodily infirmities and ailments are so common that most physicians consider aging as an unalterable predestined physiological process. Thus, insufficient attention is given to the influence of psychological and sociological factors upon geriatric changes.

A purely physiological approach to the problem is too limited. It renders an adequate understanding of the complex aging process impossible. According to modern psychosomatic field theories, changes of any component of a multipatterned entity may bring about a modification of the whole structure. Thus, we can influence the course of aging not only by manipulating its primary determinants, but also by taking action upon seemingly less relevant facets that are amenable to adjustment.

The theoretical and practical importance of studying psychological and sociological aspects of aging lies in the fact that it enables us to exert a regulating influence on accelerating or retarding trends. A number of psychological and sociological modifiers of aging have been identified in studies reported during the past decade. Of these, we propose to discuss some that are relevant to the relationship between bodily activity and behavior of aging subjects.

What do we know about psychological determinators of motor behavior and attitudes? Child psychology operates with the concept of "pleasure of function." Charlotte Buehler pointed out already in 1931 that children enjoy movement simply for the sake of moving. Having discovered a new movement they continue performing it until they reach satiation engendered through release of kinesthetic stimuli, for example, during activities such as play, sports, dancing, etcetera.

In habitually sedentary elderly subjects, this kind of pleasure which young people derive from motor action is steadily reduced, with the result that they may eventually become reluctant to move at all. The inactivity thus caused leads to muscular degeneration as well as to distinct psychological changes. One of these is a distortion of the body image (Kreitler et al., in press). Physically inactive people over fifty perceive their bodies to be broader and heavier than they are. They therefore experience their bodily activities as increasingly strenuous, thus establishing a faulty feedback between movement and body image and with it a vicious circle through which a progressive restriction of physical exercise leads to a corresponding alteration of their body image. This in turn is followed by still greater clumsiness and increased fear of physical activity, widespread characteristics of the motor behavior of aging people.

The meaning of the physical space in which we move is discovered during childhood (Lewin, 1946). Mastery of space improves continuously during youth and in early adulthood. Once the conquest of physical space is completed, the grown-up's interest turns towards the social sphere. In the second half of life, therefore, a tendency toward introversion manifests itself.

People over fifty are bent upon the exploration of the emotional or intellectual sphere. Conquest of these spheres may be exciting, but they do not involve or necessitate discharge of energy to a degree comparable to those accompanying bodily movements. Consequently, there occurs an increase in internal tension. Another cause of internal tension is pent-up aggression. The origins of human aggression have not yet been cleared up. Freud (1948) believed that aggression is due to a primary destructive drive. Lorenz, the ethologist, claimed that aggression is an instinct.

Neither theory has been proved. Both represent but metapsychological assertions.

A better understood source of aggression is frustration (Dollard et al., 1939). It has been claimed that frustration is more prevalent in old age than during youth. Yet, it is doubtful whether this hypothesis is valid. It is more likely that life confronts young people mainly with the task of overcoming external obstacles, while older people feel that they stand vis-à-vis inner barriers. Of course, aggression stemming from frustration need not increase during the second half of life. Aggressive forces may actually remain stable over many years. Nevertheless, the fact remains that young people have more occasion than old men and women to direct their aggression outwardly, to "act it out." In older people, introversion, intellectualization, social status and other factors render a like expression of aggressive trends more difficult. The result is that at least part of such trends remains without outlet, or is turned against the self.

Of course, to some extent the same statement can be made also with respect to young people who have to restrain their aggressive tendencies. However, young people have more opportunities to release their accumulated energies, largely through bodily movements which represent their most natural means of projection. There is another psychological aspect of aging which deserves to be mentioned, viz., the loss of the illusion that life is of infinite duration. Unless there is a strong belief in life after death, the threat of death is experienced by older people as more imminent. Consequently, orientation towards the future is replaced by orientation towards the past. Orientation towards the future demands preparation for action. Orientation towards the past immobilizes. The past cannot be changed. Thus, orientation towards the past engenders frustration and resignation. A further accelerating influence upon aging is derived from identification with the social image of "the old." Every person carries within himself a design of age which is patterned by the image of his parents. Younger people shape their behavior along many lines freely chosen by them. It is only with age that the parents' image acquires a vividness of its own and with it a tendency to imitate it. This tendency stems from the fact that most people remember their parents as older than they actually were; it is also true that patterns of behavior of old people which were considered adequate forty years ago are no longer appropriate models for old age behavior today.

Social roles are played according to group expectations and group demands. Every society has stereotypes about the onset of old age and about appropriate old age behavior. Such stereotypes invariably become outdated and obsolete after a few decades. Yet, society continues in its attempt to enforce outdated stereotypes. For instance, a president of a university is not expected to dance rock-an'-roll, or to bicycle to the campus. Rather he must present himself in a dignified manner, which means that he must restrain his movements.

Social stratification establishes a no-man's-land between young and old, reduces communication to the point that contact between successive generations may be lost. Many old people are eventually unable to break through the confines of social stereotypes. Though mental or physical ability does not necessarily decline with age to such an extent that the individual's usefulness comes to an end, professional retirement at a fixed age level is today expected and even enforced by many institutions with the result that many elderly but still capable people are excluded from economic and social life. Moreover, expected and available post-retirement activities are currently planned in accordance with outdated models, for social customs do not change as quickly as science progresses, and every member of the community acquires attitudes before he is afforded an opportunity to test their adequacy.

The importance of the psychological and sociological factors mentioned above, and of others which were not discussed, lies primarily in their relevance for an understanding of old age behavior; but they also have pathological implications. For instance, reduction of the "emotional reward" that is associated with physical activity and the distortion of the body image resulting from this reduction create an atmosphere of insecurity which further lessens the desire for bodily activity. Both of these tendencies are reinforced by the social stereotype of old age behavior.

It is not the task of the psychologist to deal with the problem of the relationship between reduced bodily activity and its biological sequelae, such as muscular and cardiac degeneration, but it lies within his scope to draw attention to the implications of this issue. We have mentioned that bodily activity represents an outlet for "accumulated unconsumed energy." Physical activity reduces that "free floating tension" and channels inhibited aggression. We believe it is this "free floating tension" rather than an increase in anxiety which creates geriatric symptoms such as insomnia of the old. Fretfulness and restlessness, usually considered "the cause" of insomnia of the old, are in fact neurotic symptoms resulting from tensions due to physical inactivity. Consequently the subject often turns unreleased aggressive energies against himself, using them as a self-destructive force. Such internalized aggression may lead to depression which in turn is likely to strengthen tendencies towards psychosomatic diseases, or cause sudden outbursts of rage, with all their known consequences.

Earlier in this paper we have stressed the fact that some of the psychological and sociological factors under analysis can be directed, modified and constructively re-channelled. In this context it is relevant to point out that not all behavioral manifestations of aging are "harmful." Jung (1940) has stated that introversion often enlarges the scope of "inner life space," and this trend may be looked upon categorically as a source of gain in old age.

Regular bodily exercise involves releases of kinesthetic stimuli and this in turn provides profound emotional satisfaction. Regular bodily exercise breaks the vicious circle caused by distortions in body image due to prolonged inactivity, and it re-establishes a feeling of security. Muscular exercise appropriately designed consumes "free floating energies;" it also prevents internalization of aggressive tendencies. Of course, exercise and sport are but facets of more comprehensive programs needed to activate or re-activate people. It is within the reach of social psychology to design such programs (Kreitler, H. and Sh., 1965).

The number of variables involved in the aging process is great but not beyond comprehension and management. New approaches are called for, requiring departures from post-hoc scientific principles such as that of confining research to studies of existing diseases in an attempt to understand their causes. Rather it is necessary to embark upon investigations of the feasibility of manipulating causes of degenerative changes and of premature aging, aiming at their prevention. The task seems promising. Of course, aging cannot be avoided, but people can learn to accept and live with it. Combined physiological, psychological and sociological research can, we believe, help make old age not less rewarding than youth.

References

BUEHLER, CH.: Kindheit und Jugend (Hirzel, Leipzig 1931).

DOLLARD, J.; DOOB, L. W.; MILLER, N. E.; MOWRER, O. H. and SEARS, R. R.: Frustration and aggression (Yale University Press, New Haven 1939).

FREUD, S.: Das Unbehagen in der Kultur. Gesammelte Werke, Vol. 14, pp. 419–506 (Imago, London 1948).

JUNG, C. G.: The integration of the personality (Kegan Paul, London 1940).

KREITLER, H. and KREITLER, SH.: Die weltanschauliche Orientierung der Schizophrenen (Reinhardt, Basel/München 1965).

KREITLER, H.; KREITLER, SH. and LOMRANZ, J.: Body image: the dimension of size (in press).

LEWIN, K.: Behavior and development as a function of the total situation; in CARMICHAEL, L.: Manual of child psychology; 2nd ed., pp. 918–970 (Wiley, New York 1946).

10. WOMEN'S ATTITUDES TOWARD THE MENOPAUSE

BERNICE L. NEUGARTEN, VIVIAN WOOD,
RUTH J. KRAINES, and BARBARA LOOMIS

The menopause, like puberty or pregnancy, is generally regarded as a significant event in a woman's life; one that is known to reflect profound endocrine and somatic changes; and one that presumably involves psychological and social concomitants as well. Although there is a large medical and biological literature regarding the climacterium[1], there are few psychological studies available, except those reporting symptomology or those based on observations of women who were receiving medical or psychiatric treatment. Even the theories regarding the psychological effects of the climacterium are based largely upon observations of clinicians—psychoanalytic case studies, psychiatric investigations of climacteric psychoses, and observations of their middle-aged patients made by gynecologists and other physicians (August, 1956; Barnacle, 1949; Deutsch, 1945; Fessler, 1950; Hoskins, 1944; Ross, 1951; Sicher, 1949).

Unlike the case with puberty or pregnancy, developmental psychologists have not yet turned their attention to the menopause, and to the possible relationships, whether antecedent or consequent, between biological, psychological, and social variables. (A paper by the psychoanalyst Therese Benedek [1952] is a notable exception.) Neither is there a body of anthropological or sociological literature that describes the prevailing cultural or social attitudes to be found in America or other Western societies regarding the menopause.

As preliminary to a larger study of adjustment patterns in middle age, a number of exploratory interviews were gathered in which each woman was asked to assess her own menopausal status (whether she regarded herself as pre-, "in," or postclimacteric). She was then asked the basis of this assessment; what, if any, symptoms she had experienced; what her anticipations of menopause had been, and why; what she regarded as the worst and what the best aspects; and what, if any, changes in her life she attributed to the menopause.

It was soon apparent that women varied greatly in their attitudes and experiences. Some, particularly at upper-middle-class levels, vehemently assured the interviewer that the menopause was without any social or psychological import; that, indeed, the enlightened woman does not fear, nor —even if she suffers considerable physical discomfort—does she complain about the menopause.

"Why make any fuss about it?"

"I just made up my mind I'd walk right through it, and I did . . ."

"I saw women complaining, and I thought I would never be so ridiculous. I would just sit there and perspire, if I had to. At times you do feel terribly warm. I would sit and feel the water on my head, and wonder how red I looked. But I wouldn't worry about it, because it is a natural thing, and why get worried about it? I remember one time, in the kitchen, I had a terrific hot flush . . . I went to look

---

[1] *Menopause* and *climacterium* (as well as the more popular term, *the change of life*) are often used interchangeably in the literature. In more accurate terms, *menopause* refers to the cessation of the menses; and *climacterium* to the involution of the ovary and the various processes, including menopause, associated with this involution.

at myself in the mirror. I didn't even look red, so I thought, 'All right ... the next time I'll just sit there, and who will notice? And if someone notices, I won't even care ...' "

Others confessed to considerable fear:

"I would think of my mother and the trouble she went through; and I wondered if I would come through it whole or in pieces ..."

"I knew two women who had nervous breakdowns, and I worried about losing my mind ..."

"I thought menopause would be the beginning of the end ... a gradual senility closing over, like the darkness ..."

"I was afraid we couldn't have sexual relations after the menopause—and my husband thought so, too ..."

"When I think of how I used to worry! You wish someone would tell you—but you're too embarrassed to ask anyone ..."

Other women seemed to be repeating the advice found in women's magazines and in newspaper columns:

"I just think if a woman looks for trouble, she'll find it ..."

"If you fill your thinking and your day with constructive things—like trying to help other people—then it seems to me nothing can enter a mind already filled..."

"If you keep busy, you won't think about it, and you'll be all right ..."

Underlying this variety of attitudes were two common phenomena: first, whether they made much or made little of its importance, middle-aged women were willing, even eager, to talk about the menopause. Many volunteered the comment that they seldom talked about it with other women; that they wished for more information and more communication. Second, although many professed not to believe what they termed "old wives tales," most women had nevertheless heard many such tales of the dangers of menopause, and could recite them easily: that menopause often results in mental breakdown; that it marks the end of a

woman's sexual attractiveness as well as her sexual desires; and so on. Many women said, in this connection, that while they themselves had had neither fears nor major discomforts, they indeed knew other women who held many such irrational fears or who had suffered greatly. (The investigators interpreted such responses as indicative, at least in part, of the psychological mechanism of projection.)

The Instrument

Following a round of preliminary interviews, a more systematic measurement of attitudes toward the menopause was undertaken. A checklist was drawn up containing statements culled from the exploratory interviews and from the literature on the subject. For example, the statement, "Women generally feel better after the menopause than they have for years," appears in a pamphlet about menopause for sale by the US Government Printing Office (US Public Health Service, 1959). "Women who have trouble with the menopause are usually those who have nothing to do with their time," is a statement made by a number of interviewees. "A woman in menopause is likely to do crazy things she herself does not understand" is a statement made by a woman describing her own behavior. Respondents were asked to check, for each statement, 1. agree strongly; 2. agree to some extent; 3. disagree somewhat; or 4. disagree strongly. Because of the projective phenomenon already mentioned, the statements were worded in terms of "other women," or "women in general" rather than "self" (see Table 10.2).

The checklist was then pre-tested on a sample of 50 women aged 40 to 50. Following the analysis of those responses, the instrument was revised and the number of items reduced to 35. Certain statements were eliminated because they drew stereotyped responses; others, because of overlap.

The Samples

The revised Attitudes-Toward-Menopause Checklist, hereafter referred to as the ATM, was administered as part of a lengthy interview to a sample of 100 women aged 45 to 55 on whom a variety of other data were being gathered. These 100 women, referred to here as the C, or Criterion, group had been drawn from lists of mothers of graduates from two public high schools in the Chicago metropolitan area. None of these women had had surgical or artificial menopause, and all were in relatively good health.

Once the data on the ATM had been analyzed for the Criterion group, the question arose, how do women of different ages view the menopause? Accordingly, the instrument was administered to other groups of women contacted through business firms and women's clubs. Directions for filling out the ATM were usually given in group situations, and the respondents were asked to mail back the forms to the investigators along with certain identifying information (age, level of education, marital status, number and ages of children, and health status). The proportion responding varied from group to group, with an average of about 75% responses. From this larger pool, Groups A, B, and D were drawn.

The composition of the four samples, by age and level of education, is shown in Table 10.1. All the women in all four groups were married, all were mothers of one or more children and, with the excep-

tion of a few in Groups B and D, all were living with their husbands. None of these women reported major physical illness or disability.

These groups of women, although by no means constituting representative samples, are biased in only one known direction: compared with the general population of American women, they are higher on level of education, for they include higher proportions of the college-educated. This is especially true of Group A and Group D.

Findings

Level of Education

When responses to the ATM were analyzed for differences between the women in each age group who had and those who had not attended college, only a few scattered differences appeared, a number attributable to chance.

As already indicated, however, the four samples of women represent relatively advantaged groups with regard to educational level. It is likely that in more heterogeneous samples educational level would emerge as a significant variable in women's attitudes toward menopause.

Age Differences

As shown in Table 10.2, consistent age differences were found. The statements are grouped in the table according to the pattern that emerged from a factor analysis carried out on the responses of Group

Table 10.1. The samples by age and level of education

Group	Number	Age	High School Graduation or Less	Percents One or More Years of College	No Information
A	50	21–30	8	90	2
B	52	31–44	33	50	17
C	100	45–55	65	35	0
D	65	56–65	54	46	0

Table 10.2. Attitudes toward menopause by age

Items subgrouped	Percent Who Agree[a] Age groups			
	A 21–30 (N=50)	B 31–44 (N=52)	C 45–55 (N=100)	D 56–65 (N=65)
I. *"Negative Affect"*				
28. Menopause is an unpleasant experience for a woman	56	44	58	55
32. It's not surprising that most women get disagreeable during the menopause	58	51	57	43
34. Women should expect some trouble during the menopause	60	46	59	58
30. Menopause is a disturbing thing which most women naturally dread	38*	46	57	53
20. It's no wonder women feel "down in the dumps" at the time of the menopause	54	46	49	49
33. In truth, just about every woman is depressed about the change of life	48	29	40	28
II. *"Post-Menopausal Recovery"*				
24. Women generally feel better after the menopause than they have for years	32*	20*	68	67
26. A woman has a broader outlook on life after the change of life	22*	25*	53	33*
27. A woman gets more confidence in herself after the change of life	12*	21*	52	42
16. Women are generally calmer and happier after the change of life than before	30*	46*	75	80
23. Life is more interesting for a woman after the menopause	2*	13*	45	35
17. After the change of life, a woman feels freer to do things for herself	16*	24*	74	65
31. After the change of life, a woman has a better relationship with her husband	20*	33*	62	44*
35. Many women think menopause is the best thing that ever happened to them	14*	31	46	40
21. After the change of life, a woman gets more interested in community affairs than before	24*	31*	53	60
III. *"Extent of Continuity"*				
14. A woman's body may change in menopause, but otherwise she doesn't change much	48*	71*	85	83
15. The only difference between a woman who has not been through the menopause and one who has, is that one menstruates and the other doesn't	34*	52	67	77
12. Going through the menopause really does not change a woman in any important way	58*	55*	74	83
IV. *"Control of Symptoms"*				
4. Women who have trouble with menopause are usually those who have nothing to do with their time	58	50*	71	70
7. Women who have trouble in the menopause are those who are expecting it	48*	56*	76	63
8. The thing that causes women all their trouble at menopause is something they can't control—changes inside their bodies	42*	56*	78	65
V. *"Psychological Losses"*				
29. Women often get self-centered at the time of the menopause	78	63	67	48*
25. After the change of life, women often don't consider themselves "real women" anymore	16	13	15	3*

Table 10.2. (continued)

Items subgrouped	Percent Who Agree[a] Age groups			
	A 21–30 (N=50)	B 31–44 (N=52)	C 45–55 (N=100)	D 56–65 (N=65)
1. Women often use the change of life as an excuse for getting attention	60*	69	80	68
18. Women worry about losing their minds during the menopause	28*	35	51	24*
11. A woman is concerned about how her husband will feel toward her after the menopause	58*	44	41	21*
VI. "Unpredictability"				
6. A woman in menopause is apt to do crazy things she herself does not understand	40	56	53	40
10. Menopause is a mysterious thing which most women don't understand	46	46	59	46
VII. "Sexuality"				
3. If the truth were really known, most women would like to have themselves a fling at this time in their lives	8*	33	32	24
19. After the menopause, a woman is more interested in sex than she was before	14*	27	35	21
Ungrouped Items[b]				
2. Unmarried women have a harder time than married women do at the time of the menopause	42	37	30	33
5. A woman should see a doctor during the menopause	100	100	95	94
9. A good thing about the menopause is that a woman can quit worrying about getting pregnant	64	38*	78	63*
13. Menopause is one of the biggest changes that happens in a woman's life	68*	42	50	55
22. Women think of menopause as the beginning of the end	26	13*	26	9*

[a] Those subjects who checked "agree strongly" or "agree to some extent."
[b] These statements did not show large loadings on any of the seven factors represented by the groupings in the table.
* The difference between this percentage and the percentage of Group C is significant at the .05 level or above.

C.[2] That analysis, although serving a purpose extraneous to the present report, provided groupings of the statements that are meaningful also for studying age differences.

Overall inspection of Table 10.2 shows first that, as anticipated, young women's patterns of attitudes toward the menopause are different from those of middle-aged women. When each group is compared with the Criterion group, the largest number of significant differences are found between Groups A and C; then between B and C.

At the same time, it appears that it is not age alone, but age and experience-with-menopause that are probably operating together. There are very few dif-

[2] Responses were scored from 1 to 4; and on the matrix of intercorrelations, the principal component method of factor extraction by Jacoby and the Varimax program for rotation were used. Seven factors, accounting for 85% of the variance, emerged from that analysis, factors which have been named "negative affect," "post-menopausal recovery," and so on, as indicated in Table 10.2. Within each group of statements, the order is that of their loadings on the respective factor. It should be kept in mind that a somewhat different factor pattern might have emerged from the responses of Groups A, B, or D.

ferences between Groups C and D; and relatively few between A and B. The major differences lie between the first two and the last groups—in other words, between women who have and those who have not yet experienced the changes of the climacterium. Although there is not a one-to-one correlation between chronological age and age-at-menopause, approximately 75% of the women in Group C, as well as all those in D, reported that they were presently experiencing or had already completed the "change of life." Only a few of Group B had yet entered "the period of the change."

It can be seen from Table 10.2, also, that age differences follow a particular pattern from one cluster of statements to the next. Thus, on the first cluster, "negative affect," there are no significant differences between age groups nor between statements. In each instance, about half the women agree that the menopause is a disagreeable, depressing, troublesome, unpleasant, disturbing event; and about half the women disagree.

On the second cluster of statements, however, there are sharp age differences, and in general, all in the same direction: middle-aged women recognize a "recovery," even some marked gains occurring once the menopause is past. The postmenopausal woman is seen as feeling better, more confident, calmer, freer than before. The majority of younger women, by contrast, are in disagreement with this view.

On the third and fourth clusters age differences, while not so sharp as on the second cluster, are numerous and are again consistent in direction: namely, middle-aged women take what may be interpreted as the more positive view, with higher proportions agreeing that the menopause creates no major discontinuity in life, and agreeing that, except for the underlying biological changes, women have a relative degree of control over their symptoms and need not inevitably have difficulties. This is essentially the view that one woman expressed by saying, "If women look for trouble, of course they find it."

Of the remainder of the statements, those that form the fifth, sixth, and seventh clusters as well as those that fit none of the clusters, age differences are scattered and inconsistent in direction, depending evidently upon the particular content and wording of each statement. It is interesting to note, for instance, that on No. 18, "Women worry about losing their minds," it is the Criterion group, Group C, which shows the highest proportion who agree.

It is also of interest that on Nos. 3 and 19, it is the youngest group who disagree most with the view that menopausal women may experience an upsurge of sexual impulse. In this connection, the interviews with Group C women, many of whom had not completed the change of life, showed a wide range of ideas about a woman's interest in sex relations after the menopause. The comments ranged from, "I would expect her to be less interested in sex, because that is something that belongs more or less to the childbearing period," to, "She might become more interested because the fear of pregnancy is gone." Many women expressed considerable uncertainty about the effects of the menopause on sexuality.

Discussion

That there should be generally different views of menopause in younger and in middle-aged women is hardly a surprise. Any event is likely to have quite different significance for persons who are at different points in the life line.

One reason why fewer middle-aged as compared to younger women in this study viewed menopause as a significant event may be that loss of reproductive capacity is not an important concern of middle-aged women at either a conscious or unconscious level. In the psychological and psychiatric literature it is often stated that the end of the reproductive period—the "closing of the gates," as it has been described (Deutsch, 1945, p. 457)—evokes in most women a desire for another child. If so, women might be expected to view menopause as most significant at that time in life when the loss of reproductive capacity is imminent. Yet this was not the case in these data.

There is additional evidence on the same point from our interview data. Of the 100 women in the Criterion group, only 4, in responding to a multiple-choice question, chose, "Not being able to have more children" as the worst thing in general about the menopause. (At the same time, 26 said the worst thing was, "Not knowing what to expect"; 19 said, "The discomfort and pain"; 18 said, "It's a sign you are getting old"; 4 said, "Loss of enjoyment in sex relations"; 22 said, "None of these things"; and 7 could not answer the question.) It is true, of course, that all these women had borne children; but the same was true of all the younger women in Groups A and B. Many Group C women said, in interview, that they had raised their children and were now happy to have done, not only with menstruation and its attendant annoyances, but also with the mothering of small children.

The fact that middle-aged as frequently as younger women view the menopause as unpleasant and disturbing is not irreconcilable with their view of the menopause as an unimportant event. As one woman put it, "Yes, the change of life is an unpleasant time. No one enjoys the hot flushes, the headaches, or the nervous tension. Sometimes it's even a little frightening. But I've gone through changes before, and I can weather another one. Besides, it's only a temporary condition."

Another woman joked, "It's not the pause that refreshes, it's true; but it's just a pause that depresses."

The middle-aged woman's view of the postmenopausal period as a time when she will be happier and healthier underscores her belief in the temporary nature of the unpleasant period, a belief that is reinforced perhaps by hearing postmenopausal women say, as two said to our interviewer:

"My experience has been that I've been healthier and in much better spirits since the change of life. I've been relieved of a lot of aches and pains."

"Since I have had my menopause, I have felt like a teen-ager again. I can remember my mother saying that after her menopause she really got her vigor, and I can say the same thing about myself. I'm just never tired now."

The fact that most younger women have generally more negative views is perhaps because the menopause is not only relatively far removed, and therefore relatively vague; but because, being vague, it becomes blended into the whole process of growing old, a process that is both dim and unpleasant. Perhaps it is only the middle-aged or older woman who can take a differentiated view of the menopause; and who, on the basis of experience, can, as one woman said, "separate the old wives' tales from that which is true of old wives."

Summary

An instrument for measuring attitudes toward the menopause was developed, consisting of 35 statements on which women were asked if they agreed or disagreed. The instrument was administered to 267 women of four age groups: 21–30; 31–44; 45–55; and 56–65. Differences were most marked between the first two and the last two groups, with the younger women holding the more negative and more undifferentiated attitudes.

References

AUGUST, H. E.: Psychological aspects of personal adjustment. In IRMA F. GROSS (Ed.), *Potentialities of women in the middle years* (Michigan State Univ. Press, East Lansing 1956).

BARNACLE, C. H.: Psychiatric implications of the climacteric. *Amer. Practit. 4:* 154–157 (1949).

BENEDEK, THERESE: *Psychosexual functions in women* (Ronald, New York 1952).

DEUTSCH, HELENE: *The psychology of women.* Vol. II, *Motherhood* (Grune & Stratton, New York 1945).

FESSLER, L.: Psychopathology of climacteric depression. *Psychoanal. Quart. 19:* 28–42 (1950).

HOSKINS, R. G.: Psychological treatment of the menopause. *J. clin. Endocrin. 4:* 605–610 (1944).

ROSS, M.: Psychosomatic approach to the climacterium. *Calif. Med. 74:* 240–242 (1951).

SICHER, L.: Change of life: a psychosomatic problem. *Amer. J. Psychother. 3:* 399–409 (1949).

US PUBLIC HEALTH SERVICE: *Menopause.* Health Information Series Publ. No. 179. (US Govt. Print. Off., Washington, D.C. 1959).

11. DEATH: PROCESS OR EVENT?

ROBERT S. MORISON

Most discussions of death and dying shift uneasily, and often more or less unconsciously, from one point of view to another. On the one hand, the common noun "death" is thought of as standing for a clearly defined event, a step function that puts a sharp end to life. On the other, dying is seen as a long-drawn-out process that begins when life itself begins and is not completed in any given organism until the last cell ceases to convert energy.

The first view is certainly the more traditional one. Indeed, it is so deeply embedded, not only in literature and art, but also in the law, that it is hard to free ourselves from it and from various associated attitudes that greatly influence our behavior. This article analyzes how the traditional or literary conception of death may have originated and how this conception is influencing the way in which we deal with the problem of dying under modern

conditions. In part, I contend that some of our uses of the term "death" fall close to, if not actually within, the definition of what Whitehead called the "fallacy of misplaced concreteness" (1). As he warned, "This fallacy is the occasion of great confusion in philosophy," and it may also confuse our handling of various important practical matters.

Nevertheless, there is evidence that the fallacy may be welcomed by some physicians because it frees them from the necessity of looking certain unsettling facts in the face.

In its simplest terms, the fallacy of misplaced concreteness consists in regarding or using an abstraction as if it were a thing, or, as Whitehead puts it, as a "simple instantaneous material configuration." Examples of a relatively simple kind can be found throughout science to illustrate the kinds of confusion to which the fallacy leads. Thus, our ancestors who observed the behavior of bodies at different temperatures found it convenient to explain some of their observations by inventing an abstraction they called heat. All too quickly the abstract concept turned into an actual fluid that flowed from one body to another. No doubt these conceptions helped to develop the early stages of thermodynamics. On the other hand, the satisfaction these conceptions gave their inventors may also have slowed down the development of the more sophisticated kinetic theory.

It should be quite clear that, just as we do not observe a fluid heat, but only differences in temperature, we do not observe "life" as such. Life is not a thing or a fluid anymore than heat is. What we observe are some unusual sets of objects separated from the rest of the world by certain peculiar properties such as growth, reproduction, and special ways of handling energy. These objects we elect to call "living things." From here, it is but a short step to the invention of a hypothetical entity that is possessed by all living things and that is supposed to account for the difference between living and nonliving things. We might call this entity "livingness," following the usual rule for making abstract nouns out of participles and adjectives. This sounds rather awkward, so we use the word "life" instead. This apparently tiny change in the shape of the noun helps us on our way to philosophical error. The very cumbersomeness of the word "livingness" reminds us that we have abstracted the quality for which it stands from an array of living things. The word "life," however, seems much more substantial in its own right. Indeed, it is all too easy to believe that the word, like so many other nouns, stands for something that must have an existence of its own and must be definable in general terms, quite apart from the particular objects it characterizes. Men thus find themselves thinking more and more about life as a thing in itself, capable of entering inanimate aggregations of material and turning them into living things. It is then but a short step to believing that, once life is there, it can leave or be destroyed, thereby turning living things into dead things.

Now that we have brought ourselves to mention dead things, we can observe that we have invented the abstract idea of death by observing dead things, in just the same way that we have invented the idea of life by observing living things. Again, in the same way that we come to regard life as a thing, capable of entering and leaving bodies, we come to regard death as a thing, capable of moving about on its own in order to take away life. Thus, we have become accustomed to hearing that "death comes for the archbishop," or, alternatively, that one may meet death by "appointment in Samarra." Only a very few, very sophisticated old generals simply fade away.

In many cases then, Death is not only reified, it is personified, and graduates from a mere thing to a jostling woman in the marketplace of Baghdad or an old man, complete with beard, scythe, and hourglass, ready to mow down those whose time has come. In pointing to some of the dangers of personification, it is not my purpose to abolish poetry. Figures of speech certainly have their place in the enrichment of esthetic experience, perhaps even as means for justifying the ways of God to man. Nevertheless, reification and personification of abstractions do tend to make it more difficult to think clearly about important problems.

Abstractions Can Lead to Artificial Discontinuity

A particularly frequent hazard is the use of abstractions to introduce artificial discontinuities into what are essentially continuous processes. For example, although it is convenient to think of human development as a series of stages, such periods as childhood and adolescence are not discontinuous, sharply identifiable "instantaneous configurations" that impose totally different types of behavior on persons of different ages. The infant does not suddenly leave off "mewling and puking" to pick up a satchel and go to school. Nor at the other end of life does "the justice, . . . with eyes severe and beard of formal cut" instantly turn into "the lean and slipper'd pantaloon." The changes are gradual; finally, the pantaloon slips through second childishness into "mere oblivion, sans teeth, sans eyes, sans taste, sans everything" (2). Clearly we are dealing here with a continuous process of growth and decay. There is no magic moment at which "everything" disappears. Death is no more a single, clearly delimited, momentary phenomenon than is infancy, adolescence, or middle age. The gradualness of the process of dying is even clearer than it was in Shakespeare's time, for we now know that various parts of the body can go on living for months, after its central organization has disintegrated. Some cell lines, in fact, can be continued indefinitely.

The difficulty of identifying a moment of death has always been recognized when dealing with primitive organisms, and the conventional concept has usually not been applied to organisms that reproduce themselves by simple fission. Death as we know it, so to speak, is characteristic only of differentiated and integrated organisms, and is most typically observed in the land-living vertebrates in which everything that makes life worth living depends on continuous respiratory movements. These, in turn, depend on an intact brain, which itself is dependent on the continuing circulation of properly aerated blood. Under natural conditions, this tripartite, interdependent system fails essentially at one and the same time. Indeed, the moment of failure seems often to be dramatically marked by a singularly violent last gasping breath. Observers of such a climactic agony have found it easy to believe that a special event of some consequence has

taken place, that indeed Death has come and Life has gone away. Possibly even some spirit or essence associated with Life has left the body and gone to a better world. In the circumstances surrounding the traditional deathbed, it is scarcely to be wondered at that many of the observers found comfort in personifying the dying process in this way, nor can it be said that the consequences were in any way unfortunate.

Now, however, the constant tinkering of man with his own machinery has made it obvious that death is not really a very easily identifiable event or "configuration." The integrated physiological system does not inevitably fail all at once. Substitutes can be devised for each of the major components, and the necessary integration can be provided by a computer. All the traditional vital signs are still there—provided in large part by the machines. Death does not come by inevitable appointment, in Samarra or anywhere else. He must sit patiently in the waiting room until summoned by the doctor or nurse.

Perhaps we should pause before being completely carried away by the metaphor. Has death really been kept waiting by the machines? If so, the doctor must be actively causing death when he turns the machines off. Some doctors, at least, would prefer to avoid the responsibility, and they have therefore proposed a different view of the process (3). They would like to believe that Death has already come for the patient whose vital signs are maintained by machine and that the doctor merely reveals the results of his visit. But if Death has already come, he has certainly come without making his presence known in the usual way. None of the outward and visible signs have occurred—no last gasp, no stopping of the heart, no cooling and stiffening of the limbs. On the other hand, it seems fairly obvious to most people that life under the conditions described (if it really is life) falls seriously short of being worth living.

Is a "Redefinition" of Death Enough?

We must now ask ourselves how much sense it makes to try to deal with this complex set of physiological, social, and ethical variables simply by "redefining" death or by developing new criteria for pronouncing an organism dead. Aside from the esoteric philosophical concerns discussed so far, it must be recognized that practical matters of great moment are at stake. Fewer and fewer people die quietly in their beds while relatives and friends live on, unable to stay the inevitable course. More and more patients are subject to long, continued intervention; antibiotics, intravenous feeding, artificial respiration, and even artificially induced heartbeats sustain an increasingly fictional existence. All this costs money—so much money, in fact, that the retirement income of a surviving spouse may disappear in a few months. There are other costs, less tangible but perhaps more important—for example, the diversion of scarce medical resources from younger people temporarily threatened by acute but potentially curable illnesses. Worst of all is the strain on a family that may have to live for years in close association with a mute, but apparently living, corpse.

An even more disturbing parameter has recently been added to the equation. It appears that parts of the dying body may acquire values greater than the whole. A heart, a kidney, someday even a lung or a liver, can mean all of life for some much younger, more potentially vigorous and happy "donee."

Indeed, it appears that it is primarily this latter set of facts which has led to recent proposals for redefining death. The most prominent proposals place more emphasis on the information-processing capacity of the brain and rather less on the purely mechanical and metabolic activities of the body as a whole than do the present practices. The great practical merit of these proposals is that they place the moment of death somewhat earlier in the continuum of life than the earlier definition did. By so doing, they make it easier for the physician to discontinue therapy while some of what used to be considered "signs of life" are still present, thus sparing relatives, friends, and professional attendants the anguish and the effort of caring for a "person" who has lost most of the attributes of personality. Furthermore, parts of the body which survive death, as newly defined, may be put to other, presumably more important uses, since procedures such as autopsies or removal of organs can be undertaken without being regarded as assaults.

In considering the propriety of developing these new criteria, one may begin by admitting that there is nothing particularly unusual about redefining either a material fact or a nebulous abstraction. Physical scientists are almost continuously engaged in redefining facts by making more and more precise measurements. Taxonomists spend much of their time redefining abstract categories, such as "species," in order to take into account new data or new prejudices. At somewhat rarer intervals, even such great concepts as force, mass, honor, and justice may come up for review.

Nevertheless, in spite of the obvious practical advantages and certain theoretical justifications, redefinition of abstractions can raise some very serious doubts. In the present instance, for example, we are brought face to face with the paradox that the new definitions of death are proposed, at least in part, because they provide that certain parts of the newly defined dead body will be *less dead* than they would have been if the conventional definition were still used. Looked at in this light, the proposed procedure raises serious ethical questions (4). The supporters of the new proposal are, however, confronted every day by the even more serious practical problems raised by trying to make old rules fit new situations. Faced with a dilemma, they find it easier to urge a redefinition of death than to recognize that life may reach a state such that there is no longer an ethical imperative to preserve it. While one may give his support to the first of these alternatives as a temporary path through a frightening and increasingly complicated wilderness, it might be wise not to congratulate ourselves prematurely.

As our skill in simulating the physiological processes underlying life continues to increase in disproportion to our capacity to maintain its psychological, emotional, or spiritual quality, the difficulty of regarding death as a single, more or less coherent event, resulting in the instantaneous dissolution of the organism as a whole, is likely to become more and more apparent. It may not be premature, therefore, to anticipate some of the questions that will then increasingly press upon us. Some of the consequences of adopting the attitude that death is part of a continuous process that is coextensive (almost) with living may be tentatively outlined as follows.

An unprejudiced look at the biological facts suggests, indeed, that the "life" of a complex vertebrate like man is not a clearly defined entity with sharp discontinuities at both ends. On the contrary, the living human being starts inconspicuously, unconsciously, and at an unknown time, with the conjugation of two haploid cells. In a matter of some hours, this new cell begins to divide. The net number of living cells in the organism continues to increase for perhaps 20 years, then begins slowly to decrease. Looked at in this way, life is certainly not an all-or-none phenomenon. Clearly the amount of living matter follows a long trajectory of growth and decline with no very clear beginning and a notably indeterminate end. A similar trajectory can be traced for total energy turnover.

A human life is, of course, far more than a metabolizing mass of organic matter, slavishly obeying the laws of conservation of mass and energy. Particularly

interesting are the complex interactions among the individual cells and between the totality and the environment. It is, in fact, this complexity of interaction that gives rise to the concept of human personality or soul.

Whatever metaphors are used to describe the situation, it is clear that it is the complex interactions that make the characteristic human being. The appropriate integration of these interactions is only loosely coupled to the physiological functions of circulation and respiration. The latter continue for a long time after the integrated "personality" has disappeared. Conversely, the natural rhythms of heart and respiration can fail, while the personality remains intact. The complex human organism does not often fail as a unit. The nervous system is, of course, more closely coupled to personality than are the heart and lungs (a fact that is utilized in developing the new definitions of death), but there is clearly something arbitrary in tying the sanctity of life to our ability to detect the electrical potential charges that manage to traverse the impedance of the skull.

If there is no infallible physiological index to what we value about human personality, are we not ultimately forced to make judgments about the intactness and value of the complex interactions themselves?

"Value" of a Life Changes with Value of Complex Interactions

As the complexity and richness of the interactions of an individual human being wax and wane, his "value" can be seen to change in relation to other values. For various reasons it is easier to recognize the process at the beginning than at the end of life. The growing fetus is said to become steadily more valuable with the passage of time (5): its organization becomes increasingly complex and its potential for continued life increases. Furthermore, its mother invests more in it every day and becomes increasingly aware of and pleased by its presence. Simultaneous with these increases in "value" is the increased "cost" of terminating the existence of the fetus. As a corollary, the longer a pregnancy proceeds, the more reasons are required to justify its termination. Although it may be possible to admire the intellectual ingenuity of Saint Thomas and others who sought to break this continuous process with a series of discontinuous stages and to identify the moment at which the fetus becomes a human being, modern knowledge of the biological process involved renders all such efforts simply picturesque. The essential novelty resides in the formation of the chromosomal pattern—the rest of the development is best regarded as the working out of a complicated tautology.

At the other end of life the process is reversed: the life of the dying patient becomes steadily less complicated and rich, and, as a result, less worth living or preserving. The pain and suffering involved in maintaining what is left are inexorably mounting, while the benefits enjoyed by the patient himself, or that he can in any way confer on those around him, are just as inexorably declining. As the costs mount higher and higher and the benefits become smaller and smaller, one may well begin to wonder what the point of it all is. These are the unhappy facts of the matter, and we will have to face them sooner or later. Indeed, attempts to face the facts are already being made, but usually in a gingerly and incomplete fashion. As we have seen, one way to protect ourselves is to introduce imaginary discontinuities into what are, in fact, continuous processes.

A similar kind of self-deception may be involved in attempts to find some crucial differences among the three following possibilities that are open to the physician attending the manifestly dying patient.

1. Use all possible means (including the "extraordinary measures" noted by the Pope) to keep the patient alive.

2. Discontinue the extraordinary measures but continue "ordinary therapy."
3. Take some "positive" step to hasten the termination of life or speed its downward trajectory.

Almost everyone now admits that there comes a time when it is proper to abandon procedure 1 and shift to procedure 2 although there is a good deal of disagreement about determining the moment itself. There is much less agreement about moving to procedure 3, although the weight of opinion seems to be against ever doing so.

The more one thinks of actual situations, however, the more one wonders if there is a valid distinction between allowing a person to die and hastening the downward course of life. Sometimes the words "positive" and "negative" are used, with the implication that it is all right to take away from the patient something that would help him to live but wrong to give him something that will help him to die.

The intent appears to be the same in the two cases, and it is the intent that would seem to be significant. Furthermore, one wonders if the dividing point between positive and negative in this domain is any more significant than the position of zero on the Fahrenheit scale. In practice, a physician may find it easier not to turn on a respirator or a cardiac pacemaker than to turn them off once they have been connected, but both the intents and the results are identical in the two cases. To use an analogy with mathematics, subtracting one from one would seem to be the same as not adding one to zero.

Squirm as we may to avoid the inevitable, it seems time to admit to ourselves that there is simply no hiding place and that we must shoulder the responsibility of deciding to act in such a way as to hasten the declining trajectories of some lives, while doing our best to slow down the decline of others. And we have to do this on the basis of some judgment on the quality of the lives in question.

Clearly the calculations cannot be made exclusively or even primarily on crude monetary or economic criteria. Substantial value must be put on intangibles of various kinds—the love, affection, and respect of those who once knew the fully living individual will bulk large in the equation. Another significant parameter will be the sanctity accorded to any human life, however attenuated and degraded it may have become. Respect for human life as such is fundamental to our society, and this respect must be preserved. But this respect need not be based on some concept of absolute value. Just as we recognize that an individual human life is not infinite in duration, we should now face the fact that its value varies with time and circumstance. It is a heavy responsibility that our advancing command over life has placed on us.

It has already been noted that in many nations, and increasingly in the United States, men and women have shouldered much the same kind of responsibility—but apparently with considerably less horror and dismay—at the beginning of the life-span. In spite of some theological misgivings and medical scruples, most societies now condone the destruction of a living fetus in order to protect the life of the mother. Recent developments have greatly broadened the "indications" to include what is essentially the convenience of the mother and the protection of society against the dangers of overpopulation.

A relatively new, but very interesting, development is basing the decision of whether or not to abort purely on an assessment of the quality of the life likely to be lived by the human organism in question. This development has been greatly enhanced by advances in the technique of amniocentesis, with its associated methods for determining the chromosomal pattern and biochemical competence of the unborn baby. Decisions made on such grounds are difficult, if not impossible, to differentiate, in principle, from decisions made by the Spartans and other earlier societies to expose to nature those infants born with manifest anatomical defects. We are being driven toward the ethics of an earlier period by the inexorable logic of the situation, and it may only increase our discomfort without changing our views to reflect that historians (6) and moralists (7) both agree that the abolition of infanticide was perhaps the greatest ethical achievement of early Christianity.

Issue Cannot Be Settled by Absolute Standards

Callahan (5) has recently reviewed all the biological, social, legal, and moral issues that bear on decisions to terminate life in its early stages and argues convincingly that the issue cannot be settled by appeals to absolute rights or standards. Of particular importance for our purposes, perhaps, is his discussion of the principle of the "sanctity of life," since opposition to liberalizing the abortion laws is so largely based on the fear of weakening respect for the dignity of life in general. It is particularly reassuring, therefore, that Callahan finds no objective evidence to support this contention. Indeed, in several countries agitation for the liberalization of abortion laws has proceeded simultaneously with efforts to strengthen respect for life in other areas —the abolition of capital punishment, for example. Indeed, Callahan's major thesis is that modern moral decisions can seldom rest on a single, paramount principle; they must be made individually, after a careful weighing of the facts and all the nuances in each particular case.

The same considerations that apply to abortion would appear to apply, in principle, to decisions at the other end of the life-span. In practice, however, it has proven difficult to approach the latter decisions with quite the same degree of detachment as those involving the life and death of an unborn embryo. It is not easy to overlook the fact that the dying patient possesses at least the remnants of a personality that developed over many decades and that involved a complicated set of interrelationships with other human beings. In the case of the embryo, such relationships are only potential, and it is easier to ignore the future than to overlook the past. It can be argued, however, that it should be easier to terminate a life whose potentialities have all been realized than to interrupt a pregnancy the future of which remains to be unfolded.

Once it is recognized that the process of dying under modern conditions is at least partially controlled by the decisions made by individual human beings, it becomes necessary to think rather more fully and carefully about what human beings should be involved and what kinds of considerations should be taken into account in making the decisions.

Traditionally it has been the physician who has made the decisions, and he has made them almost exclusively on his own view of what is best for the patient. Only under conditions of special stress, where available medical resources have been clearly inadequate to meet current needs, has the physician taken the welfare of third parties or "society" into account in deciding whether to give or withhold therapy. Until recently, such conditions were only encountered on the battlefield or in times of civilian catastrophe such as great fires, floods, or shipwrecks. Increasingly, however, the availability of new forms of therapy that depend on inherently scarce resources demands that decisions be made about distribution. In other words, the physician who is considering putting a patient on an artificial kidney may sometimes be forced to consider the needs of other potential users of the same device. The situation is even more difficult when the therapeutic device is an organ from another human being. In some communities, the burden of such decisions is shifted from a single physician to a group or committee that may contain nonmedical members.

These dramatic instances are often thought of as being special cases without much relationship to ordinary life and death. On the other hand, one may look upon them as simply more brilliantly colored examples of what is generally true but is not always so easy to discern. Any dying patient whose life is unduly prolonged imposes serious costs on those immediately around him and, in many cases, on a larger, less clearly defined "society." It seems probable that, as these complex interrelationships are increasingly recognized, society will develop procedures for sharing the necessary decisions more widely, following the examples of the committee structure now being developed to deal with the dramatic cases.

It is not only probable, but highly desirable, that society should proceed with the greatest caution and deliberation in proposing procedures that in any serious way threaten the traditional sanctity of the individual life. As a consequence, society will certainly move very slowly in developing formal arrangements for taking into account the interests of others in life-and-death decisions. It may not be improper, however, to suggest one step that could be taken right now. Such a step might ease the way for many dying patients without impairing the sanctity or dignity of the individual life: instead, it should be enhanced. I refer here to the possibility of changing social attitudes and laws that now restrain the individual from taking an intelligent interest in his own death.

The Judeo-Christian tradition has made suicide a sin of much the same character as murder. The decline of orthodox theology has tended to reduce the sinfulness of the act, but the feeling still persists that there must be something wrong with somebody who wants to end his own life. As a result, suicide, when it is not recognized as a sin, is regarded as a symptom of serious mental illness. In this kind of atmosphere, it is almost impossible for a patient to work out with his doctor a rational and esthetically satisfactory plan for conducting the terminating phase of his life. Only rarely can a great individualist like George

Eastman or Percy Bridgman (8) transcend the prevailing mores to show us a rational way out of current prejudice. Far from injuring the natural rights of the individual, such a move can be regarded as simply a restoration of a right once greatly valued by our Roman ancestors, who contributed so much to the "natural law" view of human rights. Seneca (9), perhaps the most articulate advocate of the Roman view that death should remain under the individual's control, put the matter this way: "To death alone it is due that life is not a punishment, that erect beneath the frowns of fortune, I can preserve my mind unshaken and master of myself."

References

1. A. N. WHITEHEAD, *Science and the Modern World* (Macmillan, New York, 1967), pp. 51–55.
2. SHAKESPEARE, *As You Like It*, Act II, Scene vii, ll. 144–166.
3. H. K. BEECHER, *J. Am. Med. Assoc.* 205, 337 (1968).
4. P. RAMSEY, in *Updating Life and Death*, D. R. Cutler, Ed. (Beacon, Boston, 1969), p. 46; H. Jonas, in *Experimentation with Human Subjects*, P. A. Freund, Ed. (Braziller, New York, 1970), pp. 10–11.
5. D. CALLAHAN, *Abortion: Law, Choice and Morality* (Macmillan, New York, 1970).
6. W. E. H. LECKY, *History of European Morals from Augustus to Charlemagne* (Appleton, New York, 1870), vol. 1.
7. H. SIDGWICK, *Outlines of the History of Ethics* (Macmillan, London, 1886; Beacon, Boston, 1960).
8. G. HOLTON, *Bull. At. Sci. 18* (No. 2), 22 (February 1962).
9. SENECA, *Ad Marciam, de Consolatione*, XX, translated by W. E. H. Lecky, in *History of European Morals from Augustus to Charlemagne* (Appleton, New York, 1870), vol. 1, p. 228.

CHAPTER TWO: SUGGESTED FURTHER READINGS

KASTENBAUM, R. *New thoughts on old age.* New York: Springer, 1964.
———. *Contributions to the psychobiology of aging.* New York: Springer, 1965.
TIMIRAS, P. S. *Developmental physiology and aging.* New York: Macmillan, 1972.
Despite a great deal of supposition about the physical aspects of aging, we were not able to locate even one good review article on this topic.

chapter three
congition

What is the mental functioning in childhood like compared to the mental functioning in adulthood? How does cognitive development take place? and does development cease at a certain stage? These are some of the questions we shall be concerned with in looking at cognition across the life span. Cognition can be defined as a combination of the understanding man has of his environment and all the inner tools he has to nurture this understanding. "Cognition" is a broad term encompassing, among other things, intelligence, learning, memory, perception, problem solving, and communication. Developmentalists have increasingly become concerned with the many areas of cognition and their relationship to the stages in human development. Traditionally, some aspects of cognitive development have been studied exclusively in relation to children, while other aspects were studied only in relation to young adults and older adults. The questions asked here are questions for a more life-span-oriented approach.

Humans are well equipped to perceive and relate to their environment. As they age, their cognitive functions become more and more sophisticated, and their ability to understand the environment undoubtedly differs accordingly. Piaget sees cognitive development as occurring in several stages, the end result of which is that adults comprehend a totally different reality than a child can.

One measure of developmental level is an analysis of the kinds of concepts that human beings are able to understand at a particular time. Consider, for example, the concept of gravity. All that young children can comprehend of it is the concrete reality they grasp from their own experience: they learn, for instance, that when they drop a toy from the crib, the object falls to the floor and out of their reach. From this experience children learn the limits of the body and the rules of the universe. As children mature, their intellectual development becomes less limited to the concrete and they are able to deal abstractly with concepts such as gravity and thereby understand the implications of the laws of gravitational force.

Cross-cultural studies facilitate a better understanding of human thought by looking at variations across cultures and suggesting the variety of forces that might shape human thought. For example, some cultures perceive the world very differently from Western industrial culture. Piaget (1974) has expressed the need for more cross-cultural research:

Psychology elaborated in our environment, which is characterized by a certain culture and language, remains essentially conjectural as long as the necessary cross-cultural material has not been gathered as a control. We would like to see cross-cultural studies of cognitive functions, which do not concern the child only but development as a whole, including the final adult stages. [p. 309.]

Just as cultures contain differences in cognitive style, so do individuals. Cognitive style develops from personal experience. Family, sex, socioeconomic situation, biological condition are all important influences on the way one thinks.

There is much research on the cognitive development in the early stages of life in the psychological literature. However, there is insufficient information on the later stages, and consequently some of our notions of later intellectual development are erroneous. Indeed, the older person is often suggested as necessarily deteriorated in mental functioning in much the same way Western scientists for years described "primitive" peoples as functioning on less able cognitive levels.

Differences in cognitive functioning at different ages could be attributed to differences between two generations, perhaps due to different educational or nutritional experiences. In the United States today, children are exposed to television, which was not so for their grandparents. All indications are that this experience will have, on the present young, profound effects that cannot be found when looking at people who are sixty or seventy today. Changes in the educational system also have strong effects on thinking: for example, being taught mathematics by a logical method rather than a memorizational one.

We think that human beings change as they age: they have different life experiences, they use their knowledge differently at different life priods, they respond differently to test situations at different ages. It is a common notion in the United States that older means dumber, that somehow the peak years for learning are over by twenty or thirty. Yet, in many other cultures only the old are regarded as wise.

Reference

PIAGET, J. Need and significance of cross-cultural studies in genetic psychology. In J. W. Berry and P. R. Dassen (Eds.), *Culture and cognition*. London: Methuen, 1974, pp. 299–309.

12. THE MYTH OF THE TWILIGHT YEARS

PAUL B. BALTES and K. WARNER SCHAIE

News reporters never tire of pointing out that Golda Meir works 20-hour days, yet is in her mid-70s, and a grandmother. *Time*, in a recent story on William O. Douglas, noted that the blue eyes of the 75-year-old Justice "are as keen and alert as ever. So, too, is [his] intellect." This sort of well-intended but patronizing compliment betrays a widespread assumption that intelligence normally declines in advanced adulthood and old age, and that people like Meir and Douglas stand out as exceptions.

In our opinion, general intellectual decline in old age is largely a myth. During the past 10 years, we and our colleagues, (particularly G. V. Labouvie and J. R. Nesselroade) have worked to gain a better understanding of intelligence in the aged. Our findings challenge the stereotyped view, and promote a more optimistic one. We have discovered that the old man's boast, "I'm just as good as I ever was," may be true, after all.

The Data on Decline

For a long time, the textbook view coincided with the everyday notion that as far as intelligence is concerned, what goes up must come down. The research that supported this view was cross-sectional in nature. The investigator administered intelligence tests to people of various ages at a given point in time, and compared the performance levels of the different age groups. Numerous studies of this type conducted during the '30s, '40s and '50s led researchers to believe that intelligence increases up to early adulthood, reaches a plateau that lasts for about 10 years, and begins to decline in a regular fashion around the fourth decade of life.

The first doubts arose when the results of longitudinal studies began to be available. In this type of study, the researcher observes a single group of subjects for a period of time, often extending over many years, and examines their performance at different ages. Early longitudinal studies suggested that intelligence during maturity and old age did not decline as soon as people had originally assumed.

As better intelligence tests became available, researchers began to realize that different intellectual measures might show different rates of decline. On measures of vocabulary and other skills reflecting educational experience, individuals seemed to maintain their adult level of functioning into the sixth, and even the seventh decade.

Resolving the Discrepancy

In 1956, one of us (Schaie) launched a major project aimed at resolving this disturbing discrepancy between the two kinds of study. Five hundred subjects, ranging in age from 21 to 70, received two intelligence tests, Thurstone and Thurstone's Primary Mental Abilities, and Schaie's Test of Behavioral Rigidity. Seven years later, we retested 301 of the subjects with the same tests.

The tests we used yielded 13 separate measures of cognitive functioning. Using factor-analysis methods, we found that the scores reflected four general, fairly independent dimensions of intelligence:

1. *Crystallized intelligence* encompasses the sorts of skills one acquires through education and acculturation, such as verbal comprehension, numerical skills, and inductive reasoning. To a large degree, it reflects the extent to which one

has accumulated the collective intelligence of one's own culture. It is the dimension tapped by most traditional IQ tests (see "Are I.Q. Tests Intelligent?" by Raymond Cattell, *Psychology Today*, March 1968).

2. *Cognitive flexibility* measures the ability to shift from one way of thinking to another, within the context of familiar intellectual operations, as when one must provide either an antonym or synonym to a word, depending on whether the words appears in capital or lower-case letters.

3. *Visuo-motor flexibility* measures a similar but independent skill, the one involved in shifting from familiar to unfamiilar patterns in tasks requiring co-ordination between visual and motor abilities, e.g., when one must copy words but interchange capitals with lower-case letters.

4. *Visualization* measures the ability to organize and process visual materials, and involves tasks such as finding a simple figure contained in a complex one or identifying a picture that is incomplete.

The Schaie study did not contain sufficient measures of fluid intelligence, which encompasses abilities thought to be relatively culture free. Other researchers, e.g., Cattell and Horn, have reported a dramatic decline with age on fluid intelligence, though on the basis of cross-sectional data only.

If we analyze the data cross-sectionally (comparing the different age groups at a given point in time), we see the conventional pattern of early, systematic decline [Figure 12.1]. But when we look at the results longitudinally (comparing a given age group's performance in 1956 with its performance in 1963), we find a definite decline on only one of the four measures, visuo-motor flexibility.

There is no strong age-related change in cognitive flexibility. For the most important dimension, crystallized intelligence,

and for visualization as well, we see a systematic *increase* in scores for the various age groups, right into old age. Even people over 70 improved from the first testing to the second.

Intellectual Generation Gap

In cross-sectional studies, people who differ in age also differ in generation, since they were born in different years. This means that any measured differences in intelligence could reflect either age or generation differences, or both. Our study, however, allowed us to compare people from different generations at the same ages, because we tested people at two different points in time. For instance, we could compare subjects who were 50 in 1956 with subjects who were 50 in 1963. Our statistical analysis revealed that the differences between scores were due mainly to generational differences, not to chronological age. In other words, the important factor was the year a subject was born, rather than his age at the time of testing. Apparently, the measured intelligence of the population is increasing. The earlier findings of general intellectual decline over the individual life span were largely an artifact of methodology. On at least some dimensions of intelligence, particularly the crystallized type, people of average health can expect to maintain or even increase their level of performance into old age.

At present, we can only speculate about the reasons for generational differences in intelligence. We believe the answer lies in the substance, method and length of education received by different generations. When we consider the history of our educational institutions, and census data on the educational levels attained by members of specific generations, it seems fair to assume that the older people in our study were exposed to shorter periods of formal education. Furthermore, their education probably relied more heavily on principles of memorization, and less heavily on those of problem-solving.

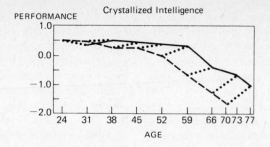

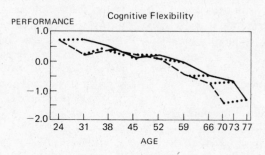

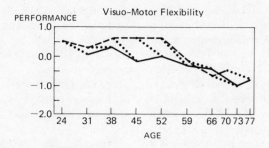

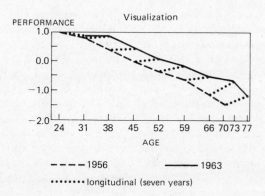

– – – – 1956 ———— 1963

•••••••• longitudinal (seven years)

Figure 12.1 Age and Dimensions of Intelligence. The broken and solid lines slope downward, indicating that in both 1956 and 1963, older people scored lower than younger ones on various dimensions of intelligence. However, the dotted lines, which show how a given age group's performance changed from the first test occasion to the second, reveal that the older groups crystallized intelligence and visualization go up, not down.
Reprinted by permission from the *Journal of Gerontology,* 1972, vol. 27.

However, there are other possibilities that must be reckoned with before we can offer a more definite interpretation. Members of different generations may differ in their sophistication in test-taking or their willingness to volunteer responses. They may differ in the extent to which they have been encouraged to achieve intellectually. And tests developed to measure the abilities of one generation may be invalid for another. In any case, the existence of differences between generations makes the search for "normal" aging phenomena a Sisyphean task.

Drop Before Death

Klaus and Ruth Riegel, psychologists at the University of Michigan, have recently suggested that when intellectual decline does occur, it comes shortly before death (see "Life, or Death and IQ," *News Line*, May 1973). In 1956, the Riegels gave intelligence tests to 380 German men and women between the ages of 55 and 75. Five years later they retested 202 of them. Some of the remainder had died, and others refused to be retested. When the Riegels looked back at the 1956 test scores of the subjects who had died, they discovered that on the average, the deceased subjects had scored lower than those who survived. Put another way, the low scores in 1956 predicted impending death.

The Riegels followed up their study in 1966 by inquiring into the fate of the people retested in 1961. Again, some people had died in the interim, and those who had died had lower scores than those who lived. Furthermore, people who had died since 1961 had declined in score from the first test session in 1956 to the second in 1961. These results pointed to a sudden deterioration during the five or fewer years immediately prior to natural death, or what the Riegels called a "terminal drop." Interestingly, the people who had refused to be retested in 1961 were more likely than the others to die before 1966. Per-

haps their refusal reflected some kind of awareness of their own decline.

The Riegels' results may offer an alternative explanation for the general decline found by cross-sectional studies: the older groups may contain a higher percentage of people in the terminal drop stage, and their lower scores would not be typical of other older people. If the researcher could foresee the future and remove from his study those subjects nearing death, he might observe little or no change in the intelligence of the remaining group. In fact, the Riegels found that elderly subjects still alive in 1966 did as well on the average, as persons at the presumed period of peak performance, 30 to 34 years, which, of course, is consistent with our own data.

While it is tempting to speculate on the reasons for terminal drop, we feel that the present state of the art is such that interpretation must be tentative at best. Most researchers would probably tend to relate the drop in intellectual functioning to neurophysiological deterioration. However, this position overlooks the possibility that psychological variables contribute both to the drop and to biological death.

Aged-Biased IQ Tests

The nature of the tests used to assess intelligence may also contribute to the apparent decline that is sometimes observed. Sidney L. Pressey (who now lives as an octogenarian in a home for the elderly and continues to make occasional but insightful contributions to psychology) first pointed out that the concept of intelligence, as well as the instruments to measure it, are defined in terms of abilities most important during youth and early adulthood. This is not really surprising, since IQ tests came into existence for the purpose of predicting school performance. The format and content of these tests may simply be inappropriate for tapping the potential wisdom of the aged. For example, older people tend to do relatively poorly on tests employing technical language such as the terminology of physics or computer programing. Their performance is better if items are worded in terms of everyday experiences.

Another problem is the distinction between a person's competence and his actual performance. Handicaps that have nothing to do with intrinsic ability may affect the way a person does on a test. For instance, Baltes and Carol A. Furry recently demonstrated that the aged are especially susceptible to the effects of fatigue; pretest fatigue considerably lowered the scores of older subjects, but did not affect the performance of younger ones.

Dwindling reinforcements may also affect the performance of the aged. Elderly individuals, because of their uncertain and shortened life expectancy, may cease to be sensitive to the sorts of long-range rewards that seem to control intellectual behavior in young people (e.g., education, career goals, and development of a reputation). Ogden Lindsley has proposed that the aged may become more dependent on immediate and idiosyncratic rewards.

Even when rewards are potentially effective, they may be unavailable to old people. Most researchers agree that the environment of the elderly is intellectually and socially impoverished. Family settings and institutions for the aged fail to provide conditions conducive to intellectual growth. The educational system discourages participation by the elderly, focusing instead on the young.

Recent work on age stereotypes indicates that some young people hold a negative view of old age. These views may influence them to withdraw reinforcements for competence in the elderly, or even to punish such competence. Aging persons may in time come to accept the stereotypes, view themselves as deficient, and put aside intellectual performance as a personal goal. In the process, the intellectual deficit becomes a self-fulfilling prophecy.

Compensatory Education for the Aged

Although educators have made massive attempts to overcome discrimination in early childhood, working through Government-funded compensatory programs, analogous efforts for the aged have barely begun. But, increasing numbers of gerontologists have felt encouraged enough by the reanalysis of intellectual decline to examine, probably for the first time in any vigorous manner, the degree to which intellectual performance can be bolstered. The results are still very sketchy, but they are promising.

Some researchers, working from a biobehavioral perspective, have looked at the effects of physical treatments. For instance, hyperbaric oxygen treatment—the breathing of concentrated oxygen for extended periods to increase oxygen supply to the brain—seems to improve memory for recent events, although the outcome of such research is not at all free of controversy. Treatment of hypertension and conditioning of alpha waves also seem to be promising, and deserve careful study. Other researchers concentrate on studying the psychological aspects of the learning process; they experiment with the pacing of items, the mode of presentation (for instance, auditory versus visual), the amount of practice, the delivery of rewards, training in mnemonics, and so on.

The speed with which a person responds, which is important on many intellectual tests, is usually assumed to be a function of biological well-being. But in a series of pilot studies, Baltes, William Hoyer and Gisela V. Labouvie were able to improve the response speed of elderly subjects rather dramatically, using Green Stamps as a reward for faster performance in canceling letters, marking answer sheets and copying words. After as little as two hours of training, women 65 to 80 years of age increased their speed as much as 20 to 35 percent. The researchers compared the performance of these "trained" subjects with that of untrained controls on 11 different intelligence tests. Although the transfer of the speed training to test performance was not earthshaking, the overall pattern was encouraging.

In the interest of rectifying some of the social injustices that have resulted from the branding of the aged as deficient, social scientists must continue to explore, with vigor and optimism, the research avenues opened during the past few years. This research should be guided by a belief in the potential of gerontological intelligence, and a rejection of the rigid, biological view that assumes an inevitable decline. We should not be surprised to find that the socialization goals and mechanisms of a society are the most powerful influence on what happens to people, not only during childhood and adolescence but also during adulthood and old age.

Social roles and resources can be assigned without regard to age only when the deleterious aspects of aging are eliminated. Toward this end, in 1971 an American Psychological Association task force on aging made some specific recommendations for eliminating the unnecessary causes of decline in intellectual functioning. They included more forceful implementation of adult-education programs; funding of research and innovative programs in voluntary (rather than mandatory) retirement, second-career training, and leisure-time activity; and better utilization of skills that are unaffected by age.

When we consider the vast spectrum of negative conditions, attributes and expectations that most Western societies impose on older people, we must acclaim the impressive robustness of our older population in the face of adversity. At the same time, we hope that society, aided by geropsychology, soon finds ways to make life for the elderly more enjoyable and effective. Acknowledging that intellectual decline is largely a myth is, we hope, a step in the right direction.

13. CROSS–CULTURAL PERSPECTIVES ON EARLY DEVELOPMENT

JEROME KAGAN and ROBERT E. KLEIN

Most American psychologists believe in the hardiness of habit and the premise that experience etches an indelible mark on the mind not easily erased by time or trauma. The application of that assumption to the first era of development leads to the popular view that psychological growth during the early years is under the strong influence of the variety and patterning of external events and that the psychological structures shaped by those initial encounters have a continuity that stretches at least into early adolescence. The first part of that hypothesis, which owes much of its popularity to Freud, Harlow, and Skinner, has strong empirical support. The continuity part of the assumption, which is more equivocal, is summarized in the American adage, "Well begun is half done."

Many developmental psychologists, certain of the long-lasting effects of early experience, set out to find the form of those initial stabilities and the earliest time they might obtain a preview of the child's future. Although several decades of research have uncovered fragile lines that seem to travel both backward and forward in time, the breadth and magnitude of intraindividual continuities have not been overwhelming, and each seems to be easily lost or shattered (Kagan & Moss, 1962; Kessen, Haith, & Salapatek, 1970). A recent exhaustive review of research on human infancy led to the conclusion that "only short term stable individual variation has been demonstrated; . . . and demonstrations of continuity in process—genotype continuity—have been rare indeed [Kessen et al., 1970, p. 297]." Since that evaluation violates popular beliefs, the authors noted a few pages later:

In spite of slight evidence of stability, our inability to make predictions of later personality from observations in the first three years of life is so much against good sense and common observation, to say nothing of the implication of all developmental theories, that the pursuit of predictively effective categories of early behavior will surely continue unabated. [p. 309.]

The modest empirical support for long-term continuity is occasionaly rationalized by arguing that although behaviors similar in manifest form might not be stable over long time periods, the underlying structures might be much firmer (Kagan, 1971). Hence, if the operational manifestations of those hidden forms were discerned, continuity of cognitive, motivational, and affective structures would be affirmed. However, we recently observed some children living in an isolated Indian village on Lake Atitlan in the highlands of northwest Guatemala. We saw listless, silent, apathetic infants; passive, quiet, timid 3-year-olds; but active, gay, intellectually competent 11-year-olds. Since there is no reason to believe that living conditions in this village have changed during the last century, it is likely that the alert 11-year-olds were, a decade earlier, listless, vacant-staring infants. That observation has forced us to question the strong form of the continuity assumption in a serious way.

The data to be presented imply absence of a predictive relationship between level of cognitive development at 12–18 months of age and quality of intellectual functioning at 11 years. This conclusion is not seriously different from the repeated demonstrations of no relation between infant intelligence quotient (IQ) or developmental quotient (DQ) scores during the first year of life and Binet or Wechsler IQ scores obtained during later childhood (Kessen et al., 1970; Pease, Wolins, & Stockdale, 1973). The significance of the current data, however, derives from the fact that the infants seemed to be more seriously retarded than those observed in earlier studies, their environments markedly less varied, and the assessment of later cognitive functioning based on culture-fair tests of specific cognitive abilities rather than culturally biased IQ tests.

Moreover, these observations suggest that it is misleading to talk about continuity of any psychological characteristic—be it cognitive, motivational, or behavioral—without specifying simultaneously the context of development. Consider the long-term stability of passivity as an example. The vast majority of the infants in the Indian village were homogeneously passive and retained this characteristic until they were five or six years old. A preschool child rarely forced a submissive posture on another. However, by eight years of age, some of the children became dominant over others because the structure of the peer group required that role to be filled. Factors other than early infant passivity were critical in determining that differentiation, and physical size, strength, and competence at valued skills seemed to be more important than the infant's disposition. In modern American society, where there is much greater variation among young children in degree of passivity and dominance, a passive four-year-old will always encounter a large group of dominant peers who enforce a continuing role of submissiveness on him. As a result, there should be firmer stability of behavioral passivity during the early years in an American city than in the Indian village. But the stability of that behavior seems to be more dependent on the presence of dominant members in the immediate vicinity than on some inherent force within the child.

Continuity of a psychological disposition is not solely the product of an inherited or early acquired structure that transcends a variety of contexts. The small group of scientists who champion that view of stability—we have been among them—envision a small box of different-colored gems tucked deep in the brain, with names like intelligent, passive, irritable, or withdrawn engraved on them. These material entities guarantee that, despite behavioral disguises, an inherent set of psychological qualities, independent of the local neighborhood and knowable under the proper conditions, belongs to each individual. This belief in a distinct and unchanging mosaic of core traits—an identity—is fundamental to Western thought and is reflected in the psychological writings of Erik Erikson and the novels of popular Western writers. Only Herman Hesse, who borrowed the philosophy of the East, fails to make a brief for personal identity. *Siddhartha, Magister Ludi,* and *Narcissus and Goldmund* are not trying to discover "who they are" but are seeking serenity, and each appreciates the relevance of setting in that journey.

A secondary theme concerns the interaction of maturation and environment, an issue that has seized academic conversation because of the renewed debate surrounding the inheritance of intelligence. But there is a broader issue to probe. The majority of American psychologists remain fundamentally Lockean in attitude, believing that thought and action owe primary allegiance to experience and that reinforcements and observations of models set the major course of change. Despite Piaget's extraordinary popularity, the majority of American psychologists do not believe that maturation supplies the major impetus for psychological growth during the childhood years. We have forgotten that many years ago Myrtle McGraw (1935) allowed one twin to climb some stairs and prevented his co-twin from practicing that skill. This homely experiment occurred only a few years after Carmichael (1926) anesthetized some *Amblystoma* embryos to prevent them from swimming. The twin not allowed to climb was behind his partner in learning this skill, but he eventually mastered it. Carmichael's embryos swam perfectly when the anesthetic was pumped out of the tank. In both instances, the organisms could not be prevented from displaying species-specific properties.

Our observations in these Indian villages have led us to reorder the hierarchy of complementary influence that biology and environmental forces exert on the development of intellectual functions that are natural to man. Seperate maturational factors seem to set the time of emergence of those basic abilities. Experience can slow down or speed up that emergence by several months or several years, but nature will win in the end. The capacity for perceptual analysis, imitation, language, inference, deduction, symbolism, and memory will eventually appear in sturdy form in any natural environment, for each is an inherent competence in the human program. But these competences, which we assume to be universal, are to be distinguished from culturally specific talents that will not appear unless the child is exposed to or taught them directly. Reading, arithmetic, and understanding of specific words and concepts fall into this latter category.

This distinction between universal and culturally specific competences implies a parallel distinction between absolute and relative retardation. Consider physical growth as an illustration of this idea. There is sufficient cross-cultural information on age of onset of walking to warrant the statement that most children should be walking unaided before their second birthday. A three-year-old unable to walk is physically retarded in the absolute sense, for he has failed to attain a natural competence at the normative time. However, there is neither an empirical nor a logical basis for expecting that most children, no matter where they live, will develop the ability to hunt with a spear, ride a horse, or play football. Hence, it is not reasonable to speak of absolute retardation on these skills. In those cultures where these talents are taught, encouraged, or modeled, children will differ in the age at which they attain varied levels of mastery. But we can only classify a child as precocious or retarded relative to another in his community. The data to be reported suggest that absolute retardation in the attainment of specific cognitive competences during infancy has no predictive validity with respect to level of competence on a selected set of natural cognitive skills at age 11. *The data do not imply that a similar level of retardation among American infants has no future implication for relative retardation on culture-specific skills.*

The Guatemalan Settings

The infant observations to be reported here were made in two settings in Guatemala. One set of data came from four subsistence farming Ladino villages in eastern Guatemala. The villages are moderately isolated, Spanish speaking, and contain between 800 and 1,200 inhabitants. The families live in small thatched huts of cane or adobe with dirt floors and no sanitary facilities. Books, pencils, paper, and pictures are typically absent from the experience of children prior to school entrance, and, even in school, the average child has no more than a thin lined notebook and a stub of a pencil.

A second location was a more isolated Indian village of 850 people located on the shores of Lake Atitlan in the northwest mountainous region of the country. Unlike the Spanish-speaking villages, the Indians of San Marcos la Laguna have no easy access to a city and are psychologically more detached. The isolation is due not only to geographical location but also to the fact that few of the women and no more than half of the men speak reasonable Spanish. Few adults and no children can engage the culture of the larger nation, and the Indians of San Marcos regard themselves as an alien and exploited group.

The Infant in San Marcos

During the first 10–12 months, the San Marcos infant spends most of his life in the small, dark interior of his windowless hut. Since women do not work in the field, the mother usually stays close to the home and spends most of her day preparing food, typically tortillas, beans, and coffee, and perhaps doing some weaving. If she travels to a market to buy or sell, she typically leaves her infant with an older child or relative. The infant is usually close to the mother, either on her lap or enclosed on her back in a colored cloth, sitting on a mat, or sleeping in a hammock. The mother rarely allows the infant to crawl on the dirt floor of the hut and feels that the outside sun, air, and dust are harmful.

The infant is rarely spoken to or played with, and the only available objects for play, besides his own clothing or his mother's body, are oranges, ears of corn, and pieces of wood and clay. These infants are distinguished from American infants of the same age by their extreme motoric passivity, fearfulness, minimal smiling, and, above all, extraordinary quietness. A few with pale cheeks and vacant stares had the quality of tiny ghosts and resembled the description of the institutionalized infants that Spitz called marasmic. Many would not orient to a taped source of speech, not smile or babble to vocal overtures, and hesitated over a minute before reaching for an attractive toy.

An American woman who lived in the village made five separate 30-minute observations in the homes of 12 infants 8–16 months of age. If a particular behavioral variable occurred during a five-second period, it was recorded once for that interval. The infants were spoken to or played with 6% of the time, with a maximum of 12%. The comparable averages for American middle-class homes are 25%, with a maximum of 40% (Lewis & Freedle, 1972). It should be noted that the infant's vocalizations, which occurred about 6% of the time, were typically grunts lasting less than a second, rather than the prolonged babbling typical of middle-class American children. The infants cried very little because the slightest irritability led the mother to nurse her child at once. Nursing was the single, universal therapeutic treatment for all infant distress, be it caused by fear, cold, hunger, or cramps. Home observations in the eastern villages are consonant with those gathered in San Marcos and reveal infrequent infant vocalization and little verbal interaction or play with adults or older siblings. The mothers in these settings seem to regard their infants the way an American parent views an expensive cashmere sweater: Keep it nearby and protect it but do not engage it reciprocally.

One reason why these mothers might behave this way is that it is abundantly clear to every parent that all children begin to walk by 18 months, to talk by age 3, and to perform some adult chores by age 10, despite the listless, silent quality of infancy. The mother's lack of active manipulation, stimulation, or interactive play with her infant is not indicative of indifference or rejection, but is a reasonable posture, given her knowledge of child development.

Comparative Study of Infant Cognitive Development

Although it was not possible to create a formal laboratory setting for testing infants in San Marcos, it was possible to do so in the eastern Ladino villages, and we shall summarize data derived from identical procedures administered to rural Guatemalan and American infants. Although the infants in the Ladino villages were more alert than the Indian children of San Marcos, the similarities in living conditions and rearing practices are such that we shall assume that the San Marcos infants would have behaved like the Ladino children or, what is more likely, at a less mature level. In these experiments, the Guatemalan mother and child came to a special laboratory equipped with a chair and a stage that simulated the setting in the Harvard laboratories where episodes were administered to cross-sectional groups of infants, 84 American and 80 Guatemalan, at $5\frac{1}{2}$, $7\frac{1}{2}$, $9\frac{1}{2}$, and $11\frac{1}{2}$ months of age, with 10–24 infants from each culture at each age level.

Before describing the procedures and results, it will be helpful to summarize the theoretical assumptions that govern interpretation of the infant's reactions to these episodes. There appear to be two important maturationally controlled processes which emerge between 2 and 12 months that influence the child's reactions to transformations of an habituated event (Kagan, 1971, 1972). During the first six weeks of life, the duration of the child's attention to a visual event is controlled by the amount of physical change or contrast in the event. During the third month, the infant shows prolonged attention to events that are moderate discrepancies from habituated standards. Maintenance of attention is controlled by the relation of the event to the child's schema for the class to which that event belongs. The typical reactions to discrepancy include increased fixation time, increased vocalization, and either cardiac deceleration or decreased variability of heart rate during the stimulus presentation. These conclusions are based on many independent studies and we shall not document them here (Cohen, Gelber, & Lazar, 1971; Kagan, 1971; Lewis, Goldberg, & Campbell, 1970).

However, at approximately eight–nine months, a second process emerges. The infant now begins to activate cognitive structures, called hypotheses, in the service of interpreting discrepant events. A hypothesis is viewed as a representation of a relation between two schemata. Stated in different language, the infant not only notes and processes a discrepancy, he also attempts to transform it to his prior schemata for that class of event and activates hypotheses to serve this advanced cognitive function. It is not a coincidence that postulation of this new competence coincides with the time when the infant displays object permanence and separation anxiety, phenomena that require the child to activate an idea of an absent object or person.

There are two sources of support for this notion. The first is based on age changes in attention to the same set of events. Regardless of whether the stimulus is a set of human masks, a simple black and white design, or a dynamic sequence in which a moving orange rod turns on a bank of three light bulbs upon contact, there is a U-shaped relation between age and duration of attention across the period 3–36 months, with the trough typically occurring between 7 and 12 months of age (Kagan, 1972).

The curvilinear relation between age and attention to human masks has been replicated among American, rural Guatemalan, and Kahlahari desert Bushman children (Kagan, 1971; Konnor, 1973; Sellers, Klein, Kagan, & Minton, 1972). If discrepancy were the only factor controlling fixation time, a child's attention should decrease with age, for the stimulus events become less discrepant as he grows older. The increase in attention toward the end of the first year is interpreted as a sign of a new cognitive competence, which we have called the *activation of hypotheses*.

A second source of support for this idea is that the probability of a cardiac acceleration to a particular discrepancy increases toward the end of the first year, whereas cardiac deceleration is the modal reaction during the earlier months (Kagan, 1972). Because studies of adults and young children indicate that cardiac acceleration accompanies mental work, while deceleration accompanies attention to an interesting event (Lacey, 1967; Van Hover, 1971), the appearance of acceleration toward the end of the first year implies that the infants are performing active mental work, or activating hypotheses.

Since increased attention to a particular discrepancy toward the end of the first year is one diagnostic sign of the emergence of this stage of cognitive development, cultural differences in attention to fixed discrepancies during the first year might provide information on the developmental maturity of the infants in each cultural group.

Method

Block Episode. Each child was shown a 2-inch wooden orange block for six or eight successive trials (six for the two older ages, and eight for the two younger ages) followed by three or five transformation trials in which a 1½-inch orange block was presented. These transformations were followed by three representations of the original 2-inch block.

Light Episode. The child was shown 8 or 10 repetitions of a sequence in which a hand moved an orange rod in a semicircle until it touched a bank of three light bulbs which were lighted upon contact between the rod and the bulbs. In the five transformation trials that followed, the hand appeared but the rod did not move and the lights lit after a four-second interval. Following the transformations, the original event was presented for three additional trials.

During each of the episodes, two observers coded (*a*) how long the infant
attended to the event, (*b*) whether the
infant vocalized or smiled, and (*c*) fret-
ting or crying. Intercoder reliability for
these variables was over .90.

Results

The Guatemalan infants were significantly
less attentive than the Americans on both
episodes, and the cultural differences were
greater at the two older than at the two

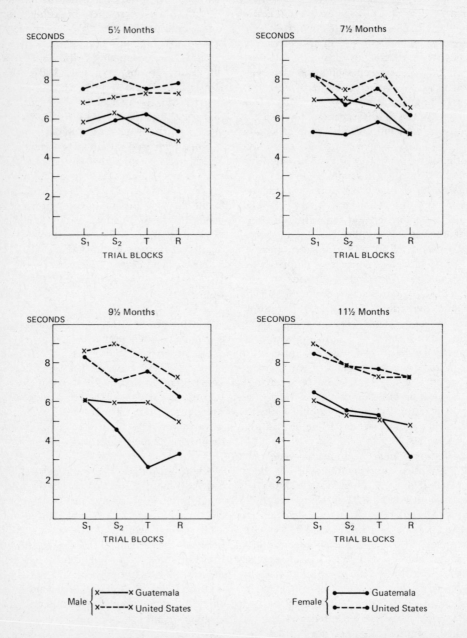

Figure 13.1. Average total fixation time to the block episode by age and culture

younger ages. Figures 13.1 and 13.2 illustrate the mean total fixation time to four successive trial blocks for the two episodes. The four trial blocks were the first three standard trials, the last three standards, the first three transformations, and the three return trials.

The American infants of all ages had longer fixation times to the block during every trial block (F ranged from 30.8 to 67.3, $df=1/154$, $p<.001$). The American infants also displayed longer fixations to the light during every trial block (F ranged from 9.8 to 18.4, $df=1/141$, $p<.01$).

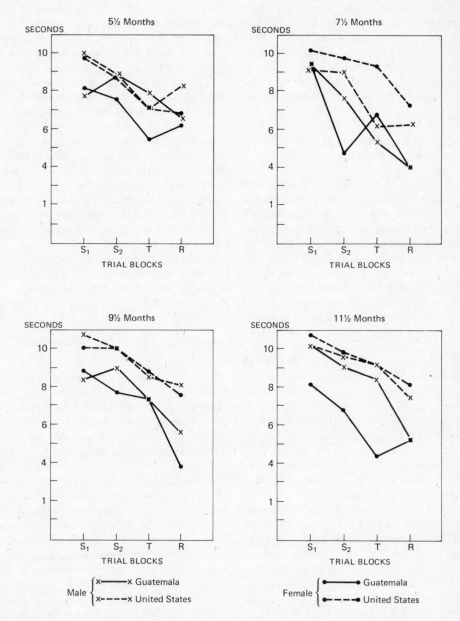

Figure 13.2. Average total fixation time to the light episode by age and culture

However, it is important to note that at 11½ months, the American children maintained more sustained attention to the return of the standard than the Guatemalans, who showed a drop in fixation time toward the end of the episode. These data suggest that more of the American than of the Guatemalan infants had entered the stage of activation of hypotheses. Since the Ladino infants appeared more mature than the San Marcos children, it is possible that the American one-year-olds were approximately three months advanced over the San Marcos children in this cognitive function.

Additional Assessments of Developmental Status

We collected, under less formal conditions in the home, additional information on the developmental status of the San Marcos infant. Not one of the 12 infants between 8 and 16 months reached for an attractive object they watched being hidden, although many would, with considerable hesitation, reach for a visible object placed close to their hands. Furthermore, none of these 12 infants revealed facial surprise following a sequence in which they watched an object being hidden under a cloth but saw no object when that cloth was removed. These observations suggest an absolute retardation of four months in the display of behavioral signs diagnostic of the attainment of object permanence.

A third source of data is based on observations of stranger anxiety. Each of 16 infants between 8 and 20 months was observed following the first exposure to a strange male (the senior author [J. K.]). The first age at which obvious apprehension and/or crying occurred was 13 months, suggesting a five-month lag between San Marcos and American infants. Finally, the information on nonmorphemic babbling and the onset of meaningful speech supports a diagnosis of absolute retardation. There was no marked increase in frequency of babbling or vocalization between 8 and 16 months among the 12 San Marcos infants observed at home, while comparable observations in American homes revealed a significant increase in babbling and the appearance of morphemic vocalizations for some children. Furthermore, many parents remarked that meaningful speech typically appears first at 2½ years of age, about one year later than the average display of first words in American children.

These data, together with the extremely depressed, withdrawn appearance of the San Marcos infants, suggest retardations of three or more months for various psychological competences that typically emerge during the first two years of life. With the exception of one 16-month-old boy, whose alert appearance resembled that of an American infant, there was little variability among the remaining children. Since over 90% were homogeneously passive, non-alert, and quiet, it is unlikely that the recovery of intellectual functioning to be reported later was a result of the selective mortality of a small group of severely retarded infants.

Resilience of Cognitive Development

The major theme of this article is the potential for recovery of cognitive functions despite early infant retardation. When the San Marcos child becomes mobile at around 15 months he leaves the dark hut, begins to play with other children, and provides himself with cognitive challenges that demand accommodations. Since all children experience this marked discontinuity in variety of experience and opportunity for exploration between the first and second birthday, it is instructive to compare the cognitive competence of older Guatemalan and American children to determine if differences in level of functioning are still present.

The tests administered were designed to

assess cognitive processes that are believed to be part of the natural competence of growing children, rather than the culturally arbitrary segments of knowledge contained in a standard IQ test. We tried to create tests that were culturally fair, recognizing that this goal is, in the extreme, unattainable. Hence, the tests were not standardized instruments with psychometric profiles of test-retest reliabilities and criterion validity studies. This investigation should be viewed as a natural experiment in which the independent variable was degree of retardation in infancy and the dependent variables were performances on selected cognitive instruments during childhood. We assume, along with many psychologists, that perceptual analysis, recall and recognition memory, and inference are among the basic cognitive functions of children (even though they do not exhaust that set), and our tests were designed to evaluate those processes.

Tests of recall and recognition memory, perceptual analysis, and perceptual and conceptual inference were given to children in San Marcos, the Ladino villages, an Indian village close to Guatemala City and more modern than San Marcos, Cambridge, Massachusetts, and to two different groups of children living in Guatemala City. One of the Guatemala City settings, the "guarderia," was a day care center for very poor children. The second group, middle-class children attending nursery school, resembled a middle-class American sample in both family background and opportunity. Not all tests were administered to all children. The discussion is organized according to the cognitive function assessed, rather than the sample studied. The sample sizes ranged from 12 to 40 children at any one age.

Recall Memory for Familiar Objects

The ability to organize experience for commitment to long-term memory and to retrieve that information on demand is a basic cognitive skill. It is generally believed that the form of the organization contains diagnostic information regarding cognitive maturity for, among Western samples, both number of independent units of information and the conceptual clustering of that information increase with age.

A 12-object recall task was administered to two samples of Guatemalan children. One group lived in a Ladino village 17 kilometers from Guatemala City; the second group was composed of San Marcos children. The 80 subjects from the Ladino village were 5 and 7 years old, equally balanced for age and sex. The 55 subjects from San Marcos were between 5 and 12 years of age (26 boys and 29 girls).

The 12 miniature objects to be recalled were common to village life and belonged to three conceptual categories: animals (pig, dog, horse, cow), kitchen utensils (knife, spoon, fork, glass), and clothing (pants, dress, underpants, hat). Each child was first required to name the objects, and if the child was unable to he was given the name. The child was then told that after the objects had been randomly arranged on a board he would have 10 seconds to inspect them, after which they would be covered with a cloth, and he would be required to say all the objects he could remember.

Table 13.1 contains the average number of objects recalled and the number of pairs

Table 13.1. Mean number of objects and pairs recalled

Age	Trial 1		Trial 2	
	Recall	Pairs	Recall	Pairs
Ladino Village				
5	5.2	2.1	5.4	2.1
7	6.7	3.3	7.8	3.7
Indian Village				
5–6	7.1	3.4	7.8	3.8
7–8	8.6	3.4	8.3	3.6
9–10	10.3	4.9	10.3	4.3
11–12	9.6	3.4	10.1	3.6

of conceptually similar words recalled—an index of clustering—for the first two trials. A pair was defined as the temporally contiguous recall of two or more items of the same category. A child received one point for reporting a pair of contiguous items, two points for three contiguous items, and three points for contiguous recall of four items. Hence, the maximum clustering score for a single trial was nine points. As Table 13.1 reveals, the children showed a level of clustering beyond chance expectation (which is between 1.5 and 2.0 pairs for recall scores of seven to eight words). Moreover, recall scores increased with age on both trials for children in both villages (F ranged from 11.2 to 27.7, $p<.05$), while clustering increased with age in the Ladino village ($F=26.8$, $p<.001$ for Trial 1; $F=3.48$, $p<.05$ for Trial 2).

No five- or six-year-old in either village and only 12 of the 40 seven-year-olds in the Ladino village were attending school. School for the others consisted of little more than semiorganized games. Moreover, none of the children in San Marcos had ever left the village, and the five- and six-year-olds typically spent most of the day within a 500-yard radius of their homes. Hence, school attendance and contact with books and a written language do not seem to be prerequisites for clustering in young children.

The recall and cluster scores obtained in Guatemala were remarkably comparable to those reported for middle-class American children. Appel, Cooper, McCarrell, Knight, Yussen, and Flavell (1971) presented 12 pictures to Minneapolis children in Grade 1 (approximately age 7) and 15 pictures to children in Grade 5 (approximately age 11) in a single-trial recall task similar to the one described here. The recall scores were 66% for the 7-year-olds and 80% for the 11-year-olds. These values are almost identical to those obtained in both Guatemalan villages. The cluster indices were also comparable. The American 7-year-olds had a cluster ratio of .25;

the San Marcos 5- and 6-year-olds had a ratio of .39.[1]

Recognition Memory

The cultural similarity in recall also holds for recognition memory. In a separate study, 5-, 8-, and 11-year-old children from Ladino villages in the East and from Cambridge, Massachusetts, were shown 60 pictures of objects—all of which were familiar to the Americans but some of which were unfamiliar to the Guatemalans. After 0-, 24-, or 48-hours delay, each child was shown 60 pairs of pictures, one of which was old and the other new, and was asked to decide which one he had seen. Although the 5- and 8-year-old Americans performed significantly better than the Guatemalans, there was no statistically significant cultural difference for the 11-year-olds, whose scores ranged from 85% to 98% after 0-, 24-, or 48-hours delay (Kagan et al., 1973). (See Table 13.2.) The remarkably high scores of the American 5-year-olds have also been reported by Scott (1973).

Table 13.2. Mean percentage of correct responses

	Americans			Guatemalans		
			Age			
Delay	5	8	11	5	8	11
0 hours	92.8	96.7	98.3	58.4	74.6	85.2
24 hours	86.7	95.6	96.7	55.8	71.0	87.0
48 hours	87.5	90.3	93.9	61.4	75.8	86.2

Note. Percent signs are omitted.

A similar result was found on a recognition memory task for 32 photos of faces, balanced for sex, child versus adult, and Indian versus Caucasian, administered to 35 American and 38 San Marcos children

[1] The cluster index is the ratio of the number of pairs recalled to the product of the number of categories in the list times one less than the number of words in each category.

8–11 years of age. Each child initially inspected 32 chromatic photographs of faces, one at a time, in a self-paced procedure. Each child's recognition memory was tested by showing him 32 pairs of photographs (each pair was of the same sex, age, and ethnicity), one of which was old and the other new. The child had to state which photograph he had seen during the inspection phase. Although the American 8- and 9-year-olds performed slightly better than the Guatemalans (82% versus 70%), there was no significant cultural difference among the 10- and 11-year-olds (91% versus 87%). Moreover, there was no cultural difference at any age for the highest performance attained by a single child.[2] The favored interpretation of the poorer performance of the younger children in both recognition memory studies is that some of them did not completely understand the task and others did not activate the proper problem-solving strategies during the registration and retrieval phases of the task.

It appears that recall and recognition memory are basic cognitive functions that seem to mature in a regular way in a natural environment. The cognitive retardation observed during the first year does not have any serious predictive validity for these two important aspects of cognitive functioning for children 10–11 years of age.

Perceptual Analysis

The Guatemalan children were also capable of solving difficult Embedded Figures Test items. The test consisted of 12

color drawings of familiar objects in which a triangle had been embedded as part of the object. The child had to locate the hidden triangle and place a black paper triangle so that it was congruent with the design of the drawing. The test was administered to rural Indian children from San Marcos, as well as to rural Indians living close to Guatemala City (labeled Indian$_1$ in Figure 13.3), the Ladino villages, and two groups from Guatemala City. (See Figure 13.3.)

The Guatemala City middle-class children had the highest scores and, except for San Marcos, the rural children, the poorest. The surprisingly competent performance of the San Marcos children is due, we believe, to the more friendly conditions of testing. This suggestion is affirmed by an independent study in which a special attempt was made to maximize rapport and comprehension of instructions with a group of rural isolated children before administering a large battery of tests. Although all test performances were not facilitated by this rapport-raising procedure, performance on the Embedded Figures Test was improved considerably. It is important to note that no five- or six-year-old was completely incapable of solving some of these problems. The village differences in mean score reflect the fact that the rural children had difficulty with three or four of the harder items. This was the first time that many rural children had ever seen a two-dimensional drawing, and most of the five-, six-, and seven-year-olds in San Marcos had had no opportunity to play with books, paper, pictures, or crayons. Nonetheless, these children solved seven or eight of the test items. Investigators who have suggested that prior experience with pictures is necessary for efficient analysis of two-dimensional information may have incorrectly misinterpreted failure to understand the requirements of the problem with a deficiency in cognitive competence. This competence seems to develop in the world of moving leaves, chickens, and

---

[2] These photographs were also used in an identical procedure with 12 Kipsigis-speaking 10- and 11-year-olds from a rural village in eastern Kenya. Despite the absence of any black faces in the set, the percentage of items recognized correctly was 82 for this group of African children.

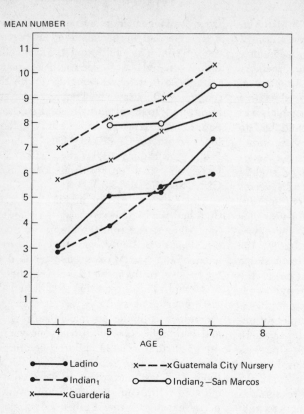

MEAN NUMBER

Figure 13.3. Mean number correct on the Embedded Figures Test

Ladino •——•
Indian₁ •– – –•
Guarderia ×———×
Guatemala City Nursery ×– – –×
Indian₂—San Marcos ○———○

Perceptual Inference

The competence of the San Marcos children on the Embedded Figures Test is affirmed by their performance on a test administered only in San Marcos and Cambridge and called Perceptual Inference. The children (60 American and 55 Guatemalan, 5–12 years of age) were shown a schematic drawing of an object and asked to guess what the object might be if the drawing were completed. The child was given a total of four clues for

water.[3] As with recall and recognition memory, the performance of the San Marcos child was comparable to that of his age peer in a modern urban setting.

each of 13 items, where each clue added more information. The child had to guess an object from an incomplete illustration, to make an inference from minimal information (see Figures 13.4 and 13.5).

There was no significant cultural difference for the children 7–12 years of age, although the American 5- and 6-year-olds did perform significantly better than the Indian children. In San Marcos, performance improved from 62% correct on one of the first two clues for the 5- and 6-year-olds to 77% correct for the 9–12-year-olds. The comparable changes for the American children were from 77% to 84%. (See Figure 13.6.)

Familiarity with the test objects was critical for success. All of the San Marcos children had seen hats, fish, and corn, and these items were rarely missed. By contrast, many American children failed these items. No San Marcos child not attending school, and therefore unfamiliar with

---

[3] This conclusion holds for Embedded Figures Test performance, and not necessarily for the ability to detect three-dimensional perspective in two-dimensional drawings.

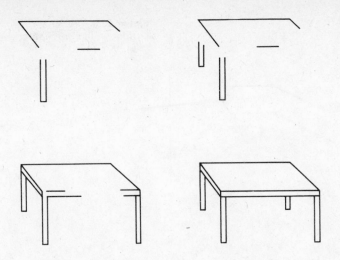

Figure 13.4. Sample item from the Perceptual Inference Test

books, correctly guessed the book item, whereas most of those in school guessed it correctly. As with memory and perceptual analysis, the retardation seen during infancy did not predict comparable retardation in the ability of the 11-year-old to make difficult perceptual inferences.

Conceptual Inference

The San Marcos child also performed well on questions requiring conceptual inference. In this test, the child was told verbally three characteristics of an object and was required to guess the object. Some of the examples included: What has wings, eats chickens, and lives in a tree?

What moves trees, cannot be seen, and makes one cold? What is made of wood, is used to carry things, and allows one to make journeys? There was improved performance with age; the 5- and 6-years-olds obtained an average of 9 out of 14 correct, and the 11- and 12-year-olds obtained 12 out of 14 correct. The San Marcos child was capable of making moderately difficult inferences from both visual and verbal information.

Discussion

This corpus of data implies that absolute retardation in the time of emergence of universal cognitive competences during in-

Figure 13.5. Sample item from the Perceptual Inference Test

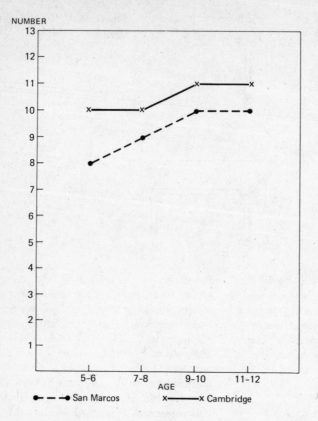

NUMBER

AGE

● – – ● San Marcos   x————x Cambridge

Figure 13.6. Number correct on the Perceptual Inference Test

fancy is not predictive of comparable deficits for memory, perceptual analysis, and inference during preadolescence. Although the rural Guatemalan infants were retarded with respect to activation of hypotheses, alertness, and onset of stranger anxiety and object permanence, the preadolescents' performance on the tests of perceptual analysis, perceptual inference, and recall and recognition memory were comparable to American middle-class norms. Infant retardation seems to be partially reversible and cognitive development during the early years more resilient than had been supposed.

One potential objection to this conclusion is that the tests were too easy for the Guatemalan 11-year-olds and that is why cultural differences were absent. There are two comments that can be addressed to that issue. First, it is not intuitively reasonable to argue that the ability to remem-

ber 60 photographs of objects, classify an object from a few sketchy lines, or detect the triangle hidden in a two-dimensional drawing is "easy" for children who rarely see photographs, pencils, crayons, or books. Second, we deliberately assessed cognitive functions that we believe all children should master by the time they are preadolescents. The fact that many 11-year-olds approached the ceiling on some tests is support for the basic premise of this article, namely, that infant retardation does not prevent a child from eventually developing basic cognitive competencies.

This result is surprising if one believes that each child is born with a certain level of general intellectual competence that is stable from infancy through adulthood. If, on the contrary, one assumes that each stage of development is characterized by a different profile of specific competences and there is no necessary relation between early emergence of the capacities of infancy and level of attainment of the quite different abilities characteristic of childhood, then these results are more reasonable. There is no reason to assume that the caterpillar who metamorphoses a bit earlier than his kin is a better adapted or more efficient butterfly.

Consideration of why the rural Guatemalan children lagged behind the urban children on some tests during the period five through nine years of age comprises a second implication of these data. It will be recalled that on the embedded figures and recognition memory tests the performance of rural children was several years behind both the American and Guatemala City middle-class children. The differences were minimal for the object recall and perceptual inference tests. The approximately three-year lag in performance is paralleled by comparable differences between lower- and middle-class children in urban Western cities. For example, Bosco (1972) found that middle-class first and third graders were able to tolerate smaller interstimulus intervals in a backward masking procedure than lower-class children, but this difference had vanished among sixth-grade children. Similarly, Bakker (1972) compared good and poor readers from urban centers in Holland on a task that required operating simultaneously on two items of information in a temporal integration task. The poor readers performed less well than the good readers at ages six to eight, but were comparable to the good readings during the preadolescent years.

We interpret these results as indicating that the urban lower-class children, like the younger, rural Guatemalans, were not able to mobilize proper problem-solving strategies necessary for task solution, but achieved that level of competence by 11 years of age. Some of these strategies include focused attention, rehearsal of task information and instructions, awareness of and understanding the problem to be solved, maintenance of problem set, and the ability to remember critical information elements in the problem and to operate on that information. It is believed that these functions may emerge a little later in some groups of children than in others, but that they are operative in all children by 11–12 years of age. In a recently completed study with Patricia Engle, we found that among rural Guatemalan children, 5 through 11 years of age, the rate of improvement in performance on three memory tasks (memory for numbers, memory for sentences, and auditory blending) was greatest between 9 and 11 years of age, whereas White (1970), using comparable data from American children, found that the greatest rate of improvement was between 5 and 7 years of age—a lag of about three years.

These data have implications for America's educational problems. There is a tendency to regard the poor test performances of economically impoverished, minority group 6-year-olds in the United States as indicative of a permanent and, perhaps, irreversible defect in intellectual ability—as a difference in quality of function rather than slower maturational rate. The Guatemalan data, together with those of Bosco and Bakker, suggest that children differ in the age at which basic cognitive competences emerge and that experiential factors influence the time of emergence. Economically disadvantaged American children and isolated rural Guatemalan children appear to be from one to three years behind middle-class children in demonstrating some of the problem-solving skills characteristic of Piaget's stage of concrete operations. But these competences eventually appear in sturdy form by age 10 or 11. The common practice of arbitrarily setting 7 years—the usual time of school entrance—as the age when children are to be classified as competent or incompetent confuses differences in maturational rate with permanent, qualitative differences in intellectual ability. This practice is as logical as classifying children as reproductively fertile or sterile depending on whether or not they have reached physiological puberty by their thirteenth birthday.

When educators note correctly that poor children tend to remain permanently behind middle-class children on intellectual and academic performance, they are referring to the relative retardation on the culturally specific skills of reading, mathematics, and language achievement described earlier. That relative retardation is the product of the rank ordering of scores on achievement and IQ tests. The fact that relative retardation on these abilities is stable from age five on does not mean that the relatively retarded children are not growing intellectually (when compared with themselves), often at the same rate as economically advantaged youngsters.

The suggestion that basic cognitive competences, in contrast to culturally specific ones, emerge at different times and that the child retains the capacity for actualization of his competence until a late age is not substantially different from the earlier conclusions of Dennis and Najarian (1957). Although the 49 infants 2–12 months of age living in poorly staffed Lebanese institutions were seriously retarded on the Cattell developmental scale (mean developmental quotient of 68 compared with a quotient of 102 for a comparison group), the 4½–6-year-olds who had resided in the same institution all their lives performed at a level comparable to American norms on a memory test (Knox Cubes) as well as on Porteus mazes and the Goodenough Draw-a-Man Test.

Of more direct relevance is Dennis's (1973) recent follow-up study of 16 children who were adopted out of the same Lebanese institution between 12 and 24 months of age—the period during which the San Marcos infant leaves the unstimulating environment of the dark hut—with an average developmental quotient of 50 on the Cattell Infant Scale. Even though

the assessment of later intellectual ability was based on the culturally biased Stanford-Binet IQ test, the average IQ, obtained when the children were between 4 and 12 years of age, was 101, and 13 of the 16 children had IQ scores of 90 or above.

Additional support for the inherent resiliency in human development comes from longitudinal information on two sisters who spent most of their infancy in a crib in a small bedroom with no toys.[4] The mother, who felt unable to care for her fourth child, restricted her to the room soon after birth and instructed her eight-year-old daughter to care for the child. One year later, another daughter was born, and she, too, was placed in a crib with the older sister. These two children only left the room to be fed and, according to the caretaking sister who is now a married woman in her twenties, the two infants spent about 23 hours of each day together in a barren crib. When the authorities were notified of this arrangement, the children were removed from the home and taken to a hospital when the younger was 2½ and the older 3½ years old. Medical records reveal that both children were malnourished, severely retarded in weight and height, and seriously retarded psychologically. After a month in the hospital, following considerable physical recovery, both sisters were placed in the care of a middle-class family who had several young children. The sisters have remained with that family for the last 12 years and regard the husband and wife as their parents. One of us (J. K.) tested the sisters five times when they were between 4 and 9 years of age, and recently interviewed and tested both of them over a two-day period when they were 14½ and 15½ years old.

The younger sister has performed consistently better than the older one over the last 10 years. The IQ scores of the

---

[4] The authors thank Meinhard Robinow for information on these girls.

younger girl have risen steadily from a Stanford-Binet IQ of 74 at age 4½ (after two years in the foster home) to a Wechsler Full Scale IQ of 88 at age 14. The older girl's scores have also improved, but less dramatically, from a Stanford-Binet IQ of 59 at age 5 to a Wechsler IQ of 72 at age 15. The author also administered a lengthy battery of tests, some of which were discussed earlier. On the Perceptual Inference Test, the percentage correct was 85 for the younger sister and 61 for the older sister. On the Recognition Memory for Photographs, the percentages were 94 for both. On the Embedded Figures Test, the percentages were 92 and 100, and on the recall memory for objects, the percentages were 92 and 83 for the younger and older sister, respectively. Moreover, the interpersonal behavior of both girls was in no way different from that of the average rural Ohio adolescent —a group the author came to know well after seven years of work in the area. Although there is some ambiguity surrounding the competence of the older girl, the younger one performs at an average level on a wide range of tests of cognitive functioning, despite 2½ years of serious isolation.

These data, together with the poor predictive relation between scores on infant developmental tests and later assessments of intellectual functioning, strengthen the conclusion that environmentally produced retardation during the first year or two of life appears to be reversible. The importance of the Guatemalan data derives from the fact that the San Marcos 11-year-olds performed so well, considering the homogeneity and isolation of their childhood environment. Additionally, there is a stronger feeling now than there was in 1957 that environmentally produced retardation during the first two years may be irreversible, even though the empirical basis for that belief is no firmer in 1972 than it was in 1957.

More dramatic support for the notion that psychological development is malle-

able comes from recent experimental studies with animals. Several years ago Harlow's group demonstrated that although monkeys reared in isolation for the first six months displayed abnormal and often bizarre social behaviors, they could, if the experimenter were patient, solve the complex learning problems normally administered to feral-born monkeys. The prolonged isolation did not destroy their cognitive competence (Harlow, Schiltz, & Harlow, 1969). More recently, Suomi and Harlow (1972) have shown that even the stereotyped and bizarre social behavior shown by six-month-old isolates can be altered by placing them with female monkeys three months younger than themselves over a 26-week therapeutic period. "By the end of the therapy period the behavioral levels were virtually indistinguishable from those of the socially competent therapist monkeys [Suomi & Harlow, 1972, p. 491]."

This resiliency has also been demonstrated for infant mice (Cairns & Nakelski, 1971) who experienced an initial 10 weeks of isolation from other animals. Compared with group-reared mice of the same strain, the isolated subjects were hyperreactive to other mice, displaying both extreme withdrawal and extreme aggressiveness. These investigators also attempted rehabilitation of the isolates by placing them with groups of mice for an additional 10 weeks, however, after which their behavior was indistinguishable from animals that had never been isolated.

By the seventieth day after interchange, the effects of group therapy were complete, and animals that had been isolated for one hundred days following weaning were indistinguishable from animals that had never been isolated [Cairns & Nakelski, 1971, p. 363].

These dramatic alterations in molar behavior are in accord with replicated reports of recovery of visual function in monkeys and cats deprived of patterned light soon after birth (Baxter, 1966; Chow & Stewart, 1972; Wilson & Riesen, 1966). Kittens deprived of light for one year recovered basic visual functions after only 10 days in the experimenter's home (Baxter, 1966); kittens who had one or both eyes sutured for close to two years were able to learn pattern discriminations with the deprived eye only after moderate training (Chow & Stewart, 1972).

If the extreme behavioral and perceptual sequelae of isolation in monkeys, cats, and mice can be altered by such brief periods of rehabilitative experience, it is not difficult to believe that the San Marcos infant is capable of as dramatic a recovery over a period of nine years. These data do not indicate the impotence of early environments, but rather the potency of the environment in which the organism is functioning. There is no question that early experience seriously affects kittens, monkeys, and children. If the first environment does not permit the full actualization of psychological competences, the child will function below his ability as long as he remains in that context. But if he is transferred to an environment that presents greater variety and requires more accommodations, he seems more capable of exploiting that experience and repairing the damage wrought by the first environment than some theorists have implied.

These conclusions do not imply that intervention or rehabilitation efforts with poor American or minority group preschool children are of no value. Unlike San Marcos, where children are assigned adult responsibilities when they are strong and alert enough to assume them, rather than at a fixed age, American children live in a severely age graded system, in which children are continualy rank ordered. Hence, if a poor four-year-old falls behind a middle-class four-year-old on a culturally significant skill, like knowledge of letters or numbers, he may never catch up with the child who was advanced and is likely to be placed in a special educational category. Hence, American parents must be concerned with the early psychological growth of their children. We live in a society in which the relative retardation of a four-

year-old seriously influences his future opportunities because we have made relative retardation functionally synonymous with absolute retardation. This is not true in subsistence farming communities like San Marcos.

These data suggest that exploration of the new and the construction of objects or ideas from some prior schematic blueprint must be inherent properties of the mind. The idea that the child carries with him at all times the essential mental competence to understand the new in some terms and to make a personal contribution to each new encounter is only original in our time. Despite the current popularity of Kant and Píaget, the overwhelming prejudice of Western psychologists is that higher order cognitive competences and personality factors are molded completely by the environment. Locke's image of an unmarked tablet on which sensation played its patterned melody has a parallel in Darwin's failure to realize, until late in his life, that the organism made a contribution to his own evolution. Darwin was troubled by the fact that the same climate on different islands in the Galapagos produced differnt forms of the same species. Since he believed that climatic variation was the dynamic agent in evolution he was baffled. He did not appreciate that the gene was the organism's contribution to his own alteration. Western psychologists have been blocked by the same prejudice that prevented young Darwin from solving his riddle. From Locke to Skinner we have viewed the perfectibility of man as vulnerable to the vicissitudes of the objects and people who block, praise, or push him, and resisted giving the child any compass of his own. The mind, like the nucleus of a cell, has a plan for growth and can transduce a new flower, an odd pain, or a stranger's unexpected smile into a form that is comprehensible. This process is accomplished through wedding cognitive structures to selective attention, activation of hypotheses, assimilation, and accommodation. The purpose of these processes is to convert an alerting unfamiliar event, incompletely understood, to a recognized variation of an existing familiar structure. This is accomplished through the detection of the dimensions of the event that bear a relation to existing schemata and the subsequent incorporation of the total event into the older structure.

We need not speak of joy in this psychological mastery, for neither walking nor breathing is performed in order to experience happiness. These properties of the motor or autonomic systems occur because each physiological system or organ naturally exercises its primary function. The child explores the unfamiliar and attempts to match his ideas and actions to some previously acquired representation because these are basic properties of the mind. The child has no choice.

The San Marcos child knows much less than the American about planes, computers, cars, and the many hundreds of other phenomena that are familiar to the Western youngster, and he is a little slower in developing some of the basic cognitive competences of our species. But neither appreciation of these events nor the earlier cognitive maturation is necessary for a successful journey to adulthood in San Marcos. The American child knows far less about how to make canoes, rope, tortillas, or how to burn an old milpa in preparation for June planting. Each knows what is necessary, each assimilates the cognitive conflicts that are presented to him, and each seems to have the potential to display more talent than his environment demands of him. There are few dumb children in the world if one classifies them from the perspective of the community of adaptation, but millions of dumb children if one classifies them from the perspective of another society.

References

APPEL, L. F., COOPER, R. G., MCCARRELL, N., KNIGHT, J. S., YUSSEN, S. R., & FLAVELL, J. H. The developmental acquisition of the distinction between perceiving and memory. Unpublished manuscript, University of Minnesota-Minneapolis, 1971.

BAKKER, D. J. *Temporal order in disturbed reading.* Rotterdam: Rotterdam University Press, 1972.

BAXTER, B. L. Effect of visual deprivation during postnatal maturation on the electroencephalogram of the cat. *Experimental Neurology*, 1966, *14*, 224–237.

BOSCO, J. The visual information processing speed of lower middle class children. *Child Development*, 1972, *43*, 1418–1422.

CAIRNS, R. B., & NAKELSKI, J. S. On fighting in mice: Ontogenetic and experiential determinants. *Journal of Comparative and Physiological Psychology*, 1971, *74*, 354–364.

CARMICHAEL, L. The development of behavior in vertebrates experimentally removed from the influence of external stimulation. *Psychological Review*, 1926, *33*, 51–58.

CHOW, K. L., & STEWART, D. L. Reversal of structural and functional effects of longterm visual deprivation in cats. *Experimental Neurology*, 1972, *34*, 409–433.

COHEN, L. B., GELBER, E. R., & LAZAR, M. A. Infant habituation and generalization to differing degrees of novelty. *Journal of Experimental Child Psychology*, 1971, *11*, 379–389.

COLE, M., GAY, J. GLICK, J. A., & SHARP, D. W. *The cultural context of learning and thinking.* New York: Basic Books, 1971.

DENNIS, W. *Children of the Créche.* New York: Appleton-Century-Crofts, 1973.

DENNIS, W., & NAJARIAN, P. Infant development under environmental handicap. *Psychological Monographs*, 1957, *71* (7, Whole No. 436).

HARLOW, H. F., SCHLITZ, K. A., & HARLOW, M. K. The effects of social isolation on the learning performance of rhesus monkeys. In C. R. Carpenter (Ed.), *Proceedings of the Second International Congress of Primatology.* Vol. 1. New York: Karger, 1969.

KAGAN, J. *Change and continuity in infancy.* New York: Wiley, 1971.

KAGAN, J. Do infants think? *Scientific American,* 1972, *226* (3), 74–82.

KAGAN, J., KLEIN, R. E., HAITH, M. M., N MORRISON, F. J. Memory and meaning in two cultures. *Child Development,* 1973, *44,* 221–223.

KAGAN, J., & MOSS, H. A. *Birth to maturity.* New York: Wiley, 1962.

KESSEN, W., HAITH, M. M., & SALAPATEK, P. H. Human infancy: A bibliography and guide. In P. H. Mussen (Ed.), *Carmichael's manual of child psychology.* (3rd ed.) Vol. 1. New York: Wiley, 1970.

KONNOR, M. J. Development among the Bushmen of Botswana. Unpublished doctoral dissertation, Harvard University, 1973.

LACEY, J. I. Somatic response patterning in stress: Some revisions of activation theory. In M. H. Appley & R. Trumbull (Eds.), *Psychological stress: Issues in research.* New York: Appleton-Century-Crofts, 1967.

LEWIS, M., & FREEDLE, R. *Mother-infant dyad: The cradle of meaning.* (Research Bulletin RB72–22) Princeton, N.J.: Educational Testing Service, 1972.

LEWIS, M., GOLDBERG, S., & CAMPBELL, H. A developmental study of learning within the first three years of life: Response decrement to a redundant signal. *Monograph of the Society for Research in Child Development,* 1970, *34* (No. 133).

MCGRAW, M. B. *Growth: A study of Johnny and Jimmy.* New York: Appleton-Century, 1935.

PEASE, D., WOLINS, L., & STOCKDALE, D. F. Relationship and prediction of infant tests. *Journal of Genetic Psychology,* 1973, *122,* 31–35.

SCOTT, M. S. The absence of interference effects in preschool children's picture recognition. *Journal of Genetic Psychology,* 1973, *122,* 121–126.

SELLERS, M. J., KLEIN, R. E., KAGAN, J., & MINTON, C. Developmental determinants of attention: A cross-cultural replication. *Developmental Psychology,* 1972, *6,* 185.

SUOMI, S. J., & HARLOW, H. F. Social rehabilitation of isolate reared monkeys. *Developmental Psychology,* 1972, *6,* 487–496.

VAN HOVER, K. I. S. A developmental study of three components of attention. Unpublished doctoral dissertation, Harvard University, 1971.

WHITE, S. H. Some general outlines of the matrix of developmental changes between 5 and 7 years. *Bulletin of the Orton Society,* 1970, *21,* 41–57.

WILSON, P. D., & RIESEN, A. H. Visual development in rhesus monkeys neonatally deprived of patterned light. *Journal of Comparative and Physiological Psychology,* 1966, *61,* 87–95.

14. LEARNING IN THE ADULT YEARS: SET OR RIGIDITY

ROLF H. MONGE

In the field of aging, Professor Raymond G. Kuhlen is probably best remembered for his contributions to the study of age trends in motivation and adjustment. I am thinking, in particular, of the chapter he wrote for Birren's *Handbook of Aging and the Individual* (1959), his chapter in Worchel and Byrne's book, *Personality Change* (1964), and the chapter he contributed to the volume entitled *Psychological Backgrounds of Adult Education* (1963) of which he was also the editor. During the last year or two of his life, his attention was focused in particular on motivation and on personality variables that might differentially influence learning during young adulthood, middle age, and the older years. At about this time he and his close friend and colleague at Syracuse University, Dr. Eric F. Gardner, obtained from the U.S. Office of Education a five-year grant to conduct a program of research in adult age differences in cognitive performance and learning. The material I am presenting here . . . comes from work done with Drs. Kuhlen and Gardner. It was my privilege to study for the doctorate with Dr. Kuhlen, and afterwards to join him and Dr. Gardner in their research program.

My intention . . . is to discuss two interrelated hypotheses regarding age deficits in performance on learning tasks. I shall refer to these as the learning set hypothesis and the rigidity hypothesis.

The learning set hypothesis asserts that, for one reason or another, older adults do not know *how* to learn as well as younger people. In this classic paper, Harlow (1949) defined learned set as "learning how to learn a kind of problem, or transfer from problem to problem." Thus, learning set refers to a nonspecific transfer of learn-

ing—the transfer of knowledge of the tools and techniques of learning, rather than the transfer of a specific subject matter. In the context of aging, it is proposed that as adults grow older they encounter fewer occasions requiring new learning, and therefore the habits of learning they developed during formal schooling and in the early years of maturity have deteriorated through lack of practice. To illustrate this concept in the classroom setting, the individual who has been out of the routine of formal schooling for any appreciable length of time is likely to have lost a substantial portion of whatever he may have known about how to learn. I am thinking here of such "tools of learning" as knowing how to study, how to concentrate or focus attention, how to organize the work, how to take notes, and a myriad of other "mental adjustments" and attitudes towards the process of *learning*.

Those . . . who have taught courses enrolling people who have been out of school routine for some time have no doubt had the experience of dealing with students who, after the first class meeting, gather at the lectern to express serious doubts about their ability to compete in an academic setting. Some of them, to be sure, are merely having problems in rearranging the priorities of their daily lives to find time for studying, but there are those genuinely concerned about recapturing their skill in the mechanics of learning.

While my original statement of the learning set hypothesis was couched in terms of chronological age, it should be noted that age, *per se*, is not the critical independent variable. The critical variable is, of course, the cognitive style of life of the individual. That is, individuals who are more or less continuously engaged in making use of the tools and techniques of learning should suffer little or no deterioration in learning set. Thus older adults who have maintained learning sets may be expected to perform more nearly like young adults than will those who have not maintained learning sets.

Some evidence bearing on this point comes from the study conducted by Levinson and Reese (1967). Those investigators compared the performance of children, college students, institutionalized and community-dwelling aged, and retired college faculty on a classic Harlow-type object-quality discrimination learning set series. Performance increased with age in the early years, reaching a peak in the college-age group, and decreased with age thereafter. Of particular interest, however, was the finding that the retired faculty were markedly superior to the other aged subjects. Levinson and Reese (1967) suggested that "an initial high IQ and/or considerable educational achievement may be more significant variables than CA. . . . Presumably the learning ability of older Ss and their capacity to deal effectively with large amounts of incoming information is maintained by large amounts of educational experience."

Now, I should like to consider some data on age differences in learning set. The first of the planned series of studies in our research program was a learning set investigation (Monge, 1967; Monge, Kuhlen and Gardner, 1968).

The major purposes of this study were to examine suggestions that there are, in addition to the deficit due to loss of *response* speed with age, deficits in concentrating or focusing upon the materials to be learned. The paired-associate paradigm was used. The anticipation interval was held constant, and the inspection interval varied, to test the hypothesis that the performance of older subjects would suffer more than that of younger subjects when the time allowed to review the stimulus-response pair was limited. Furthermore, it was felt that if the predicted defi-

cit was due to difficulty in concentrating or focusing upon the materials at a fast pace, then if subjects were given the opportunity to accustom themselves to the experimental situation—in other words, to form a learning set—the age difference should be reduced. To this end, each subject learned successively six unrelated lists of paired associates.

The subjects were 40 women, 20 in their thirties and 20 in their sixties, all recruited from women's religious organizations through the technique of offering to pay the organization four dollars for each person delivered from the membership.

Older and younger subjects did not differ at the 5% level either in mean score on a 20-item vocabulary test, nor in mean number of years of schooling. The average subject had finished high school and had some post-high school training such as business school, nurses training, or some college. The younger women were all housewives and mothers active in parochial school activities, while the older were, for the most part, either currently employed or recently retired from clerical office jobs or work of that general category. In summary, both the older and the younger subjects were active, involved, community-dwelling individuals of a reasonably high educational level.

Subjects were randomly assigned to one of two conditions of presentation of six 12-pair lists. In the slow pace condition, subjects learned the lists to a criterion of one perfect recitation, or a maximum of nine trials, at a 4:2-sec rate, that is, four seconds anticipation time and two seconds inspection time. In the fast pace condition, subjects learned to the same criteria at a 4:1-sec rate. The presentation device was a Stowe memory drum, Model 459B. The pairs of words were all two-syllable adjectives, and the six lists had been approximately equated for difficulty in a pilot study. Nevertheless, two of the six lists appeared equally often in the first and sixth positions of presentation to provide complete counterbalancing of residual inequalities in list difficulty at the endpoints of the learning sequence. The other four lists were assigned randomly to the second through fifth positions of presentation in such a way that each subject within each age by pace condition learned the six lists in a different order. Thus, the relationship between the groups and the relationship of the first to the sixth list learned were not confounded with residual inequality in list difficulties.

Figure 14.1 shows the mean number of total, omission, and commission errors, and Table 14.1 gives the results of the repeated measures analyses of variance. Individual comparisons for the total errors measure showed that the older group at the slower pace and the younger group at the faster pace improved significantly from the first to the sixth list learned, while the

other two groups did not change significantly from the beginning to the end of the series. Since the lists did, in fact, differ in difficulty in spite of the pilot work done to equate them, it is not possible to say unequivocally that the sharp improvement shown by all but the older group at the fast pace from the first to the second position was due solely to learning set formation.

The most unusual finding—for which I have no ready explanation—was that the best-performing group was the older group at the slower pace. As expected, however, the older group at the faster pace was worst, and the two younger groups did not differ substantially, although the younger at the faster pace did worse than those at the slower pace at all list positions but the sixth in total and omission errors. Surpris-

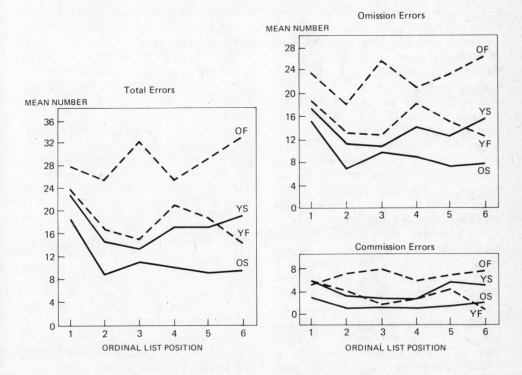

Figure 14.1. Performance of Ss on six successively-learned lists of paired associates in terms of total, omission, and commission errors. The first letter of the label refers to age (O = Old, 60–69 years; Y = young, 30–39 years) and the second to presentation pace (S = slow, 4:2-sec; F = fast, 4:1-sec)

Table 14.1. Summary of analyses of variance of errors measures over six lists

Source of Variation	df	Total Errors Mean Square	F	Omission Errors Mean Square	F	Commission Errors Mean Square	F
Between Ss							
Age (A)	1	273.1	<1	199.8	<1	5.7	<1
Pace (P)	1	5078.4	4.6[1]	3667.5	4.6[1]	175.1	2.1
A×P	1	4437.6	4.1	2059.2	2.8	451.0	5.3
Error (between)	36	1091.6		733.2		84.5	
Wtihin Ss							
Lists (L)	5	237.1	3.7[2]	170.1	3.4[2]	20.2	1.8
A×L	5	123.2	1.9	55.8	1.1	21.4	1.9
P×L	5	50.7	<1	38.0	<1	8.6	<1
A×P×L	5	154.7	2.4[1]	72.2	1.4	17.6	1.6
Error (within)	180	64.0		50.7		11.2	

Note—All figures calculated to two decimals, rounded to one. Means and variances for total and omission errors were correlated; however, there was no change in locus of significance after square root transformation of raw scores.
[1] = P<.05
[2] = P<.01

ingly, also, the main effect due to age was not significant in any analysis. In accordance with prediction, however, the main effect due to pace was significant and in the expected direction for the total and omission errors.

It was hypothesized, you will recall, that if the faster pace affected the older subjects as predicted, then the deficit might in part be due to an age-related difficulty in concentrating upon the materials to be learned, and that giving subjects the opportunity to accustom themselves to the pace, the materials, and the presentation device—in short, to form a learning set— would ameliorate the difficulty. This appeared to be the case for the older subjects at the slower, but not the faster pace. It might be conjectured that the older subjects at the faster pace did, indeed, form a learning set——but that they learned something other than what the experiment intended. That is, after a list or two they learned that the easiest way out of the situation was to simply wait out the maximum nine trials, responding only to those items that came easily. A follow-up experiment might profitably be done comparing a condition in which all subjects proceed

through a fixed number of trials with one in which subjects are instructed that they *must* reach criterion.

Now let's turn our attention briefly to the rigidity hypothesis. In his excellent interpretive review Botwinick (1967) stated the hypothesis thus:

There is a recurrent notion that advancing age is associated with a relative inability to learn new things, not so much because of a reduced learning capacity, but because of prior learning which persists even when no longer effective. . . . It is necessary to ascertain whether rigidity is really independent of the ability to learn. It may be that when older people appear more rigid than younger people it is because they are less able to learn or to perform. When [older] people find learning difficult, they may try repeatedly the same ineffective ways of acquiring information rather than do nothing. Thus, what is primary incapacity becomes secondary rigidity.

I would like to suggest that a substantial part of this "primary incapacity" is due to learning set inadequacies.

Professor Kuhlen, in an unpublished paper, suggested that the older adult who has suffered a breakdown in learning sets through disuse over long periods of time is aware of this handicap and is, accordingly, threatened by the task he faces. This is especially likely to be true in the instance of difficult material.

It strikes me that one of the consequences of inadequate learning sets, therefore, is an emotional reaction to the threat posed by the learning task, which manifests itself as rigid-appearing behavior.

A recently-completed dissertation research project done by Dr. David Hultsch (1968) in our laboratory bears, at least indirectly, on the rigidity hypothesis. Hultsch investigated the ability of men of different ages to organize material to be recalled. A 16-trial free recall task was given to men aged 16–19 years, 30–39 years, and 45–54 years. Subjects were required to write down after each trial as many of the 20 words presented as they could recall. Three instructional conditions were used: one in which Ss were just asked to recall as many words as possible; a second which suggested that recall would be easier if the words were organized in some unspecified way, and a third which told Ss to alphabetize the words as an aid to recall. As predicted, the older Ss recalled fewer words than the high school seniors, although no difference was noted between the two older groups. Also, as predicted, those of all ages with alphabetization instructions performed best, but the interaction of age and instructions which might be expected on the basis of the rigidity hypothesis did not appear. Thus, although the older men did not recall as much, what they did recall was as well-organized as the recall of the younger Ss. They were, in other words, as able as the younger to use either their own or an instruction-induced organizational scheme.

While I have no further data comparing different age groups, I should like to indicate the status of some pilot work we have done which shows promise of further illuminating both the learning set and rigidity hypotheses. It is our practice to run pilot studies uisng as subjects adults en-

rolled in courses in the late afternoon and evening division of the graduate school of education. These are, of course, people of higher than average intelligence and educational attainment, and their ages form a highly-skewed distribution. The median age is roughly 25, the mean about 30, and the oldest ages represented rarely are greater than 50–55. Nevertheless, we can get some indications as to the usefulness of our experimental manipulations and measures, thus saving the harder-to-come-by community-dwelling adults for refined investigations.

One such study tried to take advantage of the life-long habits of people to read from left to right, and to observe the results of reversing the process. In the pilot study, students of the type described above learned a list of paired associates in the usual fashion, stimulus presented on the left, and response term on the right. Another group of students learned the same list with the stimulus and response terms reversed in position, in other words, learned right-to-left. A difference significant at the 5% level favoring the left-to-right group in mean number of trials to criterion was found. We are presently running this task using adults varying widely in age to test the hypothesis that older people will find it more difficult than younger adults to overcome the left-to-right habit.

In closing, I'd like to speculate a bit on the consequences of inadequate learning sets.

One consequence might be confusion. The subject might ask himself, "What am I doing here?"—"What am I supposed to pay attention to?"—"What am I expected to say or do?" We cannot assume that the pre-experiment instructions we give filter accurately through the perceptual categories of the subject to end up as an adequate learning set. A learning set is, after all, something which is itself learned and, presumably, its acquistion is affected by motivation, by practice, by frequency and recency, etc. That instructions and, indeed pretraining, are not sufficient to establish a learning set may be deduced, I think, from the sharp increases in performance typically seen in the initial stages of learning set experiments. A substantial proportion of the sharp initial change must be due to the subject's getting a firm grip on the instructions.

A second consequence of inadequate learning set might be the perseveration of incorrect responses, a symptom of rigidity. The demand characteristics of many experimental situations require a response of some sort to be made. Indeed, it may be that one of the few elements of the pre-experimenal instructions that do filter through to the subject is that a response is required of him. And what is he to do but make wrong responses—or *no* response—if he knows not the correct response?

A third consequence, as just indicated, derives in large part from the second—for an alternative to perseveration in an incorrect response is, indeed, to make no response at all. Whether perseveration or omission is the alternative chosen may depend in a significant way on the "atmosphere" generated by the experimenter through his manner and his instructions, and upon the subject's emotional response to this atmosphere. Rosenthal's (1966) work has made abundantly clear the strength of the "experimenter effect." It is my opinion, unsupported at this time by data, that an incorrect response—that is, an error of commission—will tend to be made if the instructions strongly demand that some response be made, and that response omission will otherwise be the choice.

Although there are, I believe, a number of consequences of inadequate learning set

other than those enumerated, I should like to point to only one other, and that is stimulus-response reviewing, a matter which may also be discussed under the rubric of caution. Caution may be described as the tendency of a subject to carefully review the content both of the stimulus constellation and of his response repertory before choosing and making a response. One purpose of stimulus-response reviewing may be to avoid making an incorrect response. Reviewing is necessary, at least in part, because of genuine uncertainty on the part of the subject as to what it is to which he is expected to attend, and as to what he is expected to do—in short, to inadequacy of learning set.

In conclusion I wish to make it clear that I do not believe that every instance of rigid behavior, confusion, response perseveration, response omission, or stimulus-response reviewing is due to learning set inadequacies. Confusion can arise from many sources; persistence in an incorrect response may be due to many things, including lack of feedback of response accuracy and thus to the subject's belief that he has been making correct responses; omission of responses may not be deliberate, but due to lack of speed in making an overt response of any kind within the time limits imposed by the experimenter, possibly because the reviewing process took too much time. My purpose has been merely to indicate the possibility that a substantial proportion of these kinds of response modes are due to inadequacy of learning sets and, therefore, to propose that the state of an individual's learning sets be taken into account in the design, analysis, and interpretation of learning experiments.

References

BOTWINICK, J.: Cognitive processes in maturity and old age (Springer, New York 1967).

HARLOW, H.: The formation of learning sets. Psychol. Rev. *56:* 51–65 (1949).

HULTSCH, D. F.: Subjective organization in free recall as a function of adult age and type of instructions (unpubl. Ph.D. dissertation, Syracuse Univ. 1968).

KUHLEN, R. G.: Aging and life-adjustment; in BIRREN, Handbook of aging and the individual, pp. 852–897 (Univ. Chicago Press, Chicago 1959).

KUHLEN, R. G.: Motivational changes during the adult years; in KUHLEN, Psychological backgrounds of adult education, pp. 77–113 (Center for the Study of Liberal Education for Adults, Chicago 1963).

KUHLEN, R. G.: Personality change with age; in WORCHEL and BYRNE, Personality change, pp. 524–555 (Wiley, New York 1964).

LEVINSON, B., and REESE, H. W.: Patterns of discrimination learning set in preschool children, fifth graders, college freshman, and the aged. Monogr. Soc. Res. Child Develop. 32: 7 (1967).

MONGE, R. H.: Adult age differences in paired associate verbal learning set formation (unpubl. Ph.D. dissertation, Syracuse Univ. 1967).

MONGE, R. H., KUHLEN, R. G., and GARDNER, E. F.: Effect of variation of the inspection interval on paired associate learning at two adult age levels (Eastern Psychol. Ass., Washington 1968).

ROSENTHAL, R.: Experimenter effects in behavioral research (Appleton-Century-Crofts, New York 1966).

15. A STUDY OF THE DROPOUT RATES IN LONGITUDINAL RESEARCH ON AGING AND THE PREDICTION OF DEATH

KLAUS F. RIEGEL, RUTH M. RIEGEL,
and GÜNTHER MEYER

During recent years, an increasing number of longitudinal studies of adult and aged subjects have been reported in the psychological literature. Most of these studies are based on special subsamples of the population and have applied restricted sets of psychological measures only. Owens (1953) retested the intelligence of a group of superior adults, and Bayley and Oden (1955) reported on the longitudinal analysis of Terman's subjects. At the other end of the continuum, Kaplan (1943, 1956) and Bell and Zubek (1960) retested mentally inferior persons. In both cases it would be inappropriate to generalize the reported findings since there is, most likely, an interaction between the rate of change and the original level of functioning. This has been emphasized by Foster and Taylor (1920), Jones and Conrad (1933), and Miles (1933).

More recently, Jarvik, Kallman, and Falek (1962), Jarvik, Kallman, Falek, and Klaber (1957), Jarvik and Falek (1963), and Falek, Kallman, Lorge, and Jarvik (1960), in a number of joint publications, reported on a longitudinal investigation of intellectual functioning and longevity of senescent twins. Kleemeier (1962) and Kaplan, Rumbaugh, Mitchell, and Thomas (1963) retested the intelligence of residents in a home for the aged after various time intervals, and observed sudden and marked performance decrements preceding the death of the subjects. Among the best-matched samples of the aging population were those by Berkowitz and Green (1963), Eisdorfer (1963), and by Schaie and Strother (1964). The former two studies were restricted to the measurement of intelligence, while the latter also included some attitudinal scales applied to stratified samples ranging from 20 to 70 years of age.

In most of these studies, developmental psychologists have never questioned the superiority of the longitudinal over the cross-sectional design. Only very recently has the complementary nature of both strategies been recognized. In particular, Schaie (1959, 1965) and Schaie and Strother (1964) have provided a thorough discussion of the experimental strategies in gerontological research, in emphasizing more general designs in comparison with which the two traditional approaches are merely specialized and incomplete cases.

In a more concrete sense, the limitations of the traditional research strategies have long been recognized. In their cross-sectional study, Jones, Conrad, and Horn (1928) analyzed the performance of subjects who had originally refused to participate in their study, thus biasing the sample. More recently, Sussman (1964), Damon (1965), and Rose (1965) discussed the representativeness of samples in longitudinal research primarily concerned with the health of the subjects.

Because of systematic factors, of which sickness and death are the most obvious, the problem of sample bias is equally important for longitudinal and cross-sectional studies in psychological gerontology. Indeed, if systematic selection by dropout factors (such as selective death rates) can be detected, the concept of psychological development based on observed trends would itself be seriously challenged, because then cross-sectional or longitudinal research would represent averages for sets of systematically biased age samples only;

therefore any inferences about general developmental trends would be questionable.

The present analysis has been undertaken primarily to determine the psychological characteristics of subjects who either did not survive the time period between the two testings, were too ill, or refused to be retested. Since significant differences between the subgroups were detected, attempts have also been made to predict the ensuing death of the subjects on the basis of sociopsychological factors. The present analysis is restricted to major comparisons between the four subgroups mentioned. (In a supplementary technical report—Riegel, Riegel, & Meyer, 1967—statistical details on the 43 variables and five age groups at both testings have been provided, and differences in the distributions of test scores and the effect of multiple testing have been dsicussed.)

Method and Procedure

Subjects

The present analysis is based on the results of the first testing of a study on sociopsychological factors of aging, conducted in Germany in 1956–57 and a retest study in 1961–62.

The original sample consisted of 190 females and 190 males. These cases were drawn from a group of about 500 subjects, and were subvided into five age levels of 38 females and 38 males each. The five age levels were 55–59, 60–64, 65–69, 70–74, and over 75 years (average age=79.0 years). Aside from controlling for age and sex, each age level was matched against census statistics on the following criteria: occupation, source of income, marital status, refugees versus nonrefugees, and religious affiliation. The samples can be regarded as representative for the population of northern Germany. Fuller descriptions of the samples and the procedures are given elsewhere (Riegel & Riegel, 1959; Riegel, Riegel, & Skiba, 1962).

At the time of the second testing all

subjects had moved into the next higher age levels. Of the 380 persons originally tested, 202 participated in the second testing, 62 had died during the intervening 5 years, 32 were too ill to be retested (were in hospitals or had to remain in bed during the weeks of the testing), and 84 refused to be retested. A comparison of these four categories of subjects by age levels is given in Table 15.1 and shows that the number of subjects retested decreased rather regularly with age, whereas the number of deceased subjects increased. The number of sick subjects increased irregularly. No systematic differences in the number of noncooperative subjects existed between the age levels.

Method

The following measures were used:

1. Short forms of the Hamburg Wechsler Intelligence Test for Adults. These scales were administered to all subjects and the full test to a random subsample of 128 (see K. F. Riegel & R. M. Riegel, 1962; R. M. Riegel, 1960; R. M. Riegel & K. F. Riegel, 1959, 1962).

2. Five multiple-choice verbal tests (synonyms, antonyms, selections, classifications, analogies) as described by Riegel (1959, 1967). Though subjects were under no time stress, the duration of the test performances were recorded. Half of the items of the antonyms, selections, and classifications tests were mixed (m); the others were presented each in separate forms (s).

3. Four attitude and interest scales of the Likert type (rigidity, dogmatism, attitude toward life, interests) as described by Riegel and Riegel (1960).

4. A general questionnaire on the social and living conditions of the subjects, including inquiries on the following topics: education, financial status, health, physical activities, leisure-time activities, social activities, itemized activities, expressions of well-being, comparisons of situations, as well as many single items dealing with the conditions and habits of daily life (see Riegel et al., 1962).

Results and Discussion

Developmental Trends of Subsamples

The main problems to be analyzed can be outlined in reference to Figures 15.1 and 15.2, which represent the average scores of the various subgroups on the scale of behavioral rigidity (see Riegel & Riegel, 1960). According to Figure 15.1, which includes the data from the first testing only, rigidity increased rather steadily with age. Subjects who were later retested were less rigid than the total group, but the rate of increase was about the same for both. Subjects who died during the following 5 years were much more rigid than both the total group and the subjects to be retested. Age differences were small for nonsurvivors. The scores of subjects who were ill at the time of the second testing varied rather markedly between the age levels, but generally were far above those of the other groups. The same held for the subjects who later refused to be retested. However, this group did not deviate as much from the general trend as did the ill subjects.

Figure 15.2 compares the mean scores obtained at the second testing with total scores of the first test. Again the rigidity of the retested subjects increased with age. The trend of the means was closely parallel to that of the first testing, though the means were significantly higher ($p<.01$). Of greater importance, however, was the fact that the retest means were still below

Table 15.1. Fate of subjects from the original samples at the time of the second testing

	55–59	60–64	65–69	70–74	75+	Sum
Retested	51	48	44	34	25	202
Deceased	2	8	12	17	23	62
Too ill	4	2	6	11	9	32
Refusals	19	18	14	14	19	84

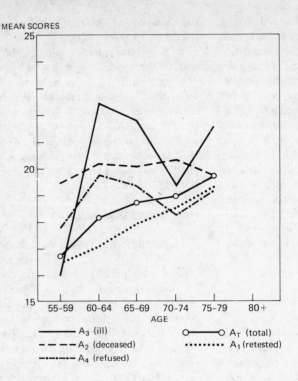

MEAN SCORES

Figure 15.1. Mean scores in behavioral rigidity at the first testing for five age levels and four subgroups of subjects

AGE

——— A₃ (ill)	—o—o— Aᴛ (total)
– – – A₂ (deceased)	·········· A₁ (retested)
–·–·– A₄ (refused)	

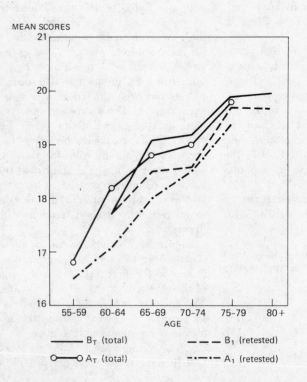

MEAN SCORES

Figure 15.2. Mean scores in behavioral rigidity for five age levels of the total group and the group of retested subjects at the first (A) and second (B) testing

AGE

——— Bᴛ (total)	– – – B₁ (retested)
—o—o— Aᴛ (total)	–·–·– A₁ (retested)

the averages of the total group at the first testing. This may be attributed to the absence of those subjects who died, became ill, or refused to be retested. If one reinstated these subjects by averaging their scores from the first testing with the second scores from the retested group, artificially complete samples would be created on the rather disadvantageous assumption that the scores of the subjects not retested would have remained unchanged during the intervening 5 years. The means of these artificial groups were comparable to those of the total group at the time of the first testing. As Figure 15.2 shows, they were above those of the first testing as well as above all other subgroups; that is, rigidity was higher during the later years than estimated in any of the other analyses. Of major concern in our discussion below will be the question of which of the various curves of Figure 15.2 would represent most appropriately the developmental trend.

Dropout Rates

Since at the younger age levels some of the four subgroups did not include enough cases to allow for reliable estimates, the five consecutive age samples were pooled using the retirement age of 65 years as the cutting point. The significance of the retirement age for changes in behavior has been strongly suggested by the authors as well as by earlier investigations. But aside from any such considerations, the age of 65 years subdivided the group of retested subjects in nearly equal sections of 99 and 103 subjects, respectively, and was selected primarily for this reason.

In the following analysis, the 43 variables tested are being regarded as a sample of measures not all of which are independent of one another but whose interdependencies—though slightly increasing with age—do not yield different correlation matrices at the two age levels. The variability in scores did not change markedly with age even though the dropout of

subjects at the earlier age levels seemed to depend on systematic rather than random factors. These results justify the following comparisons in the numbers of significant differences between the subgroups.

For each variable the differences between the means of the four subgroups at the two remaining age levels have been tested for significance by analyses of variances. Subsequently, the most important t-test comparisons between the subgroups have been made and are explained in the footnote to Table 15.2. Signs are given whenever the differences are significant at or beyond the .05 level. In particular, positive signs indicate that the direction of differences in the first group of comparisons leaned toward greater intelligence, superiority in verbal abilities, more rigidity, more negativism in their attitude toward life, less interested, better education and financial support, poorer health, greater activity, feeling of well-being, and a favorable comparison of their present situation with the past.

By adding all the significant signs for each of the two age groups, it is evident that the subsamples deviated increasingly from one another. Below 65 years there were 35 significant differences, whereas for those over 65 there were 63 significant signs. This difference was particularly marked for the three intelligence measures, where the ratio of signs for the two age groups was 3:12, as well as for the battery of verbal tests (ratio of 8:19) and the questionnaire scales (ratio of 5:13). An equal number of significant signs occurred for the two age groups on the various attitude scales (ratio of 19:19). Similar results were obtained by comparing the retested and nonretested subjects (1—N). Eleven of the 32 variables listed in Table 15.1 were significant for the younger, but 18 for the older age group.

In particular, both the deceased and the sick subjects deviated on a rather large number of variables from the retested subjects. Below 65 years, seven and eight variables, respectively, differed significantly.

Table 15.2. Significance of difference in mean scores between various subgroups of the original sample[a]

Item	Age Group 55–64						Age Group Over 65					
	1—2	1—3	1—4	2—3	A—2	1—N	1—2	1—3	1—4	2—3	A—2	1—N
Age							—	—				—
Intelligence		+					+	+	+			+
Verbal		+				+	+	+	+			+
Performance							+	+	+			+
Verbal tests	+	+		+			+	+	+			+
Synonyms							+	+	+		+	+
Antonyms	+	+		+	+		+	+				+
Selections									+	+		+
Classifications												+
Analogies					+		+	+				+
Rigidity		—					—	—				—
General	—						—	—				—
Personal	—		—				—	—				—
Dogmatism		—	—				—					
Anxiety		—					—					
Intolerance	—						—					
General				+			—		+		—	
Attitude toward life	—						—					
Proretrospect												—
Contemporary	—						—	—				
Interests												+
Receptive activity												
Productive activity							+	+	+			+
Physical activity												
Education				+			+		+			
Financial status												
Health	—						—	—				
Physical activity							+					+
Social activity												
Leisure-time activity		—					+		+			+
Itemized activity							+		+			+
Well-Being									+			
Competitive situations							+				—	
Σ signs	7	8	2	1	6	11	12	13	14	5	1	18

[a] The subgroups are denoted by the numbers and letters in the heading of the table in the following way: 1=retested subjects, 2=deceased subjects, 3=subjects too ill, 4=subjects refusing to be retested, A=alive subject (retested+ill+refusing subjects), N=not retested subjects (decreased+ill+refusing subjects). Thus, the denotation 1—2 indicates the differences between subgroup 1 and 2, etc. If any of the differences was significant (p<.05) and positive, a positive sign (+) was used; if negative, a negative sign (−) was given.

Above 65 years, the corresponding figures were 12 and 13. For variables discriminating between noncooperative and retested subjects there was also a rather marked age difference. Below 65 years these two groups differed only on two scales (dogmatism and leisure-time activity). Above 65 years, however, 14 variables were significantly different. For both age groups, there were few significant differences between deceased and sick subjects. Only one variable was significant for subjects below 65, and five for subjects above 65 years of age.

Undoubtedly of greatest importance was the finding that in the younger group the deceased subjects differed from all the survivors (including those retested or not retested) on six variables whereas there was only one significant difference at the higher age level. This finding encouraged a search for systematic differences that might have allowed the prediction of the subjects' death on the basis of their socio-psychological functioning at the time of the first testing.

Prediction of Death

Multiple-regression predictions of death were calculated on an IBM 7090 computer. Age and sex were excluded from the predictions since both of them—being known as good predictors—could have covered up the more interesting psychological variables, even though their elimination would necessarily reduce the overall degree of correlation.

The predictions were made by successively reducing the F level at which variables would enter into the equations. The F levels were set at .05 and .10, but for each variable the F values were also empirically determined. This was necessary because under the more lenient conditions of $p = .10$ the F values for some of the variables already entered could have changed, depending on their correlations with the newly entering measures. Indeed, in some cases, high-ranking predictor variables have been dropped altogether from the equations. Generally, in a new field of investigation it seems reasonable to go somewhat beyond the conventional level of $p = .05$ because additional variables will pick up unaccounted portions of the variance. Even though they will increase the likelihood of Type 2 errors, it seems more appropriate to retain hypotheses initially, which after sufficient further research turn out to be false, rather than to reject hypotheses too early that may turn out to be true.

As shown in Table 15.3, thirteen variables entered into the equation for the 55- to 64-year-old subjects at an F level of .10, but only five for the subjects above 65 years. Moreover, one of these five variables

Table 15.3. Ranks and F levels for the prediction of death at two age levels

	55 to 64		Over 65	
Variable	Rank	F	Rank	F
Personal rigidity	11	4.51*		
General rigidity	10	3.10*		
General dogmatism	2	6.91	2	9.48
Productive activities	4	5.48	4	3.13*
Classifications m			5	3.74*
Antonyms T	3	9.37		
Classifications T	5	4.42		
Total testing time m	7	4.48		
Financial status	9	3.01*		
Health	1	11.94		
Physical activity			1	8.80
Free time	8	3.16*		
Yrs. married			3	4.81
No. acquaintances	12	3.57*		
Itemized activities	6	3.91		
Widow(er) or not	13	2.76*		

* $p = .10$.

correlated highly with age, namely, the number of years married, and thus may have been excluded for the same reason for which age has been eliminated. Only two of the five variables were also predictors for the younger age group, namely, general dogmatism and productive activities (interests). The remaining variables were different for both groups. Even though the best single predictors were health for the younger, and the amount of physical activity for the older group, both the attitude and the intellectual measures entered strongly into the regression equations. Because the various intercorrelations were taken into account, the variables selected and shown in Table 15.3 were not necessarily identical with those significantly different in means between deceased and live subjects (see Table 15.2).

The point-biserial multiple correlations at the F level of .05 were .47 for the seven variables selected into the equation of the younger, and .31 for the three variables of the older subjects. When the F level was lowered to .10, the multiple correlations were raised to .60 and .35, respectively. In further lowering the F level to .50, the correlations could have been increased to .68 and .46, respectively, but at the same time the errors of estimate would have grown considerably so that this gain would not have been beneficial.

Conclusions

The present analysis was based on five cross-sectional samples of consecutive age groups above 55 years. Five years after the first testing, attempts were made to retest all subjects. However, success was not possible in these attempts because, in numbers increasing with age, some subjects had died or had become sick. Others refused to be retested, but their numbers seemed to be independent of age. If the biological determinants of death and disease interact with psychological or sociological factors—as has been shown in the present study—a number of far-reaching conclusions can be drawn.

First, a concept of development as represented by curves of growth and decline is questionable, regardless of whether these curves are based on longitudinal or cross-sectional data.

Development as reflected by trends of average test or rating scores would be a meaningful concept only if the dropout of subjects in consecutive age groups is strictly a random process. However, biologically weak subjects will die earlier or will become increasingly unable to participate in the testings. A particular occupational, financial, educational and/or social status may increase the risks and may decrease the chances of survival. According to the present study, groups of dropouts (particularly the younger ones) are also psychologically different in their abilities and attitudes.

Age samples drawn for cross-sectional studies or followed up in longitudinal studies become increasingly biased, the further one moves upward in the age scale, and thus the generalized trend will be confounded by the increasing degree of sample bias.

Second, older reports on the decline of intelligence have been received with shock or suspicion. Relief was felt when some longitudinal studies (Bayley & Oden, 1955; Owens, 1953) reported higher stabilities than originally observed, even though these studies were restricted to subjects with superior capacities. According to the present findings and aside from other psychological factors, less-able persons die earlier or are more likely to become seriously ill. Thus, the samples are increasingly loaded with highly able persons. If it had been possible to retest all of the subjects originally involved in the study, the decline would have been more marked than either cross-sectional or longitudinal studies have revealed.

A third conclusion can be added concerning the determinants of death. Even though the groups of dropouts differed on an increasing number of variables, prediction of death was more successful at the earlier than at the later age levels. This should be attributed to slightly lower intercorrelations between the predictor variables, and to the larger differences in average scores between the groups of subjects who were either sick, refused to be retested, or had died. The differences in accuracy of predictions indicate that at lower age levels nonsurvivors can be described as a subgroup wihch differs sociopsychologically from the rest in almost the same sense as victims of cancer or heart attacks may differ from healthy persons. At the higher age levels, however, death seems to strike at random, and psychological predictions become less valid. Using again the biological analogy, nonsurvivors resemble persons with general syndromes of aging rather than specific diseases which cause their death.

Summary

Intelligence, verbal abilities, attitudes, interests, and social conditions of 380 Ss above 55 years of age were measured. Five years later Ss were retested. Some refused to cooperate again, and others had died or become ill. Retested Ss differed significantly from the total group, but in particular from the other subgroups. The prediction of death on the basis of sociopsychological variables was more successful for Ss below than above 65 years of age.

It was concluded that developmental trends are based on increasingly biased samples, that previous studies have underestimated the amount of attrition, and that nonsurvivors under 65 years form a sociopsychological subgroup of different characteristics than survivors.

References

BAYLEY, N., & ODEN, M. H. The maintenance of intellectual ability in gifted adults. *Journal of Gerontology*, 1955, *10*, 91–107.

BELL, A., & ZUBEK, J. P. The effect of age on the intellectual performance of mental defectives. *Journal of Gerontology*, 1960, *15*, 285–295.

BERKOWITZ, B., & GREEN, R. F. Changes in intellect with age: I. Longitudinal study of Wechsler-Bellevue scores. *Journal of Genetic Psychology*, 1963, *103*, 3–21.

DAMON, A. Discrepancies between findings of longitudinal and cross-sectional studies in adult life: Physique and physiology. *Human Development*, 1965, *8*, 16–22.

EISDORFER, C. The WAIS performance of the aged: A retest evaluation. *Journal of Gerontology*, 1963, *18*, 169–172.

FALEK, A., KALLMAN, F. J., LORGE, I., & JARVIK, L. F. Longevity and intellectual variation in a senescent twin population. *Journal of Gerontology*, 1960, *15*, 305–309.

FOSTER, J. C., & TAYLOR, G. A. The application of mental tests to persons over 50. *Journal of Applied Psychology*, 1920, *4*, 39–58.

JARVIK, L. F., & FALEK, A. Intellectual stability and survival in the aged. *Journal of Gerontology*, 1963, *18*, 173–176.

JARVIK, L. F., KALLMAN, F. J., & FALEK, A. Intellectual changes in aged twins. *Journal of Gerontology* 1962, *17*, 289–294.

JARVIK, L. F., KALLMAN, F. J., FALEK, A., & KLABER, M. M. Changing intellectual functions in senescent twins. *Acta Genetica et Statistica Medica*, 1957, *7*, 421–430.

JONES, H. E., & CONRAD, H. S. The growth and decline of intelligence: A study of a homogeneous group between the ages ten and sixty. *Genetic Psychology Monographs*, 1933, *13*, 223–298.

JONES, H. E., CONRAD, H. S., & HORN, A. Psychological studies of motion pictures: II. Observation and recall as a function of age. *University of California Publications in Psychology*, 1928, *3*, 225–243.

KAPLAN, O. J. Mental decline in older morons. *American Journal of Mental Deficiency*, 1943, *47*, 277–285.

KAPLAN, O. J. *Mental disorders in later life*. Stanford: Stanford University Press, 1956.

KAPLAN, O. J., RUMBAUGH, D. M., MITCHELL, D. C., & THOMAS, E. D. Effects of level of surviving abilities, time of day, and test-retest upon psychological performance in seniles. *Journal of Gerontology*, 1963, *18*, 55–59.

KLEEMEIER, R. W. Intellectual changes in the senium. In, *Proceedings, Social Statistics Section, American Statistical Association*. Washington, D.C.: American Statistical Association, 1962. Pp. 290–295.

MILES, W. R. Age and human ability. *Psychological Review*, 1933, *40*, 99–123.

OWENS, W. A., JR. Age and mental abilities: A longitudinal study. *Genetic Psychology Monographs*, 1953, *48*, 3–54.

RIEGEL, K. F. A study on verbal achievements of older persons. *Journal of Gerontology*, 1959, *14*, 453–456.

RIEGEL, K. F. Changes in psycholinguistic performance with age. In G. A. Talland (Ed.), *Human behavior and aging: Recent advances in research and theory.* New York: Academic Press, 1967, in press.

RIEGEL, K. F., & RIEGEL, R. M. A study on changes of attitudes and interests during later years of life. *Vita Humana*, 1960, *3*, 177–206.

RIEGEL, K. F., & RIEGEL, R. M. Analysis of differences in test performance and item difficulty between young and old adults. *Journal of Gerontology*, 1962, *17*, 97–105.

RIEGEL, K. F., RIEGEL, R. M., & MEYER, G. Sociopsychological factors of aging: A cohort-sequential analysis. *Human Development*, 1967, *10*, in press.

RIEGEL, K. F., RIEGEL, R. M., & SKIBA, G. Untersuchung der Lebensbedingungen, Gewohnheiten und Anpassung älterer Menschen in Norddeutschland. *Vita Humana*, 1962, *5*, 204–247.

RIEGEL, R. M. Faktorenanalysen des Hamburg-Wechsler-Intelligenztests für Erwachsene (HAWIE) für die Altersstufen 20–34, 35–49, 50–64 und 65 Jahre und älter. *Diagnostica*, 1960, *6*, 41–66.

RIEGEL, R. M., & RIEGEL, K. F. Standardisierung des Hamburg-Wechsler-Intelligenztests für Erwachsen (HAWIE) für die Altersstufen über 50 Jahre. *Diagnostica*, 1959, *5*, 97–128.

RIEGEL, R. M., & RIEGEL, K. F. A comparison and reinterpretation of factorial structures of the W-B, the WAIS, and the HAWIE on aged persons. *Journal of Consulting Psychology*, 1962, *26*, 31–37.

ROSE, C. H. Representatives of volunteer subjects in a longitudinal aging study. *Human Development*, 1965, *8*, 152–156.

SCHAIE, K. W. Cross-sectional methods in the study of psychological aspects of aging. *Journal of Gerontology*, 1959, *14*, 208–215.

SCHAIE, K. W. A general model for the study of developmental problems. *Psychological Bulletin*, 1965, *64*, 92–108.

SCHAIE, K. W., & STROTHER, C. R. The effect of time and cohort differences on the interpretation of age changes in cognitive behavior. *American Psychologist*, 1964, *19*, 546.

SUSSMAN, M. B. Use of longitudinal designs in studies of long-term illness, some advantages and limitations. *Gerontologist*, 1964, *4*, 25–29.

16. SOME REFLECTIONS ON L. S. VYGOTSKY'S THOUGHT AND LANGUAGE[1]

JERRY FODOR

According to the textbook accounts, philosophy and psychology achieved an amicable divorce towards the end of the last century. Psychology assimilated the experimental method and became the science of the mind (or, in some versions, of behavior). Philosophy went on doing whatever it is philosophers do.

As often happens with textbook accounts, this one is a little lacking in its feeling for nuance. On the one hand, philosophers speculating about mental processes had never been entirely unaware of the possible bearings of experimental findings upon their theories, though it is true enough that they rarely thought of running the experiments. Thus, discussions of the Mollyneaux problem run through the Empiricist literature from Locke forward and the examples of perceptual illusions with which contemporary psychologists enliven introductory courses are sometimes borrowed from Berkeley.

If epistemology was not entirely unaware of the existence of what would now be recognized as specifically psychological problems, it is equally true that contemporary psychology has not abandoned the body of epistemological assumptions that constitute much of its philsophical heritage. The discovery that experimental research on mental processes is possible in principle (and occasionally rewarding in

fact) marks the beginning of modern psychology. But, very often, the psychological experimenter is motivated by theories which are recognizably (if unconsciously) borrowed from the philosophy of mind. Thus, the profound similarities between modern associationism and classical Empiricism have repeatedly been remarked, as has the indebtedness of Gestalt psychology to philosophical Rationalism.

The official dichotomization of philosophy and psychology has not, in short, spared psychologists the necessity of dealing with characteristically philosophical issues. Rather, the philosophy in psychology books has tended to go underground, living the life of the implicit assumption and the unstated methodological postulate. Psychologists have not been able to stop doing philosophy, for no one can think seriously about mentation without eventually dealing with the sorts of issues that presented themselves to Locke, Hume, Berkeley, and Kant. But they *have* often managed to stop noticing when they are doing philosophy, and from not doing it consciously, it is a short step to not doing it well.

Vygotsky's book is a classic example of this state of affairs. What Vygotsky *wanted* to do was pursue a straightforward "scientific" investigation of the relation between talking and thinking: one which adopted no philosophical preconceptions whatever and no generalizations except those dictated by experimental results. What, in fact, happened was that at every move Vygotsky's hand was forced by largely a priori assumptions about the nature of concepts; assumptions whose influence is evident both in the decisions Vygotsky makes about what experiments are worth running

[1] *Thought and Language* was first published in 1934 and is, of course, a classic in the literature on cognitive development. I have, however, chosen to treat it as a contemporary text rather than a period piece, both because many of Vygotsky's notions are still widespread in psychology, and because they seem to me intrinsically worth a run for their money. Page references are to L. S. Vygotsky's *Thought and Language* (1965), Cambridge, Mass., M.I.T. Press.

and in the conclusions he accepts on the basis of his experimental results. And, since the assumptions he adopts are seen to be untenable as soon as they are made explicit, it is small wonder that they eventually run him into a muddle. The present paper is a meditation on these unhappy events.

Vygotsky's book is ostensibly about the "problem of thought and language," a problem that bothered his generation more than it bothers ours. "The problem" is simply whether thought and language can be distinguished, and Vygotsky, sensibly, holds that the answer is "yes." There is every reason to suppose that some thinking is nonverbal: one need not *say* anything to oneself when one thinks how a steak tastes served medium rare. Conversely, there is abundant reason to suppose that some verbalization is unaccompanied by thought. This last point is something more than a joke. The theory that says intelligent talking is reciting aloud to the dictation of a small inner voice lacks both logical coherence (who dictates to the voice?) and introspective plausibility.

If the traditional problem of thought and language now strikes one as slightly uninteresting, that is perhaps because it was almost invariably formulated in the narrowest possible terms. Thought was identified with problem solving (as though one cannot think "Sunday will perhaps be warm") and language was identified with speech. On both grounds one is at a loss to understand what Vygotsky is up to when he argues for the phylogenetic independence of thought from language on the evidence that problem solving in apes is largely independent of vocalization. It is not self-evident that problem solving in experimental situations is a reasonable paradigm either for ape mentation or for ours. And it is still less evident why the call system of apes ought to be compared to a human language. Vygotsky's astonishing remark that human speech "certainly originated" in such vocalizations as apes produce in high motivational states (40) is presumably to be treated as a lapse.

It is worth remarking that the problem of the relation between thought and language can be disentangled from the context of phylogenetic and ontogenetic theorizing in which it has traditionally been enmeshed. For that matter, there is an important sense in which it can, and should, be freed of any specifically *linguistic* context, since it belongs with a class of problems about cognition that have nothing in particular to do with language.

For example, something psychologists worry about less than they might is the routine ability of higher organisms to interpret information in any one input mode in terms of information from any other. What we see often determines how we take what we hear. The way things smell affects the way they taste, and vice versa and so on. It is tempting (perhaps it is mandatory) to explain such interactions by assuming that sensory channels transduce stimulus data into a central computing language rich enough to represent visual, tactual, auditory, gustatory and olfactory information as well as whatever abstract conceptual apparatus is involved in thought. In such a language are performed the calculations involved in evaluating the auditory implications of visual inputs, the gustatory implications of olfaction, etc. It is, in any event, self-evident that the language in which we integrate visual and auditory information cannot be either the language of vision or the language of audition, though it must contain both.

Insofar as one accepts this sort of model, one is led to think of a natural language as analogous to a sensory mode, i.e., as providing a channel through which input data can gain access to the central information handling system. Linguistic data, like sensory data, are subject to integration and interpretation in light of memory information and current experience (for the integration and interpretation of which they are in turn available). Presumably the computations underlying these integrative processes are effected in the central code. If this is so, then the production and comprehension of speech involve translating between this central code and a natural language.

On this account, the problem of thought and language is primarily the problem of characterizing these information exchanges between natural languages and the central computing language. The distinction between the programming languages in which real computers talk to their environment and the machine languages in which they talk to themselves thus provides a precedent for a distinction between the internal code in which *our* thinking is carried out and the linguistic systems in which we exchange the results of our computations.

Nor is (anecdotal) evidence for the psychological reality of such a distinction entirely lacking. We tend to lose detail about the form and source of input information faster than we lose its content, and this would be the natural expectation if the central language is distinct from, and relatively neutral between, the various codes that the input systems use. Did you first hear or read that the sum of the angles of a triangle is 180 degrees? If you are French/English bilingual, try to remember whether you saw the dubbed or the original version of "Devil in the Flesh." Probably you have to do it by trying to recall the circumstances in which you saw the film; if so, what you have lost in memory is precisely information which specifies the original input code.

These reflections suggest aspects of the problem of thought and language which lead directly to deep questions in theoretical psychology. To what extent is the presumed internal code innate, to what extent is it labile? It bears on this question whether a natural language, once learned, can be incorporated into the computing language, thereby itself becoming a vehicle of thought. Or again, however exact the analogy between languages and sensory modes, it is important that languages are learned. If talking a language involves translating into and out of a central computing language, then learning a language

must involve constructing a system (in effect, a "compiler") for effecting this translation. It is, however, hard to imagine that we, or any other mechanism, could be able to construct compilers for *arbitrary* codes. What, then, are the innate constraints on the codes that we can learn to compile? What must a language be that a man may learn to speak it?[2]

There are, in short, a number of ways in which the problem of thought and language might profitably be revived. None of these, however, figure in Vygotsky's book which, despite its title, is primarily concerned with issues in the theory of cognitive development. There is, Vygotsky maintains, a preverbal stage in thought and a preintellectual stage in speech. Moreover, the eventual recruitment of verbal categories in the service of thought, and the corresponding acquisition of the capacity to express thought in verbalization, is by no means an instantaneous achievement on the part of the developing child. That "word meanings evolve . . . as the child develops" (124) is perhaps the central thesis of Vygotsky's book. Specifically, this is understood to mean that the type of concept a child is capable of entertaining at a given stage is characteristic of its developmental level. The mental development of a child is thus viewed as a progression which finds its terminus in the achievement of fully adult patterns of conceptualization.

Now, there is a serious prima facie objection to this sort of line which Vygotsky

---

[2] In the *Philosophical Investigations*, Wittgenstein (1953) criticizes some remarks of Augustine's on language learning: "Augustine describes the learning of human language as if the child came into a strange country and did not understand the language of the country; that is, as if it already had a language, only not this one. Or again: as if the child could already *think*, only not yet speak. And 'think' would here mean something like 'talk to itself' " (para. 32). Wittgenstein seems to suppose that the absurdity of that sort of view is self-evident. I have been arguing, on the contrary, that the Augustinian account is likely to be *precisely* correct.

fails to meet in any satisfactory way. It is that if the conceptualizations of children are radically different from those of adults, it is extremely difficult to imagine how children and adults could ever manage to understand one another. All the more so if the alleged differences are supposed to be differences in word meanings, for that is to say that adults and children are, in a fairly strict sense, talking different languages; a situation only barely disguised by the similarities of the phonological and syntactic system the languages employ.

Vygotsky's way of dealing with this objection is simply hopeless. He says, ". . . (the child's) usage of words coincides with that of adults in its objective reference but not in its meaning" (130). That is, the child and the adult are supposed to be employing terms that exhibit extensional but not intensional identity.

To see that this solution cannot be right, consider the case of witches, ghosts, goblins, and elves. Since these concepts have the *same* extension (namely, the null set), our discussions with children about which of them (e.g.) rides on broomsticks *cannot* be mediated by a merely extensional consensus. Analogously, one could hardly teach a child that Lenin was the father of the revolution if you agree on who the terms refer to but not on what they mean. On the contrary, the condition upon a statement which expresses a synthetic identity being informative is precisely that one knows what the terms mean but not what they refer to. (Cf., Frege, 1952.)

Of course, children and adults often do misunderstand one another in ways that suggest differences in the conceptual equipment each brings to the communication situation. But, prima facie, these would seem to be differences of degree, not differences of kind. For example, adult concepts form a rich and elaborately interconnected network, of which the child's developing conceptual system is at best a sketch. So that, even when parent and child use the same words, the adult may sense resonances and ironies that escape

the child. Compare the way you read *Alice in Wonderland* now with the way you read it the first time.

In fact, however, Vygotsky does not understand the differences between the adult's concepts and the child's in terms of the relative systematicity of the former. On the contrary, it is a serious objection to Vygotsky's account of the nature of concepts that he fails to realize the extent to which each obtains its identity from its position in a network which connects them all. We shall see that, like most philosophical Empiricists, Vygotsky thinks that concepts are severally related to experience by necessary and sufficient conditions for their application, so that whether a given concept applies is, at least in principle, independent of any fact about the world except those mentioned in its definition. The difficulties with this sort of view have been persuasively argued by such philosophers as Quine (1961) and Putnam (1962), and I shall not review them here.

In short, there are obvious quantitative differences between the mentation of adults and children, and one might consider how far an appeal to these might take one in explaining the occasionally startling differences in their cognitive styles. For Vygotsky, however, the differences are radical and epistemic. It is not just that the adult knows more than the child, or that he sees more of the ways in which what he knows interconnects. Rather, adults and children use different *kinds* of concepts. Hence, they *must* misunderstand each other essentially; and, insofar as they appear to communicate, the appearances must be misleading. Nothing less than this is entailed by the view that word meanings evolve.

Insofar as this is prima facie an unpalatable consequence, pretty strong evidence will be needed to support it. But the striking fact about Vygotsky's theory is that it is motivated almost entirely by his failure to find in children conceptual capacities which he assumes, on strictly a priori grounds, are paradigmatic of the mentation of adults. Of course, this finding might show that conceptualization undergoes radical developmental changes. But it might equally show (what is considerably less exciting) just that Vygotsky was wrong about the nature of *adult* concepts.

One can put this point in a way that makes the (presumptive) error sound less like an empirical mistake and more like a philosophical muddle. Vygotsky assumes a gradation of concepts from concrete-and-infantile to abstract-and-adult. Now, the question whether children's concepts are, in Vygotsky's sense, concrete is an empirical question, as is the question whether adults have concepts that are, in Vygotsky's sense, abstract. But the logically prior question whether any sense can be made of the notions of concreteness and abstractness themselves is an a priori question, not an experimental one. I think that Vygotsky has in large part created the problem he is trying to solve by unwarranted assumptions about what makes for conceptual abstractness.

What Vygotsky thinks a concept is emerges most clearly from the experimental procedures he uses to test them. According to an editorial footnote borrowed from *Conceptual Thinking in Schizophrenia*:

The material used in the concept formation tests consists of 22 wooden blocks varying in color, shape, height, and size. There are 5 different colors, 6 different shapes, 2 heights (the tall blocks and the flat blocks), and 2 sizes of the horizontal surface (large and small). On the underside of each figure, which is not seen by the subject, is written one of the four nonsense words: lag, bik, mur, cev. Regardless of color or shape, lag is written on all tall large figures, bik on all flat large figures, mur on the tall small ones, and cev on the flat small ones. At the beginning of the experiment all blocks, well mixed as to color, size and shape, are scattered on a table in front of the subject . . . the examiner turns up one of the blocks (the "sample"), shows and reads its name to the subject, and asks him to pick out all the blocks which he thinks might belong to the same kind. After the sub-

ject has done so . . . the examiner turns up one of the "wrongly" selected blocks, shows that this is a block of a different kind, and encourages the subject to continue trying. As the number of the turned blocks increases, the subject by degrees obtains a basis for discovering to which characteristics of the blocks the nonsense words refer. As soon as he makes this discovery the . . . words . . . come to stand for definite kinds of objects (e.g., lag for large tall blocks, bik for large flat ones), and new concepts for which the language provides no names are thus built up. The subject is then able to complete the task of separating the four kinds of blocks indicated by the nonsense words. Thus the use of concepts has a definite functional value for the performance required by this test. Whether the subject actually uses conceptual thinking in trying to solve the problem . . . can be inferred from the nature of the groups he builds and from his procedure in building them: Nearly every step in his reasoning is reflected in his manipulations of the blocks. The first attack on the problem; the handling of the sample; the response to correction; the finding of the solution—all these stages of the experiment provide data that can serve as indicators of the subject's level of thinking. [pp. 56–57.]

In short, what the child must learn to do in the task Vygotsky sets is think of the objects before him as being characterized by some rather small number of criterial properties. For example, he must learn to attend to the color, size and shape of the blocks, but to ignore indefinitely many such task-irrelevant properties as their weight, texture, distance from his hand, and so on. Having isolated the properties that are relevant to sorting, the child must then learn to choose those of the objects that exhibit some Boolean function of the criterial properties. Characteristically, his language provides him with words for each of the criterial properties ("large," "red," etc.) but fails to provide him with (single) words which exactly characterize the relevant Boolean functions. Since it does, however, provide him with *phrases* ("large and red" etc.), and since he has presumably got these sorts of phrases well under control prior to his experience in the experimental situation, it would seem hazardous to claim either that "new concepts for which the language provides no names are . . . built up" in the course of the experiment or that the experimental situation recapitulates the experience of the child learning word meanings in his (first) language. What seems to be going on is rather that the child is learning that "bik" translates "large and flat" in the nonce-language of the experiment.

Two points need to be stressed. First, that for purposes of this test, and, so far as I can discover, throughout Vygotsky's book, mastery of a concept requires the isolation of sensory invariants whose presence or absence determines whether an individual falls under the concept. Vygotsky repeatedly speaks of a hierarchy of abstractness in which, it appears, the defining conditions for the application of higher level concepts are to be specified as functions of lower level concepts. Second, the mathematics of concept formation is assumed to be the set theoretic operations of forming the union, intersection, complement, etc., of sets of objects exhibiting the criterial attributes. According to Vygotsky, ". . . the advanced concept presupposes more than unification (i.e., more than applicability of the concept to a variety of individuals). To form such a concept, it is also necessary to abstract, to single out elements and to view the abstracted elements apart from the totality of the concrete experience in which they are embedded" (76). The condition upon a concept is, then, that the individuals falling under it should share some Boolean function of criterial attributes and the condition upon forming a concept is that the relevant criteria should be abstracted out of the noisy attributes with which they co-occur in individual objects. Finally, criterial attributes are themselves functions of sensory invariants.

Now, the question is whether, in general, adult concepts have these characteristics. This question is important since it turns out, on Vygotsky's data, that skilled performance on his test is a rather late achievement, one which Vygotsky is disinclined to attribute to the pre-adolescent. So, if adult conceptualization is what Vygotsky thinks it is, and what the Vygotsky test presupposes that it is, the history of mental development is indeed the history of the child's gradual approximation of adult mastery of Boolean logic. If, on the other hand, adult concepts do not, in general, fit the Vygotsky model, if an adult concept isn't the sort of thing that Vygotsky supposes it to be, then there is less interest in the fact that children find it hard, and adults find it less hard, to perform with Vygotsky blocks. The same could be said, after all, of bricks.

Vygotsky himself mentions a number of adult concepts that fail to fit the model, including the concept of furniture, the concept of a family, and the concept of tableware. In each case (and one could add indefinitely more; indeed, it is difficult to think of concepts that *do* fit Vygotsky's model other than lag, bik, mur, and cev) there is no sensory attribute, and no Boolean feature of sensory attributes, characteristic of all and only the instances that fall under the concept. Hence there is no way of learning the concept by abstracting a sensory invariant from each of its instances. What knives, spoons, and forks have in common is not that they look, feel, etc. alike, but that they are used for analogous purposes. Say, if you wish, that *that* is the property abstracted out by the child. But you will hardly say that this defining property (being used for eating) is less abstractly related to sensory data than the defined concept (tableware). There is thus no point in saying that the child learns the concept by abstracting out the property, since, if there is a puzzle about how he does the one, there is the *same* puzzle about how he does the other.

Vygotsky recognized concepts which lack the appropriate kind of invariants as apparent counter-examples to his account of concepts and to his account of concept learning. But he does so only in order to castigate them (and here the vocabulary of opprobrium becomes explicitly philosophical) as merely factitious, concrete, lacking in logical unity, unreal (!) and so on.

Why the concept of family relation is less logical, more concrete, less real, more factitous, etc., than the concepts lag, bik, mur, and cev, escapes me. After all, is not the relation "father of" asymmetrical, intransitive, irreflexive, and so on? And aren't these logical relations in good standing? Indeed, they are the *same* logical relations required to define a hierarchy. What, then, could lead one to say that the child who understands why two people who look as different as James Smith and Alfred Smith are both called Smith is operating at a *less* abstract conceptual level than an adult who can learn to sort blocks into blue squares and red spheres?

If there is no reason to suppose that concepts must, in general, be defined by reference to sensory invariants, there is still less reason to suppose that such defining properties as there are must be specifiable by Boolean operations. Predictably, Vygotsky runs into serious troubles when he touches upon the child's mastery of any of the indefinitely many concepts which cannot be so specified. For example, most children presumably learn that there is no largest number. But this fact cannot be represented by the sort of finitistic mathematics with which Vygotsky hopes to treat *adult* concepts. Vygotsky's treatment of the learning of arithmetic relations is thus exhausted by the remark "at the earlier stage certain aspects of objects had been abstracted and generalized into ideas of numbers" (114). This is, of course, fudge. *What* aspects of objects could be abstracted out to provide the notion of number? Their cardinality? And how, from any finite number of such abstractive processes, could the child conceivably arrive at the notion that the number of numbers is infinite?

It would appear that Vygotsky simply has not got a clear idea of the enormous computational complexity of the concepts children are required (and normally manage) to acquire. For example, one would think it a sufficient explanation of why children find it hard to learn to write that the task involves the internalization of an extremely complex body of information, including a mapping of acoustic onto geometric objects and a refined system of motor integrations involved in producing the latter. (A better question than "why do children find it hard to learn to write" is "why do children find it easy to learn to talk.") Vygotsky, however, has to make up reasons.

Written language demands conscious work because its relation to inner speech is different from that of oral speech . . . Inner speech is condensed, abbreviated, speech. Written speech is deployed to its fullest extent, more complete than oral speech . . . etc. [p. 100.]

Does Vygotsky suppose that it would be easier to learn to write if we allowed the child to write only notes? Surely there is a profound problem about how we learn to write that is quite independent of the problem about how we learn to write grammatically, well, coherently, etc.? Analogously, if the problem about writing is only or primarily that "the motives for writing are . . . more abstract, more intellectualized, further removed from immediate needs . . ." (98) than the motives for oral speech, why can't we get a machine to do it? The fact is that the transformations of the speech signal which must be internalized in learning to read or write are so complicated that no theorist is currently able to formalize them in any very satisfactory way. But we are unlikely to be able to appreciate the character of what the child achieves in becoming literate if we assume that Boolean functions represent the upper bound on the complexity of the operations he can learn to perform.

There is a variety of different morals one might consider drawing at this point. For example, the following.

It is a fundamental assumption of Vygotsky's, and, apparently, of many Piagetians, that operations of a specified computational power are either available or absent across the board at any given developmental stage. At a given stage, a child's concepts are either concrete or they are not; Boolean operations are either "there" or they aren't. A child has "reversible" operations or he doesn't. Exigetical accuracy requires certain *caveats*. Piagetians think that a new kind of operation is likely to show first in motor tasks, whence it is "internalized" to subserve the purposes of cognition and perception. And it is in the spirit of both Vygotsky and Piaget to suppose that vestiges of "lower" levels of conceptualization are occasionally exhibited at "higher" developmental stages. As in Hegel, development involves the transcendence of early integrations, but it also involves their preservation.

Nevertheless, the general point is clear enough. Take a time slice of a child and you will find pervasive and homogeneous limits upon the type of concepts it can form. Developmental stages are to be characterized by reference to such limits; ideally, by the construction of formalisms which express them precisely. The primary goal of theories in cognitive development is thus to exhibit the changing mental capacities of the child in terms of an orderly progression of such formalisms, and to characterize the endogenous and exogenous pressures which occasion transitions between them.

There are, however, alternative views. One might suppose that computational power is quite *un*evenly distributed among the tasks with which a given child is confronted at a given time. Formally quite powerful computational processes may thus be available to the very young child, though only for the performance of quite specific sorts of computations. For example, no one rational can now doubt the formal power of the mechanisms underlying the acquisition of syntax. What is striking is that the child who is exploiting these mechanisms for language learning

apparently does not have analogously powerful systems available for "general problem solving" (e.g., for performing with Vygotsky blocks). Essentially similar remarks could presumably be made about the power, and the specificity, of the computational procedures underlying the ontogenesis of spatial orientation, face recognition, locomotion, depth perception, object constancy, and so on.

One thus considers the possibility of viewing the mental life of children in a way that is quite alien to the Vygotskyian (or the Piagetian) tradition. Classical developmental psychology invites us to think of the child as a realization of an algebra which can be applied, relatively indifferently, to a wide variety of types of cognitive integrations, but which differs in essential respects from the mathematics underlying adult mentation. The alternative picture is that the child is a bundle of relatively special purpose computational systems which are formally analogous to those involved in adult cognition but which are quite restricted in their range of application, each being more or less tightly tied to the computation of a specific sort of data, more or less rigidly endogenously paced, and relatively inaccessible to purposes and influences other than those which conditioned its evolution. Cognitive development, on this view, is the maturation of the processes such systems subserve, and the gradual broadening of the kinds of computations to which they can apply.

I will not insist upon the ethological plausibility of this view (which, however, I think is considerable). Suffice it to remark upon the increasing body of evidence that very complicated cognitive processes are in fact to be found in the young child *if you look in the right places*. See, for a variety of types of examples, recent work by Bower (1966), Bloom (1970), Eimas *et al.* (1971), etc. The moral seems to be that the young child differs from the adult not in the *kinds* of conceptual integrations it can effect, but rather, *in the areas in which it can effect them.* Adults can bring their thinking to bear on a wide area of what we call, in our ignorance, "general" problem solving. Children seem to have available [a] comparably powerful computational apparatus, but it is special purpose equipment. This too is a difference of quantity, not quality. For, there must be some structure to the types of problems that *adults* can solve, though we are hardly in an optimal position to see it. Our mentation might look, to a suitably intellectual angel, structured, task specific, and endogenously constrained in ways that differ in degree rather than in kind from the mentation of our progeny. How, after all, could this fail to be true? We are related to our children.

I have been arguing that viewing the development of the child's mental capacities as the development of the ability to do Boolean operations has some very curious consequences. First, the child's achievement of complicated conceptual integrations is consigned to relatively low developmental levels, while the test of maturity is taken to be the mastery of mathematically trivial operations. The mathematics required to characterize the structure of faces or the syntax of a language is presumably far more powerful than that required to characterize correct performances with Vygotsky blocks. Yet the child is good at talking and recognizing faces long before he is good at the Vygotsky test. A natural conclusion is that the Vygotsky test does not engage the computational procedures that are most central to the child's concept attainment; that the test results are, in that sense, artifactual. This is not the conclusion Vygotsky draws.

The second consequence of Vygotsky's curious views about the nature of mature conceptualization is that many of the remarks he makes about the way children operate at "lower" developmental stages are exactly applicable to normal adult thought. This is, of course, a way of saying that Vygotsky's stages do not correspond to anything *in rerum natura*. Thus, Vygot-

sky says: "Since children of a certain age think in pseudo-concepts, the words designate to them complexes of concrete objects, their thinking must result in participation, i.e., in bonds unacceptable to adult logic. A particular thing may be included in different complexes on the strength of its different concrete attributes and consequently may have several names; which one is used depends on the complex activated at the time" (71–72). Followed, inevitably, by talk about how similar children and primitives are in these respects. But, of course, if they are in that boat, so are we. For, *we* think a chair may be "Queen Anne," or "to low to reach the light bulb by standing on," etc. And which of these "attributes" *we* use depends precisely on the complex activated at the time: e.g., on whether we are interested in antiques or in changing the light bulb. What else *could* it depend on?

It is not only Vygotsky's remarks about intermediate levels of conceptualization that apply with full force to the conceptualizations of adults. "The young child takes the first step toward concept formation when he puts together a number of objects in an *unorganized congeries*, or 'heap' . . . at this stage, word meaning denotes nothing more to the child than a *vague syncretic conglomeration of individual objects*" (59). Now, this might mean that the child does what he does for no reason at all; not that there is a special kind of concept underlying his behavior, but that there is no concept whatever; he is simply pushing blocks around. This, however, is not Vygotsky's line. Rather, the phenomenon is ". . . the result of a tendency to compensate for the paucity of well-apprehended objective relations by an overabundance of subjective connections and to mistake these subjective bonds for real bonds between things" (60). It is interesting to note the work that words like "real," "objective," etc. do in this passage. They serve simultaneously to compare the concept allegedly governing the child's sorting with Vygotsky's notion of paradigmatic adult concepts and to castigate the former as ontologically unsound. In fact, why are not "all the things I like" or "all the things that happened to me on the way to the office," etc. perfectly acceptable *adult* concepts? And how could one possibly suppose that employing these very sophisticated notions somehow indicates a *lower* level of functioning than operating with notions like "blocks that are both blue and square"?

Once again, I do not wish to deny that there may be *some* sense in which children's thinking is relatively concrete, subjective, factitious, etc. I am claiming only that Vygotsky is driven to this conclusion less by his data than by some quite unreasonable philosophical convictions about what it is to think abstractly, logically, maturely, and so on. Indeed, once the muddle is straightened up and it is seen that the inability to deal with Boolean functions needs not, *ipso facto*, entail primitive mentation, the data that Vygotsky has left appear pretty sketchy. He says, for example, that "even abstract concepts are often translated into the language of concrete action (by children): *Reasonable* means when I am hot and don't stand in a draft" (78). But Socrates, who wanted to know what "good" means, had the same trouble with his *adult* informants: they persisted in providing him with examples of good things, acts, people, or whatever. The problem wasn't, of course, that their mental functioning was impaired; it was that they didn't have the concept of a *definition* (neither, by the way, did Socrates).

Similarly, among the anecdotes that are supposed to convince us of the concrete, etc., character of children's thinking is the following. "A pre-school child who, in response to the question, 'Do you know your name?' tells his name, lacks . . . self-reflective awareness: He knows his name but is not conscious of knowing it" (91). But this is a joke. It is, in fact, this joke:

(A road. *Vladimir and Estragon enter right*)

Vladimir: "Could you tell me the time?"
Estragon: "Yes."
(Silence. Exit left slowly. Fade.)

References

BLOOM, LOIS. (1970) *Language Development*. Cambridge, Mass., M.I.T. Press.

BOWER, T. (1966) The Visual World of Infants. *Scient. Amer.* 215/6.

EIMAS, P., SIQUELAND, E., JUSCZYK, P., VIGORITO, J. (1971) Speech Perception in Infants. *Science*. 171, 3968.

FREGE, G. (1952) On Sense and Reference. In *Transactions from the Philosophical Writings*. Oxford University Press.

PUTNAM, H. (1962) What Theories Are Not. In: Nagel, Suppes and Tarski (eds.) *Logic Methodology and Philosophy of Science*. Stanford University Press.

QUINE, W. V. (1961) Two Dogmas of Empiricism. In: *From A Logical Point of View*. Harvard University Press.

WITTGENSTEIN, L. (1953) *Philosophical Investigations*. Oxford, Blackwell.

CHAPTER THREE: SUGGESTED FURTHER READINGS

BAYLEY, N. Development of mental abilities. In P. Mussen (Ed.), *Carmichael's manual of child psychology*. (3rd ed.) Vol. 1. New York: Wiley. 1970, Pp. 1163–1310.

ELKIND, D., and FLAVELL, J. *Studies in cognitive development.* New York: Oxford University Press, 1969.

KAGAN, J., and KOGAN, N. Individual variations in cognitive processes. In P. Mussen (Ed.), *Carmichael's manual of child psychology.* (3rd ed.) Vol. 1. New York: Wiley, 1970. Pp. 1273–1365.

KOGAN, N. Creativity and cognitive style: A life-span perspective. In P. B. Baltes and K. W. Schaie (Eds.), *Life-span developmental psychology: Personality and socialization.* New York: Academic Press, 1973. Pp. 146–179.

SCHAIE, K. W. A reinterpretation of age related changes in cognitive structure and functioning. In L. R. Goulet and P. B. Baltes (Eds.), *Life-span developmental psychology.* New York: Academic Press, 1970. Pp. 486–508.

chapter four
language

All human beings have the biological capacity to produce language, and infants in all cultures seem to progress through the same early states of language development, the earliest of which is babbling. However, there is no correlation between babbling and later speech of the child; that is, early babbling does not necessarily indicate early speech or early acquisition of grammatical skills. After about the first year of life the infant begins to use one-word utterances. These are usually words that are high in content such as nouns. At about eighteen to twenty-four months the child has progressed to the two-word stage. This stage is characterized by the use of what are called pivot-open distinctions such as "see daddy." This manner of speaking is obviously different from adult speech but is related to the language of the adult. Finally the child begins to use three-word sequences. This longer sentence provides the implicit content missing from the two-word structure. An example of this is "daddy eat food." From this point on the child continues to expand his linguistic skills, using longer and more complex syntactic and grammatical sequences.

At all stages of development the child's own language system appears to be rule-governed. His sentences sound simple, but they are coherent, systematic, and lawful. They are not just patterns of words being mimicked from adult speech. Evidence of the fact that the child's speech is rule-governed is his frequent overgeneralization of language rules; for example, in forming the past tense of the irregular verb "take," the child will typically respond with "taked" rather than "took." "I runned" shows that a child is not just imitating adult speech, but has abstracted a general rule for the English past tense.

Research has found that learning-theory principles such as reinforcement and imitation play an insignificant role in language development. Parents tend to reinforce or reward the child for accuracy and truthfulness of content rather than for grammatical correctness (Brown, 1969). It is phenomenal that the child learns such complex syntactic and grammatical patterns, especially in such a short period. By five years all children seem to know most of the basic rules of their native language, even though languages differ greatly in complexity of grammar or vocabulary (Rebelsky, Starr, and Luria, 1967).

The relatedness of thought and language is an interesting developmental issue. The young child thinks and speaks in infantile terms; he has a limited world view. As he matures, he begins to think and speak about topics other than his own self-satisfaction and uses more adultlike abstract patterns. Not only do mental concepts and thought content change and develop but the way in which they are expressed does also. This is a trend which can be noted through all the stages of life. The issues that a young child thinks about and communicates are different from those which an adolescent conveys, and a middle-aged person thinks and speaks differently than an eighty-year-old does. Even during the life of an eighty-year-old, events may change drastically, necessitating the development of new thought and language skills. As the maturing individual grows,

he perceives the nature of events differently than he does at another stage; therefore, he undoubtedly reacts and verbalizes differently. Cognitive abilities do not remain stable all through life. They change and develop over the life span, and it is likely that language abilities do so too.

It is interesting to look at language development from another perspective, that of studying adults' perception of children's speech. Research has found that adults who have children can understand the speech of young children better than those who do not. It is also true that adults can understand their own children better than someone else's. In this sense, adults who can decipher the speech of the young can be regarded as bilingual (Weist and Stebbins, 1972). This ability to decipher the speech of children can also be regarded as a linguistic developmental process of adults.

Regardless of the approach to language one chooses to endorse, the central issue remains: Language development is a continuous process. It does not begin with babbling during infancy and end abruptly by age five when the child has acquired unquestionably complex grammatical skill; instead it continues to develop over the years. As cognitive abilities grow, language abilities continue to mature.

The fact that language development is a life-span issue has important implications on research in the field. After a review of the literature, we conclude that most of the prior work done on language acquisition implies that development stops at age five, and that more research is called for in the field of language development after the age of five.

References

BROWN, R. *Social psychology.* New York: Free Press, 1965. Pp. 246–350.

REBELSKY, F., STARR, R., and LURIA, Z. Language development, the first four years. In Y. Brackbill (Ed.), *Infancy and early childhood.* New York: Free Press, 1967. Pp. 289–357.

WEIST, R. M., and STEBBINS, P. Adult perception of children's speech. *Psychonomic Science,* 1972, 27, 359–360.

17. THE DEVELOPMENT OF COMPETENCE IN AN EXCEPTIONAL LANGUAGE STRUCTURE IN OLDER CHILDREN AND YOUNG ADULTS

PAMELA E. KRAMER, ELISSA KOFF,
and ZELLA LURIA

There appears to be an interesting class of exceptional linguistic structures which, because of their relative linguistic complexity and infrequency, are acquired rather late in life and may never be acquired by all adult speakers. Such linguistic structures allow the process of language acquisition to be studied not only in young children, but also in young adults.

Our work is based directly upon the work of Carol Chomsky (1969). In her research, subjects ranging in age from 5 to 10 years were tested on their ability to decode sentences involving an exceptional structure in English, the exception to the Minimal Distance Principle. "I tell him where to go" follows the Minimal Distance Principle; the subject of the complement verb phrase "where to go" is the noun phrase most closely preceding that verb phrase, or the object of the main clause. "I ask him where to go" violates the Minimal Distance Principle. Here, the subject of the complement "where to go" is the main clause subject, the noun phrase more distant from the complement.

"Ask" is an unusual verb in that it can follow the Minimal Distance Principle as in the sentence "John asked Bill to leave," or violate the Minimal Distance Principle as in the sentence "John asked Bill what to do." Presumably, children who have not learned when to apply the exception to the Minimal Distance Principle will apply the Minimal Distance Principle, the regular rule. Therefore, Carol Chomsky predicted, such children would interpret the sentence "(you) ask John what to paint" as "ask John what he should paint." Con-

sequently, these children should respond to this sentence with "John, what do you want to paint?" when "what should I paint?" is the correct response.

In addition to the above response, however, Carol Chomsky found that over half of the subjects, especially the younger children—5- and 6-year-olds—were responding to "ask" in such sentences as "Ask John what to paint" as if "ask" were synonymous wtih "tell." Subjects were responding, moreover, to "ask" in less complicated sentences such as "ask John what color this is" in a similar manner. (Subjects would respond "it's red.") While this is an understandable mistake in that "ask" in the sense of a request often does mean the same thing as "tell," it nonetheless seemed startling that the structural meaning of such common and everyday words should fail to be distinguished by such large numbers of children.

On the basis of these findings, Carol Chomsky decided to investigate structures involving "ask" and "tell" in a more general manner, with the exception to the Minimal Distance Principle as the most difficult structure tested. She tested for children's understandings of three kinds of sentences: case 1, "Ask Laura what time it is"; case 2, "Ask Laura her last name"; case 3, "Ask Laura what to feed the doll." She found five stages in the acquisition of competence in these constructions. In the first, Ss would tell rather than *ask* in response to simple sentences such as "Ask Mary what color this is" (case 1). In the second, Ss would respond correctly to the preceding sentence (where all elements of

the response are present in the complement) but would *tell* in response to sentences such as "Ask Mary her last name"
(case 2). In the third stage, Ss would
respond correctly to the simple "ask" constructions of cases 1 and 2, but would *tell*
in response to sentences calling for the
violation of the Minimal Distance Principle
in case 3. In the fourth stage, Ss would
"ask" in response to sentences calling for
the exception, but would choose the wrong
subject for the Wh-clause. Finally, in the
fifth stage, Ss would respond correctly to
all of the test sentences. Because these
stages follow an orderly progression, and
because the stage of the subject correlates
with age (younger Ss tend to be in lower
stages than are older Ss), the five stages
which have been described appear to represent developmental stages in the acquisition of competence in "ask" constructions.

The purpose of the current study was to
investigate the acquisition of the exception
to the Minimal Distance Principle in sentences with the main verb "to ask" in older
children and adults. We hypothesized that:

1. Although competence in the exception
to the Minimal Distance Principle increases with age, differences in competence will be found even in adults. No
age group should demonstrate 100%
competence.
2. Based upon the Lenneberg hypothesis
of a critical period for language learning, (*a*) after the age of 12 the proportion of Ss within any given age group
who demonstrate competence will not
vary significantly; (*b*) Ss under 12 (the
"language-plastic" period) who do not
have the competence in question will
more readily acquire the rule for the
exception after modeling by a peer than
will those over 12; (*c*) Ss who upon
first testing do not have the exceptional
structure, and who are within the language-plastic age range, will be more
likely to induce the rule than will Ss
aged 12 and over when retested some

2 years later.
3. The later developmental stages in the
acquisition of the exception to the Minimal Distance Principle found by Carol
Chomsky will be found in our sample.
4. IQ and competence in the exceptional
structure will be related.

Study 1

Method

Subjects The Ss were 122 white, middle-class children and young adults—61
boys and 61 girls—who were divided into
six age groups (mean ages: 8-10; 10-7;
12-10; 14-6; 15-8; and 19-0). Each group
consisted of 10 boys and 10 girls with the
exception of the college sample, which
consisted of 11 men and 11 women. All of
the Ss ranged in IQ from 106 to 148.

Procedure The Ss were required to
respond to a four-part interview. During
the entire interview, a second child or
helper was present in addition to S. The
"helper" was always a child who had demonstrated competence in the exception to
the Minimal Distance Principle (MDP)
on a pretest.

After instructions, Ss responded to sentences involving "to ask" in its regular,
nonexceptional use (part 1). Inasmuch as
it was not anticipated that any of the Ss
would have difficulty with this portion of
the interview, and none did, these sentences were intended primarily as a warm-
up. If there were no questions, part 2 followed.

Test Sentences
Part 1: Cases 1 and 2
  (S) ask H (helper) what time it is
    (case 1, stage A)
  (H) tell (S) how many pencils there
    are
  (S) ask (H) his last name (case 2,
    stage B)
  (H) tell (S) where you live
Part 2: Test trials (case 3, exception to
  MDP, stages C,D,E)

(S) ask (H) which book to read
(H) tell (S) which pencil to use
(S) ask (H) which comb to use
(H) tell (S) which hammer to pound with
Optional (for Ss who missed one of the above)
(S) ask (H) which cup to use
(H) tell (S) which spoon to use
If optional omitted (cue sentence, case 1)
(S) ask (H) which cup *you* should use
(H) tell (S) which spoon to use
If optional included (cue sentence, case 1)
(S) ask (H) which book *you* should read
(H) tell (S) which pencil to use

Part 2 was the critical section of the experimental interview. Here, test instruction sentences were used which tested the S's ability to decode the exception to the MDP. The helper, in turn, responded to nonexceptional sentences including the verb "to tell" rather than "to ask" (i.e., "John, tell Bill which pencil to use" [John, the helper, responds]. "Bill, ask John which book to read" [Bill, the S, responds]).

In part 3, an attempt was made to test the S's knowledge of the exceptional structure without requiring a verbal response. The Ss made a series of choices between pairs of pictures as possible depictions of sentences spoken by the E, calling for the violation of the MDP. Following each choice, the S was required to explain why the picture chosen corresponded with the sentence which had been given. Some sample sentences are: "Mother told Sally what to wear," "John asked Mary what to paint."

In part 4 of the experimental interview, S responded to sentences similar to those in part 2 after the correct response to sentences violating the MDP had been modeled by the "helper."

The Ss were scored as having demonstrated competence on any given portion of the interview if they responded correctly

to at least two out of three of the test sentences, duplicating Chomsky's requirements. The entire interview was tape-recorded. Objects referred to in the test sentences and the pictures that were correct within each pair were alternated such that half of the subjects received sentences referring to one set of objects or pictures (part A), and the other half of the Ss received sentences referring to the opposite set (part B). For each S the number and order of sibs, and IQ, were recorded.

Results

Our first hypothesis consisted of two parts: (1) that differences in competence would be found in our six age groups, and (2) that no age group would have 100% competence. Both parts of this hypothesis were confirmed, as can be seen in Table 17.1. In our sample of 122 subjects, 69 performed to criterion on part 2 of the experimental interview and 53 did not. The breakdown of the Ss according to age can be found in Table 17.1. Part 3 of the experimental interview was not used as an index of competence because it was revealed to be an inadequate test of whether or not the Ss had the exceptional structure. The Ss elaborated reasons for choosing either of the two pictures shown which seemed plausible to us.

Our second hypothesis, based on the idea of a critical period in the development

Table 17.1. *N* successes and failures for each age group for exceptioal use of "ask"

Age Group	Successes (N)		Failures (N)	Total
College	15	(68)	7	22
Sophomore high school	12	(60)	8	20
Ninth grade	11	(55)	9	20
Seventh grade	14	(70)	6	20
Fifth grade	10	(50)	10	20
Third grade	7	(35)	13	20
Total	69		53	122

Note—Percentage of successes in parentheses.

of language, stated that after the critical period the proportion of Ss who demonstrate competence in exceptional structures will remain roughly the same. Again referring to Table 17.1, it can be seen that the proportion of Ss who perform to criterion on part 2 within each age group does not vary substantially from seventh grade on. Calculation of exact probabilities for difference in two independent proportions supports this assertion in that significant differences are found when subjects over 12 are compared with all younger children. Thus, competence in the exception to the MDP may be seen as increasing in our sample until somewhere between the ages of 10 and 12, after which age most, but never all, of our subjects may be expected to demonstrate competence. It appears that for every two competent adults, there is one noncompetent adult, even in this college group.

We had predicted (hypothesis 2b) that children under 12 should more readily acquire the exception after the correct response had been modeled by a peer. While our data do *not* support this hypothesis, we also found that our method allowed Ss to parrot the model. Since Ss were often not able to supply the correct response when it was no longer available in the environment (and since we did not discover this until half the Ss had been run), we feel that this portion of the interview was not an adequate test of the hypothesis.

The follow-up testing of hypothesis 2c, that Ss who on first trial did not have the exceptional structure would be more likely on retest some two years later to have the structure *if* the original test had been given before age 12, rather than after that age, will be reported below as study 2.

A third hypothesis predicted that the responses of Ss to the test sentences in part 2 would correspond to the last three developmental stages described by Carol Chomsky. In fact, all of the incorrect responses on part 2 fell into one of two categories. First, Ss would *tell* rather than *ask* in response to these sentences (e.g., "John,

ask Bill which comb to use"; John: "Use that one"). Second, Ss would formulate a question but would choose the wrong subject (e.g., "Arthur, ask Nancy which book to read"; Arthur: "Which book do you want to read, Nancy?") A χ^2 ($df=2$) for the age of the S and the type of error made by S was significant at $p<.01$. Younger subjects tend to "tell" whereas older subjects tend to choose the incorrect subject. Thus, our data confirm Carol Chomsky's findings. We have duplicated her last three stages for a sample older than the one which she used.

A fourth hypothesis predicted that there would be a significant and positive correlation between successful performance on part 2 and IQ. With a correction for the restricted range of the IQ scores, we obtained an estimate of r of .49 for our sample (significant at $p<.01$).

Study 2

Method

Subjects   The Ss were 34 children and young adults who participated in the original study 2 years earlier and who failed to demonstrate competence in the exception to the MDP in sentences with the main verb *to ask*. There were 10 10–11-year-olds (4 girls, 6 boys), six 12–13-year-olds (3 girls, 3 boys), four 15-year-olds (1 girl, 3 boys), nine 16–18-year-olds (4 girls, 5 boys), and five 20–21-year-olds (1 girl, 4 boys). The IQ range in the original study was between 106 and 148; the IQ range of this group was 108 to 134.

Although an attempt was made to reach all 53 Ss in study 1 who had failed to meet the criterion, only 34 Ss were still available for interviewing in this follow-up study.

Procedure   Each S was required to repeat parts 1 and 2 of the original experimental interview. Part 1 was identical with part 1 of the original interview, and functioned as a warm-up. No one experienced difficulty with this part of the interview. The only change in part 2 was the inclusion of the optional sentences cited in study 1. This was done purely to make the interview, which was extremely brief, seem slightly longer. The criterion for demonstrating competence remained the same: correct responses to at least two out of three of the test sentences.

The interview was tape-recorded. Approximately one half the Ss received part A and one half part B. There was no difference between these two parts in the original study; this assignment was done only in order to replicate the conditions of the first study.

Results

In this sample of 34 SS, 19 performed to criterion in response to the test sentences in part 2, and 15 failed to do so These results, by age group, appear in Table 17.2. They give no basis for support of the hypothesis that Ss tested originally at ages 12–13 and under would be more likely to pick up the exceptional structure than would older Ss. It must be noted, however, that the group is quite small at each age. We have, however, not found any startling difference.

As found in the original study, the incorrect responses fall into one of two categories. The Ss would *tell* instead of *ask* (e.g., "use this cup") or they would phrase a question but use the wrong subject for the Wh-clause (e.g., "which pencil will you use?"), or echo the second part of the instruction sentence (e.g., "which to use?"), omitting the noun. The latter mode was used by only one S, a fifth grader.

Tell responses decreased with age, and the older Ss (eleventh grade to college) chose incorrect subjects for the Wh-clause exclusively. Of the 15 failures, seven were *tell* errors and eight were "wrong subject" errors. The distribution of types of errors duplicates the results in our original sample and in Chomsky's sample in that only the last three stages appear. Younger Ss make more third-stage errors (failing case 3) and older Ss make more fourth-stage errors (wrong subject for case 3).

In study 1, Ss tended to be highly consistent in their responses to the test instruction sentences. Out of the 15 Ss in study 2 who failed to reach criterion, 12 gave consistent responses throughout the series, and three gave inconsistent responses. If Ss switched responses, they tended to switch from the *you* (wrong subject) error to the *tell* error (to regress from the fourth to the third stage), rather than from incorrect to correct responses. There were two Ss who switched spontaneously from incorrect to correct responses after the first test sentence, and one who did so on the third sentence. Of the first two Ss, one was

Table 17.2. N successes and failures for each age group on study 2

Age Group	Successes (N)		Failures (N)	Total Tested/ Total Possible[a]
College (20–21 yr)	3	(60)	2	5/7
Twelfth grade (17–18 yr)	4	(100)	0	4/8
Eleventh2grade (16–17 yr)	3	(60)	2	5/8
Ninth grade (15 yr)	1	(25)	3	4/6
Seventh grade (12–13 yr)	5	(83)	1	6/10
Fifth grade (10–11 yr)	3	(30)	7	10/14
Total	19		15	34/53

Note—Percentages of successes in parentheses.
[a] Total possible represents the number of failures from the original study; not all were able to be found this time.

a fifth grader who switched from "which book to read?" to the correct response, and the other a college student who went from "which book would you like to read?" to the correct response. Consistency of responses is generally high as in the first study. The IQs of those succeeding in study 2 are not different from those failing on the exceptional structure.

It appears that Ss over the age of 12 who failed to demonstrate competence succeeded in doing so 2 years later in about the same proportion as those who were 12 or under at the original testing. It is not possible to perform any meaningful statistical analysis on the data due to the restrictions of the small N and the nonrandomness of the sample.

Discussion

The exceptional structure studied here is not the only complex structure with which young children have difficulty. It is clear from Carol Chomsky's work on some other exceptional structures that there are a series of such structures which have a cognitive complexity such that children over 6 are still acquiring competence.

We have found no solid evidence to confirm the hypothesis that acquisition of a structure is *more* likely for children of language-plastic ages. We have, however, some inkling from our Ss' statements during the second study that some older Ss who have mastered the exceptional structure after failure in the first study are not comfortably sure of themselves. One college student told us that she knew she had been wrong in the first study, had actively tried to figure it out, but that even now "I have to think about it; I'm never sure I've got it right." No child under 12 behaved as though the task was difficult, regardless of whether the child was competent or not. It seems possible that syntactic structures in one's native language that are learned late in life (after age 12) may be associated with longer latencies and may never

be quite as automatic as structures learned earlier. We have only hints of this, but no firm evidence.

Kessel (1970) has recently reported that by 8 years of age all of his Ss were responding to "ask" and "tell" sentences (similar to those studied here) correctly. Kessel appears to believe his results are discrepant from both Chomsky's and ours because of differing linguistic task requirements in the two Boston [studies] as compared with his Minnesota studies. Unfortunately he has not been sufficiently aware of extraneous cues which could amply account for his results.

In both Chomsky's (1969) and our study an interview situation was used. The S had to decode a stimulus utterance in the absence of extralinguistic cues. Kessel objects to this method on the grounds that the stimulus utterance is an imperative, which may encourage a set to "tell." Therefore, Kessel used a picture-choice situation in which the child must decode a simple declarative utterance by choosing and explaining which of two pictures represents the utterance. Part 3 of our interview was very much like Kessel's. We finally discarded the results because of the ambiguities of interpretation. Every child offered us reasons for his choice of picture which were thoroughly reasonable on contextual, nonlinguistic grounds. We, therefore, concluded we were not testing any psycholinguistic hypothesis after all. Unfortunately, the introduction of pictures into a linguistic comprehension task raises two additional interrelated problems.

First, on what basis does the child choose? When Kessel uses the utterance "the girl asked the boy which pencil to sharpen," the child does not need to determine that the girl, and not the boy, will be doing the action (Chomsky's stage D vs. stage E). The S need only determine *who* is asking, and *who* is telling (stage B or C vs. stage D or E). If the child looks at the pictures, the girl is clearly asking in Kessel's picture where she is holding out the two pencils, and telling in the picture where she is pointing and the boy is holding the two pencils. Therefore, a child who fails to violate the MDP and chooses the wrong subject for the complement clause can still choose the correct picture if the chlid does not confuse "ask" and "tell." Supposedly, Kessel's two follow-up questions: (1) Why did you choose that one? (2) What is she (he) saying? should detect when a child is depending upon extralinguistic cues in the manner described above. However, in response to the first question, all the child need do is parrot the original stimulus utterance ("because the girl is asking the boy"), a feat which in no way demonstrates that S has the competence in question (as we found to our chagrin in part 4 of our experimental interview). Furthermore, in response to the second question, if the child has chosen correctly, the answer may be read from the picture. The girl has the pencils; therefore, she must be planning to sharpen one of them for herself. In short, the follow-up questions do not appear to yield unambiguous information concerning the linguistic or nonlinguistic basis of the child's initial choice.

Second, implicit in the preceding is that the reasons for correct or incorrect choice of pictures are not clearly separated out by Kessel. Stage C is characterized by the achievement of the semantic distinction between "ask" and "tell" for all but complex statements ("ask John what to do"). The simple statement ("ask John his name") does not require any violation of the MDP; moreover there is no need for the S to recover a deleted subject for his answer. It is somewhat surprising that Kessel's Ss so often failed this item.

Stage D is the point where the ask-tell distinction (semantic) extends to the complex sentence with the deleted subject: "ask John what to do." Stage-D Ss ask correctly, but they fail to violate the MDP ("John, what are you going to do?"). Thus, only at stage E do Ss have both the semantic distinction and the grammatical exception: "John, what should I do?"

Our impression is that Kessel has judged Ss giving stages B, C, and D answers as incompetent and only stage E as competent. This makes it altogether more curious that he gets so many competent 8-year-olds.

We believe that his Ss are making, for the most part, semantic distinctions about ask-tell, which stage-C children can do. Kessel's failure to distinguish clearly between the semantic and grammatical has blinded him to the role of nongrammatical cues in the child's picture choices. Thus, his high-scoring 8-year-olds may well be our stage-C children, with the ask-tell distinction available for the simple but not complex distinction. In that case, Chomsky's results and ours are not so discrepant from Kessel's. Future researchers should especially take note of the difficulties of making two picture-alternatives represent, on purely linguistic grounds, large numbers of reasonable grammatical constructions.

We have wondered how an adult fares without competence in these exceptional structures and have attended to real-life situations with adults who lacked some syntactic structure. It seems to us that adult speakers have enough redundancy in their everyday speech to cover up lack of competence. They may respond incorrectly but they often continue talking, thus providing the answer to the question posed. Adults rarely correct other adults' linguistic errors. Thus, once the information requested is given, the form of the response is rarely remarked upon. Language is for communication; the redundant answer "corrects" the linguistic error.

Summary

Ss between 8 and 20 years of age were tested for competence on an exception to a grammatical rule, the Minimal Distance Principle. No age group tested was found with all Ss competent. Older groups had 2 competent Ss for every S who lacked the competence. Stages found by C. Chomsky (1969) for Ss below 8 were duplicated above age 8. Two years after the original experiment, Ss who had not been found

competent originally were retested. All age groups improved; no evidence for greater improvement of competency for the younger "language-plastic"-aged Ss was found.

References

CHOMSKY, C. *The acquisition of syntax in children from five to ten.* Cambridge, Mass.: M.I.T. Press, 1969.

KESSEL, F. S. The role of syntax in children's comprehension from ages six to twelve. *Monographs of the Society for Research in Child Development*, 1970, 35 (6, Serial No. 139).

18. LANGUAGE ACQUISITION FROM AGE FIVE ONWARD

DAVID S. PALERMO and DENNIS MOLFESE

It has become a commonplace in recent years to point to the impressive accomplishments evidenced in the developing language of the child between the ages of 18 months, when two-word utterances begin to be heard, and 4 or 5 years of age, when the child has succeeded "in mastering the exceedingly complex structure of his native language [Slobin, 1971a, p. 1]." While the accumulated observations of the language development of the preschool child do leave one with a sense of awe, especially when viewed within the theoretical framework of recent linguistic and psycholinguistic theory (e.g., McNeill, 1970), it seems to the present authors that the emphasis upon what goes on between the ages of 18 months and 4½ years has led to the relative neglect of development in language from age 5 onward.

Thus, without minimizing the important character of the language accomplishments up to age 5, this article attempts to show that considerable additional development

occurs from age 5 to adolescence. A review of the literature indicates that the 5-year-old is far from having the equivalent of an adult native speaker's facility with the language. Scattered through the literature is evidence that at the phonological, syntactic, and the semantic levels a good deal more facility needs to be acquired before the adult level is reached.

Phonological Development

Perhaps the most neglected aspect of language acquisition is that of phonological development. The relative lack of research is surprising in light of the advanced state of phonological theory in general (e.g., Chomsky & Halle, 1968; Halle & Keyser, 1971) and the recently translated developmental theory of phonology advanced by Jacobson (1968).

Our review of the literature provides us with little more than anecdotal evidence about the receptive or comprehension aspects of the phonological capacities of the child. Most of the research discussed will allow us to make statements only about the productive capacities of the child. This is an unfortunate state of affairs considering the valuable insights provided by studies of comprehension at the level of syntax. While the problems associated with the study of comprehension at the phonological level may be different than those at the syntactic level, it seems useful to examine phonological development through experiments that use methodology along the lines of the Fraser, Bellugi, and Brown (1963) study, for example, to add to what we know about the productive capacities.

Beginning with the comprehensive study of Templin (1957), we have strong evidence that the articulatory skills of the child at his fifth birthday are far from complete. Although there are other studies that preceded Templin's (e.g., Poole, 1934; Wellman, Case, Mengert & Bradbury, 1931), hers is based upon a carefully selected sample, a set of 176 sounds tested in intial, medial, and final positions, and the broad age range from 3 to 8 years. The sounds were elicited by pictures, written words, or repetition of the experimenter's oral example.[1] In general, the results show a marked increase in performance from age 3 to 4, a plateau from age 4 to 5, and then significant increases in performance from age 5 to 7. At age 8 the child's articulation is essentially the same as that of the adult. Phonemes in the initial position are articulated correctly prior to those in the medial position, and

the latter tend to precede correct articulation in the final position. Most of the errors at age 5 and beyond occurred on double and triple consonant blends. Only 14 sounds or sound combinations tested in initial position were failed by 25% or more of the children at this age, but some 50 other sounds or sound combinations in medial and final positions were failed by 25% or more of the sample.

It seems from Templin's data that while most individual phonemes in English are correctly articulated in most positions in words by age 5, there is considerably more difficulty in combining a series of consonants in clusters. Such consonant clusters are undoubtedly less frequent in the language, thus affording the child less opportunity to acquire the rules involved in their production. In addition, the phonological rules for production of such strings of consonants in English are surely more complex than those involving consonant-vowel clusters. It also apepars from these data that the consonant features +continuant and +strident tend to be late in coming into the phonological repertoires of these children.

Recently, Menyuk (1968) reported an analysis of the role of distinctive features in children's acquision of phonology. Her data are based upon the consonant substitutions produced by children while spontaneously generating sentences. She reported on the percentage of usage of six features for childern from ages 2 years, 6 months, to 5 years. The features nasality, gravity, and voicing appear to be correctly used nearly 100% of the time by 4½ years; the diffuseness feature comes in a bit later; and the features of continuancy in combination with stridency are not completely mastered until after the sixth birthday. Additional data collected from Japanese children in a narrower age range suggest the same rank ordering of the correct usage of these features.

A study by Snow (1964) analyzed the sound substitutions that 438 Grade 1 children, aged 6 to 8 years, made on an artic-

---

[1] It is of interest to note that no significant differences were obtained in the child's responses when the experimenter correctly articulated the sound in a word and the child repeated it as compared to spontaneous articulation of the same sounds. This fact is, of course, reminiscent of Ervin's (1964) report on syntactic imitation and suggests that additional study of this phenomenon, perhaps along the lines of Slobin's analysis of imitation (Slobin, 1968; Slobin & Welch, in press), may be fruitful.

ulation test. While the mean number of errors for each child was small, the large sample and number of sound tests produced a substantial set of errors upon which to base generalizations. The major findings indicate that unvoiced plosives are replaced by other unvoiced plosives, and unvoiced fricatives are replaced by unvoiced fricatives. Similarly, voiced plosives and fricatives are replaced by other voiced plosives and fricatives. Semivowels are replaced by other semivowels. If a change in voicing occurs, it is nearly always an unvoiced phoneme substituted for a voiced phoneme and seldom the reverse. The most frequent errors, /f/ for /θ/ and /v/, /θ/ for /s/, /k/ for /t/, and /n/ for /m/, are the errors most frequently made in adult perceptual confusions and in substitutions made at all ages. The fact that these substitutions reflect sounds differing on but one distinctive feature is of interest, but of greater interest would be some indication of why particular single features are confused and not other single features and why single-feature confusions occur with some phonemes and not with others.

ˑThe production difficulties that children evidence from age 5 to 8 seem to center on (a) sounds that occur in the medial or final position of a word; (b) consonant sounds that involve the features of continuancy and stridency; and (c) sounds that involve a sequence or cluster of consonants as in the case of -lfth (twelfth), which Templin found was difficult even for 8-year-olds. As Menyuk (1971) has indicated, these production difficulties may result from the fact that the sounds involved lack clear acoustic differences that the child can distinguish. If the child fails to discriminate the acoustic cues, he will fail, in turn, to articulate them. On the other hand, if he can make the acoustic discriminations, the production errors may be attributable to difficulties with the articulatory gestures involved.

While it would be helpful to have some perceptual data to resolve this question, it would seem from what little evidence we have that the difficulty resides in the articulatory gestures and not the acoustic cues. First, it would seem from casual evidence that speech sound percepiton is more advanced than production and certainly begins long before production (e.g., Eimas, Siqueland, Jusczyk, & Vigorito, 1971). Second, the fact that sounds in the initial position cause little difficulty, while the same sounds in medial or final position may lead to errors, suggests that articulatory factors associated with preceding articulatory contexts may be problematical. The child may have no difficulty in producing a sound from a resting position, but when that same sound must be produced from the position of the articulators after making another sound in the sequence composing a word, the child finds the task more difficult. Even in correct articulation by adults there is a good deal more variability in articulatory movements in medial and final positions than initial position (MacNeilage, 1970). Third, the child has difficulty with consonant blends that seem to involve a rapid series of complicated articulatory gestures unrelieved by interruption of an easier vowel sound. Fourth, the errors that do occur seem to be near misses in articulation. Plosives are replaced by other plosives, fricatives by other fricatives, and so on. Children make errors that seem to result from imprecise articulation rather than incorrect articulation. Finally, the errors that are made after age 5 seem to be made on sounds such as fricatives and liquids in which partial closure in the middle of the vocal tract is required. The bilabial sounds formed with the front of the vocal tract come in early, the sounds made at the back of the vocal tract come in somewhat later, but when rather precise control of the tongue shape and position in the region from the dental ridge to the front third of the hard palate is required, production errors persist to relatively older ages. Thus, the child can identify easily, with respect to his own motor movements, the end points of the vocal tract, and he can make more easily the grosser muscular movements associated with articulating sounds at each end of the vocal tract. However, when partial closure of the vocal tract is required with constriction in various parts of the central region, more errors are made. Thus, the target that the articulators must hit seems to be smaller for fricatives and liquids, varies with context in the case of a broader range of sounds, and requires greater muscular control in the case of consonant blends.

A somewhat different approach to the understanding of phonological development was begun by Berko (1958)[2] and expanded by Anisfeld and his colleagues. Berko was interested primarily in the acquisition of the morphological rules associated with the formation of plurals, possessives, and third-person singular of the verb, and with the inflections for the past tense of regular verbs. Since all of the sounds used in producing these inflections were within the articulatory abilities of the children, the question of concern was whether the children had acquired the phonological rules that determine the particular inflectional ending for each phonological context, that is, the three allomorphs for past tense and the three allomorphs for pluralization.

Berko's procedure involved presenting the child with pictures that were referred to with nonsense or real English names and then eliciting from the child the appropriate names with an inflection. A comparison of the 4- and 5-year-old group with the 6- and 7-year-old group of children indicates that of 28 items used in her test, there were 12 items on which significantly more adultlike performance was evidenced in the productions of the older children. Pluralization of the nonsense words was generally 70% correct or better for all ages when the /s/ and /z/ allo-

morphs were required but less than 40% correct when the /əz/ allomorph was correct, despite the fact that 99% of the older children correctly inflected *glass* for the plural form. Similarly, when the /əz/ inflection was required in forming the third-person singular of a verb or the possessive form of a noun, performance was poor. In the case of past-tense inflection, performance ranged approximately from 50% to 85% correct when the /t/ or /d/ inflection was called for, but was less than 35% correct at all ages when the /əd/ inflection was correct for the nonsense words, although the verb *melt* was correctly inflected by better than 70% of all children.

It would appear that in both the case of the pluralization rules and the past-tense inflection rules, the child at this age has collapsed the three rules involved into two rules, at least insofar as the productive extension of the rules is concerned. The child is able to extend the /s/ and /z/ plural allomorphs and the /t/ and /d/ past-tense allomorphs to new forms, but he fails to use the /əz/ and /əd/ allomorphs. Another interpretation is that the child has three rules in each case, but, for nouns ending in a sibilant or verbs ending in /t/ or /d/, pluralization and past tense, respectively, are formed by a zero allomorph. Alternatively, Berko favored the argument that there is only one rule in each case, a rule that /z/ added to a noun makes that word plural and a rule that /d/ added to a verb makes it past tense, and under certain conditions the /z/ becomes /s/ and the /d/ becomes a /t/ automatically by a more general phonological rule. Anisfeld's research reported below provides some additional data relative to these alternatives.

One other point with respect to Berko's study pertains to the fact that the plural of some nouns, for example, *heaf*, and the past tense of some verbs, for example, *gling*, were treated as irregular forms by a significant number of adults who offered the plural form *heaves* (42%) and the past form *glung* or *glang* (75%), which the

---

[2] The methodological weaknesses of this pioneering research have been pointed out by Natalicio and Natalicio (1969) and should be consulted by those interested in extensions of this work.

children seldom produced. This finding suggests that children learn some irregular forms by rote and later acquire an alternative rule that is based upon a few irregular words in the language and may be extended to new words that have a similar overall phonological form to the irregular words already known. The fact that the /əz/ plural for *glass* was used correctly by 99% of the older children but not generalized to new words suggests that rote learning may be a general initial strategy in language acquisition, at least for this aspect of language, and only when the memory load or some other factor makes rote learning unmanageable does the use of more general rules come into play. Even when the rules are acquired, Berko's data on the relatively better performance with the /əz/ allomorph, both for possessive forms and for the third-person singular verbs relative to the plural form, may imply that the rules are sensitive to other factors, such as syntactic context, before they are applied only on phonological bases.

In discussing some aspects of her data, Berko suggested that children may generalize responses on the basis of phonological similarity rather than on the basis of phonetic similarity, that is, on the basis of feature similarity and not sound similarity. This point has been cleverly investigated by Anisfeld in a series of three studies that have examined some aspects of the development of phonological rules in young children.

In the first of this series, Anisfeld and Tucker (1967) revealed a number of interesting aspects of the development of the pluralization rules. An initial experiment with 6-year-old children not only established that children of this age have difficulty with the pluralization rule in which /iz/[3] is used but that they are aware

both of the concept of plurality and the phonological problems involved with words ending in sounds that require the /iz/ plural form. These aspects of the child's conceptual as well as linguistic processes are revealed by the fact that the children tended to use numbers in their responses when they were not sure of the correct pluralization rule, usually when /iz/ was required. Thus, the children responded as if they knew that their pluralization might not convey the semantic concept, and therefore they preceded the word by the appropriate number to achieve the same effect.

A second study indicated that children seem to have a concept that the plural form of a name is the singular form with something appended. It would seem that children of this age have the concepts of one and more than one, the ability to recognize when they do not know how to correctly pluralize a word, and the concept that pluralization demands some sort of phonological addition to the word to make it plural—although they may not know what the addition should be.

Finally, the authors attempted to determine both the recognitory and productive capacities of the child at 6 years of age for the specific English pluralization rules. The results confirmed the difficulty that children at this age have with the productive use of the /iz/ inflection and the relative lack of difficulty with the /s/ and /z/ inflections. The mean error rate for the /iz/ forms was somewhat more than 50%, while it was less than 25% for the other two forms. In the recognition task, however, the error rate was high for the /s/ as well as the /iz/ form, although the overall error rate was less for recognition than production.

A study by Anisfeld, Barlow, and Frail (1968) delves specifically into the child's generalization of phonological rules in relation to the distinctive features of the sounds. Four groups of subjects, 6, 7, 8, and 19 years of age, were used. Consonant-vowel-consonant trigrams ending in /l/,

[3] Anisfeld and his collaborators use the /iz/ and /id/ phonetic symbols where Berko uses the /əz/ and /əd/. Presumably this difference reflects dialect differences of the subjects used in the experiments.

/r/, or /n/ were presented to them as a singular name, and they were asked to choose which of a pair of plural alternatives they preferred. The plural alternatives were formed by adding to the singular form one of the following sounds: /p/, /b/, /m/, /f/, /v/, /k/, /g/, /t/, /d/, /n/, and /ch/.

All of the singular forms called for the /z/ ending so that the results were tabulated in terms of the distinctive features with the same sign that the chosen consonants had in common with the correct /z/ plural form. Obviously a random distribution of choices would be expected if the generalization of phonological rules played no part in affecting the choice of responses. It was found that +continuant (/f/ and /v/) and +strident (/f/, /v/, and /ch/) sounds were preferred significantly by the first- and second-grade subjects and the adults, although not by the 6-year-old kindergarten children. Further, it was found that the older groups tended to select the artificial plural marker with the fewest feature differences compared to the regular one. The authors argued that the features of +continuant and +strident are more important than the features +diffuse, −grave, +voice, and −nasal, which also characterize /z/ because it is the two features +continuant and +strident that distinguish the plural marker /z/ from more other consonants than any of the other features. The additional fact that voicing was not an important distinguishing feature was interpreted to indicate that pluralization rules are not formulated in terms of the voiced /z/ and voiceless /s/. Rather, a more general rule, which states that an inflectional suffix has the same sign on voicing as the preceding sound, pertains to all suffixes and therefore is not an important feature distinction in a particular instance such as pluralization. The fact that the kindergarteners did not show the same systematicity as the older subjects may be attributed to the lack of development of the phonological rules involved or, as the authors suggested, to the influence

of a rule irrelevant to phonology that led them to select the second of the two alternatives presented.

A study by Anisfeld and Gordon (1968) more thoroughly examined the problem of inflectional rules. In this case, a larger number of consonantal endings were used. The subjects were first- and fourth-grade children and adults. In addition, the inflection of synthetic verbs for past tense was investigated with fifth-grade children. Otherwise, essentially the same procedures were used as in the earlier study. The use of the past-tense test was added for two reasons: First, to demonstrate that the findings of this and the previous study were not due merely to particular sound preferences regardless of the task; and, second, to show that the voicing feature is a part of a more general voicing-assimilation rule applicable to inflections in general rather than pluralization in particular.

The results showed that adults restricted their choices when possible to sounds that were +strident (/ch/ and /j/), +continuant (/th/) or both (/f/, /v/, and /sh/). The first- and fourth-grade children showed preferences only for /sh/, /ch/, and /j/, which make up the subclass of sounds that along with /s/ and /z/ are the functionally significant sounds in English pluralization in that they all take the /iz/ form for pluralization when they occur at the end of a noun. The children's rules thus seem more restrictive than those of the adults. Although they showed some tendency to prefer the /f/, /v/, and the /th/, found acceptable by the adults, their preferences for all sounds were less strong than those of the adults. Further evidence that the children's phonological rules are not as well developed nor as complete as those of the adults was reflected by the fact that the adults favored /m/ and /n/ endings often used in irregular forms of pluralization in English, while the children showed no such preferences, a finding that seems to corroborate Berko's results with *heaf* and *gling*.

In the case of the past-tense choices, the fifth-grade children showed significant preferences for /ch/ and /j/. The authors attributed this result to the fact that there are no other sounds relevant to past tense as there are in the case of pluralization. They argued that the /ch/ and /j/ sounds contain within them the regular past-tense markers /t/ and /d/; that is, in the articulation of /ch/ and /j/, the /t/ and /d/ sounds are part of the more complex /ch/ and /j/, respectively. In addition, the children showed a significant rejection of the /s/ and /z/ sounds that are relevant to the pluralization inflection and thus in grammatical opposition to the past-tense inflection.

In contrast to the efforts of Anisfeld to determine the phonological rules for appending a sound, in the form of an inflection, to an already complete word, Bruce (1964) attempted to examine the child's ability to analyze the component sounds comprising a word unit. His approach was to present a series of words to 5–7½-year-old children (from 5 to 9 years mental age) and to ask them to delete one sound from the word and pronounce the word with the sound deleted. All of the deletions resulted in other real English words. Both the sound and position of the elision were included in the instructions for each word. The strategies employed in the task by the children at various ages are perhaps most revealing of the phonological development indicated by this task. Up to about mental age 6, the children were not able to separate sound from word. They could produce isolated sounds and words, but they were unable to take from a word one of its component sounds, regardless of whether that sound was at the beginning, middle, or end of the word. At mental age 6, the child began to be able to take a part of the word and form a new word, but the relation of the word they formed and the satisfactory solution of the task was often remote. While the 6-year-old child has begun to get the idea of sounds within words, it appears that word units

merely were being substituted for word units. The last stage prior to correct performance was characterized by elision, but errors of overdeletion or incorrect deletion were prominent, and deletion from the middle of a word was particularly likely to lead to error.

These data, along with those from a study by Bryant and Anisfeld (1969) which show that children have difficulty parsing the singular form from a plural form, suggest that children take a holistic approach to words as sound units. It may be that at earlier ages the child treats whole sentences as undivided units, and as he acquires more language he parses the larger units into parts. At least in the age range from 5 to 8 years, it would appear that the word, or syllable, is the sound unit with which the child deals. He lacks the analytic abilities required to isolate and manipulate phonemic units within words. Savin and Bever (1970) presented some data that suggest that adults analyze the syllable unit prior to the phonemic unit. They argued that phonemes are abstract entities that are perceived only by an analysis of previously perceived syllables. It may be the case that young children learning inflection rules are learning new words that express semantic concepts rather than new phonemes that convert singular words to their plural form. Only at a later age, sometimes after the child generalizes the /id/ and /iz/ inflectional forms, will the children make the latter analysis. The child may have developed a complex system of phonological rules by the time he is 6 or 7 years old, but he still has not abstracted the phoneme from that system of rules and mastered the complex relationships which it has to acoustic stimuli and to articulatory movements.

Another bit of data that may relate to the same point is provided by Warren and Warren (1966). Their results indicate that compared to college-age subjects, 5- and 6-year-old children do not hear as many verbal transitions nor as many different verbal forms in a verbal transformation task. When children do report transformations, they tend to involve several sound changes at once, and sometimes additional sounds, rather than gradual single sound changes more characteristic of the older subjects. Children from 8 to 10 years of age tend to respond in a manner more similar to the adults.

Warren and Warren (1966) interpreted their results to indicate that the younger children organize the repeating stimulus in terms of individual phonemes because they report sound sequences not permitted in English. Just the opposite interpretation might be indicated since the adults tend to change only single phonemes when they report transformations while the children report fewer but larger transformations. Children cannot break up the word unit. When they do report transformations, the form of the word changes by several phonemes. These results do not seem contradictory to the hypothesis that words or syllables are the perceptual units for young children—as Savin and Bever have argued that they are for adults—and that, in contrast to the adult, the child prior to about 8 years of age has not yet developed the conceptual ability to abstract the phonemes from the word unit.

In summary, it seems that there are ample data here to allow us to agree fully with Chomsky's comment that "It is by no means obvious that a child of six has mastered his phonological system in full—he may not yet have been presented with all of the evidence that determines the general structure of the English sound pattern [Chomsky, 1964, p. 7]." It seems equally clear that the area of phonological development deserves a good deal more attention both before and after age 5 than it has received from researchers to date. In particular, the examination of the perceptual as well as the productive aspects of the system requires further research effort. Perhaps an expansion and elaboration of the sound-discrimination task, reported only briefly by Templin (1957), would be

a valuable place to start. In addition, the relationship between acoustic characteristics of sounds and the production difficulties of the child might be revealing in light of Liberman's (1966, p. 193) comments indicating that /s/, /sh/, /l/, and /r/ are some of the most stable acoustic phonemes, but they tend to cause articulatory problems for the child. Finally, little or no research has been done on the prosodic aspects of the phonology of children this age.

Syntactic Development

Turning now to syntax, we find considerably more research available and a large number of studies conceived within the general transformational-generative framework. The results of these studies have frequently been interpreted to support the contention that "All the basic structures used by adults to generate their sentences can be found in the grammar of nursery school children [Menyuk, 1963, p. 419]." The interpertation turns, of course, upon what is meant by the phrase "basic structures." Without trying to quibble about what is or is not a basic structure, some data suggest that important syntactic advances occur long after the child has passed his fifth birthday.

The first set of studies that is examined here attempted to evaluate syntactic development by the procedure of collecting a corpus of language from children of various ages, followed by an analysis of that corpus in terms of a set of grammatical rules that could be used to describe it. The rules that describe the corpus are, in turn, compared to the rules presumed to account for adult language, and evaluations of development are made. The methodological and interpretative difficulties with such an approach are, of course, serious, although they are not discussed here.

The studies of Menyuk (1963, 1964, 1968), Loban (1963, 1966), and O'Donnell, Griffin, and Norris (1967) are particularly extensive examples of this type of approach. Menyuk examined the language of children from 2 to 7 years of age. Approximately 80 to 120 sentences were collected from each child, although no indication was given of how the sentences were selected from the running speech of the child. On the basis of grammars written to describe the sentences of the children, Menyuk concluded that nursery-school children have completed the phrase structure and morphological levels of grammar. Her analyses focused upon transformation rules in which some developmental trends were observed. Menyuk suggested that nearly all transformations used in adult language are present in some of the nursery-school-aged children, but even the first graders, as well as the kindergarten children, in the age range of 5 to 7 years failed to exhibit full development of the auxiliary *have*, participial complement, iteration, nominalization, pronominalization, and conjunctions with *if* and *so*. In addition, there were some 17 types of restricted transformations used only by children and not apparent in the language of adults. For example, noun phrase redundancy, as in "She took it away the hat," actually increased significantly in frequency from nursery school to Grade 1. Finally, there were some structures used by adults that never appeared in the children's language at any age level although these were not specified. Little can be said about whether the latter failed to appear because of lack of opportunity or lack of the competence to produce such structures.

Loban (1963, 1966) conducted a longitudinal study of language development over a 10-year period for a group of 220 children carefully selected in terms of socioeconomic level and a number of other variables. The study began when the children were in kindergarten and continued through ninth grade. Each subject was individually interviewed annually, and his spoken responses recorded. The results indicate that as children get older their speech performance improves, as indicated by decreases in incomplete syntactic struc-

tures, increases in the variety of structural patterns used, and greater variation in the structures within sentences in terms of vocabulary, positions of phrases (such as adverbial modifiers), nominalizations, and so on.

In a similar study, O'Donnell et al. (1967) collected samples of oral and written language from 5- to 14-year-old children. The analyses of the data were similar to those of Loban but based upon terminal syntactic units (T units) used by Hunt (1965) in an earlier study of children's written language. Simple or complex sentences were defined as T units, but a compound sentence was analyzed in the smaller T units of which it was composed.

The length of the T units increased from about 7 words for kindergarteners to about 10 for the seventh graders. Of more interest, however, is the evidence for two periods in which sudden changes in performance appear to occur. Between kindergarten and first grade and between fifth grade and seventh grade are developmental periods when large increases in new grammatical constructions, or sudden increases in the use of constructions previously evidence at low frequences, and high error rates on some kinds of constructions seem to occur. Mean number of sentence-embedding transformations within T units increased significantly at both of these transition periods. Marked increases in nominal, adverbial, and coordinate constructions also occurred at both of these developmental points. Nominals containing adjectives and prepositional phrases particularly increased from Grade 5 to 7. Finally, frequency of coordinate nominals and coordinate predicates increased significantly from Grade 5 to 7.

In addition, O'Donnell et al. reported that only 2.6% of the seventh graders' utterances (excluding garbles) could not be accounted for by 1 of 11 common structural descriptions (e.g., subject-verb-object, etc.), while 12.5% of the kindergarten children's utterances fell outside of these categories. Most of the excluded utterances, however, did not involve gross grammatical errors. The subject-verb and subject-verb-object structural forms accounted for approximately 77% of the grammatical utterances of kindergarten children and nearly 90% of the seventh-grade children's utterances. Passive constructions accounted for less than 1% of the sentences of any of the grades, although there was a slight rise in these forms with age. These results are consistent with those of Loban and fit well with the data reported by Goldman-Eisler and Cohen (1970), who found that only 4% of adult utterances were passive, while 87% were of the simple, active, affirmative, declarative form.

In summary, the Menyuk (1963, 1964), Loban (1963, 1966), and O'Donnell et al. (1967) research provides a general overview of further language development in the child after 5 years of age. The overall results suggest that there is a general but gradual consolidation of language structures from kindergarten to seventh grade but also abrupt shifts in performance, which occur between kindergarten and first grade and between the fifth and seventh grades. More research focused upon these two periods may be of particular interest in revealing what is happening at these ages. It may be that the child is acquiring rules for different syntactic structures at these ages and that these rules affect and disrupt other structures that the child previously has dealt with in a competent manner. Language is an integrated system in which a change in one structure cannot help but affect other structures within the system. Examples of this latter phenomenon are seen in the data reported by Chomsky (1969) and Kessel (1970) using more controlled experimental procedures in which specific linguistic constructions were investigated.

Chomsky (1969) studied aspects of comprehension as a function of a number of factors including sentence complexity, selectional restrictions, and subcategorization restrictions. She was concerned with the developmental control over deep structure–surface structure relations when particular lexical items do not conform to rules that frequently relate surface structure to deep structure. She focused her attention upon the lexical entries *ask, tell,* and *promise*; pronominalization; and the syntactic comprehension of sentences in which the surface structure subject is not the deep structure subject. Her subjects ranged in age from 5 to 10 years. A Piagetian interviewing method with structured tasks and specified initial questions was used with more open questioning to evaluate the child's comprehension of the language-task relations.

In the case of *promise*, the so-called minimal distance principle applicable to most verbs is violated. In sentences that conform to the minimal distance principle, the noun phrase that immediately precedes an infinitive complement verb is the subject of that verb. Thus, in "John wanted Bill to leave" it is Bill who does the leaving, but in "John promised Bill to leave" it is John who does the leaving.

Chomsky's results indicate that while even the youngest children in this age range seem to know the meaning of *promise*, although there is some doubt as to the adequacy of Chomsky's check on this, they show systematic developmental trends suggesting that they do not correctly comprehend sentences involving both *promise* and the minimal distance principle until they are about 8 years old. The children appeared to pass through a stage in which they first applied the minimal distance principle to all cases across the board. Next, as children began to recognize exceptions to the rule, they made errors with sentences that followed the minimal distance principle as well as those that did not. In the third stage, the children finally straightened out the case to which the minimal distance principle applied but continued to mix their responses to the exceptions so that sometimes they treated *promise* appropriately and sometimes overgeneralized the principle. Only at the fourth stage was errorless performance achieved in all cases. While there was a good deal of variability with respect to the ages of the children who achieved each stage, the sequence of achieving the stages was orderly and nontransitive. Similar results were found when *ask* and *tell* were used in another experimental task in which *ask* was used both as a command and a question. *Tell* consistently follows the minimal distance principle, while *ask* is inconsistent and does not when used in the command or request form. Development of the correct interpretation of *ask* in the command form was correlated with the development of *promise*, and similar stages of confusion with *tell* were apparent. Comprehension of *promise*, which consistently violates the minimal distance principle, always preceded the comprehension of *ask*, which is inconsistent with respect to this rule.

Kessel (1970) also investigated the *ask–tell* relationships with a group of children ranging from kindergarten to fifth grade. His results were highly correlated with Chomsky's (1969). The major difference was that Kessel's subjects tended to achieve the various stages described by Chomsky at somewhat earlier ages. Like Chomsky, Kessel found that children passed through an invariant and nontransitive sequence in their acquision of *ask* and *tell*.

Chomsky's (1969) examination of the comprehension of sentences in which the surface structure subject is not the deep structure subject made use of the child's response to the sentence "Is this doll easy to see or hard to see?" in the context of a blindfolded doll. Her results indicated that 5-year-old children tend to interpret the sentence to mean that the doll is hard to see, that is, that *doll* is the deep structure subject of the sentence rather than the object of the infinitive. By ·9 years of age no child incorrectly interpreted the question.

Both Kessel (1970) and Cromer (1970) have challenged Chomsky's (1969) methodology in this task. Kessel argued that the blindfold is an unnecessarily distracting cue in the task and that poor performance may be attributed to the fact that the younger children did not recognize that the blindfold was irrelevant to the question. Further, Kessel noted that Chomsky did not test comprehension of superficially similar sentences in which the deep and surface structures are the same.

Kessel used a simulated hide-and-seek game in which the child responded to eight declarative sentences. Half of the sentences were of the form "Lucy was sure to see," and half were of the form "Lucy was impossible to see." The results indicated that 6-year-old children have little difficulty with sentences in which the deep and surface structure subjects are the same, but they do have difficulty in the comprehension of sentences in which the deep and surface structure subjects are not congruent. The children's errors indicated that the difficulty in sentences of the latter form is manifest in the assignment of the incorrect subject to the infinitive verb. In line with Chomsky's results, Kessel found that by 9 years of age children have little difficulty with such sentences. Again, a nontransitive sequence of stages was found in the acquisition of sentences of this type.

Cromer (1970) examined the comprehension of sentences in which the nouns and verbs were held constant, but adjectives, such as *eager* and *easy*, determined the relation of the deep and surface structure subjects. His subjects used hand puppets to act out the sentences uttered by the experimenter. Cromer used four adjectives that unambiguously require the noun to be interpreted as the subject of the sentence, four adjectives that unambiguously require the noun to be interpreted as the objective of the infinitive verb, and four adjectives that render the sentences ambiguous. The results indicate that children of mental age up to 5 years, 7 months, tend to interpret all sentences as if the noun were the subject of the sentence; between 5 years, 9 months, and 6 years, 6 months, the children are in a transition stage in which the first type of sentence is correctly interpreted, but there are both correct and incorrect interpretations of the second type of sentence; and children over mental age 6 years, 8 months, interpret both the first and second sentence types correctly and interpret some of the ambiguous sentences one way and some the other. Cromer divided his groups by mental age rather than chronological age because the apparent developmental trends seem to emerge more clearly. This may be an important finding that others should note more carefully in future studies plotting the course of language acquisition.

Cromer also found that all but two of the youngest children had no difficulty with comprehension of passives, indicating that these children knew that what appears to be the surface subject in sentences need not necessarily be the deep structure subject. Finally, he presented the children two nonsense words in sentence frames, which required them to be differentiated with respect to what was to be taken as the deep structure subject and then tested for comprehension of the two nonsense words. Children in the first stage failed to make the differentiation; some of the children in the transition stage correctly interpreted the two new words, but most of the children did not; and, finally, those children who were in the third stage correctly interpreted the two new nonsense words on the basis of hearing them used in only oney one repeated sentence. Thus, it would appear that Chomsky's results have generality when tested under different conditions.

In the case of pronominalization, Chomsky found that children learned the non-identity restriction for pronominalization between 5 and 6 years of age, while seven-year-olds were able to handle, in addition, the identity case. Thus, kindergarten children were able to comprehend sentences such as, "He knew that John was going to win the race," in which *he* and *John* refer to two different persons. Not until the children were older, however,

did the identity situation, as in "John knew that he was going to win the race"— where *John* and *he* refer to the same person —no longer present any difficulties. Chomsky (1969) argued that since the second form requires a more complex set of rules, because of the ambiguity involved, it would be acquired later. Since the ability to deal with pronominals in these situations is basically dependent upon two rules, she theorized that this would account for such structures being acquired relatively early, while other constructions such as the *ask-tell* distinction would require more time to be mastered because a more specific and complex set of rules is necessary to account for them.

Other investigators, however, have found that difficulties with pronominal forms persist into the junior-high-school level.[4] Loban (1963), for example, found a marked increase in errors of pronominalization at the seventh grade which did not decrease to the performance level of the sixth graders until after grade 9. Chai (1967), in a controlled experimental procedure, also reported that difficulty in comprehending pronominal referents in compound sentences extends into the junior-high-school range. It seems that the development of structures involving pronominalization are far from complete by 5 years of age, as evidenced in both production and comprehension capacities of children well beyond that age.

There are a number of studies that have focused on comprehension and production of question, negative, and, particularly, passive sentences by children in the age

---

[4] L. S. Golub, W. C. Fredrick, & S. L. Johnson. Development and refinement of measures of linguistic abilities. (Working Paper No. 33) Madison, Wisconsin: Wisconsin Research and Development Center for Cognitive Learning, 1970. Golub et al. used a multiple-choice format to test comprehension of sentences containing a pronoun and found that a large percentage of fourth and sixth graders had difficulty identifying the referents of pronouns in sentences, particularly when relative pronouns were involved.

range we have been considering, Slobin (1966) reported a rather extensive developmental study of the comprehension of various sentence structures including passives. His data for 6-, 8-, 10-, and 12-year-old children and for adults indicate a developmental trend toward increasing performance in comprehending passive, negative, and passive-negative sentences. Unfortunately he reported only latency data, and the more revealing error data collected are not reported in the published paper. It is of interest to note, however, that performance on passive sentences is superior if the subject and object of the passive sentence are not reversible, a result that was especially clear for the 6- and 8-year-old children. In fact, the nonreversible passive sentences were nearly as easy as the simple, active, affirmative, declarative sentences. Slobin argued that the difficulty in keeping track of which noun is the actor is eliminated on a semantic basis in the nonreversible passive sentence.

Turner and Rommetveit (1967a) provided support for Slobin's hypothesis. In a developmental study of active and passive sentence imitation, comprehension, and production, they found that 94.5% of the errors made in the various tasks involved inversion of the two noun elements. Most of the errors occurred on the reversible sentences, but a surprisingly large percentage (32.6%) occurred on the nonreversible sentences, which suggests that even with semantic support, children in the age range from 4 to 9 years continue to have difficulty with comprehension and production of passive sentences. Not until second grade (mean age 8.11 years) was performance with reversible passive sentences better than 60% correct on either comprehension or performance tests, although the kindergarten children (mean age 5.87 years) performed at approximately the same level on nonreversible sentences.

A second study by Turner and Rommetveit (1967b), using the same subjects as in the previous study, tried to provide contexts in which children would be likely to use the passive structure. The children were presented pictures and encouraged by the experimenter to describe the pictures with passive sentences by focusing attention upon the acted-upon noun rather than the actor noun.

The results indicated that spontaneous use of passive forms was minimal. Not until first grade (mean age 7.00 years) was it possible to induce the children to give more than 50% passive sentences even after an example had been given and the acted-upon object was shown first in the picture. When questions were asked about the object, kindergarteners gave approximately 50% passive responses. Those who did use the passive forms tended to show advanced linguistic abilities on the independent measure of imitation, comprehension, and production reported in the previous study. Thus, there appear to be individual difference variables involved, and most children do not seem to have command of passive forms until after age 5. There was a tendency to give passive constructions more frequently when nonreversible actor-object relations were involved.

Hayhurst (1967) also found that children between the ages of 5 and 9 have a great deal of difficulty producing passive constructions even when the experimenter provides passive examples in the context of describing a picture. If the passive sentences are negated, the child's difficulty is compounded, but if the passive is truncated, that is, without an expressed actor, the child's difficulty is reduced. Under no condition, however, was performance as high as 50% correct for the 5- and 6-year-old children in Hayhurst's study.

Another study confirms the difficulty that children have with passive constructions (Gaer, 1969). Not until 6 years of age did Gaer's subjects show comprehension of passives that was well above chance, and Gaer's production test yielded little evidence of ability to produce passives at that age. Gaer also found that 5-year-old children have considerable difficulty in comprehending and producing sentences with embeddings, particularly when there are two embeddings or a single center embedding.

In summary, it would appear from these data that the 5-year-old child is just beginning to fully comprehend the passive construction and very seldom uses the passive in his own spontaneous speech. The various experimental attempts to elicit passive constructions yield results that make it difficult as yet to judge when production capacity is well developed. Clearly, there are marked individual differences that are, perhaps, more evident with this construction than most others that have received research attention. It may be fruitful to examine variables that are considered to affect language acquisition in general, with the acquisition of passive forms. The technique, used with adults by Wright (1969), of giving sentences in passive (or active) form and then asking questions about the sentence in active (or passive) form might be used effectively in revealing some of the difficulties that children have with passive sentences.

Finally, in this section we consider some data pertaining to connectives, which could, perhaps, be discussed in the next section on semantics since there seems to be a strong semantic component involved in the results, although the specific words of interest are usually considered function rather than content words. A study by Katz and Brent (1968) provided some information about the comprehension and production of the connectives *because, then, therefore, but, although,* and *and.* Their data are based upon a corpus of spontaneous speech, responses to pairs of sentences in which various connectives were contrasted, and explanations for choices made in the latter situation. The subjects were first- and sixth-grade children and a college student group. Some of the data clearly suggest that the meaning of *because, then,* and *therefore* changes between first and sixth grade. While the first grader may use these words in his spontaneous speech, it would appear that the temporal relations of *because,* for example, are better understood than the causal ones, and the younger children probably do not have more than a sequential, as opposed to a causal, meaning for *because.* In other words, all three of these words are used as if they were marked semantically as *then,* with no causal relations implied. In addition, it appeared that when the adversative connectives *but* and *although* were used, children in the first grade showed little evidence of comprehending such constructions, and the sixth graders, while better in the identification of sentences correctly using the words, showed little ability to account for their choice. Finally, there was a developmental trend revealing an increase from Grade 1 to Grade 6 in the preference for the linguistic order of clauses to mirror the temporal order of cause and effect events. Thus, sixth graders seemed more aware than first graders of the cause and effect relations in such sentences as, "The benches were wet, we did not sit down" and showed a marked preference for stating the sentence in that order rather than in the order, "We did not sit down, the benches were wet." The college students showed no preference for order. These results may reflect a general cognitive developmental awareness of cause and effect by the older children and, at a somewhat more abstract level, may reflect the same kind of perceptual linguistic interrelationship showed by Huttenlocher in her studies (Huttenlocher, Eisenberg, & Strauss, 1968; Huttenlocher & Strauss, 1968) and Bever in some of his work (Bever, 1970).

In a series of studies concerned with logical thinking within a Piagetian framework, Neimark reported some surprising results related to the connectives *and* and *or*. In the first study (Neimark & Slotnick, 1970), children in Grades 3 through 9 and college students were presented with a sequence of 16 problems dealing with class inclusion and exclusion, class intersect, and class union. The results indicate that none of the subjects had any difficulty with class inclusion and exclusion, only the third-grade children had any difficulty with class intersection, but only the college students achieved success on the majority of the union problems. Children in Grade 9 responded correctly only 30% of the time when given instructions to select A or B, and performance was still poorer when the presumably clearer instruction to select A or B or both was given. According to the authors, these results are not culture bound since they replicate findings with Japanese children. An analysis of the errors revealed that most of the children interpreted *or* as *and,* a result also apparent in a study by Shine and Walsh (1971).

A second study (Neimark, 1970), conducted with children in Grades 9 through 12, indicated that correct performance on union problems increases steadily from Grade 9 to 12. A particularly interesting finding comes from the children's descriptions of the union sets in one form of the test used. It would appear from the children's own efforts to describe the sets that they do not use the word *or* spontaneously, at least under these circumstances. Only 6 of 39 subjects used *or* in describing union sets. Instead of using *or* they used *and* in describing the sets. They did not even use *except* or *all but* with any frequency. This failure of children as old as high school age to be able to comprehend a word as superficially simple and frequently used as *or* suggests that syntactic and/or semantic development extends over an unexpectedly long period and that it must be carefully examined

throughout childhood.

Along similar lines, Olds (1968) has developed a game for children which cleverly allows exploration of the comprehension of various syntactic forms. He has shown, among other things, that children as old as 9 years do not comprehend the conditional *unless.* Children of age 9 and younger interpret *unless* as if the word *if* had been used.

Finally, a study of Goodglass, Gleason, and Hyde (1970) may be mentioned here. As a part of their study, they tested normal children between the ages of 3 and 10 years for comprehension of prepositions. In one test the subject was shown sets of three pictures and asked to identify, for example, the picture with the girl standing *behind* (as opposed to *in front of* or *next to*) the car. In the other test, the subjects were asked to indicate which of two sentences involving a contrast in prepositions was a better description of a picture.

Performance was relatively good on the first test and showed a steady increase from about 73% correct for the 3- and 4-year-old children to about 97% for the 10-year-old children. The biggest increase occurred between 5 and 6 years. On the second test, however, performance was near chance level until the age of 6 when performance jumped to a level indicating full comprehension of the correct prepositional forms. Further investigation of the comprehension of prepositions will be required before firm conclusions may be drawn.

The results of these studies of syntactic development point to a close interrelationship between general cognitive development and the comprehension and production of syntactic forms. Slobin (1971b) recently has suggested that this is the case, and he has outlined a model beginning with semantic intentions, which are based upon the general cognitive developmental level of the child, and relating those semantic intentions to the means for expressing them in a linguistic form. Particular linguistic forms are not comprehended nor produced until the underlying cognitive aspects are developed. Once such cognitive development has occurred, the child will look to the language for the means to express the new cognitive structures. Thus, examination of the language development of children, which reveals errors of various kinds at different ages, indicates either that cognitive development has not reached the point where the linguistic forms in question have any meaning for the child or the child has not as yet discovered the appropriate linguistic means for expressing the meaning he does know, a point that McNeill (1970) discussed in terms of weak and strong linguistic universals. In some cases it may be quite easy to distinguish which problem the child is having, while in others a theory of cognitive development may be a more important prerequisite to the understanding of language acquisition. For example, in the previous section the research of Anisfeld and Tucker (1967) clearly indicated that 5-year-old children had the cognitive concept of plurality but did not always know how to express it in a linguistically correct form. Slobin's examples with bilingual children make this point in a particularly convincing fashion. On the other hand, the review of the studies of pronominalization present an unusually complex picture in which the child seems to grasp pronominal constructions at one age only to lose them and reacquire them again, with final errorless performance coming relatively late in language acquisition. Surely the child acquires the concept of the pronoun as a noun substitute rather early. The erroneous linguistic structures that occur at later stages result either from attempts to express more complex cognitive relations in which the pronoun and its noun substitute become confused in the form of linguistic expression, or from the development of new cognitive structures to which pronominalization is differently

related.

While the research reviewed in this section reflects a steady development of linguistic form from age 5 to adolescence, there is an indication across a number of the studies that the periods between 5 and 8 years and between 10 and 13 years are marked by instability in linguistic development, and these periods are followed by growth to new levels and subsequent stable linguistic performance. It may not be coincidental that these are precisely the periods in cognitive development marked by Piaget (1970) as transition points from preoperational thought to concrete operations in the first case and from concrete operations to formal operations in the second case.[5] It is during these two periods that large increases in new grammatical constructions and high error rates on some kinds of constructions are reported. The minimal distance principle is worked out during the first of these periods, as is the passive construction. Pronominalization performance advances during both of these periods. The work of Katz and Brent (1968) provided some specific hints about the relation between cognitive development and linguistic expression. The indication of a shift in the use of *because* from a mere expression of time sequencing to cause and effect relations, and the ordering of phrases in sentences, are two examples that seem to indicate that even when the same surface structure forms are used, the underlying syntactic and semantic relations may change as the child develops cognitively. Finally, the research of Neimark and her associates on union problems appears to fit very nicely with Piaget's notions of formal operations and gives additional support to the cognitive basis of language development.

---

[5] Sinclair-de Zwart (1969) has argued along similar lines and has noted the fact that the beginning of structured language occurs as the child's cognitive development shifts from the sensorimotor to the preoperational stage at about 18 months to 2 years of age.

Semantic Development

Since the research that might be considered relevant to semantic development has not been integrated by any particular theoretical point of view, it is difficult to interrelate it or to determine which kinds of data are of importance in the evaluation of the child's semantic system. To begin with, it is obvious that additions to the vocabulary are made throughout the life span. The fact that we add a new word to our lexicon, however, may have relatively little effect upon our semantic system. It is probably insignificant to a consideration of the semantic system if a new word merely acts as a label or shortcut for expressing something that it is possible to express using other words. For example, an unmarried male expresses adequately what is meant by bachelor, and the addition of the latter word to the vocabulary says little about language development. Thus, developmental studies of vocabulary growth, while gross indexes of semantic development, may not be very revealing of the system itself.

The problem, of course, is to identify the significant aspects of semantic change as the child develops. This problem is not limited to the nature of the semantic features in the narrow sense but must also include the interword semantic restrictions. We must examine not only the acquisition of the semantic features that mark the words *wish* and *want,* for example, as nearly synonymous but also the semantic restrictions and syntactic restrictions that allow us to say, "The man wishes that she would go home," but not, "The chair wishes that she would go home" or "The man wants that she would go home."

Thus, the expansion of the semantic system involves not merely the meaning of isolated words, however described, but the interrelations of those words with others. Research in this area, therefore, needs to be devoted to a consideration, in studies of both comprehension and production, of the development of semantic markers and selection restrictions, both syntactic and semantic.

Turning now to the data, we devote our attention to some evidence for the evolving meaning of lexical items in the dictionary, avoiding research reviewed in other discussions of the topic (e.g., McNeill, 1970). A number of studies scattered through the literature indicate that the elementary-school-aged child may have a substantial set of words in his vocabulary that have different meanings than those same words have for adults. Asch and Nerlove (1960), for example, investigated the development of what they call "double function" words. Such words as *bright, hard,* and *sweet,* for example, have both a physical and a psychological meaning in the sense that they may refer to both physical characteristics of objects and to psychological characteristics of persons. The authors studied the development of these two functions of such words in children between the ages of 3 and 12 years. In a Piagetian type of interview situation, the children were presented a series of objects and asked if any of the objects could be called *sweet,* or *cold,* or *crooked,* etc. If the child could identify correctly the object associated with the words, he then was asked if a person could be "sweet." If the child used the word in the psychological sense, he was asked about the relation of that meaning to the physical meaning.

The results indicated that the 3- and 4-year-old children could correctly use the words with respect to the physical objects, but, with the possible exception of *sweet,* they had no idea that the words could be applied to people, and, in fact, they denied specifically that these words could be so used. The 5- and 6-year-old children showed little evidence of change from the performance of the youngest children. In the 7- and 8-year-old group, however, about half of the words were correctly applied to people, but the children could not relate the physical meaning of the word to the psychological meaning with any great success. By 9 to 10 years of age, half of the children could correctly use all of the words in both contexts, and the ability to indicate the relation between the two uses began to be evident. While all of the 11- and 12-year-old groups did not perform perfectly, they did show marked advances in the comprehension of the dual function of the words.

The authors concluded that children first master the object reference of double function words, then the psychological sense of these terms as independent meanings, and, finally, the dual or relational aspects of the words are acquired. It appears that the two related meanings of these words are acquired independently by the children first, and only later are the common features of the meanings integrated. If the semantic markers associated with the two meanings of each of these words are functionally independent and, therefore, entered separately into the dictionary at first and only later unified, then these results seem most consonant with what McNeill (1970) has called vertical development of the dictionary. The latter hypothesis is that lexical items enter the dictionary list with a nearly complete set of semantic markers, and semantic development consists primarily of establishing the relations among entries through the vertical organization of common markers.

The results also may be interpreted as an indication of the relation between semantic development and general conceptual development of children who give other indications of moving from the ability to conceptualize primarily in terms of concrete operations to more abstract levels at about 11 or 12 years of age (Piaget, 1970). Additional evidence for the development of more abstract conceptualization of words, which may be conceived as the vertical organization of semantic markers, may be found in some developmental studies of word definitions (e.g., Al-Issa, 1969; Wolman & Baker, 1965), which indicate that concrete and functional definitions of words give way to abstract definitions at about 10 to 12 years of age. Similarly, in some recently reported research, Anglin (1970) emphasized the concrete to abstract developmental trend in semantic development.

At about the same time that Asch and Nerlove were studying the developmental convergence of the meanings of words, Ervin and Foster (1960) were examining the developmental differentiation within sets of words that are frequently correlated in usage but that are not synonymous. Children in Grades 1 and 6 were presented with objects that could be described in terms of weight, strength, and size and pictures of faces that could be described as *happy, pretty, clean,* and *good.* The materials within each set were presented in pairs such that one of the dimensions was contrasted in the pairs and the other dimensions held constant. The children were asked about all of the dimensions. The results revealed that both first and sixth graders indicated that the dimensions held constant also varied in addition to the one actually contrasted in the objects presented. The effects were so strong with the words *good, pretty,* and *happy* that the authors concluded that these three words are interchangeable synonyms for first-grade children. The tendency to treat the *big, strong, heavy* set as synonyms was less strong, and in both cases the effects decreased with age. In contrast with the results of the Asch and Nerlove study, these results point to the interpretation of what McNeill calls the horizontal development of semantic markers rather than vertical development. These sets of common words appear to have entered the dictionary without all of the semantic markers required to differentiate among them. As semantic development progresses, additional markers are associated with each entry so that eventually words that were once treated as synonyms are differentiated.

A more recent study by Lumsden and Poteat (1968) points to the same interpretation. They were concerned only with the concept of "bigger" in children 5 and 6 years of age and a high school control group. They presented children with pairs of geometric figures in which the area was equal but the vertical dimension was varied, and the child was asked which of the two was bigger. For example, one pair consisted of an 8 × 8 inch square and a 13 × 4.8 inch rectangle with a vertical axis of 13 inches. Two additional pairs were used in which the area as well as the vertical dimension varied.

The results indicated that the 5- and 6-year-old children selected the object with the greatest vertical dimension in approximately 72%–97% of the pairs. Even when the area of the alternate object was four times as great as the object with the greater vertical dimension, 85% of the children selected the smaller object with the greater vertical dimension. Since rectangles were used and therefore the vertical lines did not bisect the horizontal lines, there is little likelihood that these results are attributable to the vertical-horizontal illusion. This illusion actually increases from 6 years of age to adulthood when bisection is not involved (Fraisse & Vautrey, 1956).[6] If we assume that these results are attributable to a lack of the appropriate semantic markers on the lexical entry *bigger*, rather than to some factor associated with the perceptual salience of the vertical dimension in the experimental task, then these data may be interpreted as supporting the hypothesis of horizontal semantic development.

Finally, another study that attacks the same problem with still another technique is reported by Bradshaw and Anderson (1968). Their interest was in adverbial modifiers. They investigated the problem by asking their subjects to compare each of nine adverbial modifiers with all of the other modifiers using a paired-comparison procedure. The modifiers were *slightly, somewhat, rather, pretty, quite, decidedly, unusually, very*, and *extremely*, and all were modifying the word *large*. The subjects were drawn from Grades 1 through 6, 8, 10, 12, and college. The procedure proved to be highly reliable at all grades, and developmental differences in meaning were evidenced at the younger grade levels. Specifically, the modifiers *slightly* and *somewhat* were neutral modifiers for the children in the first two grades. *Slightly* shifted to the most extreme position by Grade 4, and somewhat moved into its adult position next to *slightly* more gradually and was not located where adults place it until Grade 8. *Very*, at the other end of the continuum, was considered the equivalent of *extremely* by first graders and gradually shifted toward the neutral position in ranking and was located at the adult position by fifth-grade children. The fact that *slightly large*, for example, is considered by the first-grade children as meaning larger than *rather large, large*, or *quite large* implies that the markers associated with the adverbial modifier *slightly* are either different or incomplete, relative to those that the adult has. While these data seem to support the horizontal semantic development hypothesis of McNeill, they also suggest the possibility that a third hypothesis may be tenable. It is conceivable that the young child may enter incorrect markers for some lexical entries in the dictionary, and semantic development may consist of acquiring enough knowledge about entries to not only add markers as in horizontal development but in some cases subtract markers associated with particular entries.

In summary, our examination of the literature in this area has been far from complete, but the data reviewed seem to leave us in the same position that McNeill found himself in evaluating the characteristics of a set of developmental data dealing primarily with word associations, word recognition, and recall of word strings.

[6] We are grateful to Charles N. Cofer (personal communication, May 1971) who pointed out that this illusion might be relevant here.

Both the horizontal and vertical semantic developmental hypothesis seem to be supported by parts of the data. Perhaps both processes take place, but some additional research, focused on attempting to directly test the hypothesis, is needed since it is always difficult to evaluate reseach within one framework when it was collected within another.

Conclusions

In conclusion, while this review has not been exhaustive, there are a number of general impressions that emerge. First, there are rather clear indications that language development is far from complete when the child reaches his fifth birthday. Regardless of whether we examine phonology, syntax, or semantics, we find data already in the literature that indicate that further development is required before adult language competence may be reached. Furthermore, there are numerous hints in the literature reviewed that additional research will reveal other areas, not yet fully explored, in which development is incomplete. For example, at the phonological level there are indications that adults have a set of rules that subsume subsets of the so-called irregular inflectional forms. Young children, on the other hand, evidence no such rules and seem to acquire the irregular forms by rote memory. Presumably after enough experience with enough examples within each subset of irregular forms, the child infers rules that govern subsequent inflections for new words. It also may be possible that a hierarchy of rules is acquired such that in this case, for example, the regular or more frequently used rule is applied first, but other rules are available if the regular rule is inappropriate.

Second, this review suggests that in the analysis of children's performance it is becoming more difficult to clearly distinguish phonological, syntactic, and semantic aspects of language as separate levels that can be studied independently; for exam-

ple, children seem to be aware of the semantic aspects of inflections, and when they do not know the phonological rules required to convey a semantic concept, they use some other method of conveying the concept. At the syntactic level the so-called function words, which in and of themselves are semantically empty, do involve meaning, and the analysis of the comprehension and use of these words cannot treat them from a syntactic point of view alone.

Third, the interrelationship of phonology, syntax, and semantics with overall cognitive development was continually apparent throughout our consideration of the research reviewed. It is clear that a theory of language development must be embedded within the larger context of a theory of cognitive development. While cognitive development may precede its expression in language, it is obvious that the reverse is unlikely. Thus, for example, the use of plural inflections must be preceded by a concept of number, and the full comprehension of the logical connective *or* must be preceded by the concept of set union. In addition, the suggestions in the data that the age ranges of from 5 to 7 and from 12 to 14 may be important transition points in language development [coincide with] the age ranges in which other more general cognitive changes are assumed to occur, at least within a Piagetian framework. White (1965) has documented many other changes that occur in various cognitive skills at the 5–7-year age range. Further exploration of the 12–14-year age range may prove fruitful both from a cognitive and a language point of view. The general point that cognitive development and language development are related intimately has also been emphasized strongly by Slobin (1971b) and Olson (1970) as well as Piaget (Sinclair-de Zwart, 1969). In this connection, mental age has been shown to be related closely to performance measures of language development in two studies reported here (Bruce, 1964; Cromer, 1970).

It may be appropriate in future studies to look more closely at this relationship.

Summary

The article examined the acquisition of language after 4 years of age with respect to important developmental changes that occur after the earlier dramatic initiation of language behavior. At all levels significant advances in language were found in the literature. The evidence was interpreted as indicating that phonological, syntactic and semantic levels of analysis were intimately interrelated and that language advances appeared to be correlated with developmental periods of cognitive advance.

References

AL-ISSA, I. The development of word definitions in children. *The Journal of Genetic Psychology,* 1969, *114,* 25–28.

ANGLIN, J. M. *The growth of word meaning.* Cambridge: M. I. T. Press, 1970.

ANISFELD, M., BARLOW, J., & FRAIL, C. M. Distinctive features in the pluralization rules of English speakers. *Language and Speech,* 1968, *11,* 31–37.

ANISFELD, M., & GORDON, M. On the psychophonological structure of English inflectional rules. *Journal of Verbal Learning and Verbal Behavior,* 1968, 7, 973–979.

ANISFELD, M. & TUCKER, G. R. English pluralization rules of six-year-old children. *Child Development,* 1967, *38,* 1201–1217.

ASCH, S. E., & NERLOVE, H. The development of double function terms in children: An exploratory investigation. In B. Kaplan & S. Wapner (Eds.), *Perspectives in psychological theory: Essays in honor of Heinz Werner.* New York: International Universities Press, 1960.

BERKO, J. The child's learning of English morphology. *Word,* 1958, *14,* 150–177.

BEVER, T. G. The cognitive basis for linguistic structures. In J. R. Hayes (Ed.), *Cognition and the development of language.* New York: Wiley, 1970.

BRADSHAW, W. L., & ANDERSON. H. E., JR. Developmental study of the meaning of adverbial modifiers. *Journal of Educational Psychology,* 1968, *59,* 111–118.

BRUCE, D. J. The analysis of word sounds by young children. *British Journal of Educational Psychology,* 1964, *34,* 158–159.

BRYANT, B., & ANISFELD, M. Feedback versus no-feedback in testing children's knowledge of English pluralization rules. *Journal of Experimental Child Psychology,* 1969, *8,* 250–255.

CHAI, D. T. *Communication of pronominal referents in ambiguous English sentences for children and adults.* Unpublished doctoral dissertation, University of Michigan, 1967.

CHOMSKY, C. *The acquisition of syntax in children from 5 to 10.* Cambridge: M. I. T. Press, 1969.

CHOMSKY, N. Comments for project literacy meeting. (Project Literacy Rep., No. 2) Ithaca, N.Y.: Cornell University, 1964. (Mimeo) (Also available from ERIC Document No. ED 010 308.)

CHOMSKY, N., & HALLE, M. *The sound pattern of English.* New York: Harper & Row, 1968.

CROMER, R. F. "Children are nice to understand": Surface structure clues for the recovery of deep structure. *British Journal of Psychology,* 1970, *61,* 397–408.

EIMAS, P. D., SIQUELAND, E. R., JUSCZYK, P., & VIGORITO, J. Speech perception in infants. *Science,* 1971, *171,* 303–306.

ERVIN, S. M. Imitation and structural change in children's language. In E. H. Lenneberg (Ed.), *New directions in the study of language.* Cambridge: M. I. T. Press, 1964.

ERVIN, S. M., & FOSTER, G. The development of meaning in children's descriptive terms. *Journal of Abnormal and Social Psychology,* 1960, *61,* 271–275.

FRAISSE, P., & VAUTREY, P. The influence of age, sex, and specialized training on the vertical-horizontal illusion. *The Quarterly Journal of Experimental Psychology*, 1956, 8, 114–120.

FRASER, C., BELLUGI, U., & BROWN, R. Control of grammar in imitation, comprehension, and production. *Journal of Verbal Learning and Verbal Behavior*, 1963, 2, 121–135.

GAER, E. P. Children's understanding and production of sentences. *Journal of Verbal Learning and Verbal Behavior*, 1969, 8, 289–294.

GOLDMAN-EISLER, F., & COHEN, M. Is N, P, and NP difficulty a valid criterion of transformational operations? *Journal of Verbal Learning and Verbal Behavior*, 1970, 9, 161–166.

GOODGLASS, H., GLEASON, J. G., & HYDE, M. R. Some dimensions of auditory language comprehension in aphasia. *Journal of Speech and Hearing Research*, 1970, 13, 595–606.

HALLE, M., & KEYSER, S. *English stress: Its form, its growth, and its role in verse.* New York: Harper & Row, 1971.

HAYHURST, H. Some errors of young children in producing passive sentences. *Journal of Verbal Learning and Verbal Behavior*, 1967, 6, 634–639.

HUNT, K. W. *Grammatical structures written at three grade levels.* (Research Rep. No. 3) Champaign, Ill.: National Council of Teachers of English, 1965.

HUTTENLOCHER, J., & STRAUSS, S. Comprehension and a statement's relation to the situation it describes. *Journal of Verbal Learning and Verbal Behavior*, 1968, 7, 300–304.

HUTTENLOCHER, J., EISENBERG, K., & STRAUSS, S. Comprehension: Relation between perceived actor and logical subject. *Journal of Verbal Learning and Verbal Behavior*, 1968, 7, 527–530.

JACOBSON, R. *Child language, aphasia and phonological universals.* The Hague: Mouton, 1968.

KATZ, E. W., & BRENT, S. B. Understanding connectives. *Journal of Verbal Learning and Verbal Behavior*, 1968, 7, 501–509.

KESSEL, F. S. The role of syntax in children's comprehension from ages six to twelve. *Monographs of the Society for Research in Child Deveolpment*, 1970, 35 (6, Whole No. 139).

LIBERMAN, A. M. General discussion. In F. Smith & G. A. Miller (Eds.), *The genesis of language.* Cambridge: M. I. T. Press, 1966.

LOBAN, W. D. *The language of elementary school children.* (Research Rep. No. 1) Champaign, Ill.: National Council of Teachers of English, 1963.

LOBAN, W. D. *Problems in oral English.* (Research Rep. No. 5) Champaign, Ill.: National Council of Teachers of English, 1966.

LUMSDEN, E. A., JR., & POTEAT, B. W. S. The salience of the vertical dimension in the concept of "bigger" in five and six year olds. *Journal of Verbal Learning and Verbal Behavior*, 1968, 7, 404–408.

MACNEILAGE, P. F. Motor control of serial ordering of speech. *Psychological Review*, 1970, 77, 182–196.

MCNEILL, D. *The acquisition of language: The study of developmental psycholinguistics.* New York: Harper & Row, 1970.

MENYUK, P. Syntactic structures in the language of children. *Child Development*, 1963, 34, 407–422.

MENYUK, P. Syntactic rules used by children from preschool through first grade. *Child Development*, 1964, 35, 533–546.

MENYUK, P. The role of distinctive features in children's acquisition of phonology. *Journal of Speech and Hearing Research*, 1968, 11, 138–146.

MENYUK, P. *The acquisition and development of language.* Englewood Cliffs, N.J.: Prentice-Hall, 1971.

NATALICIO, D. S., & NATALICIO, L. S. F. "The child's learning of English morphology" revisited. *Language Learning*, 1969, 19, 205–215.

NEIMARK, E. D. Development of comprehension of logical connectives: Understanding of "or." *Psychonomic Science*, 1970, 21, 217–219.

NEIMARK, E. D., & SLOTNICK, N. S. Development of the understanding of logical connectives. *Journal of Educational Psychology*, 1970, 61, 451–460.

O'DONNELL, R. C., GRIFFIN, W. J., & NORRIS, R. C. *Syntax of kindergarten and elementary school children: A transformational analysis.* (Research Rep. No. 8) Champaign, Ill.: National Council of Teachers of English 1967.

OLDS, H. F., JR. *An experimental study of syntactic factors influencing children's comprehension of certain complex relationships.* (Center for Research and Development of Educational Difficulties Rep. No. 4) Cambridge, Mass.: Harvard University Press, 1968.

OLSON, D. R. Language and thought: Aspects of a cognitive theory of semantics. *Psychological Review*, 1970, 77, 257–273.

PIAGET, J. Piaget's theory. In P. H. Mussen (Ed.), *Carmichael's manual of child psychology.* New York: Wiley, 1970.

POOLE, I. Genetic development of articulation of consonant sounds in speech. *Elementary English Review*, 1934, *11*, 158–161.

SAVIN, H. B., & BEVER, T. G. The nonperceptual reality of the phoneme. *Journal of Verbal Learning and Verbal Behavior*, 1970, 9, 295–302.

SHINE, D., & WALSH, J. F. Developmental trends in the use of logical connectives. *Psychonomic Science*, 1971, 23, 171–172.

SINCLAIR-DE ZWART, H. Developmental psycholinguistics. In D. Elkind & J. H. Flavell (Eds.), *Studies in cognitive development: Essays in honor of Jean Piaget.* Oxford: Oxford University Press, 1969.

SLOBIN, D. I. Grammatical transformations and sentence comprehension in childhood and adulthood. *Journal of Verbal Learning and Verbal Behavior*, 1966, 5, 219–227.

SLOBIN, D. I. Imitation and grammatical development in children. In N. S. Endler, L. R. Boulter, & H. Osser (Eds.), *Contemporary issues in developmental psychology.* New York: Holt, Rinehart & Winston, 1968.

SLOBIN, D. I. *The ontogenesis of grammar: Facts & theories.* New York: Academic Press, 1971. (a)

SLOBIN, D. I. Developmental psycholinguistics. In W. O. Dingwell (Ed.), *A survey of linguistic science.* College Park, Md.: Linguistics Program, University of Maryland, 1971. (b)

SLOBIN, D. I., & WELCH, C. A. Elicited imitation as a research tool in developmental psycholinguistics. In C. A. Ferguson & D. I. Slobin (Eds.), *Readings on child language acquisition.* New York: Holt, Rinehart & Winston, in press.

SNOW, K. A comparative study of sound substitutions used by "normal" first grade children. *Speech Monographs*, 1964, *31*, 135-142.

TEMPLIN, M. C. *Certain language skills in children: Their development and interrelations.* (Monographs Series No. 26) Minneapolis: University of Minnesota, Institute of Child Welfare, 1957.

TURNER, E. A., & ROMMETVEIT, R. The acquisition of sentence voice and reversibility. *Child Development*, 1967, *38*, 649–660. (a)

TURNER, E. A., & ROMMETVEIT, R. Experimental manipulation of the production of active and passive voice in children. *Language and Speech*, 1967, *10*, 169–180. (b)

WARREN, R. M., & WARREN, R. P. A comparison of speech perception in childhood, maturity, and old age by means of the verbal transformation effect. *Journal of Verbal Learning and Verbal Behavior*, 1966, 5, 142–146.

WELLMAN, B. L., CASE, I. M., MENGERT, I. G., & BRADBURY, D. Speech sounds of young children. *University of Iowa Studies in Child Welfare*, 1931, 5, No. 2.

WHITE, S. H. Evidence for a hierarchical arrangement of learning processes. In L. P. Lipsitt & C. C. Spiker (Eds.), *Advances in child development and behavior. Volume 2.* New York: Academic Press, 1965.

WOLMAN, R. N., & BAKER, E. N. A developmental study of word definitions. *Journal of Genetic Psychology*, 1965, *107*, 159–166.

WRIGHT, P. Transformations and the understanding of sentences. *Language and Speech*, 1969, *12*, 156–166.

19. ADULT PERCEPTION OF CHILDREN'S SPEECH

RICHARD M. WEIST and PAT STEBBINS

One of the most consistent themes that reoccurs in reviews of language development research (e.g., Brown, 1970; McNeill, 1970; Menyuk, 1971) is that the language of children is essentially different from the language of adults and that there are considerable regularities in the child's language development. These observations have been made on all aspects of language. One syntactic example of this claim is found in Klima & Bellugi's (1966) Stage 3 in the development of the negation and question. The auxiliary emerges in this stage independent of its former link with the negation. The interrogative transformation which involves a permutation of the auxiliary occurs in the yes/no question in a manner which is similar to the adult usage, e.g., "Does the kitty stand up," but the same transformation does not occur in the Wh question, e.g., "What he can ride in." Similar support for the above claim is found in phonological (Jakobson & Halle, 1956) and semantic (Bever, 1970) research. The present research is based on the premise that if the child is speaking a language which differs from the adult's language, and the adult can understand what the child says, then the adult shares a bilingual relationship with the child. This argument is confirmed if parents are better able to understand the utterances of children than persons without recent contact with children.

Method

The Ss were 12 parents, 6 mothers and 6 fathers, from the University of Nebraska—Lincoln community and 12 college students who were enrolled in introductory psychology classes and who had not had any recent contact with young children. The speech of 6 children was tape-recorded. One child came from each of the 6 mother-father pairs who were Ss in the experiment. The taping sessions for each child averaged about 4 h. Ten single-word and 10 multiple-word utterances were chosen for each child based on the clarity of the recording. The meaning of each utterance was determined by the context in which it occurred, and when the context was insufficient, the child was questioned. Only utterances for which a meaning had clearly been determined were used. A random sequence was determined for the 120 selected utterances, and the utterances were transferred directly to an experimental tape. The experimental utterances were spaced 9 sec apart.

The 120 stimuli were presented one at a time to an individual adult S. The Ss were told that the utterances of several children would be played and that their task was to report the meaning of what they heard. The Ss were told not to try to mimic the utterances, and it was again emphasized that S was to convey to E the meaning of the utterances. The Ss were asked to give their responses in 9 sec, but told that they could have more time if necessary. The utterances were never repeated for S. Two tape recorders were used, one to present the stimuli and one to record Ss' responses.

After the experiment was completed, E transcribed Ss' responses. One graduate student and three undergraduate psychology students rated the extent to which the 24 Ss reported the correct meaning of the 120 utterances on a 10-point scale. Interrater reliability ranged from $r = .91$ to .94. There were two dependent variables: the number of words correct and the average rated meaning.

Table 19.1. Average number of words correctly reported and average meaning ratings for parent and nonparent Ss

				Meaning Ratings				
Parent	3.32		Mother	3.71	Own	5.18	Nonparent	2.25
			Father	2.85	Other	2.99		
				Words Reported				
Parent	127.67		Mother	147.50	Own	5.55% *	Nonparent	96.33
			Father	107.83	Other	30.6%		

* Percent based on the number of words from a parent's child.

Results

All of the relevant comparisons (see Table 19.1) were significant on both dependent variables: parents were superior to nonparents [$t(22) = 5.06$, $p < .001$, on ratings and $t(22) = 3.24$, $p < .001$, on words]; mothers did better than fathers [$t(10) = 3.17$, $p < .01$, on ratings and $t(10) = 3.11$, $p <).01$, on words (not a male-female artifact)]; parents were better able to understand their own children than other children [$t(11) = 7.43$, $p < .001$, on ratings and $t(11) = 7.41$, $p < .001$, on words]. The comparison of parents vs. nonparents is complicated by the fact that one-sixth of the parents' responses were based on utterances of their own children. The parents' responses on other children were compared with those of nonparents, and parents maintained a significant advantage [$t(22) = 1.72$, $p < .05$]. Table 19.1 shows that the most accurate performance achieved by parents on their own children reached only 55.5%. This is undoubtedly a low estimate of parents' capacity to understand their children because both linguistic and nonlinguistic context were eliminated in this study.

Discussion

These results support the hypothesis that the child's language is essentially different from that of the adult. The child's language, like the language of a linguistic community, is a language that must be learned. In this experiment, the parents demonstrate that they have learned enough about children's language in general to exceed the performance of nonparents who lack experience with the language. The parent is better able to understand his (or her) own child than other children. This may indicate that the language of each child is marked by unique features. It is also possible that the children were in different stages of development and parents were responding to regularities at those stages. The corpus was not large enough, nor the analysis extensive enough, to establish stages of development. The greater experience that mothers have with the language of children was manifest in their superior performance as compared to fathers. This research demonstrates, in addition to these facts about children's language, a technique that can be used to determine what parents know about their children's language which differentiates them from other adults who have not had recent contact with this linguistic community. Further research is needed to discover the relative contribution of phonological, syntactic, and semantic aspects of children's language to the parent-child bilingual relationship.

Summary

The utterances of six preschool children were recorded and used as stimuli in a perception task. The parents of the recorded children and adults with no recent exposure to children listened to the utterances and judged the meaning of the stimuli. Parents were more proficient than nonparents, and this difference was not limited to the parents' superior knowledge of their own children's ideolects. It was argued that there is a sense in which adults with an extensive exposure to children's language may be considered to be bilinguals.

References

BEVER, T. G. The cognitive basis for linguistic structures. In J. R. Hayes (Ed.), *Cognition and the development of language.* New York: Wiley, 1970, pp. 279–362.

BROWN, R. *Psycholingustics.* New York: Free Press, 1970.

JAKOBSON, J., & HALLE, M. *Fundamentals of language.* The Hague: Mouton, 1956.

KLIMA, E. S., & BELLUGI, U. Syntactic regularities in the speech of children. In J. Lyons and R. Wales (Eds.), *Psycholinguistic papers.* Edinburgh: Edinburgh University Press, 1966, pp. 183–207.

MCNEILL, D. *The acquisition of language.* New York: Harper & Row, 1970.

MENYUK, P. *The acquisition and development of language.* Englewod Cliffs, N.J.: Prentice-Hall, 1971.

CHAPTER FOUR: SUGGESTED FURTHER READINGS

BROWN, R. *Words and things.* Glencoe, Ill.: Free Press, 1959.

———. *A first language.* Cambridge, Mass.: Harvard University Press, 1973.

PALERMO, D. S. Research on language acquisition: Do we know where we are going? In L. R. Goulet and P. B. Baltes (Eds.), *Life-span developmental psychology.* New York: Academic Press, 1970. Pp. 401–420.

SLOBIN, D. *Psycholinguistics.* Glenview, Ill.: Scott, Foresman, 1971.

chapter five
personality

One aspect of life-span study is its newness to the field of psychology. Personality growth is like other aspects of developmental psychology in this regard. Traditionally, the personality aspect has been studied only in the context of the years from infancy through adolescence. Personality development has always been perceived as occuring during the childhood years. Whether we were boisterous and active or quiet and passive, our actions as children defined our personalities. The unfortunate assumption that traditional developmental psychologists make is an obvious one, namely that our personalities are completely formed by the time we reach adolescence and do not develop beyond that point. It is the point of the following chapter on personality development to ask whether this assumption is a valid one to make.

In attempting to arrive at an answer several issues must be raised. First, are our personalities, in fact, fixed invariant structures that we carry around with us throughout our lifetime? The fact of the matter is that we know very little about how personalities develop and grow. Evidence does exist, however, as the Macfarlane article bears out, that rebellious children do not necessarily grow up to be rebellious adults, nor do low achievers in grade school fail during their college and postcollege years.

A second issue which must be dealt with concerns the methodology employed to study personality variables. One problem is definitional: How do we know that what we study and call "dependency" really is dependency? Is a frustrated child who asks for help to solve a problem being dependent because he asks for help? or is he being independent because he realizes he is unable to solve the problem and realistically needs some assistance? A second problem is, What are the changes, if any, in the assessment of the same personality variable at different ages? For example, will a fifty-year-old show dependency in the same way that a twenty-year-old does? and will a twenty-year-old show dependency with the same behaviors or needs as a two-year-old? If not, what kinds of value judgments are made? and what implications do they have for studying the developing personality? A third problem concerns the personality measurements themselves. Is it, for example, sufficient to test for a variable such as self-concept at adolescence and during middle age and then measure how self-concept changes? or is it possible that some variables, like self-concept, are more salient at one stage than another?

A third and most important issue which must be asked is, What are the personality changes that occur as a result of the aging process? There are many varied events that occur during the lifetime which surely must influence to some extent how the personality changes and develops. This is true not only of children and adolescents but of middle- and old-aged people as well. Let us briefly consider some historical events in the life span that probably influence personalities: a college student graduates; a couple gets married; a woman has a baby; a loved one dies; a man works for over thirty years and retires; a sixty-year-old housewife goes back to college. These and the many more events which we live through have a definite and unique impact on our personality development. We can read in many textbooks about the effects of parental deaths on children, but what about the effects of such deaths on older people? Is the same effect mainfested or a different one? and how?

Sigmund Freud, among others, spelled out a theory of personality which asserts that personality is firmly established by adolescence. It is only recently that this view has begun to be questioned. As future social scientists we must all share in the awesome responsibility of constructing new realities concerning psychological development.

20. ANTAGORHYTHM 2
(CHANT FOR TWO VOICES)

MORTON H. LEEDS

Young Power	*Old Power*
I look at him and I see	I look at him and I see
someone I cannot respect	someone I cannot respect
He is old	He is young
His hair is white	His hair is black
He hoards power	He covets power
Does not know how to use it	Does not know how to use it
He is an anal character	He is an oral character
and is incapable of	and is incapable of
relating to others	relating to others
I hate to think of what	I hate to think of what
has happened to us	would happen to us
under him	under him
Can you see yourself	Can you see yourself
supporting him?	supporting him?
I am young and strong	I am old and wise
Support me.	Support me.

21. PERSONALITY AND THE AGING PROCESS

BERNICE L. NEUGARTEN

Knowledge of personality changes that occur during the middle and later years is scanty. There have been relatively few empirical studies from which findings can be generalized. More important, there is not yet available a systematic body of theory on the aging personality as a framework within which isolated and fragmentary findings can be related. Existing personality theories, developed primarily for ordering observations of child and adolescent personality, appear insufficient and inappropriate for describing the changes that occur as a person moves from young adulthood to old age.

Against this background, a number of studies of personality processes from age forty to seventy have been carried out with the larger research undertakings that have come to be known as the Kansas City studies of adult life. Although these studies are still in progress, the findings are beginning to form a consistent pattern now and point to a theory that can be tested by other investigators.

Sampling

A major problem in studies of personality differences with age is sampling. Most reports have been based on groups of institutionalized old people, psychiatric patients, or volunteer samplings. The studies in this paper share one important characteristic: they all deal with subjects drawn from two large samples of adults residing in the Midwestern metropolitan area, Kansas City. The groups constituted random samples of people, age forty to seventy-one, drawn by modified area-probability techniques, but stratified by age, sex, and socioeconomic level. The first sample was drawn in 1953; the second, in 1955. (A group of ambulatory old people, age seventy to eighty-five, have recently been added to our study groups.) Altogether, in the course of the Kansas City studies of adult life, varying amounts of information have been gathered on over one thousand people forty and over, all living in their own homes and participating in the activities characteristic of functioning members of the community. They were volunteers only in the sense that, after being approached and, to varying degrees, persuaded, by a member of our field staff, they agreed to be interviewed.

All the studies in this paper were based on subsamples drawn from this pool. Each study, furthermore, involved a relatively large group of subjects—in each instance, more than one hundred. Although all these studies have been primarily concerned with age as the major variable, it should be made clear that the data are all cross-sectional, not longitudinal. Thus inferences drawn regarding changes with age are, strictly speaking, statements based on observed differences among age groups.

Social Competence and Life Satisfaction

In these Kansas City studies there are three different lines of investigation that bear on personality functioning. The first may be called the "social personality." Here attention has been focused on gross patterns of social interaction and competence, thus on relatively overt, public behavior. The second is the area that measures what, for lack of a better term, has often been called "adjustment" or "successful aging" and individual happiness or satisfaction with life. The third line of investigation, the one with which the present report is primarily concerned, relates to the more covert, less readily observed aspects of personality dynamics. These three aspects of behavior are, of course, inextricably woven into everyone's life, yet they may be investigated separately. Indeed, these studies have produced rather different findings about the significance of chronological age in each of these areas.

When the investigator's attention was focused on social aspects of behavior or competence, the findings showed neither significant nor consistent age changes from forty to sixty-five. In more exact terms, chronological age has not proved a meaningful variable in the variance in scores. Thus, Havighurst rated the performance of 240 men and women from varying social levels in roles of worker, parent, spouse, homemaker, user of leisure time, friend, citizen, club and association member, and church member. If a person was not penalized for the absence of one or more roles (the widow, for instance, by definition is no longer filling the role of spouse, so she was rated on eight, rather than nine, roles), then the quality of role performance did not vary appreciably over the age range from forty to sixty-five (Havighurst, 1957).

It is not until people reach their mid-sixties, on the average, that gross patterns of social interaction show marked changes. This is demonstrated in the study by

Cumming, Dean, Newell, and McCaffrey (1960) in which various measures of social interaction were utilized: hours of a typical day spent with other persons; total interactions with different kinds of people over one month; number of social roles the person fills. Here, with a sample of more than two hundred people from fifty through eighty-five, grouped in five-year age intervals, there were relatively consistent changes over this wide age range as age increased. At the same time, the most marked changes in score pattern appeared around sixty-five (Cumming et al., 1960). As far as our measures of social interaction are concerned, then, it appears that the period from the forties to the mid-sixties may be viewed as a plateau, relative to the periods that precede and follow. Systematic changes related to chronological age are not evident.

It should be pointed out that the behaviors described here are relatively gross. To say that a man continues to perform well on his job or that a woman continues to interact with the same number of people when she is sixty as when she was forty is not to deny that there may be measurable changes occurring in quality and mode of social interaction. More refined observations might be expected to produce different findings regarding changes with age in this area of behavior.

In the second area of investigation, adjustment and/or life satisfaction, the Kansas City studies showed no consistent relations with age, even, perhaps, to the age of eighty-five. For instance, Peck and Berkowitz rated over-all adjustment for a sample of 120 persons, age forty to sixty-four, from all social levels and found no relation to chronological age (Peck & Berkowitz, 1959). Similarly, Havighurst and Neugarten, using four rounds of interviews over a period of two years, rated more than two hundred people from fifty to eighty-five on five components of life satisfaction (zest for life; mood tone; sense of resolution or fortitude; consistency between desired and

achieved life goals; and degree to which the self is positively regarded). No correlation was found between these ratings and chronological age (Havighurst, supra). It appears, therefore, that age is not a significant variable, not only in the twenty-five years prior to sixty-five, but probably in the seventies and eighties as well. (Relative to life satisfaction at the older ages, this finding must be interpreted with caution, since the seventy- and eighty-year-old subjects did not suffer from major illness or economic deprivation, thus constituting a select group of survivors.)

Age–Related Changes in Personality

Turning now to studies that deal with the more covert, inner aspects of personality, the picture is different as regards chronological age. Here, when the investigator was concerned with such issues as the perception of the self vis-à-vis the external environment, handling of impulse, or nature of ego boundaries, the findings lead to the conclusion that there are significant and consistent age differences after forty.

These differences are not always readily discernible, however, as even some of our own investigations have produced varying results on this point. The variation has been caused, to some extent, by using different theoretical approaches and sets of personality variables; to perhaps greater extent, by the particular type of data used; and by whether an inductive or deductive approach was taken. Because the studies illustrate different points regarding method, they are described separately.

In one investigation (Gruen, 1958), an adaptation of Erikson's theory of ego development through life was used. Conceiving Erikson's eight so-called nuclear stages of ego development as independent personality dimensions, Gruen devised rating scales for them (trust versus distrust; autonomy versus shame; initiative versus guilt; industry versus inferiority; ego identity versus role diffusion; intimacy versus ego isolation; generativeness versus ego stagnation; and ego integrity versus despair) and rated 108 men and women from forty to sixty-four, of varying social classes, on the basis of interview data. The interviews contained open-ended questions about work, retirement, plans for the future, use of leisure time, health, attitude toward aging, spouse and children, religion, friends, expression of emotional states and evaluation of life. Ratings were based on the whole interview protocol, not on particular questions. An analysis of variance showed no consistent variance attributable to age.

In another study, Peck and Berkowitz (1959) used the same interview data with responses to six TAT (Thematic Apperception Test) cards for a sample of 120 men and women from forty to sixty-four. Ratings were made on seven personality variables derived from a developmental theory formulated by Peck (1956). This theory proposes that particular adaptive capacities in the personality become salient one after another as the adult attempts to resolve the psychological crises that accompany events of the middle and older years, such as widowhood or retirement. The variables are entitled flexibility of cathection, mental flexibility, ego transcendence, body transcendence, body satisfaction, and sexual integration. As in Gruen's study, statistical analysis of the ratings on these variables showed no consistent age differences.

Problems of Method

These two studies are at variance with others of our studies of personality as far as they show no significant change with age from forty to sixty-five. The discrepancy is probably related to differences of method. The next studies to be described were based on projective data analyzed blind for age, whereas the two studies just cited were based on interview data that could not be disguised for age.

The point about method is not merely that projective data and interview data may yield different orders of information about the same personality nor that research of this kind is always improved to the extent that the investigator's biases can be controlled, as they are when the data are blinded for age. The point is rather that the investigator's bias is particularly difficult to control in studying the relatively unfamiliar area of developmental differences in adulthood, as compared to studying developmental differences in childhood or adolescence. The researcher operates under special difficulties in making evaluative judgments from interview data. Not only is the adult subject more practiced than the child in controlling the information he reveals in an interview, but the investigator himself has difficulty in avoiding a shifting frame of reference in making his judgments. The same datum of behavior, when it appears in a seventy-year-old, is often differently regarded from when it appears in a forty-year-old. (As we have witnessed many times in our training sessions, a frequent thought process in the judge seems to be, "That's quite good—for a seventy-year-old!") Nor is such a bias consistent from datum to datum on the same subject.

Ensuring that the same units of measurements have been applied to all members of a sample is a problem common to all rating methods; it is a more likely source of error in handling the behavior of forty-, fifty-, and sixty-year-olds than that of two-, four-, and six-year-olds. This is because developmental psychologists have become relatively sophisticated about the characteristic behavior of children at various developmental points. Furthermore, in studies of childhood and adolescence, there are clearer concepts of what constitutes an appropriate normative population. In dealing with adults, such concepts are less clear. Are forty-year-olds and seventy-year-olds to be regarded as a single population? If not, what developmental points can be used to establish appropriate normative groupings? Such problems as these have proven to be major ones. They will be overcome only when more research has been done on normal adults and when more developmental bench marks become available. Controlling for age bias and maintaining constant points of reference are also largely avoided when responses to specific interview questions constitute the data for analysis. Such data can usually be treated in straightforward fashion, and a set of categories initially independent of age can be established. The problem lies, therefore, not with the interview method, but with making evaluations of interview data.

For the reasons implied in these comments, most of our studies of age differences in personality have been based on projective data. It has proved difficult to blind interview data for age, but relatively easy to detach, for instance, the TAT protocol from the rest of the interview and analyze it blind for age.[1]

The first of these projective studies on Kansas City subjects was one that has been reported by Neugarten and Gutmann (1958). Responses of 131 working-class and middle-class men and women aged forty to seventy to a specially drawn type of TAT picture were analyzed. Although this study was first undertaken as an investigation of age-sex roles, it became apparent that the data reflected consistent personality differences related to age. The individual's covert investment in his roles, sources of gratification, and preferred modes of action seemed to differ markedly between forty-year-olds and and sixty-year-olds. There were, for instance, different views of the nature of the external world. Forty-year-olds seemed to see themselves possessing energy congruent with the opportunities perceived in

the outer world. The environment was seen to reward boldness and risk-taking— a person gets from the world what he gives to it. For older respondents the outer world was complex and a bit dangerous. It was not to be reformed according to personal wishes; instead, one conformed and accommodated himself to its demands. To the older respondent, the individual no longer manipulated the object world forcefully, but was, instead, a rather passive object manipulated by the environment.

This study also gave evidence that, with increasing age, the ego qualities of the personality that regulate impulses and adapt to environmental demands seem to contract. With increased age, the ego seemed not only in a position of lessened mastery relative to the outer world, but also the ego seemed less in contact with and less effective in controlling and channeling impulse.

With increasing age the data suggested, "Ego functions are turned inward, as it were, and while rational thought processes are still important in the personality, thought is less relevant to action" (Neugarten & Gutmann, 1958, p. 23).

The same study suggested important differences between men and women as they age. For instance, men seem to become more receptive to their own affiliative, nurturant, and sensual promptings, whereas women seem to become more responsive toward, and less guilty about, their own aggressive, egocentric impulses. Although sex differences cannot be elaborated in the present paper, the fact should be mentioned that such differences have appeared in most of these studies. Social class has also proven to be an important variable.

Studies of Ego Functions

To follow some of the leads from the study just mentioned, several subsequent investigations of ego functions were undertaken. In one study (Gutmann, Henry,

---

[1] Our analyses have been primarily of Thematic Apperception Test data, although we have available also sentence-completion and Draw-a-Person data for some groups. Preliminary analyses of these projective data corroborate the over-all finding of consistent differences related to age.

& Neugarten, 1959) the stories told by 144 men to four standard TAT cards were analyzed. Here the individual stories, rather than individual men, were treated as the units for analysis. Stories that were similar in central focus and structure were grouped together to form categories, and the categories were then ranked on a continuum from active to passive mastery. That is, stories that reflected an energetic, motoric, or alloplastic approach to the environment were placed at the active end of the continuum; stories that reflected a passive, autoplastic attitude—where the hero was resigned, deferential, or constricted in the face of environmental pressures—were ranked at the passive end of the continuum. The percentage of stories in each category was computed for each age group, and from these percentages the psychological issues that are most prominent at each age were inferred. For instance, the most frequent stories given by men in the forty to forty-nine age group stressed virility and resistance to coercion. Intrusive energies were ascribed to the hero figures, passive and dependent wishes were denied, problems were thrashed out in combat with the environment.

Stories told by fifty-year-olds were frequently those in which passive and deferential rather than rebellious or defiant heroes were projected, although there was also a high percentage of stories reflecting striving and active mastery. Thus, both relations to the environment were given prominence—as if fifty-year-old men are conflicted more than the other age groups. They begin to favor short-range, sensual, and affiliative rewards over long-range achievement goals, yet they seem reluctant to retreat from the struggle.

In the stories of the sixty-year-olds, the conflicts seem to have been resolved. The most frequent stories were those in which the heroes conform, abase themselves, and are meek, friendly, and mild. Aggression was ascribed only to the external world, and parental figures or impersonal insti-

tutional demands are important in the outcomes.

In contrast to the study just described, Rosen and Neugarten (1960) took a deductive approach in studying changes with age in the ego process. Following the indication that ego functions seem to diminish in effectiveness with increased age, the investigators proceeded on certain formulations developed by ego psychologists (particulary Hartmann, 1951; Lustman, 1957; Rapaport, 1951) relating to the concept of ego energy. A research design was established for testing the hypothesis that during the middle and later years there is a decrease in the energy available to the ego for responding to, or maintaining former investment in, outer world events.

On the postulation that they would provide gross estimates of available ego energy, four dimensions of ego function were selected for study, and methods for measuring them by TAT data were delineated. These dimensions and the corresponding TAT measures were ability to integrate wide ranges of stimuli (measured by introducing nonpictorial characters into TAT stories); readiness to perceive or handle complicated, challenging, or conflict-filled situations (measured by introducing conflict, controversy, choice, or decision into the stories); tendency toward vigorous, assertive activity (measured by the activity-energy level ascribed to story characters); and tendency to perceive or to be concerned with emotions as these play a part in life situations (measured by the degree to which affect states are seen as playing a role in the story productions).

The sample was 144 men and women from forty to seventy-one, divided into eighteen equal cells on the bases of age, sex, and social class. The TAT stories were scored blind, then a three-way analysis of variance was carried out. Results indicated that on all four measures only the factor of age was significant in accounting for variance. Scores decreased from age group to age group in the predicted direction.

Dr. Gutmann has proceeded to investigate further the indication that problems with inner life increase as aging progresses. Using TAT data for 145 men aged forty to seventy-one and working inductively from the data, he made a formulation about each man's personality for major concerns and preoccupations, especially in the unconscious drive (impulse life); ego defenses (coping mechanisms) elaborated in response to such preoccupations; and success or failure of these coping mechanisms as indicated by the form of the TAT stories, the accuracy of interpreting the stimuli, the flexibility or rigidity of approach, the themes, and the expression of affect and energy (Gutmann, 1959). Five major personality types were established. When the data were decoded, the five types were distributed by age, and the differences in the distribution proved to be statistically significant.

We cannot define the types here, but the data indicate the older men fall off markedly in active participation with the outer world, shifting their attention to intrapsychic events. Whereas the forty-year-old man tends to ignore the inner life and strives to dominate the outer world, older respondents seem to deploy their energy inward in the attempt to master the psychic life. They also seem to have resolved autonomy-dependency problems, which preoccupied the younger men, with solutions in the direction of passivity and deference. There is an age shift from reliance on ego to reliance on superego elements of the personality—in solving issues and problems there is more concern with abstract rules and authority than with working out rational, adaptive solutions, an increased frequency of distorted and inappropriate interpretations, and other evidence of ineffective ego controls.

The findings from this study confirm and elaborate those from the earlier ones. To recapitulate, in males there are age-related differences from forty to seventy that indicate a shift from active to passive mastery in dealing with the outer world, greater preoccupation with impulse life, less efficient modes of coping with impulse life, greater emphasis on conformity and constriction, and greater dependency on superego functions in handing problems from within and without.

In a similar analysis of TAT data for women aged forty to seventy-one, five major personality types were also delineated, although the most salient psychological issues for women are not identical with those for men (Gutmann, 1960). The typology for women is based on the extent to which issues and personal conflicts are externalized and projected onto the outside world, effectiveness of ego controls over impulse, extent of intropunitiveness or extrapunitiveness, and balance between maternal and altruistic, versus domineering and retentive, motivations (the latter are usually revealed by stories dealing with children or young people interacting with older people).

When the five types were arrayed along a continuum from good to defective ego control and from maternal and altruistic orientation to egocentric and retentive orientation and when the protocols were decoded for age, there was a clear relationship between personality type and chronological age for women aged fifty to seventy. The women aged forty to fifty, however, were distributed over all five types. The meaning of this finding is not yet clear and awaits further analyses of other data on the women. It is apparent, however, that, although men's and women's personalities change differently with age, there are significant age changes in both sexes.

We are now at that point where we have demonstrated significant age differences in the period from forty to sixty-five in the more covert and private motivational and attitudinal aspects of personality. Now we are moving to the study of the relations between these personality measures and other types of information on the same individuals. Although generalizations are still premature, our first attempts in this direction are yielding meaningful findings. To illustrate, it appears that there is a positive relation between personality type as delineated by Gutmann on the basis of the TAT and life satisfaction, with those men who are high on active-mastery being those who are also high on life satisfaction. Similarly, there seems to be a positive relation between ego energy, as delineated by Rosen on the basis of the TAT, and the individual's outlook on the future, as reflected in responses to interview questions. If meaningful relationships such as these continue to appear, they will provide some valid measure for these personality assessments. At the same time, they will constitute further evidence that inductive approaches to the study of personality change in adulthood are fruitful.

Summary and Implications

In summary, these studies have demonstrated significant age differences in the period from forty to sixty-five in the covert, motivational, and attitudinal aspects of personality. These changes have been (1) in mode of relating to the environment and handling impulses, with a movement of energy from an outer-world to inner-world orientation and from active to passive mastery; (2) in the degree of effectiveness of ego functions; and (3) in the amount of energy available to the ego. These functions are obviously interrelated and may only constitute different reflections of increased constriction and turning inward as a person grows old. That these processes occur in the years from forty to sixty-five is the point to be stressed, since in these years gross measures of social competence show no age changes.

These findings are, it should be repeated, based on cross-sectional data, and it remains to be demonstrated that they represent developmental changes. If the latter can be demonstrated, however, the

implication is that we have evidence that corroborates the theory of disengagement, formulated by Cumming and Henry (Cumming et al., 1960; Henry & Cumming, 1959): "A theory of aging in which a disengaging process which may be primarily intrinsic, and secondarily responsive, leads to a disengaged state. The individual is pictured as participating with others in his social systems in a process of mutual withdrawal, rather than being deserted by others in the structure" (Cumming et al., 1960, p. 34).

Data from the Kansas City studies about patterns of social interaction show no marked differences and thus do not directly reflect disengagement until the mid-sixties. The data summarized here, however, indicate that personality changes consonant with the disengagement theory are measurable as early as the forties. With due regard for the facts that the aspects of social interaction thus far measured are very broad and that the measurements have been relatively gross, the differences in the timing of age changes are nevertheless impressive. The suggestion is that changes occur within the individual long before they are manifested in his social interactions. If this difference is borne out when more refined measures of social interaction become available, it would be justifiable to infer that disengagement does have intrinsic as well as responsive components.

The aspects of personality measured here lie closer, perhaps, to biological than to social determinants of behavior. It is true that we lack data for assessing the interrelations between biological, psychological, and social factors in the aging process and that any attempt to categorize behavior or its determinants is, at best, only a heuristic device. At the same time, no theory of aging can be attempted without giving at least some consideration to possible interactions between such classes of factors. Accordingly, we are suggesting here that, just as biological maturation is primary for the development of an adequately functioning ego in the early years of life, it may be that biological factors again take precedence in maintaining the ego functions of the aging individual. Decreased efficiency in these personality functions may be closely related to decreased efficiency in biological functions. In this connection, other investigators have pointed out that until at least the mid-sixties the average person maintains social competence in the face of considerable biological change (Havighurst, 1957). The present studies indicate a somewhat parallel phenomenon—that people maintain social competence in the face of considerable personality change.

To proceed further in these speculations, it is possible, just as it is with biological changes, that only when personality changes go beyond a certain threshold are the visible patterns of social functioning affected. Or, in different terms, the biological organism shows unmistakable signs of aging during the period from forty to sixty-five; so does the psychological organism, but within a considerable range the changes seem to remain relatively independent of social performance and personal satisfaction with life. Only when there is gross biological malfunction or illness is the independence between biological and social functions destroyed. The same may be true of the personality processes studied here. Only when there is marked distortion or gross breakdown of ego functions will there be a visible effect on everyday behavior.

References

CUMMING, ELAINE, DEAN, LOIS R., NEWELL, D. S., & MCCAFFREY, ISABEL. Disengagement—a tentative theory of aging. *Sociometry*, 1960, 23, 23–35.

GRUEN, W. An experimental application of Erikson's theory of ego development. Unpublished memorandum on file with the Committee on Human Development, University of Chicago, 1958.

GUTMANN, D. L. Personality change with age in males. Unpublished research report on file with the Committee on Human Development, University of Chicago, 1959.

GUTMANN, D. L. Personality change with age in females. Unpublished memorandum on file with the Committee on Human Development, University of Chicago, 1960.

GUTMANN, D. L., HENRY, W. E., & NEUGARTEN, BERNICE L. Personality development in middle-aged men. Paper read at the annual meeting of the American Psychological Association, Cincinnati, 1959.

HARTMANN, H. Ego psychology and the problem of adaptation. In D. Rapaport (Ed.), *Organization and pathology of thought*. New York: Columbia University Press, 1951, pp. 362–396.

HAVIGHURST, R. J. The social competence of middle-aged people. *Genet. Psychol. Monogr.*, 1957, 56, 297–375.

HENRY, W. E., & CUMMING, ELAINE. Personality development in adulthood and old age. *J. proj. Tech.*, 1959, 23, 383–390.

LUSTMAN, S. Psychic energy and mechanisms of defense. In Ruth S. Eissler, Anna Freud, H. Hartmann, & G. Kris (Eds.), *The psychoanalytic study of the child*. Vol. 12. New York: International Universities Press, 1957, pp. 151–165.

NEUGARTEN, BERNICE L., & GUTMANN, D. L. Age-sex roles and personality in middle age: A thematic apperception study. *Psychol. Monogr.*, 1958, 72, No. 17.

PECK, R. F. Psychological developments in the second half of life. In J. E. Anderson (Ed.), *Psychological aspects of aging*. Washington, D.C.: American Psychological Association, 1956, pp. 42–53.

PECK, R. F., & BERKOWITZ, H. Personality and adjustment in middle age. Unpublished memorandum on file with the Committee on Human Development, University of Chicago, 1959.

RAPAPORT, D. Toward a theory of thinking. In D. Rapaport (Ed.), *Organization and pathology of thought*. New York: Columbia University Press, 1951, pp. 689–730.

ROSEN, JACQUELINE L., & NEUGARTEN, BERNICE L. Ego functions in the middle and later years: A thematic apperception study of normal adults. *J. Geront.*, 1960, *15*, 62–67.

22. SEXUAL THOUGHT THROUGHOUT THE LIFE–SPAN

PAUL CAMERON and HENRY BIBER

Sex has been and continues to be a topic of active psychological investigation. Investigators have explored the techniques of sexual behavior (Masters & Johnson, 1966), varieties of sexual behavior (Kinsey, Pomeroy, & Martin, 1948), numerous studies of sexual attitudes ranging from premarital sexual encounters to sex in senescence, amounts of sexual conversation (Cameron, 1970a), and physiological and pharmacological correlates of sexual maturation (Reynolds & Wines, 1948, 1951). With the exception of the rather limited reports of Cameron (1967, 1970b), no normative data concerning the kind and frequency of human sexual thought are available.

It seems reasonable to proceed with the investigation of thought as a topic of legitimate scientific concern in its own right (Ginnane, 1960). It is known that much of human behavior is engaged in without thinking (Ossorio, 1966). Most of the motor skills that persons exhibit are so routinized that they are unaccompanied by thought, while the same circumstance obtains with the various emotional states (Gosling, 1962). As persons are almost always thinking, some species of human endeavor must be thought about much more than they are exhibited in observ-

able behavior. Is sex one of these species? Does sexual thought trace the same developmental pattern as interest in sex, or observable sexual behavior? Some theorists (e.g., Linden & Courtney, 1953) have contended that a resurgence of sexuality occurs in senescence. While it appears that a resurgence of observable sexual behavior does not generally occur (Kinsey et al., 1948), is this resurgence possibly expressed in greater mental investment?

Thought can be considered as occurring at two levels of activity. At one level, many kinds of thought seem to flit through the mind: often, seemingly independently of these snatches of thought, the mind is focusing in on a topic of some concern to the person. While no sharp mental "line" separates these two kinds of thought, the distinction is at least as old as William James (Boring, 1933). The present report presents normative data regarding the frequency of both ephemeral and focal sexual thought throughout the life-span.

How We Sampled Thoughts

As the contents of thought might vary as a function of time-of-day, situation, and activity, 4,420 persons ranging in age from 8 to 99 were interviewed or asked to fill out a questionnaire equally-frequently across all daylight hours in the most frequent situations of daily life—in school, while engaging in recreation, at home, or at work. The at-home sample was obtained via a strict area sample of areas of Los Angeles, Louisville, Detroit, and Evansville (762 males and 959 females, with a rejection rate of 28%); the at-work sample was obtained by college student volunteers from their co-workers in Detroit, Evansville, and Louisville (931 males and 507 females, occupying 84 different job locations with a rejection rate of less than 1%); the at-school sample was drawn by a classroom-time-grade selection process whereby certain proportions of the students in given classes had their work interrupted and the questionnaire was filled out by the subjects (244 males and 233 females, with a rejection rate of less than 1% at two different schools, one in Kentucky and the other in New Jersey); the at-church sample was obtained by the interruption of cooperating Sunday School classes and the private approaching of designated worshippers during services at four churches (12 males and 30 females, 1 rejection); the at-leisure sample was obtained by staking out certain areas in 11 different locations in Louisville, Los Angeles, and Denver, and randomly interviewing one of every so many people who entered the area (6 shopping areas, 2 beaches, 2 parks, and one organized ballgame provided 221 males and 521 females and a rejection rate of less than 1%). While persons were not assessed in all the kinds of situations and performing all the kinds of activities that are common in our culture, the vast majority of persons in our society spend the majority of their waking lives in the situations we sampled, engaging in the kinds of activity we interrupted. We interviewed 2,250 females and 2,170 males distributed over the life-span and achieved an over-all rejection rate of less than 11%.

The questionnaire was introduced "What were you thinking about over the past 5 min.?" "Did you think about sex or were your thoughts sexually colored—even for a moment (perhaps it crossed your mind)?" "What was the central focus of your thought over the past 5 min.?" (among the 14 possible responses was "about a personal problem-topic concerning sex").

What Was Found

Before reporting the results, we should like to explain the massing of the findings instead of their presentation by situation or by mode of assessment. Two hundred of the at-home sample were administered the questionnaire without interviewer assistance. No differences between self- or interviewer-administration nor between the samples drawn from the various cities were uncovered. Further, no difference in frequency of possible replies as a function of time-of-day nor situation for most variables (including frequency of thoughts of sex) was discovered (the only differences found concerned mood and situation-specific thoughts, i.e., children at-school thought more frequently about school than children at-leisure did, adults at-church thought more frequently about religion than adults at-home, etc.). The trends we uncovered evidenced themselves in each situation we sampled, hence both the combination of results and reason to regard our results with considerably more confidence than the probabilities associated with the particular outcomes.

There were no systematic variations in sexual thought as a function of marital status or race. Sexual thought varied by age and sex. Our sample consisted of 119 males and 116 females aged 8 to 11, 146 males and 177 females aged 12 and 13, 130 males and 137 females aged 14 and 15, 104 males and 207 females aged 16 and 17, 541 males and 629 females aged 18 to 25, 472 males and 443 females aged 26 to 39, 379 males and 366 females aged 40 to 55, 97 males and 95 females aged 56 to 64, and 82 old males and 80 old females. For males, the percentage of respondents in each age-grouping who reported that sex had "crossed their mind in the last 5 min." was, starting at the youngest, 25, 50, 57, 51, 48, 33, 20, 19, and 9 for the old. For females, the corresponding percentages were 27, 39, 42, 42, 33, 19, 9, 12, and 6. For males, the percentage of respondents in the corresponding age-groups who reported that sex had been the focus of their thought in the last 5 min. was 4, 16, 10, 14, 10, 8, 4, 3, and 0. For females, the percentages ran 4, 11, 11, 6, 6, 2, 2, 0, and 0. Clearly the frequency of both in-passing and focal sexual thought was curvilinearly related to the life-span, reaching a high point in the teen-age and young adult years. With but three exceptions, of the 18 comparisons, males reported more sexual thought than females (the sign test places the probability of such an outcome at less than .004).

Where Has All the Sex Gone?

Human thought broaches sex much more frequently than sexual behavior is engaged in. While investigators in both the USA and Japan (Asayama, 1957) have found relatively low amounts of sexual behavior among boys before the age of 15, the frequency of thinking about sex is essentially constant for the males of our sample from the age of 12 through 25. While US girls seldom experience coitus before the age of 16 and only by 16 have approximately half of them ever kissed or petted, the 16-year-olds in our sample are essentially indistinguishable from our 12- and 13-year-olds in amount of mental "space" devoted to sex. The co-relation between sexual behavior and sexual thought appears far from coincident, both in absolute incidence and in ages of highest frequency.

Both the Japanese and USA reports of sexual behavior concluded that males engaged in sexual behavior earlier in life, on the average, than females, and achieved and maintained a higher incidence of the various kinds of sexual behavior. Clearly our results evidence no indication that males start frequent thinking about sex at a younger age than females, but do provide evidence that males think about sex more frequently at all ages than females.

What people talk about has been theorized to follow closely what people think about (Jesus opined that what people thought generated what they talked about and said). In the only large-scale study reported to date, college students were found to talk about sex about 17% of their conversational time (Cameron, 1970b). In the present study the average amount of time spent thinking about sex in-passing averaged about 40% for young adults while focal sexual thought averaged about 8%. The rules of conversation include a demand that usually some sort of logical progression be followed, so probably most of what we have termed in-passing thought would not be mentioned, as it is so often alogical. We would expect the frequency of a subject's being the topic of conversation to fall below the in-passing rate, and somewhere close to the focal rate (possibly a little lower or higher). Our present data thus generate a reasonable match between the incidence of sex as a conversational and mental topic for young adults.

When asked to estimate what percentage of the time they thought about sex, 188 Boulder, Colorado, adults estimated a median of 20% for 18- to 22-year-olds, 8% for 28- to 35-year-olds, and 1% for those over 60 (Cameron, 1967). The average adult (about 45 years of age) reported an estimate of about 8%. In the present investigation, the middle-aged averaged about 15% in-passing sexual thought, and 3% focal sexual thought. As with conversation, the absolute percentage of time spent thinking about sex is probably closer cognitively to the focal than the in-passing estimate. Thus estimates of percentage of time spent in thought about sex approximate the frequency of what appears to be the actual time spent thinking about the topic.

Verwoerdt, Pfeiffer, and Wang (1969) have reported results of interviewing a convenience sample of older persons about certain aspects of their sexual lives four times during a 10-year longitudinal study. While the initial sample consisted of 260 persons 60 years of age or older, various kinds of attrition sharply reduced the number of subjects providing complete data over the decade (one of the last studies was concerned with 39 subjects). The questions of primary interest for the purposes of this paper were: (a) "How would you describe your sexual feelings at the present time?" (a psychiatrist rated the subject's response as indicating "strong"/"moderate"/"weak"/or "no" interest in heterosexual coitus), and (b) "How often, on the average, do you have sexual intercourse at the present time?" (the psychiatrist rated the response as indicating heterosexual sexual intercourse of "more than once per week"/"once per week"/"once every 2 weeks"/"once per month"/or "none"). Verwoerdt et al. (1969) construed the first questions as indexing sexual interest (why subjects were not asked directly about their interest in sex or heterosexual sexual intercourse instead of inferring interests from feelings is not made clear).

While Verwoerdt et al. allow that sexual outlets other than heterosexual coitus exist and were not indexed, they report that the degree of sexual interest inferred by the psychiatrists from the responses of the subjects declined for both males and females with age. They also report that the percentage of their sample whose responses the psychiatrist judged as expressing some interest in heterosexual coitus remained at 56% over the decade. Ver-woerdt et al. construed their findings as indicating that sexual interest declines with age (but, by only indexing feelings about heterosexual coitus, they ignored the possibility of increasing sexual interest in masturbation, bestiality, homosexuality, etc.). While it may correspond with the reality of sexual interest in old age, their conclusion does not necessarily follow from their results. They also reported that interest in heterosexual coitus was judged as more frequently expressed by males and to a stronger degree. The percentage of the sample who reported some heterosexual coitus declined from 44% at the beginning to 20% at the end of the decade. Verwoerdt et al. construed this as evidencing "declining sexual activity." Again, the concept sexual activity subsumes activities other than heterosexual coitus, so that their conclusion does not necessarily follow from their results. Generally males were found to more frequently report some heterosexual coitus, and more frequent coitus if sexually active in this way. Our findings of declining frequency of contemplation of sex with age and the greater mental sexiness of males at all points along the adult life-span are similar to the Verwoerdt et al. results. However, if our subjects could have reported thinking about sex when contemplating: (a) a member of their sex, (b) an attractive dog, (c) a *Playboy* centerfold, or (d) any of the varieties of noncoital heterosexual sexual behavior, there is no conceptual necessity for similarity between the two sets of findings.

We unearthed no evidence that sexuality as manifested in thought increased markedly in old age. Linden and Courtney's (1953) notion of a spurt in sexuality in old age thus finds no support in the cognitive domain.

References

ASAYAMA, S. Comparison of sexual development of American and Japanese adolescents. *Psychologia*, 1957, *1*, 129–131.

BORING, E. G. *The physical dimensions of consciousness.* New York: Century, 1933.

CAMERON, P. Note on time spent thinking about sex. *Psychological Reports,* 1967, *20,* 741–742.

CAMERON, P. The words college students use and what they talked about. *Journal of Communication Disorders,* 1970, *3,* 36–46. (a)

CAMERON, P., BIBER, H., BROWN, N., SIRO, M., & COLDEN, C. Consciousness: Thoughts about world and social problems, death, and sex by the generations. Paper read at Kentucky Psychological Association, Sept. 25, 1970. (b)

GINNANE, W. Thought. *Mind,* 1960, *69,* 372–390.

GOSLING, J. Mental causes and fear. *Mind,* 1962, *71,* 289–306.

KINSEY, A. C., POMEROY, W. B., & MARTIN, E. E. *Sexual behavior in the human male.* Philadelphia: Saunders, 1948.

LINDEN, M. E., & COURTNEY, D. The human life cycle and its interruptions. *American Journal of Psychiatry,* 1953, *109,* 906–915.

MASTERS, W. H., & JOHNSON, V. E. *Human sexual response.* Boston: Little, Brown, 1966.

OSSORIO, P. G. *Persons.* Los Angeles: Linguistic Research Institute, 1966.

REYNOLDS, E. L., & WINES, J. V. Individual difference in physical changes associated with adolescence in girls. *American Journal of Diseases of Children,* 1948, 75, 329–350.

REYNOLDS, E. L., & WINES, J. V. Physical changes associated with adolescence in boys. *American Journal of Diseases of Children,* 1951, 82, 529–547.

VERWOERDT, A., PFEIFFER, E., & WANG, H. S. Sexual behavior in senescence. II. Patterns of change in sexual activity and interest. *Geriatrics,* 1969, *24,* 137–154.

23. TRANSITION TO AGING AND THE SELF–IMAGE

KURT W. BACK

Research on aging has shown important contrasts between objective social and behavioral changes and the individual's reaction to them. Faculties and abilities as well as social rewards and objective social conditions decline rather consistently during the later years of the life cycle. On the other hand, subjective satisfaction and morale not only do not decrease correspondingly but seem to improve during old age (Riley and Foner, 1968; Back and Gergen, 1966). It is plausibe to explain this apparent contradiction by the fact that morale is a personal comparison of self-worth with a realization of loss of socially important roles.

While the loss itself may be traumatic, the new status may be acceptable later; for the aged, even social losses might be welcome adaptations to reduced capacity. It might be conjectured that physical capacity and energy decline steadily from early middle age on, while *psychological extent,* the size of the psychological life space, is maintained until a relatively sudden decline sets in at a comparatively late date. Thus, in early middle age we would find conformity between age and ability. During onset of old age, psychological extent would remain higher than actual life situation. But as psychological life space declines, the two would be rejoined again, and a high level of satisfaction is attained again (Back and Gergen, 1968).

Theoretical advance in this field must await measurement techniques that capture the personal meaning of the self-concept. We are seeking a measure not of morale in the general sense, but of evaluation of the self, the discrepancy of the self-image one holds to the way one feels he is seen by others, and the different features of the self-image which may become important. The present paper deals with the evaluation of two possible measures of self-image: one an adaptation of the semantic differential, and the other an adaptation of Kuhn's Who-Are-You test (Kuhn and McPartland, 1954). These measures had been used previously to show not only the dimensions of the self-image but also the discrepancy between ideal, real, and actual self-image and self-presentation (Brehm and Back, 1968; Back and Paramesh, 1969).

The utility of these measures can be determined by their sensitivity to adaptation to aging of varying population groups, especially those with different problems during the aging process. Among the crises which can occur during the later parts of the life cycle, some appear in almost every life. One is the loss of occupational role through voluntary of forced retirement; another, the loss of family role through the leaving home of grown children—the "empty nest" stage of the family sociologist. It can be suggested that the first crisis is of particular importance to men, while the second is of greater importance to women. A valuable use of the measures of self which we are trying to develop is therefore to assess the relative impact of chronological age, retirement, and leaving of children on men and women.

Method

The data to be reported here were collected as part of a future panel study on adaptation and aging to be conducted at the Duke Center for the Study of Aging and Human Development. The information collection involved a lengthy physical, physiological, psychological, and social assessment, lasting an entire day. The sample was designed to represent the wide middle class population. The intent was to draw an equal sample of men and women in each five-year range from 45 to 70, with some oversampling of the older ages to compensate for the higher expected loss in these age ranges during the life of the panel. The present data are based on the first wave of study in which 502 interviews were collected. This sample was a stratified random sample taken from the files of a major local health insurance company, stratified by sex and age. Refusals to be interviewed were replaced by substitutions from the same group. Almost half of the sample could not be interviewed on the first attempt and had to be substituted, partly because of the time-consuming and arduous medical procedures. The total sample actually interviewed did not differ in main social characteristics from the originally selected sample. But there is a possible bias in the direction of respondents more ready to cooperate with scientific research and less anxious about medical examination. In general, the method of selection would also oversample working women, which was fortunate for the present study.

The questions used in this paper were part of the social history section of the study. Social history gave age, sex, working status, and family situation, including separation from children. The measures of self-orientation were of two kinds: one was a semantic differential and the other the Who-Are-You test. The semantic differential consisted of a list of seven bipolar scales, each scored from one to seven, each of which rated three concepts. The concepts were, "What I really am"; "What I would like to be"; and "How I appear to others." The seven scales were, "useful, busy, effective, free to do things, respected, looking to the future, and satisfied with life." The first three (busy, effective, and useful) can be characterized as involvement, the last three (respected, looking to the future, and satisfied with life) as evaluation. Several different measures of the three concepts could be obtained from the twenty-one scales. One measure, the direct rating, could be used on each of the concepts, evaluation of self, ideal self, and self-presentation, along the seven dimensions. Second, on each of the dimensions, differences could be shown between members of each pair of the three concepts. Thus, for instance, we could determine whether the person felt he was more or less busy than he would like to be. Third, the overall difference between members of each pair of the three concepts could be computed. This was done by the difference formula suggested by Osgood, Suci, and Tannenbaum (1957), which is the square root of the sums of the squared differences of all the seven scales. It can be visualized as a simple geometrical distance in a dimensional space. We shall be concerned here with the difference between the "real self" and "how I appear to others," the reality-appearance difference.

The Who-Are-You test is simply an open-ended rating of the self: "If someone were to ask you, 'Who are you?' what would you say?" The respondent himself can fill in all the dimensions which he likes and which seem to be important. The answers were scored in three main categories: (a) answers referring to personal background, family situation, ancestry, ethnic or religious identification, i.e., ascribed characteristics: (b) personal characteristics such as character, ambition, occupation: and (c) personal values such as beliefs, opinions, and attitudes. These three categories represent Riesman's classifications into other directed, inner directed, and traditionally oriented character structure (Riesman, Denny, and Glazer, 1950; Back and Paramesh, 1969). Each respondent gave three answers to the question, so that when the answers were combined, each of the three vari-

ances (personal background, personal characteristics, and personal values) had a possible range from zero to three. If a person gave three personal background items, he would be given a score of three on this variable and zero on the other two. If he listed two personal characteristics and one value, he would be scored two on characteristics and one on value. Here again, we can use the scores for each question as a basis of self-determination of the relevant variables of the self.

We have thus two ways of measuring the self-concept: (a) a qualitative self-anchored way, which lets the respondent choose the variables which he finds critical: (b) a measure based on a predetermied set of scales, which makes mathematical transformation possible.

Results

Real Self versus Apparent Self

Let us look at one of the crises of the self-image occurring in aging-the contrast between what a person really feels about himself and the image that he presents to others. This is expressed by the difference between the semantic differential measures of the two concepts, the real self and the apparent self. An analysis of the distance measure between the two concepts, classified by sex and five-year age categories, shows significant differences by age, especially among women, although not in a monotonically increasing fashion. For women, the largest divergence between self and appearance of self occurs in the two oldest groups (60 to 64 and 65 and over), but the next is the youngest group (45 to 49), followed by the other groups (50 to 54 and 55 to 59). Among men, the sequence is almost regular, increasing with age, the only exception being a large difference in the 50 to 54 group. This sequence would indicate that the discrepancy is not due to an intrinsic effect of aging but to events in the life cycle which change the position of a person in the world.

There are two ways to learn more about the meaning of this changing reality-appearance contrast. One is by investigating the components and qualities which make up the self-image: the other is by comparing the reactions to the different crises of the later years. First, let us examine the semantic differential itself to determine which scales contribute most to the reality-appearance difference. Dividing the scales into three groups, involvement (busy, useful, and effective), evaluation (looks to future, satisfied, and respected), and freedom to do things (Guptill, 1969), only the involvement factor distinguished significantly between age groups, but this was affected by the sex of the respondent: the differences of the men were almost in the same order as the total difference; among women the youngest group (45 to 49) had the greatest difference, then the oldest, and then the intermediate groups. Overall, the interaction between sex and age was statistically significant.

Going beyond the semantic differential itself, we can find some clues to the meaning of the reality-appearance difference in the answers to the Who-Are-You question. The strongest difference is revealed in the personal background directed answers. When asked who they are, women, in general, gave more answers relating to personal background, but this *declines* with age; men give fewer answers regarding personal background and their scores remain constant over the years; thus there is a great difference between the sexes in

the youngest age group but none in the oldest group. Among women, therefore, personal background characteristics, which include family relations, become of diminishing importance with age.

Children Leaving Home

Because of the sex differences in the influence of age on the reality-appearance discrepancy, we shall investigate the particular crises which may affect the sexes differently using the semantic differential. Let us examine first the departure from home of the children. Controlling for this variable we find age differences only in men. In other words, the age difference in the discrepancy of the real self and appearance to others is due mainly to the departure of the children among women, but not among men.

The influence of age on the reality-appearance difference among women is thus partially accounted for by the fact that older women have fewer children living at home. Child separation, however, does not affect age changes in the interpretation of the meaning of the self. In response to the Who-Are-You question, the shift among women from personal background to achieved traits becomes stronger if controlled for child separation. Among men there is little change in the Who-Are-You question, while among women there is a sharp decline of personal background items by age and an increase in value items with age in each group, classified according to child separation.

Table 23.1. Distance between apparent and real self (semantic differential) by sex and age

	Under 50	50–54	55–59	60–64	65 and Over
Male	2.38	2.88	2.46	3.02	3.25
Female	2.64	2.59	2.49	2.69	2.92

Sex: $F(1,489) = 1.09$ n.s.
Age: $F(4,489) = 3.32$ p<.05.
Sex×age: $F(4,489) = .94$ n.s.

Table 23.2. Difference of three scale clusters between apparent and real self by sex and age

| | Involvement | | Evaluation | | Freedom | |
	Male	Female	Male	Female	Male	Female
Under 50	.11	.19	.30	.01	−.09	−.16
50–54	.28	.02	.12	.11	.19	−.43
55–59	.25	.26	.33	.22	.32	−.04
60–64	.36	.10	.35	.15	−.11	−.04
65 and over	.09	.32	.32	.35	.32	−.24

Sex $F(1,492)$	.39 n.s.		3.82 p<.10	4.77 p<.05
Age $F(4,492)$	.42 n.s.		1.73 n.s.	.55 n.s.
Sex×age $F(4,492)$	2.25 p<.10		1.08 n.s.	.89 n.s.

Table 23.3. Who-Are-You score by age and sex

| | Personal Background | | Personal Characteristics | | Values | |
	Male	Female	Male	Female	Male	Female
Under 50	.43	1.35	1.09	1.00	1.00	.23
50–54	.53	.98	1.16	1.27	.86	.61
55–59	.57	.81	1.02	1.00	.73	.71
60–64	.38	.67	1.40	1.20	.78	.70
65 and over	.39	.41	1.27	1.13	.85	.94

Sex $F(1,492)$	24.82 p<.01	.56 n.s.	6.67 p<.05
Age $F(4,492)$	5.00 p<.01	1.55 n.s.	1.29 n.s.
Sex×age $F(4,492)$	3.81 p<.01	.37 n.s.	3.60 p<.01

Table 23.4. Distance between apparent and real self by sex, age, and children's residence (parents only)

| | Male | | Female | |
	Children not at home	Children at home	Children not at home	Children at home
Under 50	1.92	2.43	2.83	2.64
50–54	2.45	3.21	2.40	2.67
55–59	2.33	2.37	2.29	2.43
60–64	2.95	3.33	2.66	2.18
65 and over	3.30	3.54	2.96	2.57

Sex $F(1,402)=1.97$ n.s.
Age $F(4,402)=2.68$ p<.05
Child residence $F(1,402)=.64$ n.s.
Sex×age $F(4,402)=2.20$ p<.10
Other interactions not significant

Table 23.5. Who-Are-You score by age, sex, and children's residence (parents only)

A. PERSONAL BACKGROUND

| | Male | | Female | |
	Children not at home	Children at home	Children not at home	Children at home
Under 50	.38	.46	1.13	1.63
50–54	.50	.60	1.10	1.11
55–59	:53	.75	.81	.73
60–64	.35	.63	.75	1.29
65 and over	.43	.45	.51	0.00

Sex F(1,404)=14.88 p<.01
Age F(4,404)=3.41 p<.01
Child residence F(1,404)=1.26 n.s.
Sex×age F(4,404)=3.61 <.01
Other interactions not significant

B. PERSONAL CHARACTERISTICS

Under 50	1.00	1.08	1.50	.68
50–54	1.36	1.08	1.10	1.32
55–59	1.11	1.06	.88	1.36
60–64	1.32	1.25	1.21	.57
65 and over	1.28	1.36	1.13	.80

No significant F ratios

C. VALUES

Under 50	1.23	.92	.13	.21
50–54	.93	.72	.70	.37
55–59	.74	.94	.75	.73
60–64	.91	.38	.71	.86
65 and over	.85	.73	.85	2.00

Sex F(1,404)=1.04 n.s.
Age F(4,404)=2.71 p<.05
Child residence F(1,404)=0.00 n.s.
Sex×age F(4,404)=6.05 p<.01
Sex×child F(1,404)=3.84 p~.05
Other interactions not significant

Table 23.6. Distance between apparent and real self by age, sex, and work status

| | Male | | Female | |
	Working	Not working	Working	Not working
Under 60	2.55	2.71	2.62	2.45
60–65	2.91	3.14	2.49	2.69
Over 65	3.23	3.56	1.92	3.29

Sex F(1,487)=7.00 p<.01
Age F(2,487)=2.07 n.s.
Work F(1,487)=4.51 p<.05
Age×work F(2,487)=2.35 p<.10
Other interactions not significant

Table 23.7. Who-Are-You score by age, sex, and work status

A. PERSONAL BACKGROUND

| | Male | | Female | |
	Working	Not working	Working	Not working
Under 60	.54	2.00	.88	1.20
60–65	.36	.20	.59	.67
Over 65	.59	.30	.42	.40

Sex $F(1,490)=11.63$ $p<.01$
Age $F(2,490)=1.91$ n.s.
Work $F(1,490)=.92$ n.s.
Sex×age $F(2,490)=4.92$ $p<.01$
Sex×work $F(1,490)=4.74$ $p<.05$
Other interactions not significant

B. PERSONAL CHARACTERISTICS

| | Male | | Female | |
	Working	Not working	Working	Not working
Under 60	1.07	1.57	1.26	.84
60–65	1.41	1.60	1.47	.97
Over 65	1.07	1.30	1.33	1.06

Sex $F(1,490)=2.33$ n.s.
Age $F(2,490)=.95$ n.s.
Work $F(1,490)=.13$ n.s.
Sex×work $F(1,490)=8.33$ $p<.01$
Other interactions not significant

C. VALUES

| | Male | | Female | |
	Working	Not working	Working	Not working
Under 60	.82	.71	.56	.50
60–65	.82	.70	.76	.93
Over 65	1.03	.79	.92	.90

No significant F ratios

Table 23.8. Distance between apparent and real self by age, sex, and children's residence (working only, parents only)

| | Male | | Female | |
	Children not at home	Children at home	Children not at home	Children at home
Under 50	1.92	2.43	3.24	2.62
50–54	2.45	3.21	2.29	2.49
55–59	2.30	2.37	2.62	2.61
60–64	3.03	3.16	2.13	1.38
65 and over	2.77	4.41	1.94	1.71

Sex $F(1,265)=6.76$ $p<.01$
Age $F(4,265)=.26$ n.s.
Child residence $F(1,265)=.78$ n.s.
Sex×age $F(4,265)=5.99$ $p<.01$
Sex×child $F(1,265)=5.43$ $p<.05$
Other interactions not significant

Retirement

By contrast, work and retirement affect both sexes in the same manner. Controlling for work status, we find no more differences according to age, but definite differences by sex and work status: men and non-workers claim the bigger difference between appearance and reality of the self-image. Looking at the Who-Are-You question we can see the traits that may account for these differences. Among the retirees, women mention significantly more personal background data and men more individual characteristics. Among the workers there is no difference in amount of personal background data, but women mention more individual characteristics.

In order to assess the relative importance of separation from work and child, we have to control simultaneously for work and family status. Because there are too few male non-workers in the younger ages, we cannot control for both in the whole age range. Instead we can measure the influence of child separation in the working respondents in this group: for men the reality-appearance discrepancy increases with age, and for women it declines; further, for men the discrepancy increases with child separation, and for women it declines. There are no significant differences according to the Who-Are-You question.

Discussion

The data presented here have shown the values and limitations of the two measures which we have employed in studying the changes in self-concept brought on by old age. The most consistent result has been the sex differences in the answers to the Who-Are-You question. Women are more likely to answer in terms of personal background, such as family relations and demographic characteristics, but this emphasis declines after the fifties such that in the last age groups, 60 to 64 and 65 and over,

there is no difference between the sexes in this regard. Correspondingly, personally achieved positions and characteristics, as well as personal values, become more important for women with age. This development remains constant even if controlled for varying experiences, such as retirement and child separation during aging.

Thus, neither retirement nor separation from children affects the content of the self-image as much as the aging process alone. However, the discrepancy between reality and appearance of the self is influenced by these factors. Both crises are important; but separation from children accounts only for the effect on women, while retirement or non-working affects both sexes. In general, men have a greater problem with the discrepancy between who they feel they are and what they imagine other people think about them. This is also true with non-working members of both sexes.

During the aging process, women tend to shift their self-image from their relationship to others, the social characteristics, to their own abilities and feelings; the separation from children can be viewed in this way. Freed from family obligations, they may feel that they can now much more easily be accepted for what they are. Men, on the other hand, are involved in the work role more personally, and difficulties with this role through aging may make life even more difficult for them. Separation from children may, therefore, aggravate this discrepancy, making them more dependent on the work role in which they have difficulty in presenting the right image. Hence the increase in self-image discrepancy in working men separated from children, while for women the discrepancy decreases with age and separation from children.

Measures of the self-image that can be administered in a relatively simple manner to a large sample can show some of the more subtle features of the management of crises incumbent on the aged.

References

BACK, K. W., & GERGEN, K. J. Personal orientation and morale of the aging. In J. McKinney & I. Simpson (Eds.), *Social aspects of aging.* Durham, N.C.: Duke University Press, 1966.

BACK, K. W., & GERGEN, K. J. The self through the latter span of life. In C. Gordon & K. J. Gergen (Eds.), *The self in social interaction.* New York: Wiley, 1968.

BACK, K. W., & PARAMESH, C. R. Self-image, information exchange and social character. *International Journal of Psychology*, 1969, *4*, 109–117.

BREHM, M. L., & BACK, K. W. Self image and attitude toward drugs. *Journal of Personality*, 1968, *35*, 299–314.

GUPTILL, C. S. A measure of age identification. *Gerontologist*, 1969, *9* (Summer), 96–102.

KUHN, M. H., & MCPARTLAND, T. S. An empirical investigation of self-attitudes. *American Sociological Review*, 1954, *19*, 68–76.

OSGOOD, C., SUCI, G., & TANNENBAUM, P. *The measurement of meaning.* Urbana, Ill.: University of Illinois Press, 1957.

RIESMAN, D., DENNY, R., & GLAZER, N. *The lonely crowd.* New Haven: Yale University Press, 1950.

RILEY, M. W., & FONER, A. *Aging and society, vol. I: An inventory of research findings.* New York: Russell Sage Foundation, 1968.

24. COPING

MIMI FERLEMANN

The development of human personality always has puzzled and intrigued man. When does an infant become enculturated? How do behavior patterns evolve? What is learned response and what is genetically innate?

More than 20 years ago The Menninger Foundation began to study childhood development, with Dr. Sibylle Escalona and Dr. Mary Leitch as project directors. Their findings triggered four related studies by Foundation staff who were or have since become nationally recognized for their work in this area. Researchers such as Drs. Lois Murphy, Alice Moriarty, Clyde Rousey, Gardner Murphy, Povi Toussieng and Grace Heider began a concentrated investigation of coping patterns in children. Eventually, the five projects merged into a longitudinal study which spanned two

decades and followed about 50 children from infancy to adulthood.

The study was in no way normative. Instead researchers were interested in describing how children develop individual coping styles within their subcultures. Researchers defined coping as the methods individuals use to handle the stresses of life—ways they maximize their resources and compensate for their weaknesses and vulnerabilities.

Most subjects were middle class, relatively stable, responsible, intact families— families with good parents by society's standards. No families were extremely affluent nor were any extremely poor, but were representative of the middle economic group of Topeka families between years 1950 and 1970.

The complexity and individuality of the

human personality are emphasized when one realizes the 20-year study offers no prescription for child-rearing. However, insights into what is likely typical behavior for native white, middle class groups living in cities of similar size and conservative background as that of the sampling are offered.

Dr. Alice Moriarty, senior staff psychologist, became involved with the coping studies almost from their inception. Starting as a research assistant in 1951, she worked on the pre-school and adolescent studies and has written extensively about them. In a recent interview, she talked about some of the coping patterns observed during the studies.

Dr. Moriarty and her colleagues occupied the unique position of watching a generation of children grow from infancy to adulthood—observing development and results of their behavior patterns, becoming intimately knowledgeable about their physiological and psychological responses, but never passing judgment or interfering. They offered advice only on request.

"We had no authority to intervene and we passed no critical judgments," Dr. Moriarty said. "Of course there were times when we secretly thought the child was going down the drain but most of the children made out exceptionally well."

Although hesitant to state absolute conclusions, researchers do agree that coping involves many factors. Parental acceptance, family stability, consistency of care and discipline, physiological and psychological intactness and innate personality differences are only some of the variables. Attempting to categorize and present guidelines for such intangibles is an impossible task. Prescriptions to guarantee a child will develop the strengths needed for coping do not exist. However, certain patterns seem to be important to develop the independence and internal strengths which help individuals handle everyday anxieties and stresses.

"It's hard to say just when coping patterns are established," Dr. Moriarty said,

"but in some three-year-olds we have seen consistent coping styles which have continued over time. In some children an astute observer can determine these patterns in early infancy. Actually, everyone has a complex of personality traits which tend to persist. For example, some children are very active—they want to explore and always are getting into things. Others tend to withdraw from anything which is exciting or upsetting. This activity-passivity continuum can be detected early and continues over time. The active, exploring babies become active, exploring adolescents, and the passive babies tend to retain their passivity. I believe a lot of this is inborn."

Dr. Moriarty added that although active children seem to be better copers in most situations, they also become involved in many more stressful situations than the more docile children. However, passivity may be an excellent coping mechanism for some people.

The ability to sublimate—to find other outlets—is a characteristic of better copers, Dr. Moriarty said. Although this ability has some base in innate constitutional factors, it appears that mothers can help their children to develop the trait. For example, children whose mothers were able to show them acceptable alternatives became better copers.

A mother might say, "Johnny, you may not hit your sister but you may hit your punching bag." Or she might tell him, "You can't jump on the sofa but you can jump on the lawn."

When introduced early, this approach becomes internalized and children begin to determine alternatives themselves—"I can't do this but I can do that." Dr. Moriarty said children who learn to do this are able to handle stress because they aren't stymied when they hit barriers.

Still the tolerance level for frustration differs in individuals. Whether frustration level is innate or learned or both is difficult to determine. "One can't just state a formula and say this is how it comes about," Dr. Moriarty said. "Recognizing limitations and interests is an important part of developing tolerance for frustration. A child must learn he can't do everything, and he must learn there is a sequence to learning anything. Before he can walk he must first learn to sit up, then crawl, and then stand. Learning to cope is much the same process.

"There are so many influences—the other family members, peers, church, schools, the community, plus all that the child brings with him through heredity. Most parents do the best they can but they have just so much control."

Developing psychological strengths necessary for coping is influenced by many factors. One of the most important is physiological intactness. An individual's health can determine how he reacts to situations. For example, if tlurough accident or illness a child acquires some deviancy in physical functioning, he often will be handicapped in the psychological growth process as well. He is likely to have slower speech, slower locomotion, more limited exploration of his immediate world, poor ability for abstract thinking and inadequate acquisition of academic skills. In addition he will be frustrated in developing emotional-social relationships.

Early illness sometimes can cause serious emotional restrictions and family disruption. The anxiety, doubts and fears illness generates in both children and parents contributes to life styles which can interfere with development and cause extreme pressure within the family structure. But the toll illness takes is not always immediately obvious.

For example, one young girl almost died from a severe respiratory illness when she was six weeks old. Although she fully recovered and throughout her life was in good health, she was so controlled and protected by her anxious mother that she never acquired her own individuality. She became an obedient, conforming child, one who never questioned decisions or de-

mands. Outwardly she was physically attractive, intelligent and socially and academically successful. Internally she never was able to utilize her own resources for creativity, initiative and responsibility—nor was she capable of developing close personal relationships.

Another girl was paralyzed at an early age. She, too, recovered but doctors predicted she would never walk. Through her own persistence and her mother's determination, along with constant care and rehabilitative procedures, she not only walked but also learned to dance and to ride a bicycle. Ultimately she graduated from college and married. The toll here was in a self-centered preoccupation with her physical health and in the intense hostility and resentment engendered in her younger brother, who became marginally delinquent.

Family stability also influences the ability to cope but, Dr. Moriarty pointed out, family stability does not mean absence of problems. Although families in the studies generally were physically and emotionally healthy they did experience intermittent problems. Several members of the family groups at some time or other sought psychiatric help for difficulties ranging from depression, marital conflict, and alcoholism to poor school achievement and minor social adjustment problems. But despite occasional upheavals such as these, most parents managed to rear responsible, thoughtful children who were able to assume their independence without serious adolescent rebellion. Problems are a part of living, and family stability means facing these problems and constructively dealing with them.

Dr. Moriarty said serious delinquency occurred in only one case. From birth one boy was subjected to such inconsistent care and control that he developed no sense of right or wrong. With a mother who was seriously neurotic, preoccupied with real or imaginary ills, and who was totally unable to adhere to any structure or plan, the boy was unable to direct his behavior and could not develop social coping skills.

Subjected to grossly inconsistent discipline, once given away to the church pastor, and pitted against his father, the confused child manifested difficulties in each developmental stage; weaning, toilet training, speech, school achievement and social relationships. Somewhat passive and always a loner, he began stealing from school in the early grades, progressed to drinking, spent time in a mental hospital and finally was sent to prison for committing a felony. All his life he suffered from "grossly inadequate mothering" which for him meant erratic and inconsistent care and discipline, rejection, and lack of example or demand for stable and independent functioning. Without a model of responsibility, he failed to develop responsibility for his own acts.

Unfortunately, coping ability does not increase with the number of problems one must face. Extremes in adversity can be as detrimental to developing coping mechanisms as extremes in protectiveness. One should neither be over-exposed nor over-insulated. Presumably there is a middle ground which promotes learning to face stress by mobilizing internal resources, but which is not so severe that the stresses become overwhelming.

Here again the mother plays a vital role —she must know her child to be able to give him both the independence and the reassurance he needs for healthy development. Dr. Moriarty said the best relationships in the study existed between mothers and children who were compatible in outlook and approach. This compatibility proved to be even more important than sensitivity.

Dr. Grace M. Heider, in her writings concerning the study, cites two examples of the effects of this compatibility or viability.

One mother, who was not especially sensitive, handled her infant son very roughly. He was a sturdy baby and fully satisfied his mother's wish for a boy. This mother took great pleasure in treating her son in an off-hand casual manner—giving him far less support than most mothers would give babies that age. The boy thrived on this approach. They understood each other and their relationship was solid and satisfying to both.

On the other hand, another mother did not have the same satisfying relationship with her child. This mother fit the stereotype of the ideal mother—tender, gentle, sensitive, aware. But her energetic, noisy son demanded more stimulation and rougher treatment than his mother could comfortably give. Although fully aware of her child's needs, this mother had a difficult time meeting them, and the relationship was literally a mismatch.

Dr. Moriarty said this viability between mother and child is very important for positive child development. An independent child will have a difficult time with an over-protective mother. A shy, more inhibited youngster will suffer if pushed from the nest too soon by a mother who demands more independence than the child is ready to assume.

Not much can be done about the mismatch, but if the mother is aware of it she can minimize the effects.

Time takes care of some of these difficulties since children go through various phases in which their needs fluctuate between dependence and independence. A mother who is ideally matched with her child at one stage may not be so at another, and although such conflict affects the child as he matures, it is a very normal part of the growth process.

Just how important adequate mothering can be to a child's development was stressed in Dr. Moriarty's work with ghetto children. Although parental inadequacy is not limited to low socio-economic levels, poverty, with its associated apathy, depression, and disorganization in living styles, clearly interferes with optimal social and emotional development. Dr. Moriarty notes that learning problems, poor verbal communications, difficulties in concept formation, impulsivity, low self-esteem and poor interpersonal relationships are ominously present in many ghetto children.

"Ghetto mothers are hard-pressed for time and money to devote to their children," she said. "Studies show that in lower socio-economic classes, mothers tend to be more arbitrary, coercive, restrictive and punitive in discipline, less willing to explain or to see cause-effect relationships and more concerned with keeping children out of trouble than in offering constructive outlets for children's normal curiosity and aggressive tendencies."

Lower-class mothers also marry earlier and often are extremely young when they bear children; therefore they are more likely to be emotionally immature and unready to accept the restrictions and responsibilities of parenthood.

However, poverty and racial bias are not necessarily causes of inadequate mothering, Dr. Moriarty stressed. Poor parenting is seen on all socio-economic levels, but these factors do add stress to an already anxiety-laden life situation.

Dr. Moriarty said that if one general statement can be made from her observation of ghetto and middle-class children, it is that middle-class children develop a wider range of coping mechanisms.

New situations confronting any child can be gratifying, challenging, threatening or frustrating. When a child approaches an immediately gratifying new situation, he doesn't need to cope. For example, tasting an agreeable new food does not involve coping.

However, if a situation involves some threat, the child's reaction may be an attempt to reduce the threat, postpone it, bypass it, create distance between himself and the threat, divide his attention or ignore it.

For example, different children in the pre-school studies faced difficult intellectual tasks with varying approaches. Some postponed the threat—"I can't do that right now." Some diverted it—"Do you want me to do something I *can* do?" Some children even tried to eliminate the task by breaking the toys, hiding the games or crumbling and tearing the paper they were instructed to work with.

Which mechanisms a child chooses depends on a combination of his basic genetic make-up, his learned responses, his capacity and ability to integrate knowledge, his own self-image and the degree of support he draws from his physical, social and emotional environment.

Volumes of data have been gathered through the coping studies, and although researchers now know more than ever about behavior and development, still they readily admit relatively little is known—in any precise, scientific and viable way—about how multiple forces interact to shape an individual's human personality.

Dr. Moriarty said researchers repeatedly were impressed with one finding—many behavior patterns of the children studied appeared to be innate or constitutional. It is evident that many personality characteristics already are present at birth, she said. Precisely which characteristics are innate and how they develop forms the base of a new study co-directed by Dr. Moriarty and Dr. Joseph Kovach, noted Foundation ethologist.

The 20 years Dr. Moriarty and her colleagues have spent watching children cope with the physiological, sociological psychological and environmental complexities of life, augmented by Dr. Kovach's ethological studies, have provided some of the basic knoweldge necessary for researchers to begin probing into the mechanism by which man's genetic heritage translates itself into lifetime behavioral styles.

25. ADULT CHILDREN AND THEIR AGING PARENTS

BERTHA G. SIMOS

The care of the aged is rapidly becoming a leading social issue. One of the most confusing areas in this growing field is the relationship of adult children to aging parents(1). Part of the confusion arises from myths concerning parent-child relationships. One of the most persistent myths is the belief that the nuclear family's increasing isolation has caused a lessening of filial responsibility in the past few generations. There is reason to question such a conclusion.

In fact, the aging of an individual eventually results in a crisis for every family. To ascertain the impact of parental aging on adult children, the author conducted a study whose goal was to identify the kinds of problems the children encountered, their feelings about them, ways of coping with them, the impact of memories of childhood on present attitudes toward aging parents, and the influence of the parents' aging patterns on the children's hopes and fears for their own later years. The study involved a sample of fifty adult children (thirty-six females and fourteen males) reporting on sixty aging parents (eighteen fathers and forty-two mothers) who lived in the greater Los Angeles area(2). The fifty children, selected from the clientele of a Jewish family agency, had requested information about or service for a problem concerning an aging parent or parents who lived in the same community. Data were obtained from personal interviews during the spring of 1968; these interviews had been conducted with the use of a semistructured interview schedule.

The parents ranged in age from 60 to 94. They had migrated to the United States from an Eastern European *shtetl* as children or adolescents some time prior to World War I. Their education had been mainly limited to that provided by a religious school. A majority of the fathers had been semiskilled laborers or owners of small businesses, and they had settled with their families in an eastern or midwestern city before moving to the West Coast.

By contrast, most of their children (who ranged in age from 36 to 68 years) had been born in the United States. They tended to be either professionals or businessmen. The difference in economic status, educational achievement, and social class was marked between the generations.

This article deals with only one aspect of the study, namely, the range of physical, psychological, family, social, financial, and housing problems encountered by the children in connection with their aging parents. Although the data relate to a specific group—American Jews—the enormity of the problems encountered can be generalized to all families. Thus at the end of the article the author discusses the implications of her findings for social work with the aged.

Physical Problems

Almost all the parents had physical problems. A number of these conditions could be considered serious, either because of the threat to life itself (e.g., cardiovascular disease) or because of a disability resulting from such conditions as glaucoma or severe hearing loss.

Problems of more than ten years' duration included sensory disorders, sleep complaints, and cardiovascular disease. Cardiovascular diseases were most frequently reported, followed by conditions attributed to "general physical decline." The mothers tended to have more sleep problems and more major long-standing problems than the fathers. Many of the childern had responsibility for two aging parents, both of whom had serious physical disabilities.

When a parent was rejected by his spouse because his infirmities increased, he experienced psychic pain in addition to physical pain. This was especially apt to happen in a late second marriage. The children also found it difficult to deal with parents who needed but refused protective services, especially when they could not go against their parents' wishes. In these instances children struggled with a variety of compromises—a live-in companion, taking turns caring for the daily needs of parent, having the parent live alternately with one child or another—in an attempt both to protect the parent and to permit him to retain some decision-making power.

The study clearly showed that the aging process itself was responsible for the physical problems of the parents. And these physical problems were so intense that, when combined with their psychological effects, the children had little time to deal with any other problems they might have had with their parents. For example, the children had to find adequate medical care, transport their parents to medical appointments, and make sure that prescriptions were filled and medication taken. In addition, they had to transport physically ailing parents to social and recreational activities, find suitable living facilities for them, provide general protective services, and give them physical and emotional support.

Psychological Problems

The parents' general unhappiness was the most frequent and depression the second-most frequent cause of discomfort to the children. Both conditions seemed to have developed with age. Since the children were not trained to distinguish between unhappiness and depression, the author made no attempt to validate the children's interpretations. What was significant was the parents' general feeling of sadness and its impact on the children.

Thirty-nine children considered the parents' stubbornness a major problem and did not think it was related to the aging process; they saw it as a long-standing chronic trait, especially of the mothers. Emotional coldness was reported as a chronic long-standing trait of fathers by one-fifth of the children. More than half the children reported such psychological problems as complaints against others, fears and anxieties, loneliness, complaints about physical symptoms, and feelings of hopelessness.

Although grief and mourning by parents were mentioned as psychological problems in slightly over one-fourth of the cases, the author believes that many other instances were overlooked by the children, primarily because the dynamics of loss are inadequately understood in our society. Parental mourning was recognized primarily when the loss had to do with a significant other, such as a spouse or child. When grief was recognized, it was usually responded to with sympathy. It was the rare individual, however, who could realize that the parent might also grieve over the death of a pet; the loss of a job, a social role, self-esteem, independence, a lifetime home, or the right to drive an automobile; or the failure of bodily functions or sensory acuity.

If the loss itself went unnoticed, surely the parental reaction to the loss would also tend to go unrecognized or be misunderstood. Yet many of the problems attributed to the parents, masked under the general categories of depression, repeated physical complaints, stubbornness, being demanding, and criticalness, are among the common reactions of the aged to loss(3). Isolation and denial as defenses against the pain of loss were seen by chlidren as lack of feeling on the part of the parent. Feelings of helplessness and despair, normal reactions to loss, were experienced as burdensome parental traits. A desperate attempt to hold on to remaining possessions or lifestyles was seen as stubbornness. Often the losses of a lifetime were merged in the grieving process of a mentally impaired parent. One aged mother might grieve for the baby she lost in infancy, another for the sister who died many years previously, another for the husband dead for a quarter of a century, and still another might grieve and keep forgetting for whom she was grieving. All of these were dismissed by children as evidence of parental "senility."

Parents were thus subjected to additional stress—the inability to work through grief experiences appropriately at a stage of life when losses are multiple and cumulative. With feelings of loneliness and isolation thus increased, parents were left vulnerable to the pathological potentials now becoming more and more recognized in the literature as consequences of unresolved grief(4).

All the parents in the study had psychological problems. As was mentioned in relation to physical problems, the parents' psychological problems alone were extensive enough to keep the children fully involved. Involvement could take the form of attempting to console or comfort the parent, struggling with negative feelings aroused by the parent, serving as peacemaker with caretaking personnel and others, dealing with family disruptions set off by the parent or in rare cases attempting to limit the parent's insatiable demands.

Family Relationships

One-fourth of the children reported cordial, if not warm relationships, with no serious rifts or family alignments. However, three-fourths of the children reported a variety of familial problems resulting from parental aging. Many difficulties surfaced when a parent joined the household of an adult child, particularly if the parent was overly dependent and intrusive and allowed the adult child no privacy.

Friction also occurred when the dependency of a parent, formerly masked by a long marriage with a compatible spouse who met such needs, was transferred to adult children unprepared to play a sim-

ilar role. The now-dependent parent who still persisted in advising, admonishing, and directing the very adult child on whom he might be dependent was particularly incongruous. The chronic complainer, the easily "hurt" parent, the one who gave in order to control, the one who stoically refused to give up old patterns of independent functioning despite resulting dangers or increased demands on children, or the parent caught in an unhappy second marriage—all served to stir up family conflict, especially when children reacted to the surface behavior without an understanding of the underlying dynamics.

The children usually attributed longstanding intergenerational or interpersonal problems to the personality structure of the parent himself. One example was the suspicious parent, who had caused family friction and rivalries over the years. Another was the parent who had fought the children's marriage and was now no more reconciled to their independence or marital choice than in the past. Resentment was expressed toward the parent who over the years had used the technique of "divide and conquer" to stir up rivalries among siblings or between children and the other parent in order to emerge as the understanding and sympathetic one. When family problems had begun with the parents' marriage itself, children were all too aware of parents "not being suited to one another" or "being neurotically suited to each other despite the misery it caused us during our childhood and the resulting impact on our adult lives."

A common theme in this cultural group, in which women have traditionally taken second place, was the rivalry between the sexes—e.g., the women's depreciation of men and the men's resentment of domineering women. Family problems were also found when parents were cold and ungiving or were openly hostile. The attacking, hostile parent, oblivious to his own provocation of others but nursing psychic wounds of being "hurt" by others, did not fool the adult children, even though they could not cut through this behavior.

As a rule, relationship problems did not improve with age, but tended to become more entrenched. With the added stresses of age, old defensive patterns were mobilized to meet new strains and, although surface behavior might now be different, the basic underlying pathology remained.

There were rare instances in which long-standing problems did improve with age. This occurred when the adult child had undergone psychotherapy or had otherwise increased his understanding of the parent. Some children were able to achieve a sense of competence in relation to their parents only after the parents'- strength began to fail.

Social Problems

This area disclosed surprising discrepancies between the children's perceptions and reality. Frequently children admitted being unable to distinguish between their parents' actual social problems and what they thought should be social problems. It was clear that the children felt their parents would be happier if they were socially involved and active, even if the parents did not express a need to be so.

Over one-half of the parents were seen as having social problems related to aging itself, while slightly over one-fourth were judged to have had long-standing social problems. In seven cases the parents were too ill for the question to apply. The parents' distress, whether explicit by direct demands or implicit by complaints of loneliness, angered the children more than any other problem presented.

Some children perceived social interaction with physically and mentally impaired parents as a give-and-take interaction. Yet for many parents this type of interaction had ceased, both with friends and with their children. Some children were uncomfortable even about visiting their parents and complained that "there is nothing to

do; we just sit there." It was incomprehensible to them that they might be supporting their parents emotionally, merely by their presence and interest. Others, however, were able to take pleasure in taking a walk with a parent, even though unable to converse with him.

Another major social problem was the parents' reluctance to socialize because of limited physical mobility owing to strokes, poor vision, arthritis, and so forth. Some parents were ashamed to participate in social activities because they had gnarled fingers, tremors, or even a history of heart attacks, all of which represented psychic blows to their body image and self-esteem.

Social problems were manifested in different ways. Some parents had difficulty in making new contacts. Among these were people who had spent their early years working long hours, their social life limited to family interaction. They had not developed social skills that could now be of help to them. Others had never developed a range of interests on which they could draw. A number of parents lacked a general sense of social purpose. Some refused to participate even when given the opportunity, a situation most confusing to their children. Others would respond to overtures from others but could not initiate social contacts, e.g., mothers who depended on their daughters to include them in their own social lives. Children were often puzzled by such parents, who might have been outgoing and sociable when they were younger. And long-standing social problems could certainly reflect characterological disturbances manifested by extreme hostility, fault-finding, or even psychosis.

Parents who exhibited a pattern of well-matched neurotic interaction with their spouses presented another problem. In some instances this symbiotic relationship was so well entrenched and smooth running that a casual observer did not think to analyze the part each partner played in the unified picture presented for public view. Only with the death of the more sociable partner did the plight of the more passive or withdrawn parent become apparent. His center of social gravity was now gone. Such a parent might attempt to manipulate his child into taking the role of the deceased partner and thereby fulfill his needs through this new relationship. Others became depressed and seemed to lose interest and initiative; they moved like automatons to plans made for them by their children and showed no interest in a life of their own.

Lack of Facilities

The lack of recreational facilities in many parts of the greater Los Angeles area and the inadequate public transpotration system contributed to the social isolation of many parents. The child who encouraged his parent to move into his suburban home could inadvertently subject the parent to social isolation in an area populated primarily by young families. The lack of transportation complicated many aspects of the parents lives—shopping, medical care, and recreation—and generally hampered their freedom.

Not all parents had social problems. Some functioned adequately on a social level and made good use of facilities provided for senior citizens or were content with a limited social life. Further, few children were aware that the social needs of the elderly might differ from those of the middle aged. They thought their parents were disengaged only when the parents were severly impaired, either mentally or physically.

Thus it was in the area of social problems of parents that the children were most subjective and tended to see their parents in terms of themselves. They could accept the idea of physical and psychological changes with age. They were unable, however, to grasp that social needs might also change and felt an urge to force parents into inappropriate social molds.

Financial Problems

Financial problems must be viewed not only in the context of current realities but also in terms of future expectations of need. Although twenty families indicated there were no financial problems, this response did not take into account the fact that parents might be managing financially because they could still remain in their own homes. If one parent became ill and needed placement, there might well be financial distress to care for two parents living separately.

In ten families the parents had already been forced to seek financial assistance through the state old age assistance program. The study did not explore the extent of financial distress prior to such action, but all the fathers had been financially independent during their working years. Nor did the lack of complaints about finances in any way imply that children were satisfied with the quality of medical, psychiatric, or nursing care parents were able to purchase. When medical expenses had exhausted parental savings, children were bitter about being deprived of what they considered to be their rightful inheritance from parents. Even when parents were relatively healthy, the dread of future illness with the accompanying medical expenses hovered in the minds of the children as a contnigency with which they could not deal because prediction or preparation was impossible. The children frequently remarked that saving for one's old age was useless in our society.

Twenty families did report current or anticipated financial difficulties. A typical problem involved moving a parent from an expensive or moderate-priced facility to one that would accept the state old age assistance. Such a shift could seriously affect the parent's life, although the children were unaware of this potential danger. The children did not recognize the damage that could be inflicted on a father's self-esteem by the depletion of financial reserves when his only hold on reality was his pride that "the money is still holding out." The already confused parent could become further disoriented by the loss of familiar surroundings and caretakers.

Most children did not think their parents were responsible for their financial plight. For the most part, they viewed their parents as having been hard working, highly motivated, and upwardly striving during their working lives. They blamed the "system" for making it financially prohibitive to care for the elderly and believed it was society's responsibility to support their parents as payment for past productivity.

However, the children did express anger at those parents who either had money and refused to spend it or who refused to apply for financial aid because of a "false" sense of pride or independence. They did not attribute their parents' refusal to spend or accept money to the hardships experienced in early years. Having reached maturity in the affluent years after World War II, the children were unable to identify with their parents' early deprivation in the Eastern European *shtetl*, their experience as immigrants, or the devastating impact of the depression of the 1930s, which occurred when the parents were just getting started in the new land(5).

The children did not feel guilty about their parents' financial problems as they did about psychological problems such as unhappiness or depression or of social problems such as loneliness. The children believed their primary financial obligation was to their nuclear family and then to their married children and grandchildren. Moreover, those with high incomes did not always provide for their parents. Whereas a family of moderate income might sacrifice material comforts or a vacation to pay for a parent's care, a wealthy woman might be reluctant to ask her husband to provide for her mother in a residential facility.

The parents' sources of current income varied. No one was financially dependent on social security alone. Many had been independent small shopkeepers and thus had not been included in social security until long after the program had been established. Workers who were covered in the early years had accumulated benefits when wages were low, so that the present grant level was hardly adequate. Social security payments were supplemented by present earnings and investments or savings, including pensions, state old age assistance, and/or contributions from children. Subsidization by children could be through joint living arrangements, direct monetary contributions, or services.

Housing Problems

Housing problems were found in all but five cases. Most children were reconciled to the inevitabilily of one or more housing changes as the parent advanced in age and his need for comprehensive medical and nursing care increased.

Housing problems occurred from a variety of causes. These included the breaking up of the home following the death of one of the spouses, other changes in family constellation, increasing physical and/or mental disability of parents, and financial pressures. Relatively few parents lived with children even as an intermediate step from independent living to community living. The reasons given were lack of space, fear of family dissension, lack of adequate supervision for the parent, and need for nursing care, which a congregate facility might better provide. Frequent housing changes seemed to be the result of the children's attempt to please parents who were dissatisfied with one apartment or caretaking facility after another because of paranoid tendencies.

The distress of parents who had to be separated when their physical and/or mental conditions became too divergent was also painful for the children. The healthy parent might react with grief and loss to such separation but understand the need for it. When both parents were disoriented, the separation caused further confusion and helplessness, which the child was powerless to alleviate.

Some parents had to be separated after entering a residential facility because the bickering and fighting that had characterized their marital relationship could not be tolerated by the other residents. The mutuality of the neurotic interaction became all too apparent when such a couple was separated: it was not uncommon for one or both of the partners to become depressed.

Implications for Practice

The problems described in this paper fall into three major categories: failing health of the parents and the resulting need for community resources, problems around loss, and long-standing interpersonal problems. The social work practitioner must take responsibility in all these areas. It is only too obvious that social responsibility for the steadily increasing elderly population has failed to keep pace with the demands for services of all kinds. The practitioner needs to see himself, in the front lines of practice, as one who documents unmet needs: he has the obligation to direct policy-makers and planning bodies and goad them into developing appropriate and much-needed services of all kinds.

With the exception of crisis intervention theory and practice, the concept of loss has not been dealt with adequately by the helping professions. A hopeful note is the mounting literature during the past few years on death and dying. More emphasis needs to be placed on helping practitioners deal with both normal and abnormal grief reactions and to understand and work with the dynamics of loss so central to the aged.

And finally, everyone who survives grows old and carries personality or interpersonal problems of a lifetime into old age. Without appropriate and timely intervention, these problems become more entrenched with the passage of time, creating additional stresses on the family and aged person at a critical point in the parent's life. Social services must be geared to provide a range of interventions for a variety of problems to people of all ages. Problems derived from generations of deprivation and stress are not readily or quickly undone. Unresolved, they remain ever ready to erupt at any point of strain. The aging and death of parents represent such stress points in the family and individual life cycles. The parent remains forever a most significant figure and model for identification in the life of his child. Children in their middle years begin to identify with or reject the coping styles they observe in parents. The social worker's help to the aging individual and his family can provide not only help in the present but also courage rather than despair to succeeding generations moving toward their own aging and death.

References

1. CLARK TIBBITTS, "Middle-aged and Older People in American Society." Paper prepared for the Training Institute for Public Welfare Specialists in Aging, Cleveland, Ohio, June 1965.
2. BERTHA GOLDFARB SIMOS, "Intergenerational Relations of Middle-Aged Adults with Their Aging Parents." Unpublished doctoral dissertation, University of Southern California, June 1969. For a summary of thestudy see Simos, "Relations of Adults with Aging Parents," The Gerontologist, 10 (Summer 1970), pp. 135–139.
3. ALEXANDER BRODEN, "Reaction to Loss in the Aged," in Bernard Schoenberg et al., eds., Loss and Grief: Psychological Management in Medical Practice (New York: Columbia University Press, 1970), chap. 14.

4. GREGORY ROCHLIN, *Griefs and Discontents: The Forces of Change* (Boston: Little, Brown & Co., 1965), p. viii.

5. *See* RUTH LANDES and MARK ZBOROWSKI, "Hypotheses Concerning the Eastern European Jewish Family," in Herman D. Stein and Richard A. Cloward, eds., *Social Perspectives on Behavior* (Glencoe, Ill.: Free Press, 1958), p. 58.

26. PERSPECTIVES ON PERSONALITY CONSISTENCY AND CHANGE

JEAN WALKER MacFARLANE

We are all engaged in following the over time flow of that multi-faceted complex of coherencies, simply and naively accepted by the laity as "persons." As scientists, we are not satisfied with the laity's perceptions and descriptions, nor with their simple explanatory concepts, valid as they may be. So we each take out a slice of this multi-faceted complexity; we define "objectively" our own "relevant" personality variables and constructs; and we seek empirical or construct validity; a process which, I submit, is not unrelated to our own personalities and experiences.

Some of us, who are anal reductionists by temperament and training, firmly believe that, in time, by the piling up of data from studies of small segments of this complexity and by using methods neat and clean, the major variances and coherencies can be ascertained and that, like humptydumpty in the nursery rhyme, can then be reassembled.

Others of us, who are oral incorporators by temperament, with a high tolerance for ambiguity and inclusion, and who are organismic ideographists by experience, just as firmly believe that the intensive study of individual "lives in process" over a long time span will disclose the *relevant* bio-environmental-behavioral integrations and the major sources of continuity and change within and among individual personalities. Some of us are preoccupied with the development of internal "dynamic structure," others with the impinging pressures from the outside stimulus field, e.g., with behavior settings, with social class, and with interpersonal relations, especially with family members. Others of us are concerned with the developing processes of learning, perception, cognition, and motivation; still others of us with the emergence of psychodynamic patterns out of the enlarging circles of outer-inner and inner-outer transactions.

It is well at this neonatal stage of development of a science of personality that we should vary so in temperament, selective awareness, experience, and research preoccupations. Einstein warned even in the field of physics that there is no privileged position from which to make scientific observations, but that there is a responsibility to be aware of our positions in time and space. The late Alan Gregg, of the Rockefeller Foundation, had an opening gambit for grant applicants: "The only way I can judge a research project is by appraising the applicant's awareness of where he stands . . . Let me tell you a story of the young engineer using surveying instruments for the first time. He suddenly shouted exuberantly, 'Eureka, I've found the rod!' but after a few moments quietly added, 'but where am I?'" Especially in the field of personality research it is important that investigators inspect more diligently the bases of their own selective awareness. To do so would clarify the events that have led to specific research programs from which come the data, data which in turn have led to reported findings and theoretical notions. To do so might even reduce current overgeneralization.

I shall now violate the folkways of scientific reporting by being personal and concrete in locating myself in time and space: I was an endomorph raised in a small old town where one knew everyone well; where there were many varieties; and where right was right and wrong was wrong! I was sensitized to persons, and to rigorous cultural pressures which often had very ingenious built-in escape hatches. For example, the best informed and intellectually most exciting person in town was a bachelor who got drunk every Saturday night; one of the most attractive girls had an illegitimate child; the most dignified and aristocratic man owned the houses where prostitution flourished—but each of these persons, in spite of verbal taboos and differing time lags, was accepted. In contrast, a young man of 21, from the wrong side of the tracks, was discovered in sex play with a 10-year-old boy, and within 48 hours was put into the State penitentiary. It made one wonder.

I had a mother who had been raised by five adults representing one agnostic and four differing religious affiliations, four ethnic derivations, and an array of child-rearing practices. She passed on to me three convictions: (1) that there were *many* roads to Rome; (2) that one had to gather and weigh the evidence, make up one's own mind, and take the responsibility for one's own choices; and (3) that nothing was more unrewarding than fool-

ing oneself. (This last was very helpful for an investigator in this complex field of personality.) I had a father who had the long view and whose frequent comment in discussion was, "You have a good point but it just isn't that simple," and who set up in me a belief that intellectual integrity demanded avoidance of premature closure.

Undergraduate philosophy courses, with their intellectual and aesthetic satisfactions in following the intricacies of logically coherent but mutually dissident theories, left me a skeptical pragmatist about theory *qua* theory. A theory was fine if it led to new explorations and/or pulled together what had previously been discrete and unrelated. I shall omit the details of my graduate professional training in psychology, physiology, and sociology, and my work in juvenile courts, clinics and hospitals. Certainly observing the striking individual differences in babies as yet uncontaminated by the "socialization process" during the first two weeks of life, and the differential responses they evoked, reinforced my idiographic and organismic leanings. . . .

Our data collection procedure was to repeat systematically to age 18, on a normal sample of cases serially selected from the birth certificate registry, a wide range of measurements covering what we hoped were representative arrays of biological, environmental, familial, and overt-covert behavioral aspects of the growing organism.

Direct measures such as developmental x-rays, body-build measures, mental tests, and projective tests were used; also interviews furnished materials as seen by parents, teachers, brothers, sisters, the child himself, and the professional interviewers (clinical psychologists and physicians). Classmate appraisal was secured by sociometric techniques, and cumulative achievement was assessed from yearly school records.

At age 30, a core group of measurements were repeated and the subjects and their spouses were interviewed to secure data for the appraisal of self-acceptance and morale; and competences and satisfactions on the job, as a husband or wife, and as a parent. The children of these subjects were also administered a schedule of measurements.

What one observes of change and continuity in personality depends upon the following:

1. Breadth and/or intensity of coverage.
2. Whether one's focus of attention is upon (a) the aspects in which all developing persons are like all others—the growing availability of functions with physical maturation, expanding attention span, increased learned skills and residuals, sharpened perceptual discriminations, expanding cognitive complexity, increasing ability to bind tension, and so on; (b) whether the attention is upon *the ways in which individuals are like some other individuals*—derived from analyses of subgroups or clusters of persons who are homogeneous with respect to certain behaviors or styles of coping, and by looking at the correlates of such behaviors in morphology, child-training practices, or social class; or (c) whether attention is upon the *unique patternings of coherence or change within individuals* over time, through developmental periods, and across varying situations. Our study has attempted all three types of analyses.
3. Observations reported also depend upon the ages encompassed and the time span covered. Group findings show that interage correlations are a function of the time span and the age level for physical and mental measures, with correlations between physical measures far exceeding in magnitude correlations between mental measures in earlier years. For very few of the personality and behavioral variables we used did interage correlations even approach in magnitude those obtained for physical and mental measures. Furthermore, they were often

higher for an age span which straddled marked situational and biological changes (e.g. adolescence) than for adjacent age levels. That is, the correlations for girls were higher on a number of behavior-personality variables between ages 9 and 14 years than between 11 and 12 years. Either our personality variables and measures were not as adequate as those for physical and mental growth, which is probable, and/or behavior-personality measures are more subject to variability in time of biological or situational stress and change, a point for which we have clear evidence.
4. One's findings also depend upon whether or not investigatory techniques, including interpersonal impacts, over a long time span, have added a significant new dimension to the child's and his famliy's life space. We have evidence from our two groups, the control group and intensively interviewed group, and from the adult testimony of many subjects that such new dimensions were added.
5. A fifth factor influencing what one reports is related to the nature of the organizing variables and concepts used, whether they are quantified descriptions referring to coping behaviors, specific to certain developmental stages or structural maturational levels or situations, or whether they are more encompassing inferential concepts. We tried to make our first order of analysis from quantified description. We hoped thereby to derive dimensions empirically so that we would not be left merely drawing inferences from inferences. The most consistent dimensions obtained by clusters of variables over a long time span (2 to 16 years) related to styles of behaviors: namely, reactive-expressive or retractive-inhibitive.

First, let us take an overall look at growing, developing organisms within their environmental contexts.

We found important to personality . . .

the *combinations* of biological statuses which varying organisms encompass in respect to morphology, rate of growth, sensory acuity, types of musculature, abilities, general sturdiness, state of health, natural tempo or motility level, thresholds of stimulatibility, autonomic reactivity, levels of input tolerance, and temperament—combinations which gave rise both to very differing readinesses for stimulation acceptance or evasion, and to differing styles of overt-covert response patterning.

These varying organisms were not only stimulated to response, but these responses were also subjected to the regulatory procedures of parents, siblings, playmates, and teachers. Each of these persons had his own set of values, temperament, habits of showing affection, tempo, thresholds of stimulatibility, stabilized reaction patterns; and each of these persons had his own selective use of rewards, disapprovals, and punishments which changed with the child's age and which shifted with the trainer's moods, state of health, worries, and his preoccupations with aspects of living other than child regulating. Further, these stimulating and controlling persons gave rise to confusion in cues to the child, since they both gave affection and induced frustrations; they often acted very differently when alone with a child than when present with a spouse; and they often said one thing while facial expression showed they meant another. Some of these stimulating and controlling pressures were, and others were not, appropriate to the child's developmental readinesses or his input tolerances, or congenial to the needs of his temperament. In turn, the child's temperament, motility level, and behaviors were in or out of line with the trainers' expectancies, congenial or uncongenial to *their* needs and within or beyond *their* input tolerances.

Additionally, the individual was faced with myriad behavioral settings, differing sub-cultural pressures, and shifts in circumstances as well as shifts in the state of his biological organism. The complexity of the perceptual and learning tasks is enormous in ordering the priority of cues to respond to or to evade. The individual had the additional task of responding to this complexity in ways which, hopefully, would not bring on further distress. We submit that no experimentalist of sound mind in the fields of perception, learning, or cognition would attempt to order this contextual complexity of reality which the four-year-old struggles to order. We might well ask how *anyone* achieves even *relative* coherence. Yet it is clear that a majority do, albeit each in his own way and at his own speed.

Let us consider a few findings from individual lives that have forced us to look again at some of our theoretical notions. One inescapable lesson learned from 166 lives followed from babyhood to age 30 is the almost incredible capacity of the individual to process the welter of inner-outer stimulation; to program his overt-covert responses in ways that not only permit survival but permit growth in complexities of integrations and skills within his capacities and need systems; and still to have surplus energies with which to explore, to seek stimulation, and to enjoy a wide range of activities. Obviously, if catastrophic discontinuities occur, especially at vulnerable periods, or if biological functioning becomes seriously impaired, or if he is subjected to harsh and capricious pressures beyond his tolerance levels, or if most of his coping attempts are punished or derided, the individual may explode into erratic behavior. He may become immovably resistant, may develop psychosomatic disorders, or may become immobilized.

Our adult outcome data, however, show that for many persons early roadblocks were in time bypassed; or compensatory satisfactions were secured; or changed situations permitted resumption of or change in direction of growth. In fact, many of the most outstandingly mature adults in our entire group, many who are well integrated, highly competent, and/or creative, who are clear about their values, who are understanding and accepting of self and others, are recruited from those who were confronted with very difficult situations and whose characteristic responses during childhood and adolescence seemed to us to compound their problems. Among these were chronic rebels who were expelled from school, bright academic failures, one socially inept girl with blood pressure 4+ sigmas above the mean (now one sigma below), hostile dependents, unhappy withdrawn schizoids. They include one full-blown adolescent schizophrenic, who, without benefit of psychotherapy, now functions perceptively, creatively, and competently as a wife, mother, home builder, gardener, and community participant.

From their retrospective accounts at age 30, these individuals were very convincing that behaviors we had regarded as disruptive to growth and stability had, in fact, provided them with essential maturity-inducing benefits. To quote one former rebel, "Granted that my defiance of authority precluded a college education. I desperately needed approval, even if it was from as maladjusted kids as I was. Yet I can see positive results, too. To maintain my rebel status called for a commitment that demanded my disciplined *all* of intelligence and stamina which, I believe, has contributed to my adult strength and to my self-confidence in tackling later tough problems. I hope my children find less wasteful ways to mature—but who knows?"

The following comment was made by a recovered schizophrenic: "The only stabilizing aspect of my life during that period was the undeviating and all-enveloping homicidal fantasies against my mother. I believe they prevented my complete disintegration until I could escape my home and achieve other methods of handling my strains."

Our theoretical expectations were also rudely jarred by the adult status of a number of our subjects who early had had easy and confidence-inducing lives. As children and adolescents, they were free of severe strains, showed high abilities and/or talents, excelled at academic work, and were the adulated images of success. Included among these were boy athlete leaders and good-looking, socially skillful girls. One sees among them at age 30 a high proportion of brittle, discontented, and puzzled adults whose high potentialities have not been actualized, at least as of now.

As investigators, we were not always wrong! We did have several small groups whose adult status fulfilled theoretical expectations, some with severe organic impairment or deficits, physically and/or intellectually. There were a few cases where the loss of the warm, supporting parent during the preschool years, with no adequate substitute, was accompanied by somber withdrawal that has persisted into adulthood. There were some individuals from homes of unequivocal pathology where irrational pressures made integrations impossible and induced explosive behavioral escapes or repression and denial, with their toll of strain and restriction of coping flexibility. As an example, a vulnerable organism (a boy who had acute allergies), subjected to unpredictable sado-masochistic fluctuations in one or both parents, was left with such an unresolved love-hate tie that it was carried over into his new adult family and was often accompanied by acute depressive swings and/or compulsive drinking. In one case, the incoherent ambivalences have found supportive outlet in the John Birch Society.

Next, a few statements regarding needs for theory modification as I see them.

1. It seems clear that personality theories based upon pathological samples (essentially neurotic) need modification if they are to be useful for prediction for the larger number of developing persons. The currently expanding studies of normal persons, and of the talented and creative, should help to trim our past overgeneralizations derived from

our sample limitations. This is true even though all of us are aware that the initial and basic impetus to personality theory and research has come from the study of disrupted persons.

2. We had not appreciated the maturing utility of many painful, strain-producing, and confusing experiences which in time, if lived through, brought sharpened awareness, more complex integrations, better skills in problem solving, clarified goals, and increasing stability. Nor had we been aware that early success might delay or possibly forestall continuing growth, richness, and competence. It is not clear whether early success, reinforced by the projections of others trying to identify with success, led to unreal expectations and to a disproportionate draining of energies into maintaining an image, whether early success caused fixation on goals inappropriate to adult demands, or side tracked development from other needed areas, or whether there was not enough stress to temper strength and induce development. We need to look at and to try to conceptualize the configurations of what kinds of stress, in what graded doses, with what compensating supports, at what developmental periods, and in what kinds of organisms, forestall maturity and strength or facilitate them. The recent expansion of interest in ego psychology appears as one important shift of emphasis in a useful direction.

3. Our experience confirms that the early years of family intimacy, of learning to control body functions, of discovering what overt behaviors are both permissible and useful in coping, comprise a highly important period, especially to basic self-confidence and affective trust, or their lack. Our data show that subsequent problem-solving periods (as all periods are) are also highly important.

Adolescence is reported by a substantial number of our subjects as their most confusing period and the time of lowest morale. It presented not only marked changes in biochemistry, with heightened reactivity and new sensory intensities, but was also a period of struggle to establish status with peers of the same and opposite sex. It was a period of driving urgency for independent selfhood (while being still dependent) and, simultaneously, a period of increased and anxiety-laden pressures from parents for high scholastic and/or social achievement. It was for many individuals a confusing period of establishing priorities among the competing pressures and needs. The priorities to which these adolescents gave time and energies, while accelerating certain competences, retarded or even precluded growth in other aspects. Here, too, we need better conceptualization of the dynamics of competing needs.

For many persons, parenthood turns out to be a very important period for consolidating identity and for expanding maturity. For others, it is a period marked by reactivation of unsolved problems from their early or adolescent past. For many girls, parenthood meant an expanding fulfillment, especially for those who were able to give their children a richer and a less straining environment than the one they had had. Among many of our rebels and our hostile dependent boys, parenthood offered an opportunity, not open to them when they were on the receiving end as children and adolescents, for responsibility to and nurturance of others; an opportunity which permitted dramatic modification of long established behavioral habits and induced new feelings of self-worth which liberated potentials for other adult tasks. It seems clear that learning theory which ignores differing personality needs, and personality theory which ignores adult capacity for learning in new situations, could profit by modification.

May I add a final personal note. With my strange combinations of personality characteristics and early experiences, involvement in a long longitudinal, multidiscipline study of personality has offered an intellectually exciting, frustrating, humility-inducing, but highly satisfying life. If, on the other hand, the investigator's personality is one that needs neatness and early closure, he should think long and hard before entering the field of personality, longitudinally observed.

Summary

This paper presents a few of the concepts which have survived or have been modified in the course of studying personality continuity and change in a normal sample of persons over a long time span—from infancy to age 30. In the personality field, programming of research is peculiarly related to the temperament, experience, theoretical predictions, and sensitivities of the investigator. The great advantage of long-term longitudinal research is that it permits verification, refinement, or discard of previous theories and ideas.

We have found from a review of life histories that certain deficits of constitution and/or environment, and certain unsolvable interpersonal conflicts, have long-term effects upon the individual, up to age 30. We have also found that much of personality theory based on pathological samples is not useful for prediction for the larger number of persons. Many of our most mature and competent adults had severely troubled and confusing childhoods and adolescences. Many of our highly successful children and adolescents have failed to achieve their predicted potential. It is clear that we need more sophisticated theory that will help us weight the relevant components—the types of stress, the compensating supports, in various types of organisms, at the various developmental periods—if we are to predict which combinations of factors forestall and which combinations facilitate maturity and strength.

References

It is impossible to list all the bibliographical references, theoretical, empirical, and methodological, which have sharpened our awareness in the many bio-environmental-personality aspects of our undertaking over a thirty-five year period. Even the 290 references listed in N. Sanford's recent chapter, "Personality: Its Place in Psychology" in: A study of science, Vol. 5, ed. by S. Koch (McGraw-Hill Book Company, Inc., 1963) do not exhaust the investigators to whom we are indebted in the personality field. The literature of biological growth, development, differentiation, and integration, and that of the cultural-environmental-ecological surround, are also very extensive. Instead of attempting such a bibliography, we are listing here some of the major publications from the Guidance Study. Studies incorporating the adult data are now in preparation and do not appear in this list.

ATHERTON, KARYL: A comparison of solutions obtained in factor analyses of socio-economic variables. Psychol. Reports 11: 259–273 (1962).

BAYER, LEONA M., and SNYDER, MARGARET, M.: Illness experience of a group of normal children. Child Develop. 21: 93–120 (1950).

BAYLEY, NANCY: Some psychological correlates of somatic androgyny. Child Develop. 22: 47–60 (1951).

BRONSON, WANDA C.; KATTEN, EDITH S., and LIVSON, N.: Patterns of authority and affection in two generations. J. abnorm. soc. Psychol. 58: 143–152 (1959).

BRONSON, WANDA C.: Dimensions of ego and infantile identification. J. Personality 27: 532–545 (1959).

ERIKSON, E. H.: Sex differences in the play configurations of preadolescents. Amer. J. Orthopsychiat. 21: 667–692 (1951).

HANLEY, C.: Physique and reputation of junior high school boys. Child Develop. *22:* 247–260 (1951).

HEINSTEIN, M. I.: Behavioral correlates of breast-bottle regimes under varying parent-infant relationships. Monogr. Soc. Res. Child Develop. *28* (Whole) (1963).

HONZIK, MARJORIE P.; MACFARLANE, JEAN W., and ALLEN, LUCILE: The stability of mental test performance between two and eighteen years. J. exp. Educ. *17:* 309–324 (1948).

HONZIK, MARJORIE P.: Developmental studies of parent-child resemblance in intelligence. Child Develop. *28:* 215–228 (1957).

LIVSON, N., and MCNEILL, D.: Variability in male stature as a function of adolescent maturation rate. Science *133:* 708–709 (1961).

MACFARLANE, JEAN W.: Studies in child guidance. I. Methodology of data collection and organization. Monogr. Soc. Res. Child Develop. *3:* 1–254 (1938).—The guidance study. Sociometry *2:* 1–23 (1939).—Interpersonal relationships within the family. Marriage and Family Living *3:* 25–31 (1941).

MACFARLANE, JEAN W., and TUDDENHAM, R. D.: Problems in the validation of projective techniques. In: H. H. Anderson and G. L. Anderson (Eds.), An introduction to projective techniques (Prentice-Hall, New York 1951).

MACFARLANE, JEAN W., ALLEN, LUCILLE, and HONZIK, MARJORIE P.: A developmental study of the behavior problems of normal children between twenty-one months and fourteen years. University of California Publications in Child Develop. *2:* 222 (Univ. of California Press, Berkeley 1954).

MCFATE, MARGUERITE Q., and ORR, FRANCES G.: Through adolescence with the Rorschach. Rorschach Res. Exch. and J. proj. Tech. *13:* 302–319 (1949).

NICOLSON, ARLINE B., and HANLEY, C.: Indices of physiological maturity: derivation and interrelationships. Child Develop. *24:* 3–38 (1953).

PYLE, MARJORIE K., STOLZ, H. R., and MACFARLANE, JEAN W.: The accuracy of mothers' reports on birth and developmental data. Child Develop. *6:* 165–176 (1935).

TUDDENHAM, R. D.: Studies in reputation. III. Correlates of popularity among elementary school children. J. educ. Psychol.: 257–276 (1951).—Studies in reputation: I. Sex and grade differences in school children's evaluations of their peers, and II. The diagnosis of social adjustment. Psychol. Monogr. *66:* 1–58 (1952).

TUDDENHAM, R. D., and SNYDER, MARGARET M.: Physical growth of California boys and girls from birth to 18 years. University of California Publications in Child Develop. I: 183–364 (Univ. of California Press, Berkeley 1954).

CHAPTER FIVE: SUGGESTED FURTHER READINGS

BORGATTA, E. F., and LAMBERT, W. W. (Eds.). *Handbook of personality theory and research.* Chicago: Rand McNally, 1968.

BALTES, P. B., and SCHAIE, K. W. (Eds.). *Life-span developmental psychology: personality and socialization.* New York: Academic Press, 1973.

NEUGARTEN, B. L., et al. *Personality in middle and late life.* New York: Atherton, 1964.

part two socialization issues

chapter six
general
problems

A woman's place is in the home.
Men are strong and never cry.
Sex is dirty.

Every day we are exposed to someone or
something telling us what is right or
wrong, truth or fiction, good or bad. Parents, friends, and media barrage us with
information about the world we live in.
It does not matter what the subject is,
everyone seems to have a different opinion. Some of what we are introduced to
we accept, some we reject, and some
things linger on in our minds for more
thought. Just how is it then, that we come
to the opinions, attitudes, and beliefs we
have? When do people acquire their
values, what influences them to choose
what they do, and do attitudes change
over the years or remain basically stable?
These are among the many questions that
plague researchers interested in the process of socialization.

Socialization remains a very difficult research problem. It requires a series of
interactions which has defied definition by
virtue of its extreme complexity. In the
past many psychologists concentrated
their research and theory on socialization
in the early years. Maternal and paternal
deprivation, differing styles of parenting,

the school environment, and many other facets of early life were examined to shed light on early socialization experiences. More recently, studies have examined the effect television and movies have had on children, especially in the area of violence and aggression. Yet despite these and countless other studies, the process of socialization has not been examined from the view of a whole life span. If we begin to think of socialization as a lifelong process of actions and interactions with the environment shaping our attitudes and constantly forcing us to reevaluate them, then we can begin to look at socialization in more than a superficial way.

In American society, for instance, there seems to be a timetable that controls major life events; that is, there is an expected time when people will learn sex roles and gender identity, go to school, get married, have children, retire, and die, as Neugarten, Moore, and Lowe show in their article in this chapter. Many of these norms and stereotypes are sheer fabrication built around age-old traditions.

In a more recent article Neugarten (1974) notes that the society in which we live is changing so rapidly that it is changing the rhythm of the whole life cycle. Not only do we have greater longevity, but events in the life cycle are also at a different pace. Until the last year or two, the marriage age was dropping steadily. Women and men were marrying younger and having their first child within the first year of marriage. Thus, the family cycle is developing a new rhythm . . . The image of old age is no longer that of the old person in a rocking chair; it is the old person on the golf course, [p. 38].

Beyond the rapid change in life events is the tide of change in other inputs to the socialization process. Many of our widely accepted norms and stereotypes are being challenged. The women's movement has precipitated a new appraisal of sex roles in terms of how they develop and affect our lives. Minority groups have challenged their inferior treatment in jobs, education, and health care (not to mention the validity of psychological tests, such as the intelligence tests). Older people have organized into groups like the Gray Panthers in an attempt to regain control of their lives. Changes due to automation, job retraining, and early retirement will also have their effects on our world of work. Hopefully, the pressure maintained by these active groups will spur more research on socialization over the life span, resulting in a clearer understanding of what the process of socialization is and how it works. It is a long and arduous task to find clear-cut answers to complex problems in the area of socialization, but it is necessary if we are to understand ourselves and our social system.

Reference

NEUGARTEN, B. The roles we play. In Effie O. Ellis (Ed.), *The quality of life: the middle years*. Acton, Mass.: Publishing Sciences Group, 1974, pp. 35–38.

27. AGE NORMS, AGE CONSTRAINTS, AND ADULT SOCIALIZATION

BERNICE L. NEUGARTEN, JOAN W. MOORE, and JOHN C. LOWE

In all societies, age is one of the bases for the ascription of status and one of the underlying dimensions by which social interaction is regulated. Anthropologists have studied age-grading in simple societies, and sociologists in the tradition of Mannheim have been interested in the relations between generations; but little systematic attention has been given to the ways in which age groups relate to each other in complex societies or to systems of norms which refer to age-appropriate behavior. A promising group of theoretical papers which appeared twenty or more years ago have now become classics (Benedict, 1938; Davis, 1940; Linton, 1936; Lowie, 1920; Mannheim, 1952; Parsons, 1942; Prins, 1953; Van Gennep, 1908) but with the exceptions of a major contribution by Eisenstadt (1956) and a provocative paper by Berger (1960), little theoretical or empirical work has been done in this area in the two decades that have intervened, and there has been little development of what might be called a sociology of age.

The present paper deals with two related issues: first, with the degree of constraint perceived with regard to age norms that operate in American society; second, with adult socialization to those norms.[1] Preliminary to presenting the data that bear upon these issues, however, a few comments regarding the age-norm system and certain illustrative observations gathered earlier may help to provide context for this study.

Background Concepts and Observations

Expectations regarding age-appropriate behavior form an elaborated and pervasive system of norms governing behavior and interaction, a network of expectations that is imbedded throughout the cultural fabric of adult life. There exists what might be called a prescriptive timetable for the ordering of major life events: a time in the life span when men and women are expected to marry, a time to raise children, a time to retire. This normative pattern is adhered to, more or less consistently, by most persons in the society. Although the actual occurrences of major life events for both men and women are influenced by a variety of life contingencies, and although the norms themselves vary somewhat from one group of persons to another, it can easily be demonstrated that norms and actual occurrences are closely related. Age norms and age expectations operate as prods and brakes upon behavior, in some instances hastening an event, in others delaying it. Men and women are aware not only of the social clocks that operate in various areas of their lives, but they are aware also of their own timing and readily describe themselves as "early," "late," or "on time" with regard to family and occupational events.

Age norms operate also in many less clear-cut ways and in more peripheral areas of adult life as illustrated in such phrases as "He's too old to be working so hard" or "She's too young to wear that style of clothing" or "That's a strange thing for a man of his age to say." The concern over age-appropriate behavior is

---

[1] With some exceptions, such as the work of Merton (1957), sociologists have as yet given little attention to the broader problem of adult socialization.

further illustrated by colloquialisms such as "Act your age!"—an exhortation made to the adult as well as to the child in this society.

Such norms, implicit or explicit, are supported by a wide variety of sanctions ranging from those, on the one hand, that relate directly to the physical health of the transgressor to those, on the other hand, that stress the deleterious effects of the transgression on other persons. For example, the fifty-year-old man who insists on a strenuous athletic life is chastised for inviting an impairment of his own health; a middle-aged woman who dresses like an adolescent brings into question her husband's good judgment as well as her own; a middle-aged couple who decide to have another child are criticized because of the presumed embarrassment to their adolescent or married children. Whether affecting the self or others, age norms and accompanying sanctions are relevant to a great variety of adult behaviors; they are both systematic and pervasive in American society.

Despite the diversity of value patterns, life styles, and reference groups that influence attitudes, a high degree of consensus can be demonstrated with regard to age-appropriate and age-linked behaviors as illustrated by data shown in Table 27.1. The table shows how responses were distributed when a representative sample of middle-class men and women aged forty to seventy[2] were asked such questions as: "What do you think is the best

age for a man to marry? . . . to finish school?" "What age comes to your mind when you think of a 'young' man? . . . an 'old' man?" "At what age do you think a man has the most responsibilities . . . accomplishes the most?"[3]

The consensus indicated in the table is not limited to persons residing in a particular region of the United States or to middle-aged persons. Responses to the same set of questions were obtained from other middle-class groups: one group of fifty men and women aged twenty to thirty residing in a second midwestern city, a group of sixty Negro men and women aged forty to sixty in a third midwestern city, and a group of forty persons aged seventy to eighty in a New England community. Essentially the same patterns emerged in each set of data.

The Problem and the Method

Based upon various sets of data such as those illustrated in Table 27.1, the present investigation proceeded on the assumption that age norms and age expectations operate in this society as a system of social control. For a great variety of behaviors, there is a span of years within which the occurrence of a given behavior is regarded as appropriate. When the behavior occurs

---

[2] The sample was drawn by area-probability methods (a 2 per cent listing of households in randomly selected census tracts) with the resulting pool of cases then stratified by age, sex, and socioeconomic status. Using the indexes of occupation, level of education, house type, and area of residence, these respondents were all middle class. The data were gathered in connection with the Kansas City Studies of Adult Life, a research program carried out over a period of years under the direction of Robert J. Havighurst, William E. Henry, Bernice L. Neugarten, and other members of the Committee on Human Development, University of Chicago.

[3] For each item in the table, the percentages that appear in the third and fourth columns obviously vary directly with the breadth of the age span shown for that item. The age span shown was, in turn, the one selected by the investigators to produce the most accurate reflection of the consensus that existed in the data.

The way in which degree of consensus was calculated can be illustrated on "Best age for a man to marry." Individuals usually responded to this item in terms of specific years, such as "20" or "22" or in terms of narrow ranges, such as "from 20 to 23." These responses were counted as consensus within the five-year age range shown in Table 27.1, on the grounds that the respondents were concurring that the best age was somewhere between twenty and twenty-five. A response such as "18 to 20" or "any time in the 20's" was outside the range regarded as consensus and was therefore excluded.

Table 27.1. Consensus in a middle-class middle-aged sample regarding various age-related characteristics

	Age Range Designated as Appropriate or Expected	Percent Who Concur Men (N=50)	Women (N=43)
Best age for a man to marry	20–25	80	90
Best age for a woman to marry	19–24	85	90
When most people should become grandparents	45–50	84	79
Best age for most people to finish school and go to work	20–22	86	82
When most men should be settled on a career	24–26	74	64
When most men hold their top jobs	45–50	71	58
When most people should be ready to retire	60–65	83	86
A young man	18–22	84	83
A middle-aged man	40–50	86	75
An old man	65–75	75	57
A young woman	18–24	89	88
A middle aged woman	40–50	87	77
An old woman	60–75	83	87
When a man has the most responsibilities	35–50	79	75
When a man accomplishes most	40–50	82	71
The prime of life for a man	35–50	86	80
When a woman has the most responsibilities	25–40	93	91
When a woman accomplishes most	30–45	94	92
A good-looking woman	20–35	92	82

outside that span of years, it is regarded as inappropriate and is negatively sanctioned.

The specific questions of this study were these: How do members of the society vary in their perception of the strictures involved in age norms, or in the degree of constraint they perceive with regard to age-appropriate behaviors? To what extent are personal attitudes congruent with the attitudes ascribed to the generalized other? Finally, using this congruence as an index of socialization, can adult socialization to age norms be shown to occur as respondents themselves increase in age?

The instrument A questionnaire was constructed in which the respondent was asked on each of a series of items which of three ages he would regard as appropriate or inappropriate, or which he would approve or disapprove. As seen in the illustrations below, the age spans being proposed were intended to be psychologically rather than chronologically equal in the sense that for some events a broad age

span is appropriate, for others, a narrow one.

A woman who feels it's all right at her age to wear a two-piece bathing suit to the beach:
    When she's 45 (approve or disapprove)
    When she's 30 (approve or disapprove)
    When she's 18 (approve or disapprove).

Other illustrative items were:

A woman who decides to have another child
    When she's 45, 37, 30.
A man who's willing to move his family from one town to another to get ahead in his company
    When he's 45, 35, 25.
A couple who like to do the "Twist"
    When they're 55, 30, 20.
A man who still prefers living with his parents rather than getting his own apartment
    When he's 30, 25, 21.
A couple who move across country so they can live near their married children
    When they're 40, 55, 70.

The thirty-nine items finally selected after careful pretesting are divided equally into three types: those that relate to occupational career; those that relate to the family cycle; and a broader grouping that refer to recreation, appearance, and consumption behaviors. In addition, the items were varied systematically with regard to their applicability to three periods: young adulthood, middle age, and old age.

In general, then, the questionnaire presents the respondent with a relatively balanced selection of adult behaviors which were known from pretesting to be successful in evoking age discriminations. A means of scoring was devised whereby the score reflects the degree of refinement with which the respondent makes age discriminations. For instance, the respondent who approves of a couple dancing the "Twist" if they are twenty, but who disapproves if they are thirty, is placing relative age constraint upon this item of behavior as compared to another respondent who approves the "Twist" both at age twenty and at age thirty, but not at age fifty-five. The higher the score, the more the respondent regards age as a salient dimension across a wide variety of behaviors and the more constraint he accepts in the operation of age norms.[4]

---

[4] For each item of behavior, one of the ages being proposed is scored as the "appropriate" age; another, the "marginal"; and the third, the "inappropriate" (the age at which the behavior is usually proscribed on the basis of its transgression of an age norm). A response which expresses disapproval of only the "inappropriate" age is scored 1, while a response which expresses disapproval of not only the "inappropriate" but also the "marginal" age receives a score of 3. The total possible score is 117, a score that could result only if the respondent were perceiving maximum age constraint with regard to every one of the thirty-nine items. A response which expresses approval or disapproval of all three ages for a given behavior is scored zero, since for that respondent the item is not age-related, at least not within the age range being proposed.

The "appropriate" age for each item had previously been designated by the investigators on the basis of previous findings such as those illustrated on Table 27.1 of this report. That the designations were generally accurate was corroborated by the fact that when the present instrument was administered to the four hundred respondents described here, more than 90 percent of respondents on successive test items checked "approve" for the "appropriate" one of the three proposed ages.

The sample   A quota sample of middle-class respondents was obtained in which level of education, occupation, and area of residence were used to determine social class. The sample is divided into six age-sex cells: fifty men and fifty women aged twenty to thirty, one hundred men and one hundred women aged thirty to fifty-five, and fifty men and fifty women aged sixty-five and over. Of the four hundred respondents, all but a few in the older group were or had been married. The great majority were parents of one or more children.

The only known bias in the sample occurs in the older group (median age for men is sixty-nine; for women seventy-two) where most individuals were members of Senior Citizens clubs and where, as a result, the subsample is biased in the direction of better health and greater community involvement than can be expected for the universe of persons in this age range. While Senior Citizens is a highly age-conscious and highly age-graded association from the perspective of the wider society, there is no evidence that the seventy-year-old who joins is any more or any less aware of age discriminations than is the seventy-year-old who does not join.[5] The older group was no more or less homogeneous with regard to religious affiliation, ethnic background, or indexes of social class than were the other two age groups in this sample.

Administration   To investigate the similarity between personal attitudes and attitudes ascribed to the generalized other, the questionnaire was first administered with instructions to give "your personal opinions" about each of the items; then

---

[5] On the other hand, members of Senior Citizens are more likely to be activists and to regard themselves as younger in outlook than persons who do not join such groups. If this is true, the age differences to be described in the following sections of this paper might be expected to be even more marked in future studies in which samples are more representative.

the respondent was given a second copy of the questionnaire and asked to respond in the way he believed "most people" would respond.[6]

In about half the cases, both forms of the instrument were administered consecutively in personal interviews. In the remainder of the cases, responses on the first form were gathered in group sessions (in one instance, a parents' meeting in a school), and the second form was completed later and returned by mail to the investigator.

The two types of administration were utilized about evenly within each age-sex group. No significant differences in responses were found to be due to this difference in procedure of data-gathering.

Findings

The findings of this study can be read from Figure 27.1. The figure shows a striking convergence with age between the two sets of attitudes.

1. Age trends within each set of data are opposite in direction. With regard to personal opinions, there is a highly

significant increase in scores with age— that is, an increase in the extent to which respondents ascribe importance to age norms and place constraints upon adult behavior in terms of age appropriateness.

2. With regard to "most people's opinions" there is a significant decrease in scores with age—that is, a decrease in the extent to which age constraints are perceived in the society and attributed to a generalized other.

3. Sex differences are minimal with the exception that young women stand somewhat outside the general trend on "personal opinions," with scores that differentiate them from young men but not from middle-aged women.

Discussion

The difference shown in these data between personal attitudes and attitudes attributed to the generalized other (a finding that holds true for all but the oldest respondents) implies that age norms operate like other types of norms insofar as there is some lack of congruence between that which is acknowledged to be operating in the society and that which is personally accepted as valid. It is noteworthy, on the one hand, that age norms are uniformly acknowledged to exist in the minds of "most people." While the data are not shown here, on each one of the thirty-nine behavioral items some 80 percent or more of all respondents made age discriminations when asked for "most people's opinions." In other words, general censensus exists that behaviors described in the test instrument are age-related. On the other hand, respondents uniformly attributed greater stricture to age norms in the minds of other people than in their own minds. This difference was reflected in the scores for every respondent as well as in the mean scores.

These findings indicate that there is an overriding norm of "liberal-mindedness" regarding age, whereby men and women

---

[6] The problem being studied here relates to problems of conformity, deviation, and personal versus public attitudes. As is true of other empirical research in these areas, the terms used here are not altogether satisfactory, in part because of the lack of uniform terminology in this field. For example, while age norms are in some respects related to "attitudinal" and "doctrinal" conformity as posed by Merton (1959), these data do not fit that analytical framework because age norms are less clear-cut than the norms Merton discusses, and the realms of attitudinal and doctrinal conformity are less prescribed.

Similarly, the projection of personal attitudes upon the generalized other has been studied by Getzels and Walsh (1958) but their theoretical model is not altogether applicable because in the present research the phenomenon of projection cannot be demonstrated. The same lack of fit exists with the concepts used by Rokeach (1960); and with the concepts of social norms, norms of common consent, and personal norms as used by Bott (1957). The *self, generalized other* terminology is therefore regarded as the most appropriate for describing the present data.

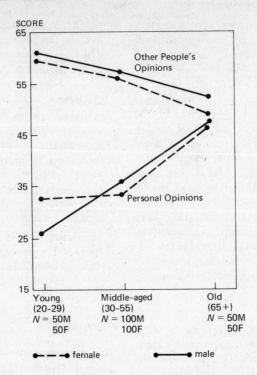

Figure 27.1. Perception of age constraints in adulthood by age and sex. An analysis of variance for the data on "personal opinions" showed that age was a highly significant variable (F is statistically reliable beyond the .001 level); and the interaction between age and sex was significant (F is reliable at the .05 level). For the data on "other people's opinions," age alone is a significant variable (F is reliable beyond the .001 level).

consistently maintain that they hold more liberal views than do others. In many ways this situation is reminiscent of the phenomenon of pluralistic ignorance, in which no respondent's personal view of the attitudes of others is altogether correct (Allport, 1924). In other ways, however, this may be a situation in which respondents tend to exaggerate, rather than to misconstrue, the opinions of others. A young person who says, in effect, "I am not strict about age norms, but other people are," is indeed correct that other people are stricter than he is (as shown in these data on "personal opinions"); but he exaggerates, for other people are not so strict as he thinks. Similarly, when an old person says, in effect, "I think this is the norm, and other people think so, too," he is also partly correct that other old peo-

ple agree with him, but he ignores what *young* people think.

These partial misconceptions have at least two implications: first, when a person's own opinions differ from the norms he encounters, he may exaggerate the differences and place the norms even further away from his own opinions than is warranted. Second, it may be that in considering age norms the individual gives undue weight to the opinion of persons who are older or stricter than himself and ignores the opinions of others who are younger or less strict. In both instances, the norm image is not the average of all opinions encountered but the image of the "ideal" norm. In the case of age norms, the "ideal" norms may well be those held by older persons.

The findings of this study are also of

interest when viewed within the context of adult socialization. Cross-sectional data of this type must be interpreted with caution since the differences between age groups may reflect historical changes in values and attitudes as much as changes that accompany increased age itself. Still, the findings seem congruent with a theory of adult socialization: that personal belief in the relevance and validity of social norms increases through the adult life span and that, in this instance, as the individual ages he becomes increasingly aware of age discriminations in adult behavior and of the system of social sanctions that operate with regard to age appropriateness. The middle-aged and the old seem to have learned that age is a reasonable criterion by which to evaluate behavior, that to be "off-time" with regard to life events or to show other age-deviant behavior brings with it social and psychological sequelae that cannot be disregarded. In the young, especially the young male, this view is only partially accepted; and there seems to be a certain denial of age as a valid dimension by which to judge behavior.

This age-related difference in point of view is perhaps well illustrated by the response of a twenty-year-old who, when asked what he thought of marriage between seventeen-year-olds, said, "I suppose it would be all right if the boy got a good job, and if they loved each other. Why not? It isn't age that's the important thing." A forty-five-year-old, by contrast, said, "At that age, they'd be foolish. Neither one of them is settled enough. A boy on his own, at seventeen, couldn't support a wife, and he certainly couldn't support children. Kids who marry that young will suffer for it later."

Along with increased personal conviction regarding the validity of age norms goes a decreased tendency to perceive the generalized other as restrictive. The overall convergence in the data, a convergence which we have interpreted in terms of adult socialization, may reflect status

and deference relationships between age groups in American society, where high status is afforded the middle-aged and where social enforcement of norms may generally be said to be vested in the mature rather than the young. The young person, having only recently graduated from the age-segregated world of adolescents, and incompletely socialized to adult values, seems to perceive a psychological distance between himself and "most people" and to feel only partially identified with the adult world. This is evidenced by the fact that when asked, "Whom do you have in mind when you think of 'most people'?" young adults tended to answer, "Older people."

Only for old people is there a high degree of congruence between personal opinions and the opinions ascribed to others. This may reflect not only the accumulated effects of adult socialization and the internalization of age norms, but also a certain crystallization of attitudes in the aged. Older respondents volunteered the most vehement and the most opinionated comments as they moved from item to item, as if to underscore the fact that their attitudes with regard to age and age-related behaviors are highly charged emotionally. Under these circumstances, there is likely to be a blurring of distinctions between what the respondent himself regards as right and what he thinks other people would "naturally" regard as right.

With regard to sex differences, the fact that young women perceive greater constraints regarding age-appropriate behavior than do young men is generally congruent with other evidence of differences in socialization for women and men in our society. Young women are probably more highly sensitized to the imperatives of age norms than are young men, given the relatively more stringent expectations regarding age at marriage for women.

It should be recalled that the present study is based upon quota samples of middle-class respondents and that accordingly the findings cannot be readily generalized to other samples. Nevertheless, the findings support the interpretation that age norms are salient over a wide variety of adult behaviors and support the view that adult socialization produces increas-ingly clear perception of these norms as well as an increasing awareness that the norms provide constraints upon adult behavior.

References

1. ALLPORT, F. H. *Social psychology*. Boston: Houghton Mifflin Co., 1924.

2. BENEDICT, RUTH. Continuities and discontinuities in culture conditioning. *Psychiatry*, 1938, *I*, 161–167.

3. BOTT, ELIZABETH. *Family and social network*. London: Tavistock, 1957.

4. BERGER, B. M. How long is a generation? *British Journal of Sociology*, 1960, *XI*, 10–23.

5. DAVIS, K. The sociology of parent-youth conflict. *American Sociological Review*, 1940, *V*, 523–535.

6. EISENSTADT, S. N. *From generation to generation*. Glencoe, Ill.: Free Press, 1956.

7. GETZELS, J. W. and WALSH, J. J. The method of paired direct and projective questionnaires in the study of attitude structure and socialization. *Psychological Monographs*, 1958, *LXXVII*, (Whole No. 454).

8. LINTON, R. *The study of man*. New York: Appleton-Century, 1936.

9. LOWIE, R. *Primitive society*. New York: Harper & Bros., 1961.

10. MANNHEIM, K. The problem of generations. *Essays on the Sociology of Knowledge*, 1952, 276–322.

11. MERTON, R. K. *Social theory and social structure*. Glencoe, Ill.: Free Press, 1957.

12. ———. Social conformity, deviation and opportunity structures: a comment on the contributions of Dubin and Cloward. *American Sociological Review*, 1959, *XXIV*, 177–189.

13. PARSONS, T. Age and sex in the social structure of the United States. *American Sociological Review*, 1942, *VII*, 604–616.

14. PRINS, A. H. J. *East-African age-class systems*. Groningen: J. B. Wolters, 1953.

15. ROKEACH, M. *The open and closed mind*. New York: Basic Books, 1960.

16. VAN GENNEP, A. *The rites of passage*. Chicago: University of Chicago Press, 1960.

28. CHRONOLOGICAL AGE IN RELATION TO ATTITUDINAL JUDGMENTS: AN EXPERIMENTAL ANALYSIS

BILL D. BELL and GARY G. STANFIELD

Cultural attitudes toward older people have long been of interest to social gerontologists (Axelrod & Eisdorfer, 1961; Ko-gan, 1961; Slater, 1963; Tuckman & Lorge, 1952a, b). Nevertheless, serious research in this area has been of relatively recent origin. The researches of Tuckman & Lorge (1952a, b; 1953a, b; 1954; 1958), for example, signaled the beginnings of an empirical thrust in this direction. In this regard, many early findings suggested old age to be a period marked by failing physical and mental powers, economic insecurity, and resistance to change. These factors, often in combination, have supposedly fostered a negative stereotype toward older adults in general.

Subsequent research has done little to either challenge or alter the above suggestions. For the most part, research attention has been focused on the development of various instruments for assessing age-stereotypical information. Axelrod and Eisdorfer (1961) and Eisdorfer (1966), for example, have attempted to shorten as well as to increase the validity of the Tuckman-Lorge scale. Generally speaking, however, these efforts have not proven fruitful. Besides scalar modifications, other techniques and devices have enjoyed popularity. Eisdorfer and Altrocchi (1961), for instance, prefer the use of the semantic differential, whereas Kogan (1961) favors a Likert scaling procedure. Aaronson (1966) and Golde and Kogan (1959), on the other hand, utilize attitude checklists and sentence completion instruments, respectively. In all instances, however, negative attitudes are observed with respect to older age groupings (Ginzberg, 1952; Slater, 1963).

The present research suggests the need for a new look at attitudes toward age. This suggestion is based on both theoretical and empirical considerations. Theoretically speaking, cultural attitudes, like cultural values, seldom remain static (McKee, 1969). The social movements of the late 60s (e.g., women's liberation, gay liberation, etc.), for example, have done much to focus attention on different value perspectives. As a consequence, a new tolerance has arisen relative to various "minority groupings" (Toby, 1971). To some extent, the aged fall within this category. From an empirical standpoint, on the other hand, local, state, and federal programs for the elderly have had an influence on the ideas and values of the young with respect to their older age counterparts. In a series of researches yet to be published, for instance, the authors observed significant shifts in the value perspectives of both young and old respondents following exposure to an extension course on aging. As a consequence of these and other observations, it seems probable that many of the previously-referenced attitudes toward age may have undergone significant changes in the last 10 years.

The most immediate reason for renewed concern involves the methodological considerations of previous research. In this regard, it is clear that the major portion of this work has been conducted in the university setting. As such, the sample survey has proven the most utilized methodological tool. For the most part, subjects are asked to evaluate certain age categories (e.g., 50–64, 65–74, 75–84, etc.) with respect to a number of personal and social characteristics. Although an "efficient" procedure for gathering data, such an approach tends to ignore such problems as response-set biases as well as errors of central tendency (Eisdorfer, 1966). In addition, a "knowledge bias" is probable. That is, a subject's reported judgment relative to a given grouping may reflect assumed "knowledge" of what is held culturally in this regard rather than any *personal* feelings relative to the group(s) in question. To the extent that such factors are or have been operative in previous methodologies, the entire issue of attitudes toward age invites a more contemporary reexamination.

The following research is an extension of an earlier study of attitudes toward age which employed an experimental format (Bell & Stanfield, 1973). This previous investigation was conducted within a college-age population (N=280). The methodology reported below is essentially the same with the exception of the measurement device employed and the consideration of a contrasting context. In the initial study of the college sample, two scales were utilized: (1) a modified Tuckman-Lorge scale, and (2) an aging semantic differential (Rosencranz & McNevin, 1969). Although the students involved in Experiment One below are the same as those previously reported, the present research concerns itself with those findings associated with the Rosencranz and McNevin instrument. In addition, the experimental procedure has been adapted to a second setting—a sample of older retired adults (N = 96). In the latter context, only the Rosencranz and McNevin device was employed.

Experiment One

Methodology

The experiment was performed in four sections of an undergraduate sociology course at the University of Missouri, Columbia. Of the 280 individuals comprising the sample, 136 were male; 144 were female. The mean age of the sample was 19 years. In each of the classes the experimenter prefaced a recorded discussion by a previously unknown stimulus person (SP) with the following explanation:

Mr. Stanfield and I are interested in the different ways and manners by which one individual forms an impression of another. To examine this process more closely we have devised the following study. We will shortly play for you a recording made by a Mr. John Cross. Mr. Cross is a real person and additional information about him appears on the booklets you will be receiving presently. Following his discussion we will ask you to give us your impressions of him utilizing the format in the impression booklet. We will pass out the booklets now and you can familiarize yourselves with them before we play the recording. PLEASE READ OVER THESE TO YOURSELVES AND DON'T TALK ABOUT THIS AMONG YOURSELVES UNTIL WE HAVE COLLECTED ALL PAPERS AT THE END OF THE STUDY.

In the experimental classes (N's = 126, 80, and 32), two kinds of information were distributed. The forms were identical except that in one the SP was described as being "25 years old"; in the other, the phrase "65 years old" was used. These descriptions reference the SP as "young" and "old," respectively. The content of the "old" version was as follows:

The following is a short recorded discussion by Mr. John Cross, a 65-year-old journalist, regarding the contemporary question of ecology. He has read rather extensively on the subject and has written several papers in this area. Listen carefully to his remarks. DO NOT EXCHANGE COMMENTS with those about you regarding either his views or his personality. At the completion of his talk we want to obtain your impressions of him.

Both young and old versions were distributed randomly within each of the experimental groups, in such a manner that no one was aware that discrepant information was being dispersed. In the control group (N = 42), no indication of age was provided. All subsequent information, however, remained the same. The experimenter then played for each class a 15-min. recording on the topic of ecology. This discussion was succeeded by the following instructions:

Now we'd like to get your impressions of Mr. Cross. We would like to emphasize that this is not a test of you personally, nor will this material be identified as belonging to particular persons. On the contrary, this information will be kept strictly confidential. It will be of most value to us if you are completely honest in your evaluation of Mr. Cross. Also, please understand that what you put down will not be used against him or cause him to lose his job or anything like that. This is not a test of him but merely a study of how persons react to different individuals on short acquaintance.

The subjects then rated the SP on the 32-item Rosencranz and McNevin semantic differential. This scale is arrayed in a seven-choice response format. An additional bipolar pair (young-old) was included as a check on the age manipulation. The point biserial correlation between experimental treatments and actual judgment provide significant at the .001 level. The analysis to follow employs the point biserial statistic instead of the t-test, since the former technique measures both level of significance and strength of association (Ferguson, 1966). The alpha level utilized was .05 or less.

The Findings

As the differences in the ratings produced by the young-old variable were consistent from one experimental section to the other, the data were combined by equating means (the SD's were essentially identical) and the results subjected to final analysis. Column two of Table 28.1 illustrates the differential ratings of the SP by subjects receiving "young" or "old" preinformation.

It will be noted that only six of the adjectives in the original scale are significantly associated with the type of preinformation presented. This was one less than observed with the use of the Tuckman-Lorge instrument (Bell & Stanfield, 1973). Contrary to the expectations of previous writers, the associations reflect a *positive* bias toward the *older* SP. That is, those subjects given "old" preinformation tended to rate the SP as significantly more progressive, strong, active, friendly, agressive, and exciting, than those provided with "young" descriptions. In the case of the Tuckman-Lorge scale, the older person was seen to possess a better memory, be less cranky, and have less respect for tradition. His younger counterpart, on the other hand, was viewed as having more friends, being more productive, worrying less about unimportant things, and in a better position from which to marry (Bell & Stanfield, 1973). In both instances, however, these relationships, although significant, were quite weak. The strongest association in the present research, for ex-

ample, accounted for only 2% of the variance in the dependent variable. For the Tuckman-Lorge measure, the strongest relationship explained only 3% of the variance. Under these circumstances, it was not possible in either instance to conclude a definite pattern of attitudinal judgment from the data. Nevertheless, it is interesting to note the trend toward a more *positive* evaluation of the SP on the part of those receiving "old" as opposed to "young" preinformation.

Column three of Table 28.1 presents the correlation of each scale item with the subject's independent judgment of age. Although nonparametric sign tests indicated a significant tendency for subjects to favor the younger SP in this condition, the associations in question are decidely weak. In only four instances did these associations prove significant. This is in contrast to the 14 significant relationships noted with the Tuckman-Lorge measure (Bell & Stanfield, 1973). In the latter instance, the tendency again was to evaluate the "old" SP more favorably than his younger counterpart. Once again, however, it should be pointed out that the degree of association between young and old impressions varied with each dimension of perception tapped. This fact argues against a "halo effect" interpretation of the findings. The young-old variable appears to be related to some scale items more than others.

The employment of a control group made possible an examination of the effect of no preinformation as well as "young-old" preinformation on the impressions formed. Column one of Table 28.1 indicates the differential effects of preinformation–no preinformation on scale ratings. As can be seen, those subjects receiving age information generally tended to rate the SP higher on the scales in question. The same finding was observed in the case of the Tuckman-Lorge measure (Bell & Stanfield, 1973). In the present study, significant relationships were noted in only two instances (optimistic and trustful). In

Table 28.1. Relationship between adjective ratings and each independent variable in the younger sample

High End of Scale	Low End of Scale	Age Indication vs. No Age Indication[a] (N=280) I	Pre-information Young-Old[b] (N=238) II	Actual Judgment Young-Old[c] (N=280) III
Progressive	Old-fashioned	−.04	−.12*	.06
Consistent	Inconsistent	−.08	.09	.04
Independent	Dependent	−.08	−.07	−.02
Rich	Poor	−.04	−.10	−.21**
Generous	Selfish	−.03	−.04	−.01
Productive	Unproductive	.06	−.09	−.04
Busy	Idle	.02	−.06	.02
Secure	Insecure	−.03	−.05	−.06
Strong	Weak	−.08	−.12*	.04
Healthy	Unhealthy	.03	.02	.14**
Active	Passive	.01	−.15**	.03
Handsome	Ugly	−.09	−.04	.14**
Cooperative	Uncooperative	−.00	−.08	−.03
Optimistic	Pessimistic	−.15**	.02	.09
Satisfied	Dissatisfied	−.07	−.02	.03
Expectant	Resigned	−.07	.04	.09
Flexible	Inflexible	−.02	−.08	.05
Hopeful	Dejected	−.08	−.05	.02
Organized	Disorganized	−.02	−.07	.02
Happy	Sad	−.03	−.04	−.02
Friendly	Unfriendly	.05	−.11*	.05
Neat	Untidy	.00	.10	.02
Trustful	Suspicious	−.10*	.08	.00
Self-reliant	Dependent	.00	−.05	−.04
Liberal	Conservative	.02	−.03	.09
Certain	Uncertain	−.09	−.01	−.02
Tolerant	Intolerant	−.06	−.07	−.03
Pleasant	Unpleasant	.04	−.09	.05
Ordinary	Eccenrtic	.09	.09	.07
Aggressive	Defensive	−.02	−.12*	.08
Exciting	Dull	−.06	−.15**	.17**
Decisive	Indecisive	−.03	.03	.07

[a] A positive correlation indicates a higher score for the subjects receiving no age information.
[b] A positive correlation indicates a higher score for those subjects receiving "young" preinformation.
[c] A positive correlation indicates a higher score for those subjects responding with "young" judgments.
* $p = <.05$.
** $p = <.01$.

the former, only three significant associations were observed (should marry; never a nuisance to others; has great potential). On the whole, however, these associations were not frequent or strong enough to warrant interpretation.

Ratings by experimental and control groups showed a weak pattern of more favorable ratings of the older SP. This tendency proved significant in six instances. On the other hand, in the case of actual age judgments, a more favorable evaluation of the *younger* SP was evidenced. Associations in this instance, however, were notably weak. Only 3 of the 21 correlations favoring younger age proved statistically significant. It is apparent from the data, therefore, that age indications *per se* are not sufficient to control strongly either positive or negative judgments of the type called for in the present research.

Experiment Two

Methodology and Findings

This experiment was performed on a sample of older adults representing retirement organizations in 15 counties in central Missouri. The meeting in question was held for the purpose of discussing the implications of the 1971 White House Conference on Aging. Thirty-two of the subjects were male; 64 were female. The mean age of the group was 66 years. Essentially the same research format was employed. On the basis of the previous analysis, however, no control group was utilized. Column one of Table 28.2 illustrates the differential ratings of the SP by subjects receiving "young" or "old" preinformation.

It will be noted that none of the adjectives in the original scale are significantly associated with the type of preinformation presented. That is, there is no significant pattern of attitudinal judgment reflected in the data. This is true for those receiving "old" as well as "young" descriptions of the SP. On the other hand, there seems a slight tendency for the present sample to rate the "younger" SP somewhat higher on the aging semantic differential scales than was the case in the college-age sample. Again, however, this finding is only suggestive and far from significant.

Column two of Table 28.2 gives the correlation of each scale item with the subject's independent judgment of age. Again, although nonparemetric sign tests indicated a significant tendency for subjects

to favor the younger SP in this condition, the associations in question were quite weak. In only four instances did these associations prove significant. Specifically, the younger SP was seen as significantly more progressive, handsome, exciting, and flexible. While the general pattern is not statistically significant, the present sample does tend toward a more positive rating of the *younger* SP than was the case in the college groupings.

Discussion

A number of things are suggested by the present study. First of all, the data do not clearly demonstrate a social change effect. While the tendency among younger age groups to rate the *older* SP higher on the aging scales is apparent, it is not reflected to the same extent among the older respondents. To the contrary, the older respondents tended to rate the younger more favorably. In addition, both young and old subjects tended to rate the younger SP more favorably in those instances where an actual judgment of age was made. Although the biserial r's are seldom significant in either instance, the trend in evaluation reversal is clear. It should be noted in this instance that these findings were consistent across the age and sex categories of both groups of subjects.

The apparent contradictions between preinformation set and actual age judgments may be endemic to the present methodology. As the manipulation of age and impression utilized a tape recorded conversation, it seems certain that in addition to the explicit information given on age, the implicit information conveyed by tone of voice, professional attainment, expressive style, etc. may have acted to influence the research findings. The tendency, for example, to rate the younger SP more favorably in instances of actual age judgments is consistent with the tendency of controls to rate the SP somewhat younger than experimental groups. It may also be the case that the age attributed to the voice in the "old age" condition may not actually have been old enough. There may very well be a point when a marked shift in attitude toward older adults occurs, and this point quite possibly is after age 65. As for the higher ratings of the older SP in the younger sample, it may be that a 65-year-old journalist, still employed, is viewed as considerably more prestigious than a younger journalist. Consequently,

prestige rather than age designations may be determinative of present judgments.

In the final analysis, it is not appropriate (as others have done) to generalize these findings and/or suggestions to the culture at large. It is certain, however, that chronological age exhibits different meanings to different individuals. It is also evident that these meanings vary both within as well as across generations. Generally speaking,

Table 28.2. Relationship between adjective ratings and each independent variable in the older sample

High End of Scale	Low End of Scale	Preinformation: Young-Old[a] (N=96) I	Actual Judgment: Young-Old[b] (N=96) III
Progressive	Old-fashioned	.10	.34**
Consistent	Inconsistent	−.12	−.09
Independent	Dependent	.00	.03
Rich	Poor	.12	.03
Productive	Unproductive	.10	.08
Busy	Idle	.09	.07
Secure	Insecure	−.04	−.01
Strong	Weak	.05	.08
Generous[c]	Selfish	.07	.13
Healthy[c]	Unhealthy	−.04	.02
Active	Passive	−.16	.02
Handsome	Ugly	.13	.36**
Cooperative	Uncooperative	.05	.09
Optimistic[c]	Pessimistic	.17	.13
Satisfied	Dissatisfied	.01	−.05
Expectant	Resigned	−.16	.03
Flexible	Inflexible	.14	.22*
Hopeful	Dejected	.19	.09
Organized	Disorganized	−.10	−.03
Happy	Sad	.04	.09
Friendly[c]	Unfriendly	.14	.16
Neat	Untidy	−.06	.01
Trustful	Suspicious	.14	.17
Self-reliant[c]	Dependent	.01	−.07
Liberal	Conservative	.07	.12
Certain	Uncertain	.04	.09
Tolerant	Intolerant	.17	.09
Pleasant[c]	Unpleasant	.17	.17
Ordinary	Eccentric	.10	.02
Aggressive	Defensive	−.07	.09
Exciting	Dull	.11	.33**
Decisive	Indecisive	−.07	.11

[a] A positive correlation indicates a higher score for those subjects receiving "young" preinformation.
[b] A positive correlation indicates a higher score for those responding with "young" judgments.
[c] These scales were reversed when presented to the subjects.
* $p = <.05$.
** $p = <.01$.

however, the effect of age designations upon attitudinal response patterns remains open to question. The present methodology, while suggestive of age effects, does not permit an extensive examination of those additional (usually implicit) factors influencing particular appraisals. It would seem essential that subsequent research build on the present model by

1. employing real stimulus individuals
2. providing a greater age span in relation to the rating of specific attitudinal judgments
3. controlling for such variables as occupation, education, income, etc.
4. giving close attention to such characteristics of voice as tonal quality and expressive style.

Summary

The present study utilized an experimental format to examine the influence of age designations upon differential ratings of a stimulus person. Two experiments were conducted—one in a college-age population (N=280); the other in a grouping of older, retired adults (N=96). In both settings, subjects heard a recorded discussion by a SP described as being either 25 or 65 years of age. Ratings were made on the 32-item Rosencranz and McNevin aging semantic differential. The data reveal a slight but nonsignificant tendency for younger subjects to rate an older SP more positively on the scales in question than do the older subjects. In the case of actual age judgments, however, all subjects, regardless of age, reflect a tendency (again, not statistically significant) to rate the younger SP more positively than the older individual. In and of itself, chronological age appeared insufficient to control strongly a pattern of judgment relative to a SP. These findings call to question (1) the employment of chronological categories in assessing age-related attitudes, and (2) that research which reports the predominately negative character of such responses. It is suggested that subsequent research incorporate real stimulus individuals when attempting to gauge the issue at hand.

References

AARONSON, B. S. Personality stereotypes of aging. *Journal of Gerontology*, 1966, *21*, 458–462.

AXELROD, S., & EISDORFER, C. Attitudes toward old people: An empirical analysis of the stimulus-group validity of the Tuckman-Lorge Questionnaire. *Journal of Gerontology*, 1961, *16*, 75–80.

BELL, B. D., & STANFIELD, G. G. The aging stereotype in experimental perspective. *Gerontologist*, 1973, *13*, 341–344.

EISDORFER, C., & ALTROCCHI, J. A comparison of attitudes toward old age and mental illness. *Journal of Gerontology*, 1961, *16*, 340–343.

EISDORFER, C. Attitudes toward old people: A re-analysis of the item-validity of the stereotype scale. *Journal of Gerontology*, 1966, *21*, 455–462.

FERGUSON, G. A. *Statistical analysis in psychology and education.* McGraw-Hill, New York, 1966.

GINZBERG, R. The negative attitude toward the elderly. *Geriatrics*, 1952, *7*, 297–302.

GOLDE, P., & KOGAN, N. A. A sentence completion procedure for assessing attitudes toward old people. *Journal of Gerontology*, 1959, *14*, 355–363.

KOGAN, N. A., & WALLACH, M. A. Age changes in values and attitudes. *Journal of Gerontology*, 1961, *16*, 272–280.

KOGAN, N. A. Attitudes toward old people: The development of a scale and an examination of correlates. *Journal of Abnormal Social Psychology*, 1961, *62*, 44–54.

LABOVITZ, S. Some observations on measurement and statistics. *Social Forces*, 1967, *46*, 151–160.

MCKEE, J. B. *Introduction to sociology.* Holt, Rinehart & Winston, New York, 1969.

ROSENCRANZ, H. A., & MCNEVIN, T. E. A factor analysis of attitudes toward the aged. *Gerontologist*, 1969, *9*, 55–59.

SLATER, P. E. Cultural attitudes toward the aged. *Geriatrics*, 1963, *18*, 308–314.

TOBY, J. *Contemporary society: An introduction to sociology.* John Wiley & Sons, New York, 1971.

TUCKMAN, J., & LORGE, I. The effect of institutionalization on attitudes toward old people. *Journal of Abnormal Social Psychology*, 1952, 47, 337–344. (a)

TUCKMAN, J., & LORGE, I. The influence of a course in the psychology of the adult on attitudes toward old people and older workers. *Journal of Educational Psychology*, 1952, *43*, 400–407. (b)

TUCKMAN, J., & LORGE, I. Attitudes toward old people. *Journal of Social Psychology*, 1953, 37, 249–260. (a)

TUCKMAN, J., & LORGE, I. When does old age begin and a worker become old? *Journal of Gerontology*, 1953, *8*, 483–488. (b)

TUCKMAN, J., & LORGE, I. The influence of changed directions on stereotypes about aging: Before and after instruction. *Educational Psychological Measurements*, 1954, *14*, 128–132.

TUCKMAN, J., & LORGE, I. Attitude toward aging of individuals with experiences with the aged. *Journal of Genetic Psychology*, 1958, 92, 199–204.

CHAPTER SIX: SUGGESTED FURTHER READINGS

BALTES, P. B., and SCHAIE, K. W. (Eds.). *Life-span developmental psychology: Personality and socialization.* New York: Academic Press, 1973.

KOHLBERG, L. Stage and sequence: The cognitive-developmental approach to socialization. In D. A. Goslin (Ed.), *Handbook of socialization theory and research.* Chicago: Rand McNally, 1969. Pp. 347–480.

WILEY, M. W., FONER, A., HESS, B., and TOBY, M. L. Socialization for the middle and later years. In D. A. Goslin (Ed.), *Handbook of socialization theory and research.* Chicago: Rand McNally, 1969. Pp. 951–982.

chapter seven
sex roles

The process of socialization is a continuous one. From birth to death, there are a myriad of social-role changes and sex-role changes to be encountered. The child learns very early in life who it is in terms of sex, and sex roles become very significant identifying elements in society. In fact, it is apparent during early childhood how culture, through institutions such as the church, family, and school, is instrumental in shaping and prescribing masculine-feminine roles. By the time adolescence occurs, sex roles become much larger than those elements identified by society as the adolescent experiments with sexuality and actually struggles in the quest for sexual identity.

After adolescence, sex roles change again for the young adult. Men and women within a marriage or an intimate relationship assume certain roles that are markedly different from their roles when they were without a partner. The young adult also assumes new roles within the framework of job, friends, community, and so forth. While being socialized themselves, the young adults who are parents are simultaneously engaged in the socialization of their children. Often by the time women and men have reached middle age, they have had to assume dual responsibilities: parents over their own children and caretakers or authorities over their aging parents. Finally, in old age, sex roles make a last change. With the birth and death of others in the family, the elderly move into grandparenthood or widowhood.

Since all humans exist within some culture which prescribes both explicitly and implicitly certain patterns for living, sex roles can be expected to change with the passing of time. Yet when a new role is imposed by circumstances beyond one's control, the change experienced is a dramatic one. If a women is married for twenty years and becomes a widow long before she is prepared for this role, the effect on her is likely to be quite startling. Parents who suddenly become childless, or children who become parentless probably experience a radical change in their sex roles, as well as in other aspects of their lives.

The change in sex roles is also dramatic if one experiences a certain landmark event at a time that is either earlier or later than the culture deems appropriate. For example, if a ten-year-old girl begins menstruation and develops the breasts and hips of a young woman, it is understandable that she is alienated from her peers, who are still allowed to be "girls," or that she attains status and expectations from others that are new to her. Perhaps when this same ten-year-old becomes a middle-aged women, she will correlate her early maturation with senescence: "Will my body begin its physical regression as rapidly as it matured?" What do developmentalists really know, in fact, about the correlation between these two periods of rapid change? At this time, they know very little.

If a man and a woman marry and have children at fifteen or marry for the first time at sixty-five, they are exhibiting behavior that is age-inappropriate in our society. If one never experiences marriage or parenthood, if one chooses to reject traditional sex roles altogether in pursuit of a viable alternative, it is concluded that such behavior is probably deviant or inappropriate. Developmentalists must examine the whole gamut of potential changes in sex roles throughout life. They must examine the various changes in sex roles in a context that transcends the traditional view to achieve a richer understanding of what is, and what might be, the liberation of human sex-role potential.

29. THE EMERGENCE OF SEX DIFFERENCES

JEROME KAGAN

The current preoccupation with psychological sex differences has generated a debate concerning the degree to which these differences are purely the result of history or the partial consequence of biological differences between the sexes. A useful strategy is to assume that the earlier a particular behavioral difference appears in the life cycle, the more likely it is influenced by biological factors. If a 7-day-old boy is more active than a 7-day-old girl, we are tempted to conclude that this variety derives from biological factors—either heredity or pre- or perinatal conditions. This paper summarizes what we have learned about sex differences in the opening two years of life.

Before beginning the discussion, it is important to note that biological differences do not place serious constraints on the kinds of vocational and social roles men and women should assume in our society. Even if a small proportion of occupations—and it is probably less than 1 percent—is biologically better suited to one sex, most roles in Western society can probably be filled with competence by men or women. Thus the reader should regard the present essay as an intellectual adventure, not a sociopolitical treatise.

Although most of the research on sex differences has been atheoretical, it is helpful to organize the knowledge we have gained along theoretical dimensions. We shall try to synthesize this discussion around the following four dimensions: susceptibility to fear, cognitive functioning, variability, and social class.

Susceptibility to Fear

Most investigations of male and female infants during the first eighteen months of life report that there is a slight tendency for the infant female to display fear and anxiety more frequently and more intensely than the male. For example, in a typical experimental situation a mother and her 1-year-old infant are brought into a strange room in a university laboratory. Under these conditions the girl is more likely to remain near her mother or in physical contact with her for a much longer period of time than the boy. If the room contains toys, the boy is likely to venture out after fifteen or twenty seconds; the girl, perhaps, only after a minute. Moreover, in more restricted laboratory situations, where unusual visual or auditory stimuli are presented to a child, the female infant under 1 year is more likely to cry and show distress than is the male. In one of our experiments we found that twice as many 4-month-old girls as boys cried in the service of fear in a strange laboratory (1).

There seems to be some generality to this finding, for the same sex difference occurs among rhesus monkeys. Mitchell found that female rhesus infants are likely to stay closer to their mothers than male infants during the first two months of life (2). Since the mother pushes her son away from her but restrains her daughter, this difference is not due solely to the fact that the male infants have a disposition to wander.

The reason for this sex difference in susceptibility to fear is not clear. One possibility is that the male is more likely to issue a response in an uncertain situation. The activation of a response tends to buffer fear. That is, beginning at around 4 months of age, girls begin to inhibit active motoric responses in a strange situation, while boys remain active. If a mother and infant are placed behind a wire barrier and the mother puts her infant on one

247

side, 1-year-old girls are more likely to freeze, while boys are more likely to initiate some action. The boy might see a piece of paper on the floor and examine it, or try to shake the barrier. Each of these responses diverts the child from the source of frustration or uncertainty and aborts the fear. We believe that action has the capability of forestalling fear when a child is in an uncertain situation. Thus, if boys have a natural disposition to action in situations that are uncertain, even though a particular behavior may have no relevance for the uncertainty, the boy may be protected from emerging fear. In any case, the girl infants' earlier display of fear, motor inhibition, and tendency to stay close to the primary caretaker are not easily interpreted as a result of differential treatment by parents and, therefore, are likely to be a partial product of biology.

A second explanation for the earlier display of fear, in addition to the suggestion that boys are more likely to act in an uncertain situation, is the fact that the infant female is biologically ahead of the male. Growth of the myelin sheath around the axons of the central nervous system and the development of bone and muscle are precocious in the female. If this known precocity in biological functions is paralleled by precocious psychological functioning, a set of important corollaries follows.

The first elements of knowledge the infant develops are called *schemata*. A schema should be viewed as an abstract representation of an experience. Before the second month has passed all infants have developed schemata for some of the events in the world around them. If a female were precocious, she might develop these schemata sooner and possess, at an earlier age, a better articulated idea of her life space. An event that is slightly different from the original one that produced the schema—called a dsicrepant event— alerts the infant and motivates him to understand the unfamiliar—that is, to resolve the uncertainty the discrepant event generated. A 4-month-old baby who has a representation for his crib and room at home becomes alerted if he is placed in a strange bed. The infant can cope with this discrepant event by assimilating it or withdrawing from it. If either of these reactions occurs, the infant will not cry. However, if the infant can neither assimilate nor withdraw, he becomes afraid. The earlier and more frequent occurrences of fear, in the girl, in discrepant situations may reflect the fact that she has developed better articulated schemata than the boy. She is alerted by new situations but cannot understand them; hence, she cries more often. This hypothesis is supported by the fact that first-born girls who were most fearful in a laboratory setting when they were 4 months old displayed the most creative play with toys when they were 13 months old. This continuity between early fear and creative play nine months later did not occur for boys(3).

In most young mammals withdrawal is the preferred response to fear. If the infant habitually withdraws as a response to fear during the first year of life, a strong tendency to display that behavior can be established. If this argument has any merit, it might help explain why girls and older women are more likely to withdraw and show more cautiousness in fearful contexts than males.

However, we must acknowledge the possibility that the more frequent female withdrawal could result from tendencies favoring retreat under conditions of uncertainty. If male and female rhesus monkeys are raised in isolation chambers from birth and brought together as adults, the females tend to withdraw, while males are likely to attack(4). These different actions cannot be the result of differential growth of schemata, since both animals had the same environment and both were subadults when tested. At the moment, we do not have enough information to allow us to choose between these two hypotheses to explain the behavioral facts. Moreover, it is possible that both arguments have some merit, and that the female not only has a stronger tendency to withdraw but is also precocious in cognitive development.

Cognitive Functioning

There is a second implication that stems from the fact that females are precocious compared with males. The paired cerebral hemispheres of the brain become increasingly asymmetric with respect to relative dominance of one over the other as the child grows. It has been suggested that, in the newborn infant, the cerebral hemispheres are of approximately equal dominance; but, with age, the left hemisphere gradually gains dominance over the right(5). For most individuals the major site of language function is in the left hemisphere, although a capacity for language comprehension is contained in the right hemisphere. If the girl were developmentally precocious, she would attain left-hemisphere dominance at a faster rate than the boy, perhaps because of precocious myelination of the corpus callosum and the medial surface of the temporal lobe. If this were true, then the important speech functions contained in the left hemisphere would develop at a faster rate among girls than boys. This deduction fits well with the fact that preschool girls generally begin to speak a few months earlier than boys, and their speech is more comprehensive, more accurate, and more complex. But since the boy eventually develops a language as complex and rich as the girl's, it is possible that the girl only has a temporary advantage.

Support for the idea that language functions do develop earlier in girls is found in an extensive longitudinal study of firstborn white children from 4 to 27 months of age(6). During the first year of life nonmeaningful vocalizations, often called babbling, are a better index of the state of excitability to interesting events among girls than boys. If a tape recorder plays a sample of human speech to 8-month-olds, the girls who are most attentive to that

speech are most likely to vocalize for a few seconds after the speech ends. No such relation exists for boys. Further, the educational level of the girl's family is an excellent predictor of the degree to which she increases her vocalizations during the last half of the first year. The boy's social class is unrelated to changes in vocalization over that same period.

In general, young girls who vocalized frequently during the last half of the first year were, at 3 years of age, more active and more excitable than quiet female infants. No comparable relation occurred among the boys. These data, as well as others, indicate that babbling in the infant girl is a sensitive index of the excitement generated by interesting experience. This inference is in accord with the fact that babbling scores on infant intelligence tests in the first year are better predictors of future intellectual functioning among preschool girls than among boys(7). The likelihood that differences in brain functioning are related to language competence is supported by an interesting study performed on adult epileptic patients who had an epileptic focus in either the right or left temporal lobe. Some adult patients had part of the left temporal lobe surgically removed, while others had part of the right temporal lobe removed. Following surgery, both language and nonlanguage tests were administered to all patients. For those who lost the left temporal lobe, verbal functioning was more seriously impaired in women than in men. Removal of the right hemisphere, which seems to be important for competence on nonverbal tasks, impaired performance on spatial reasoning more seriously for men than for women(8). This finding tentatively supports the possibility of sex differences in brain functioning. These data seem reliable enough to invite additional inquiry. Although they do not come close to proving that there are sex differences in central nervous system organization, they are sufficiently strong to suggest that this possibility should be entertained. Indeed, the special link between vocalization and attentional excitement in the infant girl may be a joint product of central nervous system organization and special caretaking practices toward daughters. Since societies are likely to adopt practices that are friendly to the biological attributes of the organism, both hypotheses may have merit.

We might note that Western culture has produced many creative women poets and writers. However, in the nonverbal art forms—music and painting—there are far fewer women than one would expect, considering their numbers in the language arts. Perhaps this asymmetry in choice of creative mode is the price women pay for their initial left hemispheric advantage. Perhaps it is woman, not man, who is the intellectual specialist; woman, not man, who insists on interlacing sensory experience with meaning. These reversal of popular homilies join other maxims that science has begun to question. For now we know that it is the female, not the male, who is most predictable; the female, not the male, who is biologically more resistant to infirmity; the female's anatomy, not the male's, that is nature's preferred form. Man's a priori guesses about sex differences have reflected an understandable but excessive masculine narcissism.

Sex Differences in Variability

In addition to sex differences in precocity, the female also shows less variability for many biological attributes. More boys than girls are extreme on dimensions like height, weight, and bone growth. There are more very tall and very short men, more very heavy and very light men. This variability in physical growth also holds for tested intelligence. We have known for many years that there are more men than women who have very high or very low IQ scores.

The greater male variability is accompanied by weaker long-term continuity for both psychological and physical variables. As indicated above, height, weight, or number of ossification centers in the wrist are more predictable from one age to another among females than among males. Analogously, IQ scores and grades in school are more predictable over time for girls than for boys.

If biological factors led to more extreme instances of lethargy or irritability among boys than girls, one would expect a different relation between familial experience and future development. This possibility forms a liaison with our last theme.

Sex Differences in Relation to Social Class

Many studies of Western children have found a closer correlation for girls than boys between indexes of cognitive development and social class. Moreover, this pattern occurs not only in the United States but also in Europe and rural areas of Guatemala. Typically the correlation between social class (as measured by education and occupation in the United States or by type of housing and sanitation in rural, primitive areas) and some index of cognitive development, be it attentiveness during infancy or IQ score during school age, is higher for girls than for boys(9). The question is, How do we interpret this replicable and provocative phenomenon?

The differences in correlation between social class of family and cognitive achievement among girls of school age is understandable if we assume that the girl is more likely to adopt the values of her family than the boy. This is a reasonable assumption. Since there is a major difference in concern with intellectual development between poor and affluent parents, we should get larger covariation between social class and indexes of cognitive achievement for girls than for boys. However, this mechanism could not operate during the first year of life, when the child does not have a motive to adopt the values or skills of his parent. At this early age, it is likely that there is a greater variability across social-class levels in a mother's reaction to her daughter than to her son. Most mothers in the United States, regardless of their social class, tend to believe their sons should develop independence, a sense of responsibility, and some vocational role. When working-class and middle-class mothers of preschool children were asked to teach their child a new task, mothers of both classes were more achievement oriented toward their sons than toward their daughters and adopted a much more businesslike posture toward their sons (10).

Poor mothers seemed to project their greater sense of impotence and inadequacy onto their daughters more than onto their sons and were less likely to encourage or give high praise to their daughters' simple accomplishments. Middle-class mothers spend more time talking to and entertaining their daughters and also chide them more often for task incompetence (11). In one of our longitudinal studies, we visited a large group of children when they were 27 months of age. The observer recorded descriptive statements that dealt with aspects of the mother-child interaction. There were no class differences for most of the dimensions that we studied. However, when a class difference in maternal behavior emerged, it was more likely to be for daughters than for sons. The most striking difference occurred for punishment of incompetent behavior. Upper-middle-class mothers were much more likely to note incompetent behavior and criticize it in their daughters than in their sons.

We noted all the incidents that provoked the mother to criticize or punish her child. Less than 1 percent involved incompetence among lower-middle-class boys, upper-middle-class boys, or lower-middle-class girls. However, 2.4 percent of the maternal criticisms of the child involved this particular violation for the middle- and upper-middle-class mothers. Well-educated mothers or daughters were three times more likely than poorly educated ones to chide the daughter for not performing up to a standard held by the mother (12). This difference was specific

to task competence, for the well-educated mothers were more tolerant of other kinds of violations in their daughters than were the working-class mothers. Other studies with older children reveal that first-born girls experience a greater pressure for competent performance on problems. Mothers of preschool daughters are more likely to remind them of incompetent performance and be intrusive while the child is working at the problems. We are suggesting that the mothers from a broad range of social and educational backgrounds differ more in their preoccupation with intellectual development in their daughters than in their sons, and this phenomenon could explain the greater correlation between maternal social class and cognitive development among girls.

In addition, the sex differences in variability alluded to earlier imply that there are more infant boys than girls who are extremely irritable, alert, or lethargic. If, as a result of biological factors, an infant is at the extreme of a psychological dimension, he should be less influenced by specific caretaking practices than a child of more normative temperament. For it is difficult to play for long periods of time reciprocally with a highly mobile, highly apathetic, or highly irritable infant. Thus the mother who initiates these caretaking actions with an infant of extreme temperament will influence the child less than one who initiates the same sequence with a less extreme child. This would lead to a poorer correlation between a mother's practices and the child's subsequent development for boys than for girls.

There is some reason to believe that social experience does affect girls' development in a more orderly fashion than that of boys. Three-month-old infants were observed in their home with their mothers, and the amount of face-to-face contact between mother and child was noted. After these observations were made in the home, the infants came to the laboratory and looked at representations of human faces, as well as geometric stimuli. The girls who experienced the most face-to-face interaction in the home were most attentive toward the faces, but this relationship did not hold for boys. Moreover, the tendency to remain quiet at 1 month and show low irritability at 3 months was a good predictor of high attentiveness among the boys but not among the girls(13). One interpretation is that specific experiences with the mother exert a major influence on the subsequent attentiveness of the girl, while congenital temperament is more influential for boys. The effect of experience in the home is more faithfully reflected in the infant girl than in the infant boy. Perhaps greater male variability in both maturational development and display of temperamental attributes is responsible for this difference.

We have summarized some of the early differences that emerge in the young infant before the first two years of life are over, and have suggested that some may be biological in origin and lead to slightly different developmental routes for boys and girls. However, these differences are subtle, not blatant, and the environment has power to modify them. Since environments accommodate to the temperamental and biological attributes of children, it is likely that there always has been and will continue to be an intimate interaction between experience and biology that tempts men and women in any society to march to slightly different pipers and to be gratified by events that the other sex disregards.

References

1. JEROME KAGAN, *Change and Continuity in Infancy* (New York: John Wiley & Sons, 1971).
2. G. D. MITCHELL, "Attachment Differences in Male and Female Infant Monkeys," *Child Development* 39 (1968): 611–20.
3. KAGAN.
4. G. D. MITCHELL, "Persistent Behavior Pathology in Rhesus Monkeys Following Early Social Isolation," *Folia Primatologica* 8 (1968): 132–47.
5. M. S. GAZZANIGA, *The Bisected Brain* (New York: Appleton-Century-Crofts, Inc., 1970).
6. KAGAN.
7. T. MOORE, "Language and Intelligence—a Longitudinal Study of the First Eight Years," *Human Development* 10 (1967): 88–106.
8. H. LANSDELL, "The Use of Factor Scores from the Wechsler-Bellevue Scale of Intelligence in Assessing Patients with Temporal Lobe Removal," *Cortex* 4 (1968): 257–68.
9. E. E. WERNER, "Sex Differences in Correlations between Children's IQs and Measures of Parental Ability and Environmental Ratings," *Developmental Psychology* 1 (1969): 280–85.
10. R. D. HESS et al., "The Cognitive Environments of Uurban Preschool Children" (report to the Graduate School of Education, University of Chicago, 1968 and 1969).
11. M. K. ROTHBART, "Birth Order and Mother-Child Interaction in an Achievement Situation," *Journal of Personality and Social Psychology* 17 (1971): 113–20.
12. C. M. MINTON, J. KAGAN, and J. A. LEVINE, "Mother-Child Interaction in 27-Month-Old Children," *Child Development* (1971), in press.
13. H. A. MOSS and K. S. ROBSON, "The Relation between Amount of Time Infants Spend in Various States and the Development of Visual Behavior," *Child Development* 41 (1970): 509–17.

30. EFFECTS OF MATERNAL EMPLOYMENT ON THE CHILD— A REVIEW OF THE RESEARCH

LOIS WLADIS HOFFMAN

In a previous review of the literature on the effects of maternal employment on the child, we pointed out that the earlier view that maternal employment had a great many effects on the child, all of them bad, had been replaced by a new outlook—that maternal employment had no effects at all (Hoffman, 1963a). We assumed that maternal employment did have an effect. What the effect was might depend on the nature of the employment, the attitude of the working mother, her family circumstances, the social class, whether employment is full or part time, the age and sex of the child, the kinds of child care arrangements that are set up, and a whole host of other conditions, but until the research questions had been properly defined and explored, we were not prepared to concede that there was no effect. While studies of maternal employment as a general concept yielded little, it was suggested that examining the effects under specified conditions might prove more fruitful. To demonstrate, we tried to show that when the relationships between maternal employment and a child characteristic were examined separately for various subgroups, interesting patterns were revealed. Thus, juvenile delinquency did seem to relate to maternal employment in the middle class, although it did not in the lower class. Part-time maternal employment seemed to have a positive effect on adolescent children, although this was not equally true for full-time employment or for younger children. The lack of consistent findings with respect to the effects on the child's independence or academic achievement was tied to the failure to examine these relationships separately for each sex. And the mother's attitude toward employment was seen as an important aspect of the situation that would affect her child-rearing behavior and thus mediate the impact of her employment on the child.

It was our hope that such speculations would give rise to new empirical investigations, but the intervening years have produced few studies of maternal employment. About the same time our review was published three others appeared: Stoltz, 1960; Siegel and Haas, 1963; and Yudkin and Holme, 1963. Perhaps the overall impression given was not that maternal employment required more careful study, but that it should not be studied at all. Most of the more recent studies reviewed here were only incidentally interested in the effects of maternal employment on the child, and the few that focused on this variable were modest in scope.

On the other hand, it was previously noted that segments of the American population that contributed more than an equal share of the working mothers—blacks and single-parent families in particular—were not studied at all. A few investigators have begun to fill this gap (Kriesberg, 1970; Rieber & Womack, 1968; Smith, 1969; Woods, 1972).

Moreover, there have been some methodological improvements. Few studies today would lump boys and girls together, and most consider relationships separately for each social class. Several studies have, in fact, focused only on one class—the professional mother being a particularly popular subject currently (Birnbaum, 1971; Garland, 1972; Hoffman, 1973; Holmstrom, 1972; Jones, Lundsteen, & Michael, 1967; Poloma, 1972; Rapoport & Rapoport, 1972). These studies have, in turn, revealed the need to consider both the education of the parents and the nature of the mother's job. The new studies indicate that the mother who works as a professional has a very different influence than one who works in a less intellectually demanding and less prestigious position. Since women's jobs often underuse their talents and training, education and the nature of the job are important singly and also in interaction.

Even methodologically, however, the studies leave much to be desired. Very few controlled on family size or ordinal position, although these variables relate to both maternal employment and most of the child characteristics studied. Failure to match on these may give an advantage to the working mother, since her family is smaller, and small family size contributes positively to cognitive abilities, particularly in the lower class (Clausen & Clausen, 1973). The need to control on more than one variable simultaneously is apparent in a number of reports, while the crudeness of the social class control is a problem in others.

But the most distressing aspect of the current research situation is the lack of theory. The typical study uses the sniper approach—maternal employment is run against whatever other variables are at hand, usually scores on intelligence tests or personality inventories. Even when a study indicates a complex pattern of findings or results counter to the accumulated research, no attempt is made to explain the pattern or reconcile the discrepancy.

Furthermore, the typical study deals only with two levels—the mother's employment status and a child characteristic. The many steps in between—family roles and interaction patterns, the child's perceptions, the mother's feelings about her employment, the child-rearing practices— are rarely measured. As previously noted (Hoffman & Lippitt, 1960), the distance between an antecedent condition like maternal employment and a child characteristic is too great to be covered in a single

leap. Several levels should be examined in any single study to obtain adequate insight into the process involved.

To help counteract the generally atheoretical aspect of so much of the maternal employment research, the present review tries to organize the data around five basic approaches.

Hypotheses About the Effects of Maternal Employment on the Child

What is the process by which maternal employment might affect the child? The ideas, whether implicit or explicit, that seem to guide the research and discussion can be classified into five general forms:

1. Because the mother is employed, she, and possibly her husband, provide a different model of behavior for the children in the family. Children learn sex role behavior largely from their parents. To the extent that a different role is carried out by the working mother than the nonworking mother, the child has a different conception of what the female role is. The self-concept of girls is particularly affected.

2. The mother's emotional state is influenced by whether or not she is employed, and this affects her interaction with her children.

3. Employed and nonemployed mothers probably use different child-rearing practices, not only because the mother's emotional state is different but also because the situational demands are different.

4. Because of her regular absences from the home, the working mother provides less personal supervision of her child than does the nonworking mother; and it is usually assumed that the supervision is less adequate.

5. Again, because of the working mother's regular absences from the home, the

child is deprived, either emotionally or cognitively, or perceives her absence as rejection.

In the sections that follow we examine each of these hypotheses and report the relevant research.

The ultimate dependent variables that have been studied—that is, the child characteristics that are the focus of attention—can be classified as follows: (*a*) the child's social attitudes and values; (*b*) the child's general mental health and social adjustment and independence or dependence specifically; and (*c*) the child's cognitive abilities, achievement motivation, and intellectual performance. . . .

The Working Mother as Role Model

Hartley (1961) has observed that one experience common to all children of working mothers is that they "are exposed to a female parent who implements a social role not implemented by the female parents of other children [p. 42]." Since the child learns sex roles from observations of his parents, maternal employment influences his concept of the female role. More importantly, since one of the earliest statuses assigned to the child is that of gender, maternal employment presumably affects the female child's concept of herself and the behavior expected of her.

There is an impressive array of data to support this theory. Hartley (1961) found that elementary-school-age daughters of working mothers, in comparison to daughters of nonworking mothers, are more likely to say that both men and women typically engage in a wide variety of specified adult activities, ranging from using a sewing machine to using a gun and from selecting home furnishings to climbing mountains. That is, the daughters of working mothers indicated more similarity in the participation of men and women. They saw women as less restricted to their homes

and more active in the world outside.[1]

That the division of labor between husband and wife is affected by maternal employment is well established. Husbands of employed women help more in household tasks including child care. While considerable traditionalism remains and working women engage in more domestic tasks than do their husbands, the division of household tasks is nonetheless more egalitarian when the mother is employed (Blood & Hamblin, 1958; Hall & Schroeder, 1970; Holmstrom, 1972; Kligler, 1954; Szoali, 1966; Walker, 1970b; Weil, 1961). Furthermore, this difference is reflected in the children's perceptions, as seen in Hoffman's (1963b) study of children in the third through sixth grades and Finkelman's (1966) more recent study of fifth and sixth graders. Children five years of age and older whose mothers work are more likely to approve of maternal employment (Duvall, 1955; Mathews, 1933), and King, McIntyre, and Axelson (1968) reported that ninth graders whose mothers worked viewed maternal employment as less threatening to the marital relationship. These investigators also found that the greater the father's participation in household tasks, the more accepting of maternal employment were the adolescent boys and girls.

Furthermore, daughters of working mothers view work as something they will want to do when they are mothers. This was reported by Hartley (1960) in her study of elementary school children and in four studies of adolescent girls (Banducci, 1967; Below, 1969; Peterson, 1958; Smith, 1969). It was also found in college women (Almquist & Angrist, 1971; Zissis, 1964) and as a background factor among working professional women (Astin, 1969;

---

[1] When asked to indicate which activities women liked and disliked, the daughters of working mothers reported more liking and less disliking of all activities—household, work, and recreation.

Birnbaum, 1971).[2] Douvan (1963) and Roy (1963) found that adolescent daughters of working mothers were, in fact, more likely to be already employed.

Another closely related group of findings dealt with the attitudes toward women's roles in general. Are working mothers' children less likely to endorse a traditional or stereotypic view of women? Douvan (1963) found that the daughters of working mothers scored low on an index of traditional femininity.[3] Vogel, Broverman, Broverman, Clarkson, and Rosenkrantz (1970) studied the relationship between the sex role perceptions held by male and by female college students and their mothers' employment. Sex role perceptions were measured by having subjects describe the typical adult male and the typical adult female by checking a point along a continuum between two bipolar descriptions. Previous work with this scale had indicated which descriptions were more typically assigned to each sex and also which traits were seen as positive or negative. In general, the positively valued stereotypes about males included items that reflected effectiveness and competence; the highly valued female-associated items described warmth and expressiveness. Both male students and female students with employed mothers perceived significantly smaller differences between men and wom-

en, with the women being more affected by maternal employment than were the men. Furthermore, the effect of maternal employment was to raise the estimation of one's own sex; that is, each sex added positive traits usually associated with the opposite sex—daughters of working mothers saw women as competent and effective, while sons of working mothers saw men as warm and expressive.

. . .

It is clear that the effects of maternal employment considered in this light must be different for males and females. For one thing, although maternal employment might affect all children's concepts of the woman's role, it should affect only the girls' self-concept, unless the mother's working also reflects something about the father. Douvan found that lower-class adolescent boys whose mothers work full time are less likely than those whose mothers do not work to name their father as the person they most admire. In the lower class, the mother's employment may communicate to the child that the father is an economic failure. McCord, McCord, and Thurber (1963) also found in their study of lower-class boys from intact families that the sons of women who were employed during the boys' preadolescent years were significantly more likely than were the sons of full-time housewives to indicate disapproval of their fathers. Since these two studies were done, maternal employment has become much more prevalent, and it might therefore be expected that the finding would no longer be obtained. However, two recent Canadian studies reported the same pattern. Kappel and Lambert (1972) found in their study of children 9 to 16 years old that the sons of full-time working mothers in the lower class evaluated their fathers lower than did the sons of other full-time working mothers and lower than did the sons of the part-time or nonworking mothers in any class.[4]

---

[2] Studies of children usually deal with maternal employment at the time of the study. Adult subjects, on the other hand, typically report past employment, for example, "when you were growing up," and one does not know how old the child was at the time of the employment. The age of the child is also ambiguous in studies in which samples have been selected in terms of a characteristic of the mothers, since the ages of the children may vary.

[3] The fact that daughters of working mothers are lower on traditional femininity should be kept in mind in evaluating studies like Nelson's (1971) that use pencil-and-paper personality inventories. Many of these inventories are biased toward the very questionable assumption that traditional femininity is the healthy pattern for girls (Constantinople, 1973; Henshel, 1971; Lunneborg, 1968).

---

[4] This finding was obtained from Tables 3 and 5 of the Kappel and Lambert study and was not discussed by the authors.

Propper (1972) found that in a predominantly working class sample, the adolescent sons of full-time working mothers were less likely than were the sons of nonworking mothers to name their father as the man they most admired. The finding by Vogel and his colleagues (1970) discussed previously suggests, on the other hand, that at least among middle-class males the father whose wife works may be seen as a more nurturant figure, possibly because of his taking over some of the child care roles. In any case, maternal employment more clearly defines the mother's role change than the father's, and thus the effect on the daughter may be more pronounced.

Nevertheless, there have been few studies of the effect of maternal employment on the daughter's self-esteem, and they have not always found the expected results. Thus, Baruch (1972b) found no relationship between maternal employment and the self-esteem of college women as measured by the Coopersmith Self-Esteem Inventory. She reported that the daughters of working mothers with positive career attitudes tended to have higher self-esteem, but this relationship was not statistically significant. Kappel and Lambert (1972) using a semantic-differential-style self-esteem measure with 3,315 9- to 16-year-old Canadian children, found that the daughters of nonworking mothers were lower in self-esteem than were the daughters of part-time working mothers but higher than were the daughters of full-time working mothers. The daughters of full-time working mothers did have higher self-esteem than did those of the nonworking group, however, when any one of the following conditions existed: The mother worked for self-oriented reasons, was very satisfied with work, or was a professional.

Despite the inconclusive findings on self-esteem, for girls maternal employment seems to contribute to a greater admiration of the mother, a concept of the female role that includes less restriction and a wider range of activities, and a self-concept that incorporates these aspects of the female role. Douvan (1963) found the adolescent daughters of working mothers to be relatively independent, autonomous, and active, and there are suggestions from other studies that this may be true for younger girls as well (Hoffman, 1963a). For boys, maternal employment might influence their concept of the female role, but what the effects are on their attitudes toward their father and themselves depends very much on the circumstances surrounding the mother's employment.

.   .   .

Nevertheless, it does seem clear that when a mother works she provides a different model of behavior for the children in the family, particularly for the girls. Further, the hypothesis that this difference is important for the daughter's concept of sex roles, and thus presumably her self-concept, makes sense. Traditional sex role stereotypes in America assign a lower status to women than to men and include the view that women are less competent. Maslow, Rand, and Newman (1960) described as one effect, "the woman in order to be a good female may feel it necessary to give up her strength, intelligence or talent, fearing them as somehow masculine and defeminizing [p. 208]." Another effect has been empirically documented by Horner (1972)—that women who dare to achieve do so with anxiety and ambivalence about their success. The role of working mother is less likely to lead to traditional sex role stereotypes and more likely to communicate competence and the value of the woman's contribution to the family. She may have higher status in the family and represent to her daughter a person who is capable in areas that are, in some respects, more salient to a growing girl than are household skills.

To summarize: Considering the four major dependent variables from the standpoint of the role-model theory, the data indicate that maternal employment is associated with less traditional sex role concepts, more approval of maternal employment, and a higher evaluation of female competence. This in turn should imply a more positive self-concept for the daughters of working mothers and better social adjustment, but there are only indirect data on this. There is some support for the idea that daughters of working mothers are more independent because of modeling their more independent mothers. Evidence also suggests that the daughters of working mothers have higher achievement aspirations, but it has not yet been demonstrated that the actual abilities of the child are affected by the different role model provided by the working mother.

The Mother's Emotional State

Morale   The assumption that the mother's emotional state is influenced by whether or not she is employed and that this affects her adequacy as a mother underlies several different approaches. One type of hypothesis, for example, relies on the commonly accepted belief that good morale improves job performance. Since this theory has validity in the industrial setting (Roethlisberger & Dickson, 1939), why not in the home? In fact, there is some support for it. Yarrow, Scott, de-Leeuw, and Heinig (1962) examined, by means of interviews with mothers of elementary school children, the child-rearing patterns of four groups of mothers: (a) mothers who worked and preferred to work, (b) mothers who worked and preferred not to work (c) nonworking mothers who preferred to work, and (d) nonworking mothers who preferred not to work. Among the nonworking mothers, satisfaction with their lot made a significant difference: The satisfied nonworking mothers obtained higher scores on a measure of adequacy of mothering. However, satisfaction did not differentiate the working mothers. One should keep in mind that when this study was conducted it was more socially acceptable to say, "Yes, I am working, but I wish I could be home all the time with my children" than it was to

say, "Yes, I am home all day with my children, but I wish I were out working." Thus, some of the dissatisfied workers may not have been as dissatisfied as they indicated. By the same token, the dissatisfaction of the homemaker may have been more extreme, and her dissatisfaction more closely linked to the mothering role itself; that is, the very role with which she was indicating dissatisfaction included mothering. Indeed, of all four groups, the lowest scores on adequacy of mothering were obtained by the dissatisfied homemaker. (The highest, by the satisfied homemaker.) Furthermore, the investigators considered the motives for choosing full-time homemaking: Those women who stressed duty as the basis for the choice had the lowest scores of all.

The question of the dissatisfied nonworking mother is interesting. Would the working mother who enjoys her work be dissatisfied as a full-time homemaker? In the practical sense, this may be the real issue; and the Yarrow et al. (1962) data suggest that the satisfied working mother may not be as adequate a parent as the satisfied nonworking mother but she is more adequate than the dissatisfied nonworking mother. Birnbaum (1971) in an interesting study compared professionally employed mothers with mothers who had graduated from college "with distinction" but had become full-time homemakers, that is, women who had the ability to pursue professional careers had they so chosen. Both groups were about 15 to 25 years past their bachelor's degree at the time they were interviewed. With respect to morale, the professional women were clearly higher. The nonworking mothers had lower self-esteem, a lower sense of personal competence—even with respect to child care skills, felt less attractive, expressed more concern over identity issues, and indicated greater feelings of loneliness. The nonworking mothers were even more insecure and unhappy in these respects than was a third sample of professional women who had never married.

Asked what they felt was missing from their lives, the predominant answer from the two groups of professional women was time, but for the housewives it was challenge and creative involvement.

The mothers were also compared with respect to orientation toward their children. In response to the question. "How does having children change a woman's life," the full-time homemakers stressed the sacrifice that motherhood entailed significantly more often than did the professional women. The professional women answered more often in terms of enrichment and self-fulfillment. Although both groups mentioned the work involved and the demanding aspects of motherhood, the homemakers stressed duty and responsibility to a greater extent. The homemakers indicated more anxiety about their children, especially with regard to the child's achievements, and they stressed their own inadequacies as mothers. In response to a projective picture showing a boy and his parents with a crutch in the background, the homemakers told more dramatic, depressed, and anxious stories. With respect to the growing independence of their children, the professional women responded postively, while the homemaekrs indicated ambivalence and regret. They seemed to be concerned about the loss of familiar patterns of their own importance.

There are no direct data in the Birnbaum (1971) study on the children themselves, but the pattern of the able, educated, full-time homemakers suggests that they would have shortcomings as mothers, particularly as their children approached adolescence. At that time, when the child needs a parent who can encourage independence and instill self-confidence, the anxieties and concerns of these women and their own frustrations would seem to operate as a handicap.

There are additional studies suggesting that when work is a source of personal satisfaction for the mother, her role as mother is positively affected. Kligler (1954) found that women who worked because of interest in the job were more likely than were those who worked for financial reasons to feel that there was improvement in the child's behavior as a result of employment. Kappel and Lambert (1972) found that the 9- to 16-year-old daughters of full-time working mothers who indicated they were working for self-oriented reasons had higher self-esteem and evaluated both parents more highly than did either the daughters of full-time working mothers who were working for family-oriented reasons or the daughters of nonworking mothers. In this study the measures of the mother's motives for working and the child data were obtained independently. In the studies by Yarrow et al. (1962), Birnbaum (1971), and Kligler, the mother was the source of all of the data. Woods (1972) found that in a study of fifth graders in a lower-class, predominantly black urban area where almost all of the mothers were employed, mothers who reported a positive attitude toward employment had children who obtained scores on the California Test of Personality indicating good social and personal adjustment.

Role strain   Another dimension of morale that has been studied focuses on the strain of handling the dual roles of worker and mother. The general idea is that whatever the effect of maternal employment under conflict-free circumstances, the sheer pressure of trying to fill these two very demanding roles can result in a state of stress that in turn has a negative effect on the child. Thus, the main thrust of Kappel and Lambert's (1972) argument is that part-time employment, and full-time employment when it involves minimal conflict, have a positive effect; full-time employment under most conditions, however, involves strain and therefore has adverse effects. In Douvan's (1963) study of adolescent children in intact families, the only group of working-mother children who indicated adjustment problems were the children of full-time working mothers in the lower class. This group of working mothers was the one for whom the strain of the dual role seemed to be the greatest.

In contrast, Woods (1972) found the children of full-time workers to be the best adjusted. Her sample, however, was all lower class from a population in which most mothers were employed and included many single-parent families. Under these circumstances, the full-time employed mothers may have been financially better off than were the others and may have had more stable household arrangements to facilitate their employment. The mother's positive attitude toward employment related to the child's adjustment, as noted above, but also her satisfaction with child care arrangements contributed to a positive attitude toward employment. In a sense then, although full-time employment of lower-class mothers did not seem to have adverse effects on the child as suggested in the other two studies, strain as manifested in dissatisfaction with child care arrangements may have exerted such an influence.[5] To some extent the attitude toward employment generally may reflect the mother's feeling of role strain.

Guilt Still another possible emotional response to employment is that the working mother feels guilty about her work because of the prevailing admonishments against maternal employment. While this may result in some appropriate compensation for her absence from home, it may also be overdone.

There is evidence that working mothers are very concerned about whether or not their employment is "bad" for their children, and they often feel guilty. Even Birnbaum's (1971) happy professional mothers indicated frequent guilt feelings. Kligler (1954) also noted that the working mothers experienced anxiety and guilt and tried to compensate in their behavior

toward their children. Some evidence for guilt on the part of the working mother and the effects of this on the child is provided in a study by Hoffman (1963b). Third- through sixth-grade children of working mothers were studied, with each working-mother family matched to a nonworking-mother family on father's occupation, sex of child, and ordinal position of the child. The data included questionnaires filled out by the children, personal interviews with the mothers, teacher ratings, and classroom sociometrics. The working mothers were divided into those who indicated that they liked working and those who disliked it. Working mothers who liked work, compared to the nonworking matched sample, had more positive interaction with the child, felt more sympathy and less anger toward the child in discipline situations, and used less severe discipline techniques. However, the children of these working mothers appeared to be less assertive and less effective in their peer interactions. Their intellectual performance was rated lower by teachers, and their scores on the school intelligence tests were lower. Also, these children helped somewhat less in household tasks than did the children of nonworking mothers. Thus, the overall pattern seemed to indicate that the working mother who liked work not only tried to compensate for her employment but may have actually overcompensated. These data were collected in 1957 when popular sentiment was opposed to maternal employment. As a result the women may have felt guilty about working. In trying to be good mothers, they may have gone too far, since the children's behavior suggested a pattern of overprotection or "smother love."

The mothers who did not like work, on the other hand, showed a very different pattern. They seemed less involved with the child; for example, they indicated less frequent disciplining and somewhat fewer positive interactions, as compared to nonworking mothers. The children helped

---

[5] The study does not indicate whether the woman's satisfaction reflected the objective conditions or not; the mother's perceptions and the child's report of the situation were significantly but not highly related.

with household tasks to a greater extent than did the children of nonworking mothers. They were also more assertive and hostile toward their peers. Their school performance as rated by their teachers was lower, although they did not perform more poorly on the school intelligence tests. The total pattern suggested that these children were somewhat neglected in comparison to the nonworking matched sample. The working mothers who disliked work had less reason to feel guilty, since they were working for other than self-oriented reasons.

Effects on the child A complicated picture is presented if the data on the working mother's emotional state are considered in relation to the child characteristics cited earlier as most often linked to maternal employment: (*a*) the child's attitudes, (*b*) mental health and social adjustment and independence-dependence specifically, and (*c*) cognitive abilities and orientations. First, with respect to the attitude toward maternal employment itself, there are some indications that the tendency of working mothers' children to have a postive attitude is enhanced when the employment is accompanied by a minimum of conflict and strain for the mother (Baruch, 1972a; King et al., 1968).

Moving on to the more complex dependent variables, it appears that when maternal employment is satisfying to the mother, either because it is more easily incorporated into her activities or because it is intrinsically gratifying, the effects on the child may be positive. The effects are more clearly positive—as indicated by various measures such as an "adequacy of mothering" score, the child's self-esteem, the child's adjustment score on the California Test of Personality, and attitudes toward parents—when this situation is compared either to that of the full-time housewife who would really prefer to work (Yarrow et al., 1962) or to maternal employment when it is accompanied by strain and harassment (Douvan, 1963; Kappel & Lambert, 1972; Woods, 1972). There are even indications that in some situations, as when the children are approaching adolescence and older or when the mother is particularly educated and able, the working-mother role may be more satisfying than is the role of full-time housewife and that this may make the working mother less anxious and more encouraging of independence in her children (Birnbaum, 1971). On the other hand, there is also evidence that the working mother with younger children who likes work might feel guilty and thus overcompensate, with adverse effects for the child in the form of passivity, ineffectiveness with peers, and low academic performance (Hoffman, 1963b). Thus the data about the mother's emotional state suggest that the working mother who obtains satisfaction from her work, who has adequate arrangements so that her dual role does not involve undue strain, and who does not feel so guilty that she overcompensates is likely to do quite well and, under certain conditions, better than does the nonworking mother.

Child–Rearing Practices

Concern here is with whether the child of a working mother is subject to different child-rearing practices and how these in turn affect his development. To some extent this topic is covered in other sections. In discussing the different role models presented in the working-mother families, for example, we indicated that the child-rearing functions are more likely to be shared by both parents. The fact that the child then has a more balanced relationship with both parents has generally been viewed with favor. The active involvement of the father has seen as conducive to high achievement in women, particularly when he is supportive of independence and performance (Ginzberg, 1971; Hoffman, 1973), and to the social adjustment of boys (Hoffman, 1961) as well as to the general adjustment of both boys and girls (Dizard, 1968).

Data also indicate that the working mother's family is more likely to include someone outside the conjugal family who participates in the child care (Hoffman, 1958; U.S. Department of Labor, 1972). This situation undoubtedly operates as a selective factor, since the presence of, for example, the grandmother makes it easier for the mother to go to work; but the effects of this pattern have not been widely examined. The specific issue of multiple mothering and frequent turnover in baby-sitters is discussed later in the article, primarily in terms of effects on the infant and the young child when these issues are most meaningful.

In discussing the guilt sometimes felt by the working mothers, it was suggested that they sometimes try to compensate for their employment, in some cases overdoing it. There is considerable evidence that working mothers particularly in the middle class do try to compensate. In some studies, this is made explicit by the respondents (Jones et al., 1967; Kligler, 1954; Rapoport & Rapoport, 1972), while in others it is revealed in the pattern of working-nonworking differences obtained. As examples of the latter, Yarrow and her colleagues (1962) found that the college-educated working mothers compensated by having more planned activities with children, and the professional mothers in Fisher's (1939) early study spent as many hours with their children as did the full-time homemakers. Finally, Jones et al. found that the mothers employed as professionals spent more time reading with their sixth-grade children than did nonworking mothers, though this was part of a generally greater stress on educational goals, not just compensation for employment.

When the working mother tries to make up for her employment, she often makes certain implicit judgments about what the nonworking situation is like. These may be quite inaccurate. The working mothers in Hoffman's (1963b) study who required less household help from their children than did the nonworking mothers are a

case in point. And, in general, the non-working mother is not necessarily interacting with her child as much as is imagined or as pleasantly. There is a great deal of pluralistic ignorance about the mothering role, and many mothers may be measuring themselves against, and trying to match, an overidealized image. It is possible that the nonworking mother spends relatively little time in direct positive interaction with her child, and thus the working mother's deliberate efforts might end up as more total positive interaction time. With respect to the amount of time spent in total child care, comparisons indicate that the nonworking women spend more time (Robinson, 1971; Walker & Woods, 1972). These reports, however, are geared toward other purposes and are not helpful in providing information about parent-child interaction. In most cases, working and nonworking women are compared without regard to whether or not they are mothers. Obviously the nonworking women include more mothers, and thus they do, as a group, spend more time in child care. Even when only mothers are compared, the number of children in the family and the children's ages are not considered, and the kind of child care is often not specified. Just how much of the day does the nonworking mother spend interacting with the child? This is an unfortunate gap in our knowledge.

Independence training   Several studies have focused on whether the working mother encourages independence and maturity in her children more than does the nonworking mother. The answer seems to depend on the age of the child and the social class or education of the mother. In the work of Yarrow and her colleagues (1962), the working mothers who had not gone to college were more likely to indicate a stress on independence training and to assign the children a greater share of the household responsibilities. The college-educated working mothers did not show this pattern and in fact showed a nonsignificant tendency in the opposite direction. The subjects in this study were similar to Hoffman's (1963b) respondents in that the children were of elementary school age; thus it is interesting that the college-educated working mothers in the former study exhibit a pattern similar to the working women who liked work in the latter study. Burchinal and Lovell (1959) reported for somewhat older children that working mothers were more likely to stress independence, and a stress on independence and responsibility can be inferred as more characteristic of the working mothers in the national sample study of adolescent girls reported by Douvan (1963), although the data rely more on what the girl is like than on parental child-rearing practices. Birnbaum's (1971) study of professionally employed mothers also suggests an encouragement of independence. The age of these children varied. The study by Von Mering (1955) is often cited as evidence that professional mothers stress independence training in elementary-school-age children, but since there were only eight mothers in the sample, such conclusions do not seem justified.[6]

A longitudinal study of lower-class boys from intact families, begun in the 1930s, suggests that the relationship between maternal employment and independence training is contingent upon the family milieu (McCord et al., 1963). Data obtained when the boys were between 10 and 15 years old showed that among the families judged to be stable by a composite index, working mothers were less overpro-

tective and more supportive of independence than were nonworking mothers. These differences were not obtained for the unstable families, and the sons of the working mothers in this group proved to be the most dependent subjects in the entire sample. Because their mothers did not seem to be the most encouraging of dependency, their dependent behavior was interpreted by the authors as a response to feelings of rejection rather than to parental patterns of independence training.

The data are quite sketchy, but the general picture is that except for the working mothers of younger children (elementary school age) who are educated or enjoy work and possibly the working mothers in unstable families, working mothers stress independence training more than do nonworking mothers. This is consistent with what one would expect. It has already been indicated that the more educated working mothers try to compensate for their employment. Thus they would be expected to avoid pushing the younger children into maturity, stressing the nurturant aspects of their role to make up for their absence at work. As the child grows older, independence is called for. To the nonworking mother the move from protector and nurturer to independence trainer is often very difficult. For the working mother, on the other hand, the child's growing independence eases her role strain. Furthermore, the psychological threat of becoming less essential to the child is lessened by the presence of alternative roles and sources of self-worth.

The evidence for the effect of this pattern on the child is not definitely established. Two of the studies, Hoffman's (1963b) and McCord et al.'s (1963), examined data at each of the three levels: employment status, child-rearing behavior, and child characteristics; but the findings are ambiguous. Hoffman did not directly examine the relationship between maternal behavior and the child characteristics; McCord and her colleagues did and failed to find a significant association between in-

---

[6] Propper (1972) found that the adolescent children of working mothers were more likely to report disagreements with parents but were not different from the children of nonworking mothers with respect to feelings of closeness to parents, parental interest, or support. The overall pattern may indicate more tolerance of disagreement by the working mothers rather than a more strained relationship. This interpretation fits well with the general picture of working mothers encouraging independence and autonomy in adolescent children.

dependence training and independence. None of the other relevant maternal employment studies obtained separate data on the child-rearing patterns and the child characteristics. On the other hand, several child development studies that have no data on maternal employment have found that parental encouragement of independence relates to high achievement motivation, competence, and achievement behavior in both males and females (Baumrind & Black, 1967; Hoffman, 1972; Winterbottom, 1958).

Household responsibilities   Most of the data indicate that the child of the working mother has more household responsibilities (Douvan, 1963; Johnson, 1969; Propper, 1972; Roy, 1963; Walker, 1970a). The exception to this generalization is again the mothers of younger children who are more educated or who enjoy work. Although working mothers may sometimes deliberately avoid giving the child household responsibilities, such participation by children has generally been found to have a positive, not a negative, effect (Clausen, 1966; Johnson, 1969; Woods, 1972). Obviously, this does not mean overburdening the child, but expecting the child to be one of the effectively contributing members of the family seems conducive to the development of social adjustment and responsibility.

Parental control   What other effects of maternal employment on child-rearing practices might be expected? One hypothesis might be that the working mother leaves her child more often without care or supervision. This is the focus of the next section, but by and large, there is little evidence that this is the case. On the other hand, because of the demands imposed by the dual role of worker and mother, the working mother might be stricter and impose more conformity to a specified standard. That is, just as reality adaptation might lead her to encourage the child in independence and to take on household

responsibilities, she might also be expected to demand more conformity to rules so that the household can function smoothly in her absence. There is some evidence for this pattern among the less educated groups. Yarrow et al. (1962) found that the children of working mothers in their noncollege group were generally under firmer parental control than were the children of nonworking mothers. Woods (1972) found more consistency between principles and practice in the discipline used by the full-time working mothers in her lower-class, predominantly black sample. However, Yarrow et al. found greater inconsistency in their college-educated working mothers.

Still another possibility is that the working mother is milder in discipline because of conscious efforts to compensate the child or because of higher morale. Hoffman's (1963b) working mothers, especially those who liked work, used less severe discipline and indicated less hostility in the discipline situation than did the nonworking mothers. It should be noted that the focus in this study was not on the content of the discipline but on its severity. Thus the data do not indicate whether the children were under more or less firm control but only that the discipline used was milder.

There are a few studies, such as those that compared the child-rearing views of working and nonworking mothers and found no meaningful differences (Kligler, 1954; Powell, 1963), that are not reviewed here, but we have included most of the available data on maternal employment and child-rearing practices. It is surprising how few investigations of maternal employment have obtained data about actual child-rearing behavior. Most of the studies have simply related employment to a child characteristic and then later speculated about any relationship that might be found. If the daughters of working mothers are found to be more independent or higher achievers, one cannot tell if this is a product of the working mother as model, the fact that the father is more likely to have had an active part in the girl's upbringing, the result of the fathers in working-mother families being more likely to approve of and encourage competence in females, or whether it is because these girls were more likely to have been encouraged by their mothers to achieve independence and assume responsibilities. All of these intervening variables have been linked to female independence and achievement (Hoffman, 1972, 1973).

Maternal Absence and Supervision

The most persistent concern about maternal employment has to do with the sheer absence of the mother from the home while she is working and the fear that this represents a loss to the child in terms of supervision, love, or cognitive enrichment. Much of the earlier research on maternal employment and juvenile delinquency was based on this hypothesis: The mother was working, the child was unsupervised, and thus he was a delinquent. There is some support for this theory, despite the fact that maternal employment and delinquency do not relate as expected. In the study of lower-class boys carried out by Glueck and Glueck (1957), regularly employed mothers were no more likely to have delinquent sons than were nonemployed mothers. However, inadequate supervision seemed to lead to delinquency whatever the mother's employment status, and employed mothers, whether employed regularly or occasionally, were more likely to provide inadequate supervision. McCord and McCord (1959) also found a tie between supervision and delinquency in their longitudinal study of lower-class boys (which, unlike the Gluecks', included only intact families), but there was little difference between the working and nonworking mothers with respect to adequacy of supervision (McCord et al., 1963). Furthermore, the tie between the adequacy of supervision and social adjustment conceptualized more generally is not conclu-

sively established. In the study by Woods (1972) of lower-class fifth-grade children, inadequate supervision did not have a statistically demonstrable adverse effect on boys, although unsupervised girls clearly showed lower school adjustment scores on tests of social relations and cognitive abilities.[7] Delinquency per se was too rare in this sample for any comparison, and the relationship between maternal employment and the adequacy of supervision was not examined.

Even less is known about the linkage of these three variables—maternal employment, supervision, and delinquency—in the middle class. Although middle-class working mothers express concern about finding adequate supervision for their children and although a number of publications stress the inadequacy of supervision in families in which the mother works (Low & Spindler, 1968), it is not clearly established that the children end up with less supervision in either social class. Furthermore, although the adequacy of supervision seems related to delinquency in the lower class, this relationship is not established for the middle class. Nye (1958), for example, found a curvilinear relationship—both high and low supervision moderately associated with delinquency. It may seem obvious that these three variables should be linked in both the middle and the lower class, but there is little empirical documentation.

---

[7] The sex differences in the Woods study are both intriguing and difficult to interpret. In most child development studies, the girls show ill effects from too much supervision or control, while the boys typically suffer from too little (Becker, 1964; Bronfenbrenner, 1961; Hoffman, 1972). This may reflect the higher level of control generally exercised over girls, so that the low end of the scale for girls is not as low as for boys, either objectively or subjectively. However, there have been very few child development studies of the lower class, and it is possible that the lack of supervision is more extreme than in the typical child development sample. Thus the middle-class girl who is unsupervised relative to other middle-class girls may not represent the level of neglect encountered by Woods.

Ignoring now the issue of supervision, what is the relationship between maternal employment and delinquency? In our previous review, we suggested that there did seem to be a relationship between maternal employment and delinquency in the middle class. This relationship was found by Nye (1963) using a self-report measure of delinquent behavior and Gold (1961) who used police contact as the measure; in both studies the relationship was obtained for the middle class and not for the lower class.[8] Glueck and Glueck (1957), studying only lower-class subjects, found no tendency for the sons of regularly employed women to be delinquent despite the fact that their sample included broken homes, a variable that relates to both delinquency and maternal employment. They did find the sons of the "occasionally" employed women to be delinquent, but the occasionally employed group was clearly more unstable than were those in which the mother worked regularly or not at all. They were none likely to have husbands with poor work habits and emotional disturbances, poor marriages, or to be widowed or divorced. The Gluecks saw the occasionally employed mother as working "to escape household drudgery and parental responsibility," but, in another view, the question is not why they went to work, since their employment was obviously needed by the circumstances of their lives, but why they resisted regular employment. The delinquency of their sons seemed more a function of family instability, the inadequacies of the father, or something about the mothers' not being employed more regularly, rather than a function of maternal employment per se.

Two studies already mentioned supplement these ideas. McCord et al. (1963)

found no tendency for maternal employment to be associated with delinquency when the family was stable, but in the unstable families the sons of working mothers did have a higher delinquency rate. The higher frequency of delinquency was clearly not simply due to the instability; family instability did relate to delinquency, but maternal employment in the unstable family further increased the risk.

Woods' (1972) study, which included results of psychological tests and information gathered from teachers and school and community records, found that the full-time, steadily working mother seemed to be a positive factor in the child's social adjustment. The subjects were 142 fifth graders, all the fifth graders in the school, and 108 had working mothers. Clearly, in this context, in which maternal employment is the common, accepted pattern, its meaning to parents and children is quite different. The author suggests that full-time maternal employment is a requirement of family well-being in the economic circumstances of these families and as such is respected and appreciated.

Woods' (1972) interpretation is consistent with our own earlier hypotheses about the meaning of maternal employment particularly among blacks (Hoffman, 1963a) and with other data (Kriesberg, 1970). A basic theme throughout both the earlier review and the present one is that the context within which maternal employment takes place—the meaning it has for the family and the social setting—determines its effects. In addition, the positive influence of full-time maternal employment in the lower class raises the question again of why some lower-class women resist full-time employment when their situation obviously calls for it. What characterizes these nonworking or irregularly employed mothers? They may have less ego strength, less competence in terms of physical or emotional health, training or intellectual ability, or more children. The Gluecks' (1957) data indicate that the occasionally employed mothers were the most likely to

---

[8] There are two other recent studies (Brown, 1970; Riege, 1972) in which no relationship was found between maternal employment and juvenile delinquency. Since there was no separate examination by social class or attention to relevant mediating variables, these studies are not illuminating in this disccusion.

have a history of delinquency themselves. In short, in addition to the value of the mother's employment to the family, the differences may reflect selective factors, and the employed mothers in these circumstances may be healthier, more competent, or in better circumstances with respect to family size.[9]

Consistent with Woods' (1972) interpretation is the fact that the children in the study with extensive responsibility for the household tasks and the care of siblings showed higher school achievement.[10] Like their mothers they were cooperating with realistic family demands. The author is aware, however, that the causality might be reversed, that is, that mothers give competent children more responsibilities. There are also other interpretations: For example, firstborn children particularly in lower income families usually show higher academic performance, and they are also the ones more likely to be given household tasks.

To summarize, the hypothesis that maternal employment means inadequate supervision has been primarily invoked to predict higher delinquency rates for the children of working mothers. There are data, although not very solid, that in the lower class, working mothers provide less adequate supervision for their children and that adequacy of supervision is linked to delinquency and social adjustment, but

there is not evidence that the children of working mothers are more likely to be delinquent. The data suggest instead that full-time maternal employment in the very low social class groups represents a realistic response to economic stress and thus, because of selective factors or effects, may be correlated with more socially desirable characteristics in the child. Adequacy of supervision has rarely been studied in the middle class, although here there is some evidence for a higher delinquency rate among working mothers' children.

Maternal Deprivation

The school-age child For school-age children, there is very little empirically to link maternal employment to maternal deprivation. Although Woods (1972) suggests that full-time employment may represent rejection to the middle-class child, there is no evidence of this. While it has been commonly assumed that maternal employment is interpreted by the child as rejection, the evidence, as indicated above, suggests that the children of working mothers tend to support the idea of mothers working. Furthermore, as maternal employment becomes the norm in the middle, as well as in the lower, class it seems even less likely that the sheer fact that a mother is working would lead to a sense of being rejected.

The evidence as to whether the working mother actually does reject the school-age child has already been covered in earlier sections of this review. The general pattern is that the working mother, particularly in the middle class, makes a deliberate effort to compensate the child for her employment (Hoffman, 1963b; Jones et al., 1967; Kligler, 1954; Poloma, 1972; Rapoport & Rapoport, 1972; Yarrow et al., 1962) and that the dissatisfied mother, whether employed or not and whether lower class or middle class, is less likely to be an adequate mother (Birnbaum, 1971; Woods, 1972; Yarrow et al., 1962). The idea that maternal employment brings

---

[9] There are data that indicate that children from large families, particularly in the lower class, show lower school performance than do children from smaller families (Clausen & Clausen, 1973). Perhaps then, it is not that full-time employment has a positive effect but that the full-time employed mothers have fewer children and the positive effect is a function of smaller family size.

[10] These findings seem somewhat inconsistent with Douvan's (1963) suggestion that the lower-class daughters of full-time working mothers were overburdened with household responsibilities. Douvan's subejcts were older, and thus it is possible that they were more heavily burdened than were the fifth graders and more resentful of their duties. Douvan's sample was also white, while Woods' was predominantly black.

emotional deprivation to the school-age child has not been supported (Hoffman, 1963a; Peterson, 1958; Propper, 1972; Siegel & Haas, 1963; Yudkin & Holme, 1963). In part this may be because the working mother is often away from home only when the child is in school; and if her work is gratifying in some measure, if she does not feel unduly hassled, or if she deliberately sets about to do so, she may even spend more time in positive interaction with the child than does the nonworking mother. While this can sometimes be overdone and compensation can turn into overcompensation (Hoffman, 1963b), it may also be one of the important reasons why maternal employment has not been experienced by the school-age child as deprivation. In drawing action conclusions from the research, it is important to keep this in mind. The absence of negative effects does not mean that the mother's employment is an irrelevant variable; it may mean that mothers have been sufficiently concerned to counterbalance such effects effectively.

Infancy More recently attention has focused on the possible adverse effects of maternal employment on the infant and the very young child. The importance of attachment and a one-to-one relationship in the early years has been stressed by Spitz (1945), Bowlby (1958, 1969), and others (Yarrow, 1964). Although most of this research has been carried out on children in insitutions with the most dramatic effects demonstrated among children whose infancy was spent in grossly deprived circumstances, it nevertheless seems clear that something important is happening during these early years and that there are critical periods when cognitive and affective inputs may have important ramifications throughout the individual's life. Concern has been generated about this issue because of the recent increase in maternal employment among mothers of infants and young children and also because of the new interest in day care

centers as a means of caring for the preschool children of working mothers. As these two patterns emerge, the effects of maternal employment must be reevaluted. In this section we review the evidence that has been cited on one side or the other of these issues. As we shall see, however, we really know very little.

The research on maternal deprivation suggests that the infant needs a one-to-one relationship with an adult or else he may suffer cognitive and affective loss that may, in extreme conditions, never be regained. The importance of interactions in which the adult responds to the child and the child to the adult in a reciprocal relationship has been particularly stressed (Bronfenbrenner, 1973). There is some evidence of a need for cuddling (Harlow & Harlow, 1966) and a need for environmental stimulation (Dennis & Najarian, 1957; Hunt, 1961). These studies are often cited as evidence for the importance of the mother's full-time presence in the home when the infant is young.

Extending these findings to the maternal employment situation may be inappropriate, however. Not only were the early Bowlby (1953, 1958) and Spitz (1945) data obtained from studies of extremely barren, understaffed institutions, but later research suggested that the drastic effects they had observed might be avoided by increasing the staff-child ratio, by providing nurses who attended and responded to the infants' cries, smiles, and vocalizations, and by providing a more stimulating visual environment. Further, the age of the child, the duration of the institutionalization, and the previous and subsequent experiences of the child all affect the outcome (Rheingold, 1956; Rheingold & Bayley, 1959; Rheingold, Gewirtz, & Ross, 1959; Tizard, Cooperman, Joseph, & Tizard, 1972; Yarrow, 1964). Most important, however, institutionalization is not the same as day care, and day care is not the same as maternal employment. The inappropriateness of the studies of institutionalized infants to maternal employment has also been noted by Yudkin and Holme (1963), by Yarrow (1964), and by Wortis (1971).

In addition, there is no evidence that the caretaker has to be the mother or that this role is better filled by a male or a female. There is some evidence that the baby benefits from predictability in handling, but whether this is true throughout infancy or only during certain periods is not clear, nor is it clear whether the different handling has any long-lasting effects. Studies of multiple mothering have produced conflicting results (Caldwell, 1964). Child psychologists generally believe that there must be at least one stable figure to whom the infant forms an attachment, but this is not definitely established, and we do not know whether the periodic absence from the infant that is likely to go along with the mother's employment is sufficient to undermine her potential as the object of the infant's attachment.

Nevertheless, a number of child development studies suggest that within the normal range of parent-child interaction, the amount of expressive and vocal stimulation and response the mother gives to the infant affects his development (Emerson & Schaffer, 1964; Kagan, 1969; Lewis & Goldberg, 1969; Moss, 1967). Furthermore, although the attempts to increase cognitive performance through day care programs have not been very successful, attempts to increase the mother-infant interaction in the home appear to have more enduring effects (Bronfenbrenner, 1973; Levenstein, 1970, 1971). While there is no evidence that employment actually affects the quantity or quality of the mother-infant interaction, the voluntary employment of mothers of infants and young children has not heretofore been common, and it has rarely been studied. It is therefore important to find out whether the mother's employment results in less (or more) personal stimulation and interaction for the infant.

In addition to the importance of stimulation and interaction and the issue of emotional attachment for the infant, there are less fully explored questions about the effects on the mother. Bowlby (1958) and others (Hess, 1970) believe that the mother-child interaction is important for the development of the mother's "attachment," that an important source of maternal feeling is the experience of caring for the infant. Yudkin and Holme (1963), who generally approve of maternal employment in their review, stress this as one of the real dangers of full-time maternal employment when the child is young:

We would consider this need for a mother to develop a close and mutually satisfying relationship with her young infant one of the fundamental reasons why we oppose full-time work for mothers of children under 3 years. We do not say that it would not be possible to combine the two if children were cared for near their mothers so that they could see and be with each other during the day for parts of the day, and by such changes in households as will reduce the amount of time and energy needed for household chores. We are only stating that this occurs very rarely in our present society and is unlikely to be general in the foreseeable future and that the separation of children from their mothers for eight or nine hours a day, while the effects on the children may be counteracted by good substitute care, must have profound effects on the mother's own relationship with her young children and therefore on their relationship in the family as they grow older [pp. 131–132].

The issue of day care centers is not discussed in this review in any detail; however, our ignorance is almost as great here. While the cognitive advances expected from the Head Start day care programs were not adequately demonstrated (Bronfenbrenner, 1973), neither were there negative effects of these programs (Caldwell, Wright, Honig, & Tannenbaum, 1970). Obviously, the effects of day care centers for working mothers' children depend on the quality of the program, the time the child spends there, what happens to the child when he is not at the day care center, and what the alternatives are.

Arguments on either side of the issue of working mothers and day care often use data from studies of the kibbutzim in Israel, since all kibbutzim mothers work and from infancy on the child lives most of the time in the child centers. Some investigators have been favorably impressed with the development of these children (Kohn-Raz, 1968; Rabkin & Rabkin, 1969), while others have noted at least some deleterious consequences (Bettelheim, 1969; Spiro, 1965). In fact, however, these data are probably quite irrelevant. According to Bronfenbrenner (1973), these children spend more time each day interacting with their parents than do children in the more conventional nuclear family arrangement, and the time they spend together is less subject to distractions. The whole living arrangement is different, including the nature of the parents' work and the social context within which interaction takes place. The mother participates a great deal in the infant care, breast feeding is the norm, and both parents play daily with the child for long periods and without other diversions even as he matures. Thus, the Israeli kibbutz does not provide an example of maternal deprivation, American day care, or maternal employment as it is experienced in the United States.

. . .

Obviously the effects of maternal employment on the infant depend on the extent of the mother's absence and the nature of the substitute care—whether it is warm, stimulating, and stable. However, while studies of maternal employment and the school-age child by and large offer reassurance to the working mother, we have very little solid evidence concerning the effect on the younger child.

. . .

Summary

Research on the effects of maternal employment on the child were reveiwed. Findings were organized around five hypotheses: (a) The working mother provides a different role model than does the nonworking mother; (b) employment affects the mother's emotional state—sometimes providing satisfactions, sometimes role strain, and sometimes guilt—and this, in turn, influences the mother-child interaction; (c) the different situational demands as well as the emotional state of the working mother affect child-rearing practices; (d) working mothers provide less adequate supervision; and (e) the working mother's absence results in emotional and possibly cognitive deprivation for the child. Accumulated evidence, although sketchy and inadequate, offered some support for the first four hypotheses. Empirical studies of school-age children yielded no evidence for a theory of deprivation resulting from maternal employment, but there were not adequate data on the effects of maternal employment on the infant.

References

ALMQUIST, E. M., & ANGRIST, S. S. Role model influences on college women's career aspirations. *Merrill-Palmer Quarterly*, 1971, *17*, 263–279.

ASTIN, H. S. *The woman doctorate in America*. New York: Russell Sage Foundation, 1969.

ATKINSON, J. W. (Ed.) *Motives in fantasy, action, and society*. Princeton, N.J.: Van Nostrand, 1958.

BANDUCCI, R. The effect of mother's employment on the achievement, aspirations, and expectations of the child. *Personnel and Guidance Journal*, 1967, *46*, 263–267.

BARUCH, G. K. Maternal influences upon college women's attitudes toward women and work. *Developmental Psychology*, 1972, *6*, 32–37. (a)

BARUCH, G. K. Maternal role pattern as related to self-esteem and parental identification in college women. Paper presented at the meeting of the Eastern Psychological Association, Boston, April 1972. (b)

BAUMRIND, D., & BLACK, A. E. Socialization practices associated with dimensions of competence in preschool boys and girls. *Child Development*, 1967, *38*, 291–327.

BECKER, W. C. Consequences of different kinds of parental discipline. In M. L. Hoffman & L. W. Hoffman (Eds.), *Review of child development research*. New York: Russell Sage Foundation, 1964.

BELOW, H. I. Life styles and roles of women as perceived by high-school girls. Unpublished doctoral dissertation, Indiana University, 1969.

BETTELHEIM, B. *The children of the dream*. London: Macmillan, 1969.

BIRNBAUM, J. A. Life patterns, personality style and self esteem in gifted family oriented and career committed women. Unpublished doctoral dissertation, University of Michigan, 1971.

BLOOD, R. O., & HAMBLIN, R. L. The effect of the wife's employment on the family power structure. *Social Forces*, 1958, *36*, 347–352.

BOWLBY, J. A. Some pathological processes engendered by early mother-child separation. In M. J. E. Senn (Ed.), *Infancy and childhood*. New York: Josiah Macy, Jr. Foundation, 1953.

BOWLBY, J. A. The nature of the child's tie to his mother. *International Journal of Psychoanalysis*, 1958, *39*, 350–373.

BOWLBY, J. A. *Attachment*. New York: Basic Books, 1969.

BRONFENBRENNER, U. Some familial antecedents of responsibility and leadership on adolescents. In L. Petrullo & B. M. Bass (Eds.), *Leadership and interpersonal behavior*. New York: Holt, Rinehart & Winston, 1961.

BRONFENBRENNER, U. Is early intervention effective? Paper presented at the biennial meeting of the Society for Research in Child Development, Philadelphia, March 1973.

BROWN, S. W. *A comparative study of maternal employment and nonemployment*. (Doctoral dissertation, Mississippi State University) Ann Arbor, Mich.: University Microfilms, 1970, No. 70–8610.

BURCHINAL, L. G. Personality characteristics of children. In F. I. Nye & L. W. Hoffman (Eds.), *The employed mother in America*. Chicago: Rand McNally, 1963.

BURCHINAL, L. G., & LOVELL, L. Relation of employment status of mothers to children's anxiety, parental personality and PARI scores. Unpublished manuscript (1425), Iowa State University, 1959.

CALDWELL, B. M. The effects of infant care. In M. L. Hoffman & L. W. Hoffman (Eds.), *Review of child development research*. New York: Russell Sage Foundation, 1964.

CALDWELL, B. M., WRIGHT, C. M., HONIG, A. S., & TANNENBAUM, J. Infant day care and attachment. *American Journal of Orthopsychiatry*, 1970, *40*, 397–412.

CLAUSEN, J. A. Family structure, socialization, and personality. In L. W. Hoffman & M. L. Hoffman (Eds.), *Reveiw of child development research*. Vol. 2. New York: Russell Sage Foundation, 1966.

CLAUSEN, J. A., & CLAUSEN, S. R. The effects of family size on parents and children. In J. Fawcett (Ed.), *Psychological perspectives on fertility*. New York: Basic Books, 1973.

CONSTANTINOPLE, A. Masculinity-femininity: An exception to a famous dictum? *Psychological Bulletin*, 1973, *80*, 389–407.

DENNIS, W., & NAJARIAN, P. Infant development under environmental handicap. *Psychological Monographs*, 1957, *71* (7, Whole No. 436).

DIZARD, J. *Social change in the family*. Chicago: University of Chicago, Community and Family Study Center, 1968.

DOUVAN, E. Employment and the adolescent. In F. I. Nye & L. W. Hoffman (Eds.), *The employed mother in America*. Chicago: Rand McNally, 1963.

DUVALL, E. B. Conceptions of mother roles by five and six year old children of working and non-working mothers. Unpublished doctoral dissertation, Florida State University, 1955.

EMERSON, P. E., & SCHAFFER, H. R. The development of social attachments in infancy. *Monographs of the Society for Research in Child Development*, 1964, 29 (3, serial No. 94).

FARLEY, J. Maternal employment and child behavior. *Cornell Journal of Social Relations*, 1968, 3, 58–70.

FINKELMAN, J. J. Maternal employment, family relationships, and parental role perception. Unpublished doctoral dissertation, Yeshiva University, 1966.

FISHER, M. S. Marriage and work for college women. *Vassar Alumnae Magazine*, 1939, 24, 7–10.

FRANKEL, E. Characteristics of working and nonworking mothers among intellectually gifted high and low achievers. *Personnel and Guidance Journal*, 1964, 42, 776–780.

GARLAND, T. N. The better half? The male in the dual profession family. In C. Safilios-Rothschild (Ed.), *Toward a sociology of women*. Lexington, Mass.: Xerox College Publishing, 1972.

GINZBERG, E. *Educated American women: Life styles and self-portraits*. New York: Columbia University Press, 1971.

GLUECK, S., & GLUECK, E. Working mothers and delinquency. *Mental Hygiene*, 1957, 41, 327–352.

GOLD, M. *A social-psychology of delinquent boys*. Ann Arbor, Mich.: Institute for Social Research, 1961.

GOLDBERG, P. Misogyny and the college girl. Paper presented at the meeting of the Eastern Psychological Association, Boston, April 1967.

HALL, F. T., & SCHROEDER, M. P. Time spent on household tasks. *Journal of Home Economics*, 1970, 62, 23–29.

HARLOW, H., & HARLOW, M. K. Learning to love. *American Scientist*, 1966, 54, 244–272.

HARTLEY, R. E. Children's concepts of male and female roles. *Merrill-Palmer Quarterly*, 1960, 6, 83–91.

HARTLEY, R. E. What aspects of child behavior should be studied in relation to maternal employment? In A. E. Siegel (Ed.), *Research issues related to the effects of maternal employment on children*. University Park, Penn.: Social Science Research Center, 1961.

HENSHEL, A. Anti-feminist bias in traditional measurements of masculinity-femininity. Paper presented at the meeeting of the National Council on Family Relations, Estes Park, Colorado, August 1971.

HESS, H. Ethology and developmental psychology. In P. Mussen (Ed.), *Carmichael's manual of child psychology*. New York: Wiley, 1970.

HOFFMAN, L. W. *Effects of the employment of mothers on parental power relations and the division of household tasks*. Unpublished doctoral dissertation, University of Michigan, 1958.

HOFFMAN, L. W. The father's role in the family and the child's peer group adjustment. *Merrill-Palmer Quarterly*, 1961, 7, 97–105.

HOFFMAN, L. W. Effects on children: Summary and discussion. In F. I. Nye & L. W. Hoffman (Eds.), *The employed mother in America*. Chicago: Rand McNally, 1963. (a)

HOFFMAN, L. W. Mother's enjoyment of work and effects on the child. In F. I. Nye & L. W. Hoffman (Eds.), *The employed mother in America*. Chicago: Rand McNally, 1963. (b)

HOFFMAN, L. W. Parental power relations and the division of household tasks. In F. I. Nye & L. W. Hoffman (Eds.), *The employed mother in America*. Chicago: Rand McNally, 1963. (c)

HOFFMAN, L. W. Early childhood experiences and women's achievement motives. *Journal of Social Issues*, 1972, 28 (2), 129–155.

HOFFMAN, L. W. The professional woman as mother. In R. B. Kundsin (Ed.), *A conference on successful women in the sciences*. New York: New York Academy of Sciences, 1973.

HOFFMAN, L. W., & LIPPITT, R. The measurement of family life variables. In P. Mussen (Ed.), *Handbook of research methods in child development*. New York: Wiley, 1960.

HOLMSTROM, L. L. The two-career family. Paper presented at the conference of Women: Resource for a Changing World, Radcliffe Institute, Radcliffe College, Cambridge, April 1972.

HORNER, M. S. Femininity and successful achievement: A basic inconsistency. In J. M. Bardwick, E. Douvan, M. S. Horner, & D. Gutman, *Feminine personality and conflict*. Belmont, Calif.: Brooks/Cole,1972.

HUNT, J. MCV. *Intelligence and experience*. New York: Ronald Press, 1961.

JOHNSON, C. L. *Leadership patterns in working and nonworking mother middle class families*. (Doctoral dissertation, University of Kansas) Ann Arbor, Mich.: University Microfilms, 1969, No. 69–11, 224.

JONES, J. B., LUNDSTEEN, S. W., & MICHAEL, W. B. The relationship of the professional employment status of mothers to reading achievement of sixth-grade children. *California Journal of Educational Research*, 1967, *43*, 102–108.

KAGAN, J. Continuity of cognitive development during the first year. *Merrill-Palmer Quarterly*, 1969, *15*, 101–119.

KAPPEL, B. E., & LAMBERT, R. D. Self worth among the children of working mothers. Unpublished manuscript, University of Waterloo, 1972.

KEIDEL, K. C. Maternal employment and ninth grade achievement in Bismarck, North Dakota. *Family Coordinator*, 1970, *19*, 95–97.

KING, K., MCINTYRE, J., & AXELSON, L. J. Adolescents' views of maternal employment as a threat to the marital relationship. *Journal of Marriage and the Family*, 1968, *30*, 633–637.

KLIGLER, D. The effects of employment of married women on husband and wife roles: A study in culture change. Unpublished doctoral dissertation, Yale University, 1954.

KOHN-RAZ, R. Mental and motor development of kibbutz, institutionalized, and home-reared infants in Israel. *Child Development*; 1968, *39*, 489–504.

KRIESBERG, L. *Mothers in poverty: A study of fatherless families*. Chicago: Aldine, 1970.

LIPMAN-BUMEN, J. How ideology shapes women's lives. *Scientific American*, 1972, *226* (1), 34–42.

LEVENSTEIN, P. Cognitive growth in preschoolers through verbal interaction with mothers. *American Journal of Orthopsychiatry*, 1970, *40*, 426–432.

LEVENSTEIN, P. Verbal interaction project: Aiding cognitive growth in disadvantaged preschoolers through the Mother-Child Home Program July 1, 1967–August 31, 1970. Final report to Children's Bureau, Office of Child Development, U.S. Department of Health, Education, and Welfare, 1971. (Mimeo)

LEVINE, A. G. Marital and occupational plans of women in professional schools: Law, medicine, nursing, teaching. Unpublished doctoral dissertation, Yale University, 1968.

LEWIS, M., & GOLDBERG, S. Perceptual-cognitive development in infancy: A generalized expectancy model as a function of the mother-infant interaction. *Merrill-Palmer Quarterly*, 1969, *15*, 81–100.

LOW, S., & SPINDLER, P. *Child care arrangements of working mothers in the United States*. (Children's Bureau Publication 461) Washington, D.C.: U.S. Government Printing Office, 1968.

LUNNEBORG, P. W. Stereotypic aspect in masculinity-femininity measurement. Paper presented at the meeting of the American Psychological Association, San Francisco, September 1968.

MACCOBY, E. E. Sex differences in intellectual functioning. In E. E. Maccoby (Ed.), *The development of sex differences*. Stanford, Calif.: Stanford University Press, 1966.

MASLOW, A. H., RAND, H., & NEWMAN, S. Some parallels between sexual and dominance behavior of infra-human primates and the fantasies of patients in psychotherapy. *Journal of Nervous and Mental Disease*, 1960, *131*, 202–212.

MATHEWS, S. M. The development of children's attitudes concerning mothers' out-of-home employment. *Journal of Educational Sociology*, 1933, *6*, 259–271.

MCCORD, W., & MCCORD, J. *Origins of crime.* New York: Columbia University Press, 1959.

MCCORD, J., MCCORD, W., & THURBER, E. Effects of maternal employment on lower-class boys. *Journal of Abnormal and Social Psychology,* 1963, 67, 177–182.

MEIER, H. C. Mother-centeredness and college youths' attitudes toward social equality for women: Some empirical findings. *Journal of Marriage and the Family,* 1972, 34, 115–121.

MOORE, T. Children of working mothers. In S. Yudkin & H. Holme (Eds.), *Working mothers and their children.* London: Michael Joseph, 1963.

MOSS, H. A. Sex, age, and state as determinants of mother-infant interaction. *Merrill-Palmer Quarterly,* 1967, 13, 19–36.

NELSON, D. D. A study of school achievement among adolescent children with working and nonworking mothers. *Journal of Educational Research,* 1969, 62, 456–457.

NELSON, D. D. A study of personality adjustment among adolescent children with working and nonworking mothers. *Journal of Educational Research,* 1971, 64, 1328–1330.

NOLAN, F. L. Effects on rural children. In F. I. Nye & L. W. Hoffman (Eds.), *The employed mother in America.* Chicago: Rand McNally, 1963.

NYE, F. I. *Family relationships and delinquent behavior.* New York: Wiley, 1958.

NYE, F. I. The adjustment of adolescent children. In F. I. Nye & L. W. Hoffman (Eds.), *The employed mother in America.* Chicago: Rand McNally, 1963.

PETERSON, E. T. The impact of maternal employment on the mother-daughter relationship and on the daughter's role-orientation. Unpublished doctoral dissertation, University of Michigan, 1958.

POLOMA, M. M. Role conflict and the married professional woman. In C. Safilios-Rothschild (Ed.), *Toward a sociology of women.* Lexington, Mass.: Xerox College Publishing, 1972.

POWELL, K. Personalities of children and child-rearing attitudes of mothers. In F. I. Nye & L. W. Hoffman (Eds.), *The employed mother in America.* Chicago: Rand McNally, 1963.

PROPPER, A. M. The relationship of maternal employment to adolescent roles, activities, and parental relationships. *Journal of Marriage and the Family,* 1972, 34, 417–421.

RABKIN, L. Y., & RABKIN, K. Children of the kibbutz. *Psychology Today,* 1969, 3 (4), 40.

RAPOPORT, R., & RAPOPORT, R. The dual-career family: A variant pattern and social change. In C. Safilios-Rothschild (Ed.), *Toward a sociology of women.* Lexington, Mass.: Xerox College Publishing, 1972.

REES, A. N., & PALMER, F. H. Factors related to change in mental test performance. *Developmental Psychology Monograph,* 1970, 3 (2, Pt. 2).

RHEINGOLD, H. The modification of social responsiveness in institutional babies. *Monographs of the Society for Research in Child Development,* 1956, 21 (2, Serial No. 63).

RHEINGOLD, H., & BAYLEY, N. The later effects of an experimental modification of mothering. *Child Development,* 1959, 30, 363–372.

RHEINGOLD, H., GEWIRTZ, J. L., & ROSS, H. W. Social conditioning of vocalizations in the infant. *Journal of Comparative and Physiological Psychology,* 1959, 52, 68–73.

RIEBER, M., & WOMACK, M. The intelligence of preschool children as related to ethnic and demographic variables. *Exceptional Children,* 1968, 34, 609–614.

RIEGE, M. G. Parental affection and juvenile delinquency in girls. *The British Journal of Criminology,* 1972, 12, 55–73.

ROBINSON, J. B. Historical changes in how people spend their time. In A. Michel (Ed.), *Family issues of employed women in Europe and America.* Leiden, Netherlands: E. J. Brill, 1971.

ROETHLISBERGER, F. J., & DICKSON, W. J. *Business Research Studies.* Cambridge, Mass.: Harvard Business School, Division of Research, 1939.

ROY, P. Adolescent roles: Rural-urban differentials. In F. I. Nye & L. W. Hoffman (Eds.), *The employed mother in America.* Chicago: Rand McNally, 1963.

SIEGEL, A. E., & HAAS, M. B. The working mother: A review of research. *Child Development,* 1963, *34,* 513–542.

SMITH, H. C. *An investigation of the attitudes of adolescent girls toward combining marriage, motherhood and a career.* (Doctoral dissertation, Columbia University) Ann Arbor, Mich.: University Microfilms, 1969, No. 69–8089.

SPIRO, M. E. *Children of the kibbutz.* New York: Schocken Books, 1965.

SPITZ, R. A. Hospitalism: An inquiry into the genesis of psychiatric conditions in early childhood. *Psychoanalytic Studies of the Child,* 1945, *1,* 53–74.

STOLZ, L. M. Effects of maternal employment on children: Evidence from research. *Child Development,* 1960, *31,* 749–782.

SZOLAI, A. The multinational comparative time budget: A venture in international research cooperation. *American Behavioral Scientist,* 1966, *10,* 1–31.

TANGRI, S. S. Role innovation in occupational choice. Unpublished doctoral dissertation, University of Michigan, 1969.

TIZARD, B., COOPERMAN, O., JOSEPH, A., & TIZARD, J. Environmental effects on language development: A study of young children in long-stay residential nurseries. *Child Development,* 1972, *43,* 337–358.

U.S. DEPARTMENT OF LABOR, Women's Bureau. *Who are the working mothers?* (Leaflet 37) Washington, D.C.: U.S. Government Printing Office, 1972.

VOGEL, S. R., BROVERMAN, I. K., BROVERMAN, D. M., CLARKSON, F. E., & ROSENKRANTZ, P. S. Maternal employment and perception of sex roles among college students. *Developmental Psychology,* 1970, *3,* 384–391.

VON MERING, F. H. Professional and non-professional women as mothers. *Journal of Social Psychology,* 1955, *42,* 21–34.

WALKER, K. E. How much help for working mothers?: The children's role. *Human Ecology Forum,* 1970, *1* (2), 13–15. (a)

WALKER, K. E. Time-use patterns for household work related to homemakers' employment. Paper presented at the meeting of the Agricultural Outlook Conference, Washington, D.C., February 1970. (b)

WALKER, K. E., & WOODS, M. E. Time use for care of family members. (Use-of-Time Research Project, working paper 1) Unpublished manuscript, Cornell University, 1972.

WEIL, M. W. An analysis of the factors influencing married women's actual or planned work participation. *American Sociological Review,* 1961, *26,* 91–96.

WINTERBOTTOM, M. R. The relation of need for achievement to learning experiences in independence and mastery. In J. W. Atkinson (Ed.), *Motives in fantasy, action, and society.* Princeton: Van Nostrand, 1958.

WOODS, M. B. The unsupervised child of the working mother. *Developmental Psychology,* 1972, *6,* 14–25.

WORTIS, R. P. The acceptance of the concept of the maternal role by behavioral scientists: Its effects on women. *American Journal of Orthopsychiatry,* 1971, *41,* 733–746.

YARROW, L. J. Separation from parents during early childhood. In M. L. Hoffman & L. W. Hoffman (Eds.), *Review of child development research.* New York: Russell Sage Foundation, 1964.

YARROW, M. R., SCOTT, P., DELEEUW, L., & HEINIG, C. Child-rearing in families of working and nonworking mothers. *Sociometry,* 1962, *25,* 122–140.

YUDKIN, S., & HOLME, A. *Working mothers and their children.* London: Michael Joseph, 1963.

ZISSIS, C. A study of the life planning of 550 freshman women at Purdue University. *Journal of the National Association of Women Deans and Counselors,* 1964, *28,* 153–159.

31. AGE–SEX ROLES AND PERSONALITY IN MIDDLE AGE: A THEMATIC APPERCEPTION STUDY

BERNICE L. NEUGARTEN and DAVID L. GUTMANN

The original purpose of this investigation was to explore the use of projective techniques in studying adult age-sex roles in the family. At least two considerations prompted the choice of the Thematic Apperception Test technique. The first was that the responses would be relatively uncensored, more closely related to the respondent's personal values and experiences than those he might feel constrained to give in answer to more direct questions. Second, fantasy material, although presenting certain difficulties of analysis as compared with questionnaire data, would have a decided advantage for exploratory research. The richness and unstructured nature of projective data enable the investigator to follow an inductive process; he can follow up clues as they appear in the data rather than check dimensions and hypotheses defined in advance.

The primary concern of the study was with the collective role images of husbands, wives, sons, and daughters, as those images emerged from the projections of different respondents. After the role images had been delineated, the investigators turned to implications in the data regarding the personalities of the respondents. Thus, this investigation broadened in scope as the research progressed, and, as will become clearer in following sections, this report deals not only with familial roles but also with the relations between role image and personality in middle age.

The Sample

The study population consisted of 131 men and women, distributed by age, sex, and social class, as shown in Table 31.1.

The middle-class men were well-to-do business executives and professionals, none of whom were retired. The working-class men were stable blue-collar workers, of whom three had retired. Of both groups of women, the large majority were married housewives, only a few of whom held part-time or full-time jobs outside the home. With only a few exceptions, all the people in the study population were native-born of north European ethnic backgrounds. The large majority grew up in Kansas, Missouri, or neighboring Midwest states. Almost all were Protestant. With regard to family status, of the total 131 cases, only four women had never married; only eight of the men and six of the women were childless. One-half of the women and one-third of the men were grandparents.

The Data and Methods of Analysis

A specially drawn picture was used, one designed specifically to evoke the sentiments and preoccupations of middle-aged respondents in relation to family roles (Figure 31.1).

Three levels of inquiry were employed in using the picture. The person was asked, first, to tell a story about the picture—a story with a beginning, a middle, and an end. Then the interviewer, mov-

Table 31.1. The sample

	40–54		55–70	
	Men	Women	Men	Women
Middle class	18	22	14	13
Working class	21	12	15	16
Total = 131				

276

Figure 31.1

ing clockwise around the picture and beginning with the figure of the young man, asked the respondent to assign an age and to give a general description of each of the four figures. Again moving clockwise, the respondent was finally asked to describe what he thought each figure in the picture was feeling about the others.

Stimulus Value of the Picture

Almost without exception, all respondents saw the picture as representing a two-generation family. One of the younger figures, most often the young man, was frequently seen as being outside the primary group, usually in the role of suitor or fiancée, son-in-law or daughter-in-law. Although always structured as a family situation, the stories varied widely. It might be a story of a young man coming to ask for the daughter's hand in marriage and being opposed by the older woman; it might be a mother, father, daughter, and son-in-law having a casual conversation before dinner; it might be a young couple asking for financial help from parents; or it might be an older couple coming to visit the younger.

It is within the setting of the two-generation family, then, that the role images of the young man, young woman, old man, and old woman emerged.

General Approach to Role Analysis

Having used the three levels of inquiry, the data for each figure can be regarded as a set of expectations as to how that category of person (YM, YW, OM, OW) relates to the social environment and to other categories of persons in the family in terms of action and affect. It is this set of expectations which were regarded operationally as the role description. The following assumption was made: granted that the different attributes ascribed by the respondent to the four figures in the picture that have roots in intrapsychic determinants, the respondent's expectations, based on his experiences with real people, will still have a highly determining effect on which aspects of the self he chooses to ascribe to each figure in the picture. In other words, the investigators took the respondent's perceptions as projections, mindful of the fact that what was given was intrapsychically determined, but trusting that the interactional social reality had called out and directed the projection.

Illustration of the Method

The first step in the analysis was to see what was the preoccupation around which the respondent had built his story, for the role descriptions took on greater meaning once the basic theme, or preoccupation, was understood.

For example, a woman tells the following story:

"I think the boy is going away to the service. He's telling the mother and father. That's his wife with him. The father is pretty downhearted about it. He has a downcast look on his face. His wife doesn't feel too good about it, but she's trying to pacify the older couple. They've just been married. I can't tell how it'll end up. If he has to go overseas to fight, there's always the possibility he won't come back.

[General description of the YM] Sort of a boy who has always been close to his parents. Looks like a nice kind of boy.

[General description of the YW] Looks very sympathetic. She's a real nice girl. She's trying to sympathize with the old people.

[General description of the OM] Looks like a nice homebody. Nice fellow.

[General description of the OW] I can't see enough of her face. I couldn't say any more, because there's no face to go by. Sort of refined, from her stature.

[YM's feelings] He thinks they're all right, or he wouldn't have sat down. . . . Well, some boys wouldn't care how their folks felt, but he seems to realize that they're hurt.

[YW's feelings] She thinks her husband is a pretty fine fellow, or she wouldn't be trying to sympathize with his folks.

[OM's feelings] He's pleased with the young folks. He's interested in what his son's going to do.

[OW's feelings] She's in a bad place—can't see enough of her. I really couldn't say."

The theme which underlies this story is the theme of family dispersion, the "empty nest." The respondent tells us, in effect, that the children are leaving home and that they "won't come back."

Looking first at the description of the young man, in the story proper we are told what his action is: to leave home, presumably for some dangerous and rigorous extrafamilial environment. His action has emotional consequences for the parents, consequences which he does not seek to mitigate. His face is set beyond the boundaries of the primary group, and his only action in the group is the rather formal one of making this position clear to his parents. "He's telling the mother and father."

We are next told about the young man that he has always been close to his parents. The implication is that an earlier relationship of the son to the parents is now ending. It is of interest that the respondent speaks of the YM's affiliation to the parents only when she discusses him in the general, nonsituational context. When she is asked to consider him in relation to the immediate situation and to the actors in it, the theme of remoteness infuses the portrayal. This point is made clear when the respondent is again asked to put the young man back into the interactive context and to discuss his feelings there. Now he emerges as one who, although essentially detached, still adheres no minimal social forms. The respondent has difficulty in ascribing any but the most qualified feeling to him: "thinks they're all right," and "seems to realize that they're hurt." The YM's reaction to the parents' feelings is a relatively intellectualized one: he "realizes" or recognizes their existence, while it is his wife who "sympathizes" with them. Even this modest affective gesture on the part of the YM is doubted, for the respondent goes out of her way to assure us that the YM is not like other boys who "wouldn't care how their parents felt." In the respondent's whole recital, then, she attributes to the YM only minimal and grudging affiliation to the parents.

We can now make this general statement about the perception of the young man's familial role—his basic orientation is to rigorous and compelling nonaffective extrafamilial concerns, and intimacy for him is to be found with peers of the opposite sex. Although not too long ago (in terms of subjective time) the primary, paternal group was a major focus of his interest, his present role there is governed by moral directives (superego demands) rather than by spontaneous warmth. These directives, coming into conflict with his more compelling extrafamilial interests, result in a posture of grudging punctiliousness, of bare attention to formal, socially defined demands. Himself barely participant in the family—although at the same time, a source of concern to the parents—he leaves to his wife the mediation of the emotional issues between himself and his parents. He is generally governed by outside demands, as though those demands were more congenial to his energies and motivations than are the demands made by the parental group.

Turing to the YW, we are given a different image. In the story proper she, too, appears as one whose actions are directed towards the parents, but whereas, the YM's action toward the parents—telling them that he is leaving—begins and ends his contract with them, her action—"trying to pacify them"—implies a continuing and multifaceted relationship with the older group. The young man only tells them about himself and at the most can only "recognize" the effects of his announcement on the parents. The young woman, although she "doesn't feel too good about it," does not deal with her own reaction but attempts to alleviate the parents' grief. The word "pacify" implies maternal behavior, as does the pattern of dealing with the woes of others rather than with her own.

Our interpretation of the young woman's strong, maternal concern with intimate human relations is strengthened when we look at the general description given of her. Here, the respondent persists in seeing the YW in relation to the current crisis. Again she is seen as a person whose actions are nurturant and consoling, but at this point an element of emotional distance enters into the description. The young woman is "trying" to sympathize with the older group. Here is an implication of some barrier against emotional rapport between the old group and the YW, a barrier which she feels impelled to overcome. The description of the YW's feelings give us a clue as to why she attempts to overcome the barrier. It is because of her regard for her husband that she feels a responsibility to his parents. We are told that her primary affiliation is to her husband and that responsibility to the parents is secondary, stemming from her marital tie. She takes form now as a person who must deal nurturantly with various aspects of the interpersonal universe, although institutional and generational barriers may exist between her and certain others. If formal ties exist between her and other people, she seeks to enrich the formal ties with empathic bonds.

Taking the role description as a whole and seeing it against the theme of "empty nest," we see the young woman's role as one of emotional liaison, operating in the widening breach between the parental and filial generations. Her husband moves off into what are viewed as distant and threatening events while she, though drawn after him, bridges the gap and maintains some version of the lost emotional ties between parents and children. Against the background of traumatic family dispersion, her role has a maternal quality: although her primary tie is to her husband, her immediate concern is for those who have been injured by the course of events, and she attempts in maternal fashion to compensate the injured through her nurturance. In sum, her role is complementary to her husband's in that, while he moves off to "do battle," she tarries behind to handle the human consequences of his actions and decisions.

Turning to the figure of the old man, we first see him as feeling sad at the news of his son's leaving. No actions are ascribed to him. He reacts to traumatic situations with feeling, but he is not seen as acting out his feelings or doing anything to alter the situation which made him sad.

At the level of general description, we are told that he is "a nice homebody," positively regarded. His major cathexis or emotional investment is to the family, and it is there that he is gratified. Values relevant to his role are those of comfort and ease in an affiliative setting.

Moving to the feelings ascribed to the old man, we notice a shift away from the initial description given of him. Where he was initially saddened, he is now "pleased" with the young people, and he will maintain a meaningful, although somewhat intellectualized interest in his son's future activity. There is still no intimation that he will act to change the course of his son's affairs—the son will "do," and the father will be interested—but a note of equanimity has entered the description. If we examine this shift in light of the theme of family dissolution, we conclude that it represents a concept of defensive adjustment, adjustment to the inescapable reality of the young man's maturity through defensive denial of strong personal feeling. After some initial depression, the old man resigns himself to the fact of the breach and returns to the emotional *status quo*. Although the young group, especially the YM, is no longer reciprocally affiliative, the old man's outward feelings toward them remain basically unchanged.

The old man's role, then, somewhat like the young woman's, is an adjustive one. He buffers the shocks of transition. Accepting the reality of change, he acts to minimize the consequent feelings and to find new bases for intimacy in the new situation. It is of particular interest that the old man attempts to maintain the *status quo* by changing himself and hiding his own feelings. At no point in the protocol does he act to change anything outside himself.

This interpretation of the old man's role gains support when we turn to the old woman. In the story proper we are told nothing about her; her presence is merely noted. At the general level of description, perception of her is again denied. In effect, we are told that she has no emotionally expressive surface ("there's no face to go by"). She is associated only with "refinement," a description which implies that she has no contact with a freely affective, spontaneous environment. (By contrast, the old man is the "homebody.") The word "refined" suggests the values of restraint, pride, and possibly a defensive rigidity.

As to the old woman's feelings, the respondent tells us, in effect, that she cannot imagine any feeling states which might pertain, because the OW is "in a bad place." Although there is a relative paucity of data about the OW, we nevertheless obtain the strong impression of rigidity and withdrawal in the figure. Viewed against the thematic background, this rigidity and withdrawal take on meaning as a possible mode of coping with crisis, but a mode which is quite different from the one defined for the old man. Faced with the trauma of family breakdown, the old man's role is to adjust to the inevitable by minimizing his own reactions. The adjustive mode ascribed to the old woman seems to stress denial of the trauma and its emotional consequences, strict control, and magical defenses against her vulnerability. The old man's adjustment, although a defensive one, still is oriented toward a social universe and untroubled contact with others in future situations. The old woman's role has a more primitive, egocentric quality, as if the vulnerability of the self were the only concern and as if this concern justifies the use of archaic defenses—such as complete denial of a painful situation.

Granted that both the old man's and old woman's roles may represent possible solutions of the respondent's own problem—her defenses against the problem she has proposed—the investigators' primary interest is with the content of the roles as they emerge from the respondent's fantasy and to which figure in the picture each role is ascribed.

Treatment of the Data

Using the method illustrated above, each protocol was analyzed for role descriptions of each of the four stimulus figures. Interpretations were recorded separately for each figure. The protocols were divided according to the sex of the respondent but were analyzed without knowledge of the respondent's age or social class.

Reliability of Interpretations

The question of reliability of interpretations was dealt with at an early stage in the research. Using nine protocols selected at random, two judges rated each of the four figures on a five-point scale for each of twelve personality characteristics, and the ratings were then correlated. The average coefficients of correlation were .81 for the YM, .88 for the YW, .83 for the OM, and .88 for the OW.

This procedure proved to be a somewhat oblique test of reliability, since it was later decided not to deal with the role descriptions on the basis of such ratings, but rather to continue to draw summary descriptions of the figures and then to categorize the descriptions according to similarity. At the same time, this test of reliability was a relatively stringent one for this type of data.

Quantifying the Data

Once all the protocols had been analyzed and decoded, the data for each figure were treated separately. The procedures with reference to the data on the old man will be described here since these were the first to be dealt with and since findings regarding the OM influenced in some ways the organization of the other sets of data.

All the descriptions were grouped on the basis of similarity into mutually exclusive categories, attempting always to judge similarity in terms of the most salient features ascribed to the OM by the respondent. This was a lengthy process since the attempt was to establish categories that would produce the least distortion of the original data. At the same time, having become aware that there were age differences in the perceptions of the OM, the investigators attempted to structure the categories in such fashion as to highlight the age differences.

Six major categories were finally delineated and arranged along a continuum termed "dominance-submission." At one end were those categories in which, whatever other characteristics were ascribed to the OM, he was always a dominant figure within the family. At the other end were those categories in which he was seen as a passive or submissive figure. Dominance or submission was judged in terms of the OM's impact on the situation; the extent to which others deferred to him; the extent to which resolutions of family issues depended upon his wishes, his judgments, or his decisions.

Dealing next with one after another subsample of respondents (middle-class men, middle-class women, working-class men, working-class women), frequency distributions were made in which the role descriptions were plotted by category and by age of respondent. The distributions were then tested for statistical significance by applying the chi-square method.

For each subsample of respondents there was a shift with age in the perceptions of the OM. The role descriptions given by younger respondents (aged forty to fifty-four) more often fell in those categories in which the OM is described as dominant; the descriptions given by older respondents (aged fifty-five to seventy) most often fell in those categories in which the OM is passive. The number of cases in each subsample was too small to establish reliable chi-square values, but the trend was present in every group. Cases were then combined into larger groupings—all male, all female, all middle class, all working class. The age trends were now even more pronounced (P values were between .05 and .01). Finally, when all respondents were grouped together, the age shift was unquestionably

reliable (P was .001).

At this point, whereas age of respondent consistently produced variation in the data, it was not clear which of the original variables—age, sex, or social status—was the most important in producing the overall variation. A further step was therefore taken. Ratings on dominance-submission were assigned to each category of role description; these ratings were then submitted to an analysis of variance. It was found that of all the variables—age, sex, social status, and the interactions thereof —only age was significant (P was beyond .001). The data on the OW were also subjected to analysis of variance, with the same result emerging.[1]

The Old Man

The figure of the OM seems to symbolize for respondents the ego qualities of the personality: the rational rather than the impulsive approach to problems, concern over the needs of others, reconciliation between opposing interests, cerebral competence.

The descriptions of the OM fall into six major categories that can be ordered along a continuum from dominance to submission.

1. "Altruistic authority." In this category the OM is seen in a position of authority in the family, and he uses his authority to benefit the young people or the family as a whole. He is the benevolent monarch, the nurturant wise man, whose actions are altruistically motivated and lead only to benevolent outcomes. He operates effortlessly and easily in this role.

2. "Assertive, but guilty." These descriptions are those in which the OM attempts to further his own ends, but is restrained by inner reluctances, doubts,

---

[1] Findings *re* the YM and YW are omitted from the present version of this paper.—Ed.

or guilt. He occupies a position of strength and asserts himself in the family, and, although he is not opposed by others, he nevertheless cannot easily and single-mindedly press for his announced goals. There is always some quality of inner doubt about the justice of his claims. He is conflicted, unsure, the insecure autocrat. "He thinks it's about time those kids left home and earned their own living—he hates to tell them, though."

3. "Formal authority." Here the father is the authority, but by default. His authority is challenged as the story progresses, or other individuals take action to decide outcomes while he acts only to approve those outcomes. He is described here not so much in terms of service to others (as in Category 1), but in terms of pliability to the wishes of others. He merely approves decisions which have already been thrashed out among more active figures.

4. "Surrendered authority." It is indicated here that the OM could be the authority if he desired—he possesses the requisite qualities—but he refuses and/or abandons the role. In some instances, he is initially described as dominant, but, as the story unfolds, he is relegated to a more submissive position. In other instances, he is ascribed the qualities associated with leadership, but these qualities are split away from action—they have no impact on the events of the story, they do not impinge on outcomes, they find no overt behavioral expression. He is inwardly "tough" but overtly passive, or he has "executive qualities" but leaves the decision up to his wife. In no instance is there an intrusion of the OM as a dominant force on the family scene.

5. "Passive, affiliative." Here the OM is described in terms of what might be called maternal qualities. He is unflaggingly and uncritically affiliative toward the others. He "loves everybody." He

accepts, resignedly, outcomes which he may not approve. He is dominated by his wife, but seems to feel no discomfort or resentment in the situation. In stories where the OW is opposing some action proposed by the young people, such as marriage, the OM's attitude is one of affiliating with both sides—of saying affectionately to the OW, "Why fight the inevitable?"

6. "Passive, cerebral." Grouped here are those descriptions which present the OM as passive and withdrawn. He lacks any announced affiliative attachments to others. The issue of authority does not even arise. His wife rules the family, and he remains remote, both in terms of action and affect, from the family drama. As this drama swirls about him, he "thinks." (The content of his thought or its relevance to the situation is rarely specified.) The OM controls events from behind the forehead, as it were, and takes a certain satisfaction in the freedom this provides him. As one male respondent put it, "He's made up his mind about the thing. He's waiting for the old woman to tell them what to do."

Age Differences

As shown in Table 31.2, there is a consistent shift, with increasing age of respondent, from seeing the OM in situations of power in the family toward seeing him as passive and submissive. (This age shift is statistically significant beyond the .005 level.)

The stimulus figure of the OM confronts the majority of younger respondents with the issue of familial authority. (If Category 4 is included, then approximately 75 percent of all younger respondents see the OM either as an authority figure or as one who possesses the potential for authority.)

Each of the first four categories in Table 31.2 represents a different resolution of the issue of male dominance. The first

Table 31.2. Role descriptions of the old man

Category	40–54 Men	40–54 Women	55–70 Men	55–70 Women
1. Altruistic authority:				
Middle class	5	9	2	1
Working class	3	3	1	3
Total	20*		7	
2. Assertive, but guilty:				
Middle class	2	0	2	2
Working class	6	1	1	1
Total	9		6	
3. Formal authority:				
Middle class	5	5	0	0
Working class	2	3	1	0
Total	15		1	
4. Surrendered authority:				
Middle class	2	3	4	3
Working class	6	1	3	2
Total	12		12	
5. Passive, affiliative:				
Middle class	0	4	2	6
Working class	3	4	3	8
Total	11		19	
6. Passive, cerebral:				
Middle class	4	1	4	1
Working class	1	0	6	2
Total	6		13	

* The chi-square test was applied to these category totals. The probability that the distribution occurred by chance is less than .001.

two represent active resolutions. If the issue is met head on—if, that is, the OM defines self-gratifying goals and uses his position of authority to achieve them (Category 2)—the ambivalence and guilt are the necessary results. If, on the other hand, the OM uses his authority nurturantly for the benefit of others, he can act easily and comfortably in his position (Category 1). The more passive solutions involve either the OM's sanctioning of the wishes of others and attempting no intervention in the family scene (Category 3) or the more outright abandonment of the authoritative status altogether (Category 4).

For our forty–fifty-four group, the issue being dealt with around the role of the OM is not only that of male dominance, however, but also that of male aggression in the family. The problem

seems to be how the OM can be an authority without being arbitrarily, and perhaps harmfully, self-assertive. How can the cultural demand—that the father is head of the family—be met without exposing the family to male aggression? The solution seems to involve the stressing of the moral function of authority: the OM must be either an active force for good, or, by "letting things happen," he passively cooperates with the others in arriving at positive outcomes.

For older respondents, the OM no longer presents the issue of masculine authority. The stories are now those in which the OM has no impact upon family events, and he presents only one or another image of passivity. (Of all respondents aged fifty-five–seventy, 55 percent are found in the last two categories. If Category 4 is included—the OM abandoning or surrendering authority—then 80 percent of all older respondents see the OM among the categories of submission and denial of authority.)

The age shift in the image of the OM from dominance to submission is elaborated in several ways. The forty-year-old respondent sees the OM as being in doubt about his own assertive tendencies; the sixty-year-old sees him as being the passive object of others' assertion. In the forties, the OM is seen as attempting to control events. In the sixties, he attempts only to control and order the cognitive environment, the symbolic traces of objects and events. In the forties, it is proposed that the OM is aware of the pressures from an impulsive and willful woman, but that he can allow the OW full expression and still wisely control the course of events. In the sixties, it is proposed that impulse, in the form of the OW, is left in charge of the field, that the OM's wisdom can control events only behind the forehead. The OM has moved from a stance of intrafamilial autonomy to "intracranial" autonomy.

In regard to the implications for personality differences in respondents, it has been said that the figure of the OM symbolizes ego qualities of the personality. With increased age of respondent, the ego, as personified by the OM, seems to contract. On the one hand, it is no longer in contact with impulse life, controlling and channeling it (the OM no longer controls the OW's impulsivity). On the other hand, the ego is no longer in a position of mastery relative to the outer world (the OM is not successful in the extrafamilial world). Ego functions are turned inward, as it were, and, although rational thought processes are still important in the personality, thought is no longer relevant to action.

The Old Woman

The old woman, by comparison to the other figures in the picture, is the key figure in the family. The family is her arena, and within it she emerges in full scope and complexity. There are, for instance, a number of stories that might be labeled "Oedipal" in theme—stories in which the YW is being claimed by the YM or vice versa and in which there is conflict between the young and the old. In these stories, it is always the OW, but not the OM, who is seen as the protagonist in the struggle.

For the OW, the major issue is around retentiveness of the young—what the extent and the nature of the tie between herself and her children is to be. This issue always has strong emotional components for her.

In contrast to the young woman, the OW is seen as standing on her own feet, a person in her own right. The psychological distance between her and the old man is much greater than that between the two young figures. Whereas the YW and YM are seen in a close, collaborative relationship, the OW and OM stand separate and apart. They are often described in polar terms—if one is dominant, the other is submissive; if one is nurturant, the other is narcissistic.

The OW is not always seen as comfortable in her role, and she is the only figure

who is as often described by respondents in negative as in positive terms.

Descriptions of the old woman were grouped into six major categories. Although the categories are ordered in Table 31.3 along the general continuum from submission to dominance, there are really two major themes which, in one or another combination, form the basis for the differentiation. The first is the theme of control over others—whether the OW is seen as submissive and controlled (categories 1, 2, 3,) or as dominant and the controller (categories 4, 5, 6). The second theme is that of the nature of impulsivity—whether the OW is viewed as benign and nurturant (categories 1, 4, 5) or self-assertive and agressive (categories 2, 3, 6).

1. "Submissive, nurturant." Here the OW

Table 31.3. Role descriptions of the old woman

Category	40–54 Men	40–54 Women	55–70 Men	55–70 Women
1. Submissive, nurturant:				
Middle class	10	6	1	3
Working class	4	2	2	3
Total	24*		9	
2. Controlled by OM:				
Middle class	1	9	1	0
Working class	5	5	1	2
Total	20		4	
3. Limited by children:				
Middle class	2	3	1	1
Working class	3	2	2	4
Total	10		8	
4. The good mother:				
Middle class	2	0	7	2
Working class	7	0	3	2
Total	9		14	
5. The matriarch:				
Middle class	1	3	0	3
Working class	1	0	1	1
Total	5		5	
6. Hostile self-assertion:				
Middle class	2	1	4	3
Working class	1	1	5	4
Total	5		16	

* The chi-square test was applied to these category totals. The probability that the distribution occurred by chance is less than .001.

is viewed as passive relative to the determination of outcomes. She is affiliative, nurturant, benevolent, but never self-assertive. She takes a position of deference to a wise, authoritative old man. She is the fluttery, "little-woman" type and never intrudes on the masculine prerogatives of thought and decision. She is dependent on her husband for guidance and for control. To the extent that she takes action at all, the action is nurturant, promoting the best interests of others, especially the young.

2. "Controlled by OM." Here the OW is seen as aggressive and impulsive, but she is controlled by the OM. Although she is something of a "battle-ax," she is more the family nuisance than the family menace. Her rages do not intimidate; they merely annoy. The wise and tolerant husband allows her free expression of her feelings, but deftly controls her. He determines outcomes and guarantees nurturant solutions to the autonomy-seeking young, often in the face of the OW's active opposition.

3. "Limited by children." Here, as in the preceding category, an aggressive, domineering OW tries to extend her control over a resistant environment. While she now dominates her husband, she is successfully opposed and limited by the YW and/or the YM. The OM cannot provide a buffer between the intrusive OW and the young, but the young take up the cudgels for themselves and win out against the OW.

4. "The good mother." Here the issue of dominance-submission is not specifically introduced, though the OW is implicitly given the decisive role in the disposition of affairs. The OW is the good, nurturant mother who guides and supports her gratified husband and children. She is mild, benign, maternal. Though she has the most effective role in the family, there is no tension between her and the others. The view is rather of harmonious interaction, where it is only right and "natural" that the mother holds the most important place in the family.

5. "The matriarch." In this category the OW is seen as a forceful and aggressive authority. While, however, she has complete sway over the others, this leads only to benign results. The family, rather than opposing her, bask contentedly in their dependent and submissive positions. Everyone benefits from her rule.

6. "Hostile self-assertion." Here the OW is a stereotyped figure, one who exercises a harsh, arbitrary, and unopposed control. Her dominance is not tempered by any redeeming strain or affiliation or nurturance, nor does she have any concern for others. The OW is either pictured as the embodiment of amoral id—all impulse and wrath—or the punitive superego who harshly judges others and rigidly defines the moral code—a superego armed, as it were, with the energies of the id.

Age Differences

As shown in Table 31.3, role definitions of the old woman, like those of the other three figures, vary consistently with age of respondent. Whereas the age shift in the perception of the old man's role is in the direction of increasing submissiveness, the OW moves from a subordinate to an authoritative family role. (The age shift is statistically stable at the .001 level.)[2]

Younger respondents view the OW as sensitive to, or checked by, outer demands and pressures. Older respondents propose that the OW has come to be the embodiment of controls, strictures, limits. She has taken over the moral and directive qualities which, for younger respondents,

---

[2] In a subsequent study of forty-seven older men in which the same TAT card was used, Margaret Thaler Singer found essentially the same perceptions of the OM and OW (Singer, 1963, pp. 230–31).

were seen as operating outside herself.

In general, with increasing age of respondent, the OW emerges more and more as the most feeling, demanding, and aggressive figure, as the other figures tend toward greater passivity, colorlessness, and conformity. In stories told by older respondents, the point at which the OW is described tends frequently to signal the breakthrough of impulsivity, as if the OW represents unchecked impulse in a scene otherwise populated by more constricted, conforming, or affiliative figures.[3]

As regards respondents themselves, the old woman symbolizes the impulsive, self-centered qualities of the personality (in contrast to the OM, who symbolizes ego qualities of the personality). The age shift in perception of the OW implies, therefore, increasing pressures from the impulse life in the face of decreasing ego controls.

Fantasy Data in Relation to Sex-Role Behavior

Since these findings have been derived from projective data, what are their implications for role behavior?

The individual, in filling real-life roles, resolves tensions between personal needs and social expectations. The task of the ego is to organize the various affective components of the personality into a personally expressive, though socially acceptable, pattern of behavior. When presented with the picture, however, a different demand is made of the respondent. He is asked not to act in the real family setting, but to breathe vitality into a representation of family life. The task of the ego is not one of integrating various aspects of the self into a coherent pattern of behavior,

but the opposite—in effect, to distribute various components of the self among the various figures in the picture.

This fractionating of the components of personality makes the thematic apperception technique a valuable clinical instrument, but it also imposes qualifications on its use in the study of social roles. In the latter case, the respondent describes a living complexity (the role of OM or OW) in terms of only one or a few facets of the self. The projected aspect of the self temporarily winnowed out of the total personality, tends to be expressed in exaggerated form. The result is a certain stereotypy and a certain overemphasis in the role descriptions. The task of the role analyst is thus made correspondingly difficult. The role patterns he wishes to describe may have been distorted into nonviable extremes as they have become the focuses for conflicting elements in the respondents' personalities. Rather than objective role descriptions, his data are the affective connotations of role behavior, those which people limit and modify in real life.

The findings presented here must be interpreted with caution, then, in applying them to actual role behavior. It should be kept in mind that, if the respondent speaks of the old man as weak and passive and the old woman as dominant and manipulative, he is describing not only two polar forms of behavior but also two aspects of himself and that both aspects will find some (though not equal) expression in his own behavior. If the respondent is an older man, he cannot be described merely on the basis of his description of the old man as passive and weak, for the respondent is a person who also has needs for strength and dominance. It is the nature of the task —responding to the picture—which allows him to describe the old man in more unitary ways than are actually true of himself.

These considerations apply equally with regard to collective role images that emerge from groups of respondents. For

[3] Perhaps the projection of impulsive elements of personality on the figure of the OW is partially stimulated by her facelessness in the picture. If impulsivity is regarded by respondents as ego-alien. It might well be ascribed to that figure in the picture which provides fewest cues regarding social interaction.

example, many older respondents seem to agree that older men are passive, affect-less, and isolated from the stream of family events. They are described as "smoking their pipes" and "thinking." It cannot be assumed, however, that the only role of older men in the family is to stand in the corner, thinking and smoking. People who live in the family setting, young or old, do interact with others and do impinge on the environments of other family members. What can be justifiably assumed from this image is not that older men never interact or relate, but that the very activities through which they express the outward forms of intimacy also tend to highlight their desire for passivity and isolated contemplation. The image does not report the daily reality of the older man's role; rather, it is a sharply drawn, condensed expression of the affective mode which underlies his activities. The sharpness of the image is derived from the condensed expression of what is seen as being central to the figure of the old man and from the affective components of the respondents' personalities identified with this central tendency.

What we have in these data, then, is centrality rather than experienced complexity of role behavior.

To take another example, in many stories, especially in those told by men, the description of the old woman provides a point at which unchecked impulse breaks into a scene otherwise peopled by more restrained or affiliative figures. She is a figure of primal omnipotence and wrath—"a devil. Very strict. Must run everything and everybody." In one sense the description functions to bring the aggressive impulse life of the respondent into the story.[4]

----

[4] In real life the respondent's wife may function so as to express elements of the respondent's impulse life that are denied expression in his own behavior. Our findings hint at the possibility that males often handle their aggression in the family by proposing that they are the passive object of attack from a woman, rather than by proposing that aggression stems from themselves.

What emerges is not an unbiased account of the old woman, but a picture of the old woman as it is filled out by aggressive energy that has its locus in the respondent himself. (It is the respondent's own denied rage, projected on to the figure of the old woman, that he calls a "devil.") Women who live in a social environment cannot act purely from unmediated primitive impulse. They would soon be hospitalized, institutionalized, or dead. What we are being told in such accounts is that older women's behavior in the family expresses, for those respondents preoccupied with such issues, a central quality of free aggression.

Bearing such considerations in mind, these findings can nevertheless be related to actual role behavior. This relationship is posited on the grounds that the affective complexes energizing the perception of the stimulus figures are indeed cued by the respondent's expectations of such figures in real life. Granted that various components of the respondent's own personality migrate toward one or another stimulus figure, the impressive fact is the consistency with which the same personality components migrate to the same figure in the picture. For instance, for both men and women respondents, it is almost always the old woman, not the old man, to whom impulsivity, aggressivity, and hostile dominance are ascribed. This consistency cannot be explained by chance. The assumption seems warranted that there is something common to the actual role behaviors of older women that elicits this consistency in respondents' fantasies.

To sum up, projective data do not yield descriptions of the total and complex role of the older woman in the family as that role is expressed in everyday, overt behavior (similarly for other other figures). What is obtained instead is a central aspect of the role, an aspect that, in one translated form of behavior or another, is being recognized by both men and women.

The role images of all four figures varied consistently with age and sex of respondent, but not with social class. Most striking was the fact that, with increasing age of respondents, the old man and old woman reversed roles in regard to authority in the family. For younger men and women (aged forty–fifty-four) the old man was seen as the authority figure. For older men and women (aged fifty-five–seventy) the old woman was in the dominant role, and the old man, no matter what other qualities were ascribed to him, was seen as submissive.

The different images of all four figures presented by men and women at the two age levels imply personality changes in the years from forty to seventy. For example, women, as they age, seem to become more tolerant of their own aggressive, egocentric impulses; whereas men, as they age, of their own nurturant and affiliative impulses. To take another example, with increasing age in both men and women, ego qualities in the personality seem to become more constricted—more detached from the mastery of affairs and less in control of impulse ilfe.

Reference

SINGER, M. T. Personality measurement in the aged. In Birren, J. E., *et al* (Eds.), *Human aging: a biological and behavioral study.* National Institute of Mental Health, PHS Publication 986. Washington, D.C.: U.S. Government Printing Office, 1963.

32. SEX–ROLE STEREOTYPES: A CURRENT APPRAISAL

INGE K. BROVERMAN, SUSAN R. VOGEL,
DONALD M. BROVERMAN, FRANK E. CLARKSON,
and PAUL S. ROSENKRANTZ

Sex-role standards can be defined as the sum of socially designated behaviors that differentiate between men and women. Traditionally, psychologists have uncritically accepted sex roles as essential to personality development and function. Thus psychopathologists have considered gender identity to be a crucial factor in personal adjustment, with disturbances in adjustment often attributed to inadequate gender identity. Developmentalists tend to focus upon the conditions and processes which facilitate successful internalization of appropriate sex-role standards. The positive values of sex-role standards have rarely been questioned.

Recently, however, investigators have expressed concern over possible detrimental effects of sex-role standards upon the full development of capabilities of men and women (Blake, 1968; Davis, 1967; Hartley, 1961; Horner, 1969; Maccoby, 1963; Rossi, 1964). Traditional sex-role patterns are also being challenged by the new feminist movement. During such a period of revaluation, there is need for a close systematic scrutiny of the actual content of sex-role standards and an examination of the influence that these standards have upon individual behaviors. For the past six years we have been engaged in programmatic research examining the nature and effects of sex-role standards in our contemporary society. As psychologists with varying theoretical backgrounds, we share the conviction that existing sex-role standards exert real pressures upon individuals to behave in prescribed ways; we share also a strong curiosity as to what these standards consist of, how they develop, and what their consequences are.

It appeared in the mid 1960s that traditional sex-role patterns were in a state of flux, and we anticipated that a corresponding fluidity would appear in definitions of sex roles. As a first step toward determining these definitions, we devised a questionnaire that assesses individual perceptions of "typical" masculine and feminine behavior (Rosenkrantz, Vogel, Bee, Broverman, & Broverman, 1968). This questionnaire has now been administered to almost a thousand subjects, providing normative indices of the content of sex-role standards. In addition, individual differences in sex-role perception have been related to a number of independent variables, thus providing some tentative answers to questions about the antecedents and consequents of varying perceptions of sex roles.

Our findings, culled from a number of studies, lead to the following broad conclusions:

1. A strong consensus about the differing characteristics of men and women exists across groups which differ in sex, age, religion, marital status, and educational level.
2. Characteristics ascribed to men are positively valued more often than characteristics ascribed to women. The positively valued masculine traits form a cluster of related behaviors which entail competence, rationality, and assertion; the positively valued feminine traits form a cluster which reflect warmth and expressiveness.
3. The sex-role definitions are implicitly and uncritically accepted to the extent that they are incorporated into the self-concepts of both men and women. Moreover, these sex-role differences are considered desirable by college students, healthy by mental health professionals, and are even seen as ideal by both men and women.
4. Individual differences in sex-role self-concepts are associated with (a) certain sex-role relevant behaviors and attitudes such as actual and desired family size, and (b) certain antecedent conditions such as mother's employment history.

These findings will be discussed in detail following a description of our instrument and its development.

Development of the Sex-Role Questionnaire

Since our concern was with measuring current sex-role perceptions, we rejected traditional masculinity-feminity scales such as the California Psychological Inventory (CPI) (Gough, 1957) precisely because these scales are based on traditional notions of sex-appropriate behaviors and interests, which we suspected might no longer be relevant. Our concern was with the traits and behaviors currently assigned to men and women. Hence we developed our own instrument. Approximately 100 men and women enrolled in three undergraduate psychology classes were asked to list all the characteristics, attributes, and behaviors on which they thought men and women differed. From these listings, all of the items which occurred at least twice ($N = 122$) were selected for inclusion in the questionnaire. These items span a wide range of content, e.g., interpersonal sensitivity, emotionality, aggressiveness, dependence-independence, maturity, intelligence, activity level, gregariousness.

Many of the earlier studies demonstrating the existence of sex-role stereotypes required subjects to select from a list those traits which characterize men and those which characterize women (Fernberger, 1948; Sherriffs & Jarrett, 1953; Sherriffs & McKee, 1957). In contrast, we conceptualized sex roles as the degree to which men and women are perceived to possess any particular trait. Therefore the 122 items were put into bipolar form with the two poles separated by 60 points.

Men and women subjects in various other samples were then given the questionnaire with instructions to indicate the extent to which each item characterized an adult man (masculinity response), an adult woman (femininity response), and themselves (self-response). The order of presentation of masculinity and femininity instructions was reversed for approximately half the Ss within each sample; however, the self-instructions were always given last in order to obtain self-descriptions within a masculinity-femininity context.

Scoring the Sex-Role Questionnaire

The scoring procedure for the instrument, developed in our first study, was based upon responses from 74 college men and 80 college women (Rosenkrantz et al., 1968). The concept of sex-role stereotype implies extensive agreement among people as to the characteristic differences between men and women. Therefore, those items on which at least 75% agreement existed among Ss of each sex as to which pole was more descriptive of the average man than the average woman, or vice versa, were termed "stereotypic." Forty-one items met this criterion. To determine the extent of the perceived difference, correlated t tests were computed between the masculinity response (average response to the male

instructions) and the femininity response to each of the items; on each of the 41 stereotypic items the difference between these two responses was significant ($p <$ .001) in both the samples of men and women. The stereotypic items are listed in Table 32.1.

Forty-eight of the remaining items had differences between the average masculinity response and the average femininity response that were significant beyond the .05 level of confidence in each sample, but the agreement as to the direction of the differences was less than 75%. These items were termed "differentiating" items. The remaining 33 items were termed "nondifferentiating."

Pervasiveness of Sex-Role Stereotypes

Numerous investigators have noted the existence of sex-role stereotypes, i.e., consensual beliefs about the differing characteristics of men and women. These stereotypes are widely held (Lunneborg, 1970; Seward, 1946), persistent (Fernberger, 1948), and highly traditional (Komarovsky, 1950; McKee & Sherriffs, 1959). Despite the apparent fluidity of sex-role definition in contemporary society as contrasted with the previous decades, our own findings to date confirm the existence of pervasive and persistent sex-role stereotypes.

In our initial study (Rosenkrantz et al., 1968) Ss were drawn from a variety of New England institutions of higher learning, e.g., a two-year community college, a four-year city college, women's and men's schools, and parochial schools. Although the subsamples clearly differed with respect to religion and social class, our analyses indicated that they did not differ substantially from each other with respect to sex-role perceptions. Furthermore, the average masculinity responses (responses to "adult man" instructions) given by the male subjects to the 122 items correlated nearly perfectly with the average masculinity responses given by

Table 32.1. Stereotypic sex-role items (responses from 74 college men and 80 college women)

Competency Cluster: Masculine Pole is More Desirable	
Feminine	*Masculine*
Not at all aggressive	Very aggressive
Not at all independent	Very independent
Very emotional	Not at all emotional
Does not hide emotions at all	Almost always hides emotions
Very subjective	Very objective
Very easily influenced	Not at all easily influenced
Very submissive	Very dominant
Dislikes math and science very much	Likes math and science very much
Very excitable in a minor crisis	Not at all excitable in a minor crisis
Very passive	Very active
Not at all competitive	Very competitive
Very illogical	Very logical
Very home oriented	Very worldly
Not at all skilled in business	Very skilled in business
Very sneaky	Very direct
Does not know the way of the world	Knows the way of the world
Feelings easily hurt	Feelings not easily hurt
Not at all adventurous	Very adventurous
Has difficulty making decisions	Can make decisions easily
Cries very easily	Never cries
Almost never acts as a leader	Almost always acts as a leader
Not at all self-confident	Very self-confident
Very uncomfortable about being aggressive	Not at all uncomfortable about being aggressive
Not at all ambitious	Very ambitious
Unable to separate feelings from ideas	Easily able to separate feelings from ideas
Very dependent	Not at all dependent
Very conceited about appearance	Never conceited about appearance
Thinks women are always superior to men	Thinks men are always superior to women
Does not talk freely about sex with men	Talks freely about sex with men

Warmth-Expressiveness Cluster: Feminine Pole is More Desirable	
Feminine	*Masculine*
Doesn't use harsh language at all	Uses very harsh language
Very talkative	Not at all talkative
Very tactful	Very blunt
Very gentle	Very rough
Very aware of feelings of others	Not at all aware of feelings of others
Very religious	Not at all religious
Very interested in own appearance	Not at all interested in own appearance
Very neat in habits	Very sloppy in habits
Very quiet	Very loud
Very strong need for security	Very little need for security
Enjoys art and literature	Does not enjoy art and literature at all
Easily expresses tender feelings	Does not express tender feelings at all easily

the female subjects ($r=.96$). The mean femininity responses (responses to "adult woman" instructions given by the men and those given by women were also highly correlated ($r=.95$). In addition, the means of the masculinity responses

given by men and women were almost identical, as were the mean femininity responses given by the two groups. Thus, we must conclude that sex-role stereotypes cut across the sex, socioeconomic class, and religion of the respondents, at least in individuals who seek education beyond the high school level.

Responses to the sex-role questionnaire have now been obtained from 599 men and 383 women, both married and single, who range in age from 17 to 60 years and in education from the elementary school level to the advanced graduate degree level. These subjects were divided by sex and into three age groups, 17–24 years, 25–44 years, 45–56 years, making a total of six groups. Educational level varied considerably in the four older groups, while it was relatively homogeneous within the two youngest. Marital status also varied among the age groups; the oldest groups were comprised predominantly of married individuals (most frequently, parents of college students), the middle age groups consisted of both married and single individuals (including priests and nuns), while most subjects in the youngest age groups were single.

Within each of these six groups, the proportion of subjects agreeing that a given pole was more characteristic of men, or of women, was calculated for each item. All items on which agreement differed significantly from chance at the .02 level of confidence or better were noted. Seventy-four of the items met the criterion in at least four of the six different groups; 17 of the items were significant in all six groups. Thus, although some variation exists from group to group, high consensuality about the differing characteristics of men and women was found on a considerable number of items, and this was independent of age, sex, religion, education level, or marital status.

Social Desirability of the Stereotypic Items

The literature indicates that men and masculine characteristics are more highly valued in our society than are women and feminine characteristics (Dinitz, Dynes, & Clarke, 1954; Fernberger, 1948; Kitay, 1940; Lynn, 1959; McKee & Sherriffs,

1957, 1959; Sherriffs & Jarrett, 1953; Sherriffs & McKee, 1957; Smith, 1939; White, 1950). Moreover, both boys and girls between 6 and 10 years express greater preference for masculine things and activities than for feminine activities (Brown, 1958); similarly between 5 to 12 times as many women than men recall having wished they were of the opposite sex (Gallup, 1955; Terman, 1938). Sears, Maccoby, and Levin (1957) report that mothers of daughters only are happier about a new pregnancy than are mothers of sons. Investigators have also found that the interval between the birth of the first child and conception of the second is longer when the first child is a boy than when it is a girl; and that the likelihood of having a third child is greater if the first two children are both girls than both boys (Pohlman, 1969).

The valuation, or social desirability, of the characteristics designated as masculine or feminine by the questionnaire responses follows this same pattern: The masculine poles of the various items were more often considered to be socially desirable than the feminine poles. This differential valuation of sex-related characteristics was observed in several different studies. For instance, two different samples of students, one from a Catholic liberal arts college for men and one from an Eastern women's college, indicated the pole of each item that they considered to be the more socially desirable behavior for the population at large (Rosenkrantz et. al., 1968). Of the 41 items defined as stereotypic, 29 had the masculine pole chosen as more desirable by a majority of each sample. We have termed these "male-valued" items; the remaining 12 items are termed "female-valued." Moreover, the men and women showed high agreement about which poles were socially desirable (r between men and women = .96).

Additional samples of men and women were given the questionnaire with instructions to indicate that point on each item scale which they considered most desirable for an adult, sex unspecified. The average response was computed for each item for the sexes separately. The point most desirable for an adult was found to be closer to the masculine pole on the same 29 stereotypic items on which the masculine pole was considered more socially desirable by the previous samples. Also, men and women once more showed high agreement about the point on each stereotypic item that was most socially desirable for an adult.

Content of the Sex-Role Stereotypes

To explore further the dimensions reflected by the stereotypic items, factor analyses were performed separately on the masculinity and feminity responses in both a sample of men and a sample of women. Each analysis produced two initial factors accounting, on the average, for 61% of the total extractable communality. The two factors in all four analyses divided the stereotypic items into those on which the male pole is more socially desirable versus those on which the female pole is more socially desirable. These results indicated that the stereotypic items consist of two orthogonal domains, i.e., male-valued items and female-valued items.

The male-valued items seem to us to reflect a "competency" cluster. Included in this cluster are attributes such as being independent, objective, active, competitive, logical, skilled in business, worldly, adventurous, able to make decisions easily, self-confident, always acting as a leader, ambitious. A relative *absence* of these traits characterizes the stereotypic perception of women; that is, relative to men, women are perceived to be dependent, subjective, passive, noncompetitive, illogical, etc.

The female-valued stereotypic items, on the other hand, consist of attributes such as gentle, sensitive to the feelings of others, tactful, religious, neat, quiet, interested in art and literature, able to express tender feelings. These items will be referred to as the "warmth and expressiveness" cluster. Men are stereotypically perceived as lacking in these characteristics, relative to women.

Self-Concepts and Sex-Role Stereotypes

These factorial distinctions between the male-valued and female-valued components of the sex-role stereotypes have important implications for the self-concepts of men and women.

The social desirability of an item is known to increase the likelihood of that item's being reported as self-descriptive on personality tests (Edwards, 1957). This tendency to align one's self with socially desirable behaviors, together with the fact that the feminine stereotype entails many characteristics that are less socially desirable than those of the masculine stereotype, implies that women ought to reject the negatively valued feminine characteristics in their self-reports. However, our findings indicate that women incorporate the negative aspects of femininity (relative incompetence, irrationality, passivity, etc.) into their self-concepts along with the positive feminine aspects (warmth and expressiveness).

In a study of college men and women (Rosenkrantz et al., 1968), the mean self-concept scores of the men over the 41 stereotypic items were significantly different from the mean self-concept scores of the women ($p < .001$), indicating that male and female Ss clearly perceived themselves as differing along a dimension of stereotypic sex differences. However, the women's self-concepts were also significantly less feminine than their perceptions of women in general. Similarly, the self-concepts of the men were significantly less masculine than their perceptions of the "average" man.

Ideal Sex-Roles

Our evidence and that of others (Elman, Press, & Rosenkrantz, 1970; Fernberger, 1948; McKee & Sheriffs, 1959) suggest that the existing stereotypic differences between men and women are approved of and even idealized by large segments of our society. One hundred thirty-seven college men were given the questionnaire with instructions to indicate that point for each item which is most desirable for an adult man, and that point which is most desirable for an adult woman. The number of Ss who agreed that a particular pole of each item is more desirable for men or women was first computed. On 71 of the 122 items agreement was significantly different from chance ($p<.001$). The masculine pole was judged more desirable ($p<.01$) for men than women on 28 of the 29 male-valued stereotypic items (competency cluster); similar agreement reaches the .07 level of confidence on the remaining stereotypic items. These data indicate that college men feel that it is desirable for women to be less independent, less rational, less ambitious, etc., than men.

The 12 stereotypic female-valued items (warmth-expressiveness cluster), however, present a different picture. On only 7 of the 12 items was there significant agreement ($p<.01$) that the feminine pole is more socially desirable for women than for men; on one item, the agreement reaches the $p<.07$ level; on the remaining 4 items there is no significant agreement, i.e., the socially desirable adult pole is rated desirable as often for men as for women. Thus these male Ss appear to reserve for men those masculine traits which are socially desirable for adults in general, and also to consider 40% of the desirable feminine characteristics as equally desirable for men.

Again it is important to know not only the extent of agreement among Ss as to whether a trait is more desirable for men or for women, but also whether there is a significant difference between the amount of each trait assigned to men and women. Hence, the mean point at which each trait was considered most desirable for men and women, respectively, was computed for each of the stereotypic items. On the 29 male-valued traits, the difference between the means was 9.82 on the female-valued characteristics, the mean difference was 4.94. The t test between these two differences was significant ($p<.01$). This sample of college men, then, perceives male-valued traits as significantly less desirable for women than are female-valued traits for men.

Elman et al. (1970) investigated ideal sex-role concepts of both men and women. Using a shortened version of our questionnaire which included 10 male-valued and 10 female-valued stereotypic items, they asked both men and women to indicate that point on each item which is ideal for men and for women, respectively. Their results indicate that the concepts of the ideal man and the ideal woman in both men and women subjects closely parallel the male and female sex-role stereotypes. The ideal woman is perceived as significantly less aggressive, less independent, less dominant, less active, more emotional, having greater difficulty in making decisions, etc., than the ideal man; the ideal man is perceived as significantly less religious, less neat, less gentle, less aware of the feelings of others, less expressive, etc., than the ideal woman. Both greater competence in men than in women, and greater warmth and expressiveness in women than in men, then, are apparently desirable in our contemporary society. Furthermore, Elman et al. and our own results suggest that the college population, a group which tends to be critical of traditional social norms and conventions, nonetheless believes that the existing sex-role stereotypes are desirable.

Sex-Role Stereotypes and Judgments of Mental Health

The literature consistently points to a positive relationship between the social desirability of behaviors and clinical ratings of the same behaviors in terms of normality-abnormality (Cowen, Staiman, & Wolitzky, 1961), adjustment (Wiener, Blumberg, Segman, & Cooper, 1959); and health-sickness (Kogan, Quinn, Ax, & Ripley, 1957). Given the relationship existing between masculine versus feminine characteristics and social desirability, on the one hand, and social desirability and mental health on the other, we expected that clinicians would maintain distinctions in their concepts of healthy behavior in men and women paralleling stereotypic sex differences. Secondly, we predicted that behavioral attributes which are regarded as healthy for an adult, sex unspecified, and presumably indicative of an ideal health pattern will more often be considered by clinicians as healthy for men than for women. This latter prediction was derived from the assumption that an abstract notion of health (adult, sex unspecified) will tend to be more influenced by the greater social desirability of masculine stereotypic characteristics than by the lesser desirability of feminine stereotypic traits (Broverman, Broverman, Clarkson, Rosenkrantz, & Vogel, 1970).

The sample in this study consisted of 79 practicing mental health clinicians: clinical psychologists, psychiatrists, and psychiatric social workers. There were 46 men, 31 of whom held PhD or MD degrees, and 33 women, 18 with doctoral degrees. Their ages ranged from 23 to 55 years, and their experience from an internship to extensive professional practice. The clinicians were given the sex-role questionnaire with one of three sets of instructions: *male* instructions asked respondents to "think of normal, adult men, and then indicate on each item that pole to which a mature, healthy, socially competent adult man would be closer"; *female* instructions were to describe "a mature, healthy, socially competent adult woman"; finally *adult* instructions asked for the description of "a healthy, mature, socially competent adult person." Ss were asked

to think of the poles of each item in terms of direction, rather than in terms of extremes of behavior.

The results of this study, concerning the stereotypic items, indicated that men and women clinicians did not differ from each other in their descriptions of adults, women, and men, respectively. Furthermore, within each set of instructions there was high agreement as to which pole reflected the more healthy behavior, indicating that these clinicians did have generalized concepts of mental health. We also found high agreement between the pole judged as more healthy for an adult by the clinicians and the pole chosen as more desirable for adults by college students ($\chi^2 = 23.64$; $p < .01$). This confirms the positive relationship between professional concepts of mental health and conceptions of social desirability held by lay people which has been reported by other investigators (Cowen et al., 1961; Kogan et al., 1957; Wiener et al., 1959).

Comparisons of the clinicians' judgments of the healthy men and the healthy women on the competency cluster indicated that the desirable masculine pole was ascribed to the healthy man significantly more often than to the healthy woman (on 25 out of 27 items). However, only about half of the socially desirable feminine characteristics (warmth-expressiveness cluster) were ascribed more often to women than to men (7 out of 11 items). On the face of it, the finding that clinicians tend to ascribe the male-valued, competency cluster traits more often to healthy men than to healthy women may seem trite. However, a consideration of the content of these items reveals a powerful, negative assessment of women. In effect, clinicians are suggesting that healthy women differ from healthy men by being more submissive, less independent, less adventurous, less objective, more easily influenced, less aggressive, less competitive, more excitable in minor crises, more emotional, more conceited about their appearance, and having their feelings more easily hurt.

The clinicians' ratings of a healthy adult and a healthy man did not differ from each other. However, a significant difference did exist between the ratings of the healthy adult and the healthy woman. Our hypothesis that a double standard of health exists for men and women was thus confirmed: the general standard of health (adult, sex unspecified) is actually applied to men only, while healthy women are perceived as significantly *less* healthy by adult standards.

Essentially similar findings were reported by Neulinger (1968), who asked psychiatrists, psychologists, and social workers to rank 20 paragraphs descriptive of Henry Murray's manifest needs according to how descriptive they were of the Optimally Integrated Personality (OIP), i.e., the mentally healthy person. Each of his Ss completed the rankings once for the male OIP, once for the female OIP. His results showed that, although the two rankings were highly correlated, there were significant differences in the mean rankings of male and female OIP on 18 of the 20 paragraphs, 14 of them at the $p<.001$ level. Neulinger's Ss ranked dominance, achievement, autonomy, counteraction, aggression, etc., as more indicative of mental health in men than in women; sentience, nurturnace, play, succorance, deference, abasement, etc., were rated as higher for the female OIP than the male OIP. These findings are strikingly similar to ours. Neulinger interprets his findings as indicating that different conceptions of mental health exist for males and females, and that "the sex orientation of this society is not only shared, but also promoted by its clinical personnel." He believes that these rankings reflect an ideal rather than an optimally functioning person, judging by the female OIP, namely: "an affiliative, nurturant, sensuous playmate who clings to the strong, supporting male [Neulinger, 1968, p. 554]."

Behavioral Correlates of Sex-Role Stereotypes

Family Size

Davis (1967) and Blake (1969) have proposed that a critical psychological factor affecting the number of children a woman has is her acceptance or rejection of the feminine social role prevalent in our society. Blake (1969) has argued that most societies hold "pronatalistic" attitudes which prescribe for women the role of childbearer and rearer. Effective functioning in this feminine role encourages childbearing and earns social approval, while acceptance of an alternative role, such as gainful employment outside of the home, tends to reduce childbearing and earn social disapproval. Several studies have reported that working women do indeed desire (Ridley, 1959) and have (Pratt & Whelpton, 1958) fewer children than do nonworking women.

Certainly the sex-role stereotypes delineated by our research appear to be pronatalistic. Women who are perceived and perceive themselves as relatively incompetent might well feel inadequate to the challenges and stresses of employment. A less anxiety-provoking course of action would be to focus one's energies on home and family for which societal approval is cerrtain, regardless of one's effectiveness in this role. Accordingly, we investigated the relationship between self-perception in the context of stereotypic sex roles and the number of children a woman has (Clarkson, Vogel, Broverman, Broverman, & Rosenkrantz, 1970).

Sixty Catholic mothers of male college students were studied. Their ages 45 to 59 years, permitted the assumption that their families were completed. Only women with two or more children were included, thus excluding women with possible fertility problems. Education ranged from seven grades completed to doctoral degrees, with the median at 12 grades; the number of years employed outside the home since completion of formal education ranged from 0 to 29 years, with the median at 7.5 years.

Mothers with high competency self-concepts, as measured by our sex-role questionnaire, were found to have significantly fewer children than mothers who perceived themselves to be low on the competency items (3.12 versus 3.93 children, $p<.025$). Number of years worked was inversely related to number of children as expected, but did not reach statistical significance ($p<.10$).

Incorporation of male-valued stereotypic traits into the self-concepts of women should not be interpreted as a shift away from the positively valued characteristics of the female stereotype. The correlation between the self-concept score based on the competency cluster and the self-concept score based on the warmth-expressiveness cluster is low and not significant. Moreover, the self-concept scores on the warmth-expressiveness cluster were not related to family size. Thus, the self-concepts of mothers with relatively fewer children differed from the self-concepts of mothers with relatively more children only with respect to the negatively valued aspects of the feminine stereotype, i.e., the competency cluster, but do not differ with respect to the positively valued feminine traits, i.e., the warmth-expressiveness cluster.

Interpretation of these findings is not without ambiguity. It is not clear whether women who perceive themselves as relatively more competent chose to have fewer children; or whether a woman's estimation of her own competency diminishes as a function of her preoccupation with home and family. Preliminary analyses of new data from unmarried women attending a Catholic women's college suggest, however, that self-concept may be primary. College women with relatively high competency self-concepts perceive their ideal future family size as significantly smaller (4.16 children) than college women who

see themselves as relatively less competent (4.89 children). Furthermore, those women who perceive themselves as more competent indicate that they plan to combine employment with childrearing, while women who perceive themselves as relatively less competent indicate that they plan to stop working when they become mothers. Self-concept in the context of stereotypic sex roles is thus related not only to the number of children a woman has once her family is completed, but apparently influences the plans of young women concerning their future sex roles.

These data clearly demonstate a predictable and systematic relationship between sex-role attitudes—specifically, self-concept in a sex-role context—and concrete sex-role behaviors.

Maternal Employment

We have conceptualized sex-role stereotypes very broadly as attitudinal variables which intervene between particular antecedent conditions and sex-role behaviors. The following study demonstrates the relationship between sex-role attitudes and the specific antecedent condition of maternal employment.

We reasoned that a person's perception of societal sex roles, and of the self in this context, may be influenced by the degree of actual role differentiation that one experiences in one's own family. Maternal employment status appears to be central to the role differentiation that occurs between parents. If the father is employed outside the home while the mother remains a full-time homemaker, their roles tend to be clearly polarized for the child. But if both parents are employed outside the home, their roles are more likely to be perceived as similar—not only because the mother is employed, but also because the father is more likely to share childrearing and other family-related activities with the mother. Evidence exists that husbands of working wives share more in household tasks (Hoffman, 1963) and decisions (Blood, 1963; Heer, 1963) than husbands of wives remaining at home. Moreover, a number of studies suggest that the mother's employment history and status do in fact minimize a daughter's perception of sex-role related behavioral differences (Hartley, 1964), increase the likelihood of her expectation to combine marriage and a career (Riley, 1963), and make her more likely to actually pursue a career (Graham, 1970).

Accordingly, we examined the relationship between mother's employment status and sex-role perceptions of college students (Vogel, Broverman, Broverman, Clarkson, & Rosenkrantz, 1970). The sex-role questionnaire was administered under standard instructions to 24 men and 23 women whose mothers had never been employed, and to 35 men and 38 women whose mothers were currently employed. For each S the mean masculinity, femininity, and self-response scores were computed, separately for the male-valued (competency) items and for the female-valued (warmth-expressiveness) items.

As expected, daughters of employed mothers perceived significantly smaller differences between men and women than did daughters of homemaker mothers, on both the competency cluster and the warmth-expressiveness cluster. Sons of employed mothers perceived a significantly smaller difference between women and men on the warmth-expressiveness cluster than did sons of homemaker mothers. However, the perceptions of the two groups of male Ss did not differ significantly on the competency cluster. Further analysis uncovered another significant difference: Daughters of employed mothers perceived women less negatively on the competency characteristics than did daughters of homemaker mothers. Thus, while the two groups did not differ in their perceptions of women with respect to the characteristics usually valued in women (warmth-expressiveness), daughters of employed mothers did perceive women to be more competent than did the daughters of homemaker mothers.

No significant differences were found between the mean self-responses of Ss with employed mothers compared to Ss with homemaker mothers for either men or women. The self-responses fall between the masculinity and the femininity responses for all Ss. However, since the difference between the masculinity and the femininity responses is significantly smaller in Ss whose mothers are employed compared to Ss with homemaker mothers, the meaning of the self-concepts of the two groups may differ as a function of the different contexts in which they occur.

The results of this study suggest that the stereotypic conceptions of sex roles are not immutable. Insofar as perceptions of sex roles are subject to variation as a function of the individual's experience, then societal sex-role stereotypes may also be subject to change.

Summary and Conclusions

Our research demonstrates the contemporary existence of clearly defined sex-role stereotypes for men and women contrary to the phenomenon of "unisex" currently touted in the media (Bowers, 1971). Women are perceived as relatively less competent, less independent, less objective, and less logical than men; men are perceived as lacking interpersonal sensitivity, warmth, and expressiveness in comparison to women. Moreover, stereotypically masculine traits are more often perceived to be desirable than are stereotypically feminine characteristics. Most importantly, both men and women incorporate both the positive and negative traits of the appropriate stereotype into their self-concepts. Since more feminine traits are negatively valued than are masculine traits, women tend to have more negative self-concepts than do men. The tendency for women to denigrate themselves in this manner can be seen as evidence of the powerful social pressures to conform to the sex-role standards of the society.

The stereotypic differences between men

and women described above appear to be accepted by a large segment of our society. Thus college students portray the ideal woman as less competent than the ideal man, and mental health professionals tend to see mature healthy women as more submissive, less independent, etc., than either mature healthy men, or adults, sex unspecified. To the extent that these results reflect societal standards of sex-role behavior, women are clearly put in a double bind by the fact that different standards exist for women than for adults. If women adopt the behaviors specified as desirable for adults, they risk censure for their failure to be appropriately feminine; but if they adopt the behaviors that are designated as feminine, they are necessarily deficient with respect tot he general standards for adult behavior.

While many individuals are aware of the prejudicial effects of sex-role stereotypes both from personal experience and hearsay, evidence from systematic empirical studies gives added weight to this fact. The finding that sex-role stereotypes continue to be held by large and relatively varied samples of the population and furthermore are incorporated into the self-concepts of both men and women indicates how deeply ingrained these attitudes are in our society. The magnitude of the phenomenon with which individuals striving for change must cope is well delineated.

On the other hand, the finding that antecedent conditions are associated with individual differences in stereotypic sex-role perceptions offers encouragement that change is possible and points to one manner in which change can be achieved. Finally, the finding that stereotypic sex-role self-concepts correlate with actual and desired family size testifies to the central role in behavior that these concepts play. One can speculate that eventual change in sex-role concepts will in fact be associated with far-reaching changes in the life styles of both women and men.

References

BLAKE, J. Are babies consumer durables? *Population Studies*, 1968, *22*, 5–25.

BLAKE, J. Population policy for Americans: Is the government being mislead? *Science*, 1969, *164*, 522–529.

BLOOD, R. O., JR. The husband-wife relationship. In F. I. Nye and L. W. Hoffman (Eds.), *The employed mother in America*. Chicago: Rand McNally, 1963.

BOWERS, F. The sexes: Getting it all together. *Saturday Review*, 1971, *54*, 16–19.

BROVERMAN, I. K., BROVERMAN, D. M., CLARKSON, F. E., ROSENKRANTZ, P., & VOGEL, S. R. Sex-role stereotypes and clinical judgments of mental health. *Journal of Consulting Psychology*, 1970, *34*, 1–7.

BROWN, D. G. Sex role development in a changing culture. *Psychological Bulletin*, 1958, *55*, 232–242.

CLARKSON, F. E., VOGEL, S. R., BROVERMAN, I. K., BROVERMAN, D. M., & ROSENKRANTZ, P. S. Family size and sex-role stereotypes. *Science*, 1970, *167*, 390–392.

COWEN, E. L., STAIMAN, M. G., & WOLITZKY, D. L. The social desirability of trait descriptive terms: Applications to a schizophrenic sample, *Journal of Social Psychology*, 1961, *54*, 37–45.

DAVIS, K. Population policy: Will current programs succeed? *Science*, 1967, *158*, 730–739.

DINITZ, S., DYNES, R. R., & CLARKE, A. C. Preference for male or female children: Traditional or affectional. *Marriage and Family Living*, 1954, *16*, 128–130.

EDWARDS, A. L. *The social desirability variable in personality assessment and research*. New York: Dryden, 1957.

ELMAN, J. B., PRESS, A., & ROSENKRANTZ, P. S. Sex-roles and self-concepts: Real and ideal. Paper presented at the meeting of the American Psychological Association, Miami, August 1970.

FERNBERGER, S. W. Persistence of stereotypes concerning sex differences. *Journal of Abnormal and Social Psychology*, 1948, *43*, 97–101.

GALLUP, G. *Gallup poll.* Princeton: Audience Research Inc., 1955.

GOUGH, H. G. *California Psychological Inventory Manual.* Palo Alto: Consulting Psychologists Press, 1957.

GRAHAM, P. A. Women in academe. *Science*, 1970, *169*, 1284–1290.

HARTLEY, R. E. Current patterns in sex roles: Children's perspectives. *Journal of the National Association of Women Deans and Counselors*, 1961, *25*, 3–13.

HARTLEY, R. E. A developmental view of female sex-role definition and identification. *Merrill-Palmer Quarterly of Behavior and Development*, 1964, *10*, 3–16.

HEER, D. M. Dominance and the working wife. In F. I. Nye and L. W. Hoffman (Eds.), *The employed mother in America.* Chicago: Rand McNally, 1963.

HOFFMAN, L. W. Parental power relations and the division of household tasks. In F. I. Nye and L. W. Hoffman (Eds.), *The employed mother in America.* Chicago: Rand McNally, 1963.

HORNER, M. F. Bright woman. *Psychology Today*, 1969, 3.

KITAY, P. M. A comparison of the sexes in their attitudes and beliefs about women. *Sociometry*, 1940, *34*, 399–407.

KOGAN, W. S., QUINN, R., AX, A. F., & RIPLEY, H. S. Some methodological problems in the quantification of clinical assessment by Q array. *Journal of Consulting Psychology*, 1957, *21*, 57–62.

KOMAROVSKY, M. Functional analysis of sex roles. *American Sociological Review*, 1950, *15*, 508–516.

LUNNEBORG, P. W. Stereotypic aspects in masculinity-femininity measurement. *Journal of Consulting and Clinical Psychology*, 1970, *34*, 113–118.

LYNN, D. B. A note on sex differences in the development of masculine and feminine identification. *Psychological Review*, 1959, *66*, 126–135.

MACCOBY, E. Woman's intellect. In S. M. Farber and R. H. Wilson (Eds.), *The potential of women.* New York: McGraw-Hill, 1963.

MCKEE, J. P., & SHERRIFFS, A. C. The differential evaluation of males and females. *Journal of Personality*, 1957, *25*, 356–371.

MCKEE, J. P., & SHERRIFFS, A. C. Men's and women's beliefs, ideals, and self-concepts. *American Journal of Sociology*, 1959, *64*, 356–363.

NEULINGER, J. Perceptions of the optimally integrated person: A redefinition of mental health. *Proceedings of the 76th Annual Convention of the American Psychological Association*, 1968, 553–554.

POHLMAN, E. *The psychology of birth planning.* Cambridge, Mass.: Schenkman, 1969.

PRATT, L., & WHELPTON, P. K. Extra-familial participation of wives in relation to interest in and liking for children, fertility planning and actual and desired family size. In P. K. Whelpton and C. V. Kiser (Eds.), *Social and psychological factors affecting fertility.* Vol. 5, New York: Milbank Memorial Fund, 1958.

RIDLEY, J. Number of children expected in relation to nonfamilial activities of the wife. *Milbank Memorial Fund Quarterly*, 1959, *37*, 277–296.

RILEY, M., JOHNSON, M., & BOOCOCK, S. Woman's changing occupational role: A research report. *The American Behavioral Scientist*, 1963, *6*, 33–37.

ROSENKRATZ, P. S., VOGEL, S. R., BEE, H., BROVERMAN, I. K., & BROVERMAN, D. M. Sex-role stereotypes and self-concepts in college students. *Journal of Consulting and Clinical Psychology*, 1968, *32*, 287–295.

ROSSI, A. S. Equality between the sexes: An immodest proposal. *Daedalus*, 1964, *93*, 607–652.

SEARS, R. R., MACCOBY, E. E., & LEVIN, H. *Patterns of child rearing.* New York: Row, Peterson, 1957.

SEWARD, G. H. *Sex and the social order.* New York: McGraw-Hill, 1946.

SHERRIFFS, A. C., & JARRETT, R. F. Sex differences in attitudes about sex differences. *Journal of Psychology,* 1953, *35,* 161–168.

SHERRIFFS, A. C., & MCKEE, J. P. Qualitative aspects of beliefs about men and women. *Journal of Personality,* 1957, *25,* 451–464.

SMITH, S. Age and sex differences in children's opinions concerning sex differences. *Journal of Genetic Psychology,* 1939, *54,* 17–25.

TERMAN, L. M. *Psychological factors in marital happiness.* New York: McGraw-Hill, 1938.

VOGEL, S. R., BROVERMAN, I. K., BROVERMAN, D. M., CLARKSON, F. E., & ROSENKRANTZ, P. S. Maternal employment and perception of sex-roles among college students. *Developmental Psychology,* 1970, *3,* 384–391.

WHITE, L., JR. *Educating our daughters.* New York: Harper, 1950.

WIENER, M., BLUMBERG, A., SEGMAN, S., & COOPER, A. A judgment of adjustment by psychologists, psychiatric social workers, and college students, and its relationship to social desirability. *Journal of Abnormal and Social Psychology,* 1959, *59,* 315–321.

CHAPTER SEVEN: SUGGESTED FURTHER READINGS

EMMERICH, W. Socialization and sex-role development. In P. Baltes and K. W. Schaie (Eds.), *Life-span developmental psychology: Personality and socialization.* New York: Academic Press, 1973. Pp. 124–245.

HILL, R., and ALDOUS, J. Socialization for marriage and parenthood. In D. A. Goslin (Ed.), *Handbook of socialization theory and research.* Chicago: Rand McNally, 1969. Pp. 885–950.

chapter eight
family

The family can be examined as a life-span issue in two ways: the natural progression through time from childhood to parenthood to grandparenthood, which brings with each stage shifting roles and modes of behavior; or the legendary nuclear family of parents and children, which exists only during one period of life, and even then its existence as an isolated unit lacks credibility. For as the life span itself has increased, so has the complexity of the family. The postparental years, followed by grandparenthood and even great-grandparenthood, are newly discovered issues. Interaction has become a multilevel affair with children now learning to establish a perceptual view of two kinds of adults: "old people" (parents) and "real old people" (grandparents). "Old people" also have encountered new issues as their awareness of the family as a slowly unwinding chain through time lengthens. Alvin Toffler has pointed out the increased time commitment involved in marriage today. An average marriage for life meant thirty years in 1900; now it involves fifty years or more of marital compatibility: "a rather astonishing bit of optimism." (Toffler, 1971).

These issues, raised in the articles by Deutscher, Townsend, and Kahanas, examine the roles within family history as they now exist. But a perceptive glance at American culture itself shakes one out of the notion that families propagate children and their life-style in a timeless world. For the whole concept of what a family is and might be has forced a re-evaluation of where we have come from. Some believe we are truly in the center of a social revolution which will radically change the family as we know it today. Such a shift will, of course, have profound effects on psychological development. Toffler's own prognosis for the future family predicts an end to the "till death do us part" formula as more couples opt for marriages of limited duration.

Certain apparently new forms of family life are really a reemergence of the same variations. Communes, for example, existed in the early 1800s in the utopian plans of the Separatists of Zoar, Ohio, the Harmonists of Economy, Pennsylvania, and the Perfectionists of Oneida, New York. Margaret Mead has found evidence of another type of commune movement among the graduate students living in trailer parks after World War II. These families helped each other with child care and shopping and, in general, were like relatives living near each other. However, after graduation, "they moved to the suburbs and never saw a friend again" (Mead, 1971).

But one "new" kind of family has emerged through the social upheaval of the past decade. The broken family, a product of divorce, has become nearly as common as the legendary nuclear version. Statistical projections predict that four out of ten marriages consummated in 1973 will end in divorce. Futurists disagree on the reasons for the increase in the number of broken families as well as its length of stay in society. Some see it as a foreshadowing of even less stable marriages to come, and others view it as a passing tremor in the recent social earthquake.

Statistician Paul C. Glick of the Census Bureau speculates that the newly loosened divorce laws may have contributed to the current record pace of breakups by loosening a logjam of hitherto unrealizable divorces. He even argues that "there is good reason to expect this thing to go down," reasoning that the present postponement of first marriages is pruning the most unstable connubial category. [Newsweek, p. 57.]

Its proposed effect on the future generation seems equally debatable, but the national rise of marital upheavals has already had unusual results.

Many women these days are happy to stop being full-time mothers. Some are a lot less responsible about the way they shed their burden. Like Nora in A Doll's House, growing numbers of them are simply running away from the carports, the barbecue pits and the washer-driers. Although there are as yet no national statistics, private detectives report a quantum leap in the number of runaway wives they are hired to retrieve by baffled and distraught husbands. Ed Goldfader, a Manhattan investigator, says that in 1969 only 2 percent of his quarry was female; today that figure has ballooned to 56 percent.

Paralleling the rise of women's lib, the phenomenon of runaway wives starkly illustrates the re-examination of marriage and parenthood that is currently gripping the U.S. Among its more striking manifestations are plunges in the first-marriage rate, now at its lowest point since the Depression, and in the birth rate, which last year reached its lowest level in the U.S. history. Equally striking is the rising number of marriages that split apart after the major child-raising chores are finished. Among couples married fifteen to nineteen years, divorces have doubled since 1960, while in the twenty-year-and-over bracket, they are up to 56 percent. The percentage of women initiating divorce proceedings is also soaring.

Alvin Toffler, author of Future Shock, suggests that American women, prodded by the mass media, are caught up in a revolution of rising expectations. "In underdeveloped countries, those aspirations are economic," he says. "For us, they tend to be psychological." [Newsweek, p. 50.]

One might interpret these ominous turns

in family life as symptomatic of general decay in American culture. But what we are seeing is more likely the effects of adjustment to an awareness that humanness does not stop with world peace, but really starts with peace from within. The social upheaval of the past decade seems less an omen than a plea for increasing humanness in our family relationships. Humanity—the best kind of charity—begins at home.

References

The broken family: divorce U.S. style. *Newsweek*, March 12, 1973, *81*, pp. 50 and 57.

MEAD, M. In family '71: is the family obsolete? *Look*, Jan. 26, 1971, *35*, p. 36.

TOFFLER, A. In family '71: is the family obsolete? *Look*, Jan. 26, 1971, *35*, p. 35.

33. THE QUALITY OF POSTPARENTAL LIFE

IRWIN DEUTSCHER

The life cycle of the family may be thought of as the sequence of realignments of family structure and relationships ranging from the time of marriage through the death of one or both partners. In a stable society, such a sequence remains relatively fixed. A body of cultural norms related to appropriate family organization and intra-family relationships develops. Obligations, responsibilities, and privileges appropriate to each phase of the family cycle become established, and anticipatory socialization for each phase takes place during the preceding period. When, however, the society itself is in a state of general transition rather than stability, the phasing of the family cycle may change, and discontinuities in socialization from phase to phase may occur.

This paper is concerned with an emergent phase of the family cycle referred to by Cavan as the postparental: "The postparental couple are the husband and wife, usually . . . in their forties and fifties. . . . The most obvious change is the withdrawal of . . . children from the family, leaving husband and wife as the family unit. . . ." (Cavan, 1963, p. 482). This new phase of the family cycle is, in large part, a consequence of the increasing longevity, coupled with a decline in the average number of children as compared with earlier generations.

In contrast to a dearth of research on the postparental period, clinical observations, speculations, and inferences from other kinds of situations are plentiful. Commentaries based on such sources tend to be polarized. On the one hand there are those who warn that this is a period which places a severe strain on both the individual adult and the husband-wife relationship; at the other extreme is the school of thought which suggests that this is the time when life reaches its fullest bloom and the husband-wife relationship is reinforced with renewed vigor.

There is, then, a substantial amount of disagreement regarding the quality of life during this newly evolving and yet largely unexplored phase of the family cycle. In addition, the opinions held by the experts are based to a considerable extent on experiences with clients or patients—a selectively disturbed segment of the population. The present paper reports the results of an attempt to locate and describe the quality of postparental life within one stratum of the urban population and among a more representative sample of that population.

Briefly, the investigator conducted a door-to-door survey in two socio-economic areas of Kansas City, Missouri. One of these areas can be described as upper-middle class and the other as lower-middle class. Approximately 540 households were contacted in these areas. A brief questioning at the door with anyone who answered was sufficient to determine whether or not the household met the operational criteria of postparental, i.e., husband and wife both alive and living together, both between the ages of 40 and 65, and having had from one to four children, all of whom had been launched.

The survey technique resulted in the identification of 33 postparental households. Efforts to obtain intensive interviews were successful in 31 of these households, with 49 of the spouses being interviewed. Most of these open-ended interviews, which lasted from one to three hours, were tape recorded. This paper examines the way in which these urban, middle-class couples orient themselves to a new phase in the family cycle: to what extent do they define the postparental situation favorably and unfavorably?

Definitions of the Situation

The clearest clues to the manner in which postparental spouses evaluate their present situation lie in the place they reserve for it in their discussion of the total life line. This place was revealed by respondents in their discussion of such questions as, "If you could divide your life into parts, which part would you say was the best time?" and "which part was the worst time?" "How is your life different now from what it was when the children were at home?" "Now that the children have left, do you notice any difference in your husband (or wife)?" "How did you feel when the last of the children left home?" "How is your life different now than it was ten years ago?"

As Table 33.1 indicates, clear evaluations of the postparental period as being "better" than life during earlier stages of the family cycle appear in 22 of the 49 interviews. Equally clear negative evaluations occur in only *three* instances. This sample provides little support for those observers who suggest that postparental life is a time of great difficulty. (It should be pointed out, however, that couples whose difficulties during this period were

Table 33.1. Evaluation of the postparental phase of the family cycle by 49 spouses according to sex

Evaluation	Total	Husbands	Wives
(+) Postparental is "better" than preceding phases	22	8	14
Postparental is as "good" as preceding phases	15	7	8
(0) Value orientation or changes not clear	7	5	2
Postparental is as "bad" as preceding phases	2	1	1
(−) Postparental is "worse" than preceding phases	3	0	3
Total	49	21	28

reflected in extreme husband-wife friction —so extreme that the couple no longer lived together—were selected out of this sample by definition.)

What kinds of comments provide the basis for the classification which appears in Table 33.1, and what lies behind the frequencies; i.e., what are the criteria by which people judge their lives as "better" or "worse"? Let us examine first the majority, for which postparental life, far from being a time of crisis, is the "good" time —or, at least, better than the periods immediately preceding it.

For such people, it is a time of freedom —freedom from financial responsibilities, freedom to be mobile (geographically), freedom from housework and other chores, and finally, freedom to be one's self for the first time since the children came along; no longer do the parents need to lead the self-consciously restricted existence of models for their children. They can let their hair down: "We just take life easy now that the children are grown. We even serve dinner right from the stove when we're alone. It's hotter that way, but you just couldn't let down like that when your children are still at home."

These new-found "freedoms" are expressed in many ways by respondents. A newly postparental wife provides the following typical summary statement in response to the inquiry concerning how life is different now that the children are gone:

There's not as much physical labor. There's not as much cooking and there's not as much mending and, well, I remarked not long ago that for the first time since I can remember my evenings are free. And we had to be very economical to get the three children through college. We're over the hurdle now; we've completed it. Last fall was the first time in 27 years that I haven't gotten a child ready to go to school. That was very relaxing.

In this group, typical male comments are "It took a load off me when the boys left. I didn't have to support 'em anymore. I wouldn't mind having a dozen if I could support 'em right." Or, as one businessman expresses it: "I think the happiest time was when our children came into the world, but I'm looking forward to our life together now; we're getting our dividends." In a manner of speaking, these become the years of the payoff.

The wives, on the other hand, respond typically in this manner:

We're not tied down with children anymore, because they're all old enough to take care of themselves now.

I don't have as many meals to prepare anymore, and my health is better now, and we have had more to live on in the past few years; our income is better now.

We have given all for the children and that was the most important thing. We lived for the children, and after they were raised we looked for comfort for ourselves. Now when I make up my mind to get something important, I get it in time.

But even more important than these "freedoms" is the re-definition of self and the marital partnership which appears to result from them. It may be this new form of interpersonal relationship and self-conception that is the real dividend for these particular families. They speak of "better" relationships with each other, of a sense of accomplishment—a job well done—and refer to postparental life as a time of "contentment" or "satisfaction." As mentioned above, the "freedoms" culminate in the freedom to be oneself. Such a freedom could, of course, lead to either a strengthening or a weakening of the husband-wife relationship. For the moment only the former cases are considered:

My husband was a very nervous, jumpy man when the children were younger. If he wanted to do something, he would do it. We would have an argument if I tried to stop him. Now he is altogether a different man. [Q.: What do you think brought about this change in him?] Well, I think that when the girls grew up and he saw how well I was trying to raise them that he was really proud of them. Of course, as a man grows older he doesn't want to go out so much. He gets to be more of a homebody.

Nor is this a one-way picture. This woman's husband also finds her more amiable now that the children are gone:

We get along better—we always got along very well but we get along so much better since we're by ourselves. I know I appreciate and enjoyed her company more in the last year or two than I did before. The main change is like with myself; she's not as nervous since the children left home.

For some of the older postparental couples, retirement has accompanied the departure of the children, but the result is the same:

The happiest time of my life? To tell you the truth, I believe it's right now. We're happier than we've ever been because we're together constantly, you know. He's home and I don't have to worry about him going out and going on the road, and I believe we're just the happiest now that we've ever been. Of course, we were happy when we had the children.

"Of course," they were happy; however, her husband, who commented that raising four children was a "hard row to hoe" agrees: "I think it's more like home since I retired. As I told you before, I'm really enjoying my life now." It is a long, hard row to hoe, not only economically, but emotionally as well. The prelaunching years are a time of uncertainty and of anticipation—will the children turn out all right? "You put part of the tension on the children in younger lives"—

Just about now we have a comfortable home, two children, a grandchild, and I feel relaxed. That is a rather comfortable feeling— to be our age—to live for each other.

Things have not always been so good for this couple: "About ten years ago, my boy came home from the service, and I had a lot of worry and responsibility. Then, I had a teen-age daughter, and there was the uncertainty of their life." As one husband puts it, "Life didn't start settling down until the kids got grown up." He feels that now is the best time in life: "I'm more content, and there is more satisfaction."

Unfavorable evaluations made by post-parents, although they rarely occur, bear examination in order to determine their quality. The difficulties appear to center around three areas: (1) the advent of menopause and other disabilities associated with the aging process: (2) the final recognition and definition in retrospect of oneself as a "failure," either in terms of the work career or the childraising process; and (3) the inability to fill the gap—the empty place in the family which results from the departure of the children.

All of the respondents are familiar with the advent of menopause. To some it had no meaning or impact on their existence; to others it was a difficult time which had to be hurdled with a conscious effort; to a few it was a disrupting force which left a permanent impression on their lives and family relationships. Survival of the menopause is described by one respondent in terms of keeping "a healthy attitude:"

I've had a little trouble with menopause. [Q.: Is menopause very bad?] Yes, it is sometimes. You just get so terribly depressed. You have all kinds of silly feelings. You hate your best friend, and you are irritable and critical and cross. You just feel crazy sometimes. But I make a joke out of it. You got to keep a healthy attitude.

Even more telling, however, is the final assessment—the summing up—which some respondents make of their own lives. Now, in late middle age, they gain some perspective on their own histories, and to a few, the story is a tragedy of unattained goals—of "failure." One kind of failure involves the shattering of hopes and ambitions for children:

Things hurt you a little deeper when you get older. [Q.: What kinds of things?] Oh, if you have real trouble, it hurts you worse. If your children have traits— [Q.: What do you mean by traits?] Maybe you've been religious and gone to church and sent the kids to Sunday School regularly and, you know, put yourself out. Well, sometimes it ends up that the kids won't go near a church. They just say, "I had all the church I need." And education—well, you can't help but feel that they are foolish there. You have to know their personality. You can't make them over; you have to find out the hard way . . . [pause] . . . He had a voice like Nelson Eddy. Just beautiful. I tried to encourage him, but it didn't do any good. He would never do anything with it.

There are couples who have clung to marriage "for the sake of the children" or some other such rationale for as long as 25 years.

There is one respondent who illustrates in extreme form the kinds of limits which can be approached during this period; here is postparental life at its worst:

[Q.: Both of your daughters are married?] Yes, both are married and have children. Yes, here I am fifty-five—fifty-five, but I don't feel old. I feel disgusted but not old. I would lay down and die if I wasn't a coward. I was kinda depressed when my first girl married. I thought that was the end. I just died. I don't even care very much how I look. Look, I'm thirty pounds overweight. My daughters were both nineteen when they married. I didn't want them not to marry, but I missed them so much. I felt alone. I couldn't play golf. I couldn't even play bridge. I don't have a profession, and I couldn't take just any job. . . . I wanted my girls to wait until they were 30 before they got married.

Conclusions

These, then, are the evaluative outlooks on postparental life, from its best face to its worst. If the sample employed for this analysis should prove to be typical of urban middle-class postparental couples, it can be concluded that the overwhelming majority of them define the situation favorably, although serious problems present themselves for a small minority. When this gross overview is examined for sex, age, and class differences, some variations appear. A larger percentage of wives evaluate the postparental period *both* more favorably and more unfavorably than do husbands. It would appear that this is a crucial time of life for the woman and that it is being clearly resolved one way or the other as far as she is concerned. It may be that the men have not yet been forced into self-evaluation or reconciliation to any major revisions in life. They are, for the most part, still employed in their occupations as they have been for many years, and the interviews reveal that in an overwhelming majority of cases, the children were closer to the mother and her primary responsibilty. Her hand has been forced; her husband's showdown may lie in the near future when retirement comes.

Any explanation of the general blandness of the husband's interviews must be qualified in terms of some of the more universalistic sex-role characteristics in our society. Whereas a woman may be expected to be volatile, emotional, expressive, and sentimental, such qualities are hardly considered masculine. The interviews with husbands were characterized by a lack of emotional quality—of expressiveness. They were not nearly as communicative as their wives. This does not mean that their tendency toward neutral responses was an artifact of the methodology; the impression of the writer (and interviewer) is that it is more likely an artifact of the culture.

Insofar as the evidence obtained in this study is concerned, there seems to be no difference between older and younger postparental spouses regarding their evaluation of that time of life. In terms of class, however, a different picture presents itself. The upper-middle-class spouses have an appreciably more favorable outlook on postparental life than do their lower-middle counterparts.

Although the sample employed in the study is small, it does not suffer from representing only those people who seek help, and it does reveal some extreme differences. In addition, what little nonclinical research is available appears to agree with the present findings. Basing her conclusions on a study of 85 upper-middle-class women between the ages of 25 and 50, Gass found that they obtained little satisfaction from childrearing and that they were glad to be freed of the confining element of homemaking: "For these women, then, the fact that they were in their middle years increased, rather than decreased, their contentment" (Gass, 1959). Axelson studied postparental couples in two "medium sized communities" in Idaho and Washington at about the same time the field work for the present study was undertaken. His mailed questionnaire returns from over 800 parents of wedding-license applicants lead him to conclude that "this period of life seems as satisfying as earlier periods" (Axelson, 1960).

These data seem to indicate that the postparental phase of the family cycle is not generally defined unfavorably by those involved in it. This finding evidently holds true despite the relative newness of this phase of the family cycle and the assumption which might be made that little opportunity for role-taking or anticipatory socialization has existed (Deutscher, 1962).

References

AXELSON, L. J. Personal adjustments in the postparental period. *Marriage and Family Living,* 1960, 22, 66–70.

CAVAN, R. S. *The American family.* (3rd ed.) New York: Crowell, 1963.

DEUTSCHER, I. Socialization for post-parental life. In A. M. Rose (Ed.), *Human behavior and social process*, Boston: Houghton Mifflin, 1962.

GASS, G. Z. Counseling implications of woman's changing role. *Personnel and Guidance Journal*, 1959, 37, 482–487.

34. WHEN I'M SIXTY-FOUR

JOHN LENNON and PAUL McCARTNEY

When I get older losing my hair,
Many years from now.
Will you still be sending me a Valentine
Birthday greetings bottle of wine.
If I'd been out till quarter to three
Would you lock the door,
Will you still need me, will you still feed me,
When I'm sixty-four.
You'll be older too,
And if you say the word,
I could stay with you.
I could be handy, mending a fuse
When your lights have gone.
You can knit a sweater by the fireside
Sunday morning go for a ride,
Doing the garden, digging the weeds,
Who could ask for more.
Will you still need me, will you still feed me,
When I'm sixty-four.
Every summer we can rent a cottage,
In the Isle of Wight, if it's not too dear
We shall scrimp and save
Grandchildren on your knee
Vera Chuck & Dave
Send me a postcard, drop me a line,
Stating point of view
Indicate precisely what you mean to say
Yours sincerely, wasting away
Give me your answer, fill in a form
Mine for evermore
Will you still need me, will you still feed me,
When I'm sixty-four.

PETER TOWNSEND

The purpose of this paper is to call attention to a little-known fact about old people in industrial societies, and to dwell upon its implications for our understanding of ageing and the aged. In 1962 a cross-national study of people aged sixty-five and over was carried out in Denmark, Britain and the United States (Shanas et al., 1968). Probability samples of around 2,500 persons in each country were interviewed during the same period of the year. Questionnaires and methods of sampling, interviewing and analysis had been standardized.

One result surprised the investigators. A substantial proportion of the elderly populations were found to have great-grandchildren—as many as 40 per cent in the United States, 23 per cent in Denmark and 22 per cent in Britain. The existence on a substantial scale of families of four generations is a new phenomenon in the history of human societies. The emergence of a different structure brings new patterns of relationships but also different experiences of ageing. How has it happened?

This development is not attributable just to improvements in longevity. Average ages at first marriage have diminshed and for women in the United States, for example, have been relatively low throughout this century. The age of parenthood has also been diminishing. In the United States the median age of women at the birth of their first children was 23 for those born between 1880 and 1890 but is down to between 20 and 21 for the latest generations to marry. Because of the decreasing number of large families the median age at the birth of the last child has fallen more sharply. Earlier marriage, earlier childbirth and fewer large families inevitably contribute towards a narrowing of the average span in years between successive generations. The larger number of great-grandparents in the United States than in the European countries is attributable in the early decades of this century to the higher rates of marriage, the younger age at marriage and the birth to a larger proportion of women in the early years of marriage of several children.

It would, of course, be profitable to study the family life-cycle in more detail. Among the British sample, for example, it seems that the women had become grandmothers on average at 54 years of age and great-grandmothers at about 72. The men had become grandfathers at 57 and great-grandfathers at 75. One immediate thought of relevance to our understanding of human personality is the scope that exists for structural variation in family-building habits. Some women become grandmothers in their late thirties, others not until their seventies.

These structural variations have been given little attention by sociologists and psychologists. If there are shifts of emphasis in family-building practices then there are likely to be big changes in the patterns of family relations and in the types of relationship and of problems experienced by the elderly. With increasing age old people tend to find themselves nearer one of two extremes—experiencing the seclusion of the spinster or widow who lacks children *and* other near relatives, or pushed towards the pinnacle of the pyramidal family structure of four generations which may include several children and their spouses and twenty or thirty grandchildren and great-grandchildren.

Previous theories about the changes that have taken place in family relations and in the care of the aged during the process of industrialization need to be qualified heavily. When we compare what the family does now with what it did a hundred years ago we are not comparing like with like. Instead of 1 or 2 per cent of the population being aged sixty-five and over there are 10 or 15 per cent. There is the same contrast between developing and advanced industrial societies. In the "older" type of society old age may have a kind of pedestal prestige. Like the population age pyramids that the demographers produce for us of pre-industrial societies and of societies like Britain in the early stages of industrialization the extended family may have only one surviving grandparent at the apex of a structure

consisting of a large number of children and other relatives. Figure 35.1 suggests how family structure is related to the age structure of the population. Nowadays there may be two, three or all four grandparents alive and often a great-grandparent too. The structure of the kinship network has changed and this had had important effects on the ways in which this network is broken into geographically proximate groupings of households and types of households.

The structure of the extended family—understood as a group drawn from the network of kin whose members meet every

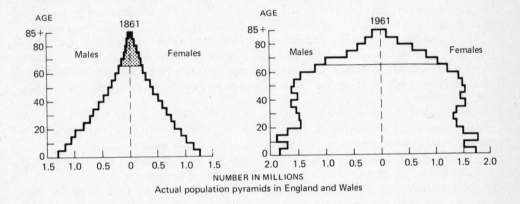

Actual population pyramids in England and Wales

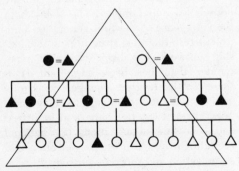

Characteristic example of kinship structure at the beginning of the twentieth century

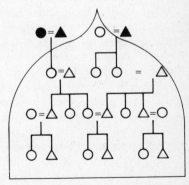

Characteristic example of kinship structure in the second half of the twentieth century

Figure 35.1

day or nearly every day and exchange a variety of services—has changed because of the pressures induced by changing mortality, birth and marriage rates. The relations between ascendant and descendant kin and affinal kin have been strengthened as compared with those with collateral kin: parents and children count more, cousins, aunts and uncles less. There is greater stability at the centre. More people marry. More marry young. More survive in married couples until an advanced age. Consequently the number of middle-aged and elderly spinsters acting as universal aunts has diminished; there are fewer "denuded" immediate families (i.e. families of parents and unmarried sibling groups where at least one member is missing) and fewer extended families of certain types—such as widowed women living in households with their brothers or sisters for the purposes of rearing children and overcoming hardship. The broken marriage and the broken "home" are no longer dominant constituents of the extended family in a group of proximate households. A model type of extended family is beginning to replace a wide variety of types of families and households ranging from lone individuals at one extreme to "kinship" tribes at the other. This family does not necessarily consist of all children and grandchildren of an old person, say, but only some of them.

What are the implications for old people in their relations with their families? They are dividing into two broad categories. Those belonging to the third generation more often have a surviving husband or wife than did persons of their age at the turn of the century. Fewer have single children remaining at home and grandchildren who are in their infancy. Since they represent the "younger" section of the elderly fewer of their children will have to look after them in infirmity, or illness, and they will have more energy to spare for their grandchildren. In various ways it is likely that the rapid relative increase in importance of the third generation, with its younger age-span, will re-

sult in much greater emphasis being placed in the future than formerly on reciprocal relations between the second and third generations. This will alter, and complicate, the whole pattern of kinship activity. Moreover, a fourth generation of relatively frail people is also being established—for the first time.

The nature of the problems of old age is therefore changing. A common instance in the past has been the middle-aged woman faced with the problem of caring for an infirm mother as well as her young children. A common instance of the future will be the woman of sixty faced with the problem of caring for an infirm mother in her eighties. Her children will be adult but it is her grandchildren who will compete with the mother for her attentions. The four generations of surviving relatives may tend to separate into semi-independent groupings each of two generations. Similarly there may be a shift of emphasis from the problem of which of the children looks after a widowed parent to the problem of how a middle-aged man and wife can reconcile dependent relationships with both sets of parents.

Changes in population structure have far wider and deeper effects than I have been able to indicate here. Insufficient attention has been paid to them in discussing relationships between parents and their children, between husbands and wives, between generations and generally among households and families. The data about the emergence of the four-generation family suggest that the structure of the kinship network has been changing more rapidly than has been supposed. It is therefore likely that changes in family organization and relationships may have been affected less by changes in industrial and economic organization, occupational recruitment and educational selection and organization and more by changes in population structure. This may constitute an argument for reviewing and revising not only theories of change in the process of ageing but also theories of urbanization and the social effects of industrialization.

Reference

SHANAS, E., *et al., Old People in Three Industrial Societies*, New York and London, Atherton and Routledge, 1968.

36. AGE GROUPING AND THE FAMILY STATUS OF THE ELDERLY

MARK MESSER

The conjugal or nuclear family structure which characterizes modern societies renders the family status of the elderly parent somewhat problematic. In terms of his relationship to those functions which define the family as a social institution, it appears that the parent whose children are themselves parents is in a position of having a family while not being in a family. His family of procreation (which clearly established his status as a parent) is now broken into as many nuclear units as the number of his children who are married. Having performed the core function of "replacing the population," his children are in a position to carry on this function themselves. He is now a grandparent—a kind of honorary parent—who, like an honorary president, is essentially functionless.

Beside the core function of procreation, however, the corollary functions of child socialization,[1] maintenance (instrumental functions), and nurturance or affection (consummatory functions) must also be considered in defining the family status of the elderly. Here again, an attrition in status seems to obtain.

With regard to the child socialization function, for instance, the fact that only a small minority of older people live in three generational households[2] reduces the possibility of sustained and significant grandchild socialization. Those studies which have investigated grandparents as socializers in modern American society have found more often than not that the consequences are dysfunctional for the child,[3] the conjugal family unit,[4] or

---

[1] Ira L. Reiss, "The Universality of the Family," *Journal of Marriage and the Family*, 27 (November, 1965), 443–53, argues that child socialization is the core function of the family. In this paper, however, we shall use the more conventional taxonomy presented by Robert F. Winch, *The Modern Family* (New York: Holt, Rinehart, and Winston, Inc., 1963).

[2] According to H. D. Sheldon, *The Older People of the United States* (New York: John Wiley and Sons, 1958), only 20 percent of people over 65 years of age in America actually live in the same household with relatives of any kind other than their spouses. For some persuasive historical data indicating that multi-generational households never have existed to any appreciable extent in America, see E. A. Friedmann, "The Impact of Aging on the Social Structure," in Clark Tibbetts (ed.), *Handbook of Social Gerontology* (Chicago: University of Chicago Press, 1960), 130–33.

[3] See, for example, B. Borden, "The Role of Grandparents in Children's Behavioral Problems," *Smith College Studies in Social Work*, 17 (1946), 115–16.

[4] H. Vollmer, "The Grandparent: A Problem in Childbearing," *American Journal of Orthopsychiatry*, 7 (November, 1937), 378–82.

the grandparents themselves.[5] It is likely, furthermore, that grandparent-grandchild interaction does not so much meet a socialization function[6] as it does a consummatory gratification function for both parties.[7]

Some recent cross-cultural research findings indicate that the vestiges of an extended kinship system are most evident in the maintenance function in the form of mutual help patterns between generations.[8] While substantial economic assistance from the older parents to the children is likely to produce more intergenerational conflict than affection,[9] there is some evidence that this sort of interchange, as with the socialization of the grandchild, is motivated more by consummatory than maintenance needs.[10] Norms of filial responsibility (economic assistance from the married children to the elderly parents) seem to be increasingly consistent with conjugal family independence. In response to the question, "Who do you think should provide for the older person who has stopped working, if he needs help?" elderly subjects in the Cornell study of aging were more likely to choose the federal government, the state govern-

ment, and the company for which they worked than the family.[11]

The corollary function of the family to provide affection and nurturance, then, seems most important in defining the family status of the elderly. The problem is whether or not a conjugal organization of the family can satisfactorily meet the consummatory needs of the elderly.

The possibility that shall be considered here is that extra-familial age grouping among the elderly is an appropriate arrangement for partially fulfilling this corollary function of the family.

Age Grouping: An Hypothesis

Some theorists have described the various phases of the life cycle in terms of appropriate patterns of role expectations and orientations.[12] These role patterns are characterized as predominantly "consummatory" for the child and old age phases, and predominantly "instrumental" for the productive middle years. Eisenstadt suggests that, in highly differentiated societies, the transition from the role patterns appropriate for the first stage of the life cycle (consummatory roles met in the family context) to that set of instrumental role patterns appropriate for the productive years is met by adolescent age grouping.[13] These age-homogeneous structures (youth cultures) are said to be universal in advanced societies which serve the function of "phasing in" a generational cohort to that sector which characterizes such societies—productivity.

It seems that the "phasing out" mech-

---

[5] Bernard Kutner *et al.*, *Five-Hundred Over Sixty* (New York: Russell Sage Foundation, 1956), 122.

[6] An important exception to this might be the American Negro family. See E. Franklin Frazier, *The Negro Family in the United States* (Chicago: University of Chicago Press, 1939); and "Ethnic Family Patterns," *American Journal of Sociology*, 53 (May 1948), 435–38.

[7] Dorrian Sweetser, "The Social Structure of Grandparenthood," *American Anthropologist*, 58 (August, 1956), 656–63; and Vollmer, *op. cit.*

[8] Ethel Shanas *et al.*, *Old People in Three Industrial Societies* (New York: Atherton Press, in press).

[9] Mirra Komarovsky, "Functional Analysis of Sex Roles," *American Sociological Review*, 15 (August, 1950), 508–16; and Marvin Sussman, "The Help-Pattern in the Middle Class Family," *American Sociological Review*, 18 (February, 1953), 22–28.

[10] Sussman, *loc. cit.*

[11] Gordon F. Streib and Wayne E. Thompson, "The Older Person in a Family Context," in Tibbits, *op. cit.*, 480.

[12] For a good review of this literature, see Leonard Caine, Jr., "Life Course and Social Structure," in Robert Faris (ed.), *Handbook of Modern Sociology* (Chicago: Rand McNally and Co., 1964), 279–309.

[13] S. N. Eisenstadt, *From Generation to Generation* (New York: The Free Press, a Division of The Macmillan Co., 1956).

anisms are not so well established.[14] There comes a time, nonetheless, when people disengage from the "productive" middle years of the life cycle. Such disengagement marks the return to consummatory role expectations and orientations.[15] The consummatory needs of the child may be thought of as "preengagement" needs and those of the elderly as "postengagement" needs. For the child, these needs can be met both by the family (of which he is still an integral part) and by his age peers. The extra-familial status of the older person, however, suggests the increased importance of age peers in meeting the appropriate expectations of disengagement. Accordingly, the following hypothesis is put forward: age grouping among the elderly might facilitate the transition from "instrumental to consummatory role patterns and thereby serve as a functional alternative to the family in satisfying some of the consummatory needs.

Method of Data Collection

Interview data from a larger study on the effects of age concentration in a sample of elderly residents of Chicago[16] were used for a preliminary test of this hypothesis. The major independent variable—relative age grouping—was operationalized by the nature of the sampling design. A probability sample of tenants of public housing projects occupied exclusively by people over 62 years of age was taken as the "age"

grouping" or age-homogeneous case. A sample of people who were themselves over 62 years old but who were living in public housing projects of mixed-age composition was used as a comparison group.

To control for differences in the feasibility of having intergenerational family contact, only those respondents who had children who were themselves parents and who lived within two hours travelling distance of these children were included in the analysis. This left a sample of 157 (51 in an age-homogeneous environment and 106 in an age-heterogeneous setting). The sample characteristics of these two groups of respondents is reported in Table 36.1.

It should be noted that eilgibility for public housing presupposes a relatively low income level (the mean annual income for the sample is $1298). The respondents are all retired (mostly from manual and factory-type jobs). For purposes of analyzing the data, this means that socioeconomic status is a controlled variable, but the limitations that this imposes on the generalizability of the findings must be considered.

Self-selection for one or the other hous-

[14] Mark Messer, "The Third Generation: An Extension of Eisenstadt's Age-Homogeneity Hypothesis," paper at The Social Science Research Institute, University of Chicago, 1965.

[15] See Lois Dean and D. S. Newell, "The Evidence for Disengagement in Attitude and Orientation Changes," in Elaine Cumming and William Henry (eds.), Growing Old (New York: Basic Books, Inc., 1961), 75–105; and Talcott Parsons, "Old Age as Consummatory Phase," The Gerontologist. 3 (March, 1963), 53–54.

[16] Mark Messer, "The Effects of Age-Concentration on Organizational and Normative Systems of the Elderly," unpublished Ph.D. thesis, Northwestern University, 1966.

Table 36.1. Sample characteristics (percentages)

	Age-Homogeneous (N=51)	Age-Heterogeneous (N=106)
Sex		
Male	35.3	29.2
Female	64.7	70.8
Age		
62–70	39.2	42.5
71–75	35.3	34.9
76–90	25.5	23.6
Race		
Negro	41.2	57.5
White	58.8	42.5
Education		
0–6th grade	35.3	38.7
7th–8th grade	39.2	39.6
9th grade or more	25.5	21.7
Health		
"Good"	49.0	47.2
"Poor"	51.0	52.8

Table 36.2. Morale by age environment and frequency of interaction with children (percentages)

	Frequency of Interaction with Children			
	Once/week or more		*Less than once/week*	
	Age Environment		*Age Environment*	
	All elderly	*Mixed ages*	*All elderly*	*Mixed ages*
Morale				
High	25.0	20.4	41.9	17.3
Medium*	55.0	55.6	45.2	51.9
Low	20.0	24.1	12.9	30.8
Total percent	100.0	100.1	100.0	100.0
Number of cases	20	54	31	52
	X^2=0.22, n.s.		X^2=6.66, P<.01	

* "medium" morale is left out of X^2 computations

ing situation is not a problem here, because the housing authority's policy is to locate applicants on the basis of their neighborhood and housing available at the time of application. Nevertheless, a measure of sampling equivalence was assured by premeasuring a subsample of people in each group before they moved into their respective housing modes. These data revealed no significant differences on the dependent variables of concern here.

The major dependent variable is the extent to which the consummatory needs of the elderly are being satisfied. No direct operational index to measure this rather ill-defined concept[17] was available, so the following indirect measures of "consummatory satisfaction" were used: morale, feelings of neglect from children, and social integration.

The conceptual hypothesis again is that age grouping will serve as a functional alternative to the family in satisfying the consummatory needs of the elderly. In operational terms, we are led to predict that those people living in an age-concentrated housing environment will show higher morale, will perceive less neglect from their adult children, and will be more integrated with the overall society than those living in mixed-aged environments.

The Research Findings

Morale was measured by the life satisfaction scale used in the Elmira and Kips Bay studies of aging.[18] A score of 0–2 on the scale was rated as "low" morale, 3–5 as "medium," and 6–7 as "high" morale. As predicted, the age-homegeneous sample showed higher morale than the mixed-age sample. This tendency was maintained when race, age, sex, and health status were added to the analysis as control variables. The data presented in Table 36.2 support our hypothesis that age grouping serves as an effective functional alternative to the family in providing such consummatory satisfactions for the elderly as are reflected in having high morale. The extent of interaction with the subjects' children is introduced to present data directly comparing the importance of age environment and family involvement for morale in the elderly.

Among those who visit their children at

[17] Instrumental and consummatory role patterns are discussed extensively in the work of Talcott Parsons. Efforts to make these concepts usable in research, however, are few. One research attempt to empirically describe role orientations and expectations (but not the satisfaction of role needs) was carried out by Lois Dean, "The Pattern Variables: Some Empirical Operations," *American Sociological Review*, 26 (February, 1961), 80–90.

[18] A complete description of this scale is available in Kutner, *et al.*, *op. cit.*, 48–54.

Table 36.3. Feelings of neglect by age environment and frequency of interaction with children (percentages)

	Frequency of Interaction with Children			
	Once/week or more Age Environment		Less than once/week Age Environment	
	All elderly	Mixed ages	All elderly	Mixed ages
Feel that children neglect them				
Yes	10.0	22.2	12.9	38.5
No	90.0	77.8	87.1	61.5
Total percent	100.0	100.0	100.0	100.0
Number of cases	20	54	31	52
	$X^2 = 144$, n.s.		$X^2 = 6.26$, P<.02	

least once a week, there is no statistically significant relationship between age environment and morale. More important for our purposes, however, among those who have less frequent familial interaction, morale goes down in the age-heterogeneous sample and up in the age-homogeneous sample. This relationship seems to suggest that the source of morale among the aged is moving away from intergenerational family interaction and toward the available age-peer group.

In response to the question, "Do you sometimes feel that your children neglect you?" those living in an age-heterogeneous setting, even though they had more frequent interaction with the children, were considerably more likely than the age-concentrated sample to answer in the affirmative (see Table 36.3).

The findings reported in Tables 36.2 and 36.3 taken together are interpreted to mean that older people living in a situation which lends itself to age-peer group formation rely less on the family for social support, but at the same time they do not feel more alienated from their families. Such a situation seems appropriate for the predominant system of conjugal family organization in complex societies.

The question arises, however, as to whether the kind of age-grading implied by separate living arrangements for the elderly might be divisive, creating feelings of detachment from the overall society. The family and other societal subsystems such as occupational groupings are said to mediate between the individual and the overall society thus creating societal integration, i.e., a kind of organic solidarity.[19] If, as is hypothesized here, age grouping is an effective functional alternative to the family for the aged, then it too should mediate between the older person and the larger society providing a sense of social integration rather than detachment.

To see if this was the case, we employed in our study Srole's scale of social integration.[20] This scale consists of five items which are said to measure the degree to which an individual feels alienated, powerless, or anomic vis-à-vis the general society. Analysis of the data indicated that age composition of the environment and race accounted for far more of the variation on social integration than any of the other variables on which we had data.

---

[19] For theoretical discussion of the mediating of societal subsystems, see Emile Durkheim, *Division of Labor* (New York: The Free Press, a Division of The Macmillan Co., 1964), 1–31; Peter Blau, "Mediating Values in Complex Structures," *Exchange and Power in Social Life* (New York: John Wiley and Sons, 1964), ch. 10; and Robert Nisbet, *Community and Power* (New York: Oxford University Press, 1962).

[20] Leo Srole, "Social Integration and Certain Corollaries," *American Sociological Review*, 21 (December, 1956), 709.

Table 36.4. Social integration by age environment and race (percentages)

	White Age Environment		Negro Age Environment	
	All elderly	Mixed ages	All elderly	Mixed ages
Social Integration				
High	63.3	26.7	33.3	23.0
Low	36.7	73.3	66.7	77.0
Total percent	100.0	100.0	100.0	100.0
Number of cases	30	45	21	61
	$X^2=9.98$, P<.01		$X^2=0.86$, n.s.	

Table 36.4 reports the findings from a simultaneous consideration of these variables.

Negroes were found to be considerably lower than whites on social integration (though they were found to be higher on morale—a topic presently under investigation). More important here, however, is that age composition of the environment has a considerable effect on social integration and in the predicted direction (though this relationship reaches statistical significance only among the white respondents). Those living in an age-concentrated situation are found to sense less detachment from the larger society than those who, in effect, are living in closer proximity to a youth and middle-age biased societal structure. A grouping, then, seems to take on certain attributes of a genuine subculture. It mediates between the individual and the overall society and at the same time decreases rather than increases social distance.

Summary

In this paper, it has been argued that, because of the dominant system of conjugal family organization in advanced societies, the elderly parent has, in many ways, an "extra-familial" status. In effect, he has a family but he is not in a family.

The last phase of the life cycle, however, is said to be characterized by consummatory needs, the satisfaction of which have traditionally been regarded as a corollary function of the family. It seems that nuclear family structure is not adequately suited for filling this function in the elderly.

Extending Eisenstadt's age-homogeneity hypothesis, we examined the possibility of age grouping among the elderly as a functional alternative to the family for consummatory gratification. Tentative findings (the severe limitation of the sample, for instance, must be borne in mind) suggest that (1) age grouping is associated with less dependence on the family as a source of morale, (2) this is not accompanied by feelings of familial neglect, and (3) age grouping serves as a mediator between the older individual and the overall society, providing a greater sense of social integration.

37. GRANDPARENTHOOD FROM THE PERSPECTIVE OF THE DEVELOPING GRANDCHILD

BOAZ KAHANA and EVA KAHANA

The purpose of this study was to examine differences in perceptions of grandparents and their significance for children of different ages and different levels of cognitive development. The child's perceptions of adult figures and especially of grandparents have seldom been studied as a function of developmental stages. Yet his changing perceptions of significant adults are essential factors which determine his relationships to the adult world. In addition, they serve as the basis for forming attitudes and stereotypes about adults and the aged. Since negative stereotypes toward the aged have been commonly observed (Becker & Taylor, 1966; Tuckman & Lorge, 1953), the development of such attitudes represents a significant problem. The child's perceptions of the elderly are also important since it has been argued that "perceptions of roles entered into in maturity are based on early learning regarding these roles [Hickey, Hickey, & Kalish, 1968, p. 22]."

Children's perceptions of age differences have been studied by Stephens, Hawthorne, and Kagan (1959) and more recently by Britton and Britton (1968). In these studies the young child's ability to discriminate age differences accurately was examined and related to social and aesthetic values about people of varying ages. In both of these studies preschool children (ages 4–6) were the subjects. Stephens et al. (1959), in his study of middle-class high IQ children, showed that about 50% of 4-year-olds were capable of fairly accurate age discriminations based on physiognomic information, that is, judging ages of individuals in pictures. Subjects who were old enough to discriminate age accurately were also found to be much more favorably disposed to younger than to older persons. Based on this finding it appears that an important relationship exists between the development of age discriminations and the development of attitudes regarding age differences.

Britton and Britton (1968) indicated in their study that young children are more able to judge younger than older persons correctly. Children were found to place all persons past the young adult level in one big category. Only 20% of children in the 4–6-age group were able to place older adults accurately in a specific age category. Both of the aforementioned investigations were based on preschool children. In Hickey, Hickey, and Kalish's (1968) study, social characteristics of older children (socioeconomic class, religion, family organization) were related to perceptions of the elderly. However, developmental studies of children's perceptions of and attitudes toward the aged could not be found in the literature.

The child's perceptions of those specific older adults who may be most directly involved in the forrmation of his perceptions and attitudes of the aged, that is, his grandparents, have also received little attention. A notable exception is Pihlblad and Habenstein's (1965) study. Those studies, touching upon the nature of the grandparent-grandchild relationship have examined the problem from grandparents' perspective, focusing on the significance of the grandparental role for the aged (Kahana, 1969; Neugarten & Weinstein, 1964). The importance of grandparents for the grandchild has been emphasized in psychoanalytic literature and in case studies of the grandparent-grandchild relationship (Abraham, 1955; Ferenczi, 1927;

Hader, 1965). The focus of these clinical investigations is on the potentially pathogenic as well as the potentially beneficial effects of contact with grandparents from the child's perspective.

The child's relationship to his grandparents may be conceptualized as a function of several factors. These include the extent of his contact with them, the grandparents' behavior toward him, the parents' relationship with the grandparents, the child's percetpions of old people in general, and of his grandparents in particular. The greater the congruence between the child's needs and those of the grandparent, the more rewarding one may expect the relationship to be. Thus, if very young children enjoy receiving favors and gifts and being given candy and other signs of affetcion, it is likely that the aged grandparent whose own affectional needs or passive indulgent qualities make him shower love and presents on the grandchild will have good rapport with young grandchildren. As the child gets older, however, concrete gifts and signs of affection may be valued less and he may enjoy a grandparent who will share his activities and have "fun" with him far more. If the grandparent retains his old styles of relating, rapport may decrease and distance may grow.

Neugarten and Weinstein, in their 1964 study of grandparenthood, found several styles of performing the grandparental role among middle-class grandparents in the United States. The role was found to vary from formal to fun seeking, parent surrogate, reservoir of family wisdom, and to distant figure. It is possible that different styles of grandparenthood fit in best with the child's needs at different stages in his development.

The present study represents a quantifiable inquiry into the changing meaning of the grandparent as a function of normal developmental stages of the grandchild. Questions were also raised about the relative importance of various styles of grandparent-grandchild relationships for children of different ages.

Method

Subjects

The sample consisted of 19 children aged 4–5, 33 children aged 8–9, and 33 children aged 11–12 divided about equally on sex. All of the children were white, of middle-socioeconomic-class background and attended a coeducational suburban nursery and elementary school.

Procedures

The youngest children (ages 4–5) were interviewed individually in their homes. Questions were administered in groups during a class period to the older children. These children were closely supervised and given individual help in understanding questions and in filling out questionnaires so as to make individual and group administrations of questionnaires as comparable as possible. It is recognized, nevertheless, that the two administrations were not strictly similar.

The questionnaire included open-ended and precoded questions, regarding frequency of contact with each one of the grandparents, activities done with each grandparent, favorite grandparent, reasons for preference of a grandparent and concepts about characteristics of the aged.

Questionnaires and interviews were coded and/or rated along the following dimensions.

1. Concepts of old age (i.e., How can you tell when someone is old?) were rated with regard to (a) structural aspects of thought (concrete, functional, abstract). These ratings were based on Rapaport's (1945) conceptual system, and (b) content categories in perceptions of the aged (specific physical characteristics,

behaviors, psychological or social characteristics).

2. Relationships with grandparents were coded in terms of (a) frequency of contact with grandparents (ranging from weekly or more often to once a year or less frequently), (b) favorite grandparent (mother's mother, mother's father, father's mother, father's father), (c) age of grandparent, and (d) reasons for preferring a particular grandparent (value or significance of grandparent) in terms of egocentric versus mutually oriented reasons and styles of grandparenting (indulgent, intimate, fun sharing, familiar, instructive).

Reliabilities of ratings were computed for those items requiring judgment. Twenty records were independently rated by two investigators. Percentages of exact agreement were: 95% in rating thought processes (see Table 37.1), 90% in rating significance of grandparent (see Table 37.4) and 85% classifying reasons for favoring a particular grandparent (see Table 37.5). In data analyses, frequencies of different categories of response for each variable were compared for children in the three age groups. Chi-square statistics were computed to determine the degree of association between ages of children and frequency of different response categories.

Results

Age-related differences appear consistently both in perceptions of the aged and in the characteristics and significance of the grandparent-grandchild relationship.

Although there is evidence from other studies (Stephens et al., 1959) that by about age 5, children are able to discriminate age-related differences, 70% of the children in the youngest age group were unable to place the age of their grandparents in the appropriate decade. These results are consistent with Britton and Britton's (1968) findings which indicated that young children find it especially difficult to accurately discriminate older ages. Among the youngest children, 83% could not report any criteria or signs of old age. In contrast, older children (8 years and up) estimated grandparents' ages realistically. Significantly more of the older children than younger ones were able to state reasons for viewing someone as old (see Table 37.1).

For the two older age groups, specific perceptual physical characteristics reflecting concrete forms of reasoning comprised the majority of responses. Wrinkles, white hair, and other specific physical signs were offered as the major indexes of old age in all age groups. Although the majority of responses were concrete even among older children, higher levels of

Table 37.1. Age-related differences in children's concepts of old age

Concepts of old age	Ages 4–5 N=18	Ages 8–9 N=28	Ages 11–12 N=28	χ^2
Wrong answer and I don't know	83.3	39.3	14.2	24.68*
Concrete	11.1	46.4	46.4	
Functional	5.6	10.7	25.0	
Abstract	0.0	3.6	14.2	
Total	100.0	100.0	99.8	

Note—All values are percentages but χ^2.
* $p < .001$.

thought progressively emerged with age; that is, functional and abstract responses were found to be more frequent among older children. Functional responses, that is, behaviors or activities signifying old age, were mentioned by 5.6% of the youngest group. 10.7% of the 8–9-year-olds and by 25% of the oldest age group. Such functional responses usually centered around declining abilities, for example, "To be old means to sit around," "They cannot hear and see you," "Old people don't play with you." Abstract responses referring to generic characteristics or constructs regarding physical, psychological, or social characteristics were relatively infrequent among this sample. Nonetheless, the emergence of abstract responses at the oldest ages is clearly present (see Table 37.1). Abstract responses typically referred to generic physical or personality characteristics, for example, "Older people are weak, sick, experienced, friendly, nice to children, etc." Data from other studies (Coe, 1968) point to adults' use of combinations of physical, social, and psychological characteristics as indicators of old age.

Age-related differences were also apparent in descriptions of the relationship between grandparent and grandchild and in the significance of the grandparent for the growing child.

Frequency of contact with grandparents was ascertained separately for each living grandparent: mother's mother, mother's father, father's mother, and father's father. Older children tended to report more frequent contact with all four groups of grandparents than did the youngest group. However, age-related differences in reported frequency of contact were significant only for paternal grandafthers (see Table 37.2).

It is also interesting to note that more frequent contact was reported by all age groups with maternal rather than paternal grandparents. These findings may reflect an actual increase in contact with grandparents as the child gains independence and mobility with increasing age. It is also possible, however, that younger children perceive elapsing time periods as longer and, hence, erroneously report less frequent contact. Data from grandparents regarding contact with grandchildren of various ages may elucidate this problem.

Systematic differences between younger and older groups also appeared in the reasons for valuing a particular grandparent. The youngest children found it difficult to verbalize any reason for their preferences, although they overwhelmingly chose a favorite (see Table 37.3).

Among the oldest children, 48% declined a preference for any particular grandparent. In explaining their reluctance to choose a favorite, these children usually gave moralistic reasons, for example, "You have to love all your grandparents the same," or, "It is not right to pick a favorite," or "I love them all the same." Whenever older children indicated a preference, they were usually able to verbalize the reasons for their choice.

It is interesting to note that the maternal grandmother was most frequently favored by the children of all ages (see Table 37.3). This finding is consistent with those of several anthropological and sociological studies which point to a close and warm relationship between mothers, daughters, and grandchildren (Kahana, 1969; Wilmott, 1960) and suggest that the grandparents' place in the kinship system is an important determinant of their relationship with their grandchildren.

Reasons for preferences for particular grandparents were categorized in terms of their mutual or reciprocal versus their egocentric nature. Young children (ages 4–5) view the preferred grandparent almost exclusively in egocentric and concrete terms. that is, what the grandparent gives to the child in the forms of love, food, and presents. Their responses indicated no mutuality in the relationship (see Table 37.4). In contrast, responses of 8- and 9-year-olds focused on mutuality in the relationship, with some focus on

Table 37.2. Age-related differences in frequency of reported contact with grandparents

Frequency of contact	Maternal Grandmother			Maternal Grandfather			Paternal Grandmother			Paternal Grandfather		
	Ages 4–5 (N=12)	Ages 8–9 (N=28)	Ages 11–12 (N=26)	Ages 4–5 (N=8)	Ages 8–9 (N=22)	Ages 11–12 (N=17)	Ages 4–5 (N=8)	Ages 8–9 (N=23)	Ages 11–12 (N=21)	Ages 4–5 (N=8)	Ages 8–9 (N=15)	Ages 11–12 (N=17)
Every few weeks or more	50.0	60.7	69.2	75.0	63.6	70.6	37.5	56.5	57.1	12.5	53.3	52.9
Every few months	8.3	17.9	15.4	12.5	13.6	17.6	12.5	17.4	38.1	12.5	20.0	35.3
Once a year or less	41.7	21.4	15.4	12.5	22.7	11.8	50.0	26.1	4.8	75.0	27.7	11.8
Sum	100.0	100.0	100.0	100.0	99.9	100.0	100.0	100.0	100.0	100.0	100.0	100.0
χ^2		3.5 (ns)			1.07 (ns)			9.02 (ns)			11.1*	

Note—All values are percentages but χ^2.
* $p < .025$.

325

Table 37.3. Favorite grandparent

Favorite Grandparent	Ages 4–5 N=19	Ages 8–9 N=33	Ages 11–12 N=33	χ^2
Mother's mother	42.1	36.4	21.2	15.40*
Mother's father	15.8	15.2	6.0	
Father's mother	15.8	3.0	6.0	
Father's father	5.3	6.0	6.0	
No preference	15.8	18.2	48.3	
No information	5.3	21.2	12.1	
Total	100.1	100.0	99.8	

Note—All values are percentages but χ^2.
* $p<.05$.

Table 37.4. Significance of grandparent

Significance of Grandparent	Ages 4–5 N=16	Ages 8–9 N=28	Ages 11–12 N=28	χ^2
Egocentric	37.3	10.7	10.7	19.95*
Mutual	0.0	21.4	7.1	
Grandparent directed	0.0	7.1	14.3	
No favorite or only one living	6.3	25.0	35.7	
No information	56.3	35.7	32.1	
Total	99.9	99.9	99.9	

Note—All values are percentages but χ^2.
* $p<.01$.

grandparental characteristics and some egocentric responses. Mutual responses usually involved shared activities, for example, "We go to the ball game together," "We play cards." Grandparent-oriented responses focused on some quality of the grandparent which was independent of his grandchild, for example, "He is a good man," "I look up to him because he is so smart." These responses were completely absent among the youngest children and increased linearly with age although they continued to represent the small minority of responses. The major difference in reasons for valuing grandparents appeared between the youngest and middle groups. The oldest group did not differ from 8- and 9-year-olds in proportion of egocentric responses and gave somewhat fewer mutual responses. This may, in part, be due to their low response frequency in expressing preferences.

In describing their interaction with their favorite grandparent, children referred to styles of grandparenting which overlap the styles of grandparenting described by Neugarten and Weinstein (1964) (see Table 37.5). Young children preferred indulgent grandparents who buy them treats and gifts. This fits in with the "formal" grandparenting style portrayed by 32% of Neugarten and Weinstein's sample of grandparents. Children in the 8- and 9-year-old groups expressed preferences for "fun-sharing" grandparents, who join them in playful leisure activities. Interestingly, in the oldest group (11- and 12-year-olds) a preference for the indulgent grandparent emerged once again with less emphasis on the mutual aspects of the relationship.

Other specific categories of grandparenting style included references to physical expressions of affection (intimate-

Table 37.5. Reasons for favorite—styles of grandparenting

Styles of Grandparenting	Ages 4–5 N=19	Ages 8–9 N=33	Ages 11–12 N=33	χ^2
Indulgent	42.1	18.2	33.3	45.75*
Intimate-affective	5.3	3.0	6.1	
Fun sharing	5.3	30.3	9.1	
Instructive	0.0	3.0	0.0	
Familiar	10.6	3.0	12.1	
Global nonspecific	10.6	0.0	21.2	
No information or preference	26.3	42.4	18.2	
Total	100.2	99.9	100.0	

Note—All values are percentages but χ^2.
* $p<.001$.

affective), references to the teaching functions of grandparents (instructive), and references to frequency of visiting or contact (familiar). These response categories appeared infrequently in all ages. An additional nonspecific response category (global responses) was included to classify highly general global, or poorly articulated responses for choosing a favorite grandparent, for example, "He is nice," "I like her." Such global responses occurred frequently among both the youngest and the oldest children. It appears, however, that their meaning was different for the different age groups. Global responses given by very young children may represent undifferentiated forms of thinking which is characteristic of them. On the other hand, among the oldest group, global responses may imply an attitude of distance which is complementary to Neugarten and Weinstein's "distant" grandparents. There is evidence from other studies (Kahana & Coe, 1969) that grandparents feel increasingly distant from their grandchildren as the grandchildren grow older.

Discussion

In considering age-related differences in children's concepts and attitudes toward grandparents, major differences appeared between children in the youngest (4–5) and middle (8–9) age groups. These

results may be explained by the cognitive stages characteristic of these age groups (Piaget, 1954). Whereas the youngest children are just approaching the important shift to the age of concrete operations and thinking, children in the middle group have already mastered concrete operations and exhibit thought processes which are characteristic of a higher developmental stage. The oldest children, on the other hand, manifest thinking which is not qualitatively superior to the 8- and 9-year-olds, since children in this group have not yet undergone the latest shift in thinking, but are just approaching the critical point of transition to the stage of formal operations in thinking. Findings of this study call attention to the importance of considering differential needs of children as well as differences in their level of cognitive maturity in determining their perceptions of significant others.

In this study, some pilot data were reported in the much neglected area of the developmental aspects of grandparent-grandchild relationships. The focus was on the grandchild's changing perceptions of his grandparents. Such data are valuable in their own right since perceptions of significant others are crucial in shaping one's behavior toward them. In future studies, however, independent data from parents and grandparents regarding the overt nature of grandparent-grandchild relationships would provide important information for understanding the potential influence of grandparents on personality development of children of different ages. Such information would also be helpful in determining to what extent grandparental styles reported by grandchildren are actually experienced. A most fruitful approach of future investigations would be a simultaneous consideration of the changing needs of grandchildren and of their grandparents and their perceptions of one another. Data from such a study would yield information regarding potential areas of conflict or misunderstanding and would lead to a better understanding of the generation gap.

The sample for the present investigation consisted of middle-class, white suburban children. Studies of children of other social class, cultural, and ethnic groups, with presumably different family constellations, would provide most interesting data about the extent to which observed developmental differences in perception of grandparents are invariant in different cultures. Findings of the present study regarding differences in children's perceptions and attitudes toward paternal and maternal grandparents could also be followed up in different social and cultural groups.

Children's views of and relationships to their grandparents may change as they grow older for many different reasons. Their perceptions of signs of aging are indications of maturational differences paralleling general cognitive shifts. It is possible, however, that differences between children of different ages are also affected by factors such as differential contact with grandparents, changing characteristics of the grandparent as the child gets older, changing equilibrium between needs of the grandparent and the grandchild. In the present study, the relative contributions of these factors could not be specified but attention was called to their presence. The importance of considering the complex set of factors which determine the nature of the relationship of the aging grandparent and his developing grandchild was underscored.

Summary

Studies of grandparenthood are usually focused on the grandparent and his views of the grandparental role. In this study grandparenthood was examined from the perspective of the other partner in the role relationship, the grandchild. The changing meaning of the grandparent for children of different ages (4–5, 8–9, 11–12) was explored. Children's views of grandparents paralleled developmental cognitive changes ranging from concrete perceptions of physical characteristics by the youngest children, through functional views of behaviors in the middle group, and finally to the emergence of an abstract interpersonal orientation among the oldest children. Major differences in quality of perception occurred between the youngest and middle-age groups. Young children valued grandparents mainly for their indulgent qualities, the middle group preferred the fun-sharing active grandparent, and the oldest group reflected distance from their grandparents. It is suggested by the findings that the meaning of the grandparental role for the aging grandparent must be understood in the context of the changing needs of the developing grandchild.

References

ABRAHAM, K. Some remarks on the role of grandparents in the psychology of neuroses. In H. C. Abraham (Ed.), *Selected papers: Clinical papers and essays in psychoanalysis.* Vol. 2. New York: Basic Books, 1955.

BECKER, L. D., & TAYLOR, C. Attitudes toward the aged in a multigenerational sample. *Journal of Gerontology*, 1966, *21*, 115–118.

BRITTON, J. O., & BRITTON, J. H. Age discrimination of children and adults through projective pictures. Paper presented at the meeting of the American Psychological Association, San Francisco, September 1968.

COE, R. M. *Physicians' attitudes toward preventive health care services.* (Final Report No. 1) St. Louis, Mo.: Medical Care Research Center, 1968.

FERENCZI, S. The grandfather complex. In J. Rickman (Ed.), *Further contributions to the theory and technique of psychoanalysis.* New York: Boni & Liveright, 1927.

HADER, M. The importance of grandparents in family life. *Family Process*, 1965, *4*, 228–240.

HICKEY, T., HICKEY, L., & KALISH, R. A. Children's perceptions of the elderly. *Journal of Genetic Psychology*, 1968, *112*, 227–235.

KAHANA, E. Grandparenthood as a function of the family structure. Paper presented at the meeting of the Society for Research in Child Development, Santa Monica, California, February 1969.

KAHANA, E., & COE, R. M. Perceptions of grandparenthood by community and institutional aged. *Proceedings of the 77th Annual Convention of the American Psychological Association*, 1969, *4*, 735–736. (Summary)

NEUGARTEN, B. L., & WEINSTEIN, K. K. The changing American grandparent. *Journal of Marriage and the Family*, 1964, *26*, 199–204.

PIAGET, J. *The construction of reality in the child.* New York: Basic Books, 1954.

PIHLBLAD, T., & HABENSTEIN, R. W. Social factors in grandparent orientation of high school youth. In A. Rose & W. Peterson (Eds.), *Older people and their social world.* Philadelphia: Davis, 1965.

RAPAPORT, D. *Diagnostic psychological testing.* Chicago: The Yearbook Publisher, 1945.

SMITH, H. E. Family interaction patterns of the aged: A review. In A. Rose & W. Peterson (Eds.), *Older people and their social world.* Philadelphia: Davis, 1965.

STEPHENS, J. W., HAWTHORNE, F. M., & KAGAN, N. Young children's perceptions of age differences. Paper presented at the meeting of the Eastern Psychological Association, Atlantic City, April 1959.

TUCKMAN, J., & LORGE, J. Attitudes toward old people. *Journal of Social Psychology*, 1953, *37*, 249–260.

WILMOTT, P. *Family and class in a London suburb.* London: Routledge & Kegan Paul, 1960.

CHAPTER EIGHT: SUGGESTED FURTHER READINGS

ANTHONY, E. J., and BENEDEK, T. *Parenthood.* Boston: Little, Brown, 1970.

HARPER, L. V. The young as a source of stimuli controlling caretaker behavior. *Developmental Psychology*, 1971, *4*, 73–88.

HILL, R., and ALDOUS, J. Socialization for marriage and parenthood. In D. A. Goslin (Ed.), *Handbook of socialization theory and research.* Chicago: Rand McNally, 1969. Pp. 885–950.

SKOLNICK, A. S., and SKOLNICK, J. H. (Eds.). *Family in transition.* Boston: Little, Brown, 1970.

chapter nine
friendship

The family life of the growing infant profoundly affects the extent and intensity of friendship patterns throughout life. All schools of psychology recognize the strong relationship between early experience with others and affection for others in later years. So parents, the visual representatives of family, serve as the first ambassadors of friendship to the infant. Erik H. Erikson, in his essay "Eight Stages of Man," describes the initial stage as the time in which the first relationship with another human being, usually the mother, is developed. A successful program for future friendship patterns is based on the amount of "trust vs. basic mistrust" developed by the infant. The basic signs of trust and of positively developing interpersonal relationships must apparently occur within a certain period of early development. Robert and Ruth Munroe gather evidence for this notion in their studies of isolated and institutionalized children.

There are many kinds of institutions, and those that supply a level of physical and social stimulation approximating home environments turn out children not very different from the ordinary.

But in institutions where caretaking is restricted to physical needs, where infants spend long hours with little environmental stimulation, and where this low level of care continues over a period of years, the adverse effects include apathy, unresponsiveness, and even general retardation in extreme cases [Munroe and Munroe, in press].

Cross-culturally, those few societies that rear infants with a minimum of indulgence seem to produce adults incapable of achieving free and open friendship patterns. The recent trend in society of mothers with careers away from home has brought with it the search for a replacement to the biological "first attachment." Day-care centers may resolve the problem of where to put the child, but their adequacy as an alternative teacher of building interpersonal affect remains unproven. Cross-cultural studies support both arguments. Margaret Mead (1928) proposed that a diffusion of affective ties in infancy ended in shallow emotional attachment in adulthood, but Schaffer (1971) sees this diffusion as a later guide to choosing certain people as friends, and not others. Kibbutz children who spend the first several years of their lives together tend not to marry within the group, but to form lifelong friendships with kibbutz members of the opposite sex. The long-term effects of day-care centers should provide interesting data in this area.

Researchers in United States have attempted studies of friendship throughout the life span only on a fragmentary basis, focusing on infants, young children, and college-age subjects. Many questions have yet to be asked. Why do some acquaintances become friends? What makes children choose new "best friends" every other week? Does birth order unconsciously affect the choice of friends? How can we adequately explain the inseparability of some adolescent friends, contrasted with the ability of some adults to maintain solid friendships over distance for long periods of time? Is there a gradual shift from school friends to work friends? How does marriage expand or limit the choices? What effect does the death of a spouse have on maintaining and shifting friendships? And throughout life, how do our friends help us to clarify our own self-image, and help us to learn about ourselves? This area of socialization, more than any other, seems ripe for research. Most of what we now know comes from poets and writers who have always delved into the human struggle for acceptance and power that characterizes friendship.

References

MEAD, M. *Coming of age in Samoa.* New York: William Morrow, 1928.

MUNROE, R. L., and MUNROE, R. *Cross-cultural human development.* Monterey, Calif: Brooks-Cole, in press.

SCHAFFER, H. R. *The growth of sociability.* Baltimore: Penguin Books, 1971.

* * *

Getting to know someone, entering that new world, is an ultimate, irretrievable leap into the unknown. The prospect is terrifying. The stakes are high. The emotions are overwhelming. The two people are reluctant really to strip themselves naked in front of each other, because in doing so they make themselves vulnerable and give enormous power over themselves one to the other. How often they inflict pain and torment upon each other! Better to maintain shallow, superficial affairs; that way the scars are not too deep. No blood is hacked from the soul.

But I do not believe a beautiful relationship has to end always in carnage, or that we have to be fraudulent and pretentious with one another. If we project fraudulent, pretentious images, or if we fantasize each other into distorted caricatures of what we really are, then, when we awake from the trance and see beyond the sham and front, all will dissolve, all will die or be transformed into bitterness and hate. I know that sometimes people fake on each other out of genuine motives to hold onto the object of their tenderest feelings. They see themselves as so inadequate that they feel forced to wear a mask in order continuously to impress the second party.

If a man is free—not in prison, the Army, a monastery, hospital, spaceship, submarine—and living a normal life with the usual multiplicity of social relations with individuals of both sexes, it may be that he is incapable of experiencing the total impact of another individual upon himself. The competing influences and conflicting forces of other personalities may dilute one's psychic and emotional perception, to the extent that one does not and cannot receive all that the other person is capable of sending.

* * *

39. FRIENDSHIP AND THE LIFEBOAT

HERBERT GOLD

Because I must, I accept that there are people who don't care too much about those they bump on the journey, just want to enjoy a beer or a joint, go to the game or watch it on the box, float through a life that is difficult enough already, and justify any companion on a part of this haphazard voyage: "Well, he makes me laugh."

That's enough. They don't ask too much of friends. A relative, a buddy, what difference; so long as it's reasonable fun to drift in his company.

And then there are the others, maniac souls, who demand perfect friendship. They are loyal and true when the friend grows sick or needful. but vindictive and creepy with night hatreds if the friend lets them down. They love. They hate. They treasure injustice with the sweaty focus of adolescent concupiscence. An evil word behind the back, a lazy dismissal of obligation—the sort of thing human beings do all the time, because they are human, evil, and lazy—calls down the maledictions of the injustice collector. He sleeps in a bed of worms. There are many such. Alas, I find myself among their number. The element of disease in this pursuit of perfect loyalty and the continual discovery of failure is not a treat. A doomed ideal is no joy, even to fanatic idealists. Anything that gives so much pain must be given a more pejorative psychological name than quixotic: love of disappointment. Masochism. Mea culpa.

Survival is everyone's aim; survival *conveniently* is what it mostly comes to. A true friend gives up some of his convenience for his buddy. When the laughter stops is when the ambiguity of survival stops being abstract. The contradictions between pleasure and obligation are crucial. Here is where depth is defined. And so friendship often has its knuckles broken as it tries to climb into the crowded lifeboat.

Let us now introduce the Dump. There comes a time when most friendships are strained by ambition (I pass him by) or love (I rob him of his girl) or a frivolous moment (I make a joke behind his back about his paunch, his ambition, his love). There are saints, true; a few of them, who never sin. I used to know a couple, but they appear, on closer study, to be feebly protecting themselves from being dumped on by never giving way to human weakness. That's more calculating than saintly, and it's a calculation from fear. One, a writer, seemed so lovable and innocent and depressed that everyone wanted to protect him. He made no enemies. He

was touchingly confident of his own weakness and tremulousness; no need to scorn or attack others.

The result was that he became exceptional in a way I'd never have predicted. Now he is certain of his saintly and generous character. His work celebrates his own self in a way that still, astonishingly, preserves some of the original innocence. He hasn't experienced much risk and shame since his frightened childhood. That was all he could bear. Grown-up abuse, withheld from the air he breathes, has resulted in a pale and babyish middle age, a swollen head, a habit of incantation. If he had been punctured regularly, there would be less gas.

Another similar case began as a man of great virtue, a natural virtue, great suffering in his past. Because nobody dumped on him, he came to believe in his virtue. He never dumped either. That confirmed what people said about him: *a truly good man.* Oh, equal pomposity and self-love. He dims into righteousness with an inward glow, shivering plumply like cherry Jello.

My interest in the subdivision of friendship and loyalty called Betrayal and Disloyalty can be classified under the heading Interested Curiosity and Implicated Science. It is not exactly abstract, despite its dry tone, any more than the famous question posed by the scientists of the medieval Salerno Medical School is scientific: "Why does the savage unicorn curb his fierce wrath with the virgin's embrace?" (I've sometimes made the same mistake as the unicorn.)

Let me describe three related crises that friendships founder on. There are other troubles, but these are the Lifeboat ones. I had a friend whom I protected. He was younger, perhaps weaker; I indulged fatherly pleasures. Along came an opportunity to do himself good while passively standing by as harm was done to me. He wished me no grief. He even wished me well. He regretted that he didn't find it in his heart to help me. He remains, as always, sensitive and good-natured, and he wanted me to prosper. But his own career on earth is constantly in danger—or so he sees it; his welfare, his pride; and here, where his interest crossed mine, he did me ill. It was risky not to. It made him feel terrible all the while he was euphoric and blissful with his momentary success at my cost. In his happiness he wrote me a despairing letter, to this effect:

Please don't think worse of me, he begged, *because hurting you did me so much good. And you are doing fine, you can bear the harm from little me, paltry me. Don't let our friendship suffer, I beg you. I am grateful, I will always treasure* . . . and so on.

Now, have I the right to be irked with him? Whence this malevolence? After all, it was his very weakness that stirred the protective and fatherly feelings in me. I knew he needed help through life, I knew he had no energy or power to spare for other than his own protection, I knew his charm and wit were ways of ingratiating himself with helpers in a world filled with dreadful challenges. I had understood him and treasured him.

And yet I was angry, and have not yet forgiven him. I have gone on collecting this injustice in memory over the years, accumulating it, savoring it, bite by bite. While now I feel no rage against him, and the harm is long past, I retain a certain spite. I speak ironically against him. I write these words. I see that his life and career are small, and I am content that they be so. His wife has a certain meanness. Good. His children are hard on him. Excellent. I am amused when someone else tells an anecdote to his discredit. He was my friend. He surely is no longer.

Was he ever my friend? I thought so, and therefore it was so. We traveled together, and poured out the overflowing hearts of youth, and laughed and dreamed together. His face made me feel fond. My little pal. Our secrets. I thought I was immune to his weakness, though of course

his sort of weakness spares no one, parents, wives, children, friends. My fatherliness expired in a petty harm done—a convenience to him. I wrote to him at the time: You would chop my fingers off if you were in the lifeboat and I in the sea. You are always afraid of foundering. You can be no one's friend.

Another time, another friend, another injustice. This is complicated. A friend asked me to do something he would later regret. Very complicated. We were college kids and I listened to what he said, not what he meant, but felt uneasy, because I sensed he would be sorry; yet it was convenient for me at the time, and, after all, he did ask me; it was his idea. So uneasily I complied.

A year later he forgot his request to me, but his deepest passions were aroused by jealousy. (Okay, be specific: we were young men, he asked me to keep his lady company while he was away, he sought freedom, he asked me to remove his obligation to her.) I had betrayed him, he thought, by doing what he asked. He had betrayed me, I thought, by asking me to pull his chestnuts from the fire, and then by forgetting he had asked, and then by jealous fury. But he was desperate, and therefore semed right, even to me. Lies? Amnesia? Mere logic-chopping. He screamed and I cringed. There was no defense I believed in. After all, he was in love.

Because of all this turmoil, my friend and the lady came back together a couple; they married. He doesn't like me much and doesn't quite remember why. Too hard for him to sort out the reasons. I remain aggrieved. Another injustice in my sack.

I don't find myself innocent here either. But no explanation helps me to understand how what was friendship, trust, and sharing congeals to a necessary ugliness. I still wish I had my old friend, with whom I laughed at the Marx Brothers and whom I called my brother. The warmth of friendship makes one forget how even friends who call each other brother can use each other.

And now a most complex friendship, the way they usually are—this one more than the usual. Hank was generous, tense, intelligent, a bit weird; he clung to his friends with the sinewy stubbornness of a lifelong orphan; sometimes I felt crowded, but his need was very real and strong. We were close. I felt pleased to answer his need.

Then his marriage broke up and he cracked. All divorcing men become a little mad, but he was having other delusions than the usual ones that he was free, he was good, she was bad, civilization was specializing in detailed annoyance of him. He was Christ. She was anti-Christ. The CIA, the Mafia, and the New Testament took roles in his foundering marriage. Phantoms watched him from helicopters. He laughed at miseries and wept over nothing. To me, across the continent, he mostly telephoned in the middle of the night. He spoke his visions, which were not the visions of anyone else who tried to look at what he saw. He began a sentence with giggles and ended it with sobs. He insulted my wife because she sounded sleepy at 2:00 A.M.: "You wish I'd go away. You don't care." His voice grew metallic when I said it was time to go back to bed. He said over the telephone from New York: "I'd like to come and stay with you a while till I get my head together. You're my only friend. The rest are working for . . . you know, Herb."

He knew he was in trouble. He knew his visions, delusions, hatreds, scenes— that floating irrelevance in his confused brain—made him a difficult man. Sometimes he had fistfights in bars. An intelligent man doesn't do that, and he was intelligent, and he had been beaten up twice on Third Avenue, just because he tried to explain to tall, morose, muscular men that they had taken a bad turn when they chose to be stupid pigs. He didn't

want to be alone, and a bar brawl wasn't really company. He wanted to be with me, his old friend, and to live like my son along with my wife and children.

"Uh," I said, which is already the beginning of the way you don't talk to a friend—thinking of ways to escape. "Uh, we're kind of busy right now."

"But I can't stand it anymore! They tell me to go to a hospital! I just need a rest. I'll clean up my room, I'll just hang around a week or two."

I tried to make a joke while I thought, Old Italian proverb: houseguest is fish, stinks after three days.

"Ha ha. I'm dying here, Herb. I've got to get away."

"Maybe you ought to get to a beach, just lie in the sun a while."

"All the resorts are controlled from Washington. The Penta—you know." He whispered: "They got a flag on me, buddy."

"Uh," I said again.

This was the young man with whom I had walked the nighttime streets of many cities, talking of our future, girls, careers, the meaning of life. At times we had been inseparable; we wrote letters faithfully through the years; and when we met again, it was as it had always been. He was a part of my early time, the best and purest part, just comradeship, warmth, hope, trust, generosity. He knew what I was thinking. I knew what he was thinking. We had traveled together with ladies, drunk wine, played tennis, strolled on beaches.

And now he was in bad trouble.

And, uh, I didn't want him around.

Being crazy, he didn't quite feel my reluctance. He was coming to San Francisco, he said. I said: "Hank, I can't have you here now. It's too complicated. They're right; you should check into a hospital for a while."

Just because strangers were following him, spying through the television, trying to break his arm by psychic power?

"I'm sorry, Hank," I said.

There was a long pause. "You think I'll do harm to you or your family," he said. "You were my friend."

The notion that friendship matters implies that we are not just a swarm of midges, invisibly devouring each other—an identical organism in shaded motion, if our planet were to be seen from afar. The notion that others are not merely occasional helpmates and collaborators, to be discarded when necessary, implies some continuity of the organism: memory, in which we live; nostalgia, in which we live; love—something permanent in the flesh that we know to be forever rotting, whatever lovely glow it emits in the process. I, like others, stubbornly insist there might be a meaning. There may be no God. There may be no Intention. But there is a divine pattern in tradition and memory. In the duration of our lives, the jostling uncertainty of the times, we cling to trust. And it is betrayed. And we cling again. Friendship and love mean more than someone to chatter with, someone to stroke, someone to couple with.

The man who dumped on me out of convenience to himself was my friend, he thought. The man who forgot the trouble he put himself in, and blamed me for his trouble, was my friend, we both thought. The man whom I dumped on in his time of trouble was my friend, I thought. I saw no alternative at that moment to letting the madman, my friend, be treated by paid nurses and doctors. The man who dumped on me also saw no alternative. Nothing was convenient; still these acts seem to be betrayals.

And still friendship matters; it seems to matter more than most things, and to have moral connections to the will more deeply human than mere connection by blood. After all, wolves are loyal to their cubs; many species protect their nests. Only men and women aspire to lifelong loyalty to friends whose bodies do not commingle. We choose. Until we are composed decently by death, we long for company unobliged by blood. The loneliness of the friendless is a special horror, and family does not fully mitigate it. Blood is fatal, inevitable, never to be denied; it demonstrates nothing about choice. But friendship, an act of pure intention, can be denied. There are no guarantees other than that most fallible one, the human heart. We choose to have friends because we must; else we'll have no hearts, we'll not feel alive. Sweet and dangerous defiance forever.

40. DETERMINANTS OF FRIENDSHIP ACROSS THE LIFE SPAN

ENID GAMER, JOHN THOMAS, and DEBBIE KENDALL

This article reviews the studies dealing with the determinants of friendship across stages of the life span. Two areas of research are examined: studies which address the common characteristics found between friends, and studies which are concerned with social cognition.

Preschoolers

Characteristics Common to Friends

There is some indication that young friendship pairs are characterized by similarity of sex, age, cooperation, and activity level. Challman (1932) analyzed peer preferences in nursery-school youngsters. His measure of friendship was the number of times per hour that two children were together. His conclusions were as follows:

1. Sex was a major factor for both a younger group (27 to 45 months old) and an older group (46 months to 59 months); boys played with boys and girls played with girls.
2. Children tended to make friends with others of the same age. This was more true for boys than for girls.
3. Children formed friendships with others who engaged in cooperative activities.
4. Children who were similar on a measure of physical activity and of energy output played together more frequently.

Mental age, IQ, height, extroversion, laughter, or attractiveness of personality had no influence on the closeness of friendship formation.

Hartup, Glazer, and Charlesworth (1967) demonstrated that social acceptance in four-year-old nursery-school youngsters was related to children responding positively to social approaches and that, rejection was related to negative behavior during social interaction. Similarly, Lee (cited in Hartup, 1975) found that peer preferences in one-year-old infants also appeared to be based upon positive responsiveness to social interaction.

The most preferred infant was "a responsive, adaptive social partner who interacted non-assertively . . . her involvements were reciprocal." The least preferred infant was "almost asocial in his behavior. . . . Both the intensity and degree to which his involvements

were mutual depended on whether or not he himself had initiated them." [p. 5.]

Social Cognition

Both experimental and anecdotal evidence indicate that the majority of three- and four-year-old children are highly egocentric, that is, they are unable to see events from another's perspective even under simple conditions (Flavell, 1966). Studies on empathy suggest that although three-year-old children are able to accurately label another child's emotion (Borke, 1971), it is probably by virtue of projection rather than through a true understanding of how another feels (Chandler and Greenspan, 1972). However, studies by Mueller (1972) and Lee (1974) demonstrated a high social interest by preschool children in one another. Although such children tend to be highly egocentric, talking mainly about themselves and their activities, they make a concerted effort to understand each other's attempts at communication. It should also be noted that, in spite of the difficulty preschoolers have with cognitively understanding another child, these early relationships can be fully as intense as those that are formed later in life. A. Freud and Dann (1951) described how young peers can provide emotional support for one another in the absence of stable adult caretakers. Sigmund Freud also remarked upon the lasting effect his relationship with a cousin John, one year his senior, had upon his character.

Until the end of my third year we had been inseparable; we had loved each other and fought each other, and, as I have already hinted, this childish relation has determined all my later feelings in intercourse with persons of my own age. [Jones, p. 8.]

Influence of Social Cognition upon Friendship Choice

How preschool children think about friends or friendship has not yet been explored. However, we might anticipate that such conceptions would be rudimentary and poorly defined. It is likely, as the studies reported suggest, that preschoolers are attracted to others who show similar play skills and who receive them with positive affect.

Early School-aged Children

Characteristics Common to Friends

Perhaps the most important factor determining friendship formation of early school-aged children is proximity. Furfey (1927) reported that among a population of nine-year-old boys, 89 percent of the friendship pairs were from the same schoolroom and 45 percent lived in the same neighborhood. This has been found for all early school grades (Gallagher, 1958; Seagoe, 1933) as well as for junior-high students (Jenkins, 1931).

Studies generally indicate that the majority of school friends are with others of the same age but that greater variability of age occurs with "outside" friends. Seagoe (1933) reported that 64 percent of all friendships made in school were between children of the same grade, whereas 57 percent of all friendships outside of school were with children in another grade. Similarly, Jenkins (1931) found a correlation of .53 between school friends and a correlation of .46 between friends outside of school. Generally, girls tended to have friends in either the same or higher grades, whereas boys had friends in both higher and lower grades as well as their own. Thorpe (1955) reported a nonsignificant trend for best friends to be closer in age than other friends and for other friends to be closer in age than nonfriends. This was the case for both boy-boy and girl-girl pairs.

Several other factors have been examined but by only one or two investigators. Physical maturity (Seagoe, 1933), size (Furfey, 1927), and athletic ability (Seagoe, 1933) bear some relationship to friend-

ship with correlations in the low 30s. Best friends have somewhat more common play interests than do nonfriends, but the differences are surprisingly small. Seagoe (1933) found that of 115 friendship pairs, 27 percent of the children had one of their three greatest interests in common, whereas 19 percent had one of their interests in common with another child picked at random.

Social Cognition

There are only a few studies concerned with the growth of social understanding in early school-aged children, but they have uncovered similar developmental trends.

Scarlett, Press, and Crockett (1971) asked first- and third-grade boys to describe liked and disliked friends. Children in both grades primarily described what their friend did in a particular context (concrete constructs). Both egocentric references, for example, "He hits me," and non-egocentric references, for example, "He plays baseball," were included in the concrete descriptions. Peevers and Secord (1973) asked kindergarteners and third graders to describe three liked friends and one disliked person. The kindergarteners and third graders gave primarily simple differentiating responses. These responses differentiated the person from his background, but did so in terms of superficial characteristics, global judgments, or gross relationships to the child, for example, "She has red hair," "He's nice," or "I've known him since kindergarten."

Both these studies, although using different terminology, concrete constructs versus simple differentiating responses, have found essentially the same results: children from kindergarten through the third grade describe and conceptualize their friends on the basis of simple observable characteristics. The rudimentary ability to differentiate others on the basis of global internal or psychological traits is present; however, early school-aged children tend not or prefer not to use such conceptualizations (Flavell, 1974).

A study by Flapan (1968) further supports the notion that children six- to eight-years old tend to interpret their world on the basis of surface characteristics, and have a difficult time coordinating psychological motivations with events. Flapan studied sixty girls of average intelligence at ages six, nine, and twelve. The girls were presented with sound film clips portraying episodes of social interaction. First they were asked to give an account in their own words of what happened in each episode, and then they were asked a set of uniform questions designed to elicit explanations of the events in each episode. Results showed that the six-year olds tended to report rather than explain or interpret what happened. No six-year old mentioned feelings that were not obviously expressed or specifically labeled by the actors. Only 3 of the 20 six-year olds inferred thoughts or intentions; none inferred feelings or interpersonal perceptions. Further, it was difficult for them to give explanations when asked about specific events.

In answering questions that called for an explanation of behavior, the six-year olds often said they did not know or gave answers that were not appropriate to the action of the film, or even explained an antecedent action by something that happened subsequently. In addition, they gave many explanations in terms of the existing situation or the just-preceding action. [p. 39.]

Influences of Social Cognition upon Friendship Choice

The data suggest that early school-aged children form impressions on the basis of external characteristics. Thus we might anticipate that friendships are formed on the basis of observable qualities. A study by Dymond, Hughes, and Raate (1952) supports this idea. They asked second graders to choose five of twenty-five phrases which best described the children

they most liked. The three items most frequently selected were "has a nice home," "is good looking," and "has lots of spending money." Thus appearance and possessions are salient features influencing friendship choice.

Middle School-aged Children

Starting at about age nine there is a major advance in social understanding; children begin to attribute psychological traits to others and to infer causation based upon internal motivation. Once again the few studies related to social cognition show rather good agreement as to the emergence of these interpersonal and inferential skills.

Descriptions of friends begin to include references to psychological traits. Scarlett, Press, and Crockett (1971) observed that fifth graders emphasized abstract traits; however, they still tended to be global and diffuse, for example, "He's good" or "She's nice." Peevers and Secord (1973) found that seventh graders showed an increased use in both differentiating items, descriptions of fairly personal characteristics such as "He smokes" or "She gets straight A's," and dispositional items, descriptions of behavioral traits such as "He's talkative." Also, descriptions now include a discussion of personal characteristics that are conditional upon situational, temporal, or internal states—an indication that the child sees complexity and fluctuation in behavior, for example, "When he is with older people he acts very immature" (Secord and Peevers, 1974).

Sensitivity to affects, motives, and psychological causations shows dramatic growth for both boys and girls during the middle-school ages. In the study by Flapan (1968), an interpretation of a movie episode by a six- and a twelve-year-old girl clearly illustrates the changes taking place.

At the beginning her daddy was sitting in the chair in the living room looking at the paper, and the little girl got out of her bed and said, "Pa, will you kiss me goodnight?" And the daddy said, "Go to bed," and the little girl went to bed crying. And he tore up the paper and he threw it down on the floor. Then he went into the kitchen and was getting ready to go out to the barn. And the lady said, "Where are you going?" And he said, "Out to the barn." And the lady said, "At this time of the night?" And the man said, "Yes."

The father was reading the newspaper, but he was thinking about something else. He couldn't really read it. And the little girl was looking down and asked her father if he didn't want to kiss her good night. The father wanted to say good night, but then he thought she did something bad, so he said, "No. Go back to bed." And the girl was crying and did go back to bed. And the father tried to read the newspaper again, but he couldn't read it, so he threw it away. He wanted to go up to her and say it wasn't so bad. But he decided he better not. So he went to the kitchen and said to his wife he was going out. And the mother said, "I think you just want to be by yourself." And he said, "Yes." And the mother said, "There is a circus coming to town tonight." I think he is going to go to the circus with the girl now. [pp. 31–32.]

It should be noted that most of the social interpretive skills evidenced by the twelve-year olds were also found for the nine-year olds. There were no significant differences between the use of such skills for these two groups, although there was a progression toward the more frequent and sophisticated use of interpretation, inference, and labeling of emotions.

Boys show similar growth. By nine years, boys are able to coordinate external behavior with an internal motivational state, an ability absent in the seven- to eight-year olds (Feffer and Gouervitch, 1960).

Influence of Social Cognition upon Friendship Choice

When children understand that there is a psychological, or internal, reality, their descriptions of friends emphasize psychological traits rather than external characteristics (Dymond et al., 1952). These psychological traits become an important determinant of friendship. Byrne and Griffitt (1966) demonstrated that at least as early as the fourth grade, children's attraction to strangers was directly related to the similarity of attitudes between the stranger and child. They asked children in grades four through twelve to fill out an eight-item scale dealing with various topics such as poetry, comic books, sports, brothers, and sisters. Each topic was arranged as a six-point attitude item. After the scales were collected, the children were given a bogus scale, filled out, so they were told, by someone of the same age and sex. The subjects were asked to rate the stranger on four seven-point evaluation scales with respect to intelligence, morality, liking, and desirability as a work-partner. The latter two evalutions were added together to get a measure of attraction. The results indicated that by nine years of age, attraction was directly and positively related to similarity of attitudes—the greater the similarity of attitude, the greater was the attraction to the "bogus" stranger.

Throughout the school years, proximity exerts a strong influence upon friendship formations. However, since we do not become friends with everyone with whom we come into contact, we have to ask about other determinants. The studies suggest that external characteristics such as appearance and possessions play an important role in friendship choice among early school-aged children. And as with preschoolers, similarity in skills and play-preference probably continue to influence friendship choice.

By middle school-age, however, attitude similarity influences friendship choice. Children now understand that others have internal or psychological traits as well as external behavior. Thus, friendships can be based upon similarity of thoughts and feelings rather than upon skills or play-preferences. It is no accident that about this age, close relationships, characterized by the sharing of perceptions, ideas, feelings, and imaginings, develop between members of the same sex (Sullivan, 1953).

Adolescence Through Adulthood

Characteristics Common to Friends

The strong influence that proximity exerts upon adult friendships has been demonstrated in several studies (Martin, 1974; Newcomb, 1956; Rubin, 1973). Athanasiou and Yoshioka (1973) studied the effect of multiple variables upon the friendship formation of approximately 275 women living in a large housing complex. The subjects were for the most part white, young (average age was 29 years), married, and over 70 percent had children. The results indicated:

1. Proximity influenced the intensity of the friendship; closest friends were most frequently found to be next-door neighbors.
2. The number of children under three-years old and the amount of time the children of two households played together were important factors in determining which of the closest neighbors became friends.
3. Husband's occupation and education, wife's education, and race did not differentiate friendship choice for next-door neighbors; however, differences in household income worked against friendship formation.
4. Age, marital status, and number of children were related to friendship choice regardless of distance. Also, husband's occupation and schooling of husband and wife were significant predictors of friendships at greater distances.

Thus this study supports the notion that proximity strongly influences the choice of friends so long as some life cycle similar-

ities are present. In this study, marital and maternal status as well as proximity were determining factors. For friendships to be maintained over longer periods additional similarities such as social class and education had to exist.

After proximity, attitude similarity appears to be the best predictor of friendship formation (Lindzey and Byrne, 1969). Izard (1960) found that pairs of close friends of high school and college subjects were more similar in affective needs than were subjects paired at random. Duck (1972, 1973) suggested that similarity of personal constructs underlies friendship. The term "personal constructs" was coined by Kelly (1955) and presumably refers to those psychological dimensions with which one structures his view of others and situations. Duck's work (1973) with university women suggested that early attraction was based upon thinking similarly about general issues, whereas, established friendships were characterized by similarity in subjective ways of viewing others. Indeed, the chances of a friendship being maintained or strengthened are enhanced by the extent to which the two members perceive themselves to be similar in the psychological constructions of their world.

Social Cognition

The social-cognitive skills developed in the middle school age become refined with continued social experience. Explanations for behavioral characteristics appear about mid-adolescence, for example, "She's a snob because she is trying to hide something about herself" (Peevers and Secord, 1973). Gollin (1958) found that boys and girls were unable to integrate satisfactorily contradictory behavior patterns evidenced by an individual until they were sixteen-years old. Thus with age we become increasingly sophisticated about the psychological motivation behind external behavior.

Conceptualizations of Friendship

The first empirical study which has attempted to conceptualize adult friendship was done by Weiss and Lowenthal (1973). They interviewed over two hundred men and women at four stages of their adult life-cycle: high school seniors, newlyweds (couples recently married and not yet parents), empty nesters (parents whose youngest child was about to leave home), and a preretirement group. Each subject was asked to discuss three separate friends. The analysis produced five specific dimensions of friendship. They were as follows:

1. Commonality—A common or sharing base was explicitly related to the relationship. Friends were viewed as being similar in personality, values, or attitudes. The sharing of activities or experiences might also be emphasized.
2. Reciprocal—Supporting or helping behaviors were characteristics of the friendship. Understanding, acceptance, and dependence were acknowledged. Emotional expressiveness and accessibility of the friend were central to the relationship.
3. Role-modeling—The friend was perceived as embodying certain ideal qualities or attributes that the respondent admired or respected.
4. Compatibility—The relationship was marked by comfort, ease, and pleasure in being together.
5. Continuity and proximity—The salient elements were spatial distance, length of time of acquaintance, and convenience of the friendship.

The investigators found that commonality provided the most frequent base to the friendship, although reciprocity was idealized as the most important dimension upon which a relationship could be built. Men placed greater emphasis upon commonality across all ages studied than did women. Women reported reciprocity to be the more important factor in their relationships. Also, as one grew older, commonality was generally viewed as less important to the relationship.

A consistent notion across sex and ages was that different friends serve different functions; respondents generally attributed a dimension of friendship to only one friend. However, with age appears to come increasing differentiation with respect to friends. The older respondents tended to relate more attributes and functions to their friends than did the younger subjects. So, as one grows older, friends become more differentiated, and friendship is based upon something other than common interests.

Another study conducted by Boston University undergraduates in 1974 sheds some light upon how adolescents and adults view friends throughout the life span. It should be noted that these interviews were not specifically designed to collect information about friends or friendship. The subjects were asked to compare their present life with what it was ten years ago and how they expected it to be ten years hence. The comments referring to friends in these interviews are of interest.

Friends were most frequently mentioned by subjects in the teenage years. Adolescents felt that it was important to have many friends as well as to have "good" friends. Respondents in their twenties and thirties spoke about being selective in their choice of friends. The great variability among people was recognized and commented upon. For some, social life was seen as more satisfying with closer relationships. For others, disruption in life style, such as divorce, resulted in the loss of friends. With the forties, two themes appeared: the first was that friendships have stabilized; the second was that more time was available for friends. Interestingly, it was not until the fifties (and then only infrequently) that friends were mentioned as offering support through difficult times. In the sixties, friends were barely mentioned. The main concerns were with retirement and health of self and spouse. The responses of the fifty-year olds suggest that, by and large, friends are not seen as a resource in difficult times, but are primarily associated with pleasant or happy social events. Subjects seventies and older spoke more often about friends than did those in their sixties. Once again, friends were mentioned as a vehicle through which one has enjoyed or can still enjoy life.

Influence of Social Cognition upon Friendship Choice

With experience we become more aware of psychological motivation behind behavior and become more sensitive to the varieties of people and behavior. During the school years it is important to have friends since they are tangible proof of social acceptance. However, as we grow older and more certain of ourselves, we become more selective and want close friends who can share and understand our perceptions and reactions to events. There are indications that as we grow older and become more differentiated, so do our friends show increasing differentiation. We select friends for different purposes and needs.

Conclusions

Strong friendships can occur throughout all stages of life-span development. The finding that proximity plays such an important role in friendship formation across all ages suggests that we make a major effort to become friends with those who are available to us. Friendships are formed with others varying in age, intelligence, size, social class, and education. However, underlying seemingly diverse friendships appears to be the one important variable of attitude similarity. After age nine or ten we tend to judge others by their attitudes and values; we feel closest to others who think like we do. Before this time, friendships appear to be based on play preferences. However, this conclusion must be offered tentatively since so little research on friendship has been done.

As we mature into and throughout our adulthood, our selves beocme more differentiated, and so do our conceptions of our friends. Again, a tentative conclusion from the research that has been done is that we learn to select different friends for different needs. Thus the determinants for friendship can be as varied as our own personalities and can change with life experiences.

References

ATHANASIOU, R., and YOSHOIKA, G. A. The spatial character of friendship formation. *Environment and Behavior*, 1973, 5, 143–165.

BORKE, H. Interpersonal perception of young children. *Developmental Psychology*, 1971, 3 (2), 263–269.

BYRNE, D., and GRIFFITT, W. A developmental investigation of the law of attraction. *Journal of Personality and Social Psychology*, 1966, 4, 699–702.

CHALLMAN, R. C. Factors influencing friendship among preschool children. *Child Development*, 1932, 3, 146–158.

CHANDLER, M. J., and GREENSPAN, S. Ersatz egocentricism: a reply to H. Borke. *Developmental Psychology*, 1972, 2, 104–106.

DUCK, S. W. Personality similarity and friendship choice: similarity of what, when? *Journal of Personality*, 1973, 41 (4), 543–558.

DUCK, S. W., and SPENCER, C. Personal constructs and friendship formation. *Journal of Personality and Social Psychology*, 1972, *23*, 40–45.

DYMOND, R. F., HUGHES, A. S., and RAATE, V. L. Measurable changes in empathy with age. *Journal of Consulting Psychology*, 1952, *16*, 202–206.

FEFFER, M., and GOUERVITCH, V. Cognitive aspects of role taking in children. *Journal of Personality*, 1960, *28*, 383–396.

FLAPAN, D. *Children's understanding of social interaction.* New York: Teachers College Press, 1968.

FLAVELL, J. H. Role-taking and communication skills in young children. *Young Children*, 1966, *21*, 164–177.

FLAVELL, J. H. The development of inferences about others. In T. Mischel (Ed.), *Understanding other persons.* New York: Rowan and Littlefield, 1974.

FREUD, A. and DANN, S. An experiment in group upbringing. R. Eisler et al. (Eds.), *The psychoanalytic study of the child* (Vol. 6). New York: International Press, 1951.

FURFEY, P. Some factors influencing the selection of boys' "chums." *Journal of Applied Psychology*, 1927, *11*, 47–51.

GALLAGHER, J. J. Social status of children related to intelligence, propinquity and social perception. *Elementary School Journal*, 1958, *58*, 225–231.

GOLLIN, E. S. Organizational characteristics of social judgment; A developmental investigation. *Journal of Personality*, 1958, *26*, 139–154.

HARTUP, W. W. The origins of friendship. To appear in M. Lewis and L. Rosenblum (Eds.), *Friendship and peer relations: the origins of behavior* (Vol. 3). New York: Wiley & Sons, 1975.

HARTUP, W. W., GLAZER, J. A., and CHARLESWORTH, R. Peer reinforcement and sociometric status. *Child Development*, 1967, *38*, 1017–1024.

IZARD, C. E. Personality similarity and friendship. *Journal of Abnormal and Social Psychology*, 1960, *61*, 47–51.

JENKINS, G. G. Factors involved in children's friendships. *Journal of Educational Psychology*, 1931, *22*, 440–448.

JONES, E. *The life and work of Sigmund Freud* (Vol. 1). New York: Basic Books, 1953.

KELLY, G. A. *The psychology of personal constructs* (Vol. 1). New York: Norton, 1955.

LEE, L. C. Conclusion of the symposium on the development of interpersonal competence: Strategies of social exchange. In H. A. Moss (Chair), The development of interpersonal competence: Strategies of social exchange. Symposium presented at the meeting of the American Psychological Association, New Orleans, August 1974.

LINDZEY, G., and BYRNE, D. Measurement of social choice and interpersonal attractiveness. In G. Lindzey and E. Aronson (Eds.). The handbook of social psychology (Vol. 2). Reading, Mass.: Addison-Wesley, 1969.

MARTIN, R. D. Friendship choices and residence hall proximity among freshman and upper year students. *Psychological Reports*, 1974, *34*, 118.

MUELLER, E. The maintenance of verbal exchanges in young children. *Child Development*, 1972, *43*, 930–938.

NEWCOMB, T. M. The prediction of interpersonal attraction. *American Psychologist*, 1956, *11*, 575–586.

PEEVERS, B. H., and SECORD, P. F. Developmental changes in attribution of descriptive concepts to persons. *Journal of Personality and Social Psychology*, 1973, 27, 120–128.

ROTHENBERG, B. B. Children's social sensitivity and the relationship to interpersonal competence, intrapersonal comfort and intellectual level. *Developmental Psychology*, 1970, *2*, 335–350.

RUBIN, Z. *Liking and Loving: An invitation to social psychology.* New York: Holt, Rinehart, & Winston, 1973.

SCARLETT, H. H., PRESS, A. N., and CROCKETT, W. H. Children's descriptions of peers: a Wernerian developmental analysis. *Child Development*, 1971, *42*, 439–453.

SEAGOE, M. V. Factors influencing the selection of associates. *Journal of Educational Research.* 1933, *27*, 32–40.

SECORD, P. F., and PEEVERS, B. H. The development and attribution of person concepts. In T. Mischel (Eds.), *Understanding other persons.* New York: Rowan & Littlefield, 1974.

SULLIVAN, H. S. *The interpersonal theory of psychiatry.* New York: Norton, 1953.

THORPE, J. G. A study of some factors in friendship formation. *Sociometry*, 1955, *18*, 207–214.

WEISS, L., and LOWENTHAL, M. F. Perceptions and complexities of friendship in four stages of the adult life cycle. In *Proceedings of the 81st Annual Convention of the American Psychological Association* (Vol. 8), Montreal, Canada, 1973.

WHITEMAN, J. Children's conceptions of psychological causality. *Child Development*, 1967, *38*, 143–155.

CHAPTER NINE: SUGGESTED FURTHER READING

HARTUP, W. Peer interaction and social organization. In P. Mussen (Ed.), *Carmichael's manual of child psychology.* (3rd ed.) Vol. II. New York: Wiley, 1970. Pp. 361–456.

There is no mention of friendship in most books on the life span, and no review of this topic in the literature.

chapter ten
work

Work, to paraphrase most dictionary definitions, is the expenditure of physical and mental energy in order to accomplish some sort of task. The simplicity of the definition, however, is belied by the significance and complexity of work in the real world. Work does involve exertion; but some work is meaningful, some is not; some work pays well, some does not; some work is enjoyable, some is despicable. The study of people at work is a fascinating field because it is the study of the entire world of human actions.

Each year new workers enter the labor force. Many of them work side by side with people twenty to thirty years their senior. Some psychologists have studied the differing characteristics of the young and the older worker, although the results of their studies have been somewhat ambiguous and paradoxical. For instance, Clay (1960) found that older workers are more accurate and stable than young workers and that older workers do not have as good muscle control as younger workers. Yet studies by Fozard and Carr (1972) and Arvey and Mussio (1973), rating job performance, indicate that older workers are either as good or better than younger workers. The commonly accepted notion that younger workers are superior to older ones does not hold water in light of these studies. How, then, did young workers come to be regarded so highly? What, if any, changes do occur if a person stays at the same job for a long period of time? If longitudinal studies were done, would there be an increment in job performance? These are the questions that scientists are now beginning to ask.

There are other aspects of work which have not been explored. At different ages or points in the life span, it seems likely that people view work from different perspectives. The high school student earning spending money, the collegian working his or her way through school, the thirty-five-year-old supporting a family, the people facing retirement—all do not work to achieve the same objectives. The interrelationship of age, personality, family situation, and socioeconomic class have a great impact on each individual's perspective toward work. Studies, both longitudinal and cross-sectional, should provide interesting data on these relationships.

As people grow older, the issue of retirement looms larger and larger. In this country, retirement has generally been fixed at about age sixty-five, at which point people are considered to be old and unproductive. For many people retirement is something to look forward to; for others it is a traumatic event. Here again, other issues, such as age and personality and especially economic status, bear heavily on the individual's demeanor. However, none of these interrelating factors indicates that a person must retire. In most cases there is no real breakdown in ability or productivity, only a cultural age norm that constrains these people into a different life from what they had been leading. It is an outrage that productive and creative people over sixty-five are cut off from transferring their knowledge to others. One can only hope that groups such as the Gray Panthers, the organization aimed at regaining older people's rights and dignity, will flourish and bring the elderly back into the mainstream of society.

Work is, indeed, more than the expenditure of mental and physical energy to accomplish a task. It is part of the interrelating system of age, personality, economics, and performance (to mention only a few), which encompasses the entirety of human thought and action. Obviously work is one of the central issues of our lives.

References

ARVEY, R., and MUSSIO, S. Test discrimination, job performance, and age. *Industrial Gerontology*, 1973 *16*, 22–29.

CLAY, H. M. *The older worker and his job*. London: Her Majesty's Stationery Office, 1960.

FOZARD, J. L., and CARR, G. D., JR. Age differences and psychological estimates of abilities and skills. *Industrial Gerontology*, 1972, *13*, 75–96.

41. THE ROLE OF WORK IN STRUCTURING THE LIFE CYCLE

WILLIAM E. HENRY

The central portion of man's lifespan is spent at work. This sector of life, for the man and for the woman who works, can be seen as a period when a central activity is that of earning a living—or, for some women and some men, supplementing other income by partial or occasional work. It has always been of interest to psychologists that some people are better at one kind of work than another. The concept of intelligence (as well as special education and training) has been used to account for many of these differences. Motivation and the will to get ahead have also been useful ideas, mainly in accounting for differentials in success within given occupational fields.

Other investigators, usually sociologists and the anthropologists, have been more impressed by the way in which the values and mores of the immediate work setting have influenced the flow of work, or have directed the nature of interpersonal relations in the work place. This latter group of investigators has also related particular lines of work, not so much to individual capacities as to societal structure, observing not only that different occupations may be assigned different prestige or social status, but that certain occupations recruit their members selectively and, one might say, according to patterns of prejudice and discrimination.

We have available, then, various sets of explanations aimed either at understanding work competence or at understanding social system influences upon particular work performances. These explanations contain 2 useful elements, but are seriously lacking in a third. They propose, on the one hand, that certain attributes indigenous to the person account for some aspects of work—the person's intelligence and other native attitudes and skills, or the facts of his birth as reflected in the social status of his family of origin. And, secondly, they take account of the fact that conditions at the workplace, above and beyond the attributes of the individual, will direct and influence the interpersonal character of an occupational setting and will further modify the individual's options in the use of his native attributes.

But the significant feature that is lacking in these explanations is the conceptual apparatus necessary to see work, not only as a way of earning a living, and not only as a job analogue of one's father's occupation, but as *a life style, as the central and most binding continuity of the years between age 20 and 70.* Those activities we call work serve to create a directing and guiding network of relationships which structures, permits, limits, sets time schedules, reduces options, opens options, and in general provides the central social and psychological framework for some 40 or 50 years of the life cycle. In this sense, and notably for men, work is *living.* With the possible exception of bad health, when it occurs, work is the most central determiner of the conditions of life that most people in modern society ever encounter.

It is true that current theories provide some concepts that focus upon work as a continuous coping system. At the societal level, social and job mobility is one such concept, one that permits some type of trajectory and some type of directionality over time—for instance, a time line based on the desire to better one's situation, or to win out over one's colleagues. (For certain types of studies, of course, such motives become less useful in explaining job mobility than information on economic level, technological need, or occupation-wide salary movements.)

From the more personalistic perspective, there is a body of ideas which relate occupational choice to early childhood dynamic relationships. In presuming direct connections between early family events and later work choices, one is proposing a trajectory with a describable direction—a course set by early experience which finds its end point in some later vocational behavior or choice. This view tends to stress difference in early life events from one occupational group to another.

But actual examples of such relationships are hard to find; and such theories tend to suffer from lack of evidence regarding the events and circumstances that intervene between the early family events and the presumed later adult outcome. In other words, a gap exists in such theories, a gap which permits the intrusion of the most extensive set of alternative events and theories, or which presumes that, in effect, no such intervening events occurred.

Work is a continuing engagement with the human community, a community presenting changing patterns of options and contingencies. The realities of the work community keep changing with social and economic conditions, with changes of policy and personnel, and with accumulations of experience and competencies on the part of the individual. Man at work is not merely a reflection of his early life, although indeed some useful analogues may be sugegsted. Man at work *is* at work—working through, on a daily basis, his views of himself, the tasks set by his work environment, his hopes for future relationships and rewards. And in his work he is also actively engaged with his family—lending major direction to the lives of his wife and children, permitting the choices he must make at work to limit the options and to set the circumstances of the lives of those he loves. Work is the living scene in which man's sense of competence waxes and wanes and he conducts his extended social and personal interactions.

Work as a Socializing Force

As a socializing agent, the family is quite legitimately referred to as primary. It is primary in many senses—it appears first in the life of the individual; the young are maximally impressionable; for several years there is no meaningful competitor. One of the significant end points of the socialization by the family is the gradual ceding of its tasks to the school, which then becomes the second main socializing force in the person's life. Whether it occurs earlier or later, one of the school's main tasks is to prepare the individual for the adult world of work.

Here, of course, we have a choice. Should we conceive of people—of each of us as individuals—as having been "finished" at the end of school, of having ended our significant cognitive and emotional development? Or should we think of the period after formal schooling as a further period of interaction between the person, as he exists at that moment, and the world of work? Previous learning at any age, is in an important sense preparatory for later life, and it is reasonable to think of the end of formal schooling as a particularly relevant termination of some forms of preparation. But it is not appropriate to think of this as the end of all preparation and new learning.

It seems far more appropriate to see the adult years, and in particular the work aspects, as a period of further socialization. In this sense, work is the third major socialization force—and its effect is to train us in the values and mores of a significant sector of the adult social system and the world of reality. This interaction exercises and develops our competencies, permitting us to articulate these life realities. Family and school socialization is over in the 20s, but the preparation for adult life that occurs in the work setting has only begun.

Continuities in adult work life occur for several reasons. One stems from the work scene itself, for each work context has its own stabilities. Secondly, many jobs set a ceiling upon work skills and individual attributes, so that individual change is limited. A third type of continuity is clearly that which comes from the residues of early childhood learning—fears of change, attachment to certain kinds of people, perhaps a ceaseless ambition and restlessness—all of which lend a consistent character to the adult, at work or at home.

In these same factors lie the forces of discontinuity and change. The work scene itself alters, and one can change jobs. Intelligence can be applied to new problems, or tried out in a new climate. And the residues of early experience may push for change—in any event, they can be made responsive to new contingencies. The end result stems from the interaction of these factors over time—from the interaction of the socializing work scene, the cognitive flexibilities of the individual, and his emotional preferences regarding interactive styles. The *lifespan* is more than the passage of years. As a concept in social science, it should be seen as reflecting a *developmental interaction* between psychodynamics based on early experience, skills and cognitive attributes, and the distinctive influences of family, school, and work, each of the latter seen as a major socialization context.

Childhood Experience and Occupational Choice

As one set of data to which these concepts seem relevant, I would like to comment briefly upon a group of mental health professionals whom we have been studying, a group of some 4,000 experienced practitioners of psychotherapy in New York, Chicago, and Los Angeles. In roughly equal proportions, these are psychoanalysts, psychiatrists, clinical psychologists, and psychiatric social workers.

Each of these groups has its separate professional association and public identity, and each offers a course of training which differs markedly from other. While the psychoanalyst and the psychiatrist start on similar pathways in medical school, even these 2 diverge in significant ways as the analyst not only continues training but comes early to develop a quite specialized sub-set of theory and skills. At the point of entry into the *parent* profession—medicine, social work, or psychology—each of these groups is embarking on what appears to be quite distinct careers. The dominant public image of each parent profession would seem to attract recruits of quite different character. The appeal of medicine has the aura of science; that of social work, the alleviation of social ills; and that of psychology, the fascination with inner-life processes. It is only after a period of time in the parent profession that the individual chooses to follow the path toward the psychotherapeutic goal, a choice that characterizes his later training and adult work.

It is traditional in studies of occupations to consider the possibility that early childhood experiences are related to the choice of occupation. Yet in the present instance of these 4 professions of different public images and different training patterns, there are no significant differences in the reports of early development and family dynamics given us by our respondents. Their reports, in interview and questionnaire, are highly repetitious regarding their relationships to parents during childhood and adolescence. And the 4 groups are similar with regard to birth order, family size, parental influences upon interests and career, childhood illnesses and trauma, and in experiences in dating and adolescent sex behavior.

At the point of initial choice of the parent professional, then, there are no discernible family and early background differences that would account for their choices. Predicting from early experiences to occupational choice would have been a complete failure. In spite of early background similarities in factors that are normally considered relevant in the psychodynamics of occupational choice, our subjects made 3 quite distinctly different choices.

Training and Early Work Years

During their training years and in the years of their subsequent therapeutic work, there occurred some marked changes which led our subjects—initially physicians, psychologists, and social workers— into pathways that turned them all into psychotherapists. These experiences, occurring in the later phases of training and in their subsequent work as therapists, are among the crucial experiences of their young and middle adult years. Although they were initially in different pathways in their profession of origin, in the early career years they made choices which moved them toward a highly overlapping set of lifestyles and social interactions. As we see them as adult practising psychotherapists, the most marked feature is their *similarity* in *current* beliefs and ways of behaving. It is not the early differences in occupational choice, not the adherence to any profession-specific convictions that is outstanding. In spite of these manifest differences in early choices and in professional identity (as a psychiatrist, or a psychiatric social worker, or clinical psychologist), there exists a truly remarkable degree of similarity in their adoption of the psychotherapeutic stance. These similarities reside in such issues as a common ideology which supersedes any beliefs of specific schools of psychological thought; similarities in the use of their work and leisure time; similarities in the patterns of their interests at work; similarities in their patterns of social interaction both at work and at home, in their systems of belief and explanation of behavior, and in fact, in the kinds of people they meet as patients.

At the point in their training when it was possible for direct clinical experience to occupy more of their time than formal didactic training, patterns of interaction styles similar across professions began to be characteristic. These experiences constitute the first and perhaps most crucial similarity across professional lines. It is, we believe, these developing patterns of styles of social interaction that contribute most significantly to the similarities of adult therapeutic stance. These styles, initially occurring during graduate school practice, clerkships, field placements, and internships, serve as the first examples of that form of personal interaction which is later to characterize their work years. That these clinical interaction styles are indeed perceived by therapists as crucial is clearly reflected in their reports of the training years. When asked what elements of their training were most useful to them in their current work, they definitely choose these clinical experiences. Regardless of profession of origin, formal didactic courses and non-clinical interactions are assigned only minor roles.

There are, of course, other elements which contribute to these socialization processes. Belief systems, the way one thinks and explains one's work, are not significantly different from one group to another. The rationale for the therapist who is a social worker is not notably different from the rationale of his colleague therapist who is a psychiatrist. And there is a set of sustaining beliefs characteristic of their professional associations which also impinges upon the developing psychotherapist. These beliefs serve as additional guiding forces and have, across professions, many elements of similarity—about professional ethics, about styles of relating to other professionals, about ways of dealing with patients, about how to handle minor and major problems which arise in the course of being a therapist. These factors reinforce that style of belief and interaction which constitutes therapeutic behavior, and they continue their socializing effect during the work years.

The similarity across all 4 groups in early family experience, as we have noted earlier, begins to suggest some effect of early influence, especially now as we note these later professional similarities. Unfortunately, however, we do not have the data needed to show that that which is common to these 4 groups is in some systematic way *different* for *non*-therapists or for other unrelated professions. What impresses us most, however, is the emergence of the cross-professional psychotherapeutic behavior, originating during the training and early work years. While it seems reasonable to believe that there are some early experiences which characterize those persons who later are able to learn the therapy role, it is the socialization forces of the adult years, in the training setting, and in the work setting, that are crucial and, we suspect, necessary parts of that process.

At each point in the lifespan, there are undoubtedly processes emerging from the interaction of previously instilled styles and contemporary environmental forces. This is a view which is familiar to us all as it applies to the pre-adult years. It is our central point here that the same is also true of the adult years, and in those years, applies especially to the world of work. The world of our work takes our time,

molds our daily interactions, structures our beliefs and values. As such, it is a significant socialization complex necessary to our understanding of the adult years, a force that contributes significantly to the character of the adult phase of the lifespan.

Summary

Work is a major socializing force in giving form and content to adult life. The prominence of work in the life cycle, and of the values, habits, and personal contacts made at the work place, suggest a compelling relationship between work and adult personality. In a study of mental health professionals (psychoanalysts, psychiatrists, clinical psychologists, psychiatric social workers) there were no significant differences in family or early childhood experiences to account for the differences in initial occupational choice. Similarities in training and in styles of early professional social interaction contributed significantly to the striking current similarities across the 4 groups in ideology, values, interests, and general life-styles.

42. EXAMINATION OF THE MEANING OF WORK TO OLDER WORKERS

EDWARD A. POWERS and WILLIS J. GOUDY

The time has already arrived when people are no longer employed for all of their adult lives. With increasing industrialization and greater longevity, many workers can expect periods of underemployment followed by retirement. There is current discussion about whether certain segments of an industrial society need ever work.

Yet, before nonemployment becomes a *fait accompli* through a shorter work week, underemployment, and longer retirement, it is necessary to determine what meaning, if any, work has for the employed individual. If it is determined, as some assert, that work is becoming simply a means of earning a living, then the absence of work should have few detrimental effects on the society. If, on the other hand, working serves more than just an economic meaning for the worker, structural alternatives will have to be provided if current trends continue.

Unfortunately, little attention has been given to conceptual clarification in this area. Authors at various times have made references to the meaning of work, the function of work, work motivation, work satisfaction and the significance of work. These, however, tend to be rather generic discussions of the concepts, with few precise definitions. Terms are often used interchangeably by the same author, and several authors use different concepts when referring to the same social phenomenon or reporting the same research findings (Morse and Weiss 1955).

One notable exception is the research of Friedmann and Havighurst (1954). They separate the "work function" from the "work meaning" in keeping with the distinctions of both Linton (1936) and Merton (1957). To Friedmann and Havighurst, the *function* of work is the contribution work makes to the satisfatcion of the needs and adjustment of a given system. The *meaning* of work, on the other hand, is the personal evaluation of work made by the individual and the functions of the job *for the individual*. Thus, in considering the meaning of work, they are discussing "both . . . the individual's recognition of the part the job has played in his life and . . . the type of affective response he has made to it" (p. 6).

For Friedmann and Havighurst, "work meanings" are related to the more universal functions of work in society. Through the study of the meaning of work, however, they only indirectly shed light on the "function" of work.

In the actual investigation into the meaning of work, there have been three basic approaches (Lofquist and Dawis 1969). The first has been the analysis or comparison of the meaning of work in pre-industrial (especially Calvinist and Renais-

sance) and industrial societies (Weber 1930; Tilgher 1930). A second category includes recent studies of the effects of taking work out of the lives of workers through retirement, unemployment or a hypothetical offer of an inheritance (Bakke 1940; Friedmann and Havighurst 1954; Morse and Weiss 1955). The third approach consists of studies of job satisfaction, vocational interests, work interests and work motivation (Vroom 1964; Darley 1955). Although each approach has provided understanding of the meaning of work to the worker, it is the second approach, the study of the effects of taking work out of the lives of workers, that will be considered here.

Morse and Weiss (1955) analyzed the meaning of work by trying to determine to what degree working serves functions for the individual other than just an economic one.[1] They attempted to hypothetically remove the economic function of work to the individual by asking workers the question, "If by some chance you inherited enough money to live comfortably without working, do you think you would work anyway or not?"

Morse and Weiss then asked those workers who said they would rather than accept the hypothetical inheritance why they would do so. Their contention was that the reason given would be some indication of the meaning of work for these individuals.

Friedmann and Havighurst approached the meaning of work through studies of older and recently retired workers in five occupational groupings: steelworkers, coalminers, salespersons, skilled craftsmen, and physicians. But, unlike Morse and Weiss,

---

[1] It appears that "meaning" and "function" are at times equated by Morse and Weiss. Although they do not clearly define either concept, they do seem to use the terms interchangeably. Morse and Weiss are careful to distinguish between "work" and "job." In fact, one of the questions they asked their subjects was whether they would keep working at *some* job, having given up their present occupation, if they accepted the hypothetical inheritance.

they did not distinguish between the importance of a particular occupation in the life of an individual and the place working has in the life of that person. Both their definition of "meaning of work" and their operationalization of this concept equates work and job.

Unfortunately, there has been no recent systematic consideration of the meaning of work to older workers, particularly across age categories. Morse and Weiss did look at the willingness of workers to continue working as related to the age of the respondent. They did not, however, report the reasons workers gave for being unwilling to accept the hypothetical inheritance. Friedmann and Havighurst's studies, conducted almost twenty years ago, only occasionally indicated the relationship of the age of the respondent to his reported meaning of work. However, this was for selected age categories and selected occupational groupings of older workers.

An understanding of the meaning of work to older workers would have several important uses. First, it would tell us what meaning, other then an economic one, work has for the older worker. It is the older worker who is fast approaching a permanent nonworker status. He is unable to consider his pending condition temporary and therefore will be in the process of making basic adjustments in what he considers to be the role of work in his life if such adjustments are made before retirement. Second, such an investigation would shed some light on the variables affecting the willingness of workers to accept retirement, adjustment in later retirement, and activities suitable for retired persons.

Procedure and Results

To this end, two questions were raised in our study: (a) In what way does the meaning of work differ between workers approaching the traditional retirement age (65) and those who exceed the retirement age? and (b) Are there any differences between pre-retirement and post-retirement age workers in the perceived advantages of quitting work?

To provide a partial answer to these questions, data were analyzed from a recent study conducted of employed males, aged 50 and older, residing in towns of 2,500 to 10,000 in a midwestern state. More than 1,900 respondents in five occupational categories—farmers, factory workers, owner-merchants, salaried professionals, and self-employed professionals—were interviewed extensively about their work histories and their attitudes toward a number of variables, including work. Approximately 2 percent of the sample came from each of the five occupational groupings. The respondents were asked the question: "Assume you were offered an annuity that would provide a comfortable living equal to what you have now for the rest of your life, with no strings attached except that you had to quit doing any work for pay or profit, would you take it?" This question is similar to the one asked by Morse and Weiss, but the Morse and Weiss question did not state what constituted a "comfortable level of living." Thus, it is likely that respondents defined the standard in different ways. By stating that the annuity would be "equal to what you have now," an attempt was made to remove the arbitrary definition of "comfort" probably applied by the respondents.

Table 42.1 indicates that pre-retirement age workers (50–64) were more willing to quit work and accept the annuity than were the post-retirement age workers (65+). This finding is similar to that observed by Morse and Weiss. The proportion of the sample in the present study who would continue to work in each age category, however, was less than that observed by Morse and Weiss. It is possible that the observed differences in the proportion willing to accept the annuity between these two studies may be a function of the population sampled. Morse and Weiss' investigation was based on a national sample of over 400 workers, while our sample was

Table 42.1. Percentages choosing to remain working or to take an annuity by age of the respondent

Percentage of respondents who would:	Age Category				
	50–54	55–59	60–64	65+	Totals
Quit working (or take the annuity)	58.2	61.2	58.1	48.7	57.3
Remain working (or not take the annuity)	41.8	38.8	41.9	51.3	42.7
Total N	591	551	408	343	1893

selected from small towns in one midwestern state. There are perhaps regional differences in the willingness to continue to work when offered a hypothetical inheritance or annuity; Morse and Weiss, however, did not present data on regional variations. Thus, we can only note that such variations possibly could account for the differences between these two studies.

It also seems likely that an important source of the observed differences stems from the questions asked. Morse and Weiss used a situation in which the respondents were offered the opportunity to live "comfortably," while our study, which offered an annuity equal to one's present income, was seen as more justly deserved. Thus, the proportion accepting the offer was greater in the present study.

No matter what their response to the first question, the respondents were then asked why they would accept or reject the annuity. Three responses—"something for nothing," "I enjoy my job," and "life would lose its meaning"—accounted for over 70 percent of all responses of those stating they would not quit even if they were offered an annuity (Table 42.2). The number of workers who would not accept an annuity because it was something for nothing was rather unexpected by the authors. This category contains approximately two-fifths of the respondents and is almost twice as high as the second most-cited reason for not accepting the annuity. Past examinations of the meaning of work have tended to limit discussion of the importance of work to occupational conditions with either tangible products of work, such as pay and hours, or the intrinsic qualities, such as how interesting the

work is and how highly the occupation is regarded (e.g., Kohn and Schooler 1969). Yet, in this sample, at least a third of the workers in each age category did not respond either in terms of the factors inherent in the nature of the occupation (intrinsic factors), or in terms of the job environment (extrinsic factors). To these workers, evidently, the annuity is unearned and, thus, not deserved. Therefore, it appears that there is a sizable number of older workers who feel active employment is a basic aspect of living and that it is important to earn their own way and care for themselves and their families.

It is notable that no older workers stated that they would quit working because termination of work would interfere with established social relationships in the work sphere. The importance of informal relationships on the job has frequently been noted. Indeed, it has been stated that a person may often receive his most gratifying social interaction at work: e.g., customers, clients, the work group (Vroom 1964). That no older worker considered this an impediment to removing himself from the work force indicates to us that, although social relationships may be important on the job, they do not provide the basic meaning of work to older workers.

This result is at variance with the findings of Friedmann and Havighurst. Their studies indicated that almost 20 percent of older or recently retired workers in each occupational group considered interpersonal association (friendship relations, peer-group relations, and subordinate-superordinate relationships) a basic meaning of work. Yet, no older worker in our

Table 42.2. Reasons given for not accepting an annuity (not quitting work) by age of the respondent, in percentages

	Age Category				
Reasons given for not quitting:	50–54	55–59	60–64	65+	Totals
Something for nothing	33.6	44.9	45.6	39.27	40.2
"No incentive to work without pay," "don't believe in handouts," "couldn't take that I didn't earn," "it would not be fair," "I'm suspicious of such an offer."					
Enjoy work	23.9	22.0	22.2	19.3	22.0
"I like work," "I want to have an active interest," "I want to die with my boots on."					
Meaning to life	21.5	21.5	12.9	11.9	17.6
"You wouldn't have a reason for being alive," "lose all incentive," "want to remain active."					
Independence provided by work	6.1	2.3	4.1	13.6	6.3
"I prefer to be my own boss," "would rather do as I please."					
Restricts freedom	6.5	3.3	8.2	6.3	5.9
"Wouldn't want that restriction on my freedom," "wouldn't want to be tied to those terms," "I want to be able to work and play as I want."					
Don't need it	0.4	0.9	5.8	6.8	3.1
Not enough present money	5.3	3.7	0.0	1.1	2.8
"Because of recent circumstances present living is inadequate."					
Other responses	2.8	1.4	1.2	1.1	1.7
No response		.5		.6	.2
Total N	247	214	171	176	808

Note—This table contains those responses the respondents mentioned first; some respondents did mention other reasons in further probes.

study indicated that established interpersonal associations would prevent him from retiring. Likewise, Morse and Weiss noted that only 1 percent of all employed males they studied considered the interruption of informal reltaionships at work a reason to continue working. Admittedly, occupational associations may play a significant role in the older workers' life *while employed*. Yet is also appears that the interruption of such relationships will not prohibit the worker from quitting.

It is further indicated in Table 42.2 that the independence that working allows becomes increasingly important as workers exceed the retirement age. Not unexpectedly, this was the only reason for continuing to work which increased to any great extent when pre-retirement-age workers in

the sample are compared with those 65 and older.

Finally, the greatest difference between pre-retirement- and post-retirement-age workers, as measured by this study, occurs among those who state that work gives meaning to their lives. Approximately 21 percent of both the 50–54- and 55–59-year-old workers would not accept an annuity for this reason. Less than 12 percent, however, of the post-retirement-age workers refused the annuity because work gives meaning to their lives.

In sum, it seems that there are many similarities in the meaning of work between pre-retirement- and post-retirement-age workers who would not accept a hypothetical annuity. First, it has been indicated that (*a*) to many older workers, work is not simply a means of earning a living, and (b) the proportion responding in this manner is fairly stable across age cohorts. Even if there were no economic need to work, a sizable minority of older workers would continue to do so. For these men, work is important for the basic satisfaction it provides. Second, all age categories emphasize the necessity of actually performing a task as a necessary aspect of work, that one should work to "earn his own way." It is also observed that all age categories of older workers are equally likely to emphasize that they enjoy their work. However, pre-retirement-age workers are more likely than post-retirement workers to feel that work gives meaning to life. On the other hand, post-retirement workers are more likely to emphasize that only if they work will they have the independence to do as they please or to decide their own style of life.

To this point, discussion has centered on the relationship between the age of the older worker and his stated reason for not retiring with annuity. As previously mentioned, several studies have investigated the meaning of work for older workers by use of the same or a similar question, although seldom across age categories. Past investigations, however, have overlooked a sizable number of workers in our society: those who would be willing to quit working and accept an annuity. It could be assumed such workers are unlikely to be motivated to work because of work's intrinsic satisfactions. Rather, such individuals are employed because work is a means to earn a living rather than an end in itself. For younger employed males, economic gain from working may provide social mobility or a desired consumption pattern, but the concern in this study is the function of work for the older worker. Therefore, a brief look at the distribution of responses of older workers basically motivated by remuneration may provide information about the meaning of work to the majority of older workers in our society—those willing to quit work.

There were no major differences in the responses of pre-retirement-age workers. Table 42.3 presents the reasons older workers gave for being willing to accept an annuity. Perhaps the most striking aspect of the table, particularly when comparing the pre-retirement-age and post-retirement-age workers, is the high degree of agreement in perceived advantages of accepting an annuity. In each age category, three responses—"security," "freedom to do what I want," and "can finally take it easy"—account for most of the responses. These three responses constitute almost two-thirds of all responses in each age category.

Finally, the reasons given by workers willing to quit work are also sometimes given by workers not willing to quit. For example, a predominant reason given by older workers willing to quit and accept an annuity was "freedom to do what I want," stated by 26 percent of this sub-sample of older workers. On the other hand, 6 percent of older workers who would not quit felt that work gives a person independence, while another 6 percent indicated that, to them, the annuity would restrict their freedom. Thus, it appears that some rationales may be given as justification either to work or to stop work.

Discussion and Summary

The findings reported here indicate that older workers willing to quit work if assured an annuity do so because such an arrangement would guarantee an income, would free the individual to do as he wants, and would finally allow him to "take it easy." On the other hand, older workers not willing to quit feel that employment gives meaning to life, provides enjoyment, or that to accept an annuity would be to get something for nothing.

What is significant is that this has been observed for all workers 50 and older. There appear to be no major differences between pre-retirement- and post-retirement-age workers in their reasons for desir-

Table 42.3. Reasons given for accepting an annuity (quitting work) by age of the respondent in percentages

Reasons given for quitting:	Age Category				
	50–54	55–59	60–64	65+	Totals
Security "Security," "like the assured income," "it would be freedom from financial worries."	27.6	31.8	30.4	28.1	29.6
Give freedom "Free to do what you want to do," "like to do the things you don't have time for now," "more time of my own."	26.2	24.9	20.7	25.7	24.5
Would be like retirement "Couldn't retire early," "I could take things easy," "have worked long enough."	12.2	10.1	9.3	11.4	10.8
Able to travel "I desire to travel," "I would be free to travel."	2.0	3.6	2.1	2.4	2.6
Could help others "I would use the time to help someone else."	7.6	8.3	7.2	3.6	7.1
Would reduce responsibilities "Reduced responsibility," "easier living," "not much responsibility."	4.4	5.0	7.6	4.8	5.3
Younger people could take over "Give someone else a job," "make job for a younger person."	4.1	2.4	5.1	2.4	3.5
Poor health "Health," "work is not healthful."	2.3	1.8	4.6	1.8	2.6
Would release me from worry "Would relieve worry and tension."	1.5	3.3	1.7	2.4	2.2
Other	10.2	8.3	10.1	16.8	10.6
No Response	1.0	.6	1.3	.6	1.2
Total N	344	337	237	168	1085

ing to work or not to work. An exception to this is that workers 65 years of age or older are more likely to continue working because of the independence gained through continued employment, while preretirement-age workers are more likely to indicate that work gives meaning to life.

Thus, it is true that working is a means of earning a living for a sizable number of the older workers studied, but there is still a large minority for whom work serves other than an economic function. Second, there is no major difference between age cohorts in the willingness of older workers to accept retirement as measured by the willingness of older worker to accept a hypothetical offer of an annuity up to the traditional age of retirement. After 65, workers are much less willing to accept the hypothetical offer. Finally, if there are basic changes in what workers consider to be the role of working in their lives, it occurs either before age 50 or after they finally retire.

Unfortunatley, this is not a longitudinal investigation. Therefore, one cannot generalize from existing information to *changes* in motivation to work experienced as a worker approaches and then exceeds retirement age. One qualification to the previous discussion must be made perfectly clear: workers of post-retirement age may be a select population in that they may be in better health than those who quit, they may be better adjusted to work, they may be more skilled, have better jobs and so on. Given this first attempt to systematically consider the relationship of the age of the worker and the meaning of work, it now seems appropriate that longitudinal studies be directed to the meaning of work to workers during the entire life cycle. Nevertheless, it remains necessary and important that we continue to examine this select group of post-retirement-age workers.

References

BAKKE, E. W. *The unemployed worker.* New York: Yale University Press, 1940.

DARLEY, J. G., & HAGENAH, T. *Vocational interest measurement.* Minneapolis: University of Minnesota Press, 1955.

FRIEDMANN, E. A., & HAVIGHURST, R. J. *The meaning of work and retirement.* Chicago: University of Chicago Press, 1954.

HALL, RICHARD H. *Occupations and the social structure.* Englewood Cliffs: Prentice-Hall, 1969.

KOHN, M. L., & SCHOOLER, C. Class, occupation, and orientation. *American Sociological Review,* 1969, *34,* 5, 659–678.

LEVY, S. J. The meaning of work. Unpublished paper for the Center for the Study of Liberal Education for Adults, 1963.

LINTON, R. *The study of man.* New York: Appleton-Century-Crofts, 1936.

LOFQUIST, L. H., & DAWIS, R. V. *Adjustment of work.* New York: Appleton-Century-Crofts, 1969.

MERTON, R. K. *Social theory and social structure.* Glencoe: Free Press, 1957.

MILLER, D. C., & FORM, W. H. *Industrial sociology.* New York: Harper & Row, 1964.

MORSE, N. C., & WEISS, R. S. The function and meaning of work and the job. *American Sociological Review,* 1955, *20,* 2, 191–198.

TAYLOR, L. *Occupational sociology.* New York: Oxford University Press, 1968.

TILGHER, A. *Work: what is has meant to men through the ages.* New York: Harcourt, 1930.

VROOM, V. H. *Work and motivation.* New York: Wiley, 1964.

WEBER, MAX. *The Protestant ethic and the spirit of capitalism.* New York: Scribner, 1930.

43. "RETIREMENT! WHAT A DISTRESSING WORD!"

GEORGE A. PERERA

I am over 60 and most distressed, not only by failing vision, missing teeth, barnacles on the spine, aching joints, gray hair and wrinkles, but because every effort is being made to separate and isolate me from a portion of my life and the rest of the living.

Some of my younger friends note that I am retired—and turn away. I read of "adult communities" and condominiums for those of "mature" years where I will not be disturbed by the sounds of children at play. I receive frequent announcements of retirement homes attached to which are information on the infirmaries that will serve as way-stations to my ultimate demise.

My mail contains almost daily reference to "senior citizens" and "the golden years," together with colorful illustrations of gracious, white-haired couples, hand-in-hand, basking by the golf course or eating picnic lunches on rustic tables by shaded lawns at the edge of trout-filled streams.

In addition, I am urged to take vitamins and minerals, correct my irregularities, avoid excess of any kind, walk briskly or jog gently, and watch out lest bed, bathtub, stress, influenza, avoirdupois or cholesterol prove my undoing.

Cards are handed me so that I may qualify for reductions in fees, fares, taxes and insurance (if permitted by the small print). Finally, such remarks as "How young you look!" and "My, you look well!" are countered by advice to procure bonds for income, avoid equities like the plague and set my house in order.

Retirement! What a distressful word! It smacks of retreat, withdrawal, seclusion, removal from circulation, elastic stockings and Windsor rockers cushioned with foam pillows to protect bony prominences.

Must I pursue some creative art or hobby merely to keep my mind and body occupied ? Must I volunteer my services for some charitable cause, whether or not I have the interest or ability? Must I engage in occupational or physical therapy?

Sometimes I wish my status was called "refirement" rather than "retirement" for I am still mobile, and my engine—although it misses a beat on occasion and emits some extraneous groans and grunts —still functions rather well.

The happy reality that comes after job severance because of age has to do with independence. No longer is one bound by boss, hierarchy, tradition, the careful ascent of promotional ladders, nor apprehensions regarding duties, obligations, pay and pensions.

One is free to say yea or nay, to work half as hard or twice as hard, or intermittently or not at all—free to moonlight or to quit if disenchanted.

To be in this capacity provides an unusual degree of liberty. Decisions are personal and based on aptitudes and inclinations. No longer are there fetters and one is no longer obligated or required to undertake a task. Little stands in the way of being true to oneself, to one's own philosophy and ideals.

44. SECOND CAREERS—A GROWING TREND

CAROL H. KELLEHER

This bibliographic essay introduces and examines some of the trends, issues and problems of career change as reflected in recent literature.

Three kinds of mid-career changes are discussed: voluntary switches, those forced on an individual by displacement from a first occupation and new careers that begin after retirement at 65, providing activity, stimulation and income for the later years.

The topic of women who take outside jobs after a period of childrearing is considered to be a separate and extensive subject and is not dealt with here, except incidentally.

Mid-Career Change

"A rcent BLS study found that about five and a half million of the almost 70 million Americans employed in January 1966 were working in an occupation different from the one they were in January 1965." Forty percent were over 35 years of age (Saben 1967).

Since middle-aged workers with family responsibilities and a certain standard of living to maintain have a vested interest in job stability, the motivation for career change during these years must be powerful. Many who voluntarily change jobs do so to improve their financial or personal status. One obvious path is the shift from blue-collar to white-collar jobs (Johnson and Stern 1969).

But more often the pattern of a career change is not so obvious and calls for analysis of motivational factors. There are certain personal or occupational "push" or "pull" factors that may lead a worker to seek a second career. Some "push" phenomena are structural determinants of an occupation, such as the age when a commercial pilot must cease flying; the early end to a first career, as in the military; elimination of an occupation by rapid social or technological change, or dissatisfaction and a desire for change. Some "pull" factors are status, pay, security or a minimal entrance requirement of specialized training for the new field (Haug and Sussman 1970).

Some social scientists feel that job mobility will increase greatly in the future and that professional employees will seldom remain long in a static job situation. Such mobility will result from managers' desire for efficiency and vitality in a department and from employees' demands for job satisfaction. Changes in corporate structure and programs, plus rapid advances in technical information, require adaptable workers who find job security in their own ability to add to their knowledge and market their skills. Professional mobility should be encouraged by such measures as portable pensions, flexible organization and workload and assistance with job finding (Kimball 1972).

The literature on second careers abounds with case histories of people who have found satisfaction and success in new positions. Stetson (1971) gives hundreds of examples of persons who have changed their careers and their lives. He includes cases of men who left the metropolitan "rat race" for a small-town job or philanthropic service at lower pay; he catalogues career changes among advertising men, financiers, university presidents and public officials. The great variety of case examples reveals an equal variety of motivations and methods. Some career changes are planned for years, others result from instantaneous decisions.

Avocation Becomes Career

For some, a lifelong avocation becomes a career (Hearn 1972). Many second-career artists are interested and trained in their art form (music, acting, painting or sculpture) from childhood, but most find that the exigencies of supporting a family make it ncessary to rely primarily on another career for financial support. At middle age or later, when the artist is financially secure, he may retire to work exclusively in his art—viewing this retirement as the beginning, rather than the end, of his creative life.

The so-called "mid-life crisis" is becoming more and more prevalent (Constandse 1972), producing a number of positive or negative forces that may impel a person to change careers. Some studies (Sheppard 1971 and 1972) reveal that a longer lifespan and extended working years, plus changes in technology and required skills, combine to create dissatisfaction and a feeling of personal obsolescence in mid-career workers. Such reactions have previously been considered a white-collar and professional syndrome, but these studies show a marked dissatisfaction among blue-collar workers who, in middle age, feel a discrepancy between their aspirations and their achievements. In a survey of white male union members aged 40 or more, Sheppard found that 35 percent were second-career candidates, based on variables of achievement values, aspiration-achievement discrepancy and autonomy on the job.

Successful People Go On

Many studies made of second careerists show that they are not unsusccessful men but persons of at least average achievement looking for upward mobility or personal satisfaction. One article (Lachter 1971) surveys executives who have left administrative management to make a new start. Many can be characterized as highly motivated, to whom salary is not a major factor, but for whom job challenge and personal fulfillment are of prime importance.

Beyond personal or immediate job factors that may dictate a career change, there is the problem of a declining industry. Probably the most vivid example of the last few years is the aerospace industry, whose retrenchment forced many highly skilled worker into unemployment. The need of aerospace workers for assistance has brought into existence a number of programs of financial and educational aid. The Technology Mobilization and Re-employment Program (TMRP) of the U.S. Department of Labor's Manpower Administration (Aun 1971) moves displaced aerospace engineers, scientists and technicians into new jobs. Grants may be made to engineers for job-seeking expenses or training, and counseling and placement services are available. A study identified 55,000 professional jobs that could be filled through 1975 by laid-off engineers

and scientists. In programs of short-term supplementary education to aid in transition to a new career, the average age of the participants was 48.

The knowledge and skills of these displaced aerospace workers, if used imaginatively, could benefit themselves and the entire country. Senator Alan Cranston (1972) illuminates many areas where scientific and engineering skills can be usefully and profitably applied. He points to pollution control, marine biology and oceanography, aviation, mass transit and computer system to aid education, health and crime fighting.

Education for a Second Career

Often it is necessary to return to school to become qualified for a second career. Dale L. Heistand (1971) surveyed a group of men and women who made a major career shift after the age of 35, requiring at least a year of graduate or professional education to complete. In examining the motives, aims, problems and achievements of such students, he sheds some light on the variable and often arbitrary admissions policies of universities toward older students. Another report (Troll and Schlossberg 1971) surveys college counselors who work with adults seeking advice on higher education and career change. The study examines the extent to which these counselors are biased against middle-aged and older students, particularly as they wish to make a career switch. While these professional counselors are less biased than the general population, more than half the sample showed some age bias. These studies and others point up the need for improved help and more liberal attitudes if educational centers are to be open to adults.

Some specific programs have been open to middle-aged persons wishing to change careers. The New Careers Program (Entine 1972) at Columbia University enrolled such persons in university graduate programs to provide them with training and accreditation in a new profession. The program proved extremely successful, and the experiment revealed three necessities for adult education of this nature: adequate financial support for the student; full counseling on academic and employment problems, and possible redesigning of courses and licensing by schools and professional accrediting associations to shorten training for the middle aged.

Retiring Military Personnel

One of the largest and most distinct groups of second careerists is the military. Even after a 20 or 30-year career in the service, retiring men are still in middle age, with the majority seeking a new civilian career. Many find pensions inadequate, or they are simply too young to retire.

A number of studies have been made on attitudes of retiring servicemen, their employment expectations and experiences and problems in seeking a second career. One article (Sharpe and Biderman 1967) is based on studies made by the Bureau of Social Science Research and the Department of Defense. It notes the aims and employment patterns of the retired military, finding that about 85 percent had found a job within four months after retirement—an encouraging figure for workers considering a second career.

Part II of the same article studies types of jobs sought by the retired military, the coordination of military skills and civilian jobs, income and job stability, and utilization of skills. Many servicemen felt that civilian jobs poorly utilized their skills acquired in the military, pointing to a need for retraining or aid in relocation and placement. The general conclusion was that the retired serviceman is evaluated in common-denominator civilian terms, such as educational achievement, rather than on the basis of specific skills.

Servicemen have been surveyed in the period just prior to their retirement (Stanford 1971) to investigate their attitudes toward retirement and how these are affected by personal, social and environmental factors. Some articles and books (Collings 1971; Quartley 1963) are intended to illuminate problem areas for the retiree and to aid in preretirement planning. Among difficulties the serviceman may face in civilian life are:

Inadequate military pensions

Age discrimination

Anti-military bias of colleges and employers

Labor market competition in areas where there are many military retirees

Legal restrictions on employment in certain fields, such as the civilian defense industry, to avoid conflict of interest.

Aid programs have been set up by the Department of Defense in an effort to smooth the employment path for the retiring serviceman (Mailler 1968). The military branches work with the U.S. Employment Service and state employment agencies in second-career counseling for these men.

Studies of retired military men (Biderman and Sharpe 1968) show that skills and experience acquired in the military with proper counseling and planning can be successfully transferred to civilian jobs. Large numbers of servicemen seek to find jobs in the governmental and institutional areas. One employment study (Angel 1971) is really an extensive catalogue for the retiring serviceman. It classifies jobs for which high school, junior college, vocational or college education is necessary, matches training of the several military branches to civilian employment and includes advice on resumes, job-finding techniques and financial aid.

Post-Retirement Careers

Earlier retirement and longer life expectancy for many people can pose the problem of boredom in the years after work. To provide the stimulus of worthwhile activity and to earn needed income, many persons retire from one career and take up a second—often in a completely different field. A number of social agencies and civic groups have organized programs of employment for older persons.

Different reports focus on the varying types of employment provided (Institute for Local Self-government 1971; Rush 1971; Aun 1971 and 1972). Some community programs establish corporations of senior citizens or organize social work, child care and landscaping activities. Some nonprofit employment agencies provide job training and counseling for older persons and develop job openings for such workers in public or private agencies or firms.

Small businesses and self-employment are popular post-retirement careers; many businessmen can use their career knowledge to start their own business or as advisors to others in consulting firms or with voluntary agencies like SCORE (Service Corps of Retired Executives) (Forbes 1970; Shloss 1970).

A unique example (Dutton 1958) is the University of California's Hastings College of Law in San Francisco, where all full-time faculty members must be 65 or over.

Volunteer service is a form of the second career ideal for retired persons whose income is adequate for their support. It services a dual purpose by providing meaningful activity and contributing to society.

"Retire To Action" (Arthur 1969) is a guide to voluntary service which encourages older people to embark on post-retirement careers and cites numerous persons who have been successful in new careers. It also offers information and advice about service organizations in urban and rural areas and lists scores of addresses of government and private agencies engaged in volunteer service.

References

ANGEL, JUVENAL L. *Matching Armed Forces Training to Civilian Jobs,* New York: World Trade Academy Press, 1971.

ARTHUR, JULIETTA K. *Retire to Action: A Guide to Voluntary Service,* Nashville: Tennessee, Abingdon Press, 1969.

AUN, EMIL MICHAEL. "New Horizons for Aerospace Engineers," *Manpower,* January 1971, pp. 2–8.

———. "No One Under Sixty Need Apply," *Manpower,* August 1970, pp. 28–32.

———. "Senior Aides: Fighting Stereotypes," *Manpower,* February 1972, pp. 7–12.

BIDERMAN, ALBERT D., and LAURE M. SHARPE. "The Convergence of Military and Civilian Occupational Structures—Evidence from Studies of Military Retired Employment," *American Journal of Sociology,* January 1968, pp. 381–399.

COLLINGS, KENT J. *The Second Time Around: Finding A Civilian Career in Mid-life,* Cranston: Rhode Island, Carroll Press, 1971.

CONSTANDSE, WILLIAM J. "A Neglected Personnel Problem," *Personnel Journal,* February 1972, pp. 129–133.

CRANSTON, ALAN (U.S. Senator). "Aerospaced Out," *Playboy,* March 1972, pp. 99, 106, 162ff.. (Reprinted in *Congressional Record,* pp. S3215–S3218.)

DUTTON, WILLIAM S. "A College Where New Careers Begin at 65," *National Parent-Teacher,* January 1958.

ENTINE, ALAN. "Second Careers: Experience and Expectations." *Where Have All the Robots Gone? Worker Dissatisfaction in the '70's,* Harold L. Sheppard and Neal Q. Herrick, New York: The Free Press, 1972, pp. 161–165.

HAUG, MARIE R., and MARVIN B. SUSSMAN. "The Second Career—Variant of *Where Have All the Robots Gone? Worker Dissatisfaction in the '70's*, Harold L. Sheppard, ed., Cambridge, Massachusetts: Schenkman Publishing Co., 1970, pp. 123–131.

HEARN, HERSHEL L. "Aging and the Artistic Career," *The Gerontologist*, Winter 1972, pp. 357–362.

HEISTAND, DALE L. *Changing Careers After 35*, New York: Columbia University Press, 1971.

Institute for Local Self-government. "Second Careers," *Aging in California*, Berkeley, The Authors, 1971, Section E., pp. 142–163.

JOHNSON, DAVID B. and JAMES L. STERN. "Why and How Workers Shift from Blue-Collar to White-Collar Jobs," *Monthly Labor Review*, October 1969, pp. 7–13.

KIMBALL, RICHARD T. "Planned Professional Manpower Mobility," *Conference Board Record*, September 1972, pp. 54–58.

LACHTER, LEWIS E. "Are You Considering a Second Career?" *Administrative Management*, April 1971, pp. 28, 32.

MAILLER, JAMES R. "Army and Labor Program for 'Second Careerists,'" *Employment Service Review*, September 1968, p. 28–31.

QUARTLEY, CHRISTOPHER J. "A New Challenge: Placing Retired Military Personnel," *Journal of College Placement*, February 1963, pp. 69–78.

RUSH, DIANE H. "Where No Science Exists," *Business and Economic Dimensions*, May 1971.

SABEN, SAMUEL. "Occupational Mobility of Employed Workers," *Monthly Labor Review*, June 1967, pp. 31–38.

SHARPE, LAURE M. and ALBERT D. BIDERMAN. "Out of Uniform" Part I, "The Employment Experience of Retired Servicemen Who Seek a Second Career," *Monthly Labor Review*, January 1967, pp. 15–21. Part II, "Educational Attainment Seen as a Key Factor for Retired Servicemen in the Establishment of a Second Career," *Monthly Labor Review*, February 1967, pp. 39–47.

SHEPPARD, HAROLD L. "Mid-Career Blues," *Where Have All the Robots Gone? Worker Dissatisfaction in the '70's*, Harold L. Sheppard and Neal Q. Herrick. New York: The Free Press, 1972, pp. 153–160.

————. "The Emerging Pattern of Second Careers, *New Perspectives on Older Workers*, Kalamazoo; Michigan, The W. E. Upjohn Institute for Employment Research, 1971, pp. 71–80.

SHLOSS, LEON. "One for the Weak Side: Unique Governmental Aid for Small Business," *Government Executive*, March 1970, pp. 57–60.

STANFORD, E. PERCIL. "Retirement Anticipation in the Military," *The Gerontologist*, Spring 1971, pp. 37–42.

STETSON, DAMON. *Starting Over*, New York: Macmillan, 1971.

TROLL, LILLIAN and NANCY SCHLOSSBERG. "How Age Biased are College Counselors?" *Industrial Gerontology*, Summer 1971, pp. 14–20.

"Why Not Start a Bank? Or a Candle Factory? Or Make Key Rings?" *Forbes*, October 15, 1970, pp. 43–47.

CHAPTER TEN: SUGGESTED FURTHER READING

MOORE, W. E. Occupational socialization. In D. A. Goslin (Ed.), *Handbook of socialization theory and research*. Chicago: Rand McNally, 1969. Pp. 861–884.

appendix

Interview Form

Interviewer's name _____ Date_____Age_____

Each interview report should have four parts: I and II are the data provided by the informant in unstructured questions; III and IV are your comments on the interview process and on implications of the data obtained.

For parts I and II, introduce yourself, saying, "I am a participant in a course at _____ University on development over the life span. We discover that we know very little about how people change throughout life, so we're asking people to help us learn what issues to think about."

How old are you? _____

(Time interview began _____)

I. Unstructured questions. Record as much as you can of what the informant says. Interpret, paraphrase, and make inferences as little as possible. Indicate whether you are quoting the source or paraphrasing by using or not using quotation marks. Indicate with an asterisk those informant's comments elicited by direct questioning or probing. Use back of this sheet if necessary.

    A. Please compare how you are now with ten years ago. Are things the same or different? Are they better or worse? How? (Try to get them to give you at least five aspects of life for each—same, different/better, worse.)

    B. Now try to think ten years from now. What do you imagine about yourself and your life then? Will things be the same or different, better or worse? How?

    C. Is there anything else that you think is important to note about this present part of your life?

D. What would you consider to be your "prime of life"? (Record answers and any comments.)

II. Structured questions. These questions need not be asked if the information was given in Part I. In any case, the interviewer should fill in this information.

A. Sex
   F_____   M_____

B. Marital status
   _____single (S)
   _____married (M)
   _____separated (SP)
   _____divorced (D)
   _____widowed (W)
   _____other (O)
   _____no data (N)

C. Children
   _____no
   _____yes
   _____number

D. Grandchildren
   _____yes
   _____no
   _____number

E. Occupation
   _____a. steady, full-time
   _____b. part-time, irregular
   _____c. not working outside home
   _____d. student
   _____e. no data

Other comments prompted by these questions:

(End of interview:_____)

F. Length of interview_____

G. What was *your* impression of the informant's overall view of the past?
  _____same (S)   _____better (B)   _____Mixed (M)
  _____different (D)   _____worse (W)   _____no data (O)

H. What was *your* impression of the informant's overall view of the future?
  _____same (S)   _____better (B)   _____Mixed (M)
  _____different (D)   _____worse (W)   _____no data (O)

III. *Interview process*

  A. How did you find the informant? (Through whom, difficulty, etc.)

  B. Setting of interview:

  C. Ease of interviewing:

  D. What were your feelings of generational differences between yourself and your informant?

  E. Other process issues?

IV. *Hypothesis*

What questions does this interview raise concerning such variables as age and sex, and concerning particular issues? Generate two hypotheses from the data you obtained from this informant:

A.

B.

C. Other comments or questions raised by the data:

Life Span Interview Code

1. Age
1, 2, 3, 4, 5, 6, 7, 8

2. Sex
F   M

3. Marital status
S single
M married
SP separated
D divorced
W widowed
O other (e.g., cohabiting)
N no data

4. Children
Y yes
N no
O no data

5. Grandchildren
Y yes
N no
O no data

6. Occupation
a. steady, full-time
b. part-time, irregular
c. not working outside home
d. student
e. no data

7. Prime: years
1, 2, 3, 4, 5, 6, 7, 8
O no data

8. Prime: length
a. one or more specific years
b. five years to a decade
c. longer than a decade
d. always the present
e. there is no prime
O no data

9. Overall view of past
B better
W worse
S same
D different
M mixed
O no data

10. Overall view of future
same as #9

Interview material was coded into the following categories if mentioned in reference to past, present, or expected in the future, regardless of positive or negative attitudes toward the issue. The coders tried to keep inference to a minimum, although coding in a category may mean that the words used in the title of the category were not mentioned specifically. Some examples of this are given below in the category descriptions.

11. Activities and skills: specific recreational, cultural pursuits, hobbies, and talents, as more general references to qualities or pursuits, such as "creativity," "things to do."

12. Aging and/or change: references to occurrences or thoughts that are attributed to getting older or to changes that are seen to be a function of time.

13. Body image: references to the individual's or other's perceptions of the S's body, e.g., loss or gain of weight, "sexiness," hair style, etc.

14. Children: mention of the S's offspring.

15. Death of others: self-explanatory.

16. Death of self: self-explanatory.

17. Education, intellectual pursuits: reference to any schooling or learning processes.

18. Grandchildren: mention of S's children's children.

19. Health: references to individual's physical well-being or mention of illnesses.

20. Home: nonspecific reference to S's place of residence, e.g., mention of "the house" or "my home."

21. Independence/dependence: mention of these words, plus any references to "freedom" or "being on one's own."

22. Interpersonal relations, friendship: includes relations with significant others, excluding spouses and family members.

23. Marriage, spouse: includes references to specific partner or marriage in general.

24. Maturity: use of this term in nonspecific way without reference to content or type of maturity. If the word "maturity" was used with reference to a specific content area, it was coded as that content area; e.g., "I have a more mature way of dealing with my parents" was coded as reference to primary family.

25. Money: any mention of personal financial matters.

26. Moves: reference to changes in location of residence.

27. Occupation, career: self-explanatory.

28. Primary family: reference to family in which S was a child, i.e., parents, siblings; as opposed to mention of family in which S is parent or grandparent, which was coded under "marriage," "children," and/or "grandchildren."

29. Problems, worries: use of these terms in nonspecific way without reference to content of problems, e.g., "I have more to worry about now," or "I handle problems differently." If these terms were used with reference to a specific content area, the remark was coded as that content area; e.g., "Money is a big problem now" would be coded as "money."

30. Religion: reference to organized religion or spiritual issues.

31. Responsibility: any use of the word in any context.

32. Retirement: reference to S's own or spouse's retirement.

33. Security: nonspecific mention without reference to content of security, e.g., "I have

more security now." If the content was mentioned it was coded under that specific content area; e.g., "financial security" was coded as "money."

34. Self-concept, -discovery, -awareness: mention of S's reflecting on his own "personality," "self-image," "identity."

35. Social, political issues: mention of social or political problems, movements, trends, or attitudes.

36. Success, achievement, goals: nonspecific mention without reference to content, e.g., "I'm beginning to achieve my goals." If the content area was mentioned, it was mentioned, it was coded under that content area; e.g., "I'm successful in my job" was coded as "occupation."

37. Worldview: view of nonspecific others and/or "philosophy of life," e.g., "I'm more tolerant of people now," "I'm a pessimist," "I trust in fate."

38. Length of interview_____

name index

Aaronson, B. S., 237, 243
Abraham, H. C., 328
Abraham, K., 321, 328
Aldous, J., 329
Al-Issa, I., 172, 175
Allen, L., 18, 20, 23, 223
Allport, F. H., 234, 236
Almquist, E. M., 255, 270
Alston, J., 52, 58, 60
Altrocchi, J., 237, 243
Anderson, H. E., Jr., 173, 175
Anderson, J. E., 19, 22, 191
Angel, J. L., 363, 364
Anglin, J. M., 172, 175
Angrist, S. S., 255, 270
Anisfeld, M., 158, 159, 160, 161, 170, 175
Anthony E. J., 329
Appel, L. F., 108, 117
Appley, M. H., 118
Aquinas, Saint Thomas, 87
Aronson, E., 344
Arthur J. K., 364
Arvey, R., 346, 347
Asayama, S., 194, 195
Asch, S. E., 171, 172, 175
Astin, H. S., 255, 270
Athanasiou, R., 341, 343
Atherton, K., 222
Atkinson, J. W., 270, 275
August, H. E., 75, 82

* A boldface page number refers to the page
on which a reprint in this text begins.

Augustine, St., 137
Augustus, 90
Aun, E. M., 362, 364
Ax, A. F., 296, 301
Axelrod, S., 236, 237, 243
Axelson, L. J., 255, 273, 310

Back, K. W., vi, xii, **196**, 197, 198, 204
Baker, C. T., 16, 23
Baker, E. N., 172, 177
Bakke, E. W., 353, 359
Bakker, D. J., 113 117
Baldwin, A. L., 60
Baltes, P. B., v, xii, **93**, 97, 145, 180, 223, 244, 302
Banducci, R., 255, 270
Bardwick, J. M., 273
Barke, H., 337, 343
Barker, R. G., 17, 22
Barlow, J., 159, 175
Barnacle, C. H., 75, 82
Baruch, G. K., 257, 261, 270, 271
Bass, B. M., 271
Baumrind, D., 264, 271
Baxter, B. L., 115, 116, 117
Bayer, L. M., 222
Bayley, N., v, xi, 11, **13**, 16, 18, 20, 21, 125, 132, 133, 144, 222, 268, 274
Becker, L. D., 321, 329
Becker, W. C., 265, 271
Bee, H., 290, 293, 294, 301
Beecher, H. K., 84, 90

Freedle, R., 102, 118
Frege, G., 138, 144
Freud, A., 191, 337, 344
Freud, S., 3, 10, 33, 36, 72, 74, 98, 182
Freund, P. A., 90
Friedmann, E. A., 315, 353, 354, 355, 359
Furfey, P. H., 20, 22, 338, 344
Furry, C. A., 97

Gaer, E. P., 167, 168, 176
Gallagher, J. J., 338, 344
Gallup, C., 293, 301
Gamer, E., vii, xiv, **336**
Gardner, E. F., 119, 120, 125
Garland, T. N., 253, 272
Gass, G. Z., 310, 311
Gay, J., 117
Gazzaniga, M. S., 249, 252
Geber, M., 20, 22
Gelber, E. R., 103, 117
Gergen, K. J., 196, 197, 204
Getzels, J. W., 233, 236
Gewirtz, J. C., 268, 274
Ginnane, W., 192, 196
Ginzberg, E., 261, 272
Ginzberg, R., 237, 243
Gitter, A. G., 58, 59, 60
Glazer, J. A., 337, 344
Glazer, N., 198, 204
Gleason, J. Berko, 169, 176
Glick, J. A., 117
Glick, P. C., 304
Glueck, E., 265, 266, 272
Glueck, S., 265, 266, 272
Gold, H., vii, xiv, **332**
Gold, M., 266, 272
Goldberg, P., 269, 272
Goldberg, S., 103, 118, 273
Golde, P., 237, 243
Goldfader, E., 304
Goldman-Eisler, F., 164, 176
Gollin, E. S., 341, 344
Golub, L. S., 166
Goodenough, F., 114
Goodglass, H., 169, 176
Gordon, C., 204
Gordon, M., 160, 175
Goslin, D. A., 60, 244, 302, 329, 365
Gosling, J., 192, 196
Goudy, W. J., vii, xiv, **352**
Gouervitch, V., 340, 344
Gough, H. G., 290, 301
Goulet, L. R., 145, 180

Graham, P. A., 299, 301
Green, R. F., 126, 133
Greenhouse, S. W., 71
Greenspan, S., 337, 343
Gregg, A., 216
Griffin, W. J., 162, 177
Griffitt, W., 340, 343
Gross, I. F., 82
Gruen, W., 185, 191
Guptill, C. S., 199, 204
Gutmann, D. L., vii, xiii, 187, 189, 190, 191, 273, **276**

Haas, M. B., 253, 268, 275
Habenstein, R. W., 321, 329
Hadar, M., 322, 329
Hagenah, T., 359
Haith, M. M., 99, 118
Hall, F. T., 255, 272
Hall, R. H., 359
Halle, M., 155, 176, 178, 180
Hamblin, R. L., 255, 271
Hanley, C., 223
Harlow, H. F., 98, 115, 118, 119, 124, 268, 272
Harlow, M. K., 115, 118, 268, 272
Harper, L. V., 329
Harris, D. B., 19, 22, 60
Hartley, R. E., 255, 272, 289, 301
Hartmann, H., 10, 188, 191
Hartup, W. W., 337, 344, 345
Haug, M. R., 361, 365
Havighurst, R. J., 52, 60, 184, 185, 191, 230, 353, 354, 355, 359
Hawthorne, F. M., 321, 329
Hayes, J. R., 175, 180
Hayhurst, H., 167, 176
Hearn, H. L., 361, 365
Heer, D. M., 298, 301
Hegal, G., 142
Heider, G., 204, 207
Heinig, C., 258, 259, 261, 262, 264, 267, 275
Heinstein, M. I., 223
Heistand, D. L., 362, 365
Hendrick, I., 30
Henry, W. E., vii, xiv, 187, 190, 191, 230, 317, **348**
Henschel, A., 256, 272
Herrick, N. Q., 364, 365
Hess, B., 244
Hess, H., 269, 272
Hess, R. D., 251, 252

concept index

about the author

Freda Rebelsky is currently a Professor of Psychology at Boston University, where she also directs the doctoral proram in Developmental Psychology. She received her B.A. and M.A. degrees at the University of Chicago and her Ph.D. from Radcliffe. Professor Rebelsky has previously held research and teaching positions at the University of Chicago, Harvard University, and Massachusetts Institute of Technology. From 1965 to 1967, Professor Rebelsky was a visiting lecturer at Utrecht University in Holland and also lectured at universities in Germany and England. She has contributed articles to *Child Development, Journal of Genetic Psychology, Contemporary Psychology,* and many other journals. In 1970 Professor Rebelsky received the Distinguished Teacher of Psychology Award from the American Psychological Foundation. She also received the 1971 E. Harris Harbison Award for Gifted Teaching from the Danforth Foundation.

a note on the type

The text of this book is set in CALEDONIA, a Linotype face designed by W. A. Dwiggins. It belongs to the family of printing types called "modern face" by printers—a term used to mark the change in style of type-letters that occurred about 1800. Caledonia borders on the general design of Scotch Modern, but is more freely drawn than that letter.

The book was composed by Cherry Hill Composition, Pennsauken, N.J. It was printed and bound by Halliday Lithograph Corp., West Hanover, Mass.